LET'S

Ecua

& The Galápagos Islands

"Its yearly revision by a new crop of Harvard students makes it as valuable as ever." **—*The New York Times***

"Value-packed, unbeatable, accurate, and comprehensive." **—*The Los Angeles Times***

"A world-wise traveling companion—always ready with friendly advice and helpful hints, all sprinkled with a bit of wit." **—*The Philadelphia Inquirer***

"Lighthearted and sophisticated, informative and fun to read. [Let's Go] helps the novice traveler navigate like a knowledgeable old hand." **—*Atlanta Journal-Constitution***

"All the essential information you need, from making a phone call to exchanging money to contacting your embassy. [Let's Go] provides maps to help you find your way from every train station to a full range of youth hostels and hotels." **—*Minneapolis Star Tribune***

"Unbeatable: good sight-seeing advice; up-to-date info on restaurants, hotels, and inns; a commitment to money-saving travel; and a wry style that brightens nearly every page." **—*The Washington Post***

■ Let's Go researchers have to make it on their own.

"The writers seem to have experienced every rooster-packed bus and lunar-surfaced mattress about which they write." **—*The New York Times***

"Retains the spirit of the student-written publication it is: candid, opinionated, resourceful, amusing info for the traveler of limited means but broad curiosity." **—*Mademoiselle***

■ No other guidebook is as comprehensive.

"Whether you're touring the United States, Europe, Southeast Asia, or Central America, a Let's Go guide will clue you in to the cheapest, yet safe, hotels and hostels, food and transportation. Going beyond the call of duty, the guides reveal a country's latest news, cultural hints, and off-beat information that any tourist is likely to miss." **—*Tulsa World***

■ Let's Go is completely revised each year.

"Up-to-date travel tips for touring four continents on skimpy budgets." **—*Time***

"Inimitable.... Let's Go's 24 guides are updated yearly (as opposed to the general guidebook standard of every two to three years), and in a marvelously spunky way." **—*The New York Times***

Let's Go Publications

Let's Go: Alaska & The Pacific Northwest
Let's Go: Britain & Ireland
Let's Go: California
Let's Go: Central America
Let's Go: Eastern Europe
Let's Go: Ecuador & The Galápagos Islands
Let's Go: Europe
Let's Go: France
Let's Go: Germany
Let's Go: Greece & Turkey
Let's Go: India & Nepal
Let's Go: Ireland
Let's Go: Israel & Egypt
Let's Go: Italy
Let's Go: London
Let's Go: Mexico
Let's Go: New York City
Let's Go: Paris
Let's Go: Rome
Let's Go: Southeast Asia
Let's Go: Spain & Portugal
Let's Go: Switzerland & Austria
Let's Go: USA
Let's Go: Washington, D.C.

Let's Go ***Map Guide:*** *Boston*
Let's Go ***Map Guide:*** *London*
Let's Go ***Map Guide:*** *New York City*
Let's Go ***Map Guide:*** *Paris*
Let's Go ***Map Guide:*** *San Francisco*
Let's Go ***Map Guide:*** *Washington, D.C.*

LET'S GO

The Budget Guide to
Ecuador
& the Galápagos Islands
1997

Katherine R. Unterman
Editor

Pogen MacNeilage
Associate Editor

Macmillan

HELPING LET'S GO

If you want to share your discoveries, suggestions, or corrections, please drop us a line. We read every piece of correspondence, whether a postcard, a 10-page e-mail, or a coconut. All suggestions are passed along to our researcher-writers. Please note that mail received after May 1997 may be too late for the 1998 book, but will be retained for the following edition. **Address mail to:**

Let's Go: Ecuador & the Galápagos
67 Mt. Auburn Street
Cambridge, MA 02138
USA

Visit Let's Go at **http://www.letsgo.com,** or send e-mail to:

Fanmail@letsgo.com
Subject: "Let's Go: Ecuador & the Galápagos"

In addition to the invaluable travel advice our readers share with us, many are kind enough to offer their services as researchers or editors. Unfortunately, the charter of Let's Go, Inc. enables us to employ only currently enrolled Harvard-Radcliffe students.

Published in Great Britain 1997 by Macmillan, an imprint of Macmillan General Books, 25 Eccleston Place, London SW1W 9NF and Basingstoke.

Published in the United States of America by St. Martin's Press, Inc.

ISBN: 0 333 68684 5

First edition
10 9 8 7 6 5 4 3 2 1

Let's Go: Ecuador & the Galápagos is written by Let's Go Publications, 67 Mt. Auburn Street, Cambridge, MA 02138, USA.

Printed in the USA on recycled paper with biodegradable soy ink.

Contents

Maps

About Let's Go

THIRTY-SIX YEARS OF WISDOM

Back in 1960, a few students at Harvard University banded together to produce a 20-page pamphlet offering a collection of tips on budget travel in Europe. This modest, mimeographed packet, offered as an extra to passengers on student charter flights to Europe, met with instant popularity. The following year, students traveling to Europe researched the first, full-fledged edition of *Let's Go: Europe*, a pocket-sized book featuring honest, irreverent writing and a decidedly youthful outlook on the world. Throughout the 60s, our guides reflected the times; the 1969 guide to America led off by inviting travelers to "dig the scene" at San Francisco's Haight-Ashbury. During the 70s and 80s, we gradually added regional guides and expanded coverage into the Middle East and Central America. With the addition of our in-depth city guides, handy map guides, and extensive coverage of Asia, the 90s are also proving to be a time of explosive growth for Let's Go, and there's certainly no end in sight. The first editions of *Let's Go: India & Nepal* and *Let's Go: Ecuador & The Galápagos Islands* hit the shelves this year, and work toward next year's series has already begun.

We've seen a lot in 37 years. *Let's Go: Europe* is now the world's bestselling international guide, translated into seven languages. And our new guides bring Let's Go's total number of titles, with their spirit of adventure and their reputation for honesty, accuracy, and editorial integrity, to 30. But some things never change: our guides are still researched, written, and produced entirely by students who know first-hand how to see the world on the cheap.

HOW WE DO IT

Each guide is completely revised and thoroughly updated every year by a well-traveled set of 200 students. Every winter, we recruit over 120 researchers and 60 editors to write the books anew. After several months of training, Researcher-Writers hit the road for seven weeks of exploration, from Anchorage to Ankara, Estonia to El Salvador, Iceland to Indonesia. Hired for their rare combination of budget travel sense, writing ability, stamina, and courage, these adventurous travelers know that train strikes, stolen luggage, food poisoning, and marriage proposals are all part of a day's work. Back at our offices, editors work from spring to fall, massaging copy written on Himalayan bus rides into witty yet informative prose. A student staff of typesetters, cartographers, publicists, and managers keeps our lively team together. In September, the collected efforts of the summer are delivered to our printer, who turns them into books in record time, so that you have the most up-to-date information available for *your* vacation. And even as you read this, work on next year's editions is well underway.

WHY WE DO IT

At Let's Go, our goal is to give you a great vacation. We don't think of budget travel as the last recourse of the destitute; we believe that it's the only way to travel. Living cheaply and simply brings you closer to the people and places you've been saving up to visit. Our books will ease your anxieties and answer your questions about the basics—so you can get off the beaten track and explore. Once you learn the ropes, we encourage you to put Let's Go away now and then to strike out on your own. As any seasoned traveler will tell you, the best discoveries are often those you make yourself. When you find something worth sharing, drop us a line. We're Let's Go Publications, 67 Mt. Auburn St., Cambridge, MA 02138, USA (e-mail: fanmail@letsgo.com).

HAPPY TRAVELS!

Acknowledgements

For late-night perks and early-morning kicks in the ass, we want to thank the Master ME, Touch-man Travelli. Also, thanks to our four intepid RWs, who exceeded all expectations to bring us copious quantities of killer copy. *Muchas gracias* to a selfless army of last-minute proofers, our fast-fingered typists, the productive production staff, and finally, thanks to an office staff that brought pleasure to the pain of an indoor summer. **—KT&P**

Thanks all around to Team Ecuador for being so kick-ass. Who would've though that two bums splashing around in Tamarindo's phosphorescence could've written a book? But Pogen, after months of late nights and smokey treats, you've kicked the most ass of all. Amy, a toast to a mutual restoration of faith. Ash, for giving me my purple-haired perspective. JK, ML siempre through sweet showdowns and spontaneous slime. And to Robyn, but solely under the condition that we can still stand each other by the time this book comes out (well, there's always Vancouver...). **—KÜ**

First and foremost, a billion thanks to my beloved editor, Katie, for late nights in the office, ramen dances, and breakfast at IHOP. Despite late night/early morning computer psychosis, always ready with a smile. We chopped, spiced, shaped and smoothed our way to quite a book, so just talk to the hand! Dependable for a quality breakfast, my dear friend the Danimal. Matt the man for alpine, mountaintop, frisbee adventures. The women of Walker, the men of Exeter (esp. Diplomat Dave), the rest of the office, and Mom, Dad, Shannon, and Romanoff, many, many thanks. **—PM**

Researcher-Writers

Chandler Arnold *The Galápagos Islands, Far Southwest Coast*

Enthusiastic in the extreme, Chandler delved into the ecology of the Galápagos Islands without reserve, swimming with sharks and taming wild tortoises. A whirlwind of Southern charm, Chandler jumped from island to island, always volunteering a helping hand and a hug to Ecuadorians of all ages, from Galápagos grandparents to Onofreo, his 10-year-old tour guide. Upon arrival, he lost his luggage, but he never let go of his cheery disposition. Even after weeks of research, Chandler persisted unfazed, honing his uncanny ability to communicate with sea lions purely through eye-contact. Come nightfall, you always knew where to find him, admiring a romantic sunset from the oh-so-perfect spot, *jugo de mora* in hand. This congenial Carolinian left his distinctively Chandlerian mark upon the islands, and the islands taught him a thing or two about the world as well.

John Bamford *North of Quito, Cotopaxi, Pacific Coast*

Kickin' his way from Cotopaxi to the coast, John overcame a hellish first two weeks to bring us his hyper-humorous and helluv-long copybatches. He was tested early on in Otavalo, where he suffered substantial losses to a swift local thief. Tapping an overflowing pool of resourcefulness, he quickly restored his lost identity (and his traveler's checks) and pushed on through sadistic markets of leather and wood, past mysteriously deserted villages and curious canines to his true homeland on the Pacific Coast. Restored by those familiar coastal breezes, he kicked his way down from Esmeraldas to Playas, devouring mountains of *ceviche* and teaching the locals a thing or two about soccer along the way. Intensely immersed in his work, John even forgot to call home, but we didn't mind; his thorough and detailed descriptions of every bend in the road made Ecuador spring to life from the page.

Robin Goldstein *Quito, Riobamba to Vilcabamba, Southern Oriente*

A veteran explorer, Robin selflessly dropped everything else when he got the chance to spend a summer in the Ecuadorian highlands. Chugging out copy like a researching machine, we always thanked our lucky stars that the competition didn't have him. All the Ecuadorian eyes seemed to turn to Robin, from the fluttering lashes of a certain *chica* with wedding bells ringing in her ears to the (friendly) stares of the incredulous Oriente *indígenas.* But nothing fazed stalwart Robin, not even a windstorm that almost blew his bus off a mountain cliff. Left high and dry, he used his logical know-how and spent the stormy night with locals, waking up in the morning untouched by a single raindrop. This intrepid intellectual thirsted for adventure and lived out many—chillin' with the Shuar, riding the roof of the bucking Alausí-Bucay train, and shaking hands with El Loco himself.

Gavin Steckler *Guayaquil, W. Lowlands, Latacunga to Baños, Northern Oriente, Near Quito*

Gavin brought us unbelievably meticulous prose pregnant with savvy sentiment and wonderfully wacky wit. During his first days in Guayaquil, Gavin was force-fed a filthy taste of the worst stuff Ecuador has to offer. He choked it down with Gavinesque grace and diligently worked his way through the western lowlands. At long last he reached the highlands, only to loop through Latacunga, bathe briefly in Baños, and descend once again, this time into the steamy Oriente, where he stewed for two weeks. Falling ill in the muddiest reaches of the Oriente, Gavin sucked it up, stuck it out, and trucked it north, only to be thwarted once again at the gates of Cuyabeno. By this time we worried for Gavin's sanity, but his work only got more inspired. After bathing in the "orgasmic" hot springs of Papallacta, he conquered the sights near Quito, then fled to the coast for some well-deserved rest. Ah, Olón at last.

How to Use This Book

Let's Go: Ecuador and The Galápagos Islands 1997 is not a manual; it's an adventure companion. Read it, revel in it, but don't let it confine you in your journey to one of the most exhilarating, eye-popping, exciting, engaging countries in South America ... nay, the world. Ecuador is the kind of spontaneous, rough 'n' tumble place that doesn't follow the rules—so neither should you. Here, nobody can guarantee that the buses will run on time or that the volcano looming overhead won't spew its stuff tomorrow—hell, with a president nicknamed "El Loco," who knows what could happen? While little can be taken for granted here, Ecuador does guarantee one thing—amazing diversity, both ecologically and culturally, from the summit of Chimborazo to the shores of Isla Santa Cruz, from Montañita's monster waves to Otavalo's markets. Ecuador's charisma comes from all that is pristine and un-gringo-fied about it. National parks and reserves preserve flora and fauna species found nowhere else in the world, traditional indígenas live in relative isolation in the Oriente, and some Pacific beaches go for days without a single footprint disturbing their sands. It's possible to experience the best Ecuador has to offer and leave it just as spectacular as it was when you arrived. Hopefully this book will help you do that.

A Let's Go jaunt into South America has been long overdue, and here we present a brand-spankin' new introduction to one of the hottest up-and-coming off-road adventure destinations around. Our four researchers bravely journeyed where no Let's Goers have gone before, and smoothly came away wiser and wilder—but not after working their butts off writing savvy, spunky copy.

The book begins with the **Essentials** section, information on all those things it's not so easy to figure out in a developing nation. How to get there, safety precautions, health information—it's all there. Ecuador is rich in history, culture, and wildlife, and all that's laid out for you too, so you know exactly what treasures you're experiencing when you see them. We've explored every region of the country too, starting with **Quito,** the country's civil, cultural, and cosmopolitan capital, as well as some killer sights nearby, like Mitad del Mundo. Then we head up **North of Quito** to the slow-paced, misty villages of many *artesanía*-making *indígenas.* Jumping back over the capital, the **Central Corridor** between Quito and Cuenca soars between some of the tallest (and sometimes active) volcanoes in Ecuador. After a mountain climb and a soaking session in the hot springs, it's on to colonial **Cuenca and the Southern Highlands** that surround it. From there it's a hop, skip, and a jump to a sunny surfing scene on the country's **Pacific Coast.** Ecuador's nitty-gritty commercial capital, **Guayaquil ... and the Western Lowlands** to its north, run the length of the country just east of the coast. After that, the only regions that remain to be explored are the country's jungle provinces of the **Oriente,** which offers off-the-beaten-track adventures at every turn. Our mainland Ecuadorian odyssey at its end, we finally jump ship for the enchanting **Galápagos Islands,** 600 miles west off of the country's coast. *¡Buena suerte!*

A NOTE TO OUR READERS

The information for this book is gathered by *Let's Go*'s researchers during the late spring and summer months. Each listing is derived from the assigned researcher's opinion based upon his or her visit at a particular time. The opinions are expressed in a candid and forthright manner. Other travelers might disagree. Those traveling at a different time may have different experiences since prices, dates, hours, and conditions are always subject to change. You are urged to check beforehand to avoid inconvenience and surprises. Travel always involves a certain degree of risk, especially in low-cost areas. When traveling, especially on a budget, always take particular care to ensure your safety.

Essentials

PLANNING YOUR TRIP

When to Go

Despite Ecuador's location at zero degrees latitude, the climate varies greatly across the country's three geographic regions. On the Pacific coast and in the Oriente region you'll find sweltering heat typical of the tropics, but in the highland's it's a different story; **the higher you get, the cooler you'll be.** Ecuador's seasons do not cycle from summer to winter as in temperate regions, but instead from wet to dry. **Coastal** and **lowland weather** is affected by the currents of the Pacific. Warm waters bathe Ecuador's shores from January to April, bringing torrential downpours and daytime temperatures around 88°F (31°C). In May, cooler currents flow north from the antarctic, meaning less heat and less rainfall for the rest of the year.

Sun worshippers and beach crawlers come and go with the seasons. Expect crowds during the *temporada* from December to April, especially on weekends and holidays. The rest of the year you'll most likely have the beach to yourself. In the **highlands,** temperatures remain more or less constant year-round, averaging 70°F (21°C) during the day and 47°F (8°C) at night. The driest time of year in the highlands is from June to September, but the variation in rainfall in not extreme. Variation in rainfall in the **Oriente** is not extreme either; you can count on rain year-round, with especially heavy rains from June to August. However, as long as you come prepared with adequate rain gear, a shower or two won't ruin your trip. The rain should just make your jungle tour that much more authentic. Year-round temperature and humidity approximates that of the coast during the wet season.

In short, there is no perfect time to visit all three regions of the country. Seasonal variation is less marked in the highlands and the Oriente, while the coast has the *temporada* from December to April. Also keep local festivals and holidays in mind when planning your trip. The most important nationwide holidays are Christmas, *Semana Santa* (Easter week), and Ecuadorian Independence Day, May 24. While these times of year are very festive, holiday destinations tend to be quite crowded. For information on other festivals and holidays see the Appendices (p. 285).

Useful Organizations

TRAVEL ORGANIZATIONS

South American Explorer's Club (SAEC), 126 Indian Creek Rd., Ithaca, NY 14850 (tel. (607) 277-0488; fax 277-6122; http://www.samexplo.org; e-mail explorer@sameplo.org), and Jorge Washington 311 y L. Plaza, Apartado 17-21-431, Eloy Alfaro, Quito, Ecuador (tel./fax (593) 2-225-228; e-mail explorer@saec.org.ec). A nonprofit organization with extensive information about traveling, working, volunteering, and researching in Latin America. Clubhouses in Ithaca, New York; Quito, Ecuador; and Lima, Perú have trip reports and compiled information packets. They also have an extensive library with books on all topics Latin American. Check out the catalog of travel gear and books on Latin America. Their knowledgeable staff and mountains of resources are at your disposal for the U.S. tax-deductible membership fee of US$40 a year.

Council on International Educational Exchange (Council), 205 East 42nd St., New York, NY 10017-5706 (tel. (888) COUNCIL (268-6245); fax (212) 822-2699; e-mail info@ciee.org; http://www.ciee.org). A private, nonprofit organization, Council administers work, volunteer, and academic programs around the world. They

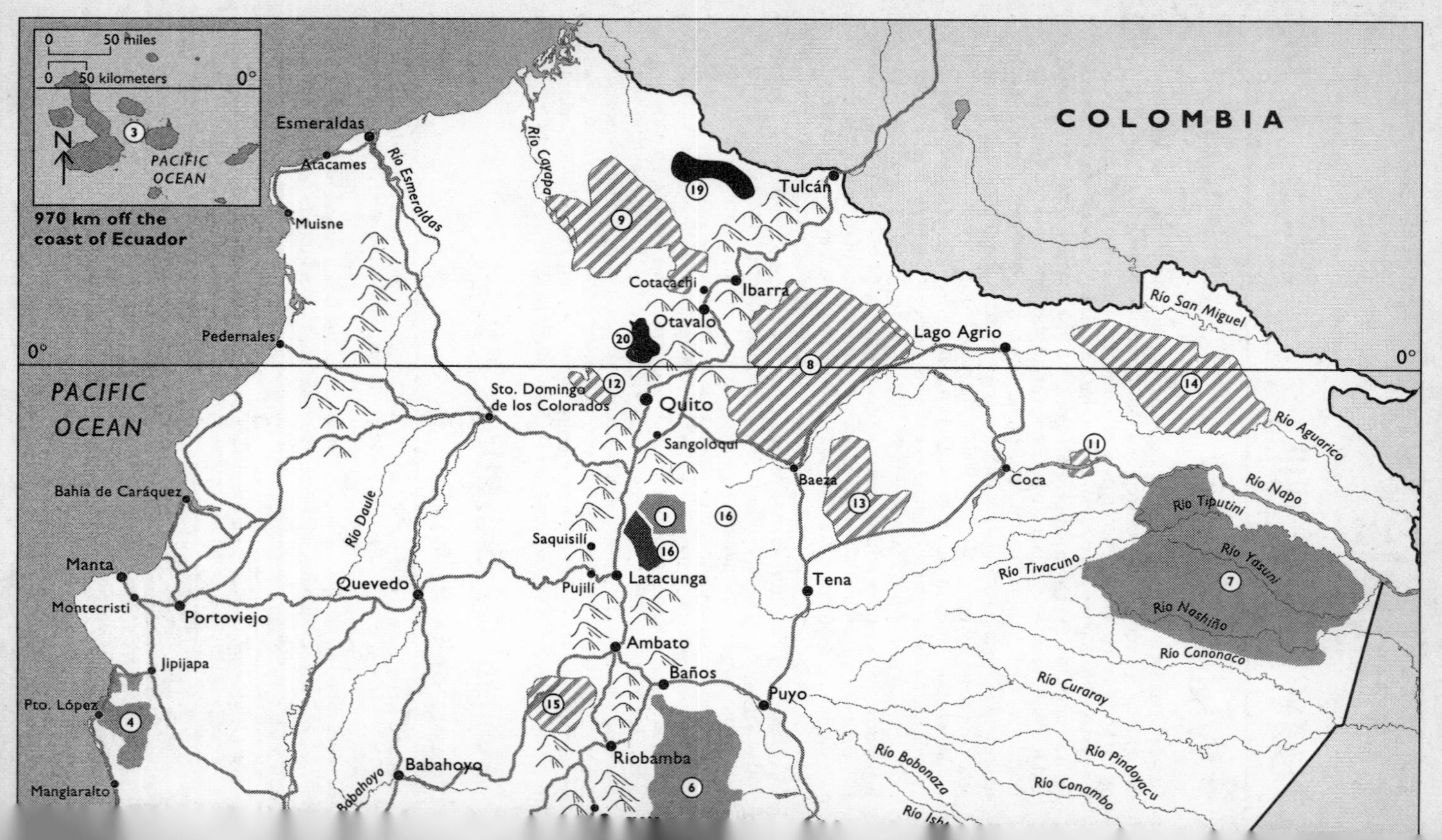
0 50 miles
0 50 kilometers
0°
N
PACIFIC OCEAN
970 km off the coast of Ecuador
COLOMBIA
PACIFIC OCEAN
0°
0°
Esmeraldas
Atacames
Muisne
Pedernales
Río Esmeraldas
Río Cayapa
Tulcán
Cotacachi
Ibarra
Otavalo
Lago Agrio
Río San Miguel
Río Aguarico
Sto. Domingo de los Colorados
Quito
Sangolquí
Baeza
Coca
Río Napo
Río Tiputini
Río Yasuní
Río Nashiño
Río Cononaco
Río Tivacuno
Bahía de Caráquez
Manta
Montecristi
Portoviejo
Río Daule
Quevedo
Saquisilí
Pujilí
Latacunga
Tena
Ambato
Baños
Puyo
Jipijapa
Pto. López
Riobamba
Babahoyo
Babahoyo
Mangiaralto
Río Curaray
Río Pindoyacu
Río Bobonaza
Río Conambo
1
3
4
6
7
8
9
11
12
13
14
15
16
16
19
20

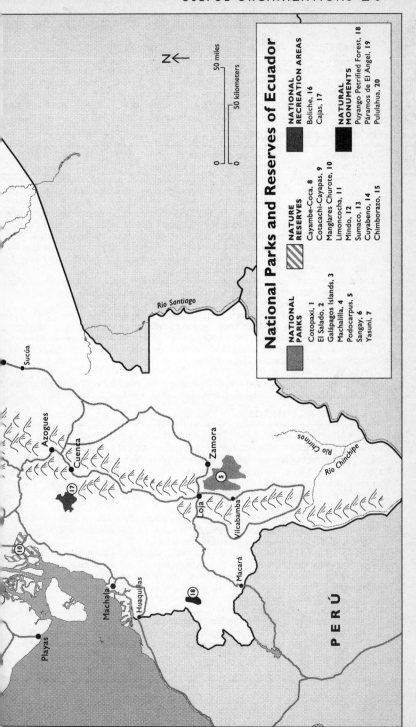

National Parks and Reserves of Ecuador

NATIONAL PARKS

Cotopaxi, 1
El Salado, 2
Galápagos Islands, 3
Machalilla, 4
Podocarpus, 5
Sangay, 6
Yasuní, 7

NATURE RESERVES

Cayambe-Coca, 8
Cotacachi-Cayapas, 9
Manglares Churote, 10
Limoncocha, 11
Mindo, 12
Sumaco, 13
Cuyabeno, 14
Chimborazo, 15

NATIONAL RECREATION AREAS

Boliche, 16
Cajas, 17

NATURAL MONUMENTS

Puyango Petrified Forest, 18
Páramos de El Angel, 19
Pululahua, 20

N

0 50 miles
0 50 kilometers

Río Santiago
Sucúa
Azogues
Cuenca
Zamora
Loja
Vilcabamba
Río Chinchipe
Río Chirinos
Machala
Huaquillas
Macará
Playas
PERÚ

also offer identity cards, including the ISIC and the GO25, and a range of publications, including the magazine *Student Travels* (free).

International Student Travel Confederation, Herengracht 479, 1017 BS Amsterdam, The Netherlands (tel. (31) 20 421 2800; fax 20 421 2810; e-mail istcinfo@istc.org; http://www.istc.org). The ISTC is a nonprofit confederation of student travel organizations whose focus is to develop, promote, and facilitate travel among young people and students. Member organizations include Student Air Travel Association (SATA), ISIS Travel Insurance, and the International Association for Educational and Work Exchange Programs (IAEWEP).

USEFUL PUBLICATIONS

Adventurous Traveler Bookstore, P.O. Box 1468, Williston, VT 05495 (tel./fax (800) 282-3963; tel. (801) 860-6776; fax 860-6607; e-mail books@atbook.com; http://www.gorp.com/atbook.htm). Free catalog upon request. Specializes in outdoor travel books and maps. The web site offers extensive browsing opportunities.

Bon Voyage!, 2069 W. Bullard Ave., Fresno, CA 93711 (tel. (800) 995-9716, from abroad (209) 447-8441; e-mail 70754.3511@compuserve.com). Annual mail order catalog offers a range of products for everyone from the luxury traveler to the die-hard trekker. Books, travel accessories, luggage, electrical converters, maps, videos, and more. All merchandise may be returned for exchange or refund within 30 days of purchase, and prices are guaranteed. (Lower advertised prices will be matched and merchandise shipped free).

Latin American Travel Consultants, P.O. Box 17-17-908, Quito, Ecuador (fax (593) 2-562-566). Publishes the 15-page quarterly *Latin American Travel Advisor,* about safety and politics in Latin America. US$39 for 1-year subscription.

Superintendent of Documents, U.S. Government Printing Office, P.O. Box 371954, Pittsburgh, PA 15250 (tel. (202) 512-1800; fax 512-2250). Open Mon.-Fri. 7:30am-4:30pm. Publishes *Your Trip Abroad* (US$1.25), *Health Information for International Travel* (US$14), and "Background Notes" on all countries (US$1 each). Postage is included in the prices.

Wide World Books and Maps, 1911 N. 45th St., Seattle, WA 98103 (tel. (206) 634-3453; fax 634-0558; e-mail travelbk@mail.nwlink.com; http://nwlink.com/travelbk). Good selection of travel guides, accessories, and hard-to-find maps.

INTERNET RESOURCES

Along with everything else in the 90s, budget travel is moving rapidly into the information age. The Internet itself can be used in many different forms, but the most useful to 'net-surfing budget travelers is the **World Wide Web.** It is often better to know a good site, and start "surfing" from there, through links from one web page to another. Below are some of our favorite sites. In addition to these, we also list relevant web sites throughout different sections of the Essentials chapter.

City.Net (http://www.city.net) is a very impressive collection of regional or city-specific web pages. Just select a geographic area, such as Ecuador, and it provides you with links to web pages related to that area.

The CIA World Factbook (http://www.odci.gov/cia/publications/95fact) has tons of vital statistics on the country you want to visit. Check it out for an overview of Ecuador's economy, or an explanation of their system of government.

Shoestring Travel (http://www.stratpub.com) is a budget travel e-zine, with feature articles, links, user exchange, and accommodations information.

The Student and Budget Travel Guide (http://asa.ugl.lib.umich.edu/chdocs/travel/travel-guide.html) is just what it sounds like.

The Interactive Travel Guide (http://www.developnet.com/travel) began as The Cheap Travel Page and has expanded its scope some, but is still useful for the budget traveler.

Documents and Formalities

Be sure to file all applications several weeks or months in advance of your planned departure date. Remember, you are relying on government agencies to complete these transactions. A backlog in processing can spoil your plans.

When you travel, always carry on your person two or more forms of identification, including at least one photo ID. A passport combined with a driver's license or birth certificate usually serves as adequate proof of your identity and citizenship. If you plan an extended stay, register your passport with the nearest embassy or consulate.

U.S. citizens seeking information about documents, formalities and travel abroad should request the booklet *Your Trip Abroad* (US$1.25) from the **Superintendent of Documents** (see Useful Publications, p. 4).

ENTRANCE REQUIREMENTS

For most nationalities, all that is required for entrance into Ecuador is a **passport** valid through the duration of your planned visit, and **proof of financial independence.** This can be in the form of a plane ticket to leave Ecuador, or evidence that you have sufficient funds (US$20 per day) to support yourself in the form of travelers checks, cash, or a credit card. Tourists are allowed to stay for a total of **90 days** in a one-year period.

Depending on your nationality, the duration of your stay, and what you will be doing in Ecuador, you may need an additional **visa.** Citizens of China, Costa Rica, Cuba, France, Guatemala, Honduras, North and South Korea, and Vietnam must acquire a 12-X visa from an Ecuadorian embassy or consulate before they will be allowed to enter Ecuador. Tourists who wish to stay longer than 90 days must acquire a 12-IX visa, good for up to **six months** in a one-year period, from an Ecuadorian embassy or consulate before they arrive. Those planning to work or study for longer than 90 days in Ecuador must also acquire a visa. To obtain a **study visa,** you must provide a letter of acceptance from the institution at which you are planning to study; for a **work visa** you must provide an employment contract.

For more information, consult the nearest Ecuadorian consulate or embassy. You may also consult *Foreign Entry Requirements* (US$0.50) published by the **Consumer Information Center,** Pueblo, CO 81009 (tel. (719) 948-3334), or contact the **Center for International Business and Travel (CIBT),** 25 West 43rd St. #1420, New York, NY 10036 (tel. (800) 925-2428 or (212) 575-2811 from NYC). This organization secures visas for travel to and from all countries. The service charge varies.

Customs when entering Ecuador is generally a pretty laid-back process. Officials are more likely to stop Ecuadorian nationals returning with loads of foreign merchandise than a backpacking *gringo.* Nevertheless, they do sometimes search bags and you don't want to be busted, so here are your allowances: you may not enter or leave the country with firearms, ammunition, narcotics, fresh meat or live plants or animals. You may bring in 300 cigarettes, 50 cigars, and a bottle of liquor tax-free.

EMBASSIES AND CONSULATES

For most matters you will want to contact the nearest consulate. Embassies can provide you with the address and phone number of the consulate nearest you.

United States Embassy of Ecuador, 2535 15th St. N.W., Washington, D.C. 20009 (tel. (202) 234-7200; fax 667-3482).

Canada Embassy of Ecuador, 50 O'Conor St., Suite 1311, Ottawa, Ontario K1P 6L2 (tel. (613) 563 8206; fax 235 5776).

United Kingdom Embassy of Ecuador, Flat 3B, 3 Hans Crescent, Knightsbridge, London, SW1X OLS, United Kingdom (tel. (071) 584 8084; fax 823 9701).

Ireland The nearest embassy is in London, but there is a consulate in **Dublin**: 27 Library Road, Dun Laoghaire, CO, Dublin (tel. (01) 280 5917).

Australia The nearest embassy is in Tokyo, but there are consulates. In **Melbourne:** 2nd Floor, 405 Burk St., Melbourne 3000, Victoria (tel. (03) 600 0866; fax 600

0414). In **Sydney:** 388 George St., Ste. 1702 A, American Express Tower, N.S. 2000, Sydney (tel. (02) 223 6266; fax 223 0041).

New Zealand The embassy is in Tokyo, but there is a consulate in **Auckland:** Ferry Building, 2nd Floor, Quay St., Auckland (tel. (09) 309 0229; fax 303 2931).

PASSPORTS

Before you leave, photocopy the page of your passport that contains your photograph and identifying information, especially your passport number. Carry this photocopy in a safe place apart from your passport, and leave another copy at home. These measures will help prove your citizenship and facilitate the issuing of a new passport if you lose the original document. Consulates also recommend you carry an expired passport or an official copy of your birth certificate in a part of your baggage separate from other documents. You can request a duplicate birth certificate from the Bureau of Vital Records and Statistics in your state or province of birth.

If you do lose your passport, it may take weeks to process a replacement, and your new one may be valid only for a limited time. In addition, any visas stamped in your old passport will be irretrievably lost. If this happens, immediately notify the local police and the nearest embassy or consulate of your home government (see Embassies and Consulates, p. 28). To expedite its replacement, you will need to know all information previously recorded and show identification and proof of citizenship. In an emergency, ask for immediate temporary traveling papers that will permit you to re-enter your home country.

United States citizens may apply for a passport at any federal or state **courthouse** or **post office** authorized to accept passport applications, or at a **U.S. Passport Agency,** located in Boston, Chicago, Honolulu, Houston, Los Angeles, Miami, New Orleans, New York, Philadelphia, San Francisco, Seattle, Stamford, CT, or Washington, D.C. Refer to the "U.S. Government, State Department" section of the telephone directory, or call your local post office for addresses. Parents must apply in person for children under age 13. You must apply in person if this is your first passport, if you're under 18, or if your passport is more than 12 years old or was issued before your 18th birthday. Various materials outlined on the passport application must be submitted with it. The cost is US$65 (under 18 US$40). You can **renew** your passport by mail or in person for US$55. Processing takes two to four weeks. Passport agencies offer **rush service** for a surcharge of US$30, with proof that you're departing within 10 working days (e.g. an airplane ticket or itinerary). Abroad, a U.S. embassy or consulate can usually issue a new passport, given proof of citizenship. For more info, contact the U.S. Passport Information's **24-hour recorded message** (tel. (202) 647-0518).

Canadian citizens can obtain application forms in English and French at all **passport offices, post offices,** and most **travel agencies.** You may apply in person at any regional Passport Offices across Canada. Canadian citizens residing abroad should contact the nearest Canadian embassy or consulate. The application form describes in English and French all materials that must be submitted to obtain a passport. Processing takes five business days for in-person applications and three weeks for mailed ones. Children under 16 may be included on a parent's passport, though some countries require children to carry their own passports. If a passport is lost abroad, Canadians must be able to prove citizenship with another document. For additional info, call (800) 567-6868 (24hr.; from Canada only) or call the Passport Office at (819) 994-3500. In Metro Toronto, call (416) 973-3251. Montréalers should dial (514) 283-2152. Refer to the booklet *Bon Voyage, But ...* for further help and a list of Canadian embassies and consulates abroad (available free from any passport office).

United Kingdom citizens, U.K. Dependent Territories citizens, U.K. nationals (overseas), and U.K. overseas citizens may apply for a **full passport.** Apply in person or by mail to a passport office, located in London, Liverpool, Newport, Peterborough, Glasgow, or Belfast. The fee is UK£18. Children under 16 may be included on a parent's passport. Processing by mail takes four to six weeks. The London office offers same-day, walk-in rush service; arrive early.

Irish citizens can apply for a passport by mail to either the Department of Foreign Affairs, Passport Office, Setanta Centre, Molesworth St., Dublin 2 (tel. (01) 671 16 33), or the Passport Office, 1A South Mall, Cork (tel. (021) 627 25 25). Obtain an application at a local Garda station or request one from a passport office. The new Passport Express Service offers a two week turn-around and is available through post offices for an extra IR£3. Passports cost IR£45 and are valid for 10 years. Citizens under 18 or over 65 can request a three-year passport that costs IR£10.

Australian citizens must apply for a passport in person at a post office, a passport office, or an Australian diplomatic mission overseas. Passport offices are located in Adelaide, Brisbane, Canberra City, Darwin, Hobart, Melbourne, Newcastle, Perth, and Sydney. Parent may file applications for children under 18. Application fees are adjusted frequently. For more info, call toll-free (in Australia) 13 12 32.

New Zealand citizens can obtain application forms for passports from travel agents and Department of Internal Affairs Link Centres in New Zealand, and overseas from New Zealand embassies, high commissions, and consulates. Completed applications may be lodged at Link Centres and at overseas posts, or forwarded to the Passport Office, PO Box 10-526, Wellington, New Zealand. Processing time is 10 working days from receipt of a correctly completed application. An urgent passport service is also available. The application fee for an adult passport is NZ$80 in New Zealand, and NZ$130 overseas for applications lodged under the standard service.

South African citizens can apply for a passport at any Home Affairs Office. Two photos, either a birth certificate or an identity book, and a US$12 fee must accompany a completed application. South African passports remain valid for 10 years. For information, contact the nearest Department of Home Affairs Office.

CUSTOMS: GOING HOME

Upon returning home, you must declare all articles you acquired abroad and must pay a duty on the value of those articles that exceed the allowance established by your country's customs. Goods purchased at duty-free shops abroad are not exempt from duty or sales tax at your point of return; you must declare these items as well.

United States Citizens returning home may bring US$400 worth of accompanying goods duty-free and must pay a 10% tax on the next US$1000. Goods are considered duty-free if they are for personal or household use (this includes gifts) and cannot include more than 200 cigarettes (1 carton), and 1L of alcohol. You must be over 21 to bring liquor into the U.S. If you mail home personal goods of U.S. origin, you can avoid duty charges by marking the package "American goods returned." For more information, consult the brochure *Know Before You Go,* available from the U.S. Customs Service, Box 7407, Washington D.C. 20044 (tel. (202) 927-6724).

Canada Citizens who remain abroad for at least one week may bring back up to CDN$500 worth of goods duty-free once per calendar year. Citizens of legal age (which varies by province) may import in-person up to 200 cigarettes, and 1.14L wine or alcohol. For more information, write to Canadian Customs, 2265 St. Laurent Blvd., Ottawa, Ontario K1G 4K3 (tel. (613) 993-0534).

Britain Citizens returning to the U.K. must declare any goods in excess of the following allowances: 200 cigarettes, 1L strong liqueurs over 22% volume or 2L other liqueurs, and UK£136 worth of all other goods including gifts. You must be over 17 to import liquor or tobacco. For more info about U.K. customs, contact Her Majesty's

Customs and Excise, Custom House, Nettleton Road, Heathrow Airport, Hounslow, Middlesex TW6 2LA (tel. (0181) 910-3744; fax 910-3765).

Ireland Citizens must declare everything in excess of IR£34 (IR£17 per traveler under 15 years of age) above the following allowances: 200 cigarettes, 1L liquor or 2L wine. For more information, contact The Revenue Commissioners, Dublin Castle (tel. (01) 679 27 77; fax 671 20 21; e-mail taxes@ior.ie; http:\\www.revenue.ie) or The Collector of Customs and Excise, The Custom House, Dublin 1.

Australia Citizens may import AUS$400 (under 18 AUS$200) of goods duty-free, including 1.125L alcohol and 250 cigarettes. You must be over 18 to import either of these. For information, contact the Regional Director, Australian Customs Service, GPO Box 8, Sydney NSW 2001(tel. (02) 2132000; fax 2134000).

New Zealand Citizens may bring home up to NZ$700 worth of duty-free goods intended for personal use or gifts, including not more than 200 cigarettes (1 carton), 4.5L of beer or wine, and 1.125L of liquor. Travelers under 17 may not import tobacco or alcohol. For more information, consult the *New Zealand Customs Guide for Travelers,* available from customs offices, or contact New Zealand Customs, 50 Anzac Ave., Box 29, Auckland (tel. (09) 377 35 20; fax 309 29 78).

South Africa Citizens can address their inquiries to the Commissioner for Customs and Excise, Private Bag X47, Pretoria 0001. South Africans in the U.S. should contact the Embassy of South Africa, 3051 Massachusetts Ave., NW, Washington, D.C. 20008 (tel. (202) 232-4400; fax 244-9417), or the South African Home Annex, 3201 New Mexico Ave. #380, NW, Washington DC 20016 (tel. (202) 966-1650).

YOUTH, STUDENT, AND TEACHER IDENTIFICATION

Though international students do not receive discounts as frequently in Ecuador as in the U.S. or European countries, it is still worth your while to carry identification and flash it whenever you get the opportunity, even if no discount is advertised. Aside from your school's ID card, consider carrying the **International Student Identity Card (ISIC).** It is one of the most widely accepted form of student identification. It also provides accident insurance of up to US$3000 with no daily limit. In addition, cardholders have access to a toll-free Traveler's Assistance hotline whose multilingual staff can provide help in medical, legal, and financial emergencies overseas.

Most student travel offices issue ISICs. The card is valid from September to December of the following year. The fee is US$18. Applicants must be at least 12 years old and degree-seeking students of a secondary or post-secondary school. The US$19 **International Teacher Identity Card (ITIC)** offers similar but limited discounts, as well as medical insurance coverage. For more info on these handy cards consult the organization's new web site (http:\\www.istc.org).

Money Matters

All prices in this book are listed in sucres, except where payment is expected in US dollars. Prices were acccurate in the summer of 1996, but due to the high inflation rates and frequent devaluation of the sucre they may have risen since.

US$1 = 3205 sucres	**1000 sucres = US$0.31**
CDN$1 = 2333 sucres	**1000 sucres= CDN$0.43**
UK£1 = 4966 sucres	**1000 sucres = UK£0.20**
IR£1 = 5160 sucres	**1000 sucres = IR£0.19**
AUS$1 = 2495 sucres	**1000 sucres = AUS$0.40**
NZ$1 = 2193 sucres	**1000 sucres = NZ$0.46**
SARand = 707 sucres	**1000 sucres = SARand$1.41**

CURRENCY AND EXCHANGE

The cost of living in Ecuador is far lower than that in most western countries. Meals can cost from $1-$4, a night's lodging from $2-$5, and transportation is on the whole dirt cheap. Don't sacrifice your health or safety for a cheaper tab, though. No matter how low your budget, if you plan to travel for more than a couple of days, you will need to keep handy a larger amount of cash than usual. Carrying it around with you, even in a money belt, is risky; personal checks from home will usually not be acceptable no matter how many forms of identification you have.

In Ecuador, as in most Latin American countries, U.S. currency is widely accepted, and in many cases even preferred over the local currency of sucres. Other foreign currency, such as New Zealand or Australian dollars, is difficult or impossible to change. Upon arrival it is a good idea to have U.S. dollars with you to use until you can get your hands on some of those sweet sucres. Despite the versatility of U.S. dollars, it is good to avoid using them when you can. Throwing dollars around to gain preferential treatment is offensive and can attract theft. Also, it labels you as a foreigner and invites many locals to jack up prices.

When changing money, observe commission rates closely and check newspapers to get the standard rate of exchange. Banks generally have the best rates, but this is by no means a hard and fast rule; sometimes tourist offices or exchange kiosks have the best rates. Shop around for a few rates before exchanging money. Since you lose money with every transaction, convert in large sums (unless the currency is depreciating rapidly), but don't convert more than you need, because it may be difficult to change it back to your home currency.

If you are using traveler's checks or bills, be sure to carry some in small denominations (US$50 or less), especially for times when you are forced to exchange money at disadvantageous rates. However, it is a good idea to carry a range of denominations, since charges are sometimes levied per check cashed.

TRAVELER'S CHECKS

Traveler's checks are one of the safest means of carrying funds since they can be refunded in case of loss or theft. When cashing your checks in Ecuador, keep in mind that in small towns, traveler's checks are less readily accepted than in cities with large tourist industries. However, even if the banks in a town will not cash your checks, you may be able to find a hotel or supermarket that will. It is good to carry a small reserve of dollars in case of emergencies.

Several agencies and many banks sell traveler's checks, usually for face value plus a 1% commission. (Members of the American Automobile Association can get American Express checks commission-free through AAA.) American Express and Visa are the most widely recognized. If you're ordering your checks, do so well in advance, especially if large sums are being requested. Remember that it will be far easier to cash your traveler's checks in Ecuador if you purchase them in U.S. currency.

Each agency provides refunds if your checks are lost or stolen, and many provide additional services. (Note that you may need a police report verifying the loss or theft.) Inquire about toll-free refund hotlines, emergency message relay services, and stolen credit card assistance when you purchase your checks.

Keep your check receipts separate from your checks and store them in a safe place or with a traveling companion; record check numbers when you cash them and leave a list of check numbers with someone at home; and ask for a list of refund centers when you buy your checks. American Express and Bank of America have over 40,000 centers worldwide. Be sure never to countersign your checks until you're prepared to cash them. Also, bring your passport with you when you plan to use the checks.

American Express: In the **U.S.** and **Canada,** call (800) 221-7282; in the **U.K.** tel. (0800) 52 13 13; in **Australia** tel. (008) 25 19 02; in **New Zealand** tel. (0800) 44 10 68. Elsewhere, call U.S. collect (801) 964-6665. American Express traveler's checks are now available in 11 currencies, but U.S. dollars will be the most useful in Ecuador. They are widely recognized worldwide and the easiest to replace if lost or stolen. Checks can be purchased for a small fee at American Express Travel Service Offices, banks, and American Automobile Association offices (AAA members can buy the checks commission-free). Card-holders can purchase checks at American Express Dispensers, at Travel Service Offices, at airports and by ordering them via phone (tel. (800) ORDER-TC/673-3782). American Express offices cash their checks commission-free, although they often offer slightly worse rates than banks.

Citicorp: Call (800) 645-6556 in the **U.S.** and **Canada;** in the **U.K.** tel. (44) 181 297 4781; from elsewhere, call U.S. collect (813) 623-1709. Sells both Citicorp and Citicorp Visa traveler's checks. Commission is 1-2%. Checkholders are automatically enrolled for 45 days in the Travel Assist Program (hotline (800) 250-4377, or U.S. collect (202) 296-8728) providing travelers with English-speaking doctor, lawyer, and interpreter referrals as well as check refund assistance and general travel information. Citicorp's World Courier Service guarantees hand-delivery of traveler's checks when a refund location is not convenient. Call 24hr.

Thomas Cook MasterCard: Call (800) 223-9920 in the U.S. and Canada; elsewhere call U.S. collect (609) 987-7300; from the U.K. call (0800) 622 101 free, or U.K. collect (1733) 502 995, or (44 1733 318 950) collect. Commission 1-2% for purchases. Try buying the checks at a Thomas Cook office for potentially lower commissions. If you cash your checks at a Thomas Cook Office they will not charge commission.

Visa: Call (800) 227-6811 in the U.S.; in the U.K. (0800) 895 492; from anywhere else in the world call (01733 318 949) which is a pay call, but they can reverse the charges. Call any of the above numbers, if you give them your zip code, they will tell you where the closest office to you is to purchase their traveler's checks. Any kind of Visa traveler's check can be reported lost at the Visa number.

CREDIT CARDS

Credit cards are relatively widely accepted in Ecuador. Fancier hotels, restaurants, and shops in cities and bigger towns will accept major credit cards. While this is often not much use to the budget traveler, many banks in cities and bigger towns allow **cash advances** on **MasterCard** and **Visa** credit cards. You can also withdraw money from certain ATMs in bigger cities if you have your credit card's **Personal Identification Number (PIN).** Ask your credit card company to assign you a PIN before you leave if you wish to use this service. Cash advances can be a bargain because credit card companies get the wholesale exchange rate, which is generally 5% better than the retail rate used by banks, and other currency exchange establishments.

Credit cards are also invaluable in an emergency—an unexpected hospital bill, ticket home, or loss of traveler's checks—which may leave you temporarily without other resources. Furthermore, credit cards offer an array of other services, from insurance to emergency assistance—these depend completely, however, on the issuer. Some even cover car rental collision insurance.

American Express (tel. (800) CASH-NOW/528-4800) has a hefty annual fee (US$55), but offers a number of services. AmEx cardholders can cash **personal checks** at AmEx offices abroad, up to US$1000 worth every 21 days, with no service charge and no interest. U.S. Assist, a 24-hour hotline offering medical and legal assistance in emergencies, is also available; call U.S. collect (301) 214-8228. Cardholders can also take advantage of the American Express Travel Service; benefits include assistance in changing reservations; sending mailgrams and international cables; and **holding your mail** at one of the more than 1700 AmEx offices around the world.

MasterCard (tel. (800) 999-0454) and **Visa** (tel. (800) 336-8472) are issued in cooperation with individual banks and some other organizations.

GETTING MONEY FROM HOME

Money can also be wired to **Western Union** (tel. (800) 325-6000) offices in Quito and Guayaquil. The rates for sending cash from a local U.S. office is US$10 cheaper than charging your credit card over the phone. The money is usually available for the recipient within an hour.

In emergencies, another way to send money abroad in cash is via **Federal Express.** While this is very illegal and involves an element of risk, it is reasonably reliable, avoids transmission fees and taxes, and is doable with minimum fuss. It requires that you remain at a set address for a while to wait for the money's arrival.

BARGAINING, TIPPING, AND TAXES

In some places it's okay to **bargain,** and a little practice at playing "the game" can make it well worth the effort. Bargaining for rooms works best in the low season, and it's not hard to get prices lowered at markets or from street vendors (though vendors at markets are most certainly going to be better at bargaining than you are). The basic technique is to expect the first offered price to be higher than what the seller actually wants; pick a lower price, and marvel at the magic of compromise.

As far as **tipping** goes, relatively affluent foreigners are generally expected to tip. At fancier restaurants a 10% tip is included on the bill. When it is not included, consider leaving that much anyway. Tips may also be expected for other services, such as guided tours or maid service; in many cases, these people count on a small bonus.

It will come as no surprise that the Ecuadorian government takes its share of tourist dollars as well. The more fancy restaurants, hotels, and shops of Ecuador's cities and bigger towns charge a **10% sales tax,** which you should expect to appear on the bill. The real whammy hits you when you try to leave the country (they don't want you to be bitter until you're on your way); there is a US$25 **airport/departure tax.**

Safety and Security

PERSONAL SAFETY

Tourists are particularly vulnerable to crime for two reasons: they often carry large amounts of cash and they are not as street savvy as locals. To avoid such unwanted attention, try to **blend in** as much as possible. Respecting local customs (in many cases, this means dressing more conservatively) can often placate would-be hecklers. The gawking camera-toter is a more obvious target than the low-profile local look-alike. Walking directly into a café or shop to check your map beats checking it on a street corner. Look over your map before leaving the hotel room so that you can act as if you know where you are going. Muggings are more often impromptu than planned. Walking with nervous, over-the-shoulder glances can be a tip that you have something valuable to protect. An obviously bewildered bodybuilder is more likely to be harassed than a stern and confident 98-pound weakling.

When exploring a new **city,** extra vigilance may be wise, but no city should force you to turn precautions into panic. When you get to a place where you'll be spending some time, find out about unsafe areas from tourist information, from the manager of your hotel or hostel, or from a local whom you trust. Especially if you are traveling alone, be sure that someone at home knows your itinerary. Never say that you're traveling alone. Both men and women may want to carry a small **whistle** to scare off attackers or attract attention, and it's not a bad idea to jot down the number of the police if you'll be in town for a couple days.

When walking at **night,** you should turn day-time precautions into mandates. Stick to busy well-lit streets and avoid dark alleyways. Do not attempt to cross through parks, parking lots, or any other large and deserted areas. A blissfully isolated beach can become a treacherous nightmare as soon as night falls. Whenever possible, *Let's Go* warns of unsafe neighborhoods and areas, but only your eyes can tell you for sure if you've wandered into one; buildings in disrepair, vacant lots, and general desertion are all bad signs. Pay attention to the neighborhood that surrounds you. A district can change character drastically in the course of a single block. Simply being aware of the flow of people can tell you a great deal about the relative safety of the area. Many notoriously dangerous districts have safe sections; look for children playing, women walking in the open, and other signs of an active community. If you feel uncomfortable, leave as quickly and directly as you can, but don't allow your fear of the new to close off whole worlds to you. Careful, persistent exploration will build confidence and make your stay in an area that much more rewarding.

There is no sure-fire set of precautions that will protect you from all of the situations you might encounter when you travel. A good self-defense course will give you more concrete ways to react to different types of aggression, but it might cost you more money than your trip. **Model Mugging,** a national organization with offices in several major cities, teaches a very effective, comprehensive course on self-defense. Contact Lynn S. Auerbach on the East Coast (tel. 617-232-7900), Alice Tibits in the Midwest (tel. 612-645-6189), and Cori Couture on the West Coast (tel. 415-592-7300). Course prices vary from $400-500. Women's and men's courses are offered. Community colleges often offer courses at more affordable prices.

For official **United States Department of State** travel advisories, including crime and security updates, call their 24-hour hotline at (202) 647-5225. To order publications, including a pamphlet entitled *A Safe Trip Abroad,* write to Superintendent of Documents (see Useful Publications, p. 4).

FINANCIAL SECURITY

Many cities and towns in Ecuador have more than their share of hustlers. Those who speak some English will try to use this to their advantage. Fast-talking men frequently confront tourists, strike up a conversation, and soon begin demanding money. Con artists and hustlers often work in groups as well, and children, unfortunately, are among the most effective at the game. These hucksters use tricks that are innumerable and adaptable. Be aware of certain classics: sob stories that require money, rolls of bills "found" on the street, mustard spilled (or saliva spit) onto your shoulder distracting you for enough time to snatch your bag. You should give strangers the cold shoulder if they seem overly effusive or if they offer to accompany you. It's not unusual for tourists to be called racist if they refuse to give money, or if they are cool to advances. Ignore the epithets and head into a bank or restaurant for safety. Contact the police if a hustler is particularly insistent or aggressive.

Don't put money in a wallet in your back pocket. Never count your money in public and carry as little as possible. If you carry a purse, buy a sturdy one with a secure clasp, and carry it crosswise on the side, away from the street with the clasp against you. As far as packs are concerned, buy some small combination padlocks that slip through the two zippers, securing the pack shut. A **money belt** is the best way to carry cash; you can buy one at most camping supply stores. The best combination of convenience and invulnerability is the nylon, zippered pouch with belt that should sit inside the waist of your pants or skirt. A **neck pouch** is equally safe, although far less accessible. Refrain from pulling out your neck pouch in public; if you must, be very discreet. Avoid keeping anything precious in a fanny-pack (even if it's worn on your stomach): your valuables will be highly visible and easy to steal. In city crowds, in markets, and especially on public transportation, pick-pockets are amazingly deft at their craft. Making **photocopies** of important documents will allow you to recover them in case they are lost or filched. Carry one copy separate from the documents and leave another copy at home. Keep some money separate from the rest to use in an emergency or in case of theft.

Label every piece of luggage both inside and out. Be particularly watchful of your belongings on **buses** (for example, carry your backpack in front of you where you can see it), don't check baggage if you can help it, and don't trust anyone to "watch your bag for a second." **Never leave your belongings unattended;** even the most demure-looking hostel may be a den of thieves. If you feel unsafe, look for places with either a curfew or a night attendant. When possible, keep expensive jewelry, valuables, and anything you couldn't bear to part with at home. Keep your valuables on your person if you're staying in low-budget hotels where someone else may have a passkey, and always in dormitory-style surroundings.

DRUGS AND ALCOHOL

Drinking in any part of Latin America is not for amateurs; non-*gringo* bars are often strongholds of *machismo.* When someone calls you *amigo* and orders you a beer, bow out quickly unless you want to match him glass for glass in a challenge potentially lasting several days.

Drugs and traveling are not a good combination. If you carry **prescription drugs** while you travel, have a copy of the prescriptions themselves readily accessible at country borders. As far as **illegal drugs** are concerned—marijuana, cocaine, and hallucinogenic drugs are all around, but don't be dopey. Drug users and carriers are never treated leniently, so expect the worst. Ecuadorian jails are probably worse than your worst hostel nightmare, but you don't want to find out. Similarly, don't bring drugs back into the U.S.; customs agents and their perceptive K-9s are not to be taken lightly. For the free pamphlet *Travel Warning on Drugs Abroad,* send a self-addressed, stamped envelope to the Bureau of Consular Affairs, Public Affairs #5807, Dept. of State, Washington, D.C. 20520 (tel. (202) 647-1488).

Health

Common sense is the simplest prescription for good health while you travel: eat well, drink and sleep enough, and don't overexert yourself. Travelers complain most often about their **feet** and their **guts,** so take precautionary measures. Drinking lots of fluids can often prevent dehydration and constipation, and wearing sturdy shoes and clean socks, and using talcum powder can help keep your feet dry.

BEFORE YOU GO

Though no amount of planning can guarantee an accident-free trip, preparation can help minimize the likelihood of contracting a disease and maximize the chances of receiving effective health-care in the event of an emergency. For minor health problems, bring a compact **first-aid kit.** It should include bandages, aspirin, or another type of pain killer, antibiotic cream, a thermometer, a Swiss Army knife with tweezers, moleskin, a decongestant for colds, a motion sickness remedy, medicine for diarrhea or stomach problems, sunscreen, insect repellent, and burn ointment.

In your passport, write the names of any people you wish to be contacted in case of a medical emergency, and also list any allergies or medical conditions you would want doctors to be aware of. If you wear glasses or contact lenses, carry an extra prescription and pair of glasses or arrange to have your doctor or a family member send a replacement pair in emergencies. Allergy sufferers should find out if their conditions are likely to be aggravated in the regions they plan to visit, and obtain a full supply of any necessary medication before the trip, since matching a prescription to a foreign equivalent is not always easy, safe, or possible. Carry up-to-date, legible prescriptions or a statement from your doctor, especially if you use insulin, a syringe, or a narcotic. While traveling, keep all medication in carry-on luggage.

Those with medical conditions (e.g. diabetes, allergies to antibiotics, epilepsy, etc.) may want to obtain a stainless steel **Medic Alert** identification tag (US$35 the first year, and US$15 annually thereafter), which identifies the disease and gives a 24-hour collect-call information number. Contact Medic Alert at (800) 825-3785.

If you are concerned about being able to access medical support while traveling, contact one of the following two services. **Global Emergency Medical Services (GEMS)** provides 24-hour international medical assistance and support, including access to medical records, and a worldwide network of screened, credentialed English-speaking doctors and hospitals. For more information call (800) 860-1111, fax (770) 475-0058. The **International Association for Medical Assistance to Travelers (IAMAT)** offers a membership ID card; a directory of English-speaking doctors around the world; and detailed charts on immunization requirements, various tropical diseases, climate, and sanitation. Membership is free, though donations are appreciated and used for further research. Contact chapters in the **U.S.** (tel. (716) 754-

4883; fax (519) 836-3412; e-mail iamat@sentex.net; http://www.sentex.net/iamat), **Canada** at (tel. (519) 836-0102) or (tel. (416) 652-0137; fax (519) 836-3412), or **New Zealand,** P.O. Box 5049, Christchurch 5.

VACCINATIONS AND OTHER DISEASE PREVENTION

You can minimize the chances of contracting a disease while traveling by taking a few precautionary measures. Take a look at your **immunization** records before you go to make sure your "childhood" vaccines (e.g. measles, mumps, tetanus) are up to date. Hepatitis A vaccine and/or an Immune Globulin injection (IG) is recommended for travelers to Ecuador. If you will be spending more than four weeks there, you should consider the typhoid vaccine as well. Check with a doctor for advice and recommendations for immunization, and try to remember that no matter how bad the needles are, they're better than the diseases they prevent.

Taking precautions while on the road is a good idea as well. It is wise to avoid contact with animals. Often dogs are not given shots, so that sweet-faced pooch at your feet might very well be disease-ridden. **Rabies** is a concern in Ecuador, so if you are bitten be sure to clean your wound thoroughly and seek medical help immediately to find out whether you need treatment.

Many diseases are transmitted by **insects**—mainly mosquitoes, fleas, ticks, and lice. Insect bites are always annoying, but they can also be dangerous and sometimes life-threatening. Be aware of insects in wet or forested areas, while hiking, and especially while camping. **Mosquitoes** are most active from dusk to dawn. Wear long pants and long sleeves (fabric need not be thick or warm; tropic-weight cottons can keep you comfortable in the heat), and buy a bednet for camping. Wear shoes and socks, and tuck long pants into socks. Use insect repellents; DEET can be bought in spray or liquid form, but use it sparingly, especially on children. Soak or spray your gear with permethrin, which is licensed in the U.S. for use on clothing. Natural repellents can also be useful: taking vitamin B-12 or garlic pills regularly can eventually make you smelly to insects. Still, be sure to supplement your vitamins with repellent. Calamine lotion or topical cortisones (like Cortaid©) may stop insect bites from itching, as can a bath with a half-cup of baking soda or oatmeal.

Malaria is transmitted by Anopheles mosquitoes, which bite during the night. These pesky bloodsuckers are present in the coastal and Oriente regions of Ecuador. Preliminary symptoms include fever, chills, aches, and fatigue. Since early stages resemble the flu, you should see a doctor for any flu-like sickness that occurs after travel in a risk area. Treatment drugs are available, but left untreated, malaria can cause anemia, kidney failure, coma, and death. Malaria poses an especially serious threat to pregnant women and their fetuses. The risk is greatest in rural areas. If hiking or staying overnight in certain areas (whether camping or not), you may want to take weekly anti-malarial drugs. Contact your doctor for a prescription.

Other insect diseases that are more rare include the following: **Filariasis** is a round worm infestation transmitted by mosquitoes. Infection causes enlargement (elephantiasis) of extremities; there is no vaccine. **Leishmaniasis** is a parasite transmitted by sand flies. Common symptoms are fever, weakness, and a swollen spleen. There is a treatment, but no vaccine.

For more information on vaccinations and region-specific health data, try the **United States Centers for Disease Control and Prevention,** which maintains an international travelers' hotline (tel. (404) 332-4559; fax 332-4565; http://www.cdc.gov). The CDC publishes the booklet *Health Information for International Travelers* (US$14), an annual global rundown of disease, immunization, and general health advice, including risks in particular countries.

FOOD- AND WATER-BORNE DISEASES

To ensure that your food is safe, make sure that everything is cooked properly (deep-fried is good, the fresher the grease the better), and be positive the water you drink is

The Rise, Fall, and Spiritual Renaissance of Dengue Fever

Dengue fever, also called "breakbone fever," is painful, relatively easy to catch, and spreading fast. It is present wherever its carriers swarm, the dread diurnal mosquitos *Aedes aegypti* and *Aedes albopictus*, and these little guys give it a potential range of over two billion human targets. Breakbone can provoke a wide range of symptoms, and its early stages are easily confused with influenza, measles, typhoid, and a slew of other fever-inducing illnesses. "Classic" dengue is characterized by an abrupt onset of high fever after an incubation period of three to 15 days. Victims often experience one of more of the following: lower back pain, headaches, malaise, severe pain in the bones or joints, nausea, vomiting, diarrhea, blurred vision, and bleeding of the gums—classic! In severe cases of dengue hemorrhagic fever (DHF), patients can also suffer a large, painful rash, circulatory failure, and system-wide bleeding: these advanced cases can be fatal.

Although dengue has been breaking out and busting ass since at least the late 18th century, DHF did not emerge until the 1950s, in Southeast Asia. It was first spotted in the New World in 1975, and it has since spread to at least 12 countries in South and Central America, including Ecuador. Attempts to create a vaccine have not yet been successful and epidemiologists expect the disease to spread. DHF seems ripe to rip through Ecuador sometime soon.

If you have been in possible contact with mosquitoes anywhere in the Americas and experience dengue-like symptoms, seek medical assistance as soon as possible. Because of the lengthy incubation period, it is possible to develop symptoms up to two weeks after your travels. Until you can get to a hospital, treat the dengue like an ordinary fever, but be sure to use acetominophen and not aspirin. But best get yourself to a hospital and avoid mosquitoes in the first place—it is discourteous to spread dengue to your hometown.

clean. Don't order meat "rare," and eggs should be thoroughly cooked, not served sunny-side up.

Cholera is an intestinal disease caused by a bacteria found in contaminated food; the disease has recently reached epidemic proportions in parts of South America, including Ecuador. The first severe symptoms of cholera are lots of watery diarrhea, dehydration, vomiting, and muscle cramps. Untreated, cholera can be fatal. Antibiotics are available, but the most important treatment is rehydration. Consider getting a (50% effective) vaccine if you have stomach problems (e.g. ulcers), or if you will be camping a good deal or living where water is not always reliable.

Typhoid Fever is more of a concern to those visiting villages and rural areas of Ecuador. While mostly transmitted through contaminated food and water, it may also be acquired by direct contact with another person. Symptoms include fever, headaches, fatigue, loss of appetite, and constipation; antibiotics treat typhoid fever. The Center for Disease Control and Prevention recommends vaccinations (70-90% effective) for those going off the "usual tourist itineraries," that is, those hiking, camping, and staying in small cities or rural areas.

Parasites (tapeworms, etc.) also hide in unsafe water and food. *Giardia,* for example, can be acquired by drinking untreated water from streams or lakes all over the world. It can stay with you for years. Symptoms of parasitic infections in general include swollen glands or lymph nodes, fever, rashes or itchiness, digestive problems, eye problems, and anemia. Boil your water, wear shoes, avoid bugs, and eat only cooked food.

Hepatitis A (distinct from B and C) is a risk to all travelers, including those visiting Ecuador. It is a viral infection of the liver acquired primarily through contaminated water, ice, shellfish, or unpeeled fruits, and vegetables (as well as from sexual contact). Symptoms include fatigue, fever, loss of appetite, nausea, dark urine, jaundice, vomiting, aches and pains, and light stools. CDC recommends vaccination, or an injection of immune globulin (IG; formerly called Gamma Globulin). Risk is highest in rural areas and the countryside, but is also present in urban areas.

Hepatitis B is a viral infection of the liver transmitted by sharing needles, having unprotected sex, or coming into direct contact with an infected person's lesioned skin. If you think you may be sexually active while traveling or if you are working or living in rural areas, you are typically advised to get the vaccination for Hepatitis B. Vaccination should begin six months before traveling.

Hepatitis C is like Hepatitis B, but the methods of transmission are different. At risk are intravenous drug users, those with occupational exposure to blood, hemodialysis patients, or recipients of a blood transfusion; doctors aren't sure if you can get it through sexual contact.

TRAVELER'S DIARRHEA

Traveler's diarrhea, also known as *turista,* is the biggest health risk for visitors to Ecuador. It is the dastardly consequence of consuming contaminated food and water. It often lasts two or three days; symptoms include cramps, nausea, vomiting, chills, and a fever as high as 103°F (39°C). If the nasties hit you, have quick-energy, non-sugary foods with protein and carbohydrates to keep your strength up. Over-the-counter remedies (such as Pepto-Bismol© or Immodium©) may counteract the symptoms, but they can complicate serious infections; avoid anti-diarrheals if you suspect you have been exposed to contaminated food or water; they put you at risk for other diseases. The most dangerous side effect of diarrhea is dehydration; the simplest and most effective anti-dehydration formula is eight oz. of (clean) water with ½ tsp. of sugar or honey and a pinch of salt. Down several of these mixtures each day, rest, and wait for the disease to run its course. If you develop a fever, or your symptoms don't go away after four or five days, consult a doctor.

To avoid *turista,* **never drink unbottled water;** ask for *agua purificada* in restaurants and hotels. To purify your own water, bring it to a rolling boil (simmering isn't enough), or treat it with iodine drops or tablets. Don't be fooled by the clever disguise of impure water—the ice-cube. Stay away from salads—uncooked vegetables (including lettuce and coleslaw) are a great way to get *turista.* Other culprits are raw shellfish, unpasteurized milk, and sauces containing raw eggs. Peel all fruits and vegetables, and beware of watermelon, which is often injected with impure water. Watch out for food from markets or street vendors that may have been washed in dirty water or fried in rancid cooking oil. Always wash your hands before eating. A golden rule in Latin America: boil it, peel it, cook it, or forget it, but don't get so paranoid about the water that you get dehydrated.

HOT, COLD, AND HIGH

Equatorial heat is no small concern. Common sense goes a long way toward preventing **heat exhaustion:** relax in hot weather, drink lots of non-alcoholic fluids, and lie down inside if you feel awful. Continuous heat stress can eventually lead to **heatstroke,** characterized by rising body temperature, severe headache, and cessation of sweating. Wear a hat, sunglasses, and a lightweight long-sleeved shirt to avoid heatstroke. Victims must be cooled off with wet towels and quickly taken to a doctor.

Always drink enough liquids to keep your urine clear. Alcoholic beverages are dehydrating, as are coffee, strong tea, and caffeinated sodas. If you'll be sweating a lot, be sure to eat enough salty food to prevent electrolyte depletion, which causes severe headaches. Less debilitating, but still dangerous, is **sunburn.** If you're prone to sunburn, bring sunscreen with you (it's often more expensive and hard to find when traveling in Ecuador), and apply it liberally and often to avoid burns and risk of skin cancer. If you get sunburned, drink more fluids than usual.

Despite the fact that the country is named for the equator, temperatures can get quite cold high in the Andes. Extreme cold is just as dangerous as heat—overexposure to cold brings the risk of **hypothermia.** Warning signs are easy to detect: body temperature drops rapidly, resulting in the failure to produce body heat. You may shiver, have poor coordination, feel exhausted, have slurred speech, feel sleepy, hallucinate, or suffer amnesia. **Do not let hypothermia victims fall asleep**—their body temperature will drop more, and if they lose consciousness they may die. Seek medical help as soon as possible. To avoid hypothermia, keep dry and stay out of the wind. In wet weather, wool and most synthetics, such as pile, will keep you warm, but most other fabric, especially cotton, will make you colder. Dress in layers, and watch for **frostbite** when the temperature is below freezing. Look for skin that has turned white, waxy, and cold. If you find frostbite, do not rub the skin. Drink warm beverages, get dry, and slowly warm the area with dry fabric or steady body contact. Take serious cases to a doctor as soon as possible.

The extreme variation in altitude in Ecuador means that **altitude sickness** is a risk as well. Travelers to the highlands should avoid exertion during their first day or two, until their bodies have adjusted to the lower level of oxygen in the air. Ignoring this advice can result in symptoms such as headache, nausea, sleeplessness, and shortness of breath, even while resting. It is best treated with rest, deep breathing, and moving to a lower altitude. If the symptoms persist or worsen, or if the victim begins to turn blue, *immediately descend to a lower altitude and proceed to a hospital if necessary.* Those planning to climb some of Ecuador's taller peaks should take a week in the highlands to adjust to the altitude before attempting the climb, and should remember to climb slowly. You should also be careful about alcohol, especially if you're used to U.S. standards for beer—many Ecuadorian brews and liquors pack more punch, and at high altitudes, any alcohol will do you in quickly.

WOMEN'S HEALTH

Women traveling in unsanitary conditions are vulnerable to urinary tract and bladder infections, common and severely uncomfortable bacterial diseases which cause a burning sensation and painful and sometimes frequent urination. Drink tons of vitamin-C-rich juice, plenty of clean water, and urinate frequently, especially right after intercourse. Untreated, these infections can lead to kidney infections, sterility, and even death. If symptoms persist, see a doctor. If you often develop vaginal yeast infections, take along an over-the-counter medicine, as treatments may not be readily available in Ecuador. Women may also be more susceptible to vaginal thrush and cystitis, two treatable but uncomfortable illnesses. Tampons and pads are sometimes hard to find when traveling; certainly your preferred brands may not be available, so it may be advisable to take supplies along. Some women also use diaphragms or cervical caps to temporarily trap menstrual flow. Refer to the *Handbook for Women Travellers* by Maggie and Gemma Moss (published by Piatkus Books) or to the women's health guide *Our Bodies, Our Selves* (published by the Boston Women's Health Collective) for more extensive information specific to women's health on the road.

BIRTH CONTROL

Reliable contraceptive devices may be difficult to find while traveling. Women on the pill should bring enough to allow for possible loss or extended stays and should bring a prescription, since forms of the pill vary a good deal. The sponge is probably too bulky to be worthwhile on the road. If you use a diaphragm, be sure that you have enough contraceptive jelly on hand. Though condoms are available, you might want to bring your favorite national brand with you; availability and quality vary. **Abortion** is illegal in Ecuador, except in cases in which a woman's physical health is threatened by the pregnancy, cases of fetal defects, and cases of rape or incest.

AIDS, HIV, AND STDS

Acquired Immune Deficiency Syndrome (AIDS) is a growing problem around the world. The World Health Organization estimates that there are around 13 million people infected with the HIV virus. Well over 90% of adults newly infected with HIV acquired their infection through heterosexual sex; women now represent 50% of all new HIV infections. The easiest mode of HIV transmission is through direct blood-to-blood contact with an HIV+ person; *never* share intravenous drug, tattooing, or other needles. The most common mode of transmission is sexual intercourse. Health professionals recommend the use of latex condoms; follow the instructions on the packet. Casual contact (including drinking from the same glass or using the same eating utensils as an infected person) is not believed to pose a risk.

For more information on AIDS, call the **U.S. Center for Disease Control's** 24-hour hotline at (800) 342-2437; in Spanish (800) 344-7332 (daily 8am-2am). In Europe, write to the **World Health Organization,** attn: Global Program on AIDS, 20 Avenue Appia, 1211 Geneva 27, Switzerland (tel. (22) 791-2111), for statistical material on AIDS internationally. Or write to the **Bureau of Consular Affairs,** CA/P/PA, Department of State, Washington, D.C. 20520.

Sexually transmitted diseases (STDs) such as gonorrhea, chlamydia, genital warts, syphilis, and herpes are a lot easier to catch than HIV, and can be just as deadly. It's wise to *look* at your partner's genitals before you have sex. If anything looks amiss, that should be a warning signal. During sex, condoms may protect from certain STDs, but oral and even manual contact can lead to transmission.

Insurance

Beware of buying unnecessary travel coverage—your regular policies may well extend to many travel-related accidents. **Medical insurance** (especially university policies) often covers costs incurred abroad, so check with your provider. In addition, your **homeowners' insurance** (or your family's coverage) often covers theft during travel. Homeowners are generally covered against loss of travel documents (passport, plane ticket, railpass, etc.) up to US$500.

ISIC and **ITIC** cards provide US$3000 worth of accident and illness insurance and US$100 daily for up to 60 days of hospitalization. They also offer up to US$1000 for accidental death or dismemberment, up to US$25,000 for injuries due to an airline, and up to US$25,000 for emergency evacuation due to an illness. The cards give access to a toll-free Traveler's Assistance hotline (in the U.S. and Canada call (800) 626-2427; elsewhere call collect to the U.S. (713) 267-2525), whose multilingual staff provides help in emergencies overseas. To supplement ISIC's insurance, **Council** (see Travel Organizations, p. 1) offers the inexpensive Trip-Safe plan with options covering medical treatment and hospitalization, accidents, baggage loss, and charter flights missed due to illness; they and **STA** also offer more comprehensive and expensive policies. **American Express** cardholders receive automatic car rental (required to decline collision insurance) and travel accident insurance on flight purchases made with the card. Call Customer Service at (800) 528-4800.

Remember that insurance companies usually require a copy of the **police report** for thefts, or evidence of having paid medical expenses (doctor's statements, receipts) before they will honor a claim, and may have time limits on filing for reimbursement. Always carry policy numbers and proof of insurance. Check with each insurance carrier for specific restrictions and policies. Most of the carriers listed below have 24-hour hotlines.

The Berkley Group/Carefree Travel Insurance, 100 Garden City Plaza, P.O. Box 9366, Garden City, NY 11530-9366 (tel. (800) 323-3149 or (516) 294-0220; fax (516) 294-1096). Offers two comprehensive packages including coverage for trip cancellation/interruption/delay, accident and sickness, medical problems, baggage loss, bag delay, accidental death and dismemberment, and travel supplier insolvency. Trip cancellation/interruption may be purchased separately for US$5.50 per US$100 of coverage. 24-hr. worldwide emergency assistance hotline.

Globalcare Travel Insurance, 220 Broadway Lynnfield, MA 01940 (tel. (800) 821-2488; fax (617) 592-7720; e-mail global@nebc.mv.com; nebc.mv.com/globalcare). Complete medical, legal, emergency, and travel-related services. On-the-spot payments and special student programs, including benefits for trip cancellation and interruption. GTI waives pre-existing medical conditions with their Globalcare Economy Plan for cruise and travel, and provides coverage for the bankruptcy or default of cruiselines, airlines, or tour operators.

Travel Assistance International, by Worldwide Assistance Services, Inc., 1133 15th St. NW, Ste. 400, Washington, D.C. 20005-2710 (tel. (800) 821-2828 or (202) 828-5894; fax (202) 828-5896; e-mail wassist@aol.com). TAI provides members with a free 24-hr. hotline for emergencies and referrals. Their Per-Trip (starting at US$52) and Frequent Traveler plans (starting at US$226) include medical, travel, and financial insurance; translation; lost document/item assistance.

Travel Insured International, Inc., 52-S Oakland Ave., P.O. Box 280568, East Hartford, CT 06128-0568 (tel. (800) 243-3174; fax (203) 528-8005). Insurance against accident, baggage loss, sickness, trip cancellation and interruption, travel delay, and default. Also covers emergency medical evacuation and automatic flight insurance.

Alternatives to Tourism

STUDY

Many students come to Ecuador to learn Spanish from one of the language schools around the country. Prices and programs vary, but they usually cost around US$200 a week and often include 4-7 hours daily of instruction, a homestay with a local family, and weekly excursions to surrounding cultural and ecological sites. In Quito, these schools are as abundant as shoeshiners, and sifting through the available options can be a daunting task. The South American Explorer's Club can help narrow down the options. The resources listed below can also be of help. Arrangements can be made before leaving your home country or after you arrive in Ecuador.

Council sponsors over 40 study abroad programs throughout the world. Contact them for more information (see Travel Organizations, p. 1). In addition to these schools, American universities and other more global organizations have different academic programs in Ecuador. Local libraries and bookstores can be helpful sources for current information on study abroad. The Internet has a study abroad website at **http://www.studyabroad.com/liteimage.html**.

American Field Service (AFS), 220 E. 42nd St., 3rd floor, New York, NY 10017 (tel. (800) AFS-INF0/237-4636 or 876-2376; fax (212) 949-9379; http//www.afs.org/usa). AFS offers summer, semester, and year-long homestay international exchange programs for high school students and graduating high school seniors and short-term service projects for adults in Ecuador (as well as other countries). Financial aid available.

College Semester Abroad, School for International Training, Admissions, Kipling Rd., P.O. Box 676, Brattleboro, VT 05302 (tel. (800) 336-1616 or 258-3279; fax 258-3500). Runs semester- and year-long programs featuring cultural orientation, intensive language study, homestay, and field and independent study. Programs cost US$8200-10300, all expenses included. Financial aid available and U.S. financial aid is transferable. Most U.S. colleges will transfer credit for semester work done abroad. Runs programs in Ecuador as well as many other countries.

Institute of International Education (IIE), 809 United Nations Plaza, New York, NY 10017-3580 (tel. (212) 984-5413 for recorded information; fax 984-5358). For book orders: IIE Books, Institute of International Educations, P.O. Box 371, Annapolis Junction, MD 20701 (tel. (800) 445- 0443; fax (301) 953-2838; e-mail iiebooks@iie.org.). A nonprofit, international and cultural exchange agency. IIE's library of study abroad resources is open to the public Tues.-Thurs. 11am-3:45pm. Publishes *Academic Year Abroad* (US$43 plus US$4 shipping) detailing over 2300 semester and year-long programs worldwide and *Vacation Study Abroad* (US$37 plus US$4 shipping) which lists over 1,800 short-term, summer, and language school programs. Write for a list of publications.

World Learning, Inc., Summer Abroad, P.O. Box 676, Brattleboro, VT 05302 (tel. (800) 345-2929 or (802) 257-7751; http://www.worldlearning.org). Founded in 1932 as The Experiment in International Living, it offers high school programs in Ecuador (among other countries), as well as language-training programs with elective homestays. Programs are 3-5 weeks long. Positions as group leaders are avail-

able worldwide if you are over 24, have previous in-country experience, are fluent in the language, and have experience with high school students.

Youth For Understanding (YFU) International Exchange, 3501 Newark St. NW, Washington, D.C. 20016 (tel. (800) TEENAGE /833-6243 or (202) 966-6800; fax 895-1104; http://www.yfu.org). As one of the oldest and largest exchange organizations in the world, FYU has placed over 175,000 high school students between the ages of 14 and 18 with families worldwide for year, semester, summer, and sport homestays.

VOLUNTEER AND WORK

Volunteering is an excellent way to immerse yourself in Ecuadorian culture and the Spanish language while improving the lives of others. The good news is that it's very easy to find volunteer positions, especially if you are willing to shell out a few bucks; the bad news is that paid work can be exceedingly difficult to find. Countries are reluctant to give up precious jobs to traveling *gringos* when many of their citizens are unemployed. It's not impossible, though, as some businesses are eager to hire English-speaking personnel for prestige or for the convenience of their patrons.

If you are a full-time student at a U.S. university, one easy way to get a job abroad is through work-permit programs run by the **Council on International Educations Exchange (Council)** and its member organizations (see Travel Organizations, p. 1). Some of the most readily available jobs are for English teachers. A work permit from the government may be an obstacle to employment, but less official arrangements can often be made. For more information, see Entrance Requirements, p. 5. The following is a list of useful publications and organizations.

Addison-Wesley, Jacob Way, Reading, MA 01867 (tel. (800) 822-6339). Published *International Jobs: Where They Are, How to Get Them* in 1993-1994 (US$16). Jobs in Ecuador are included, but they are listed by job, not by country.

Council (see Travel Organizations, p. 1) offers 2- to 4-week environmental or community service projects in over 30 countries around the globe through its Voluntary Services Department (US$195 placement fee). Participants must be at least 18 years old. Council publishes *Work, Study, Travel Abroad: The Whole World Handbook,* which covers specific programs on all continents. Includes both summer and long-term work abroad. Published by St. Martin's Press (US$14).

Global Volunteers, 375 E. Little Canada Rd., St. Paul, MN 55117-1628 (tel. (800) 487-1074 or (612) 482-1074; fax 482-0915). The organization sends groups of volunteers all over the world. The programs in Ecuador are with Camp Hope, a local organization in Quito that works with orphaned and abandoned children, 50% of whom have disabilities. Programs last for 2 weeks and include day care, health care, teaching, and construction. The cost is $1695 without airfare.

Office of Overseas Schools, A/OS Room 245, SA-29, Dept. of State, Washington, D.C. 20522-2902 (tel. (703) 875-7800). Offers teaching jobs in countries worldwide, including Ecuador.

Peace Corps, 1990 K St. NW, Washington, D.C. 20526 (tel. (800) 424-8580; fax (202) 606-4469; http://www.peacecorps.gov). Write for their "blue" brochure, which details applicant requirements. Opportunities in a variety of fields, from agriculture to business, in developing nations worldwide. Volunteers must be U.S. citizens willing to make a 2-year commitment.

Transitions Abroad, 18 Hulst Rd., P.O. Box 1300, Amherst, MA 01004-1300 (tel. (800) 293-0373; fax (413) 256-0373; e-mail trabroad@aol.com). This invaluable magazine lists publications and resources for overseas study, work, and volunteering. Also publishes *The Alternative Travel Directory,* a comprehensive guide to living, learning, and working overseas (US$20; postage US$4).

World Teach, HIID, 1 Eliot St., Cambridge, MA 02138-5705 (tel. (617) 495-5527; fax 495-1599; e-mail worldteach@hiid.harvard.edu; http://www.hiid.harvard.edu). Volunteers teach English, math, science, and environmental education to students of all ages in developing areas of many countries, including Ecuador. Teachers must usually have a bachelor's degree and are provided with room and board during their period of service. Rolling admission.

Specific Concerns

WOMEN TRAVELERS

Women exploring on their own inevitably face additional safety concerns. Always trust your instincts: if you'd feel better somewhere else, move on. Stick to centrally located accommodations and avoid late-night treks. Hitching is never safe for lone women, or even for two women traveling together. In general, dress conservatively, especially in rural areas. Avoid shorts and short skirts. Observe the way local women dress and try to follow suit as much as possible. You may be harassed no matter how you're dressed. Your best answer to verbal harassment is no answer at all (a reaction is what the harasser wants). In worse situations, don't hesitate to seek out the police or passersby. In crowds, you may be pinched or squeezed; wearing a wedding band may help prevent such incidents. Note: The northwest region of Ecuador, particularly the province of Esmeraldas, is reported to be unsafe for lone women travelers. *Let's Go* does not recommend that women travel alone here. For more genral advice see Personal Safety, p. 11. Women also face additional health concerns when traveling (see Women's Health, p. 17). All of these warnings and suggestions should not discourage women from traveling alone. Don't take unnecessary risks, but don't lose your spirit of adventure either. For additional information, try consulting one or more of the resources below:

National Organization for Women (NOW), boasts branches across the country that can refer women travelers to rape crisis centers and counseling services, and provide lists of feminist events. Main offices include 22 W. 21st St., 7th Fl., **New York,** NY 10010 (tel. (212) 260-4422); 1000 16th St. NW, 7th Fl., **Washington,**

D.C. 20004 (tel. (202) 331-0066); and 3543 18th St., **San Francisco,** CA 94110 (tel. (415) 861-8960).

Directory of Women's Media, available from the National Council for Research on Women, 530 Broadway, 10th Fl., New York, NY 10012 (tel. (212) 274-0730; fax 274-0821. The publication lists women's publishers, bookstores, theaters, and news organizations (mail orders, US$30).

A Foxy Old Woman's Guide to Traveling Alone, by Jay Ben-Lesser (Crossing Press, US$11), encompasses practically every specific concern, offering anecdotes and tips for the solitary female adventurer. No travel experience necessary.

A Journey of One's Own, by Thalia Zepatos (Eighth Mountain Press, US$17). The latest thing on the market, interesting and full of good advice. Includes a specific and manageable bibliography of books and resources.

Women Travel: Adventures, Advice & Experience by Miranda Davies and Natania Jansz (Penguin, US$13). Info on specific foreign countries plus a decent bibliography and resource index. The sequel, *More Women Travel,* is US$15.

BISEXUAL, GAY, AND LESBIAN TRAVELERS

Not the most liberal country, Ecuador punishes homosexual acts by up to 8 months in prison. Bars and meeting points are reportedly raided by the police from time to time. The existence of a few gay bars and clubs in Quito and Guayaquil proves that there is a small homosexual community in Ecuador; however, gay and lesbian travelers should be aware that being "out" here is a drastic statement, and may not be a good idea. Many Ecuadorians tend to think of homosexuality as a sickness or a lower-class phenomenon. For more information, consult the organizations and publications listed below:

Ferrari Guides, PO Box 37887, Phoenix, AZ 85069 (tel. (602) 863-2408; fax 439-3952; e-mail ferrari@q-net.com). Gay and lesbian travel guides: *Ferrari Guides' Gay Travel A to Z* (US $16), *Ferrari Guides' Men's Travel in Your Pocket* (US $14), *Ferrari Guides' Women's Travel in Your Pocket* (US $14), and *Ferrari Guides' Inn Places* (US $16). Available in bookstores or by mail order.

Giovanni's Room, 345 S. 12th St., Philadelphia, PA 19107 (tel. (215) 923-2960; fax 923-0813; e-mail gilphilp@netaxs.com). International feminist, lesbian, and gay bookstore with mail-order service. Carries many of the publications listed here.

International Gay Travel Association, P.O. Box 4974, Key West, FL 33041 (tel. (800) 448-8550; fax (305) 296-6633; e-mail IGTA@aol.com; http://www.rainbow-mall.com/igta). An organization of over 1100 companies serving gay and lesbian travelers worldwide. Call for lists of travel agents, accommodations, and events.

Spartacus International Gay Guides, published by Bruno Gmunder, Postfach 110729, D-10837 Berlin, Germany (tel. (30) 615 00 30; fax 615 91 34). Lists bars, restaurants, hotels, and bookstores around the world catering to gays. Also lists hotlines for gays and homosexuality laws in various countries. Available in bookstores and by mail order from Giovanni's Room (listed above). US$32.95.

VEGETARIAN AND KOSHER TRAVELERS

Vegetarians should have no problem finding suitable cuisine. Most restaurants will have vegetarian selections on their menus (rice, beans, fresh fruits and vegetables are always an option), and if they don't you can ask for it. In addition, many crunchy expatriates have made a place for themselves in Ecuador. As a result, there are quite a few restaurants that cater specifically to vegetarians. For more information, contact the **North American Vegetarian Society,** P.O. Box 72, Dolgeville, NY 13329 (tel. (518) 568-7970), which stocks numerous helpful publications.

There is a Jewish community in Quito, with a synagogue at 18 de Septiembre y Versalles. Services are on Fridays at 6pm and Saturdays at 9am. As far as keeping kosher, most meat in Ecuador is probably not, so stick to vegetarian dishes. If you are strict in your observance, consider bringing your own disposable plates and utensils, or preparing your own food on the road.

OLDER TRAVELERS

Senior travelers should bring a medical record that includes up-to-date information on conditions and prescriptions; the name, phone number, and address of a regular doctor; and a summary of recent medical history. *Travel Tips for Older Americans* (US$1) provides information on passports, health, and currency for those traveling abroad; contact the Superintendent of Documents (see Useful Publications, p. 4). The following organizations and publications can also be helpful:

Elderhostel, 75 Federal St., 3rd Fl., Boston, MA 02110-1941 (tel. (617) 426-7788, fax 426-8351; http://www.elderhostel.org). For those 55 or over (spouse of any age). Programs at colleges, universities, and other learning centers in over 50 countries, including Ecuador, on varied subjects lasting 1-4 weeks.

National Council of Senior Citizens, 1331 F St. NW, Washington, DC 20004 (tel. (202) 347-8800). Memberships are US$12 a year, US$30 for 3 years, or US$150 for a lifetime. Individual or couple can receive hotel and auto rental discounts, a senior citizen newspaper, use of a discount travel agency, supplemental Medicare insurance (if you're over 65), and a mail-order prescription drug service.

Unbelievably Good Deals and Great Adventures That You Absolutely Can't Get Unless You're Over 50, by Joan Rattner Heilman. After you finish reading the title page, check inside for some great tips on senior discounts and the like. Contemporary Books, US$10.

DISABLED TRAVELERS

Ecuador is not very well prepared to meet the needs of disabled travelers. Rainforests, volcanoes, and beaches rarely have smooth paths, and wheelchair-accessible buildings are rare. Still, there are exceptions, and the region is not off-limits to disabled tourists. Those with disabilities should inform airlines and hotels of their disabilities when making arrangements for travel; some time may be needed to prepare special accommodations. Travelers with seeing-eye dogs need to inquire as to the specific quarantine policies of Ecuador. At the very least, they will need a certificate of immunization against rabies. The following organizations provide helpful information and publications, or help to organize trips for the disabled:

American Foundation for the Blind, 11 Penn Plaza, New York, NY 10011 (tel. (212) 502-7600; open Mon.-Fri. 8:30am-4:30pm). Provides information and services for the visually impaired. For a catalogue of products, contact Lighthouse at (tel. (800) 829-0500).

Directions Unlimited, 720 N. Bedford Rd., Bedford Hills, NY 10507 (tel. (800) 533-5343, in NY (914) 241-1700; fax 241-0243). Specializes in arranging individual and group vacations, tours, and cruises for the physically disabled.

Mobility International, USA (MIUSA), P.O. Box 10767, Eugene, OR 97440 (tel. (514) 343-1284 voice and TDD; fax 343-6812). International Headquarters: Rue de Manchester 25, Brussles, Belgium, B-1070 (tel. (322) 410 6297; fax 410 6874). Contacts in 30 countries. Information on travel programs, international work camps, accommodations, access guides, and organized tours for those with physical disabilities. Membership US$25 per year, newsletter US$15. Sells the periodically updated and expanded *A World of Options: A Guide to International Educational Exchange, Community Service, and Travel for Persons with Disabilities* (US$14, non-members US$16). In addition, MIUSA offers a series of courses that teach strategies helpful to travelers with disabilities. Call for details.

Society for the Advancement of Travel for the Handicapped (SATH), 347 Fifth Ave. #610, New York, NY 10016 (tel. (212) 447-7284; fax 725-8253). Publishes quarterly travel newsletter *SATH News* and information booklets (free for members, US$13 each for non-members) with advice on trip planning for people with diabilities. Annual membership US$45, students and seniors US$25.

Packing

If you don't **pack lightly,** your back and wallet will suffer. The more you have, the more you have to lose. The larger your pack, the more difficult it is to store safely. Before you leave, pack your bag, strap it on, and imagine yourself walking uphill on hot asphalt for the next three hours. A good general rule is to lay out only what you absolutely need, then take half the clothes and twice the money.

If you plan to cover most of your itinerary by foot, the unbeatable piece of luggage is a sturdy **backpack.** Many are designed specifically for travelers, while others are for hikers; consider how you will use the pack before purchasing one or the other. Get a pack with a strong, padded hip belt to transfer weight from your shoulders to your hips. When purchasing, avoid excessively low-end prices—you get what you pay for. High-quality packs cost anywhere from US$150 to US$420. Bringing a smaller **day-pack** in addition to the mother-pack allows you to leave your big bag in the hotel while you go sight-seeing. It can also be used as an airplane carry-on. Guard your money, passport, and other important articles in **moneybelt or neck pouch,** and keep it with you *at all times.* They are available at any good travel or camping store.

As far as **clothing** is concerned, packing lightly does not mean dressing badly. Aim for versatility and comfort, and avoid fabrics that wrinkle easily. Remember that solid colors mix best. Bring along something besides the basic shorts, t-shirts, and jeans. Shorts can be inappropriate, jeans can be uncomfortable, and loud t-shirts may offend. For dressier occassions, remember that simple is elegant, not boring. Black is ideal because it is always in fashion and you can't tell if it's been worn five times. Women should bring a simple, solid-colored dress made of cotton or another versatile fabric. Men should bring a pair of khakis, which can be both dressy and casual, and the essential white button-up shirt. Be sure to bring enough warm clothing, especially if you plan to visit the Sierra. **Good shoes** are essential, not a place to cut corners. Well-cushioned sneakers are good for walking, but if you plan to do any hiking, a water-proofed pair of hiking boots is better. Whatever kind of shoes you choose, break them in before you leave. **Rain gear** is also essential. A waterproof jacket and a backpack cover will take care of you and your stuff at a moment's notice. Gore-Tex® is a miracle fabric that's both waterproof and breathable.

If you plan on doing any camping, a sturdy, compact, lightweight **sleeping bag** will serve you well. Otherwise, a **bedsheet** can come in handy; you may have to crash somewhere that does not have sheets. In terms of **washing clothes,** *Let's Go* attempts to provide information on laundromats, but in case you have to use a sink, bring detergent soap, and a rubber squash ball to stop up the drain. Ecuador uses the same **electric current** as North America (110 volts, 60 cycles). A **camera** is always good, but consider bringing a disposable one rather than an expensive, permanent one. **Film** is expensive; bring lots from home. Also, Airport security X-rays *can* fog film; always pack it in your carry-on luggage, and either pack it in a lead-lined pouch (sold at camera stores) or ask the security to hand inspect it. **Additional items** are: resealable plastic bags (for damp clothes, and spillables, like shampoo), alarm clock, hat, needle and thread, safety pins, a personal stereo (nothing too valuable), pocketknife, water bottle, compass, towel, padlock, flashlight, insect repellant, sunscreen, vitamins. Items not readily available on the road include: deodorant, razors, condoms, tampons. For other important packing tips see Health: Before You Go, p. 13.

GETTING THERE

Flying to Ecuador

The airline industry attempts to squeeze every dollar from customers; finding a cheap airfare in their deliberately mysterious and confusing jungle will be easier if you understand the airlines' systems. Call every toll-free number and don't be afraid to ask about discounts. Have a knowledgeable **travel agent** guide you.

Students and "youth" (people under 26) with proper ID qualify for enticing reduced airfares. These are rarely available from airlines or travel agents; instead, look to **budget travel agencies,** many of which specialize in student travel (listed below). Student travel agencies can also help non-students and people over 26, but probably won't be able to get the same low fares. Sunday newspapers often have travel sections that list bargain fares from the local airport. *The Airline Passenger's Guerrilla Handbook* (US$15) is a renegade resource for finding the best fares. On the web, try the **Air Traveler's Handbook**(http://www.cis.ohio-state.edu/hypertext/faq/usenet/travel/air/handbook/top.html).

Most airfares peak between mid-June and early September. During midweek (Mon.-Thurs. morning), roundtrip flights run about US$40-50 cheaper than those leaving on weekends. Traveling from hubs is usually cheaper than flying from smaller cities. Miami, Houston, and Los Angeles are the biggest hubs for travel to Latin America. The two Ecuadorian cities with international airports are Quito and Guayaquil. Return-date flexibility is usually possible for budget travelers; "open-return" tickets can be pricier than paying to change a set return date (for studetns, only around US$25 per segment through Council or Let's Go Travel). Pick up tickets well in advance of the departure date, have the flight confirmed within 72 hours of departure, and arrive at the airport at least two hours before your flight departs.

COMMERCIAL AIRLINES

Both U.S. and Latin American commercial airlines fly to Ecuador. While the U.S. airlines are typically more expensive, they allow you to fly from anywhere in the United States. The Latin American airlines, on the other hand, fly only to and from Miami,

Houston, Los Angeles, and sometimes New York. U.S. airlines that fly to Ecuador are **American** (tel. (800) 433-7300), **Continental** (tel. (800) 231-0856), and **United** (tel. (800) 241-6522); the Latin American ones are **LACSA** (tel. (800) 225-2272), **SAETA** (tel. (800) 827-2382), **VIASA** (tel. (800) 468-4272), and **Avianca** (tel. (800) 284-2622). Roundtrip fares normally run around US$700 (give or take US$100), but may drop closer to US$400, depending on the season and other more mysterious factors.

The commercial airlines' lowest regular offer is the **APEX** (Advance Purchase Excursion Fare), which provides passengers with confirmed reservations and allows passengers to land in and return from different cities. Reservations must be made seven to 21 days in advance, with seven- to 14-day minimum and up to 90-day maximum stay limits, with hefty cancellation and change penalties (fees rise in summer). Book APEX fares early during peak seasons, as they fill up quickly.

Even if you pay an airline's lowest published fare, you may spend hundreds of unnecessary dollars. For the adventurous or the bargain-hungry, there are other, perhaps more inconvenient or time-consuming options. But before searching through them, it is a good idea to find out the average commercial price in order to measure just how great a "bargain" you are being offered.

CONSOLIDATORS AND COURIER COMPANIES

Ticket consolidators, also known as "bucket shops," resell unsold tickets on commercial and charter airlines at unpublished fares. Consolidator flights are the best deals if you are traveling on short notice (since you aren't tangled in the airline bureaucracy of advance purchases) or in the peak season, when published fares are jacked way up. Restrictions are not always the same as those on commercial flights, which can sometimes be convenient. Look for tiny ads in weekend papers (the U.S., the Sunday *New York Times* is best). In London, the Air Travel Advisory Bureau (tel. (0171) 636 5000) provides a list of consolidators.

For destinations worldwide, try **Airfare Busters,** with locations in Washington, D.C. (tel. (800) 776-0481); Boca Raton, FL (tel. (800) 881-3273); and Houston, TX (tel. (232-8783); or **Pennsylvania Travel,** in Paoli, PA (tel. (800) 331-0947); or **Cheap Tickets** (tel. (800) 377-1000), in Los Angeles, CA; San Francisco, CA; Honolulu, HI; Overland Park, KS; and New York, NY; or **Moment's Notice,** in New York, NY (tel. (718) 234-6295; fax 234-6450). For a processing fee, depending on the number of travelers and the itinerary, **Travel Avenue,** in Chicago, IL (tel. (800) 333-3335), searches for the lowest international airfare, offering rebates on fares over US$300.

Kelly Monaghan's *Consolidators: Air Travel's Bargain Basement* (US$7, plus US$2 shipping charges) is a valuable source for more information and lists of consolidators by location and destination. Cyber-resources include **World Wide** (http://www.tmn.com/wwwanderer/WWWa) and the incredibly informative **Airline ticket consolidators and bucket shops** (http://www.gnn.com/gnn/wic/wics/trav.97.html).

Traveling as a **courier** can get you some of the cheapest flights around, but there are many restrictions. Courier flights to Ecuador leave only from Miami, and you have to travel light. Fares are between US$200-300, and maximum length of stay ranges from 21 to 60 days. The company hiring you will use your checked luggage for freight; you're only allowed to bring carry-ons. You are responsible for the safe delivery of the baggage claim slips (given to you by a courier company representative) to the representative waiting when you arrive. You will probably never see the cargo you are transporting—the company handles it all—and airport officials know that couriers are not responsible for the baggage checked for them. The following companies handle courier flight to Ecuador: **Discount Travel International** (tel. (212) 362-3636), **Line Haul Services** (tel. (305) 477-0651), **Martillo Express Travel** (tel. (305) 822-0880), and **Trans-Air Systems, Inc.** (tel. (305) 592-1771).

Budget Travel Agencies

Council Travel (http://www.ciee.org/cts/ctshome.htm), the travel division of Council, is a full-service travel agency specializing in youth and budget travel. They offer discount airfares, hosteling cards, guidebooks, budget tours, travel gear, and student (ISIC) and teacher (ITIC) identity cards. For the U.S. office nearest you: (tel. (800) 2-COUNCIL/226-8624). In the U.K.: 28A Poland St. Oxford Circus, London, W1V 3DB (tel. (0171) 437 7767).

STA Travel, 6560 Scottsdale Rd. #F100, Scottsdale, AZ 85253 (tel. (800) 777-0112; fax (602) 922-0793). A student and youth travel organization with over 100 offices worldwide, including 16 in the U.S., and others in Australia, New Zealand, and the U.K. Offers discount airfares, accommodations, tours, insurance and ISICs.

Let's Go Travel, Harvard Student Agencies, 67 Mt. Auburn St., Cambridge, MA 02138 (tel. (800) 5-LETS GO/553-8746) or (617) 495-9649). HI-AYH memberships, ISICs, ITICs, FIYTO cards, guidebooks, maps, bargain flights, and a complete line of travel gear. All items available by mail; call or write for a catalog.

Campus Travel, 52 Grosvenor Gardens, London SW1W 0AG (http://www.campustravel.co.uk). Has 41 branches in the U.K. Student and youth fares on plane travel. Flexible airline tickets. Discount and ID cards for youths, travel insurance for students and those under 35, and maps and guides. Publishes travel suggestion booklets. Telephone booking service: in **Europe** (tel. (0171) 730 3402), in **North America** (tel. (0171) 730 2101), **worldwide** (tel. (0171) 730 8111).

Journeys, 4011 Jackson Rd., Ann Arbor, MI 48103 (tel. (800) 255-8735; fax (313) 665-2945; e-mail journeysni@aol.com; http://www.journeys-intl.com). Offers small-group, guided explorations of 32 different countries in Asia, Africa, the Americas, and the Pacific. Free newsletter for prospective travelers.

Travel CUTS (Canadian Universities Travel Services Limited), 187 College St., Toronto, Ont. M5T 1P7 (tel. (416) 979-2406; fax 979-8167; e-mail mail@travelcuts). Canada's national student travel bureau with 40 offices across Canada. Also in the U.K. (tel. (0171) 637 3161). Discounted domestic and international airfares open to all; special student fares to all destinations with valid ISIC. Issues ISIC, FIYTO, GO25, and HI hostel cards. Offers free *Student Traveller* magazine, as well as information on the Student Work Abroad Program (SWAP).

Usit Youth and Student Travel, 19-21 Aston Quay, O'Connell Bridge, Dublin 2, Ireland (tel. (01) 602 1200; fax 671 2408). In the USA: New York Student Center, 895 Amsterdam Ave., New York, NY, 10025 (tel. (212) 663 5435). Other offices in Cork, Galway, Limerick, Waterford, Maynooth, Coleraine, Derry, Athlone, Jordanstown, Belfast, and Greece. Specializes in youth and student travel. Offers cheap tickets and flexible travel arrangements all over the world. Supplies ISICs.

ONCE THERE

Embassies and Consulates

IN QUITO

U.S., Patria 120 y Avenida 12 de Octubre (tel. (2) 562-890; fax 502-052).

Canada, Avenida Corea 126 y Amazonas, Edificio Belmonte, 6th fl. (tel. (2) 458-102).

U.K., Avenida Gonzáles Suárez 111, Casilla 314 (tel. (2) 560-670; fax 560-730).

Rep. of Ireland, Montes 577 y Las Casas (tel. (2) 503-674; fax 501-444).

Israel, Eloy Alfaro 969 y Amazonas (tel. (2) 565-510; fax 504-635).

Colombia, Colón 133 y Amazonas, 7th fl. (tel. (2) 221-679 or 222-486; fax 566-676).

Perú, Amazonas 1429 y Colón, Edificio España, penthouse (tel. (2) 520-134; fax 562-349).

IN GUAYAQUIL

U.S., Avenida 9 de Octubre y García Moreno (tel. (4) 323-570; fax 325-286).

Canada, Córdova 810 y Víctor Manuel Rendón, 21st fl., office 4 (tel. (4) 563-560 or 566-747; fax 314-562).

U.K., Córdova 623 y Padre Solano (tel. (4) 560-400; fax 562-641).

Australia, Calle San Roque y Av. Francisco de Orellana (tel. (4) 298-823; fax 293-822)
Israel, Avenida 9 de Octubre 729 y García Aviles (tel. (4) 322-555; fax 328-196).
Colombia, Córdova 812 y V.M. Rendón, 2nd fl., office 11 (tel. (4) 563-308; fax 563-854).
Perú, Avenida 9 de Octubre 411 y Chile, 6th fl. (tel. (4) 322-738; fax 325-679).

Getting Around

BY BUS

Only the most fatalistic can enjoy Ecuador's buses. If you are among the many budget travelers who actually care about their well-being, you will know fear on Ecuadorian roads. Bus travel in Ecuador means whipping around **hairpin turns** through **thick clouds** on **cliffs,** dropping into oblivion as you **pass another bus** on a one-lane dirt highway. One technique for coping with the constant feeling of impending doom is to give in to the experience. Consider it a ride at an amusement park and make believe that no matter how scary it gets, the car is still attached to the tracks (even though it's not). Whether or not this strategy works, every budget traveler in Ecuador will eventually have to come to grips with the realities of bus travel, as it is by far Ecuador's **cheapest** and **most ubiquitous** means of transportation.

Buses of some kind or another travel to practically every part of Ecuador. They leave town from the *terminal terrestre* (bus station), or from a particular street with a high density of *cooperativos* (bus companies). The **bus fare** is usually paid upon entering the bus, or collected en route by an *ayudante* (helper). Occasionally, tickets must be purchased in advance at the *cooperativo* office. Departure times are usually approximate, and buses run between most destinations frequently enough that it is practical to just show up at the *terminal terrestre* and board the next bus headed your way. The destination is usually indicated on the bus itself, as well as advertised by a man yelling the town's name over and over again. The vehicles themselves vary greatly in quality, from open-air converted trucks *(camionetas)* to second-hand school buses to sparkling new Mercedez-Benz mega-buses. A general guideline: the longer the route, the nicer the bus will be, so it may be worthwhile to board a long-distance bus even if you plan to get off before the final destination.

A particularly peculiar aspect of Ecuadorian bus travel is that the buses rarely get "full;" drivers are often happy to pack as many passenger as they can into the aisles or even hanging out the door. If the buses get *really* full (and occasionally even if they don't), drivers will let passengers ride on the roof, an especially amazing experience in the Sierra. It is a good idea to keep your belongings with you if at all possible.

BY CAR

Taxis can be a convenient way to get around, especially when you are in a hurry or traveling to places where buses don't venture. They are commonly used for travel between towns or to outlying destinations, and they are not outrageously expensive. For example, it is usually cheaper to arrange for a taxi to drop you off and pick you up at an out-of-the-way spot than it is to rent a car and drive there yourself. If you do decide to take a taxi, try to find out a fair price for the trip before hailing a cab. Once you do stop one, be sure to settle on a price before entering; if you don't, the driver might try to take advantage of you and charge more than the ride is worth. You can also travel by **colectivo;** these Volkswagon vans travel regular routes and pick up numerous passengers, falling in-between taxis and buses in price, speed, and size.

Car rentals in Ecuador can be a real nightmare, but the convenience of having you own wheels can also be truly liberating. The drawbacks are that it will cost at least US$25 a day, the roads and drivers in Ecuador can be quite scary, and a car is one more (big) thing to worry about getting stolen. All you need to rent a car is a passport, a valid driver's license from your home country, and a credit card. Most credit cards cover standard insurance, but you may also have to purchase additional insurance

from the rental company. Information on particular companies can be found in the Practical Information of Quito, Guayaquil, and Cuenca. Budget, Avis, and Hertz are all represented in Ecuador; you may want to make arrangements before you leave home.

BY TRAIN

Railroad travel within Ecuador is not the most convenient, cheapest, nor quickest way to get around. However, some are willing to make these kinds of sacrifices for the strangely soothing sensation of traveling by train. Not only do Ecuadorian trains travel through some of the most spectacular terrain in the world, but as an added bonus, roof-riding is permitted. While the tracks run the length of the country, much of this distance is in disrepair due to mudslides and other natural damage. Nevertheless, there are several stretches that have been repaired and maintained. The most well-traveled stretches lie between Guayaquil and Alausí in the south, and Ibarra and San Lorenzo in the north. Both of these routes travel from the coast into the Sierra and give passengers the opportunity to see the land change with the altitude. Another train also runs between Quito and Riobamba. For information on prices and travel times, check the Practical Information sections of these towns.

BY PLANE

Air travel within Ecuador is definitely more expensive than traveling by bus or train, but much, much quicker. If time really *were* money, flying might actually be worth it. Flights within Ecuador are relatively cheap excursions, except to the Galápagos. Ecuador's two main airlines, **SAN/SAETA** and **TAME,** have daily flights between Quito and Guayaquil (US$46), Cuenca (US$58), Loja, Macas (US$50), Coca (US$50), and Lago Agrio (US$50). All prices are one-way and simply doubled for a roundtrip. These airlines are listed in the Practical Information sections of each of these towns. For flights to the Galápagos, see the Galápagos Essentials, p. 244.

BY BOAT

In the **Oriente,** motorized dugout canoes travel the murky, winding rivers that connect many towns. While this may seem like a glamorous way to travel, hours under the hot equatorial sun and the constant threat of torrential downpours add up. Also, since the riverbanks are just about the most accessible parts of the jungle, hopes of seeing more isolated and untouched areas by river are rarely realized. On top of these minor inconveniences, traveling by river is more expensive than going by bus on the roads that now connect many Oriente towns. If you still want to travel by river, ask about regular boat schedules and prices at a local marina. Public transportation boats regularly run up and down the **Río Napo** between Tena and Coca, and from Coca to the Peruvian border at Nueva Rocafuerte. It is also possible to charter a canoe and customize your boat itinerary, but this is only economically feasible for larger groups.

Roads run along most of **Pacific Coast,** making boat travel unnecessary and thus quite rare. One exception is the stretch between the undeveloped northern coast towns of Muisne and Cojimíes; the only way to travel between these is a cheap and frquent, one-and-a-half-hour, wet-and-wild ride boat trip. Lastly, though it is not commonly done, it is possible to travel to the **Galápagos Islands** by boat. For more information, see Travel by Boat in the Galápagos Essentials, p. 244.

BY THUMB

> *Let's Go* urges you to use common sense if you decide to hitch, and to seriously consider all possible risks before you make that decision. The information listed below and throughout the book is not intended to recommend hitchhiking; *Let's Go* does not recommend hitchhiking as a means of transportation.

Buses travel almost everywhere in Ecuador and cost very little, so it is rarely necessary to hitchhike. However, there are more remote places where buses don't travel, and hitchhiking is a common way of getting around. Trucks will often pick up passengers to make a little extra money. Usually they cost about the same as taxis, but don't be surprised if the truck driver charges a little more; settle on a price before getting in.

Suspicion is often warranted. Hitchhikers should find out where the driver is headed before getting in. Think twice if the driver opens the door quickly and offers to drive anywhere. If any cause for concern arises, make an excuse and wait for another ride. Women should never hitchhike alone. Never accept a ride without sizing up the driver. Before getting in, make sure the passenger window or door opens from inside, perhaps by stalling so the driver opens the door for you. If there are several people in the car, do not sit in the middle. Assume a quick-exit position, which rules out the back seat of a two-door car. Keep backpacks and other baggage where they are easily accessible—don't let the driver store them in the trunk. If trouble arises for any reason, affecting the pose of someone about to vomit works wonders.

Accommodations

Most budget accommodations in Ecuador are in the form of basic **hotels.** Rooms are small and simple, bathrooms may be private or communal, and there is often a lounge area, be it a plant-filled courtyard, sparsely-decorated TV-room, or dining area. These places may have laundry service for a fee, they may have a place where guests can do their own laundry, or there may be no laundry facilities at all. It is expected everywhere that after you've finished your business, you throw your toilet paper into the waste basket—*not* the toilet. Otherwise, the rules vary. There is a generally a lockout time before which you must return to the hotel. If you get locked out, you can try to wake the owner or receptionist, but don't expect their usual cheery selves.

There are also numerous **hostels** in Ecuador. Many of the same general hotel rules apply to hostels as well, but as in hostels elsewhere in the world, they may be more like dormitories. Multiple guests may have to sleep in the same room, perhaps even on bunkbeds. Some of these hostels are part of **Hostelling International (HI),** a worldwide hostel organization that guarantees a certain level of quality in terms of cleanliness, comfort, and friendliness. A Hostelling International membership (US$25 adult, US$10 under 18) will get you discounts at the 16 HI hostels in Ecuador. Many travel agencies sell HI memberships. Contact HI in the U.S. (tel. (202) 783-6161; fax 783-6171) or in Quito, Ecuador at the *Asociación Ecuatoriana de Albergues,* Pinto 325 y Reina Victoria (tel. 226-271; fax 543-995).

Camping is definitely possible in Ecuador, even though it is not terribly common nor very well organized. Some parks and reserves have designated camping areas, and some more frequently climbed mountains have *refugios* (rustic shelters) at various altitudes. Some landowners may allow camping on their property, but be sure to ask. Be cautious camping in non-designated spots, especially in isolated areas. It's best to bring equipment with you, since buying it in Ecuador will be much more expensive. There are shops in Quito should you lose equipment or need repairs.

Long-term accommodations should not be difficult to find in Ecuador. Many organizations can arrange for you to stay with an Ecuadorian family (see Alternatives to Tourism, p. 19). Classified ads in local newspapers (*El Comercio* in Quito) contain the most complete information on apartment rentals. Also consult the bulletin boards of any prime *gringo* hangouts, (in Quito: the Magic Bean, Cafecito, Super Papas (a restaurant on Mera near Foch), and, the South American Explorer's Club). Otherwise, housing advertisements may be found in or around university campuses.

Outdoor Activities

Ecuador is one of the most geographically and ecologically diverse countries in the world, which makes for excellent outdoor adventure opportunities. The Pacific coast and the Galápagos Islands are good for saltwater fun, from surfing to snorkeling with seals. The Andes provide mountains of possibilities for outdoor recreation, from refreshing scenic walks to hardcore mountain climbing. And in the Oriente, there's the Amazon experience, with more species of plants and animals than you can count on all the fingers and toes of a small army. Whatever your particular interests may be, from ocean shores to jungle tours, Ecuador's out-of-doors have something in store.

MOUNTAIN CLIMBING

With 10 peaks standing over 5000m tall, Ecuador has long been considered one of the premier mountain-climbing destinations in the world. A French expedition of the *Académie des Sciences* visited Ecuador in 1736, and after calculating the distance from the equator to the North Pole (the calculation that forms the basis of the metric system of measurement), they determined that Ecuador's 6310m Mt. Chimborazo (20,703ft.) was the highest mountain in the world, a misconception that was not challenged until the 1820s.

In 1880, the famous English climber, Edward Whymper (the first man to climb the Matterhorn), conquered five of the Ecuador's most formidable virgin peaks, including the mighty Chimborazo. His expedition put Ecuador on the map; since then, more and more adventurers have been scrambling up and down her bodacious peaks. As a result, refuges *(refugios)* have been built on many of the mountain trails to shelter climbers, and numerous national parks and reserves have been created to protect the mountains and surrounding areas. There are routes for climbers of all abilities, and numerous organizations can help arrange and lead trips. Should you decide to attempt any of the more challenging climbs, finding a competent guide is very important, especially since many who call themselves guides are actually quite inexperienced. There is an Ecuadorian Guide Association, the *Asociación Ecuatoriana de Guías de Montaña* (ASEGUIM), that certifies guides. Another good place to look for a guide is at one of the climbing shops in Quito. These shops can put you in touch with a guide and often rent gear as well. The South American Explorer's Club can provide useful information about climbing and guides (see Travel Organizations, p. 1). The book *Climbing and Hiking in Ecuador* (Bradt Publications, US$15.95), is an excellent resource, offering everything from advice on equipment to trail specifics, as well as details about some of the more mellow hikes through the mountains.

JUNGLE TOURING

Tourists mainly visit Ecuador's Oriente to take a jungle tour through the Amazon basin. While the different tours vary greatly, they typically include treks through dripping rainforests, canoe rides down muddy Oriente rivers, visits to remote indigenous communities, and overnight stays in jungle *cabaña* outposts. Some regions of the jungle have less primary growth and smaller wildlife populations, mainly because oil companies have built roads opening the jungle up to colonization, deforestation, and the destruction of native habitats. Other sections are still more or less intact, but this is precisely because they are more isolated and harder to reach.

Tours operate out of just about every town in and around the Oriente, but to reach the most remote parts, you'll want to head out of either **Coca** or **Lago Agrio.** These northern Oriente towns sit just west of Ecuador's most undeveloped rainforests and provide access to the country's most impressive protected jungle areas, including the prominent **Cuyabeno Reserve** and the enormous, remote **Parque Nacional Yasuní.** To the south and west of Coca, the pleasant town of **Tena** and the tourist village of **Misahuallí** send trips into the less pristine but still impressive jungle wilderness that stretches out just to the east of them. The undisputed base for southern Oriente jungle tours is **Macas,** which offers access to remote Shuar villages, the nearby Cueva de los Tayos, and the rugged expanse of the *zona baja* of **Parque Nacional Sangay.**

After deciding which area you want to explore, you must make the equally important decision about who you want to guide you through it. You might end up having an excellent time with a tour guide who knows what he's doing, points out interesting wildlife, and respects the land and the people, or you could go along silently as your guide mentally counts his profits and stares out into a jungle he doesn't know much about. The South American Explorer's Club can be helpful, providing trip reports that offer recommendations and warnings about various companies. The companies listed in this guide are generally quite reliable, but don't come guaranteed. In general, it pays to ask a lot of questions and follow your gut feeling; after all, there are plenty of companies. If you plan on visiting any nationally protected areas, make sure the company you choose is approved by the National Park Administration (INEFAN) to lead tours through the areas you want to visit. Check the list of INEFAN-approved companies in the appendix (p. 284).

RAFTING AND KAYAKING

Wherever you've got a wet climate with geography as extreme as Ecuador's, you're going to get some killer whitewater rafting. Aside from the adrenaline rush provided by crashing down a raging river, the views from the river are often spectacular, since river-running enables you to get to places that cannot be reached otherwise. Ecuador's recently discovered whitewater pours down from the jungle mountains west of Tena in the country's Oriente region. With a higher density of whitewater than almost anywhere else in the world, the rivers here run year-round, beckoning tourists to enjoy their frothy fun. With sections ranging from class II (easy/mild) all the way up to class VI (virtually impassable), these waters were discovered so recently that only one company has risen up make them accessible to the masses: **Ríos Ecuador.** This outfit offers rafting and kayaking trips as well as a week-long kayaking course. See Tena's Sights section for more information, p. 218.

TOUR COMPANIES

Ecuador overflows with tour companies eager to show you the wonders of their extraordinary country. Most companies are fairly small, based in towns near the sights they visit. Below are some bigger-scale companies based in Quito that lead all-inclusive tours to destinations throughout the country.

Safari Tours (tel. (02) 552-505 or 223-381; fax 220-426), at Calama and J. L. Mera in the New Town, is reputedly the biggest climbing agency in the city of Quito. This famously dependable company conquers Cotopaxi, Cayambe, Chimborazo, Pichincha, and the Ilinias (to mention a few), and organizes a huge list of other trips to Ecuadorian destinations (open Mon.-Fri. 10am-7pm, Sat. 10am-2:30pm).

Etnotur, Luis Cordero 1313 y J. L. Mera (tel. 564-565; fax 502-682), has a team of guides decked out with the latest gear that leads trips to most of Ecuador's national parks and protected areas, including climbs up Cotopaxi, treks in the Oriente with overnight stays at their camp in Cuyabeno, and boat tours in the Galápagos Islands. Prices depend on the trip and number of people.

Keeping in Touch

MAIL

The Ecuadorian postal service is functional, but not always reliable. Airmail usually reaches the U.S. in around two weeks, but can easily take a month or more. Mail to Europe and other destinations takes even longer. If you choose to send something via surface mail (or simply forget to specify airmail), be prepared to give it time. Official estimates average 40 days by boat, but in reality, it may take months. Important documents should be sent via certified mail, or else duplicates should be sent.

You can have letters sent to you in Ecuador through **Lista de Correos,** a letter-holding service similar to the General Delivery service in the U.S. and Canada, or *Entrega General* or *Poste Restante* in other countries. Address letters as follows:

Theodore KACZYINSKI
Lista de Correos
Quito
Ecuador

The letter should also be marked *"Favor de retener hasta la llegada"* ("Please hold until arrival"). The mail will go to the central post office unless you specify a post office by street address. When picking up mail sent to you via *Lista de Correos,* give your name and explain that you are expecting mail. Try to keep names as simple as possible on the envelopes. Because Latin American *apellidos* (paternal last names) fall in the middle of the written name, confusion arises for foreigners with more than a simple first and last name. A letter could be filed under any misspelled permutation of the recipient's names. To avoid confusion, the last name should be capitalized and underlined. Check for mail under both your first and your last name, just to make sure. Bring a passport or other ID to pick up mail through the *Lista de Correos.* Letters and packages will be held for varying lengths of time, usually around two weeks.

It's wise to use the Spanish abbreviations or names for countries (EEUU or EUA for the U.S.). Write *Por Avión* on all postcards and letters not otherwise marked, unless you don't mind it arriving sometime in the next millennium. While it is possible to send packages from smaller towns, larger cities provide more reliable service.

If you have friends or family in the area, using their address may be preferable. You may be able to receive mail at a hotel where you expect to stay, but call ahead to arrange it in advance. **American Express offices** will also hold mail for 30 days for cardholders before returning it; just write "Client's Mail" on the envelope. There are two AmEx offices in Ecuador, in Quito and Guayaquil. You don't need to be a cardholder to receive this service as long as you purchase traveler's checks from AmEx. Call American Express customer service for more information (tel. (800) 528-4800). Ask for the free directory of traveler service offices. **The South American Explorer's Club** in Quito will also receive and hold mail for its members.

TELEPHONES, FAXES, AND E-MAIL

Calling home is a hard nut to crack in Ecuador. The national phone company goes by two names, EMETEL and IETEL, and has offices in most cities and towns. These offices are usually open daily from 8am-10pm for local and national calls, though times may vary slightly from town to town. However, their policies on **international calls** vary widely. Some offices can't do them at all, some only do them for exorbitant rates, others allow collect and calling-card calls for a fee or with the use of tokens *(fichas),* and the nicest ones allow collect and calling-card calls for free. In cases where collect and calling-cards calls are not allowed, try making a short call and arrange to be called back at a number in Ecuador.

Collect and calling-card calls are by far the cheapest ways to call home. Many phone companies have toll-free access numbers that you can dial from Ecuador to get an operator from your home country. These can be dialed from some EMETEL/IETEL offices, from pay phones, and from fancy hotels for a fee. Some companies will be able to connect you to numbers only in your home country; others can provide other worldwide connections. If calling the U.S., there are several options: the **AT&T USA Direct** access number from Ecuador is 999-119, the **MCI World Phone** access number is 999-170, and **Sprint** has a U.S. toll free number that can be used to make a collect or calling-card call (tel. (800) 877-8000). If you are not from the U.S., call your phone company in your home country; they may offer similar services. Phone rates tend to be highest in the morning, lower in the evening, and lowest on Sundays and at night (AT&T's and MCI's phone rates remain constant).

To call Ecuador, you must first dial your country's international access code (011 in the U.S.), followed by Ecuador's country code (593), followed by the two-digit area code for the part of Ecuador you are trying to reach (listed in the appendix and in individual towns' practical information), followed by the six-digit phone number.

Faxes are not uncommon in Ecuador, especially in larger towns and cities, though the fee for sending or receiving an international fax may be outrageously high. Some EMETEL/IETEL offices offer fax service, and hotels and businesses may also allow you to use their fax machines for a fee. **Electronic mail** (e-mail) is also possible, for a fee, from a few select locations, such as the South American Explorer's Club and the British Council in Quito (see Quito Practical Information, p. 59).

Let's Go Picks

We wandered and wondered through the width and depth of this small South American country, loving it and loathing it. Here's what we found:

Best Artesanía: Otavalo (see p. 86), 'cuz it's got it *all.* And more. **Cotacachi** (see p. 91), with its loads and loads of lovin' leatherwork. **Agato** (see p. 90), for its weavings at the Tahuantinsuyo weaving workshop. Witness the weavers' acrobatic feats with the *telaros de español;* just take a shower first. **Montecristi** (see p. 181), to find out where Panama hats are *really* made. **San Antonio de Ibarra** (see p. 97), home of the whittlers who aspire to the *artesanía* elite.

Best Mud Baths: Vilcabamba (see p. 152), a.k.a. Hostal Madre Tierra, for its hammocks, mud baths, and colon therapy ... what more could a traveler's intestine ask for? **Baños de San Vicente** (see p. 196), for filthy good massages using all-natural *savila.* **Roads in Coca** (see p. 223); when you see them, you'll know why. Remember your knee-high rubber boots.

Best Surfing: Montañita (see p. 189), means bare feet, bronzed skin, unclad torsos, rolling barrels, and killer swells, especially from December to June. **Alandaluz** (see p. 188), one of Ecuador's premier surfing locales, with 10- to 12-ft. waves in winter.

Best Mountain Climbing: Volcán Cotopaxi (see p. 108), because you've got to respect the tallest active volcano in the world. Plus, it's got an awesome *refugio.* **Volcán Chimborazo** (see p. 127), whose summit is the farthest point from the earth's center, due to the equatorial bulge. As they can tell you at Mitad del Mundo, that means weight loss.

Best Nightlife: Guayaquil (see p. 206), because who wants to go to sleep when there are *chivas* roaming loose? **Montañita** (see p. 190), whose beachside bars open around 6pm and don't close until everyone's lying face-down in the sand.

Best Tree-Top Lodging: Cabaña del Arbol (see p. 188), the Alandaluz honeymoon suite that sways with love (and private bath). **La Casa del Ceiba** (see p. 267), at El Progreso in the Galápagos, in a gigantic ceiba tree 40 ft. off the ground, furnished with two beds, a bathroom, hot water, music, television, a refrigerator, and a bar.

Best Roof-top Rides: Train-top, surf up or down the Andes from Alausí to Bucay, and even pick the Devil's Nose (see p. 129). **Bus-top,** soak up the jungle mountain views from Papallacta to Quito (see p. 233). **Boat-top,** lather up for a shower and a half on the wet 'n' wild waves between Cojimíes and Muisne (see p. 170).

Best Ceviche: Salinas (see p. 193), gateway to Cevichelandia, a magical world of raw seafood and *more* raw seafood. **Puerto Bolívar** (see p. 156), the best Machala has to offer. **Puerto López** (see p. 185), and the *ceviche de spondyllus* at Spondyllus Bar and Restaurant, if only for the name.

Best "Galápagos Experience": The Galápagos Islands (see p. 241), the genuine article, the real McCoy, the cream of the crop, the bee's knees, the enchanted isles. **Isla de la Plata** (see p. 185), in Parque Nacional Machalilla: the "Poor Person's Galápagos" for nature-lovers lacking the *plata.* **Guayaquil's Parque Bolívar** (see p. 205), with iguanas nearly as numerous as on the islands, and just as much fun as the sea lions!

Best All-Around Resource: The South American Explorer's Club (see p. 1), friendly and knowledgable to boot.

Ecuador: An Introduction

History

THE EARLIEST ECUADORIANS

While the Incas may have left the biggest mark on Ecuadorian indigenous life today, **pre-Columbian civilizations** actually thrived in the region long before the Inca's 1463 arrival. Archeological evidence shows that the earliest cultures in Ecuador lived on the southern coast, in the Loja area, and near Quito, over 12,000 years ago. Auspicious ocean currents and winds made the coast especially ideal for agriculture, and for 8000 years, an industrious settlement thrived there. The oldest extensive archeological findings are remnants of the **Valdivia culture,** a people who lived along the coast of the Santa Elena Peninsula roughly between 3500-2000 BCE. Early Valdivians were hunter-gatherers; later they developed farming techniques. Villages consisted of wood and straw huts arranged in a semi-circle around a central plaza, paved with shells for ceremonial purposes. Valdivian culture even foreshadowed a major schism in later Ecuador; when some moved to nearby river floodplains to farm, a differentiation between urban and rural lifestyles arose for the first time.

By about the year 0, various tribes dotted the Andes and settled on the northern coast, in what are now known as the Manabí and Esmeraldas provinces. Little is known about the different pre-Inca tribes, except that each had its own language and all declared frequent war on each other. Groups in the coastal lowlands—the Esmeralda, Manta, Huancavilca, and Puná tribes—were hunters, fisherman, agriculturalists, and extensive traders. The sedentary and mainly agricultural Sierra tribes—the Pasto, Cara, Panzaleo, Puruhá, Cañari, and Palta—used irrigation to cultivate corn, quinoa, beans, many varieties of potatoes and squash, and fruits, like pineapples and avocados. Local chieftains raised armies, distributed communal lands, and united different villages in political confederations headed by single monarchs.

THE INCA EMPIRE

Based in their capital in Cuzco (in modern-day Perú), the Incas had an itching to expand their empire, moving north into Ecuador in the late 15th century. The Inca conquest began in 1463 under the leadership of the warrior **Pachacuti Inca Yupanqui.** Several Ecuadorian tribes met the Inca troops with fierce resistance, and it took nearly four decades before both the Sierra and the coastal populations surrendered. **Huayna Cápac,** grandson of Pachacuti Inca Yupanqui and son of a Cañari princess, became ruler of the entire extended Inca empire.

Though the Incas only controlled Ecuador for about a half-century before the Spanish conquest, they left a tremendous mark. Some aspects of life among the native Ecuadorian tribes, such as their traditional religious beliefs, did not change much, but nearly every other area of society was greatly influenced by the Incas. The new dominators introduced crops from Perú, such as yucca, sweet potatoes, cocoa, and peanuts; the use of llamas and irrigation increased greatly as well. But the biggest change involved the possession of land. Instead of the previous system of private ownership, land became the property of the Inca emperor, held collectively by the **ayllu,** a kinship-based clan. Each *ayllu* alloted individual families a piece of land to cultivate for its own consumption, as long as it gave tribute payments to the **kuraka,** or chieftain.

Huayna Cápac grew up in Ecuador, and throughout his rule he adored his childhood homeland, naming Quito the second capital of the Inca empire. Still fearful of unrest in his ever-expanding kingdom, he spent many years traveling all over the empire, putting down uprisings and strengthening unions whenever he could—sometimes by marriage, other times by replacing troublesome populations with colonists from more peaceful parts of the empire. These colonizations helped spread the traditionally Peruvian language of Quichua into Ecuador, a language still used today by *indígenas* in the Ecuadorian Andes.

Huayna Cápac's sudden death in 1526 brought on a bitter power struggle. Rather than leaving the empire to one heir, he split the kingdom between two sons. Cuzco and the southen empire were left to to Huáscar, a son by Huayna Cápac's sister and therefore the legitimate heir. Ecuador and the northern empire went to **Atahualpa,** borne by a lesser wife, but his father's favorite. In 1532, Atahualpa decisively defeated Huáscar near Riobamba in central Ecuador, a victory that still remains a source of great national pride as one of the rare occasions when Ecuador defeated a hostile neighboring power. The Inca empire was left weakened and divided, unprepared for the arrival of the Spanish conquistadors a few months later.

THE SPANISH CONQUEST

The Spaniards landed near Esmeraldas in northern Ecuador on September 21, 1526, but the first conquering mission, led by **Francisco Pizarro,** did not get underway until 1532. Spain's King Carlos I granted Pizarro the titles of governor and captain-general of Perú, so Pizarro set out determined to conquer the troublesome Incas, whose independence kept him from his fame and fortune. At a pre-arranged meeting between Atahualpa and Pizarro in the town of **Cajamarca** in northern Perú, the Inca emperor disdainfully rejected both the Spanish crown and the Christian god, and was promptly attacked. Thousands of Incas were killed and Atahualpa was taken captive by the Spaniards and held for ransom.

Although Atahualpa's loyal followers poured enough riches into Cajamarca to completely fill his cell once with gold and twice with silver, Pizarro had no intention of setting the Inca emperor free. Instead, he set him up in a corrupt trial at which Atahualpa was convicted of every single one of numerous accusations, including polygamy, worship of false gods, and crimes against the king. The punishment: execution, on August 29, 1533.

Yet despite the loss of their leader, some Inca warriors continued to defend their empire. The general **Rumiñahui,** with the help of Cañari tribesmen, continued the struggle against the Spanish conquistadors. **Sebastián de Benalcázar,** one of Pizarro's lieutenants, defeated Rumiñahui near Mount Chimborazo and began pushing the Incas north. In mid-1534, when Rumiñahui realized that the Spaniards would soon conquer Quito, he set it ablaze, prefering to destroy this secondary Inca capital rather than surrender it to the conquistadors. The defeat of Rumiñahui marked the final victory in the Spanish conquest. Quito was refounded by the Spaniards on December 6, 1534 (a day that is still celebrated with parades, bullfights, and dances in the modern city). Guayaquil, which had been founded by Benalcázar in 1533 but taken by local tribesmen, was reconquered and refounded on July 25, 1537.

THE COLONIAL ERA

Initially part of the **Viceroyalty of Perú,** Ecuador was tightly controlled by the Spanish crown, subject to the king's major administrative agencies: the **viceroy,** the **audiencia** (court), and the **cabildo** (municipal council). In 1563, Ecuador gained a separate status from Perú, attaining its own **Audiencia of Quito,** meaning that it could deal more directly with Madrid on certain matters, especially matters of jurisdiction. In 1720, in an attempt to tighten Spanish control over the colonies, Ecuador became part of the new **Viceroyalty of Nueva Granada,** and central authority shifted from Lima to Bogotá.

Spanish **encomenderos** created huge plantations for themselves and depended on Indian agricultural labor, which thay obtained peacefully and indirectly by making deals with the *kurakas.* The *kurakas* really had no choice but to acquiesce to the more powerful Spaniards, and agreed to hand over their *ayllu*'s tribute payments, supposedly in exchange for the order and Christianity that the Spanish brought them. During the 1570s, however, Spanish officials began tightening their control over the Incas, abolishing the *encomiendas* and establishing a social system known as the

repartamiento de indios, which made the entire indigenous population vassals of the Spanish crown. It also introduced the **mita,** a system of forced labor that required all men between the ages of 18-50 to work for the Spanish crown for at least two months each year. Enforced by **corregidores,** new Spanish officials in charge of administering the *mita,* Ecuadorian **mitayos** (workers) mainly labored on huge agricultural **haciendas** or in **obrajes,** primitive textile sweatshops. As treacherous as the *mita* was for Ecuadorians, they were actually fortunate; in Perú, where there were much heftier deposits of valuable minerals, miner *mitayos* experienced even more brutal conditions. Disease, however, hit the Ecuadorian indigenous population severely. **Smallpox and measles** virtually wiped out the coastal population and drastically reduced the Sierra population, especially during an epidemic of the 1690s.

The seeds of the independence movement were planted during the 18th century. European scientists, who spent time in the Audiencia de Quito while measuring the circumference of the earth around the equator, introduced the ideas of the Enlightenment. The works of Voltaire, Jean-Jacques Rousseau, and Thomas Paine taught such revolutionary concepts as universal equality and freedom. One of the most famous early revolutionaries was **Eugenio de Santa Cruz y Espejo,** an intellectual who advocated independence from Spain and a democratic system of government.

THE INDEPENDENCE MOVEMENT

Ecuador's struggle for independence was part of a larger independence movement mobilizing throughout Spanish America. During the 18th century, tensions escalated as the **criollos** (people of pure European descent born in the New World) resented their limited access to Indian labor, high taxes to the Spanish crown, trade restrictions, and the privileges the Spanish-born **peninsulares** had in gaining political office. Tensions heightened further after Europe's **Seven Years War** (1756-63), when the defeated and bankrupt Spanish kingdom passed the **Bourbon Reforms,** increasing control and taxes in the colonies.

Ironically, the first revolts against colonial rule were actually expressions of support for the Spanish king. The independence movement gained steam when Napoleon Bonaparte invaded Spain in 1808 and deposed **King Ferdinand VII** to assume control of the New World colonies. The general consensus among the colonists advocated support for Ferdinand, and many conservatives formed **cabildos abiertos,** town councils organized to pledge their support for the rightful king. In some areas, these councils even seized authority. One of the first patriot uprisings in all of Latin America is believed to have occurred when a group of leading citizens took control of Quito in August 1809. However, as troops threatened the city, the rebels returned power to the *audiencia* authorities.

But after Ferdinand VII returned to the throne in 1814, his severe and absolutist restriction of colonial autonomy caused even the conservatives of the New World to turn against him. In Guayaquil, a patriotic junta under the leadership of poet **José Joaquín Olmedo** proclaimed the city's independence in October 1820. Troops from both the independence movements of the Argentine **José de San Martín** in the south and the Venezuelan **Simón Bolívar** in the north helped fight for Ecuador's independence in the struggle against the royalist forces. Led by Lieutenant **Antonio José de Sucre,** a string of patriotic victories culminated in the decisive victory at the **Battle of Pichincha,** just outside of Quito, on May 24, 1822.

Yet independence did not mean an end to the struggle. For the next eight years, Ecuador was part of the **Confederation of Gran Colombia,** along with the modern-day nations of Colombia and Venezuela, part of Bolívar's grand plan of a united Latin America. Yet this tumultuous confederation was plagued by regional rivalries, and split up in 1830, with a small section of its southwest finally becoming the independent Republic of Ecuador.

THE EARLY REPUBLIC (1830-60)

America is ungovernable. Those who have served the revolution have plowed the sea.

—Simón Bolívar

So Ecuador suggested during its early, tormented years. The chaotic process of its governance seemed nearly impossible. Various rivalries plagued the nation, causing divisive hostilities between politicians, ideologues, and even regions. Quito and the Sierra region emerged as conservative and clerical, dominated by semi-feudal estates still using Indian labor. The cosmopolitan, commercial port of Guayaquil, on the other hand, had more exposure to the ideas of 19th-century liberalism. These coastal bourgeoisie favored free enterprise and anticlericalism. A common division in 19th-century Latin America, the liberal-conservative split made it impossible for the people of Ecuador to peacefully agree on a national leader.

The most natural leader was **General Juan José Flores,** whom Bolívar appointed governor of Ecuador when it was part of Gran Colombia. One of the *criollo* elite, Flores found his support with the conservative *quiteños,* while the liberal **José Vicente Rocafuerte** became the rival leader of the *guayaquileño* forces. For the next 15 years, the two politicians struggled for power, taking turns in the presidency. While Rocafuerte considered himself an enlightened despot, condemning civil liberties violations and developing the nation's public school system, Flores put more effort into commanding the military and securing his hold on power.

Starting with an overthrow of Flores's regime in 1845, Ecuador experienced 15 years of further chaos. The government constantly changed hands between various weak leaders through a series of coup d'états, while the role of the military became increasingly important. One of the stronger, more influential leaders, **General José María Urbina,** ruled from 1851-56. As soon as he came into office, Urbina emancipated the nation's slaves, and later played a large role in ending the Indian population's required tribute payments. But by 1859, a year known in Ecuadorian infamy as the **Terrible Year,** the country again stood in a state of near-anarchy after one local *caudillo* stirred up anger by trying to cede some Ecuadorian territory to Perú.

THE CONSERVATIVE REGIMES (1860-95)

A strong leader was exactly what Ecuador needed at this point, and a strong leader is what it got. Coming into power in 1860, **Gabriel García Moreno** is known as the father of Ecuadorian conservatism, both hailed as the country's greatest nation-builder and condemned as its worst tyrant. Once a liberal politician from Guayaquil, García Moreno married into Quito aristocracy and shifted his ideology sharply to the right. During the 1840s and 50s, he watched disappointedly as his country seemed to fall deeper into a pit of chaos. García Moreno's diagnosis: the nation needed more cohesion, some sort of a unifying social cement. At first, he believed that incorporation into the French empire could provide this cohesion, but when the French appeared more interested in Mexico, he decided that the strongest unifying force was the general population's adherence to the Roman Catholic church.

From that point on, devotion to Catholicism was the magic ingredient in García Moreno's social cement; he believed that the order, hierarchy, and discipline cultivated by the Church could unify the nation's population. After coming to power in 1860, García Moreno based his 15-year regime on two things: his personal authoritarian rule and a strict abiding by Roman Catholic orthodoxy—education, welfare, and other matters of government were placed in the hands of the Church. An 1861 charter declared Catholicism the exclusive state religion, ties to the Vatican strengthened in 1863, and a decade later the republic was officially dedicated to the Sacred Heart of Jesus. In this respect, Ecuador deviated from the path of most other Latin American nations at the time, which had military rather than Church-based dictatorships and passed many anticlerical measures.

Yet despite the conservative nature of García Moreno's ties to the Church, his accomplishments were actually quite progressive—the **construction of a railroad from Guayaquil to Quito,** ending the isolation of the Sierra; the building of many new roads, schools, and hospitals; the planting of Australian eucalyptus trees in the highlands to combat erosion; and a greater sense of nationalism in the cities.

In 1875, while standing on the steps of the presidential palace, García Moreno was hacked to death with a machete by disgruntled peasants. Realizing the power of his words, liberal journalist and long-time critic **Juan Montalvo** exclaimed, "My pen has killed him!" Yet even without the man himself, the era of García Moreno's conservativism did not die, continuing weakly, for the next 20 years. Yet by 1895, the progressive conservative leaders were plagued with scandal, and the liberals finally saw the chance to make their move. Led by **General José Eloy Alfaro Delgado,** the **Partido Liberal Radical (PRL)** stormed Quito, emerging victorious after a brief civil war.

THE ERA OF LIBERALISM (1895-1925)

If García Moreno was the leader who best personified the conservative years, Alfaro (president from 1897-1901 and 1906-11) exemplified the next 30 years of liberal rule. In an attempt to erase anything that even smelled like it came from the right, one of his first moves as president was the creation of a new secular constitution—removing the Church's privilege of censorship, exiling some of the most prominant clergy members, secularizing education, instituting civil marriage as well as divorce, seizing church lands for the state, breaking the concordat with the Vatican, and ending the nation's dedication to the Sacred Heart of Jesus. Another item on Alfaro's agenda was the creation of stronger connections between Ecuador and the rest of the world, including the construction of ports and roads, as well as the completion of the Guayaquil-Quito railroad. Yet because of his close ties with the United States, Alfaro's plan of reform and development was condemned by some to be "delivering the Republic to the Yankees."

Yet Alfaro's accomplishments—his roads, ports, and railroads—could do no good as long as Ecuador had no profitable export to transport on them. The liberals failed in other areas as well; oppression of the Indians did not change, and Alfaro's attempts to hold onto power were just as ruthless and brutal as those of any of his predecessors. In fact, when he refused to step down to a hand-picked sucessor after his second term term ended in 1911, Alfaro was forced into exile in Panamá. The new president, however, died only four months later, and when Alfaro returned and tried to regain his following, a lynch mob killed him.

In the next 13 years, the government changed hands four times among liberal leaders and their respective constitutions. Yet after Alfaro, the presidency held little real power in Ecuador; rather, a plutocracy of coastal agricultural and banking interests known as **la argolla** (the ring) called the shots from Guayaquil. During World War I and the short economic boom following, cocoa became Ecuador's dominant export, and the country's economy thrived briefly. Yet disaster struck in the early 1920s, when a fungal disease ravaged Ecuador's cacao trees and the British colonies in Africa became a major cocoa-growing competition. The resulting inflation and unemployment hit the poor and the working class especially hard. In the **July Revolution** of July 1925, a group of young military officers overthrew the government in a bloodless coup, believing they could start a new program of national regeneration and unity.

THE TURBULENT YEARS (1925-48)

Although many of the leaders of the July Revolution preached socialist ideology, to their chagrin they soon discovered that most other army officers envisioned a new regime based more on Mussolini than Marx. The 1926-31 military dictatorship of **Isidro Ayora** turned out to be exactly that type of iron fist. Attempting economic reform, Ayora created the Central Bank of Ecuador, which took the power to issue currency away from private banks. Other reforms included the devaluation of the sucre to help highland exporters, labor legislation such as the regulation of hours and conditions of work, and the establishment of a pension program for state workers. Yet the living conditions of the poor still did not improve; one social critic claimed that Ayora's "public cleansing" reforms put "prohibitions on entering markets, public buildings, schools, parks, and theaters without wearing shoes—but no reforms which gave the unshod means to buy them."

With the **stock market crash** of 1929, nearly every Latin American government came crashing down with it—including Ayora's. Overthrown in 1931, Ayora was the first of 14 presidents during the turbulent 1930s. In fact, between 1931 and 1948, none of Ecuador's 21 presidents succeeded in completing a full term in office. Ecuador fared no better than the rest of the world during the **Great Depression;** global demand of cocoa dropped drastically, the price fell by 58%, and Ecuador's exports decreased by nearly 50%. The country's other major crops, coffee and palm nuts, experienced similar plunges. To add to the strife and instability, a four-day bloody civil war broke out in Quito in August 1932.

The scene was perfectly set for a charismatic leader like **José María Velasco Ibarra,** who took on his first of five presidential stints in 1934-35 (also president 1944-47, 1952-56, 1960-1, and 1968-72). A master of 20th-century populist politics, Velasco later went on to create his own personal movement, **Velasquismo,** centered around a combination of his charisma, a carefully cultivated image of honesty and sincerity, and fiery oratory. Yet during Velasco's first term in office, his strong personality was apparently not yet appreciated, and the military overthrew him after less than a year for trying to assume dictatorial powers.

The nine years before Velasco returned to office were marked by fiscal crisis, political coups, and fraudulent elections. The transitory regimes represented the struggle for power between the elites, the middle class, and the military. **Carlos Alberto Arroyo del Río** claimed victory in the 1940 presidential elections, though it was popularly believed that Velasco had actually been the victor. Yet Arroyo del Río's government fell apart when a border dispute with Perú became a disastrous 1941 military defeat. Perú's occupation in Ecuador continued until January 1942, when both countries met in Rio de Janeiro and signed a treaty known as the **Rio Protocol,** ceding about 200,000sq.km of Ecuadorian territory in the Oriente. The Rio Protocol ignited national pride, completely discrediting the Arroyo del Río government in the eyes of the Ecuadorians, and is still a cause of dispute between Ecuador and Perú today.

Velasco returned to power in 1944 accompanied by whopping bipartisan demonstrations of support. Fine-tuning his populist rhetoric, Velasco managed to enchant the masses, regardless of their party or ideology. Yet instead of dealing with the country's pressing economic problems, Velasco obsessed over restoring Ecuador's morality and social justice. Inflation and the standard of living worsened, and by the time he was ousted in 1947, Velasco had alienated his supporters so much that nobody rose to defend him.

THE RISE OF THE MILITARY (1960-79)

Between 1948 and 1960, Ecuador experienced something with which it had little familiarity—a period of political stability. This calm was mostly due to the onset of another atypical event—economic prosperity, due to a **banana boom.** Ecuador became the U.S.'s main banana supplier when disease ravaged the Central American crop in the late 40s. Prosperity led the people back to Velasco, re-elected in 1952, who became so popular that he got away with referring to himself as "the National Personification." By the time Velasco began his fourth term in 1960, however, lower export prices initiated a rise in unemployment and general social discontent.

The 1959 **Cuban Revolution** had profound reverberations throughout Latin America. Suddenly, the presence of Communism was very real, either as a threat or an attraction, and the Latin American nations had to decide where their loyalties fell. Steering towards Communism, Velasco began including more leftists in his government and consciously antagonizing the United States. The National Congress's debate over Ecuador's ideological future became so heated and hostile that gunshots were even fired in the Chamber of Deputies. In 1961, Vice-president **Carlos Julio Arose-**

Overstepping Their Boundaries

Wondering why this book's map of Ecuador doesn't look like the same one you see in CETUR offices? That's because of a pesky little dispute over some land in the Oriente that has soured relations between Ecuador and Perú for nearly 150 years. Ecuador insists on its rightful claim to over 200,000sq.km of Amazon basin because of its initial exploration of the great river, but most of the controversy has focused on a stretch of border in the Cordillera del Cóndor. Nobody really cared about who technically owned these 78sq.km of pure jungle until 1854, when Ecuador made an agreement with private creditors to use this border stretch of border. Sporadic mini-wars ensued for decades to come—and each time Perú emerged as the victor. But Ecuador refused to give in. In 1941, the issue's worldwide attention backfired; the 1942 **Rio Protocol Treaty,** designed to end the tiff once and for all, forced the world to recognize the land as Perú's. Ever since, the border issue has aroused Ecuadorian national pride and fury, the stuff presidential campaigns are made of. Leader after patriotic leader promises to get the land back, and every January (the month the Rio Protocol was signed), the inevitable border shootings occur. On a few occasions, the catfight has erupted into full-scale war—for a few days in 1981, and for an entire month in January-February 1995. This last time, it cost Ecuador 10 lives, US$680 million, and a lot of pride—President Sixto Duran-Ballen vowed early on, "Ecuador will not withdraw"... but two months later, the land was back in Perú's hands.

mena Monroy ousted his superior and immediately sent a goodwill mission to Washington, eager to renew good terms with the U.S. Yet Ecuador grew dangerously tumultous, and with every terrorist act Arosemena was accused either of weakness or Communist sympathies.

So in July 1963, a four-man military junta seized power, vowing to implement basic socio-economic reforms and to take a hard-line against Communism. The junta jailed or exiled prominent leftist leaders, and even tried to cut down left-wing student activism by reorganizing the nation's two leading universities. However, the military junta was unable to gain much popular support; its land reforms actually accomplished very little, and the economy worsened with a continuing deterioration in banana exports. In 1966, after a bloody attack on the students of the Central University in Quito, the military reformers stepped down. A non-partisan banana grower held the presidency for the one and a half years.

When in doubt, Ecuadorians could always vote for Velasco, and in 1968 this master of charisma began an unprecedented fifth term. Disillusioned with the gridlock caused by an uncooperative Congress, Velasco assumed dictatorial powers in June 1970 with a self-seizure of power, known as an **autogolpe.** Until his overthrow in 1972, he held onto these dictatorial powers primarily with the support of the military. His controversial policies generally caused protest and social unrest; his continued hostile behavior towards the United States reached the point where the U.S. withdrew almost all economic and military aid to Ecuador.

The military coup in 1972 was not due to the army's lack of support for Velasco; rather, it was provoked by the army's fear that **Asaad Bucaram Elmhalim** might be elected after Velasco's term ran out a few months later. The leader of the populist Concentration of Popular Forces (CFP) and twice an extremely popular governor in Guayaquil, Bucaram was considered by both the military and the business community to be dangerous, unpredictable, and unfit for the presidency. For the next seven years, Ecuador was ruled by military leaders determined to introduce structural changes to the country and encourage development. Yet they were not prepared for the **1970s oil boom.** After joining the Organization of Petroleum Exporting Countries (OPEC), the minister of natural resources tried pricing Ecuadorian oil well above the world market price. Combined with a lack of infrastructure reforms, exports fell and the country's economic problems simply worsened. Pure madness. Military leaders were unable to find a stable equilibrium; just about the only thing they could agree on was that they were bound to be divided, and the only hope for a stable government lay with civilian rule.

Originally, the creation of a new constitution and the democratic election of a president was supposed to happen in 1976, but it was delayed due to disagreements, and to ensure that the popular Bucaram would not be elected. Bucaram was eventually barred from running, but the second-in-command of the CFP, **Jaime Roldós Aguilera,** with his reformist platform, won a run-off election in 1979 with 68.5 percent of the vote, on a popular ticket that included **Osvaldo Hurtado Larrea,** leader of the Christian Democratic Party (PDC), as his running mate.

A RETURN TO DEMOCRACY (1979-PRESENT)

The Roldós-Hurtado regime began under auspicious circumstances. The oil boom was finally having positive repercussions for Ecuador, with the country's preferential treatment as part of the Andean Common Market. Unfortunately, this new wealth only increased the domestic gap in income distribution. To make things worse, a rivalry developed between Roldós and Bucaram, and the president became at odds with his own party. In 1981, Roldós died in a plane crash near Loja.

Ecuador's economic luck didn't last long. Oil reserves ran dry, and massive foreign borrowing led to a debt of almost US$7 billion by 1983. The warm ocean currents from **El Niño** in 1982-3 brought drastic climate changes, resulting in a cost nearly US$1 billion in infrastructure damage. Hurtado's regime responded to the minus-3.3% GDP change and record-high 52% inflation in 1983 with austerity measures. Steps such as ending government food subsidies helped devalue the sucre but hurt the poor terribly. Unemployment skyrocketed to 13.5%, and the **United Workers Front (FUT)** launched three riotous strikes during Hurtado's term in office.

Elected in 1984, **León Febres Cordero Ribadeneyra** believed in free-market economics and a pro-U.S. policy, attempting to emulate and ingratiate his government to Reagan's. Understandably, Febres Cordero was not popular in Ecuador. Oil prices continued to fall, and Febres Cordero continued to have troubles with the National Congress and the military. A March 1987 earthquake left 20,000 homeless and destroyed a stretch of the country's main oil pipeline, forcing the president to suspend interest payments on Ecuador's US$8.3 billion foreign debt.

In late 1988, Ecuador's inflation grew so bad and the government's austerity measures so painful, that large-scale protests ensued. The recently-elected president, **Rodrigo Borja Cevallos,** made agreements with various paramilitary protest organizations, guaranteeing their civil rights in exchange for demilitarizaion of his government. However, one guerilla organization, **Montoneros Patria Libre (MPL),** refused and continued violent action. Cevallos not only faced opposition from outside the government, but from within it as well. In 1989, the vice-president's plans to organize a coup were exposed. Another overthrow attempt came to the public light in 1990, when the President of Congress unsuccessfully tried to stage a legislative coup that actually resulted in the impeachments of multiple members of Congress. The year 1990 also saw a rise in indigenous protests. The **National Confederation of the Indigenous Population of Ecuador (CONAIE)** planned a seven-province uprising, seizing oil wells and taking military hostages. Their demands included the return of various traditional community lands, recognition of Quechua as an official language, and compensation for the environmental damage caused by petroleum companies. Though the protests ended when the government agreed to consider CONAIE's demands, tensions heightened again in April 1992, when thousands of *indígenas* from the Oriente marched to Quito, demanding that their territorial rights be recognized.

During his 1992-96 presidency, **Sixto Durán Ballén** dealt with many of these same problems on a larger scale. Austerity measures designed to cut inflation continued to cause widespread protest and general strikes, especially with a 70% price increase in fuel in 1994. CONAIE and other indigenous movements caused an even bigger stir with widespread demonstrations in June 1994, when they protested the **Land Development Law,** which allowed commercialization of indigenous lands for farming and resource extraction. The next month, the law was modified to protect the rights of landowners. Disaster hit when many top government officials, including the vice-president, were indicted in financial scandals. So many top authorities were impeached that demands even arose for Ballén to resign, voiced through student demonstrations throughout 1995 and early 1996. Plans to privatize the petroleum industry also caused strikes in the energy sector in late 1995.

LAST YEAR'S NEWS

An **earthquake** measuring 5.7 on the Richter scale occurred on March 28, 1996 at 6:03pm. The epicenter was in the town of Salcedo, 15km west of Latacunga, the capital of the Cotopaxi province. Roads in the area were closed down, electricity shut off, and the Defensa Civil sent in to help. The terrible *terremoto* caused the most devastation around the village of Pujilí, where narrow adobe walls and more than 240 buildings fell. In the tiny neighborhood of San Juan, 1km from Pujilí *centro,* every single house collapsed. The communities of Isinche, La Glória, Cachi, and Cuturibí were also devastated. The earthquake caused 16 deaths, relatively few in comparison to the widespread destruction.

Abdala Bucaram of the Partido Roldolista Ecuatoriano (PRE) defeated **Jaime Nebot** of the Partido Social Cristiano (PSC) in the presidential run-off election of July 7, 1996. Bucaram, the former mayor of Guayaquil, lost to Nebot in Ecuador's two biggest cities—Guayaquil (63% to 37%) and Quito (52% to 48%)—but overwhelmingly defeated him in the tiny towns and the Oriente. The conservative Nebot simply did not inspire enough confidence within the *pueblos* that things would change with his slogan, *"Primero La Gente"* (People First). Bucaram, clearly the more liberal of the two, looked nothing like a typical presidential candidate in his gold chains and untucked shirts. He fought back with the motto, *"Primero Los Pobres"* ("The Poor First"), advocated mass nationalization, and insisted that the country's poor would come first when rebuilding the gubernatorial structure. Campaigning was brutally negative: Nebot commercials showed videotape of Bucaram covered in blood and beating up rivals; Bucaram accused Nebot of hiring professional assassins to try to kill him. Bucaram's anti-oligarchy platform scared the bourgeoisie so much that many threatened to leave the country if he won. Reactions to the election were emotional; revelers from poor neighborhoods caroused on the city streets all night after Bucaram's final 54-46% victory was confirmed. Whether anything will really change remains to be seen. Bucaram took the office from Sixto Durán Ballén amid much hoopla on August 10, 1996, and took his first presidencial measure by devaluing the sucre a few weeks later.

The People

The people of Ecuador are the result of a process of continuous biological and cultural infusion, beginning with the arrival of the first *indígenas* in the country's coastal region over 12,000 years ago. Since then, many other groups have mixed in their genes and cultures. First the Quechua-speaking Incas conquered and assimilated the natives, and then the Spanish did the same. Other groups have also mixed themselves in along the way—African slaves came to work plantations on the coast, and small but thriving communities of Chinese and Lebanese immigrants live in Ecuador today.

The majority of today's diverse racial, ethnic, and cultural population of 11 million lives in the highland and coastal regions; the urban centers of Quito and Guayaquil each hold between 2 and 2.5 million. The Amazon is still sparsely populated, but more colonists move there every day. Issues of race and ethnicity are closely intertwined; an individual's identity as white, black, *mestizo* (mixed white and indigenous), or Indian is a combination of biological and social factors. Since the elite has always been predominantly white, and the working class mainly *mestizo* and Indian, a biological *mestizo* of high social rank may be called white, while a biological white with a low social rank may be called *mestizo*. This kind of ambiguity makes it is

"Y este hombre quiere ser presidente?!"

"No puede ser," cried the television commercials of the Socialcristiano candidate Jaime Nebot before his narrow defeat at the hands of "El Loco," Abdala Bucaram. With an uncanny resemblance to the Adolf Hitler—mini-mustache, arm sweeps, and all, Abdala marched on the campaign path, with "una sola ideología: derrotar a la oligarquía" (one ideology: tear down the oligarchy). However, his resemblance to Hitler may not have been merely incidental: Abdala (he is known by his first name) once cited *Mein Kampf* as his favorite book. However, his antics put him in his own class entirely; in his unsuccessful 1988 campaign, Abdala once showed up in a helicopter in a Batman costume. Traveling with an Uruguayan rock band on the trail, Abdala would pack the working class into squares and sing "boleros" on demand. But when it came to speaking, Bucaram was all business: his charismatic content matched his throaty shouts, and he somehow motivated almost all of Ecuador's poorer areas to vote for him (in the provinces of Zamora and Morona-Santiago, he won by approximately three to one). One reason may have been the female vote: Rosalía Ortega, his running mate, is the first female vice-president of Ecuador, but once elected, she seemed to have little place in the actual running of the country. Abdala's brothers have gotten more attention since: one, who was rumored to be Abdala's new minister of finance, has studied to be a witch doctor; and an Abdala brother was detained in Guayaquil the day after the election for driving a stolen vehicle.

Disinterested onlookers secretly hoped for a Bucaram victory because he would be more fun to watch, but scared members of Ecuador's upper classes fled the country the day after the results were announced (one hour late, because exit polls revealed a difference below the margin of error). Perhaps they fled for good reason; it is revealing that the man actually lost by two to one in the city he was mayor of—Guayaquil. In any case, though, the continuing development and class struggles of modern Ecuador and the reaction of its economy to Abdala's presidency will certainly be interesting to keep an eye on.

impossible to know exactly how the population breaks down racially; however, the estimate is 5% black, 15% white, 40% *mestizo*, and 40% indigenous.

The small **black population** lives mostly in the northern coastal province of Esmeraldas and in the Chota Valley of the northwest. A slave ship supposedly wrecked on the coast of Esmeraldas in the 17th century, and the survivors lived in this remote region, independent of the rest of Ecuador for many years. The residents of the Chota Valley are the descendants of slaves brought during the 1600s to work the sugar plantations of the coastal region. Today, both of these regions and their inhabitants clearly maintain a distinct culture and ethnicity. The country's **white population** is made up predomiantly of the descendants of Spanish conquistadors and colonists. Just like their ancestors, they make up the majority of the country's elite, concentrated primarily in urban centers such as Quito, Guayaquil, and Cuenca. **Mestizos** or *cholos,* with mixed white and indigenous heritage, is a kind of catch-all group that includes all Ecuadorians who are not black, white, nor affiliated with any particular indigenous ethnicity. They make up the bulk of Ecuador's urban population, and also inhabit rural areas that sometimes overlap with indigenous communities. But the *mestizos* of Ecuador are far from a homogenous group. Their cultures and lifestyles are the complex result of many different influences, and they vary greatly from coastal lowland, to highland, to Oriente.

The ancestors of the **indigenous peoples,** or *indígenas,* lived on the land that became Ecuador when the Spaniards arrived. The largest indigenous group (numbering over 2 million) are the highland **Quichua,** collectively referred to with this name because they speak dialects of the Inca Quechua language. There are many regional distinctions among the Quichua people. Some of the better known groups are the **Otavalos** who live in and around the town of Otavalo (north of Quito), the **Salasacas** who live south of Ambato, and the **Saraguros** who live north of Loja in southern

Ecuador. In the coastal lowlands, only a few small groups remain: the **Awa,** the **Cayapas,** and the **Colorados.** These groups are dwindling in number and they regularly put their dress and customs on display simply to earn a few tourist dollars. The Amazon also has its share of autochthonous groups. The largest of these are the **Jívaro,** who live in the central and Southern Oriente and number over 70,000. Within the Jívaro are the **Achuar** and the **Shuar.** Other smaller Oriente groups, some of which continue to live in relative isolation, are the **Cofán,** the **Siona,** and the **Secoya** in the Northern Oriente, and the **Huaorani** (or Auca), who live primarily in and around Yasuní National Park.

INDIGENOUS IDENTITY

Each of these groups has a distinct ethnic identity, and all of their members identify more strongly with their ethnicity than with the Ecuadorian state. It's no wonder—until the middle of this century, the government of Ecuador paid little attention to the needs of the indigenous and *mestizo* majority of its population, mainly catering to the interests of its white, mostly urban, elite. As in most of Latin America, this imbalanced socio-political order is the legacy of colonial times, when indigenous peoples were made to labor in the *haciendas,* mines, and factories of the Spanish and Creole elites. This exploitation continued even after independence. With the beginning of the 20th century, however, there was a move by a more liberal government to try to incorporate the Indian into the national community, mainly because the ruling class saw the Indians as an obstacle to development. Under the guise of fighting for equality, the liberals attempted to pass legislation that would free the Indians from ties to the church or private land-holders by dissolving their communal lands. The ulterior motive of these liberals was to gain access to the Indian land and labor for themselves. Indian groups resisted the division of their lands, and in 1937, two laws were enacted to reinforce the Indians' right to own land communally.

Beginning in the 60s, various indigenous and human rights organizations began to demand changes that would alleviate the subordinate status of the Indian in Ecuadorian society. A Quito demonstration in 1961 by 12,000 indigenous peasants demanded social change, and in 1964 an agrarian reform bill was passed. Though the reform was more developmentalist than redistributive, it still effectively weakened the political power of the land-holding elite.

Around this time, one of Ecuador's most successful and well-known indigenous groups, the **Shuar Federation,** was founded in response to new pressures from outside forces, including missionaries, colonists from the highlands, and later, oil companies. The Shuar have organized themselves into groups of about 30 families called *centros,* who hold land communally in order to prevent the break-up and loss of indigenous land. They have also instituted a health-care program and radio schooling system independent of the government. A move from their traditional subsistence farming to cattle ranching, however, has been criticized as a danger to the environment and incompatible with their traditional way of life. While their new practices deviate from tradition, they allow the Shuar to preserve their ethnic identity, rather than lose it to the more heterogenous national Ecuadorian one. This has happened in other indigenous communities of Ecuador as well. The northern highland town of **Otavalo** has become world-renowned for its weaving industry, with people coming to its Saturday market from all around. Some would argue that such commercialism is contrary to their traditional ways, but their weaving industry is actually the only thing that has allowed them to maintain their ethnic identity. Like the Shuar, they have adapted and thus kept an indigenous identity in the face of nationalist domination.

More recently, the Ecuadorian government has attempted to incorporate aspects of indigenous experience and tradition into collective national identity. The Roldós-Hurtado administration (1979-84), concerned with winning the approval of the Indian masses, expressed a desire to include formerly marginalized groups in national political life. They created the **Fund for Rural Development for Marginalized Groups (FODERUMA),** which intended to integrate peasant labor and products into the national market. However, outsider administrators disagreed with the *indígenas* on how funds should be used, and the organization received the nickname JODERUMA (*jodear* being the verb "to screw someone over"). Such resistance to integration attempts is common and understandable, given the people's history of subordination, oppression, and manipulation by the state. A report from 1975 found that 60% of an indigenous community only 100km from Quito did not know the colors of the Ecuadorian flag. Polls from 1980 revealed that the majority of highland *indígenas* did not know who Ecuador's president was, and thought the term *la patria* (the country) refered not to the state, but to a local bus company.

In other cases, populations have shown more active resistance to the integration of local, ethnic identity into a national one. A number of state-sponsored celebrations of popular culture, aimed at fostering national identity, have received mixed responses. Many indigenous people value the attention being given to their dance and music. However, more radical groups recognize the state's agenda behind such events and criticize them as fictionalized versions of Indian culture. Some new celebrations are grounded in local tradition but lose their original meaning through celebration in a national context. One such celebration, Otavalo's festival of Yamor, was boycotted by a group of *indígenas* in 1983 and 1984. The festival was originally a celebration of the corn harvest but today is promoted by the tourism industry and includes parades and fireworks. The offended indigenous group objected that this traditional ritual must not be manipulated by outside interests. Otavalo's economic success allows locals to protest high-profile nationalist projects, but less-affluent communities often accept them for lack of a better option. In another instance, the government issued a series of stamps celebrating Ecuador's Indian heritage, a move clearly intended to link the Indian with the nation. The town of Quimsa, whose culture was shown on one of the stamps, denounced the stamps because their traditions had been wrongly depicted. Such tactics angered *indígenas* by implying that their culture can function like a collectible item. Inaccurate depictions have done more to alienate native peoples than to embrace them.

Aggravated that the government has never wanted Indian support, only Indian assimilation, the indigenous peoples have developed a number of organizations to voice their desires and complaints. In 1986, these organizations came together under an umbrella organization called the **Confederation of Indigenous Nationalities of Ecuador (CONAIE).** In 1990, CONAIE organized the largest indigenous uprising in Ecuador's history, paralyzing the country for a week. Their rallying cry, "500 years of resistance and survival," was a protest against the upcoming 1992 quincentenary celebration of Columbus's landing in the Americas. Their agenda included 16 demands to help create a satisfactory relationship between indigneous people and the state, including more indigenous autonomy and a proposed constitution amendment making Ecuador a multi-national state. These demands run contrary to the state's national vision, mainly because they threaten the current socio-political stucture. Granting indigenous people the lands that they claim, particularly in the Oriente, would prevent the government from following its own policies for developing the resources there—namely oil. It remains to be seen whether CONAIE and the indigenous people of Ecuador will acheive their goal.

Religion

An enormous influence of the Spanish on indigenous life, a product of centuries of subordination, was their conversion of the Indians to **Catholicism.** The earliest colonists were granted groups of Indians on the condition that they convert them before working them to death. The Spanish justified this cruelty by reasoning that they had at least saved the Indians' souls before they took their lives. As Indian labor became slightly more scarce, missionaries headed into the wilderness and established missions there. Often this resulted in peaceful conversion, but as soon as the missionaries had done their work, others used the trails they had blazed to enslave and exploit the Indians (as depicted in the movie *The Mission*). Today in Ecuador, as in the rest of Latin America, the population is mostly Roman Catholic. As a result of missionary activities during this century, a small percentage of the population is also **Protestant.** Even these modern-day missions can be quite coercive, offering medical services or other aid only to those who visit their churches. No one seems happy to let the indigenous people alone with their own beliefs.

However, in many cases the indigenous populations have not given up their own traditions, but have simply incorporated Catholicism into their own belief systems. The resulting **hybrid religion** intertwines identities of indigenous gods or spirits with those of Christian saints. Indigenous celebrations are now often held on Saints' Days; for instance, the June 24 festival of Saint John the Baptist is thought to have replaced the Inca festival of *Inti Raymi,* held on the summer solstice. In other cases, a given situation (e.g. an illness) requires an offering to a certain saint instead of to an Indian spirit. Still other traditions have remained completely distinct from Catholicism. The indigenous people of the Andes have always worshipped the mountains, which they believe are the homes of mighty spirits that control fertility and the rain. In addition, **shamans** (*curanderos* in Spanish) are often called upon to cure the sick. Many techniques are used to diagnose and treat illnesses, including **rubbing a guinea pig** all over the sick person's body and then using the convoluted pattern of its entrials to learn something about the ailment. Another involves rubbing the person with a **raw egg** and then interpreting the noise the egg makes when shaken. Alcohol and tobacco are often consumed in bulk in some shamanic practices.

Festivals and Holidays

Semana Santa, the Holy Week just before Easter, occasions the most parties in Ecuador. Quito is the biggest party-mecca on Good Friday, but its processions are rivaled by those in some Chimborazo province towns, like Chambo, Chunchi, Tixán, and Yaruquies. Plan well in advance for accommodations at the more popular destinations. The festivities aren't confined to the hotspots, though; you're bound to find something going on during this week wherever you are.

Keep your eyes and ears peeled for local *fiestas* wherever you are, as they can be fascinating and exceptionally fun. Most towns celebrate a different **Independence Day,** the day they were liberated from Spain. Quito, Guayaquil, and Cuenca's independence days are national holidays, but many of the lesser-known celebrations take on more of a local flavor—Esmeraldas's August 3-5 Independence Day festivities include African music and marimba dancing. Even familiar holidays are given a new twist; unlike the hyper-commercialized **Father's** and **Mother's Day** celebrations common to the United States, there is no gift-giving or flower-sending in Ecuador. Instead, mothers and fathers simply get to take the day off from work to relax or party with other mothers or fathers.

Regional festivals, such as those dedicated to patron saints of local communities, are another common reason to cut loose; usually they're celebrated by drinking, dancing to local music, and sometimes a beauty pageant or two. Don't worry if you think you hear some gun shots; most of the time, it's just some celebratory firecrackers. Men doll up in drag and blackface for Latacunga's **La Virgen de las Mercedes** holiday on September 24, in honor of the city's dark-skinned statue of the Virgin Mary, known as La Mama Negra. For more information on other local holidays, as well as a list of Ecuadorian National Holidays, see the appendices, p. 285.

Customs and Manners

As a traveler, it doesn't take long to figure out that local customs and manners aren't always what you're used to. No one bats an eye when an elderly woman hawks a loogie on a public bus, but a traveler might be frowned upon for having a stubbly beard. You'll be more likely to earn the respect of the people you encounter if you take a moment to familiarize yourself with their social norms.

Foreign visitors are often shocked by the overwhelming *machismo* in some parts of Ecuador, especially rural areas. Women in bars—and foreign women in general—

are often believed to be lascivious. If you are female, drinking, becoming raucous, or even just expressing your opinions may shock men who believe women should be quiet and meek. Whether you're a man or woman, be sensitive to rising testosterone levels. Never, ever say anything about another man's mother, sister, grandma, aunt, daughter, wife, or girlfriend. Never.

Personal hygiene and appearance are often difficult to maintain while traveling, but your appearance definitely affects how you are treated by locals. Clean-shaven men with short hair and women who don't show much skin are more likely to be well-received than scruffies and smellies or women without bras. Men should remove hats when entering a building.

Punctuality isn't as important as it is in Europe and the United States (as you'll quickly confirm after riding the buses), but there are limits, of course. A different perspective on time is also apparent during meals, which are rarely hurried in Ecuador. Enjoy the ingenious tradition of *siesta,* a time in the afternoon when it's just too hot to do anything but relax, have a drink, and maybe nap. Don't expect much to happen during the mid-afternoon, as banks and businesses often shut their doors. While eating at a table with Ecuadorians, keep your hands on the table and not in your lap.

Ecuadorians hold politeness in high esteem, both to acquaintances and strangers. Jaded foreign travelers, ingrained in cultures that consider urban indifference the highest virtue, need to adjust if they expect to be treated with respect. When meeting someone for the first time, shake hands firmly, look the person in the eye, and say *"Mucho gusto de conocerle,"* (pleased to meet you). When entering a room, greet everybody, not just the person you came to see. Females often greet each other with a peck on the cheek or a quick hug. Sometimes men shake hands with women in a business situation, but the standard greeting between a man and a woman—even if they are meeting for the first time—is a quick kiss on the cheek.

Salutations in passing are considered common courtesy in smaller towns, particularly in the Oriente. *"Buenos días"* in the morning, *"Buenas tardes"* after noon, and *"Buenas noches"* after nightfall should be said to almost anyone with whom you come in contact. This charming Latin American custom epitomizes a general feeling of *amistad* on the streets, even between strangers. A similar custom: saying *"buen provecho"* ("bon appetit") to everyone in a restaurant upon entering or leaving.

Finally, be sensitive when taking photographs. Devotees at a shrine might be interesting to look at, but their religiosity is no novelty. If you must take pictures of locals, first ask if they mind. Indigenous peoples tend to object most strongly to being photographed, so just preserve the moment mentally.

Pabulum and Potables

> **pab•u•lum** 1: FOOD; esp : a suspension or solution of nutrients in a state suitable for absorbtion 2: intellectual sustenance 3: an insipid piece of writing
> **po•ta•ble** : a liquid that is suitable for drinking; *esp.* : an alcoholic beverage
>
> *Webster's Ninth New Collegiate Dictionary*

FOOD

From conventional stand-bys to exotic local dishes, Ecuador's got something to satisfy people of all tastes. The fruits encountered here are as succulent and varied as those grown anywhere in the world. Distinctive grains and tubers abound, and a plethora of vegetables are cultivated and cooked. As for meat, just about anything is considered fair game, and every part of that game is used somehow, from hoof to heart and tentacle to testicle. Despite this variety, certain things are encountered much more often than others. For the most part your culinary experience will be determined by the region you're in and type of restaurant you choose to visit.

There are a number of dishes that are peculiar to Ecuador. Perhaps the most shocking to westerners is the mouth-watering delicacy known as **cuy** (guinea pig). A specialty dating back to Inca times, the dish gets its name from the sound the animal makes just before it getting skewered and roasted, *"Cuy, cuy, cuy ..."* The more vegetarian-friendly **llapingachos** (Andean potato and cheese pancakes) also date back to ancient times, and get their name from the sound the potatoes make when being boiled and mashed, *"Llapingacho, llapingacho, llapingacho ..."* Andean natives really know their potatoes; they were first cultivated in the Andes before becoming a starchy staple the world over. Another Andean starch favorite is the **yucca root** (also called *manioc*). As a vegetable dish it is served boiled, but fermented it becomes the alcoholic beverage know as *chicha.*

Ecuador also boasts **bananas** and **plantains** *(plátanos)* in every size, shape, color, and flavor. There are also truckloads of other **tropical fruit;** papayas, passion fruit, avocados, tangerines, pineapples, melons, and tamarinds are all found here, mostly in the fruit-friendly lowland, coast, and jungle regions. If things seems fishy, you're probably on the coast or Oriente, where **gill-endowed aquatic organisms** are served *frito* (fried), *enpanado* (breaded), and *a la plancha* (grilled). Fish is often referred to as *corvina* (sea bass), or *trucha* (trout) instead of the generic *pescado* (fish). In the Oriente you may find yourself dining on Amazonian gill-breathers, such as *balgre* (catfish) or piranha. One last way to enjoy the fruit of the sea is in **ceviche**, a dish made from raw seafood marinated in lemon and lime juice with cilantro and onions. While you may enjoy some of these delicacies at a marketplace or back in you hotel, chances are you'll do most of your eating in small, local diners known as **comedores,** or in pricier Ecuadorian restaurants.

The most commonly served meal at the *comedores* is the **almuerzo,** with similar meal deals commonly referred to as the **merienda** or **menú del día** (meal of the day). This is a set two-course plate with various extras, which has been prepared in advance and is served at a special price (usually s/3,000-6,000). The first course is **soup** (*sopa* or *caldo*); you may luck into a creamy potato and cheese soup, a catfish soup *(caldo de balgre),* or a hearty beef stew *(caldo de res).* Vegetables from spinach and asparagus to corn and carrots are all possible ingredients, as are various cuts of meat, like *higado* (liver) and *tripa* (tripe). The second, main course (**segundo** or **plato fuerte**) is based on some kind of meat (usually chicken, beef, or pork), often smothered in some kind of savory sauce. Along with the *carne* comes rice, a vegetable, and perhaps a salad or french fries. In every town there is a *comedor* or two known and loved by the locals, the perfect place to get an *almuerzo.* Fancier restaurants serve *almuerzos* as well, often at a higher price with extras like coffee, dessert, cloth napkins, and tuxedoed waiters.

If the *menu del día* doesn't do the trick, check out the menu for ***a la carta*** selections. These will almost always cost more and provide less food than the *almuerzo,* but sometimes it's worth the extra sucres to be able to choose your own meal. The food is often the same kind of thing you will find in the *almuerzo:* creamy soups, potato pancakes, chicken, fish, and *lomo* (a plain cut of meat, *not* a real steak). The fancier restaurants may serve veal *(ternera),* or more quality cuts of steak *(lomo fino)* with fancy wine or mushroom sauces. Good **steakhouses** in bigger cities will serve choice Argentinian beef in all its various forms (a satisfying splurge for meat-lovers). You may choose to try the **parilla** or **parillada,** a sizzling grill heaped full of 10 or more different kinds of meat: steak, pork chop *(chuleta de chanco),* liver, kidney *(riñon),* sausage *(chorizo),* and more unusual cuts such as intestine, udder, heart, or blood sausage (mmmmmm, my favorite).

But blood sausage just doesn't cut it first thing in the morning. Luckily, breakfast food abounds in Ecuador. Most common are eggs *(huevos),* which can be prepared just about any which way, from *frito* (fried) to *revuelto* (scrambled). Breakfast is commonly served with toast *(pan tostado),* juice, coffee, and sometimes rice and beans. For a lighter (and cheaper) breakfast just visit the local *panadería* (bakery). *Empanadas* (bread stuffed with cheese), *cachos* (croissants), *pan dulce* (sugar coated rolls), and *pan de sal* (salted rolls) all go unbelievably cheaply. Meatier, *almuerzo*-like breakfasts can also be had. Well-touristed areas may offer a *Desayuno Americano,* which includes a bit more food, for the voracious American appetite.

While traditional Ecuadorian cuisine does have a fair bit of variety, travelers staying more than a couple of weeks should prepare for **gustatory monotony.** The same things tend to turn up on every menu. However, with a little searching more international cuisine can be found in the form of burgers, pizza, or Ecuador's own version of chinese food, served at *chifas* (Chinese restaurants) throughout the country. In addition, most well-touristed areas have a few *gringo*-oriented establishments that cater more to foreign tastes. These can be a refreshing break from traditional Ecuadorian fare. If you're *really* feeling homesick, Quito and Guayaquil both offer miraculous **portals into First World life,** such as Burger King, KFC, and Pizza Hut.

DRINK

If frequent and urgent visits to the toilets of Ecuador is not your idea of fun, try to avoid drinking the tap water. Water advertised as *purificada* (purified) may have just been passed through filter. While this may be comforting, these filters do not necessarily catch all of those diarrhea-causing demons. Water that's been boiled or treated with iodine is safe to drink, but aside from that it is wisest to stick to the bottled water that can be found everywhere. Make sure the cap is the original, and that you're not just buying well water.

Sweeter, more effervescent options are Ecuador's soft drinks, always referred to as **colas.** Flavors include the worldwide Coke, Sprite, and Fanta, as well as various types of *fiorivanti* (including strawberry, apple, and pineapple), and the occasional Pepsi. Another option is the uniquely fruity Inca Kola, made from an ancient recipe that was deciphered from the hieroglyphics of the Macchu Picchu ruins in Perú.

Juices made from Ecuador's abundance of exotic fruits are common and delicious, but almost always made with water. Before consuming, make sure the water used to make the juice has been purified. **Coffee** is not as good as it should be, considering the fact that Ecuador is a coffee-producing country. It is usually served as *esencia* (boiled down concentrated coffee that is mixed with water or milk). Otherwise, you may just be served Nescafé instant coffee. **Milk** is also readily available but is much creamier than the skim milk many foreigners may be accustomed to. Before downing a tall, cold glass of the white stuff, make sure it's been pasteurized.

If you're looking for something a little more intoxicating than milk, try one of Ecuador's beers, **Pilsener** or **Club,** both of which are light lagers. Club has a little bit of an edge, while Pilsener is smoother. One of these beers will set you back a mere s/1,500-3,000 (a little more in fancier places). At these prices, why hold back? Most **wine** is Chilean and tends to be quite expensive, not really a budget beverage. If you really want drown your sorrows, liquor is readily available at almost every corner store at absurdly cheap prices (s/3,000-6,000 for a liter of decent rum). But beware, prices rise dramatically if you wish to consume your beverage in a nice bar or restaurant. Ecuador's local firewater is **aguardiente,** a sweet, tangy, and delicious sugar cane alcohol. Many a tasty drink is made from *aguardiente.* The *caneliza,* made from boiling water, *aguardiente,* cinnamon, and lemon juice, is guaranteed to warm your insides on those cool, misty highland evenings (just make sure that the water came to a boil). Another local liquor, **chicha,** is popular in the Oriente. Made from fermented yucca plant, the recipe also includes a special treat—human saliva.

The Arts

Ecuadorian art is a complex blend of influences—indigenous and European, ancient and modern. The legacy was laid by the Incas and other pre-Columbian groups, with their *artesanía* (arts and crafts) and distinctive Andean music. When the Spanish arrived, they mixed the artistic influences and technology of the Old World with the indigenous art. *Artesanía* was modernized, colonial buildings went up, and cobblestones laid down. The religious art so well-known in the Old World began being produced in a distinct new style by the Quito School. With time, the art of Ecuador followed modern trends more and more. Indigenous artisans, combining ancient and modern techniques, began making products for an international market. A number of talented painters, in touch with worldwide artistic currents, began producing modern art with Ecuadorian subject matter. Today's art scene in Ecuador is as active as ever, and numerous museums, festivals, and markets continue to celebrate the country's artistic tradition. Whether you seek the holy splendor of a colonial cathedral, or the mellifluous notes of the Andean *zampoñas,* Ecuador's got the cultural color to further decorate your cerebral canvas.

ARTESANÍA

Crafts of all kinds are produced in Ecuador, but the country is best known for its large variety of **textiles,** almost all of which are produced by various indigenous groups. The most prolific and well-known center of textile production is **Otavalo,** an Indian community 96km north of Quito. *Otavaleños* have been in the textile business for centuries; when the Incas conquered the area in the late 15th century, they forced the inhabitants to pay tribute with their textiles. A few decades later, the Spanish brought new technology in the form of the treadle loom, hand carders, and new materials, like silk and wool. Under one guise or another, they forced the Indians to work under horrible conditions in *obrajes* (textile workshops) well into the 19th century. In the early 1900s, the *otavaleños* got their start in the modern textile industry by producing imitations of British tweeds (called *casimires*). Since then, the region continues to put out quality textiles, with almost all production taking place in indigenous households. Most weaving is done with the treadle loom, but some families still use the backstrap loom, a pre-Columbian design, with one end attached to the weaver's back. All kinds of their products, from ponchos to belts and tapestries, are exported to markets around the world. The **Saturday market** in Otavalo is one of the most popular attractions in all of Ecuador. Some regions of northern Ecuador have taken to **embroidery** and ply their wares at the Otavalo and Ibarra markets. Most striking are their blouses, along with exquisite napkins, dresses, and tablecloths.

Other regions of the country are also known for their weavings. **Cuenca** and the nearby region make **ikat** textiles. This technique involves dying the threads, usually with indigo, before weaving takes place. *Paños* (elaborate shawls) are common *ikat* items, as are *macanas* (carrying cloths, commonly made in the town of Salcedo). Ponchos and wool blankets are also made using the *ikat* technique. **Salasaca** is the country's other main tapestry producer. Along with **Cañar**, it is also known for its fine wool **belts** *(chumbis),* which are decorated in various indigenous motifs. **Hand-knitted** sweaters, socks, gloves, and hats are made throughout the highlands and are sure to keep you roasty-toasty. Before buying, make sure the size is right. Most foreigners are quite large compared to the average highlander.

The leatherwork capital of Ecuador is **Cotacachi,** just north of Otavalo. Wallets, purses, belts, whips, and leather underwear can all be found in the many shops lining the town's main street. The handiwork of the Cotocachicans can also be found in less abundance at the market in Otavalo. Ecuador's highest-quality **woodwork** is made in **San Antonio de Ibarra**. Locals carve wood products of all kinds, from intricately carved wooden boxes and sculptures to furniture. Many artisans work and sell goods right out of their homes. Listen for the sounds of saws and chisels and look out for the trails of sawdust.

Pre-Hispanic metal work is amazing and in some places the tradition of hand-crafting **jewelry** lives on. Elaborate **shawl pins** (called *tupus*) are made and worn by the Indians of **Saraguro.** These pieces are often family heirlooms passed from one generation to the next. **Chordeleg** is also well known these days for its contemporary jewelry stores. Much Ecuadorian jewelry incorporates beads into the design, a tradition that began before the Spanish conquest. Beads made of red Spondylus shell were traded throughout the Andes, and to this day red is the favored bead color.

Ceramics are made throughout Ecuador. The Quichua *Sacha Runa* (jungle people) who inhabit the Oriente between the Pastaza and Napo rivers produce fine hand-coiled pots with paintings of Quichua life and mythology on the sides. Other well-respected ceramics are made in the area around **Latacunga.** The small town of **Pujilí** is known for its **painted ceramic figurines.** Shops in Quito and the market at Otavalo also have reputable ceramics for sale.

MODERN ART

The unifying theme of 20th-century Ecuadorian art is its indigenous subject matter, and this common thread lends the movement the name **indigenísmo.** Ecuador's most famous member of this school, by far, is **Oswaldo Guayasamín.** The son of an *indígena,* his paintings are strongly pro-Indian, carrying social and political messages with not-so-subtle symbolism—typically rather abstract depictions of down-trodden *indígenas* suffering in one way or another. He worked for a time with the Mexican muralist José Clemente Orozco, and was also influenced by cubism, as evidenced by the choppy style of *La Edad de la Ira (The Age of Anger), Los Turturados (The Tortured Ones),* and *Cabezas (Heads).* In 1988, Guayasamín painted a 23-panel mural in the meeting hall of the Ecuadorian Congress, depicting episodes from Ecuador's history in his trademark anti-establishmentarian manner. Most shocking was a black-and-white panel of a skeletal face wearing a Nazi helmet, with the letters CIA marked across the front. The U.S. Ambassador demanded that the letters be painted over, and members of the U.S. Congress even considered cutting off economic aid to Ecuador. The best place to see Oswaldo's work today is at his museum in Quito (p. 73).

Eduardo Kingman, another indigenist, is considered by some to be the trail-blazer of the movement. The figures in Kingman's paintings are stylized and sorrowful, often depicting scenes of oppression. His 1985 work, *Jugetería (Toy Store),* shows a young Indian girl painted in dark, shadowy colors peering into a brightly-colored toy store. **Camilo Egas** was part of the early indigenous movement, though his style was much more variedand influenced by French surrealist currents. In the 50s, he started painting indigenous subjects in a very different realist style. His figures conveyed a feeling of strength and dignity instead of the sadness and abuse depicted by other indigenists. Egas has his own museum in Quito as well. **Manuel Rendón,** another well-known Ecuadorian painter, was not especially indigenist, but is still considered part of the movement. He grew up in Paris, the son of the Ecuadorian Ambassador, and like Egas, was influenced by the modern art there. His works use various modernist styles, such as cubism and pointillism.

Of the more recent generation of painters, **Ramiro Jácome** is the most famous. Not a part of the indigenist movement, he instead prefers to paint abstract human figures using deep colors. Paintings by Jácome and other modern Ecuadorian artists are on display at the Casa de la Cultura in Quito (p. 73).

MUSIC

The music of Ecuador is the result of the confluence of two distinct musical streams: Spanish and pre-Columbian. This tranquil hybrid music of the Andes, rife with fife, strings and other things, has been popularized around the world by traveling musicians from Ecuador, Perú, and Bolivia. Often the music is just instrumental, but when there's singing, it is usually in Quichua. Bands frequently play at festivals, and recently, people have begun holding music competitions. Get into the groove at one of the many folk music clubs (called **peñas**), where locals get together to celebrate and have a good time.

Indigenous contributions to the typical Andean band include wind instruments, drums, and rattles. The first instrument that pops into most minds when thinking of Andean music is the **panpipe** or **rondador.** This ancient instrument is believed to be over 2000 years old, and where would **Zamfir** be without it? A relative of the *rondador,* originating from the southern Andes but commonly played in Ecuador, is the *zampona,* with two rows of pipes instead of just one. This instrument, along with the five-note scale on which the tunes are based, gives the Andean music its distinctively haunting sound. Two **flutes** of different sizes are also used quite often—the larger *quena* and the smaller *pingullu.* The flutes and the panpipes are both carved from Ecuadorian bamboo. **Bells, drums,** and **rattles** made from gourds *(maracas)* comprise the rest of the indigenous contributions to the modern Andean band.

When the Spanish arrived, they brought with them **stringed instruments** of all shapes, sounds, and sizes, including the *guitarra* (guitar), *violín, bandolín* (mandolin), *charango* (a uekulele-type instrument commonly made from an armadillo shell), and *arpa* (harp). These have added even more variety and texture to the already rich local music.

ARCHITECTURE

The oldest architecture around is, of course, what the Incas left behind. The ruins of **Ingapirca,** just north of Cuenca, are Ecuador's best. Located on an old Inca road, the complex is believed to have served as an inn, a fortress, a temple, or some combination of the three. The ruins exhibit the fine stonework and carving for which the Incas are famous (see Ingapirca, p. 129). Little else of Inca origin remains, primarily because the Spanish either destroyed or co-opted their buildings. A number of important Ecuadorian towns are built on the rubble of the Inca civilization; in many cases, the Spaniards even used the very same stones. Many colonial churches are perched on hilltops because they were built over foundations of Inca temples.

Colonial architecture is a blend of the Old and New Worlds; the style of religious art and architecture that resulted from the mix is called the **Quito School.** The Spaniards commissioned the works to be in the popular **baroque** style, but the indigenous peoples who executed them added their own distinctive touches. Churches and convents in the older towns of Quito and Cuenca are decorated with intricately carved facades and statuaries. The ornate interiors sparkle with gilt; leafy stone vines wrap around classically styled columns as archangels peer down from vaulted ceilings. Municipal buildings and private residences are usually more modest. Large wooden doors open onto rather blocky two-story buildings with high ceilings, interior courtyards, and covered verandas. Simple stonework and elegant wrought-iron decorate whitewashed interiors, while ancient wooden beams and weathered red tiles make up the roofs above. While Riobamba and Latacunga are old cities, they have been destroyed by earthquakes and volcanos, so few to none colonial structures remain. Much of Ecuador has been built in the 20th century, when building costs have assumed a position primacy in the architectural mind; blocky cement and rebar buildings crowd each other on the more modern streets of New Quito and Guayaquil.

LITERATURE

Ecuador's earliest literature, its **pre-Columbian oral tradition,** was mainly indigenous stories, songs, poetry, and theater intimately linked with religious practices. With the arrival of the Spanish and the forceful conversion of the indigenous peoples to Catholicism, much of this tradition was lost. One notable exception are the preserved stories of the war between Atahualpa and his brother Huascar for control of the Inca Empire just before the Spanish Conquest.

The first textual works were the writings of various clergymen during the 17th century, including poetry and discourse on social and political issues in the Spanish colony. The most well-preserved authors of the following century were three Jesuit clergymen, **Antonio Bastidas** (1615-81), **Xacinto de Evia** (1620-?) and **Gaspar de Villarroel** (1590-1665). In the 18th century, bourgeois professionals began to express discontent with the state of affairs that eventually led up to the independence movement. Called "the literature that did not yet have a country," these writings were the first to explicitly focus on what was to become Ecuadorian society. **Juan de Velasco** (1727-92), a historian and narrator, is considered by many to be the most talented writer of this time. A journalist, physician, and philosopher, **Eugenio Espejo** (1747-95) advocated sweeping societal reform and wrote on a vast array of topics including education, theology, politics, health, and the economy. He also started Quito's first newspaper, though it lasted only three months. **Juan Bautista Aguirre** (1725-86), is best known for his *Brief Design of the Cities of Guayaquil and Quito,* which examines the still-present rivalry between the two cities.

The 19th century brought Ecuador its independence from Spain, and with that a distinctive national literature established by the founding fathers, **Juan León Mera** (1832-94) and **Juan Montalvo** (1832-89). Though their Romantic style was influenced by Spanish literature, the content was very anti-monarchic and attempted to create a uniquely Ecuadorian national identity. The most important work is Mera's *Cumandá,* the first Ecuadorian novel. Mera also published other short novels, articles, poetry, and collections of Ecuadorian folklore. Known as the favorite novelist of Ecuador's liberal movement, Montalvo was more intellectual in his writing. His fictional *Chapters that Cervantes Forgot* narrates Don Quixote's adventures through the Americas, dotted with criticisms of intellectual and political enemies. The work of these influential authors contributed greatly to the literary outpouring during the 20th century.

Since then Ecuadorian literature has taken on a life of its own, dealing with uniquely Ecuadorian social, political, cultural, and historical topics. One of the most marked differences between the writings of the 19th and 20th centuries is the move away from a romanticization of Indian traditions to **Indigenism,** in which indigenous struggles are treated more realistically. One of the first Indigenist works is the 1934 *Huasipungo,* by **Jorge Incaza** (1906-78), a story of the Indian resistance to their exploitation. Another important work of the 1930s is the collection of short stories by different authors, *Los que se van (Those Who Leave)*. Subtitled "Tales of Half-breeds and Hillbillies," the stories use crude language and themes that deviated from traditional literary norms and shocked the readers of that time. **Pablo Palacio** (1906-47) was active during 20s and 30s, laying the foundations of a writing style that would become more widespread in the 60s and 70s. His writing is filled with irony and a questioning of reality; subjective descriptions, existentialism, and psychic trauma run throughout. Two authors of the 60s, **Miguel Donoso Pareja** and **Pedro Jorge Vera,** wrote anti-imperialist works reflecting Ecuador's frustration with its dependency on foreign powers. In 1978, the first Meeting on Ecuadorian Literature made the country's lit that much more legit. Ecuadorian literature has continued to flourish since.

Environmentally Responsible Tourism

Visitors inevitably affect a country's ecology, especially in poor nations where rapid development has taken place in order to encourage tourism. Nevertheless, there is not a cut-and-dried list of activities that do or do not make you an environmentally responsible tourist, and no objective criteria exist that can be used to judge your fellow traveler's guilt or innocence. Being responsible does not mean never going on a jungle tour or only using biodegradable shampoo. Rather, responsible tourism means understanding the short- and long-term effects of your actions, seriously considering these effects, and realizing you are responsible for them. Only looking at part of the picture does not lead to a responsible decision. This is especially true with spending your money. When purchasing a good or service, a sucre does much more than simply provide for you—it influences the growth of industries and the lives of those who work in them. Responsible tourism means being aware of these factors and weighing them in such a way as to make a responsible decision.

As a traveler, there are certain measures you can take to minimize your impact on the countries you visit. Always turn off the lights and the air-conditioning when you leave a room, and make sure that the doors and windows are shut when the air-conditioning is on. Better yet, stay in a place without air-conditioning; most Ecuadorians do this their entire lives. Don't accept excess packaging, particularly non-biodegradable styrofoam boxes. Women can buy feminine hygiene products with minimal packaging; O.B. brand tampons have no applicators. Choose glass soda bottles over drinking boxes or marginally recyclable aluminum cans. Reuse plastic bags. It's hard to convince Ecuadorian market vendors not to give you three plastic bags where one would suffice, but with a little extra effort, you'll surely succeed.

To be water-friendly, carry a refillable water bottle or canteen. While the water in Ecuador does present a credible health hazard, you can bring purifying tablets or iodine drops from home to treat it. This method will save you from buying countless plastic water bottles which will probably end up floating down the Napo or (not) decomposing next to the railroad tracks. Not a pretty sight.

One of the best ways to undo some of the effects of environmental destruction in Ecuador and to minimize your own impact is to volunteer for one of many environmental organizations (see Alternatives to Tourism, p. 19). Should you happen to uncover a great "ecotourism" operator or have further ideas on how to be a low-impact tourist, we at *Let's Go* would love to hear of them. Please call or write to us.

Ecotourism

As recently as a decade ago, tourism to Ecuador and the Galápagos Islands destroyed natural resources as quickly as any other industry did. Cruise ships brought littering foreigners to beaches, where they bought ornaments fashioned from the shells of endangered tortoises. Developers paved roads through the jungle, and scuba resorts encouraged divers to feed the fish and fondle the coral. Since then, countries around the world have faced strong demands for more responsible, sustainable tourism—"ecotourism" is the pop-name for this trend. The fastest-growing sector of the tourist industry, ecotourism is intended to be environmentally friendly, to encourage enjoyment and appreciation of nature while contributing to its continued existence. While few can object to the goal of encouraging respect for the environment, ecotourism has still garnered its share of criticism. Some say "eco" has come to mean economics rather than ecology, pointing to greedy entrepreneurs who lead ecotours with little or no concern for nature; others warn that increased traffic in natural settings, no matter how "low-impact" it is, can only harm the ecology in the long run.

Since the early days of the movement, ecotourists have flocked to Ecuador and the Galápagos for their bevy of natural beauties. In 1991, 364,585 foreign visitors to Ecuador handed over nearly US$200 million in revenues. The **Jatún Sacha Biological Station** was founded in 1986 with the intent to conserve the incredible biodiversity of the land and to provide a window for researchers. Located on the Río Napo, this wet tropical rainforest has 70% primary growth. It has been such a conservation success that in 1993, it was named the second International Children's Rainforest (the first was the groundbreaking Monteverde Cloudforest in Costa Rica). While Jatún Sacha limits its number of human visitors, the hundreds who cannot enter look elsewhere for some other sort of environmental experience. Such numbers tantalize entrepreneurs and experienced tour leaders alike, who readily grasp that tagging their services as "eco" could yield huge profits. The most legit tour companies have government-issued licenses (see INEFAN-Approved Tour Companies, p. 284). But no certification is required to simply call oneself an "environmental" tour guide. True eco-devotees should seek out organizations that actively support conservation efforts and strive to minimize their impact on the environment.

The recent discovery of oil in the Oriente region puts the rainforest at risk. For the first time, water and air pollution are serious threats *outside* of the cities. The effects of oil drilling have been even more destructive, as they ravage the regional wildlife and environment. Indigenous peoples such as the Huaorani and the Cofan, who live in the rainforest, have turned out to be the biggest allies of the environmentalists, their lands and lifestyles also pillaged by the multi-national oil companies. Political protests have been enough to save some areas—the **Limoncocha Biological Reserve** downriver from Coca was founded with the help of angry birdwatchers determined to push oil companies away from their haven. **"Debt-for-nature swaps,"** in which foreign creditors allow lending nations to pay off their debts by protecting areas of the rainforest, has also helped save parts of Ecuador's environment. But the **Parque Nacional Yasuní** has been the source of the most controversy; while it houses hundreds of bird, animal, and fish species, it is also potentially one of the most valuable oil-drilling areas—a serious consideration in a country with a dwindling economy.

Though progress may occur slowly, environmental awareness is on the rise. Overall, the new wave of environmental consciousness has been immensely rewarding for Ecuador's economy, to tourists with a thirst for adventure and immersion in nature, and most importantly, to the environment itself, which will only continue to serve visitors if Ecuador continues to pursue the vision of minimum-impact ecotourism.

The Land

Ecuador lies on the western coast of South America, north of Perú and south of Colombia. Its topography is dominated by the volcanic Andes, which span the country lengthwise. The earth's surface is made up of a number of **tectonic plates,** each of which is constantly being pushed and pulled by the plates around it. The Andes were formed as an **uplift** that resulted from a particularly brutal collision of two of these plates several million years ago.. Because the mountains are so young, geographically speaking, wind and water have had little time to work their erosive magic on the rugged peaks. In addition, the country's geology is far from static. The entire South American coast lies on the edge of a **continental plate** that is being subducted by the **oceanic plate** of the Pacific, making for some heavy-duty geologic action. The interaction of these two plates causes Ecuador's volcanic activity and frequent earthquakes.

This dramatic geology makes for some pretty intense geography. Only the size of the state of Oregon (just bigger than Great Britain), Ecuador is as diverse a country as you'll find anywhere in the world. In the west is the **Pacific coast,** characterized by sparsely populated sandy beaches, swampy areas, and fishing and shrimp farming industries. Just east of the coast are the **lowlands.** Fertile and humid, this land was once completely forested, but now most of it is cleared and cultivated with cacao and bananas. In fact, Ecuador was on of the first banana republics and remains the world's largest exporter of the yellow fruit. East of the banana country stretches the highlands, or the **Sierra.** Here, two mountain ridges run from north to south with a high, fertile valley between them. All of the land that is not too vertical is cultivated with cereal crops such as barley, wheat, and corn. This results in a typically Andean landscape of patchwork fields dominated by snowcapped volcanoes, with an occasional lake thrown in for good measure. Finally, to the far east is the western Amazon basin or **Oriente.** Sparsely populated for most of Ecuador's history, this region is presently booming because of the oil discovered there in the 70s. Like the rest of the Amazon, flora and fauna are diverse and mind boggling, but threatened by development.

Flora and Fauna

Ecuador hosts an unbelievably diverse range of plants and animals, especially given the region's relatively compact size. This variety is packed into less than a 400km span, from palm-lined beaches, to the lowland banana plantations, to the low-growing vegetation of the Andean highlands, to the wet rainforest of the Amazon basin. The rainforest has by far the greatest biodiversity; of the two million plant and animal species known to exist in the world today, half live exclusively in rainforests. Activists around the world have recently stepped up efforts to protect the biodiversity of these forests, where tall, enveloping trees form a several-story-high canopy under which smaller ferns, palms, and other plants grow. Thousands of animal species thrive in the Oriente, from the familiar deer, squirrels, and bats, to the powerful tapirs and jaguars, to the comically exotic guatusa, capybaras, and three-toed sloths. The high-altitude cloudforests of the Sierra are remarkable for their strange combinations of cool, moist air and fairy-tale flora. Wizened trees are covered in bright moss and colorful mushrooms, and one can't help thinking that area must be home to at least a few gnomes or pixies. The spectacled bear, the only species of bear found in South America, resides in the highland region, as do the domesticated alpacas. The palm-lined coasts, meanwhile, are a dream come true for fishermen and divers alike, and bird-watchers will delight at the tropical species found in the western lowlands, where banana, coffee, and cacao crops thrive.

Quito

Though Ecuador's capital is home to over 1.1 million people, it's hard to call Quito immense. Nature overshadows what man has created, even though man first created it over 1400 years ago. Carved into a narrow plateau towering 9405 feet (2,850m) above deep Andean valleys, Quito is still dwarfed by the cloud-topped peaks above and the looming Volcán Pichincha to the west.

Even Quito's own long and varied history makes the modern city seem small. The peaceful Quitu, Cara, Shyri and Puruhá Indians inhabited the valley since at least the sixth century. Conquered by the expansionist Incas from the south, Quito became part of their gargantuan empire around 1500, just as the Spanish began their own binge of ruthless exploitation to the northeast. Wars between the Incas and the long-standing residents of the northern Sierra continued until Francisco Pizarro's 1532 invasion, when he captured the Quito-born Incan emperor Atahualpa. *Quiteños* today celebrate Sebastián de Benalcázar's 1534 arrival as the "founding" of their city, but it was in fact the third or fourth resettling of the short-lived Inca capital. Rumiñuahi, a general of Atahualpa, had torched the city a few months earlier as Spanish troops approached, preferring to bury the Incan architectural achievements under ashes than have them used in the conquistadors' exploitation of the natives.

Little remains of the pre-Columbian people today other than their blood, flowing through the veins of 80% of Quito's population, and the subsequent social stratification reflected in the city's geography. Separated into two sections—tattered Old Town *(La Parte Colonial)* and opulent New Town *(Quito Moderno)*—the divided capital aptly reflects the economic split of most of modern South America. Predictably, the Old/New dichotomy has also developed along ethnic lines.

Old Quito has changed little since colonial days, maintaining the classic narrow cobblestone streets, steep inclines, and bustling traditional markets. But as the Ecuadorian economy continues to divide the population into more distinct classes, this home to Quito's poor becomes increasingly decrepit. The wrought-iron balconies of its traditional Spanish dwellings are slowly losing their luster while struggling to maintain their character. As the sunset sends the market vendors home, it invites out the city's underbelly—its drunkards and prostitutes. But Old Quito retains its charisma; the United Nations declared it a "World Cultural Heritage" site in 1978, prohibiting skyscrapers and thus protecting the grand churches and government palaces from being overshadowed. Though pollution-ridden, Colonial Quito's sloping alleyways and plazas, as well as the Río Machángara flowing south of town, remain quite charming by day and elegantly haunting by night.

A busy commercial and social center, Quito's New Town is not beautiful by any known architectural standard—though one need only look up past the modern mini-skyscrapers to the misty peaks of the wooded Andes for aesthetic enjoyment. Despite its relative lack of architectural beauty, the New Town is brought to life by the many universities located here. This town has had more than its fair share of radical student uprisings—just another mark of the vitality of its people and the importance of its place in Ecuador's diverse landscape and population. The New Town offers most of what there is to do in this vital, densely-populated mecca, giving a small taste of everything. Wealthy businessmen step over toothless beggars, antique colonial palaces and gaudy ultramodern constructions line the same streets, all surrounded above and below by green peaks and valleys. It is as if all of humanity and nature are captured here in one honest glimpse.

Practical Information

Tourist Office: CETUR (tel. 514-044), in the Old Town at Venezuela and Chile. CETUR can provide maps, basic tourist information, and some friendly advice (in English). The New Town CETUR (tel. 224-970), at Alfaro and Carlos Tobar, in a slightly out-of-the-way business area across the street from Parque La Carolina, is not quite as helpful or accessible (both offices open Mon.-Fri. 8:30am-5pm). To get to the New Town office, take a bus north on Av. 6 de Diciembre and get off at the Los Shyris intersection; walk west on Los Shyris and take a left on Alfaro. CETUR is on the left. The South American Explorer's Club, however, is a far better resource.

Tourist Resource: The **South American Explorer's Club,** Jorge Washington 311 y Leonidas Plaza (tel./fax 225-228, e-mail explorer@saec.org.ec for club information) is an absolutely indispensable resource for the traveler visiting any part of Ecuador. A friendly, helpful English-speaking staff will help you make the most of your vacation with trip reports, a huge guidebook with up-to-date information library, a large selection of maps, used guide books and trekking equipment, an English-language lending library of novels and travelogues, and much much more. Membership isn't cheap (US$40 for one, US$20 for each additional member), but it's certainly worth it if you're spending much time in Quito. Membership services include free tea, nice restroom facilities, lounge and chat rooms, consultation on just about any matter Ecuadorian, and fax, e-mail, and reliable mail service. Non-members can spend up to ½hr. at the club, which is actually a wonderfully restored colonial house.

British Council: Amazonas 1646 y Orellana (tel. 540-225), a 5-min. walk from downtown. The council also offers a vegetarian restaurant and tea room (open Mon.-Fri. 8am-7pm), a language school for U.K. students, a photocopier (s/100 per page), and rare e-mail service with telnet (US$0.17/min.). English-language newspapers, like the *London Times,* and *Times Higher Education Supplement,* are available up at the well-stocked library. Non-members can browse, but loans are made only to those with a membership (s/60,000 per year, plus US$20 deposit). Good video library as well (membership s/80,000 per year). Both libraries are open Mon.-Fri. 8:30am-1pm and 2-7pm.

Immigration Office: The **Oficina de Migración,** Amazonas 2639 y Republica, third floor (open Mon.-Fri. 8am-12:30pm). This is where you get a tourist card extension (for a length of stay) or a "Certificate of Exit" (rarely needed).

Embassies: United States, Av. 12 de Octubre y Patria 120 (tel. 562-890; fax 502-052). Open Mon.-Fri. 8am-12:30pm and 1:30-5pm. **Canada,** Av. 6 de Diciembre 2816 y Ortom (tel. 543-214; fax 503-108). Open Mon.-Fri. 9:30am-12:30pm. **United Kingdom,** Av. Gonzáles Suárez 111, Casilla 314 (tel. 560-670; fax 560-730). Open Mon.-Fri. 8:30am-12:30pm and 2-5pm. **Ireland,** Montes 577 y Las Casas (tel. 503-674; fax 501-444). Open Mon.-Fri. 9:30am-12:30pm. **Israel,** Eloy Alfaro 969 y Amazonas (tel. 565-510; fax 504-635). Open Mon.-Fri. 8:30am-4:30pm. **Colombia,** Colón 133 y Amazonas, 7th floor (tel. 221-679 or 222-486; fax 566-676). Open Mon.-Fri. 8:30am-1pm and 2:30-6pm. **Peru,** Amazonas 1429 y Colón, Edificio España, penthouse (tel. 520-134; fax 562-349). Open Mon.-Fri. 8:30am-1:30pm.

Money exchange: *"Casas de Cambios"* all over town, as well as banks, will always exchange cash. **VAX,** on the New Town's main thoroughfare at Amazonas and Roca, exchanges travelers checks as well, both at good rates (open Mon.-Fri. 8:30am-6pm, Sat. 9am-1pm). VAX's hours are typical for exchange houses, though many close at 5:30pm and for an hour in the early afternoon. **Multicambio** has four offices—at Colón 919 y Reina Victoria, Roca 720, Venezuela 689, and the airport. **Casa Paz** has two—at Sucre and García Moreno in the Old Town, and at Amazonas 370 y Robles in the New.

Banks: Av. Río Amazonas is filled to the brim with banks, mostly open Mon.-Fri. 9am-1:30pm. Reliable banks include: **Banco Guayaquil,** at Colón and Reina Victoria; **Banco Pichincha,** Amazonas and Colón; **Banco Popular,** Amazonas 648; and **Banco del Pacífico,** at Amazonas and Veintinilla. Cash **traveler's checks** at any bank, and buy them at **Lloyd's Bank,** Amazonas 580 y Carrión.

ATMs: Plentiful in the New Town and non-existent in the Old, but most will only take Visas or MasterCards that have been PIN-enabled. Normal ATM cards (Cirrus, Plus, etc.) only work at **BanRED** machines, located at **Banco de Prestamos** on Amazonas at Veintimilla, **Hotel Oro Verde** at Av. 12 de Octubre and Cordero, and **Filanbanco** smack in the middle of Amazonas at Robles, among other places.

Credit Card Offices: MasterCard head office, Av. Naciones Unidas 825 y Los Shyris. **Visa** head office, at Banco de Guayaquil, Colón and Reina Victoria. **American**

New Quito

GENERAL INFORMATION
British Council, **35**
Casa Paz money exchange, **3**
CETUR, **38**
EMETEL, **34**
Immigration Office, **37**
Libri Mundi, **15**
Multicambio, **23**
Post Office, **36**
SAETA/SAN Office, **31**
South American Explorer's Club, **2**
TAME Office, **30**
United States Embassy, **1**
VAX money exchange, **4**

ACCOMMODATIONS
El Cafecito Hostal, **22**
Hostel Rincón de Castilla, **5**
Hostelling International, **14**
Hotel Ambassador, **33**
Hotel Pickett, **16**
Hotel Viena, **10**
Magic Bean Hostel, **19**

FOOD
Café Moka, **13**
Columbia Steak House, **32**
La Terraza del Tártaro, **18**
Mama Clorinda, **7**
Mona Lisa, **20**
Puerto Manabí, **21**
Restaurante Mare Nostrum, **11**
Restaurant Tanquito, **6**
Rincón Cubano, **17**
Trattoria El Chianti, **21**

SIGHTS AND ENTERTAINMENT
Alcatraz, **25**
Ana María, **12**
El Hueco, **9**
El Pobre Diablo, **28**
Museo Amazonico Abya-Yala, **8**
No Bar, **29**
Papillón, **24**
Tequila Rock, **26**
Vivarium, **27**

TO THE AIRPORT (5km)
Parque La Carolina
Av. Mariana de Jesus
← MARIANA DE JESUS
Av. Gral. Eloy Alfaro
LA PRADERA
Circulo Militar
Av. Francisco de Orellano
LA COLÓN
J. León Mera
Reina Victoria
Diego de Almagro
Santa María
Av. Colón
Cordero
Baquerizo Moreno
García
Calama
Foch
Pinto
Presidente Wilson
Av. 6 de Diciembre
Gral. Baquedano
Veintimilla
J. Carrión
Av. 10 de Agosto
Páez
Av. 9 de Octubre
Av. Río Amazonas
Versalles
Murillo
Roca
Robles
Gutierrez
Tamayo
Jorge Washington
Av. 18 de Septembre
Av. 12 de Octubre
Av. Patria
Parque El Ejido
Universidad Católica
SEE OLD QUITO MAP
0 300 yards
0 300 meters

QUITO

Express office, Amazonas 339 y Jorge Washington (tel. 560-488), at Ecuadorian Tours, on the fifth floor.

Faxes: It's easiest to send and receive faxes at the **South American Explorer's Club** (tel. 225-228) on J. Washington at Leonidas. They cost s/1,000 per page plus phone costs (members only). Otherwise, **Faxtel,** Av. 12 de Octubre 1805 y Cordero, across from Hotel Oro Verde, offers SAEC members a 5% discount.

Telephone Service: Quito is probably the easiest place in the country from which to make international calls. Nearly everything can be done from **EMETEL,** which has three locations: Av. 10 de Agosto and Colón, Benalcázar and Mejía, and the Terminal Terrestre. EMETEL lets you make free calling-card calls from private booths, but you may have to wait in quite a line. **Pay phones** do not exist, at least not those of the coin variety—small-phone operators working out of stands on the street offer sometimes-overpriced local service (don't even think about making international calls there). In general, **AT&T** (toll-free tel. 999-119) and **MCI** (toll-free tel. 999-170) calling-card calls can be made from any direct-dial phone, including those in the lobbies of most expensive hotels (s/1,000-3,000 for the service). These include the **Hotel Amaranta** (tel. 238-385), across from the South American Explorer's Club at J. Washington and Leonidas, and the **Hotel Oro Verde** (tel. 566-479), at Av. 12 de Octubre and Cordero. Collect calls and local calls (for around s/1,000-2,000 per 3min.) can also be made at these posh hotels.

QUITO

Airport: Quito's international airport is **Aeropuerto Mariscal Sucre,** on Amazonas to the far north of town, near Av. La Florida. You may be a bit disoriented walking off the plane and right onto the runway, Air Force One-style, but simply follow the crowd inside, and be sure to get your tourist card and passport stamped. Save yourself some cash by hailing a cab a few blocks away from the airport, instead of getting one right out front. Taxis shouldn't charge more than s/15,000 to or from the airport. To get to the airport on public transportation, take the #1 or "Aeropuerto" bus heading north from the New or Old towns, or grab the trolley and change to Rumiñuahi at Estación Norte.

Airlines: **SAETA/SAN** (tel. 564-969 or 542-148), at Colón and Amazonas in the Edificio España; **TAME,** Amazonas 13-54 y Colón (tel. 509-382 or 509-388); **Aerogal,** Italia 241 y Alfaro (tel. 563-646 or 560-867).

Trains: Buses #1 or #2 heading south will take you to the station on Maldonado, past the Old Town. Trains are not a prominent mode of transportation in Ecuador, but the one weekly departure to Riobamba offers fantastic mountain views (every Sat., 8am, 8hr., s/24,000 to Ambato or Latacunga, s/30,000 to Riobamba). Tickets go on sale Fri. at 8am at the station (tel. 656-142). For the best views, ride on the roof. Another tourist route runs from Quito to Cotopaxi (every Sun., 8am, s/60,000). Tickets are on sale Mon.-Fri. 8am-4:30pm at Bolívar 443 y Benalcazar (tel. 513-422), in the Old Town.

Local Buses: Local buses are ubiquitous and confusing. Not to worry: once you're familiar with the system, you'll be far more confused than you were before. Perhaps the most daunting initial hurdle to local bus-riding is the fact that the buses don't actually stop—they merely slow down to around 5mph, at which point passengers must jump onto the moving bus. Once you're prepared both mentally and physically for this task, you'll have to decide which class to take. All buses are cheap, but some buses are cheaper than others. The cheapest are the ridiculous schoolbus-style **"Servicio Popular,"** at s/240, next are the over-crowded but more comfortable **"Servicio Ejecutivo,"** at s/510, and finally the **"Selectivo,"** slightly less crowded and a bit quieter, at s/600. Buses always have names of streets and/or landmarks on their front windows, and sometimes numbers as well. A common route is the **Old Town-New Town pathway,** traversed by the #2 (Colón-Camal) on 10 de Agosto, the #10 (San Bartolo-Miraflores) on 10 de Agosto, the #11 (El Tejar-El Iaca) on Av. 6 de Diciembre, and other buses on Av. 12 de Octubre. Buses to the **airport** (#1) can be caught on Amazonas (marked "aeropuerto"), and buses to the Parque La Carolina section of the New Town can be caught on Av. 6 de Diciembre—these are often also marked "Estadio" and continue on to the Olympic Stadium on Av. 6 de Diciembre and Naciones Unidas. If you have luggage, you'd be better off with a taxi—it's not expensive, it's safer, and most public buses don't even allow big backpacks or suitcases.

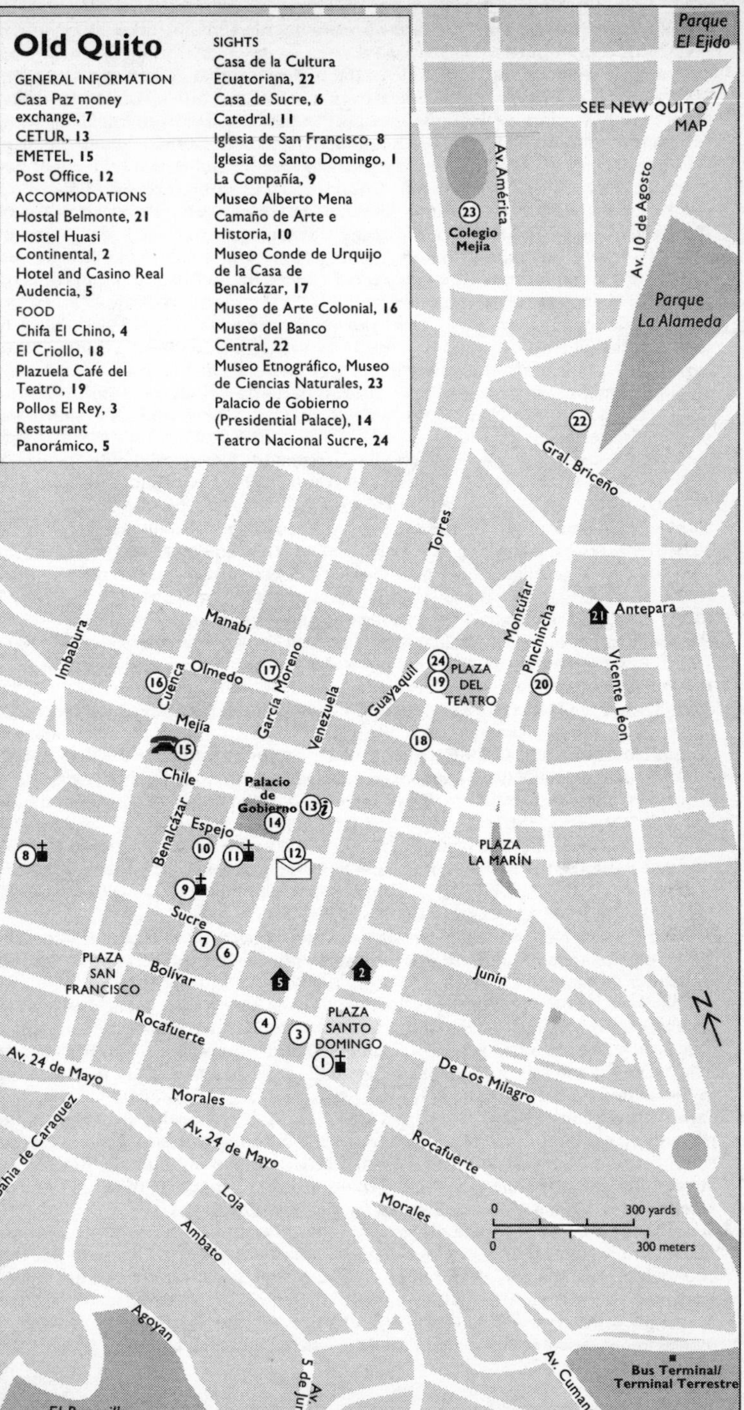
Old Quito
GENERAL INFORMATION
Casa Paz money exchange, 7
CETUR, 13
EMETEL, 15
Post Office, 12
ACCOMMODATIONS
Hostal Belmonte, 21
Hostel Huasi Continental, 2
Hotel and Casino Real Audencia, 5
FOOD
Chifa El Chino, 4
El Criollo, 18
Plazuela Café del Teatro, 19
Pollos El Rey, 3
Restaurant Panorámico, 5
SIGHTS
Casa de la Cultura Ecuatoriana, 22
Casa de Sucre, 6
Catedral, 11
Iglesia de San Francisco, 8
Iglesia de Santo Domingo, 1
La Compañía, 9
Museo Alberto Mena Camaño de Arte e Historia, 10
Museo Conde de Urquijo de la Casa de Benalcázar, 17
Museo de Arte Colonial, 16
Museo del Banco Central, 22
Museo Etnográfico, Museo de Ciencias Naturales, 23
Palacio de Gobierno (Presidential Palace), 14
Teatro Nacional Sucre, 24
Parque El Ejido
SEE NEW QUITO MAP
Av. América
Colegio Mejía
Av. 10 de Agosto
Parque La Alameda
Gral. Briceño
Torres
Antepara
Manabí
Imbabura
Olmedo
Cuenca
García Moreno
Venezuela
Guayaquil
PLAZA DEL TEATRO
Montúfar
Pinchincha
Vicente Léon
Mejía
Chile
Palacio de Gobierno
Espejo
Benalcázar
PLAZA LA MARÍN
Sucre
PLAZA SAN FRANCISCO
Bolívar
Junín
Rocafuerte
PLAZA SANTO DOMINGO
Av. 24 de Mayo
De Los Milagro
Morales
Bahia de Caraquez
Av. 24 de Mayo
Rocafuerte
Loja
Morales
Ambato
0
300 yards
0
300 meters
Agoyan
El Panecillo
Av. 5 de Junio
Av. Cumanda
Bus Terminal/ Terminal Terrestre

QUITO

Long-Distance Buses: The *terminal terrestre* lies next to a highway at the end of **Av. 24 de Mayo** in the Old Town. Take the trolley to the Cumandá stop, then descend the stairs on the north side of the highway and keep walking. Inside the several-story *terminal* are a police station, an EMETEL office, and an excessive number of bus company windows offering frequent departures to just about wherever you want to go. **Transportes Ecuador** runs to **Guayaquil** (every hr., 5:30am-12:20am, 7½hr., s/20,000), with buses leaving 40min. earlier from the new town office at Mera 330 and Washington. **Cooperativa Chimborazo** (tel. 570-601), is one of many that constantly go to **Riobamba** (5:30am-7pm, 3½hr., s/8,500), via **Ambato** (2hr., s/6,000). **Transportes Latacunga** (tel. 583-316), strangely enough, serves **Latacunga** (every 10min., 6am-8pm, 1¾hr., s/4,000). **Transportes Putumayo** goes to **Lago Agrio** (every hr., 9:30am-9:30pm, 8hr., s/20,000). **Transportes Amazonas** (tel. 571-747), travels to **Baños** (every hr., 2:35pm-7:25pm, 3hr., s/7,000). **Transportes Esmeraldas** (tel. 572-985), heads to **Esmeraldas** (at least every 1½hr., 7:30am-11pm, 6hr., s/16,000) via **Santo Domingo** (3hr., s/8000). **Cooperativa Sucre** (tel. 612-826) hits **Cuenca** (13 per day, 7:30am-midnight, 8hr., s/18,000). **Cooperativa Reina del Camino** (tel. 572-673), makes a beach run to **Manta** (16 per day, 6:30am-11pm, 10hr., s/18,000) and plenty of other places en route.

Trolleys: The spanking-new **trole (trolley)** system in Quito is fast, efficient, sparkingly modern, and crowded. You can't miss the glass-walled, arched *trole* stops—at s/700 (s/400 for children under 18, seniors, or handicapped people) it costs slightly more than a bus, but the *trole* stops! The *trole* runs along one street in the New Town (10 de Agosto) and two in the Old (Guayaquil and Montufar), so it's hard to get lost as long as you know in which direction you want to go. The *trole* zips way out to Quito's outskirts, branching out into several routes, but unless you're going to the airport or to a suburb, you won't need to go that far. To get to the **airport,** get on the Rumiñuahi route at Estación Norte at the end of the New Town. Buy for 10 trips at once and get a discount (s/640 per ride), and for 50 a slightly greater discount (s/600 per ride).

Taxis: With **TeleTaxi** (tel. 220-800; open 24hr.), s/120,000 buys a driver for an entire day. Other recommended services are: **Taxis Lagos de Ibarra,** Asunción 381 and M. Larrea (tel. 562-992); **Juan José Mejía,** Receptor 136 (tel. 570-882, 570-558, 570-986, or 570-779); **Transporte y Comercio Manuel Bucheli,** Cesar Chiriboga 451 y Inti (tel. 260-423); **Rosa Jácome A.,** Bustamente 153 y Zaldumbide (tel. 451-590 or 503-180).

Car Rental: Horozontes Ecuatorianos, Pinto 560 y Amazonas (tel. 230-463), rents cars and minibuses with or without drivers. **Budget Rent-a-Car,** Colón 1140 y J. Luis Mera (tel. 237-236 or 548-237; airport 459-052 or 240-763). **Avis Rent-a-Car,** Colón 1741 y 10 de Agosto (tel. 550-238 or 550-243).

Lost-and-Found Center: On Montufar between Olmedo and Manabí. Come with your police statement and see if your lost item has been turned in. The Second Coming is more likely.

English Bookstore: Confederate Books, Calama 410 y León Mera, has a good selection of used books—General Lee would be proud (open Mon.-Fri. 10am-7pm). The **South American Explorer's Club** (see Tourist Resource, p. 60) has Quito's best selection of English guidebooks, available for borrowing (free to members; US$30 deposit), and some used books for sale.

Spanish Bookstores: Libri Mundi is a stellar chain, though not bargain-basement priced, with a large store at León Mera 851 and Veintimilla, and another in the Hotel Colón, Amazonas and Patria (open Mon.-Fri. 8am-6pm, Sat.-Sun. 8am-2pm). **Atenea Librería,** on Alfaro and Suiza, offers an elegant and extensive selection of Spanish books (open Mon.-Fri. 9:30am-7:30pm, Sat. 10am-2pm).

Shopping: The major shopping district is on and around **Avenida Río Amazonas,** the main thoroughfare of the New Town. Buy anything from Panama hats to cheesy tourist souvenirs, electronics to clothing. Half the fun is just looking.

Computer Rental: Old IBMs with printers can be used for s/2,000 and s/2,500 per hr. at Luis Cordero and 9 de Octubre. Cheap services are also available at Av. Belmonte opposite Hotel Belmonte in the Old Town.

Photocopies: Copies can be made at approximately 2 places on every block, reflecting the curious infestation of photocopy services in all of Latin America. Among the many choices are **Copifull** at Av. 6 de Diciembre 1045 y Jorge Washington (tel. 228-473), and at Amazonas 3147 y Guayas (tel. 447-163); **Tecnocopy,** one of the cheapest in town, at Av. 12 de Octubre 1129 y Ventimilla (tel. 503-597 or 223-269); and **Copy Cad,** Ventimilla 325 y Av. 12 de Octubre (tel. 544-140). Prices range between s/60 and s/120 per copy. Hours are generally Mon.-Fri. 8am-6pm, Sat. 8am-1pm (some places close 1-2pm).

Supermarkets: Lark, at the corner of Dávalos and Versalles, offers a huge selection of clean meats and cheeses, as well as liquor and other standard supermarket fare (open Mon.-Sat. 8:30am-7:30pm, Sun. 9am-1:30pm). The high-quality, all-purpose **Supermaxi** chain has branches at the airport Centro Comercial, Centro Comercial El Bosque on Occidental, and Multicentro (Av. 6 de Diciembre and La Niña), among other locations (open Mon.-Sat. 9:30am-8pm, Sun. 9:30am-1pm).

Laundry: Most hotels offer some sort of laundry service, from complete machine service to a wash-basin and clothesline (beware daily afternoon rainfall, however). Another option is the laundromat route; *lavanderías* are readily available every couple of blocks. Options include: **Lavanderías Lavalimpio,** Tamayó 420 y Roca; **Lavanderías Modernas,** Av. 6 de Diciembre 24-00 y Colón; **One Hour Martinizing** (yes, the same one), Av. 12 de Octubre 1486, among other locations. Prices at laundromats tend to be higher than hotel prices. Most laundromats are open Mon.-Fri. 7:30 or 8am-6pm, Sat. 8am-1 or 3pm.

Hospitals: Hospital Voz Andes, Villalengua 267 (tel. 241-540 or 241-541), on the "Iñaquito" bus line, is English-speaking and highly recommended. This is the best place to come for a rabies vaccination (5 shots, over 1 month, US$185). Visiting fee US$8. **Hospital Metropolitano** (tel. 431-520, 431-521, or 431-457), at Av. Mariana de Jesus and Occidental. Get there on a "Quito Sur-San Gabriel" bus from El Tejar downtown. Also English-speaking, but expensive.

Clinics: Private medical practitioner **Dr. John Rosenberg,** Foch 476 y Almagro (tel. 223-333 or 521-104, pager 506-856 beeper 135, home 441-757), at the medical center bearing his name. Fluent in English, German, French, and Hebrew. Fee US$20. **Dr. Wallace Swanson** (tel. 449-374, home 470-830), an American doctor at the Hospital Voz Andes. **Clínica Pichincha,** Veintinilla 1259 y Paez (tel. clinic 561-643, lab 562-296), is also recommended for emergency care.

Emergency: tel. 111.

Police: The **Criminal Investigation Office** is in the Old Town at the intersection of Cuenca and Maderas (open daily 9am-midnight).

Post Offices: In the **Old Town** (no tel.), on Espejo between Guayaquil and Venezuela, ½ block towards Guayaquil from the Palacio de Gobierno (open Mon.-Fri. 7:30am-7pm, Sat. 7:30am-2pm). In the **New Town,** Eloy Alfaro 354 y 9 de Octubre. If you want mail sent to this branch, mark it "Correo Central, Eloy Alfaro;" otherwise it will be sent to the Old Town office. Stamps are sold on the seventh floor (open Mon.-Fri. 7:30am-7:30pm, Sat. 7:30am-2pm). **Packages** should be sent via **Correo Maritimo Aduana,** Ulloa 273 and Ramirez Dávalos, located next to the Santa Clara market (open Mon.-Fri. 7:30am-3:30pm). **EMS** (Express Mail Service), is centrally located on Reina Victoria 1325 between Cordero and Lizardo García (tel. 543-468 or 569-741). **FedEx** is at Amazonas 5340 between Tomás de Berlanga and Isla Floreana (tel. 251-356, 251-357, 251-552, or 251-553). The best place to receive mail in Quito—if you're a member—is the **South American Explorer's Club** (see Tourist Resource, p.60).

Telephone Code: 02

Accommodations

NEW TOWN

Hotels and hostels abound in the New Town. Just because a place calls itself a hostel does not necessarily mean that it meets any particular standards; the main distinction between the two types of accommodations is this: in hotels, single rooms are guaranteed, while in hostels, rooms are usually shared between two to 10 people. Many of the hostels are *gringo*-run or at least *gringo*-populated, tending to congregate in prime locations—either right in the middle of New Town activity near Amazonas, or in the posh-hotel district near Av. 12 de Octubre and the grand Hotel Oro Verde. Budget *hotels*, on the other hand, tend to lie slightly outside the main strips. Watch out for the definite price-location correlation among hotels.

Hotels

Hotel Viena, Tamayó 879 y Foch (tel. 235-418). More centrally located than any other budget hotel in the New Town, this friendly spot's got everything going for it. Climb the stone stairs and cross the threshold to homey rooms, complete with spotless private bathrooms and hot water. An economical choice at s/20,000 per person.

Hotel Pickett, Wilson 712 y León Mera (tel. 551-205 or 541-453). On the high end of the budget price scale, the little touches make it worth the extra couple sucres. The rooms aren't sparklingly new, but their large beds, phones, color TVs, spacious feel, and nice bathrooms have that upper-crust feel. Call ahead to make sure this centrally located hotel isn't entirely taken up by a tour group. Rooms with double beds s/15,000, with bath s/30,000.

Hostal Rincón de Castilla, Versalles 1127 y Carrión (tel. 224-312; fax 548-097). Stay here if you're visiting Ecuador to explore, not to lounge. Very basic rooms—with a bed, table, window, and little else—are clean enough and can be had for next to nothing (s/13,000). Not a place where you'd want to spend the day hanging out in your room, but that's not what you came for, is it? A communal table, sparsely-populated bookshelf, and usable kitchen add to the fun. Under 10min. from most New Town activity.

Hotel Ambassador, Av. 9 de Octubre 1052 and Colón (tel. 561-777, 562-054, or 561-993), is a 10-min. walk to the bustling center of everything, as well as the best deal among the better-than-budget hotels. Beautifully-kept, voluminous double rooms (s/70,000). Some center around a central garden; all have sparkling spotless bathrooms, color cable TV, and direct-dial phones.

Hostels

La Casona de Mario, Andalucía 213 y Galicia (tel. 544-036 or 230-129). Comfort couldn't come from a nicer guy. Mario, the Argentinean owner, sets guests up in his delightful house, a bit out of the way but in a safe and quiet residential area. Nobody interior decorates quite like Mario, who has decked out rooms with aesthetic wonders such as Indian weavings and avant-garde furniture. Very social atmosphere—after all, all rooms are shared: the bedrooms, hot-water bath, living room, dining room, kitchen, and patio. Laundry and barbeque facilities round out the amenities. S/18,000 per person; 10% discount on stays of 15 days or longer.

El Cafecito, Luis Cordero 11-24 y Reina Victoria (tel. 234-862). Coffeehouses are popular, but have you ever wanted to *sleep* in one? El Cafecito recreates the feel of the fad, complete with cigarette smoke and *gringos* galore. The rooms, with their funky wall hangings, are just as cool as the vegetarian café downstairs. A youthful, largely European crowd populates this Canadian-owned lodging, where English is spoken better than Spanish. Great window views of the neighborhood, which is vibrant though mildly red-light after dark. One double-bed room; other rooms with four or five beds. S/18,000 per person.

Centro del Mundo, Liz. García 569 y Reina Victoria (tel. 229-050). This bustling hostel calls itself "the backpacker's hang-out," and lives up to its motto. Mostly twenty-somethings pour into the Canadian-Ecuadorian owned establishment, whose loose, liberal, international atmosphere is a mix between a dormitory, an alternative café, and a halfway house. Dim, futon-strewn living room has a homey fireplace, cable TV, tables, and cheap gourmet meals cooked-to-order. Showers steam, refreshingly hip music plays, and sun deck simmers on sunny days. Lower ("party") room, decked out with tapestries and wood chests for locking up backpacks, bunks 10 for only US$4 apiece. More tranquil rooms upstairs go for US$5 a bed. Huge crowd lets loose on weekends. Rooftop kitchen offers meals under the stars.

The Magic Bean Hostel, Foch 681 y León Mera (tel. 566-181). Perhaps the best known of Quito's *gringo* hostelling hotbeds, the Magic Bean enchants with an absolutely *prime* location—amidst the New Town's activity and popular nightspots. The friendly management has conjured up well-maintained, inviting wood-paneled rooms, shared among three or more. Communal bathroom has hot water. The slightly expensive restaurant and coffeehouse downstairs have a tranquil, new age feel. Continental breakfast included in the price: s/21,000 per person. Private rooms also available at steeper rates: singles s/60,000, doubles s/72,000.

Hostelling International (HI), Pinto 3-25 y Reina Victoria (tel. 543-995). Part of the huge HI chain, this branch dutifully provides what you've come to expect in the chain: meticulous cleanliness, virtually identical rooms with those familiar thin mattresses, immaculate tiled bathrooms, and that classic standardized institutional, er, hostel feel. A safe choice, though the management can be less-than-amiable, but lacking the character of some other centrally-located New Town accommodations. HI members s/21,0000 with shared bath, s/24,000 with nearly equally crowded "private" bath. Non-members s/25,500 with shared bath, s/27,000 with private bath. Includes continental breakfast.

OLD TOWN

Hotels in the Old Town tend to be lower in both price and quality than their New Town counterparts. Price is generally the biggest reason why tourists stay here, but as budget spots open in the New Town, the benefits of staying in the Old Town are dwindling. Little of interest goes on in the Old Town after about 9pm, and as the area worsens by night, safety is a concern in the Old Town's budget hotel districts. If you choose to stay here, you'll either be confined to your room shortly after the sun sets, or else face a wee-hour cab ride back to the neighborhood (trolleys and buses stop at midnight). However, not all Old Town accommodations are as decrepit as one might imagine, and all are most definitely cheaper.

Hostel Huasi Continental, Flores 332 y Sucre (tel. 517-327 or 518-441). Usually lighting this poor is a bad omen, conjuring images of skeletons in the shadows. But the spotless Huasi Continental has nothing to hide, with its immaculate stucco-walled rooms, comfortable (if squeaky) beds, and tidy private bathrooms. Hot water from 5am-noon and 5pm-midnight. Squint a little and note the narrow mahogany desks, mirrors, and thumbtack-sized wastebaskets in each room. Ask for a back room if you mind noise. Needless to say, the lighting is shoddy throughout. Singles s/18,000, color TV s/2,000 extra.

Hotel & Casino Real Audencia, Bolívar 220 y Guayaquil (tel. 512-711), at the corner of Plaza Santo Domingo. Although the fanciest hotel in the Old Town, the Real Audencia actually offers some rooms at amazing bargains. Enjoy the same comfort, cleanliness, cold air, and breathtaking view as guests paying twice as much. Ask for a third floor room to fully appreciate the sweeping panorama of Old Quito, El Panecillo, and the surrounding residential highland hills. "Budget rooms" (which are almost identical to non-budget ones) cost only s/27,000 per night. Only about five of these cheap rooms exist, but if you show a student ID or belong to a club, the staff may make more available. Services also include free luggage storage for weeks. Blow the money you saved at the casino downstairs, or splurge with a gourmet meal at the scenic restaurant on the third floor.

Hostal Belmonte (tel. 519-006), at Antepara and León near the New Town border. The manager brags that the cozy four-story house has "tourists only," and for once the staff's boasts are indeed true—this place just oozes *gringos.* The bright colors of the house's interior are the most exiting thing about the bare-bones rooms (with thin pad-mattresses) and common bathrooms. The *real* perks are in the common room, where there's a TV, radio, tape player, and endless free coffee. Check out the view from the roof, also home of a wash basin and small kitchen. S/12,000 per person.

Hostal Residencial Marsella (tel. 575-884), at Castro and Los Ríos in a quiet section near the New Town. Basic, small rooms cost next to nothing. Common bathrooms are open-air—look on the bright side, that means they probably won't smell too bad. Just watch out for birds. Hot water from 6:30am-2pm and 8pm-6am. S/15,000 per person, s/12,000 for two or more, with private bath s/30,000.

Food

NEW TOWN

Predictably, New Town Restaurants tend to be pricier and more upscale than their Old Town counterparts, but it's still possible to eat on a reasonable budget here. The low value of the sucre means that even the ritziest joints are practically budget spots by first-world standards; travelers can "splurge" and get a classy gourmet meal for the price of average grub meal back home. Be aware that much of most of the extra cost at the ritziest New Town restaurants simply covers the frills around the edges: tuxedos on waiters, chandeliers—the food is not necessarily better than that in the *comedor* around the corner.

For cheap eats, hit the *almuerzo* (lunch) spots, mostly on the the side streets off of **Av. Río Amazonas**. Restaurant Row, the informal name for another strip of eateries, is between León Mera and Reina Victoria, in the area around **Calamá.** Fancy restaurants tend to cluster here, but there are some less expensive options as well. On Amazonas itself, **sidewalk cafés** are good for people-watching and a moderately-priced drink or two.

Cheap Eats

Restaurante Tanquito (tel. 543-565), on Carrión between 10 de Agosto and Murillo. The locals know where to go, and this is where the hungry flock. Worth the stray off the beaten path; just follow the army of loyal lunchtime regulars. Tanquito serves up an absolutely mouthwatering *almuerzo* with soup, rice, meat, and vegetables. The atmosphere aims to please: a congenial staff, attractive green tablecloths—all in a two-story structure reminiscent of a comfortable coffeeshop (open daily 8am-6:30pm).

Mini Bar Francisco, 1526 Wilson (no tel.), a typical *almuerzo* spot with a difference: a charming outdoor covered garden with umbrella tables. Palm trees and tropical blossoms serve as the canopy for three-course *almuerzos* (s/3,000). Only serves breakfast and lunch (open daily 8am-4pm).

Cevichería Viejo José, on Veintimilla between Paez and 10 de Agosto. Only a pleasant 10min. walk from the New Town center, this local favorite in the school district bursts with lunchtime activity between 1-2pm. Old José gladly brings Brobdingnagian portions of *camarones y arroz* (s/6,000) or delicious *sopa de mariscos* (seafood soup with all sorts of marine creatures, s/6,000) to an outdoor or indoor table. Everyone starts out with a bowl of popcorn and fried plantain chips (open daily 8am-9pm).

Rincón Cubano (tel. 236-844), on Amazonas at Wilson, serves up a cheap *almuerzo* (s/4,000), including dessert, with that oh-so-Cuban touch. Try to figure out what unites the bizarre collection of black-and-white wall adornments and photos, to the tune of catchy Cuban melodies. Also serves dinner (Cuban entrées, s/8,000 and up). Tuxedoed waiters contribute to a much classier atmosphere than the average *almuerzo* diner (open Mon.-Sat. 10am-10pm, Sun. 6-10pm).

Restaurant Row

Mama Clorinda, Reina Victoria 1144 y Calamá (tel. 544-362). She's the Ecuadorian *mamacita* you never had, serving traditional dishes in a room as lively, bustling, and warm as a maternal kitchen. You haven't lived until you've tried Ecuadorian specialties like cattle stomach (s/7,000), pork hide soup (s/7,000), cattle legs broth (s/6,000), and lamb belly soup (s/6,000). But don't worry, Mama Clorinda also serves less adventurous meat and seafood dishes for the not-so-Ecuadorian at heart. Wine (s/5,000) and beer (s/2,000-3,000) flow freely (open Tues.-Sun. 10am-8:30pm, Mon. 10am-5pm).

El Cafecito (tel. 234-862), at Cordero and Reina Victoria. Straight out of New York's West Village, it's where the trendy alternative scene hit Ecuador. Munch vegetarian dishes off coffee tables adorned with wrought-iron candles. Cappuccino-lovers soak up the thick, dimly-lit atmosphere; classic rock floats through the smoke-filled air. Steamy windowpanes complete the scene. Serves breakfast (s/5,000), lunch (s/

5,000), and dinner (s/6,000). Full bar, less-than-stellar coffee drinks (open daily 7am-10pm, Fri.-Sun. 7am-midnight).

Puerto Manabí, L. García 1238 y León Mera (tel. 226-206). Mainly a lunch spot most active from 1-2pm, Puerto Manabí's varied menu features nearly every creature under the sea. Shrimp, fish, and calamari *cerviches* (s/10,000-s/15,000); mixed rice and shrimp (s/10,000). Lentils are a surprisingly popular garnishing (lentils with sea bass, s/10,000). Enjoy this maritime meal the way sailors do—on informal picnic tables and benches. Sailors wouldn't pay extra just to eat on Restaurant Row, though (open daily 9am-8pm, Sun. 9am-5pm).

Trattoria El Chianti, L. García 668 y León Mera (tel. 544-683). The best pizza west of Naples, or was that the Río Napo? Either way, a native Florentine cooks up authentic, gustatorily satisfying pizzas (s/11,000-s/15,000) at this inexpensive but upscale Italian spot. Pastas (s/11,000-s/14,000) and entrées such as veal scaloppine (s/16,000) are also served on quaint coffee tables. Bourgeois locals and *gringos* populate the trattoria most heavily (open Mon.-Sat. 12:30-10:30pm; coffee only 3:30-7pm).

The Magic Bean Restaurant and Coffeehouse (tel. 566-181), at Foch and León Mera. Like the hostel upstairs, the Magic Bean eatery is an absolute *gringo* stronghold in Quito. Eager to please, it's just as its patrons would have it: a homey, two-room dining area, wood-paneled and dimly-lit, housing an almost entirely English-speaking bohemian crowd. Coffee drinks s/1,500-s/3,000. Huge salad entrées s/9,000-s/15,000—you pay for the safe lettuce. Dinner specialities include veggie kabobs (s/12,000) and grilled tuna steak (s/15,000). But really, the Magic Bean is best known for its inexpensive breakfast selection, featuring eight varieties of pancakes (s/4,000-s/6,000). Open for breakfast Mon.-Fri. 7:30-11am, Sat.-Sun. 7:30am-1pm; dinner daily 6:30-10pm.

Mona Lisa, Calama 336 y León Mera (no tel.), right in the middle of Quito's Restaurant Row, is yet another spot in the New York-coffeeshop vein. Delectable smells are the source of most mysterious smiles here. Fine art graces the walls; bright white-and-purple tablecloths greet anyone peeking in the door. Mostly *gringos* enjoy coffee drinks (s/3,000) and entrées (chicken curry s/9,000, vegetarian platter with pasta or rice s/7,000). Vegetarian lunch special s/7,000 (open Mon.-Fri. 9:30am-11pm, Sat.-Sun. 6-11pm).

On the Expensive Side

Restaurante Mare Nostrum, Tamayó 172 (tel. 237-236), on the corner of Foch. Perfect for a special occasion, this outstanding seafood restaurant inhabits a beautifully-restored 1930s mansion, with stunning hardwood floors and castellar ceiling beams. Solid pewter plates and the occasional suit of armor add to the awe. Owner Gonzalo Dávila whips up the delectable house specialties himself: *paella de manscos* (s/20,000); heavenly *menu marino,* with huge langostina shrimp, octopus, squid, and fish crepes (s/53,000); huge shrimp dishes (s/32,000). Reasonably-priced gourmet fish entrées (s/12,000-19,000), for the strictly budget-minded, round out the menu (open daily 12:30-11pm).

La Terraza del Tártaro, Veintimilla 1106 y Amazonas, on the top of a modern office building. Though this elegant restaurant serves first-rate steaks, its true attraction lies in the unparalleled view of modern Quito through the huge picture windows. Spend your last night in Quito dining by the fireplace, gazing down at the illuminated city below, while enjoying a fine cut of Argentinian beef and Chilean wine in crystal goblets. Entrees aren't cheap (about s/17,000 per plate), but considering the food and setting, they're very reasonable. Or just stop by to enjoy a beer and the view (pilsener, s/4500 per glass). Open daily noon-11pm.

Columbia Steak House, Colón 1262 (tel. 551-857), just past Amazonas. Weary after a rough day of Quito sightseeing, you spot a big neon cow on a sign overhead. Fearing it only a mirage, you stumble blindly to the entrance—and suddenly discover steak heaven. Argentinean cuts of beef fill the kitchen landscape. T-bones the size of Andorra (s/16,500) and red wine (s/3,000 a glass) will satisfy any meat-eater. Enticing salads for the herbivores among us (but remember the risks of eating raw vegetables). The entryway doubles as a fast-food stop. Hamburgers and sandwiches s/4,000- s/9,000 (open daily 9am-midnight).

La Choza, Av. 12 de Octubre 1821 y Cordero (tel. 230-839), across the street from the Hotel Oro Verde. Nowhere in Quito, or in all of Ecuador, is traditional fare served up more elegantly than it is here. Finally, you can try *llapingachos* (potato and cheese croquettes served with rice, beef, and eggs, s/11,000) without worrying about the quality of the street vendor's oil. Ecuadorian meat and fish entrees (s/12,000-18,000), along with traditional *caldos* (broths) with every part of the pig but the squeal, are also whipped up in style (open Mon.-Fri. noon-3pm and 6:30-9:30pm, Sat.-Sun. 2-4pm.)

Sidewalk Cafés and Coffeeshops

Usually small, crowded, and overflowing with trendy drinks like espresso and cappuccino, coffeeshops can't be beat in terms of atmosphere and a good place to chat. But don't come hoping for any deals—coffeehouses are notoriously overpriced, and the same finger food can be easily be found elsewhere for less. After all, you're paying for the ambience here as well.

El Chacarero Pizzeria-Cafeteria, Amazonas 430 y Robles (tel. 550-449), typifies the sidewalk cafés lining Amazonas, but may be the best choice among them. Yuppify your life—sip a tasty cappuccino (s/2,000) while watching the cellular-phone-toting bourgeois *licenciados* (educated elites) of Quito saunter by. Savor *churros rellenos* (pastries stuffed with chocolate or vanilla cream, s/2,000), but beware of the overpriced pizza (s/7,500-33,000). Waiters in tuxes let patrons sit at outdoor tables as long as they like (open daily 7am-11pm).

El Escocés, Amazonas 410 y Robles (tel. 554-704). Another sidewalk café right in the thick of things, this one with a corner location. Slightly smaller, cheaper, and less classy (i.e. fewer cell phones) than El Chacarero. Cappuccino s/2,000. Some overpriced entrees (*manscos* s/13,000 and up). *Churros* s/2,700.

Grain de Café (tel. 234-340 x14), on Baquedano between Reina Victoria and León Mera, offers a huge selection of imported coffees and teas. Espresso, cappuccino, and other caffeine-loaded drinks s/1,500-3,000. Despite its French-sounding name, Grain de Café maintains an upscale Italian feel. Tasty set-price *almuerzos* (s/7,000) come with soup, rice, and a meat entrée. Hamburgers s/7,000, pizza s/9,000-15,000 (open Mon.-Fri. 7:30am-11pm, Sat. 9am-11pm, Sun. 9am-8pm).

Café Cultura, Robles 513 y Reina Victoria (tel. 224-271). Part of a posh hotel, this coffee-and-pastry shop serves only that—coffee, tea, and pastries—but does it in style. Caters to homesick *gringos* with a supply of the latest in American magazines and a crackling fire to heat those not yet accustomed to mountain temperatures. Straight out of London, a continental breakfast of scones, jam, and tea or coffee (s/4,000). Giant cookie (s/2,500). Fruit salad and reliable water round out the thirst-quenching selections (open daily 7:30-11:30am and 3-6pm).

Café Moka, Calama 247 (tel. 520-931), between Reina Victoria and Almagro. Look carefully for this tiny café, sandwiched by more prominent upscale restaurants. This cozy yellow room provides the perfect intimate atmosphere for chatting, but good luck getting a seat at one of the three tables. Serves overpriced cappuccino (s/4,000) and natural juices (s/7,000). Open daily 9am-11pm.

Café Bangalô, Carrion 185 y Tamayó, a laid-back three-room Brazilian teahouse offering standard café fare—tea, coffee, pastries, scones, and cakes. Lose yourself in cups of gourmet imported tea (s/2,900) and romantic Brazilian beats; admire the tasteful art on the walls for hours from your flowery seat—you won't be asked to leave until closing time. A great spot for avoiding afternoon downpours. Pastries aren't cheap (s/6,000 and up). Open Mon.-Sat. 4-8pm.

OLD TOWN

The Old Town's plethora of small *almuerzo* and *merienda* (afternoon snack) restaurants makes it the perfect place to explore for that tasty, local s/3,000 three-course lunch. These restaurants are so plentiful, so similar, and change so often that it makes little sense to try to list them individually. Look around for a clean lunch spot filled with locals and no flies, and more often than not you'll come away satisfied. Otherwise, just try one of the dependable favorites below.

El Criollo, Flores 825 y Olmedo (tel. 219-811). A traditional Old Town restaurant with a classy touch: nicely furnished tables illuminated by red lanterns, surrounded by copper-plate wall ornaments complementing the full bar in back. *Gringos* aplenty congregate here; sometimes the management tries to take advantage of it by raising prices on the weekends. *Almuerzo* s/4,300-s/5,100. *Bistek con papas* (steak and fries) s/7,800. Pork chops s/9,400. Open daily 8am-10pm.

Restaurant Panorámico, in the Hotel Real Audiencia, Bolívar 220 y Guayaquil (tel. 512-711), on the corner of Plaza Santa Domingo. The name says it all—nowhere else in Quito will you find such an amazing view of the colonial city to entertain you as you eat. Feast your eyes on the statue of *El Panecillo* watching over the bustle of Santo Domingo square and the shack-covered countryside, while feasting your palate on *filet mignon* (s/10,000). Prices are surprisingly cheap, considering the high quality of the crystal, the tasty food, and the incredible view (open Mon.-Sat. 7:30am-10pm).

Pollos El Rey (tel. 516-373), on Guayaquil near the Plaza Santo Domingo. One of many Old Town *pollo* spots, this place fixes chicken so many ways it'll leave you dumbfounded. It is particularly popular with the locals due to its cheap, quality food. *Almuerzo* (s/3,500) and rotisserie-roasted chicken (¼ chicken s/7,000) are served up on faux-wood tables and benches beneath truly tasteless wall decorations (open daily 10am-7pm).

Chifa El Chino, Bólivar 256 (tel. 513-435), between Venezuela and Guayaquil. This bustling *chifa* (Chinese restaurant) actually serves only a few Chinese entrées; mostly it dishes out local specialties and seafood. The service...speedy and impersonal. The *almuerzo* (s/3,000)...decent, if unspectacular. The menu's *a la carte* items are a tastier choice: *Corvina* (local fish) with vegetables s/5,500. Chinese pepper steak s/5,500. Spring rolls s/6,000. Open daily 9am-11pm.

Plazuela Café del Teatro Cafeteria & Bar, on the corner of Manabí and Flores at the Plaza del Teatro. Prices at this small café and sandwich shop are clearly not aimed at locals; sandwiches are a steal only for the proprietors at s/5,000-7,000. *Gringos* who can afford it, however, rave about the outstanding coffee and espresso (s/1,900). Sit inside amid European-style decor, or better yet, enjoy your caffeinated drink outdoors amidst the hustle and bustle of the Old Town plaza.

Bakeries

Panaderías and *pastelerías* line the streets of Quito, both in the Old and New Towns, with amazing abundance. It is virtually impossible to walk two blocks without coming to one. All are of approximately equal quality (the bigger ones tend to be fresher and more reliable; bakeries inside supermarkets are sometimes overpriced and slightly stale). Filling breads and pastries can be had for less than pocket change—bakeries are one place where Ecuador will seem inconceivably inexpensive. Try *cachos* or *cachitos* (croissants, s/200-400), or *empanadas* (sugar-topped bread filled with either cheese or marmalade, s/500). Rolls of various varieties are good but vary in freshness (s/100-250), and French loaves and *baguettes* are amazingly cheap (s/500-1,000).

Sights

Throughout its long and varied past as an Incan, Spanish, and Ecuadorian capital, Quito has always taken the role as jet-setter of the country's culture. The city has an abundance of museums, with collections ranging from ancient artifacts to cutting-edge modern art. Anything but monotonous, much of Quito's Old Town architecture is a unique mix of indigenous and Spanish baroque styles, and it creates a striking juxtaposition against the contemporary highrises of Quito Moderno.

LA PARTE COLONIAL (OLD TOWN QUITO)

When the United Nations declared Old Quito a "World Cultural Heritage" site in 1978, scores of 300-year-old plazas, churches, and government palaces were guaranteed both longevity and a high profile. Strict zoning and construction laws have kept much of the architecture in the well-preserved Old Town more or less the way it looked in the days of Spanish colonization. Most of Quito's interesting plazas and cathedrals are found on the Old Town streets, but so are many of the city's dirtier neighborhoods and poorer inhabitants. Exercise caution in Old Quito, even by day. Pickpockets roam the streets, particularly around the market area and the *terminal terrestre.* By night the streets are even more dangerous, and tourists should retreat to the New Town, as the economically-able Ecuadorians do.

The centerpiece of colonial Quito, the **Plaza de la Independencia** wows with its stunning **Palacio Presidencial** (presidential palace) and colossal **catedral,** but is best-loved by *quiteños* as a relaxing retreat with shady palm trees and meticulously-maintained gardens. Few locals realize the true historical significance of their favorite rest stop. Built in 1667, the plaza's cathedral contains the grave of Independence hero Antonio José de Sucre, the namesake of the country's currency. A statue commemorating Quito's August 10th Independence Day dynamizes the center of the plaza, but old men engaged in the art of people-watching make sure the plaza's energy level remains low. Sitting counts as a fulfilling pastime among the Spanish wrought-iron balconies and majestic stone pillars here; weary wanderers often stay awhile to take in the air of Quito's colonial days before moving on.

A few blocks away, the gorgeous, gigantic **Monastery of San Francisco,** constructed from 1535 to 1605, flanks **Plaza San Francisco.** The bare concrete area known as **Plaza Santo Domingo** serves as an important *trole* stop near the *terminal terrestre,* but not much else. Though it houses an attractive gilt statue, the accompanying **Church of Santo Domingo** has seen better days as well. The **Plaza del Teatro,** at Guayaquil and Manabí, drapes the backdrop for the grand **Teatro Nacional Sucre,** constructed in 1878. Though the landmark theater no longer stages many plays, a free symphony plays here from time to time.

Visible from the Plaza del Teatro, as well as most other locations on the outskirts of the Old Town, the majestic statue of **La Virgen de Quito** surveys her domain from the summit of **El Panecillo.** From the top of the hill, the views of Quito and its surrounding mountains and volcanoes are as fantastic as the elaborate iconography that decorates the virgin. The trip up El Panecillo involves a long and dangerous walk up the stairs at the end of García Moreno. Even groups get robbed frequently; to be safe, have a taxi take you up and wait at the top to bring you back down (roundtrip runs around s/12,000).

One of Quito's narrowest and most colonial streets, **Calle La Ronda,** also called Juan de Dios Morales, forks off of Av. 24 de Mayo at Benalcázar. Though it has become a bit destitute and stinky, it still smells of the charm from way back when the street was known for its many serenaders.

The abundance of **churches** that clutter the streets of Old Quito is astonishing: one stands tall on practically every other block. **La Compañía,** at Benalcázar and Sucre, is perhaps the most beautiful—it was under restoration in 1996 and may or may not be open. Its stone exterior features exquisite carving and gargoyles, and the ornate gold-leaf walls and façades inside consumed over seven tons of gold during their 163-year construction, which lasted from 1605 to 1768. Other churches of note are the simple **La Merced,** on Cuenca between Chile and Mejía, **La Concepción,** on Moreno between Chile and Mejía, **El Sagrario,** on Moreno between Sucre and Espejo, **Carmen Alto,** at Moreno and Rocafuerte, and **San Agustín,** at Chile and Guayaquil, where Ecuador declared her independence.

MUSEUMS

Quito has such a plethora of museums that anyone who ever took the time to visit them all would end up a bona fide Ecuadorian, satiated with loads of information about archeology, history, indigenous groups, flora and fauna, and colonial and modern art. If you really are a student, be sure to show your ID at every opportunity, and you may gain entrance for the national rate despite your lowly foreign status.

New Town

The New Town is where the money is, and so not so coincidentally it boasts the best museums. **Museo Nacional del Banco Central,** in the huge circular, metallic building at Av. Patria and Av. 6 de Diciembre (tel. 223-258), is a recent consolidation of several separate Banco Central museums in the city, and by far the most extensive and high-class museum in Quito. Enormous winding rooms, many dim and glass-partitioned, contain exhibits of archaeology, pre-Independence paintings, religious portraits by colonial Ecuadorians, modern art, pre-Columbian gold works, and indigenous *artesanía* (open Tues.-Fri. 9am-5pm, Sat. and Sun. 10am-3pm; admission for foreigners s/10,000, with student ID s/5,000).

As part of the same building, the **Casa de la Cultura Ecuatoriana** (tel. 565-808) presents a collection of 19th- and 20th-century art and musical instruments that would impress anywhere else in the city, but pales next to its neighbor (open Tues.-Fri. 10am-6pm, Sat.-Sun. 10am-3pm; admission s/3,500, weekends free). A hangout for college students and Quito's cultural elite, movies and plays are shown here from time to time. The outside café has excellent atmosphere and coffee.

Another fine museum in an entirely different part of town, the museum of the **Fundación Guayasamín,** José Bosmediano 543 (tel. 446-277), is in the Bellavista neighborhood. Take Av. 6 de Diciembre north to Eloy Alfaro, where Bosmediano begins, and start climbing—the museum is way up the hill (they don't call it Bellavista for nothing). The entrance opens into a spacious garden with metal statues rising into the cool suburban air. Housed in several white *casas,* the collection includes an extensive exhibit of pre-Incan artifacts, all found in Ecuador. The rest of the museum is dedicated to the riveting, magnificent paintings of foundation's namesake, Oswaldo Guayasamín. Part of the indigenist movement, his images capture the problems and pains of racism, poverty, and class stratification in South America, with plenty of references to the original Spanish conquest of the *indígenas* (see Modern Art, p. 54, and Indigenous Identity, p. 47). The 77-year-old artist was president of the Organization for Human Rights in Latin America in 1980. Includes a library, cafeteria, and jewelry store (open Mon.-Fri. 9am-1pm, 3-6:30pm, and Sat. 9am-1pm; admission s/3,000).

The **Vivarium,** Reina Victoria 1576 y Santa María (tel. 230-988), is not the place for people who fear snakes. These, as well as other reptiles and some amphibians, are all that's on display in this miniature zoo. Pythons, cobras, snapping turtles, iguanas, and other scaly friends are caged and numbered so that you can follow along with a guiding pamphlet in English. Ask nicely to hold the python (open Tues.-Sun. 9am-1pm, 2:30-6pm; adults s/4,000, children s/2,000).

Relatively close to each other on Av. 12 de Octubre are two other museums, both of a more or less ethnographic nature. The **Museo Amazonico Abya-Yala,** at Av. 12 de Octubre 1430 y Wilson (tel. 562-622), is a one-room exhibit on Oriente life, but the room's a big one. Exhibits about indigenous culture, wildlife, musical instruments, and photos of oil exploitation are all on display. Downstairs in the bookstore, a huge variety of publications are available on the foundation's main interest, indigenous anthropology (open Mon.-Fri. 8:30am-1pm and 2-6pm; admission for foreigners s/1,500, nationals s/1,000). A few blocks north, **Museo Centro Exposiciones y Ferias Artesanales,** at Av. 12 de Octubre 1738 y Liz. García (tel. 503-873), has bunches of interesting Ecuadorian handicrafts, including strangely Tim Burton-esque metal sculptures in the front yard (open Mon.-Fri. 9am-4:30pm; free).

Instituto Geográfico Militar (tel. 522-066), at Calles Paz and Miño, is on a hill overlooking Quito, southeast of the city center. Getting there is a taxing uphill walk or a s/5,000 taxi ride. The Instituto boasts the best maps for every region of Ecuador. Political, topographical, Sierra, Oriente...you name it. Many are for sale, starting at around s/10,000. There is also a planetarium (call for hours; admission s/1,000) and a geographical museum. Great photos of Ecuador's volcanic craters are on display in the main room. Open to the general public, but Spanish skills are helpful for getting past the military guards at the entrance (open Mon.-Thurs. 8am-4pm, Fri. 8am-1pm).

Old Town

Not surprisingly, many of the museums in the Old Town are of a historical nature. Colonial Quito comes alive at these exhibitions, housed at times in buildings as old as the artifacts themselves. One of the highlights is the **Museo del Convento San Diego,** Calicuchima 117 (tel. 512-516), overlooking the city from the south, next to the cemetery west of El Panecillo. To get there, follow Calle Imbabura south from Old Quito until it dead-ends in the plaza in front of the convent. The religious institution was established 400 years ago by Spanish colonists, and the 45-minute guided tour through the complex (given in Spanish, and necessary to enter the museum) reveals many an intimate window into the distant past, including original murals, cooking facilities, and a chamber where bones are buried deep in the earth. The walls are decked out with religious artwork: one painting shows a rendition of the Last Supper, with the indigenous delicacy *cuy* (guinea pig) substituted in for Christ's main course (open Tues.-Sun. 9:30am-12:30pm, 2:30-5pm; admission s/5,000 for foreigners, nationals s/500).

Farther down in the traffic-heavy blocks of Old Quito, the Casa de la Cultura lives up to its cosmopolitan name with the **Museo de Arte Colonial,** Cuenca 901 y Mejía (tel 212-297). The impressive artwork dates back to the 16th through 18th centuries and includes a collection of miniature sculptures and carvings. Christ, monks, saints, and other religious figures abound (open Tues.-Fri. 10am-6pm, Sat. 10am-3pm, Sun. 10am-2pm; admission for foreigners s/5,000, nationals s/2,000). Two blocks east and two blocks south lies the **Museo Alberto Mena Camaño de Arte e Historia,** at Calle Pasaje Espejo 1147 y García Moreno (tel. 510-272). Follow Espejo about 10m west of Moreno where it is a footpath, and the entrance is on the left. The museum's permanent exhibit is an historical journey that descends into the maze-like basement where wax figures lie in murdered positions, and then surfaces in a courtyard near the entrance. There's also a ground-level room for temporary art exhibits (open Tues.-Sat. 9am-4:45pm; free).

Two blocks east and two more south, the **Museo Casa de Sucre,** Venezuela 573 y Sucre (tel. 512-860), celebrates Ecuador's battle for independence (The Battle of Pichincha) in the house of one of its key participants, Mariscal Sucre. Weapons, painting, and fighting uniforms all emphasize the military influence. The museum includes a library and a free tour (open Tues.-Fri. 8am-noon and 1:30-4pm, Mon., Sat. 8am-1pm; admission for foreigners s/3,000, nationals s/500). The continuation of this museum, **Museo Templo de la Patria,** is located way up the hill of Pichincha, under the monument to the Independence fighters of Ecuador: it was here that Mariscal Sucre triumphed and independence was won on May 24, 1822. A monument to the event, the museum contains an eternal flame, among other things. Definitely a hike (or a taxi ride; open Tues.-Fri. 9am-4pm, Sat. and Sun. 10am-2pm).

The **Colegio Nacional Mejía,** on Ante between Varga and Venezuela, has two separate museums behind the school's high walls. The **Museo Etnográfico** (tel. 583-412), entered on Venezuela, presents a series of dioramas of different indigenous peoples throughout Ecuador, as well as a taxidermy exhibit of animals that were once found throughout the country but have since been killed, cut open, and stuffed with dry material. Check out the two live tortoises in the yard. Guided tours are offered (open Mon.-Fri. 8am-noon, and 2-6pm, Sat. 8am-noon; free). **Museo de Ciencias Naturales** (tel. 583-412), accessible via the school's main entrance on Vargas, contains a thorough collection of birds, sharks, and other animals, including several bats captured in a Quevedo movie theater (open Mon.-Fri. 7am-3pm and 5-8pm; free).

The **Museo Conde de Urquijo de la Casa de Benalcázar,** Olmedo 968 y Benalcázar (tel. 218-102), resides in the historical home the founder of Quito, but doesn't devote itself to the glorification of Sebastian de Benalcázar. Instead, it houses a collection of sculptures from the 16th to 18th centuries, donated in 1966 by the Conde de Urquijo, then the Spanish ambassador. The art is devoutly religious, the library devoutly intellectual (open Mon.-Fri. 9am-1pm and 2-6pm; free).

Ecuador Strikes Gold

July 26, 1996. It was a mild summer morning. More than 80,000 people watched with bated breath as 22-year-old Jefferson Perez, decked out in slinky shorts and honest-to-God professional walking shoes, wobbled into the Olympic Stadium in Atlanta, Georgia to claim the first gold medal of the '96 Track and Field competition, **Ecuador's first Olympic medal ever.** Walking 20km in one hour, 20 minutes, and seven seconds, he beat his best time by 14 seconds, and the rest of the field by 25m. The closest Ecuador ever came to medaling before this was in 1972, when Jorge Delgado Panchama came in fourth in the 200m butterfly. In interviews after the race, Perez reminisced, "When I took the lead, I felt very tired, as if I was asleep. It felt like a dream. Then I thought that *this* is my dream. I have to go for it, even if I died."

Back in Quito, patriots filled the streets, celebrating the momentous occasion into the wee hours of the morning. Then president-elect Abdalá Bucaram announced, "This triumph has to help the country!" and declared that a special postage stamp will be issued in Perez's honor. Congrats, Jeff!

Entertainment

SPORTS AND RECREATION

In Quito, as in all of Latin America, **fútbol** (soccer) is king. Giant crowds flock to the weekend *fútbol* games at the enormous **Estadio Atahualpa,** at Av. 6 de Diciembre and Naciones Varidas, near Parque La Carolina. Take a bus marked "Estadio" on Av. 6 de Diciembre. Teams from the intra-Ecuador *liga* compete on this field; matches between Quito and its vicious rivals from Guayaquil or Cuenca are the norm. Tickets run about s/10,000 and are readily available the day of the game if you arrive a bit early. If you're lucky, you might get to see the **Selección Nacional** (Ecuadorian national squad) play another South American country in hopes of qualifying for a coveted spot in the 1998 World Cup in France. While Ecuador has never qualified, a 1996 victory over Argentina has raised hopes for '98. Ecuador isn't known for its **corridas de toros** (bullfights), but those hungry for some real bloodsport can contact **Unión de Toreros** on Amazonas at Casa Paz bank (tickets around s/20,000).

Ready for an afternoon of frisbee and pickup soccer? **Parque La Carolina,** north of the city center on Amazonas, is Quito's answer to all recreational desires. A Sunday afternoon at the park is perfect for kids, athletes, and dawdlers; it may not be *Grande Jette,* but Seurat would nevertheless be charmed by the carousels, benches, open fields, trees, and even a pond with pedal boats. The central **Parque El Ejido,** sandwiched between the Old and New Towns, has similar greenery, but not nearly as much tranquil charm. Go **swimming** at the beautiful pool in **Hotel Quito,** on Gonzalez Suárez outside the city. Non-guests pay a small fee.

SHOPPING

Quito's most cosmopolitan thoroughfare, New Town's **Avenida Río Amazonas** is the most popular (but not necessarily the cheapest) place to buy souvenirs and Ecuadorian handicrafts. Keep in mind, if you plan to buy much, that markets in neighboring towns like Otavalo offer both lower prices and a more cultural shopping experience. Even so, it's a good idea to check out some of the shops on Amazonas, if only to browse, check out prices, and get an idea of the *artesanía* Ecuador has to offer in a more comfortable, aestheticized setting than the hectic local markets. Directed at tourists, these Río Amazonas shops aim to please, stocked with the most popular handmade crafts Ecuador has to offer: Panama hats, tagua-nut carvings, hand-painted pottery, and *lots* of handwoven rugs, shawls, wall hangings, and bags. Unless prices are marked or it is explicitly stated that prices are fixed, bargaining is expected. If you don't bargain, you will most likely be ripped off. At the same time, squabbling over sucres that mean much more to the poor vendor can be petty. Every shopper must strike a comfortable balance. But remember—the best bargaining is done by the person who's perfectly ready to walk away if the price isn't right.

MOVIES

The many movie theaters in Quito generally screen American movies in English, with Spanish subtitles. The best movie listings are in the newspaper **El Comercio; Hoy** also lists the movies playing in town. Some theaters have matinees, but most screen twice during the evenings, around 6:30pm and 8:15pm. Tickets range from s/2,000 to s/8,000, with a definite correlation between price and movie quality or age (most new releases in Ecuador came out in the U.S. six months to one year earlier). Incredibly cheap, s/2,000-3,000 shows are usually pornos or chintzy action flicks. Some of the highest-quality theaters in New Town Quito are **Universitario,** at Av. Américas and Verez Guerrero at the Universidad Central; **Colón,** at Av. 10 de Agosto and Colón; **Benalcázar,** at Av. 6 de Diciembre and Portugal; **24 de Mayo,** at Grunaderos and Av. 6 de Diciembre; and the **Casa de la Cultura** (see p. 73). In the Old Town, **Cinema Central,** on Venezuela, is decent, though New Town films are generally of a much higher caliber.

THEATER

Although **Teatro Nacional Sucre** (p. 72) was built to satisfy cultural Quito's dramatic desires, more people visit it today to see the ornate exterior than the performances inside. Though music and dance concerts and plays are still performed on Sucre's stage, **Teatro San Gabriel,** on Av. América at Mariana de Jesus, has taken over as the place to see theater in Quito. North of the city center, San Gabriel has **ballet folklórico** (traditional ballet) twice weekly. The **Casa de la Cultura** (see p. 73) also offers occasional theater performances. Check *El Comercio* for all listings.

NIGHTLIFE

Compared to Guayaquil, after dark Quito yawns and then goes to sleep. The law sets a bedtime curfew at 2:30am, so the city closes up relatively early even on popular Thursday, Friday, and Saturday nights. Despite this setback, Quito still gushes with bars and dance clubs *(discotecas),* catering to the city's flocks of young people and tourists who just wanna have fun. One block north of Colón, Calle Santa María claims some of Quito's most jammin', traveler-friendly nightclubs, including **Tequila Rock, Papillón, Diego de Almagro,** and **Cafecito.** Lesbian and gay travelers have options in Quito as well... two of them. Ecuadorian law makes homosexuality a crime (see Bisexual, Gay, and Lesbian Travelers, p. 23), so gay hang-outs are a quiet, cautious phenomenon. A confusing number of club names makes it hard to keep track of any of these silent legacies.

Stick to nightlife in the New Town; not only is the scene hipper, but Old Town's streets are too dangerous for night wandering, especially if you're a bit *borracho.* But New Town's not such a safe haven either; recent reports of robberies and assaults have put the revelers of the night on guard. Follow their example, especially around Reina Victoria, and take a taxi back to your hotel.

No Bar, Calama 442 y Av. Amazonas (tel. 546-955), on Calama's Restaurant Row. The blue-and-red sign atop the roof shouts "NO," but by all means come on in to one of the trendiest night spots in Quito. A mixed crowd of locals and travelers pack the narrow, compact floor, so revelers often stand on the tables on either side of the bar. Beer s/6,000 (open daily 6pm-2:30am; no cover).

Aleatiay (tel. 238-324), on Santa María near Reina Victoria. Rock in this jailhouse-themed club, where prisoner mannequins toast above the dance floor and graffiti claim that the only way to become free is to go to jail. You probably won't experience a Camus-ian liberation here, but let loose with this international crowd anyway (open Thurs.-Sat. 6pm-2:30am, Sun.-Wed. 6pm-1:30am; no cover).

El Pobre Diablo (tel. 224-982) on Mera and Santa María. For a more relaxed evening, head to this 6-room café/bar. Sometimes it turns on the 2 fireplaces and other times it turns up the jazz. *¡Qué suave!* Beer s/4,000 (open Thurs.-Sat. 4:30pm-1am, Tues.-Wed. 4:30pm-midnight).

El Huero, Baquedano 188, a little east of Reina Victoria. This gay club is "members only," which means you'll have to meet an Ecuadorian member beforehand and enter together. The white-and-pastel interior doesn't dazzle, but the dance floor is bigger than most in Quito. Fits crowds up to 300, mostly male but with some lesbian and heterosexual women. Grinds techno tracks straight out of a NYC palace (open Fri. and Sat. 9pm-2:30am; cover s/15,000, including 2 drinks).

Ana María, Liz. García 345 y Av. 6 de Diciembre (tel. 226-714), hiding past a restaurant sign that says, *"Menestras."* A more intimate gay bar that goes by a number of other names, this boys' club has a tiny square dance floor and typical techno dance music. Bright, pink, festive, and complete with balloons shaped like big bananas (open Wed.-Sat. 8pm-3am; no cover, but a drink minimum).

Near Quito

MITAD DEL MUNDO

Latitude 0°0'0''. Yes, you're on the Equator, the namesake of the entire country and arguably the most famous thing about Ecuador. Since the equatorial monument known as Mitad del Mundo ("Middle of the World") was erected 15km north of Quito, Equator-mania has transformed this spot into an amusement park of Ecuadorian culture, history, and capitalist ventures. Perhaps more than any other location in the country, Mitad del Mundo has become a bona fide, First-World-style tourist attraction, emitting a kind of Disney World feel. A sprawling complex of museums, restaurants, gift shops, banks, and various other tourist facilities form a self-contained, overpriced tourist "village" with bleach-white sidewalks, smooth stone pathways, and a landscape that clearly gets constant upkeep. In the center of it all, the main attraction is the 30m-high monument, a wide obelisk perfectly aligned with the cardinal points of the compass. The Equator itself is denoted by a red stripe on the ground, extending from the eastern face of this structure, host to armies of straddling tourists enchanted by the idea of simultaneously standing in both hemispheres.

Ironically enough in this land of overpriced souvenirs, visiting the monument itself is free. The pathway past the parking lot leads through two rows of busts, pointing directly toward the obelisk. As multiple inscriptions explain, the structure was built in commemoration of a French-Spanish scientific expedition that measured the equator's location here between 1736 and 1744. Simply straddling the well-worn red line outside the monument can be entertaining enough story fodder, but panorama-seeking visitors can also take an elevator up the observation deck at the top of the monument itself. A set of stairs winds back down through an ethnographic museum with excellent displays of Ecuador's past and present. Free guides in Spanish or English. To enter the monument, buy a ticket from the **boletería** across the way, below the EMETEL office (admission s/1,000). The monument is open daily 10am-4:30pm.

The centerpiece is simply the high-profile start of the sightseeing experience. The Mitad del Mundo complex contains several more discreet museums; most impressive is the outdoor, thatched-roof **Museo de Sitio Intiñan,** to the northeast of the obelisk. This tribute to the sun includes a carefully-positioned model of the sun's path, sundials, replicas of indigenous culture, and some Galápagos tortoises with no obvious solar connections (open daily 8am-6pm; admission s/1,000). On the other side of the complex, a spiffy modern **planetarium** waits for at least 15 tourists to arrive before beginning its shows (open daily 10am-5pm; admission s/2,000, children s/1,500). A nearby building houses **miniature city models** of colonial Quito, downtown Guayaquil, and Cuenca (open daily 9:30am-5pm; admission s/2,000, children s/1,000). A recent addition to the complex, the monument dedicated to the **Heroes del Cenepa,** near the entrance, honors soldiers who died in the recent battles with Perú. A **scale** across from the post office lures weight-watching tourists to marvel at the pounds they seem to lose on the equator. They haven't really trimmed any inches; rather, the equatorial bulge causes them to be farther from the center of the earth, so gravity has a weaker pull and they consequently weigh less. A picture of **Don King** boasts of his visit; it seems he may have been the last to invest money in the machine. The **plaza de toros** hosts bullfights on weekends and holidays, and killer roosters compete in savage cockfights at the **gallera** on the same occasions. Predicably, the major festival days in these parts are March 21 and September 23, the **equinoxes.**

Above Mitad del Mundo's main information building resides **CETUR,** ready to hand out brochures and answer equatorial questions (open Wed.-Sun. 10am-4pm). Make phone calls from **EMETEL** (tel. 394-032), also above the main information building (open Tues.-Sun. 10am-2pm and 2:30-5pm). **Banco del Pacífico** (tel. 396-307) is on the eastern side of the village, adjacent to the bullfighting stadium (open Tues.-Fri. 10am-5pm, Sat. 9:30am-2pm). **Buses** leave Quito for Mitad del Mundo from the **El Tejar** bus area in the northern part of Old Town, around J. López and El Tejar (every 5min., 5am-8pm, 45min., s/1,000). You can also flag buses down along Av. de las Américas; try the intersection of Colón and Américas. Returning buses leave from the base of Equinocial near Av. 13 de Junio in San Antonio de Pichincha (every 5min. until 6pm). The post office, **Correos del Ecuador,** is in the main information building on the plaza, directly in front of the monument, on the first floor (open Tues.-Fri. 9am-5pm, Sat.-Sun. 10am-2pm).

If you plan to stay the night, don't count on Disney-quality luxury hotels; most tourists return to Quito for the night. **Hostal Residencial La Mitad del Mundo** (tel. 394-952), on Av. Equinoccial, is 10m down the cross-street Shrigua, on the right. Second-floor rooms have private baths; rooftop rooms share a communal one. A private home with plenty of rooms, the hostel has a warm, domestic atmosphere. Don't be surprised if single men are denied a room. S/15,000, with bath s/25,000. Farther up the road, next to Mitad del Mundo, the cleverly-named **Complejo Dos Hemisferios** clearly lies in the southern hemisphere. This resort comes complete with a bar, restaurant, sauna, heated pool, conference room, and hefty price tag.

Catering to international tastebuds, Mitad del Mundo's restaurants, cafeterias, and ice cream stores consistently overcharge in true tourist-mecca form. **Restaurante Rincón Manabita** serves heaping helpings of moderately-priced munchies. At s/3,500, the *almuerzo* is the best deal on the menu; other entrees cost about twice as much (open daily 9am-8pm). As the fanciest, priciest eatery in town, the **Restaurante Equinoccio** (tel. 394-128) occupies its own chunk of the village near the entrance to town, with mostly garden and wooden paths. Breaded fried shrimp with *tamarindo* sauce s/38,000, *llapingachos* (potato and cheese pancakes) with beef, fried egg, and peanut sauce s/17,900. Vegetarian-friendly dishes too (open daily 9am-6pm). For cheaper eats, follow the distinguished budget path down Av. Equinoccio to San Antonio and scout out a *comedor.*

PULULAHUA AND RUMICUCHO

Two nearby outings are sometimes combined with the almost obligatory Mitad del Mundo visit. The volcanic crater **Pululahua,** whose rising ridge is visible from the equatorial extravaganza nearby, is the more worthwhile. But don't expect any smoking fumaroles: this flat, inactive depression now sustains an expansive series of farms, with houses and patches of land that seem miniature from the steep edge of the crater above. The crater wall opens to the west, letting in the parade of dense clouds that hangs over the agricultural community and very often fogs out the views. Watching the mist trembling up the crater walls is almost as fascinating as the momentary glimpses you're allowed into the crater's green depths.

From Mitad del Mundo, the crater is about 5km away. There are two paths that reach it, both of which continue as trails down to the crater floor. The paths turn off the highway between San Antonio de Pichincha and the town of Calacalí, 8km to the west. Both trailheads are marked with signs, one 4km from Mitad del Mundo, the other 3km farther. The first trail is steeper and takes more than an hour to hike. There are several ways to get to the trailheads; the cheapest way is to hike, but why do that

Straight Flush

When 18th-century French explorers came to Ecuador in search of the "middle of the Earth," they (or rather their huffing lackeys) hauled along the finest compasses and astrolabes that the king's court could provide. Their find wasn't worth all the fuss, though—the Frenchmen could have done the job with a bidet. Among the odd phenomena that occur at the Earth's equator, which include feeling lighter than at any other spot on Earth, is the strange fact that toilets don't know which way to flush. A toilet in a house to the north will flush counterclockwise, while a porcelain pal to the south will flush as the clock flies. The query: what is a poor potty to do when it's set squarely in the middle? Scientists claim that something called the **"Coriolus effect"** causes the swirly switcharoo, but even they can't predict which way an equatorial whirlpool will turn. Rumor has it that, in order to dispel the mystery, a group of experts has set up a make-shift laboratory of 10 toilets, one bathtub, and a lava lamp in the basement of Mitad del Mundo's obelisk. These gurus of bowl mechanics follow a strict daily regimen (reposition toilet, pull cord, reposition, pull cord) all in search of one thing—the mythical straight flush. No one knows if they've seen it, some believe they never will, but if you want to see for yourself, grab a toilet on wheels, head towards Mitad del Mundo, and keep on flushin'.

when you can catch one of the **buses** that pass through Mitad del Mundo's traffic circle (every 45min., 6am-7pm, 20min., s/350), headed for Calacalí. Buses run back to Mitad del Mundo, often continuing to Quito, with the same frequency (5am-5pm). **Taxis** also run tourists to the first trailhead for s/5,000-s/10,000; it's three times that price if you want the driver to wait and drive you back.

The other jaunt close to Mitad del Mundo is to **Rumicucho,** a pre-Incan set of ruins atop a hill to the northeast. The roughly rectangular arrangement of rocks is barely visible from the equator lookout, but there's really not much more you need to see. Rumicucho isn't too impressive a site; the low-to-the-ground ruins are in a suburb of a suburb of a suburb, surrounded by various half-built cinder block projects. Take Avenida Equinoccial to Av. 13 de Junio, the principal strip of San Antonio de Pichincha that runs north-south. Head north for 30 to 45 minutes; when you see a sign that says "Rumicucho" pointing to the right, the ruins are close. A museum accompanies the ruins, managed by the Banco Central de Ecuador (open 7:30am-6pm; admission for foreigners s/3,000, nationals s/1,000). *Camioneta* drivers at the Mitad del Mundo traffic circle are eager to spare you the hike for s/5,000 each way.

VOLCÁN PICHINCHA

Dominating the landscape west of Quito dwells a rather explosive family. **Rucu** is the old, craggly one with antenna peaks, frequently observed from amid the busy intersections and puny buildings of Quito below. Back when he was a young volcano, Rucu shook loud and active, but the time has come when his lava just doesn't flow anymore. Now he rests, covered in hardened souvenirs from his glory days. West of Rucu sits **Padre Encantado,** the calm patriarch of the peaks, while 15km farther west steams and groans the restless **Gua Gua.** Rising above its relatives at 4794m, Gua Gua's eruptive orifice continues to inspire the awe and the twinge of fear that goes with the family's surname: **Pichincha.**

The double-cratered Volcán Pinchincha achieves most of its fame simply due to its proximity to Ecuador's distinguished capital city. (It turns out that Padre Encantado isn't really a part of the family; he's just a rock formation.) The younger, energetic Gua Gua Pichincha erupted in 1660, 1881, 1931, and 1981, to name a few fiery occasions. While the volcano rumbles alarmingly close to Quito, it does not pose an enormous threat; the closer crater, Rucu, is utterly inactive, and Gua Gua fires off in a western direction, foreshadowing doom for the tiny town Mindo but greatly relieving the distraught *quiteños.* As history has shown, the most severe threat to Quito itself is ash. The October 27, 1660 eruption piled more than a foot of volcanic soot atop the city, causing rooftops to collapse.

Despite its disastrous reputation, Pichincha's proximity to Quito makes it one of the most popular climbs in Ecuador. Less strenuous than some of Ecuador's other choice peaks, Pichincha serves as a convenient acclimatization trek before visitors venture on to higher peaks farther south. Also worthwhile in and of itself, Pichincha provides amazing views of Quito, the valley, and a slew of other mountains.

The closer crater, **Rucu,** tempts tourists simply to start scambling straight up the hillside from the city. Theoretically this is possible, but quite dangerous—not for mountain-climbing reasons, but because of thieves from the bad neighborhoods that lie at the foot of the mountain. However, trip reports from the South American Explorer's Club attest that some paths up Rucu are relatively safe. One heads west from **Avenida La Gasca** and turns south on **Occidental** into the Miraflores neighborhood. Before the tunnels, look for a road that turns off to the right and heads up the mountain. This is the trail to the antenna peaks, where a ridge leads west to the peak of Rucu. Climbers warn that the path has loose vegetation at times, and that the hike is a full and exhausting day, up and back. Start early and time the trek so that nightfall doesn't catch you on the way down. Alternatively, a road leads up to the antenna peak, **Cruz Loma,** from the **Monumento de la Libertad** in the south end of the city near the mountain (accessible by taxi). This takes three hours, and from here a ridge continues to Rucu (another 2-3hr.). Again, strike out early to avoid nightfall. Before attempting these or any other trails up Rucu, visit the South American Explorer's Club to find out the most current, reliable information from other climbers' reports.

The baby **Gua Gua** outdoes the elder Rucu in terms of altitude and scenery. From its peak, vistas stretch to the uninhabited west and south, and when clouds don't get in the way, climbers can see down into its plummeting crater. The summit is accessed from the village of **Lloa** (Yo-a), an hour drive away from Quito at the southern base of the volcano. There are two roads to Lloa; the first route heads out **Av. Venidores de Pichincha** to the military batallion, where the greatly damaged and almost impassable **Avenida Chilibulo** begins its bumpy way up. The other route continues farther down Venidores to the neighborhood of **Mena Dos,** where a street named **Angamarca** (also called "Via Lloa") begins to ascend. At the junction of Venidores and Angamarca, a constant stream of **volquetas** (yellow dump trucks) runs toward Lloa from about 7am to 5pm, and the drivers will often give climbers a lift for a minimal price. In the town of Lloa, signs point the way to the road that winds up to the **refuge,** which sits just shy of the crater's edge. The refuge can be reached by 4WD vehicles in one and a half hours or by foot in six to eight. The refuge provides a bathroom, some rainwater barrels, and several mattresses. S/5,000 per person. The sometimes snow-covered summit towers close by, a one- to two-hour roundtrip hike. It's cold up there, so warm clothing is a must. It is possible but generally discouraged and officially prohibited to hike down into the crater, as some climbers were asphyxiated by gaseous emissions several years ago while camping down there. A memorial has been erected at the edge of the crater. While the hike up Gua Gua is nothing too difficult, transportation can be quite difficult to coordinate and taxi fares may start to add up. Without a 4WD vehicle to take you to the refuge from Lloa, you'll be hard-pressed to complete the climb up and back in a day. It might be worth the bucks to hire a guide to worry about the transportation and food (see Tour Companies, p. 34).

SANGOLQUÍ

Two hours to the north, the town of Otavalo hosts Ecuador's most famous outdoor market, full of sensational Saturday steals. If you just can't get enough of all the bargains, head out to the town of Sangolquí the next day for its smaller, but still bustling, **Sunday market.** The village itself is a bit more modern than most places of its size, mostly because it's less than 20km southeast of the capital. The outdoor market spills over several blocks in the middle of Sangolquí, starting next to the principal avenue **Enriquez,** where the buses drop their loads. The majority of shoppers are local, and the market looks so typical that it could easily be from any Sierra town. Vendors wait under tarps next to piles of their goods: banana bread, rubber gloves, chicken heads, jello, jeans, bras, razor blades, chocolate bears. The selection is eclectic, the tourists rare, and Quito nearby, so there's no reason to stay the night. The Sunday market offers its first cow intestine at 5am and persists relentlessly until about 9pm. **Buses** leave Quito from the south end of **Plaza La Marín,** on the west side of a traffic circle (every 5min., 4am-11pm, 30min., s/600). The same buses return to Quito until about 9pm, leaving from where they dropped passengers off.

BOSQUE PROTECTOR PASOCHOA

Long, long ago, before man arrived to ravage this land and then set aside tiny fragments of it to protect from himself, the volcano Pasochoa violently erupted. The explosion was so powerful that the mountain collapsed, tearing the crater inward and downward, leaving a slanted, lava-steaming remnant for a peak. In the 100,000 years that followed, the ash-enriched ground sprung to life with a dark green forest. The relative inaccessibility of the crater's interior kept human interference to a minimum for many a millenia. Nevertheless, somehow man pushed in, and it took the destruction of part of the area's primary growth before Ecuador's Ministry of Agriculture proclaimed the area a protected forest in 1982. Today the area is managed by the **Fundación Natura,** Av. América 5653 y Vozandes (tel. 447-341, 342, 343 or 344), in Quito. Visitors pour into the extinct crater to hike the well-groomed, mapped trails winding across the floor and slopes of the crater reserve, from the 2700m rock-bottom to the 4200m toothlike projections of the Pasochoa peak. The forest includes plenty of rare plant species like the *podocarpus,* the only conifer native to the Andes. Aside from that, you've got your orchids, 120 species of birds, pumas, butterflies, and a whole slew of other critters. The area receives the most rain in April, and is especially dry and dusty from July to September.

QUITO

Facilities are a cross between plentiful and basic. No restaurant, no food stores, but **Hostelling International**-affiliated lodgings provide a roof over your head. The accommodations consist of stark cots in two attic-like lofts; don't forget your sleeping bag, because rooms get chilly at night. Bathrooms have hot water, and a kitchen is at your disposal, complete with fridge and stove (foreigners US$5 per night, nationals s/6,000). You can also pitch a tent in the campground, which has bathrooms and charcoal grills (foreigners US$3, nationals s/4,000). Entrance fees into the reserve aren't cheap: *extranjeros* US$7 (s/5,000), *extranjeritos* US$3 (s/3,000). The forest is a popular Quito getaway for the jeep-endowed, *gringo* and Ecuadorian alike. Reservations requested for groups over 15, at least eight days ahead of time; contact Fundación Natura. Without a car, the best way to get here is by **bus;** take it to **Amaguaña** (every 7min., 5am-8:30pm, 45min., s/850) from the very south end of Plaza La Marin, past the buses to Sangolquí. If you're in Sangolquí, intercept the buses en route to Amaguaña on Av. Enriquez, about 25 minutes out of town, away from Quito, a block past the giant statue of Rumiñahui. Amaguaña is about 6km away from the reserve's entrance. *Camionetas* cost about s/15,000, but bargain. Otherwise, hike along the highway in the direction the bus was heading, to a turn-off on the left indicated by a sign. Other signs guide you the rest of the way to the entrance, a path that is at times downhill but mostly up and not too strenuous. It's a long hike, though; some beg a departing party in the parking lot to take them to Quito, or at least as far as Amaguaña. From there, the buses return to the city.

RESERVA MAQUIPUCUNA

In the northwestern region of the Andes, just a 40km crow's flight from Quito, the Reserva Maquipucuna protects a true ecological gem. Its borders contain 4546 hectares of land, with altitudes rising from 1200m to 2800m, about 80 percent of which is primary cloud forest. Inaugurated in 1988 with a total of 3000 hectares, the reserve has since taken over much of the abandoned surrounding farmland. Researchers have swarmed into the reserve in its short decade of existence, and their work has produced numbers to brag about: in Maquipucuna's boundaries, they have found 1160 species of plants, 45 mammals, 320 birds, and 250 butterflies. The warm-blooded creatures include pumas, spectacled bears, bats, agoutis, pecaries, tapir, and deer. In addition to wildlife, Maquipucuna shelters a number of archaeological sites left by the **Yumbo,** a people who inhabitated this forest 1000 years before the Incas arrived.

Maquipucuna is one of the strictest reserves around in terms of the standards it sets for tourists. The **Thomas H. Davis Ecotourist Center** provides an open-aired, thatched-roof ecotourist oasis that can accommodate 22 people. The little piece of heaven includes dining and living areas, three meals a day, and bathrooms with hot water (foreigners US$45, children US$36; nationals US$26, national children $US21). The reserve also provides researchers in the science station with a bed and three meals for stays over one month (foreigners US$20 per day, nationals US$15). For daily entrance only (which is a rather difficult schedule): foreigners US$5, nationals US$2.

Getting here and away is by far the hardest part. The roundabout route from Quito goes through the towns of **Calacalí, Nanegalito, Nanegal,** and **Marianitas,** 4km from the reserve's entrance. **Buses** run to Nanegal (Mon.-Wed. at 1pm, Thurs. at 2pm, Fri. at 1pm, Sat. at 10am and 2pm, Sun. at 9am and 2pm, 2½hr., s/5,000) from the **San José de las Minas** terminal near Parque Alameda on José Antepara, passing through Plaza Cotocollao in north Quito 45 minutes after departure. Alternatively, **Aloag** bus line does the trip (Mon.-Fri., 2pm) for the same price, leaving from the **Terminal del Cumanda** (and passing through Plaza Cotocollao at 2:45pm). Get off the bus 2km short of Nanegal at the big green house called **La Delicia.** From here, it's a 2km hike to Marianitas, and another 4km to Maquipucuna (total walking time 1¼hr.). From December through May, when it's excessively muddy, walking is not recommended. Truck drivers Octavio, Alejandro, Diogenes, and Norton can be hired in Marianitas to go the remaining 4km (s/10,000-s/20,000). To get back, a milk truck leaves Marianitas each morning between 7:15 and 7:45am, and will give you a lift to Nanegalito for s/ 1,500. In Nanegalito buses pass by on the way to Quito (every 30min., s/4,000). For more information, contact Fundación Maquipucuna in Quito at Baquerizo 238 y Tamayo, P.O. Box 17-12-167 (tel. 507-200; fax 507-201; e-mail root@maqui.ecx.ec).

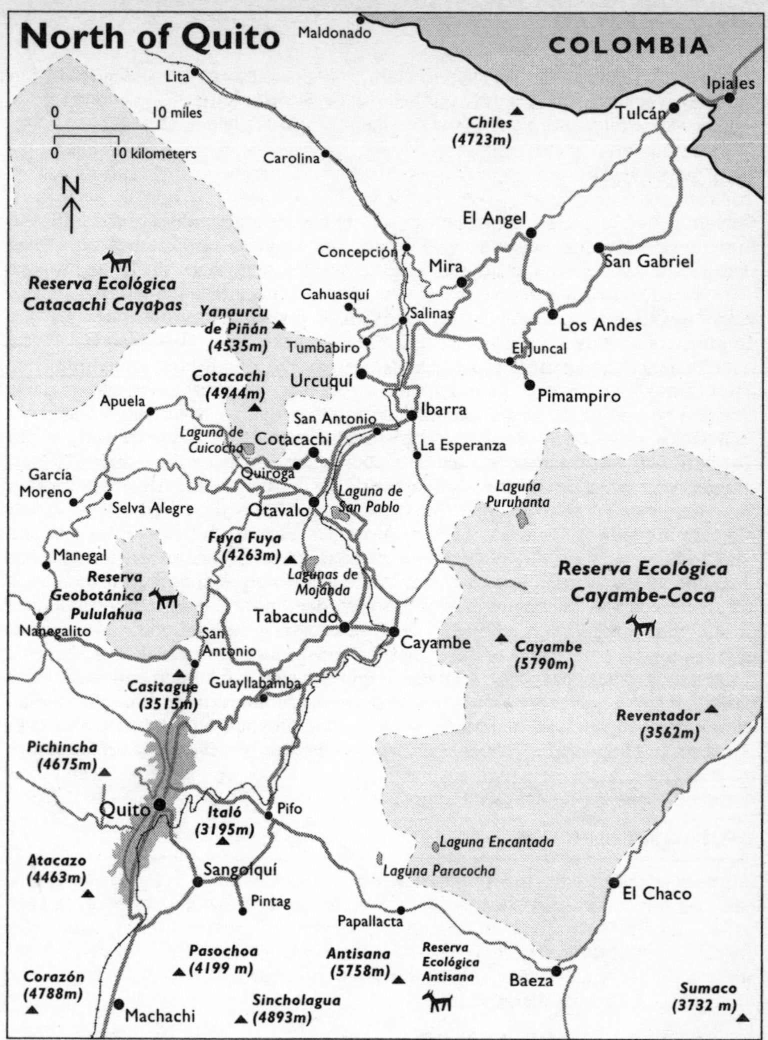

North of Quito

North of the hustle and bustle of Quito, try to sit back and enjoy life. Placid lakes like the mystical Lagunas de Mojanda, neatly tucked in the highlands of the Andes, enchant with their serene charm. The pace slows down as you head north, where indigenous villages back out of the public eye, prefering to maintain their traditional lifestyles (see Indigenous Identity, p. 47). Locals speak Quechua on the streets, wear traditional indigenous clothing, and often specialize in handcrafted *artesanía,* much of which is sold in the famous Saturday markets at Otavalo. Packed with tapestries and leather, wood carvings and hand paintings, the hopping market draws crowds not just from all over Ecuador, but from all over the world. But in the midst of the highland cloud forests, even the larger communities like this one barely show up as specks on the steep mountain cliffs. The misty cloud forest seems to dominate all, but in reality is severely endangered; protected areas like the Intag Cloud Forest are the only havens for the endangered flora and fauna of the northern Sierra.

Otavalo

Otavalo is one of the most prosperous and respected indigenous communities in Latin America, but its success hasn't come easily. Restrained by a history of oppression and racism, the local *indígenas* have been persecuted since the Incan invasion of 1496. The Spanish took the brutality to grim new heights, forcing *otavaleños* to work 15-hour days under dangerous conditions in textile sweatshops called *obrajes.* This form of tyranny gradually dissipated and, eventually, in 1964, an agrarian reform law returned much of the Otavalan land back to its indigenous residents. Most *mestizos,* however, still treated the *indígenas* like second-class citizens until *otavaleños* began to be recognized worldwide for the beauty of their weavings and music in the early 1980s. Now *otavaleño* products are sold internationally, and foreigners flock to Otavalo's **Saturday market** specifically to buy locally-made goods. A feast of sights, sounds, and smells, this frenzied fanfare overflows with Ecuador's largest selection of handmade indigenous handicrafts (see Artesanía, p. 53).

As the *indígenas* became more and more prosperous, they came to dominate Otavalo life. Today the city of Otavalo is a testament to the strength, determination, and talent of the indigenous *otavaleños.* No longer simply weavers, many *indígenas* are now leaders in the community, as lawyers, doctors, and politicians. The indigenous youth continue to reach higher levels of education and promise to surpass the awe-inspiring achievements of their parents. Perhaps most impressive is the fact that despite economic success, the *otavaleños* remain grounded in their traditions. Local women staunchly wear their traditional outfits of white blouses, blue skirts, blue shawls, and elegant gold necklaces, while men sport calf-length white pants, dark ponchos, felt hats, and rope sandals. Some accuse the *otavaleños* of selling out to tourism, but it is precisely their adaptability that has allowed them to maintain their distinct indigenous identity (see Indigenous Identity, p. 47).

ORIENTATION

Buses drop visitors off in the southeast corner of town, in front of the **Plaza Copacabana,** on the corner of **Atahualpa** and **Calderón.** Every bus company uses the east-west Calderón as a runway for its daily departures and arrivals, making it the most chaotic street in this relatively peaceful market town. The town's major north-south artery is **Sucre,** which runs past both **Parque Rumiñahui** and **Poncho Plaza,** the site of the famous Saturday market.

PRACTICAL INFORMATION

Travel Agencies: A number of travel agencies offer tours to neighboring towns and ecological reserves. Several are situated on Sucre between Calderón and Salinas, including **Inty Express,** Sucre 4-06 (tel. 921-436; fax 920-737), and **Diceny Viajes Zulay,** Sucre 10-14 y Colón (tel./fax 921-217).

Banks: Banco del Pichincha, Bolívar 6-14 (tel. 020-214), exchanges money and traveler's checks and has a 24-hr. ATM. **Banco Presivara,** Sucre 10-07 (tel. 921-212), has a 24-hr. ATM but does not change cash or traveler's checks. Some hotels and travel agencies will also change cash or traveler's checks, including **Hotel Otavalo,** Roca 504, and **Diceny Viajes Zulay** (listed above).

Telephone: IETEL, on Calderón between Sucre and Jaramillo, offers phone and telegram service. Pay phones can also be found in various shops around town.

Buses: There are 3 major bus lines in Otavalo. **Trans Otavalo,** Calderón 3-06 (tel. 920-405), and **Cooperativa Los Lagos,** Calderón 2-16 y Roca (tel. 920-302), go to **Quito** (every 20min., 3:50am-7:10pm, 2½hr., s/4,700), **Ibarra** (every 5min., 4:50am-7:30pm, 30min., s/8,500), and smaller towns. **8 de Septiembre,** on

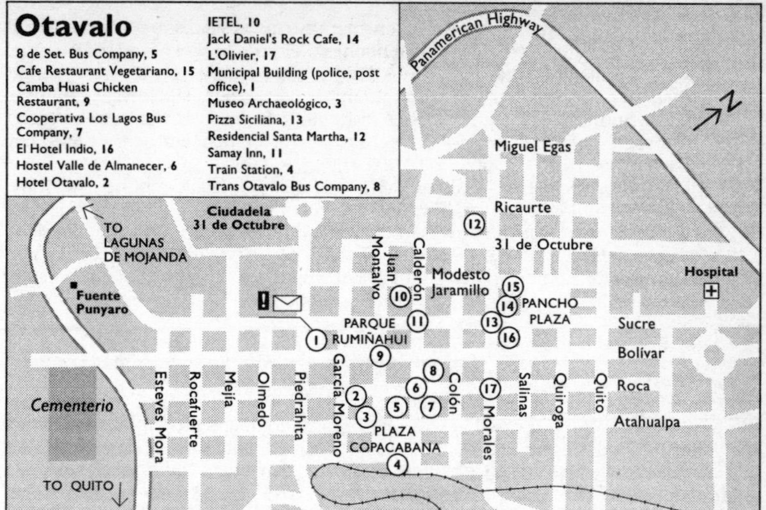

Atahualpa at Plaza Copacabana, goes to **Peguche** (every 20min., 10min., s/400) and **Agato** (every 20min., 15min., s/600).

Taxis: Taxis tend to congregate around the parks and plazas. Otavalo's 2 main companies are **Cooperativo de Taxis Copacabana** (tel. 920-438) and **Cooperativa de Taxis de la Ciudad de Otavalo** (tel. 920-301).

Laundromat: New Laundry Lavandería, Roca 9-42 (open Mon.-Sat. 8am-1pm, Sun. 3-6pm). Many hotels also have laundry service.

Pharmacies: La Dolorosa, Calderón 3-05 y Bolívar (tel. 921-817). **Farmacia Modesna** (tel. 920-395), at Moreno and Bolívar, to the left of the main entrance of the municipal building.

Medical Services: Hospital San Luis de Otavalo (tel. 920-444, 920-600, 920-700, or 922-461), on Sucre at the northern edge of town. Emergency medical care can also be handled in the municipal building. All emergency treatment is free.

Police: Policía Nacional (emergency tel. 920-101), on the northern outskirts of town. Though they normally don't handle inner-Otavalo problems, they have the only emergency telephone. The **Policía Municipal,** at Sucre and García Moreno, in the municipal building, serve Otavalo. They do not have a telephone number, but can be seen on motorcycle and on foot throughout town.

Post Office: Along Piedrahita, between Bolívar and Sucre, in the back of the municipal building (open Mon.-Fri. 8am-7pm, Sat. 8am-2pm).

Telephone Code: 06.

ACCOMMODATIONS

Hostal Valle del Almanecer (tel. 920-990; fax 920-216), at Roca and Calderón. Constructed of sturdy avocado trees and bamboo ceilings, El Valle is a refreshing organic escape from the conventional plaster and cement. Quichua-named rooms are big enough to be comfortable, but small enough to make mingling in the courtyard more pleasurable. Singles s/10,000, with bath s/15,000; 1-bed matrimonial s/20,000; doubles s/20,000, with bath s/30,000.

Hotel Otavalo, Roca 5-04 (tel. 920-416), between García Moreno and Montalvo. Welcoming rooms have 15-ft. ceilings and gargantuan beds, some of the softest in Otavalo—just try to ignore the heinous yellow-green tint of the walls. Spigots struggle to supply hot water. All rooms have private bath except a few s/30,000 doubles. Singles s/20,000, doubles s/40,000, triples s/54,000, quads s/80,000.

Samay Inn, Calderón 0-05 y Sucre (tel./fax 922-871), 2 blocks from the bus stops. All 14 rooms have 24-hr. hot water and private baths. At the snap of a finger you can have a color TV in your room for no charge. Plain as vanilla, but beds are big and rooms are cleaned daily. International phone and fax. S/15,000 per person.

Residencial Santa Martha, Colón 7-04 y Av. 31 de Octubre (tel. 923-046). Penny-pinchers need look no farther for all the basic necessities. Thick walls mute the outside world, and sagging mattresses make for soft slumber. Common bath and shower shared between every 4 of the 16 rooms. Sleep tight and save your money for Sat. Singles s/6,000, doubles s/12,000, triples 18,000.

El Hotel Indio, Sucre 12-14 y Morales (tel./fax 920-060). Don't confuse it with the bigger Hotel Indio on Bolívar. This one can be a bit pricey too, but the location, just a jump from the market, helps justify the fee. Disparate rooms either overlook Av. Sucre or Mt. Imbabura. Remove your shoes and enjoy the carpet, a rare pleasure. Hot water 24hr. Singles s/8,000, with bath and TV s/25,000; doubles s/15,000, with bath and TV s/45,000; triples s/50,000.

FOOD

Cafe Restaurant Vegetariano (no tel.), on Salinas on the south side of Poncho Plaza. Typical indigenous food with a twist. Relax man, it's organic; no fertilizers, pesticides, or parasites will get you here. All ingredients grown organically, all water purified. Veggie rice s/7,000, daily special s/6,800. Andean music perpetually piping, live on Sat. 12:30-7:30pm (cover s/2,000). Open daily 7am-9:30pm.

Jack Daniel's Rock Cafe, Sucre 12-12 y Salinas (tel. 922-185). Originally named Hard Rock Cafe, the name was changed after legal battles, and so far no whiskey companies have caught on. Listen to classic rock as you munch mouth-watering crepes (s/5,000), sip blackberry shakes, and peruse notebooks filled with the haiku, political commentaries, and apocalyptic predictions of previous diners.

L'Olivier, Morales 9-08 y Roca (no tel.). As the only representative of French cuisine in town, L'Olivier has much to live up to, and so far it has charmed even the toughest critics. The sparsely-decorated ambience doesn't overwhelm, but the enormous rumpsteaks (s/9,000-11,000) and Chilean wine might. Some dishes blend French and Latin American cuisine, like the Crepe Guacamole (s/5,500). Open daily 7:30am-1am.

Pizza Siciliana, Morales 15-01 y Sucre (tel. 922-439). Near most of the nightlife, this place prepares patrons for foodless *peñas* by packing their paunches with pizza and pasta. Outfitted with full bar, fireplace, and live Andean music on weekends, Siciliana is a scene of its own. Huge pasta servings (s/10,000) and extra large pizzas (s/18,000-34,000) blend eclectically yet harmoniously with indigenous tapestries and music (open noon-late night).

Camba Huasy Chicken Restaurant, at Bolívar and Montalvo (tel. 920-359). Meets all dining moods with its 2 dining rooms. One's dandified with Daffy Duck paintings, the other embellished with stained glass. Swing by in the morning for a *mochachino* (s/2,500) and cheese omelette (s/2,000), or drop in at lunch for a basic ham-and-cheese sandwich (s/3,000). It's always service with a smile.

SIGHTS

There are no rules when it comes the overwhelming **Saturday market.** The uncontainable fanfare starts in Poncho Plaza, but overflows onto the surrounding streets, stretching as far as 3 blocks away. **Local weavings** are concentrated in the plaza and all along Sucre, where many *indígenas* simply set up booths in front of their shops. **Wood carvings** and **leather goods** are found all over, but some of the best are sold on Sucre and in the southeast end of the market. The fried egg, pork, and potato aroma that permeates the entire market originates on Quiroga where streetside stands cook up **market munchies** for all. Av. Jaramillo is the most eclectic area, selling American goods like Air Jordans and Levi's jeans, as well as purely South American stock, such as Incan jewelry and chirping baby chickens. Although this advice holds true everywhere in the market, be especially careful with valuables while walking along Jaramillo. It is by far the most crowded street on market day, and thieves position themselves here deviously. Carry all important items in a money belt; if you don't have one, keep your hands on your valuables at all times.

Vendors usually begin selling as early as 6:30am and pack up around 5pm. An intriguing phenomenon occurs about an hour before the market starts. The **animal auction,** located just outside of town, is possibly the most peculiar event in Otavalo. An added benefit to the early-morning auction is that you'll definitely beat the crowds to the main market, and you'll probably arrive more bright-eyed and bushy-tailed than the masses.

Most tourists begin to arrive around 10am, but it is a good idea to purchase goods earlier, as bargains *(gangas)* and discounts *(discuentas)* are more readily available before demand escalates. Another good bargaining time is just before 5pm, when most vendors close up shop and eagerly try to dispose of their inventory. If you're really bargain-hungry, try shopping in the Friday market. In most cases, the starting price offered on Friday is lower than that on Saturday, but of course, then you miss out on the spectacular carnival that is Otavalo's main market.

For such a popular tourist draw, Otavalo has relatively few sites of interest aside from the market. The **Museo Arqueológico,** at Montalvo and Roca, on the second floor of Hosteria Los Andes, has over 6,000 fossils, including parts of the rib of **El Hombre de Otavalo,** a 28,000-year-old *Homo sapiens* skeleton found in Otavalo but kept (for the most part) in Quito (admission s/5,000). The **Museum of Anthropology,** on the northern outskirts of town across the Panamerican Highway, has English and Spanish information on the history and culture of the Otavalo's *indígenas* (open Tues.-Fri. 8am-noon and 2-6pm, Sat. 8am-noon; free). The **Parque Rumiñahui,** in front of the municipal building, is a great place to rest your legs under shady trees and admire **Volcán Imbabura** (4609m) towering over the town's rooftops to the east. Across the street, on the corner of Sucre and Montalvo, locals play volleyball on a dusty **playground.** You can sip a drink and just watch, or test your spiking skills and join the match. On Saturday afternoons, wander out to the coliseum along the Panamerican Highway and witness **cockfighting** at its finest. Across the highway is a small dirt **soccer field** where local teams often compete on Sundays. They won't let you play, but you're welcome to stay and watch.

The indigenous villages and Andean landscape surrounding Otavalo also offer a multitude of diversions. Daytrips to Peguche, Agato, and Lagunas de Mojanda, to name a few, are well worth the time. They can be visited independently (see below), but tourist agencies also offer tours to these and other destinations. **Zulay Tour Agency** arranges a two-day excursion to Apuela, which also visits Nalgumbi natural springs, an ecological reserve, and local pyramids in Gualiman. Horseback riding, lodging, and meals are included (US$80 per person). They also offer an Indian village tour that visits local homes in La Compañía, Agato, Peguche, Cotacachi, and finishes at Laguna de Cuicocha (lasts from 8:30am-4:30pm; s/35,000). **Inty Express** offers hik-

Sheep's Clothing

Remember some basic facts when examining textile pieces in the Otavalo market. There are three types of wool: **lana borrego** (lamb), **lana alpaca,** and **lana sintética** (synthetic). *Lana borrego* is generally considered the highest quality wool, and goods made from it tend to be more expensive. *Lana alpaca* is used solely on tapestries *(tapices)* and creates an entirely different-looking tapestry than those made of synthetic or lamb's wool. *Tapices* of *lana alpaca* resemble paintings, with rich colors depicting local scenery or indigenous peoples. Pieces constructed of *lana borrego* have duller colors, but the best way to determine the type of wool is to examine the back side of woven goods. If you pull on the wool and a thick fluffy strand emerges, it is *lana borrego;* if the strand that emerges is thin and stringy, it is *sintética.* Both are durable, but if you're a perfectionist, go with the real stuff. Most market vendors are extremely ethical and will answer questions concerning wool type and quality honestly, but a little knowledge of the materials goes a long way toward enriching the market experience.

ing tours with English-speaking guides to Lagunas de Mojanda or Lake Cuicocha, jeep ride included (US$20). Their Indian village tour costs s/32,000.

ENTERTAINMENT

Though Otavalo's nightlife is not wild and crazy by any standard, there are a few quality *peñas* that can make any weekend night a memorable one. **The Peña Tucano,** Morales 8-10 y Sucre (tel. 920-033), heats up on Friday and Saturday nights when local Andean groups play. The dancing never stops; in between bands, a DJ thumps salsa and reggae. Bands are so close you could reach out touch their authenticity. Beer s/2,000, margarita s/5,000 (open daily 9:30pm-3am; cover s/3,000). The one and only bamboo palace in Otavalo, at Morales and Av. 31 de Octubre, goes by the name **Peña Tuparina.** Speakers are so big they threaten to shake the hut to the ground. Local Andean bands play on Fri. and Sat. from 9:30pm-2am (cover s/3,000). **Peña Amauta,** at Jaramillo and Salinas, is the funkiest of 'em all: an underground cellar with dim lighting, massive *tapices,* and a fireplace. It has a small dance floor, but plenty of tables with good views of the local groups. This is the one and only home of a mysterious, potent brew known as *runallacta.* Sip it slowly and float away into the forests of the Andes (open Fri.-Sat. 8pm-2am; cover s/3,500).

■ Near Otavalo: Lagunas de Mojanda

Located 17km south of Otavalo, the Lagunas de Mojanda provide all the peace and quiet any strung-out traveler could desire. Tucked between the extinct volcano **Fuya Fuya** and a range of smaller rolling mountains, these placid lakes make an ideal retreat. A demanding trail winds through the mountains, gracefully unveiling all three lakes on its way past breathtaking views and first-rate fishing and camping.

The trail begins to the right of **Laguna Grande,** the only lake immediately visible. As you follow the trail upward, admire the spectacular scenery, but also watch the less-scenic ground, as many horses travel this path. Campers should avoid the *refugio* like the plague, as there literally may be one brewing in the depths of its muddy, littered floors. Careless guests have left heaps of trash here, and enough graffiti mar the walls to embarrass even the most ardent vandal. The path diverges near the far end of the great lake, but be calm Anxious Traveler, both paths lead to enlightenment. The trail that cuts to the left winds around the backside of **Montaña Pequeña,** leading to an amazing view of the **Laguna Negra,** so named because it is tightly surrounded by mountainous cliffs that keep the waters eternally shadowed. The other path leads downhill to a view of the minuscule **Laguna Chiquita,** providing incredible glimpses of the misty mountaintops of Fuya Fuya and Montaña Pequeña along the way.

Taxis to Mojanda charge s/40,000 roundtrip, but this price increases rapidly the longer you make the driver wait. A cheaper option is to take a cab up to the lakes and hike back, a three-hour walk. You could walk the whole way, but the trip there is all uphill and so steep that buses can't even cut it. *Camionetas,* found in Otavalo's Poncho Plaza, will generally charge the same fare as a taxi, but will probably be more reasonable concerning the wait at the lakes. Hitching is also a possibility, but *Let's Go* does not recommend hitchhiking. If this is your only option, walk south on the Panamerican Highway just outside of Otavalo for a few hundred yards. A dirt road, the only route to Mojanda, heads up to the right. When the road ends, you'll know it, as you'll be face-to-face with the immense Laguna Grande.

■ Peguche

An indigenous community well known for the vibrance and quality of its tapestries, Peguche is regarded as the most prosperous of Otavalo's satellite towns. Its affluence is not seen so much as it is heard. Strange rumblings emanate from Peguche's tiny homes. These are the sounds of electric weaving machines, commonplace here but unheard of in poorer communities. While the people are prosperous, the success has not gone to their heads. Aside from the belligerent ankle-biting dogs, everyone in town radiates friendliness.

Orientation and Practical Information Peguche is situated roughly 4km northeast of Otavalo, between the Panamerican Highway and the community of Agato. The quiet central plaza, **Centro Pachacutic,** is home to the Santa Lucia Church and will soon be the site of an indigenous cultural center. There are no real street names in town, so don't look for signs. With your back to the church, the road running from right to left in front of you, is called **Calle Cascada.** The cross street heading directly away from you is called **Calle Principal.** On the corner of Principal and Cascada, **José Cotacachi's folklore shop** sells tapestries and leather bags made by various locals. An unofficial, one-man tourist office, José will answer any questions you have regarding the history and culture of Peguche, provided you speak decent Spanish. Ask nicely and he'll escort you to a house to observe weaving in progress. If you don't have the courage to ask, or if your Spanish isn't strong enough, the best way to experience backstage weaving excitement is to visit Peguche with a tour group from Otavalo. The bus line **8 de Septiembre** routinely travels between Plaza Copacabana in **Otavalo** and the central plaza of Peguche (every 20min., 10min., s/400). Some buses from Otavalo continue on to **Agato** (s/600). Calle Principal leads to the local **dispensario,** the next best thing to Otavalo's hospital. Peguche's **police station** (tel. 920-234), on Calle Cascada just before the train tracks, also serves and protects neighboring *pueblos,* such as Agato.

Accommodations and Food Although there are no restaurants in Peguche, the two hostels in town more than pick up the slack. **Hostal and Cafeteria Aya Huma** (tel. 922-663) is on the train tracks, where the road splits near Loma Pucará. The soothing sound of the trickling stream below and the enormous jugs of purified water in each room make this a refreshing place to catch your breath. The wool comforters are straight off the sheep's back, and the blankets are the finest woven in Peguche. Phone/fax, storage of valuables, laundry service, mini-library, and hiking maps available. Spanish lessons for the highly motivated. Singles s/20,000, with bath s/36,000; doubles s/30,000, with bath s/50,000; triples s/45,000, with bath s/75,000. Restaurant has delectable treats everyday and live music on Sat. (open daily 7am-10pm). **Peguche Tio Hosteria** (tel. 922-619; fax 922-619), is across the tracks near the police station. Take a left when the road ends; the *hosteria* is around the corner on the right. Built in November 1995, it still looks spankin' new. Rooms ensure your feet won't get cold, with fireplaces and locally-woven blankets. Overflowing with cultural flair, the enthusiastic Muenala Vega family bombards visitors with classes and workshops on indigenous heritage. Gaze at monstrous Mt. Imbabura as you acquaint yourself with the llamas out back. Private hot-water bath in all rooms. Singles s/20,000; doubles s/38,000; triples s/56,000; quads s/76,000. Restaurant open Sun.-Fri. 8am-8pm, Sat. 8am-10pm.

Sights The well-shrouded waterfalls, **Las Cascadas de Peguche,** provide a nice pit stop near the entrance to town. *¡Qué refrescante!* Tell the bus driver to drop you off at Loma Pucará. Here women wash clothes in the river below the road and corn fields grow slowly on the steep hill across the way. If you see a sign for Hostal Aya Huma, you've gone too far. The waterfall is straight up the hill. When you come to the ruins of Bohio, take a right through the archway and follow signs for the waterfalls through a dense forest of blackberry bushes, pines, and *obcalito* trees. It's a five-minute walk until the waterfall emerges through the misty air.

■ Near Peguche: Agato

At first glance, Agato seems to be a ghost town. The dusty streets of this village, 3km southeast of Peguche and 8km northeast of Otavalo, are empty except for the usual scattering of young children, roosters, and pigs. A barrage of questions may enter your mind. Where is everybody? Whose children are these? And why is this dog sniffing my leg? The answers are quite simple. The parents of these children, along with the rest of the town, are either hard at work on the looms within their homes or out in the fields tending crops of wheat, barley, corn, and potatoes. Furthermore, the dog is sniffing your leg because you probably smell worse than he does.

Near the center of town, the **Tahuantinsuyo weaving workshop,** Rumiñahui 9 y Atahualpa, is run by the jovial Miguel Andrango. He's usually happy to demonstrate Agato's unique hand-weaving process. Locals of Agato, unlike their high-tech neighbors in Peguche, use old-fashioned looms. These are either of the sit-down, backstrap variety, or they're **telaros de español,** larger looms that require the use of both feet and hands at once. The tapestries, blankets, and sweaters produced in Agato are generally considered to be more carefully crafted than those of other towns, but are also more expensive. Miguel can also be persuaded to show how vegetables are used to dye wool yellow and orange, and how chemicals imported from Germany are used to create a red, pink, or blue hue. Wool that is off-white, black, or brown is usually natural. Miguel doesn't sell his goods in Otavalo, so if you're interested in making a purchase, you'll have to pay him a visit in his workshop.

The bus lines **8 de Septiembre** and **Coop Imbaburapaq** both go to Agato (s/600), but Imbaburapaq is generally faster because it doesn't always stop in Peguche. Walking is the slowest way of all, but it can be fantastic. Remember that the hike is mostly uphill and can take up to one and a half hours from Otavalo. If you're up for the exercise, head northeast out of town and up the same hill that leads to Las Cascadas de Peguche from Loma Pucará. At the ruins of Bohia, keep going straight up the hill. A simple rule when hiking to Agato: if a fork in the path appears, always go right. If you take a bus, consider walking back into town. The stroll provides glimpses of glistening **Laguna San Pablo** an other picture-perfect views of the countryside.

Cotacachi

Endowed with more leather than a sadomasochist's wet dream, Cotacachi is Ecuador's leatherwork capital. Planted under the watchful eye of **Mount Cotacachi** (4939m), this melting pot of indigenous and *mestizo* peoples, 15km northwest of Otavalo, stirs with well-dressed businessmen, devout nuns, and rambunctious schoolchildren. Av. 10 de Agosto, the main street in town (actually the *only* real street in town), runs towards the guardian mountain and is blessed with most of the leather shops in town.

Orientation and Practical Information There is only one road into Cotacachi, cleverly named **Av. Cotacachi.** Once in town, it's impossible to get lost—**Av. 10 de Agosto** is always in view, no matter where you roam. **Buses** to **Otavalo** can be picked up at the west end of Av. 10 de Agosto, or on Peñaherrera near the park (every 20min., 20min., s/600). A **taxi** ride from Otavalo is only five minutes faster, but much more expensive (15min., s/8,000). There are few phones in town, but there is an **IETEL** office on Calle Sucre to the north of town. **Farmacia Familiar,** Bolívar 13-06, is known to close sporadically when the owner gets hungry (supposedly open Mon.-Sat. 8am-7pm). There is a small emergency **hospital** with the scary name *El Servicio de Laboratorio,* Bolívar 12-34 (emergency tel. 915-342 or 915-932; open Mon.-Sat. 8am-6pm). The Cotacachi **police** have their home at Rocafuerte 10-36 y Av. 10 de Agosto (tel. 915-101). The **post office,** at Modesto Peñaherrera and Bolívar, is near the old church.

Accommodations and Food Cotacachi has only one true budget accommodation. The **Hostal Cotacachi,** Bolívar 12-26 y Av. 10 de Agosto (tel. 915-327), is certainly not elegant, but their cots won't leave you hunched and hobbling. Service is amicable, but polish up on your *español* because they don't speak a lick of English. Rooms are decorated with enormous sets of rosary beads for convenient prayer before bedtime. Private baths with hot water and towels. Washing machines, luggage storage. Singles s/10,000; doubles s/20,000; triples s/30,000.

Dining options in Cotacachi are scarce as well. For a quick and affordable filler-up, try the **Oediciasa Casesa,** Sucre 11-23 (tel. 915-161). Entertain yourself with fake fruit and ponder the juxtaposition of a Last Supper reproduction with a poster of a woman in a g-string. Rejuvenate with a mammoth soda for s/2,500. Not exactly the healthiest fare—hamburgers (s/2,000), fried eggs and french fries (s/2,000). For a slower-paced, more indigenous meal, you'll have to pay a bit more. The **Restaurante Inty Huasi** (tel. 915-789), at Bolívar and Av. 10 de Agosto, next to Hostal Cotacachi, has an appearance that implies reservations, but they're not actually needed. *Inty Huasi* means "house of the sun" in Quechua, but thankfully this shady dining room houses *from* the sun. *Platos típicos* of chicken, pork, and beef cost s/10,000; a delectable seafood dish with rice and shrimp is s/8,000.

Sights and Entertainment The grand happening in Cotacachi is the **shopping.** The leather products here are of sublime quality and, even though they are more expensive than the local weavings, they're a steal as far as leather goods go. Much of the leather found elsewhere in Ecuador is made from sheep, but the leather in Cotacachi comes only from the finest steers. There are over 50 different leather shops in this small town, selling everything from briefcases to women's heels. Most places accept credit cards, but give discounts of up to 10% for customers with cold, hard cash. One of the largest shops in town, **El Palacio del Cuero** (tel. 915-490; fax 915-286), along Av. 10 de Agosto, has gregarious employees who speak a fair amount of English. None of the Cotacachi leather goods are sold in Otavalo.

Near Cotacachi: Laguna de Cuicocha

Strange stories surround the Laguna de Cuicocha, 18km west of Cotacachi. Perhaps part of the mystique comes from its curious location inside the mouth of a live volcano crater. A common fear among locals is that the volcano will soon erupt and flood the town with lava and water. While nobody is packing up and leaving town, one can almost sense the anxiety lurking just below the surface of their smiles and leather. Strange stories have grown up around this most unusual of places. According to local lore, an enormous condor makes a sweeping flight to the two islands in the middle of the lake between 4-5pm every day. You can try to catch the Loch Cuicocha Monster on film, but locals assert that this colossal condor somehow avoids being captured by the usually dependable camera lens. Another legend claims that at midnight the corpses within the lake begin to howl and make ghoulish noises. While it might be romantic if the lake were an ancient burial ground, supposedly the only dead people in its depths are two suicides. When a multi-millionaire and his mistress drove off a cliff into the lake, millions in gold sank with them. Unfortunately, scuba diving lessons aren't offered, but a boat service does take visitors around the lake (30min., s/50,000).

You can walk to the lake from Cotacachi, but it's all uphill and can take up to two and a half hours. Buses from Cotacachi go to Quiroga, which is much closer to the lake (every 20min., s/400), but when the road gets too steep they go no farther. From Quiroga, either walk the last half-hour or take a taxi (around s/10,000). The hike all the way around the lake is picturesque, but can take up to six hours. Who knows, if you stay long enough, perhaps you'll glimpse the elusive condor of Cotacachi.

Apuela

Apuela's attractions begin with the bus ride there. As the bumpy road approaches town, the scenery becomes more and more staggering, with jaw-dropping views of the western Andean cloud forests. Vehicles nimbly tread inches from the steep mountain cliffs as the occasional waterfall cascades by. Depending on the time of day and the season, you may even find yourself riding high over the clouds. Don't fall asleep on the bus to Apuela; even a five-minute nap would be enough to miss the town entirely. Nested 2000m high in the lush, green mountains to the west of Otavalo, Apuela supports itself with agricultural activity. Visitors come to this mellow mountain town to go for a hike and simmer down in the piping hot springs.

Orientation and Practical Information Apuela is laid out symmetrically. Two similarly-sized *montes* (small mountains) lie on either side, and two parallel rivers run along their bases, forming Apuela's natural boundaries. The town follows suit, with two parallel roads running its length. The road entering town is referred to as **Av. 20 de Julio** by some locals (the others simply shrug their shoulders and comment that it's never needed a name). The **bus stop,** as well as all the places to sleep and eat, are on this street. The dusty **central plaza** behind the bus stop has a volleyball court and a small, dilapidated church. Apuela's other street, **García Moreno** (about this name most Apuelans are confident), runs across the plaza. **Trans Otavalo** buses run to **Otavalo** (8am, 10am, 2pm, 3hr., s/4,800), **Cotacachi** via **Gualimar** (11:30am, 3pm, 1hr., s/1,000), and the scenic, elevated village of **García Moreno** (11am and 1pm, 1hr., s/2,000). Along García Moreno, directly across from the bus stop, is the **police station** (no tel.; open 24hr.). The only phone in town is at the **EMETEL** next door (tel. 957-657), which also functions as the town's **emergency line** and **post office** (open Mon.-Sat. 8am-5pm). The **hospital** is on Av. 20 de Julio, 30m up the road from the bus stop (open Sun.-Fri. 8am-5pm).

Accommodations and Food The accommodations in Apuela are so unimpressive that your best bet is probably to stay at the pricier *cabañas* just outside of town. If the sun's setting and you're still in the *centro,* **Residencial Don Luis** provides a cheap night's stay and not much else. Beds are stiff and rooms are protected by the world's smallest locks, which would be a problem anywhere but in Apuela. If you want a cold shower, go outside to the communal bathroom. A definite change of pace, the **Cabañas Río Grande** (Otavalo tel. 920-442 or 920-545, Quito tel. 534-196) are a 45-minute walk away, next to the hot springs. Head east out of town on García Moreno. After crossing the second bridge, take a left on a road that leads to the cabañas and the pools. Surrounded by papaya, avocado, guava, and mango trees, the cabañas are a fruit-picking paradise. The spotless wood cabins, all built to fit three people, have electricity and meticulously-maintained private baths with 24-hour hot water. Cabins cost around s/50,000, but rates vary by season.

There are a couple of places to get a quick bite to eat before heading out for the day. The **Restaurant La Estancia,** on Av. 20 de Julio across from the bus stop, serves an appetizing San Gacho soup, filled with bananas, potatoes, and meat (s/1,500). Striving for a cosmopolitan feel, Estancia is decorated with posters of London and Niagara Falls (open 7:30am-9pm). Just up the road, **Doña Emmita's Restaurant** has posters that are a different type of cosmopolitan; these pin-up monuments may offend. Emmita's specialty is a well prepared *cuy* dish (s/20,000). The price is steep, but the food is good. Turkey dishes go for s/6,000. The restaurant at **Cabañas Río Grande** offers deals for breakfast, brunch, or dinner (s/16,000). The servings are adequate and food is excellent. Giant trout freshly caught from the nearby river, garnished with French fries and salad, costs s/8,000.

Sights There is not much to see *in* town, but there are many amazing spots *outside.* The hills that surround Apuela are criss-crossed with paths that make for good **hiking,** and the rivers on either side of town are known for their **trout fishing.** Buses going to Cotacachi also serve a **museum of archeology** and some **minor ruins** in Gualimar. A set of natural **hot springs,** 7km from Apuela, make for an easy-going day of sun and relaxation. Locals pipe hot water from a nearby volcanic crater into three jacuzzi-like wading areas and a sweltry 15-m pool. An even bigger pool is kept cold, to provide a refreshing plunge when the hot tub gets too hot. The pools are kept in decent shape, and it costs only s/1,000 to lounge in the mineral water all day.

■ Near Apuela: Intag Cloud Forest

Situated on the verdant western slopes of the Andes mountains, this reserve protects a portion of Ecuador's endangered cloud forests. While the better-known rainforests of the Amazon receive worldwide attention, these threatened cloud forests are disappearing at an even more dangerous rate. A visit to Carlos and Sandy Zorilla's majestic reserve is the ideal experience for anyone who either doubts or fanatically appreciates the cloud forest's value and importance. Most people come here to fish the rivers or to hike the multitude of five-minute to five-hour trails.

With elevations of 1850-2000m (6000-9240 ft.) and temperatures ranging from 12-27°C (55-80°F), Intag Cloud Forest is a far-from-static place. Particular combinations of clouds, fog, and constant humidity produce an incredible variety of flora and fauna. The plethora of epiphytes (plants that grow on other plants and trees) includes orchids, bromeliads, and araceas. The many mammals that live in the region—spectacled bears, pumas, spider monkeys, and mountain tapirs—tend to elude observation, as most are nocturnal and afraid of humans. All are threatened by deforestation and in danger of extinction. While mammals are a rare sight, the farm is a birdwatcher's paradise; its 22 species of hummingbird outnumber the 16 total found in North America. The plate-billed mountain toucan, toucan Barbet, and Andean cock-of-the-rock also flutter around the reserve. On the brink of extinction, the yellow-billed parrot has only been sighted once in the past year.

A stay on the farm costs US$40 per person per night and includes lodging, food, and a bilingual guide. The purely vegetarian fare is almost as raved over as the scenery. Delicious dishes include veggie-burgers (made from local grain), *culzoma,* potato and cheese casserole, and vegetable soups. The rooms are all-organic as well—simple wood cabins have sturdy straw roofs and straw mats for the floors. All beds come equipped with thick blankets for those chilly mountain nights. Carlos and Sandy only accept groups of six or more. The minimum stay is two nights, and while there is no maximum length of stay, keep in mind that this is a family-run farm and these people have lives of their own. If you don't have a group to go with, contact them a few weeks in advance so that they can place you in a group. Carlos and Sandy are not big fans of unexpected visitors, but as kind and generous people they never turn any traveler away. If you plan to visit, they ask that you write to them a couple of months in advance at Casilla #18, Otavalo, Imbabura, Ecuador. Alternatively, you may be able to contact them through a nearby tour agency. If you are not interested in staying at the farm, but still want to help, write to the above address to receive more information about the Intag preservation projects.

Ibarra

A peculiar balance between past and present exists in Ibarra. After a violent earthquake destroyed much of the city in 1868, the survivors were left with the monumental task of piecing the rubble back together. Whether by chance or premeditation, they happened to build many of the public buildings and business centers in the southern half of the city, and most of the colonial-styled, white-with-red-tile homes in the northern half. This balance persists today; as the people of Ibarra race forward into modernity in taxis, buses, and Mercedes Benzes, the city gently pulls them back with the clatter of horse-drawn buggies on cobblestone avenues. Even this provincial capital's culture has reached a balanced equilibrium. Ibarra is one of the few Ecuadorian cities that successfully integrates all three major ethnicities—black, Indian, and *mestizo.*

ORIENTATION

Buses from Quito and Otavalo drop visitors off along Borja and Enrique Vacas, on the western outskirts of town. To get to town, walk south toward Mt. Imbabura, and take a left on **Mariano Acosta.** The immense **obelisk,** visible from a good distance, serves as a good landmark. Three blocks north of the obelisk, east-west **Av. Flores** passes both major parks in Ibarra, **Parque La Merced** and, two blocks to the east, **Parque Pedro Moncayo.** One block north of the obelisk, east-west **Av. Moncayo** runs the width of the city, splitting Ibarra into two manageable halves. North of Moncayo, the city is a bit slower and you're more likely to find interesting architecture and historical monuments. To the south, buildings tend to be gray and menacing, the people move at a more frantic pace, and establishments go in and out of business in the time it takes to stop for a drink.

PRACTICAL INFORMATION

Tourist Information: CETUR (tel. 958-754 or 958-547; fax 955-711), at Acosta and Flores, above Banco Pichincha (open Mon.-Fri. 8:30am-12:30pm and 1-5pm).

Banks: Banco La Previsora, Oviedo 8-13 y Olmedo (tel. 955-900, 957-294, or 956-225; fax 957-295), has 24-hr. ATM, Visa cash advances, and cash exchange, but doesn't accept traveler's checks (open Mon.-Fri. 9am-6pm). **Banco Continental,** Olmedo 11-87 y Guerrero, accepts traveler's checks and gives Visa cash advances, but does not convert currency (open Mon.-Fri. 9am-2pm; ATM open Mon.-Fri. 9am-7pm, Sat. 9am-1pm).

Telephone: IETEL, Sucre 4-48 y Moreno. There are also public phones throughout the city that can only be used to make local calls (open daily 8am-10pm).

Trains: The **train station** (tel. 915-390) is just southwest of the obelisk as you enter town. The train goes to **San Lorenzo** daily (7am, 8hr., US$15). It can fit 42 people and is usually full, so call the day before to make a reservation. When you've made a reservation, your name should be on a permanent list of soon-to-be ticket holders, but it's still a good idea to show up 1hr. early, as names have been known to mysteriously disappear from reservation lists. The 8-hr. trip can sometimes turn into a 12-hr. one, depending on the number of stops and weather conditions. If Mother Nature is cooperative, it's best to **sit on the roof** of the train, where views are at their finest. Don't worry about getting thrown from the train; it moves very slowly and is likely the smoothest ride you'll get in Ecuador. Make sure your passport is within arm's reach, as there is a routine check in Lita and historically there have been periodic checks elsewhere along the way. Before you get your heart set on riding the train, call the office to make sure the train is functioning, as mud and rockslides often discontinue service for months. A final note regarding safety: do not follow children at either Ibarra or San Lorenzo bus stops. Often they pretend to innocently escort you to the nearest hotel, but actually lead you into a den of thieves who will leave you penniless. Before you get off the train, ask drivers for directions to the nearest, safest hotel.

Buses: Andina Bus Lines (tel. 950-832), at Acosta and Borja, serves **Quito** (every 15min., 6am-10pm, 2½hr., s/5,500). **Trans Otavalo** (tel. 920-405), at Enrique Vacas and Mariano Acosta, sends buses to **Otavalo** (every 15min., 4:15am-10pm, s/850). **Cooperativo Espejo** (tel. 952-190), at the train station, goes to **San Lorenzo** (7, 10am, 1, 2:30pm, 7hr., s/12,000). **Valle del Chota** (no tel.), at the train station, also goes to **San Lorenzo** (7, 9am, noon, 3pm, 6hr., s/12,000). **Expreso Turismo** (tel. 955-730), at Pedro Moncayo and Carvajal, goes to **Tulcán** (every hr., 5:15am-5:15pm, 2hr., s/5,500).

Taxis: Taxis abound, especially in parks and near bus stations. **Taxis Lasos,** Flores 9-24 y Cifuentes (tel. 955-150), chauffeurs to **Otavalo** (around s/18,000) and **Quito** (around s/90,000).

Library: At Bolívar and Flores, on the 1st floor of the municipal building (open Mon.-Fri. 8am-2:30pm and 3-5:30pm).

Pharmacies: Farmacia Ross, Velasco 8-108 y Narváez (tel. 952-220; open daily 7:30am-10pm). **Farmacia Estrada,** Cifuentes 11-43 (tel. 955-691; open daily 7:30am-10pm).

Medical Services: Hospital San Vicente de Paul, Luis Vargas Torres 1-156 (emergency tel. 131 or 950-333, tel. 958-272, 958-273, 958-274, or 958-275). All emergency treatment is free (open 24hr.). **Clínica Mariano Acosta,** Mariano Acosta 11-20 (emergency tel. 950-924), is a small 24-hr. emergency clinic.

Emergency: tel. 101.

Police: (tel. 950-444), on Auldos Alguilera.

Post Office: Salinas 6-62 y Oviedo (tel. 950-412 or 953-295; fax 958-038). Open Mon.-Fri. 8am-6pm, Sat. 8am-1pm.

Telephone Code: 06.

ACCOMMODATIONS

While there is certainly no shortage of rooms in Ibarra, quality rooms at moderate prices can be hard to come by. If you have no qualms about slumming it (i.e. enduring cold water, cracked ceilings, and rusted bathrooms), then you'll be like a kid in a candy store here. Most low-rent-type places congregate near the train station and provide pole position for the race to the morning train.

Hotel Imbabura, Oviedo 9-33 (tel. 950-155), between Narváez and Cifuentes, ½ block west of Parque La Merced. Wood-panelled floors and cot beds decorate barren but immaculate rooms. Flair found elsewhere, like in the courtyard with a flowing fountain and the cozy lounge with invaluable information on tours and trips from past visitors. Meticulously-maintained common showers and toilets. Singles s/8,000; doubles s/16,000; triples s/24,000.

Residencial Colón, Narváez 862 y Velasco (tel. 950-093), just north of the obelisk. Popular for its ideal location and the only all-you-can-eat breakfast in town (s/7,000). Simple rooms all have large windows that open up to a flower garden. Slumber safely, with huge locks on doors and a safe for valuables in the front office. Wood floors are patchy in places, but hot water bathrooms are in excellent condition. Doubles s/9,000, with bath s/11,000.

Hotel Nueva Colonia, Olmedo 5-19 y Grijalva (tel. 955-543; tel./fax 952-918), just north of the Parque La Merced. Sacrificing aesthetic appeal for technology and comfort, rooms are not much to look at but they do have wall-to-wall carpeting, color TVs, and phones. Same goes for the bathrooms, which could be cleaner but have 24-hr. hot showers. Giant breakfast included in the price. Singles s/25,000; doubles s/40,000; triples s/50,000; quads s/60,000.

FOOD

Ibarra's dining options are severely limited, a sad state of affairs for a busy provincial capital. There are relatively few sit-down restaurants, but the town is inundated with sidewalk vendors, tiny bakeries, and snack food establishments. Ask Ibarrans where to find a good restaurant, and they'll probably be as stumped as you are. A few establishments, however, endeavor to redeem the culinary failures of this colonial town.

El Chagra Restaurante, Olmedo 7-48 y Flores (tel. 952-114; fax 958-637), ½ block south of Parque La Merced along Olmedo, is perhaps the best budget place in town. Come in for a serving of sports on the big screen, or the s/1,500 soup of the day. Serving both Ecuadorian and indigenous dishes, El Chagra's chummy service and low prices go unmatched in Ibarra (open daily 9:30am-10pm).

Bar/Restaurant El Dorado (tel. 950-699 or 958-689; fax 958-700), on Oviedo just east of Sucre, 2 blocks south of Parque Moncayo. Feeling flabby from all the fried Ecuadorian food? Try a low-fat chicken dinner (s/7,000), then throw your 15-min. diet out the window with *cordon bleu* (s/10,000) and other rarities. The decor screams "70s," but tables come equipped with fine china and sparkling silverware (open 9am-10pm).

Deli/Café Express, Moncayo 6-14 y Bolívar (no tel.), 2 blocks south of Parque Moncayo. Decorated with U.S. license plates, this place is almost as American as its apple pie (with ice cream, s/2,500). Multinational breakfasts s/5,000 each. If your game on the chessboard-painted tables lasts long enough, have a lunch sandwich (s/5,000). Open Mon.-Fri. 7:15am-1pm and 4-10pm, Sat. 7:15am-8pm.

Restaurant Ajaui, Mariano Acosta 16-38 (tel. 955-221, 955-555, or 955-787; fax 952-485), 6 blocks from the obelisk. Inconveniently located unless you're heading out of town, the fact that Ajaui is still in business is a testament to its food and service. Chicken in wine sauce s/10,000, pork chop creole s/10,000. Weekend piano player and seafood specials (open 7am-midnight).

SIGHTS AND ENTERTAINMENT

Ibarra is home to many incredible historical and architectural structures. Rising more than 100-ft. high, the stunning white **obelisk** at Narváez and Velasco couldn't be a sorer thumb in its surroundings. The landmark looks more like a monument to Cleopatra than a dedication to Miguel de Ibarra, the man who founded this Spanish colony in 1606. A small **museum of archeology,** Moreno 7-58 y Cifuentes, is located above the Restaurant Estancia (open Mon.-Fri. noon-5pm, Sat. noon-2pm). Ibarra also has two remarkable parks, both surrounded by outstanding architecture. **Parque La Merced,** on the corner of Flores and Cifuentes, exhibits a statue of Dr. Victor Manuel Peñaherrera looking awfully bookish and distinguished. Peñaherrera (1865-1930) was a judge on the Ecuadorian Supreme Court and Deacon of the Faculty of Law in the Universidad Central. On the west side of the park, the **Basílica La Merced** supports a portrayal of the Virgin Mary adorned with a crown of silver. Within the *basílica* is an elaborate altar of gold, which reaches up to the 70-ft. high arched ceilings. The **Parque Moncayo,** at Flores and Bolívar, is a magnificent place for mundane activities; lying around on the shady grass tops the list. The surrounding architecture is exceptional, especially the **cathedral** and the municipal building. While the golden altar outshines most everything else in the cathedral, the church also houses huge portraits of all 12 apostles, painted by a local artist Rafael Troya. If you follow Moncayo to its easternmost point, you'll run right into the **Iglesia de San Francisco,** home of Ibarra's Franciscan fathers.

Tired of walking? Bored of parks and churches? Try the **Cine Grand Columbia,** on Moreno between Sucre and Rocafuerte. They have no fear of low-brow entertainment, usually showing Jean-Claude Van Damme flicks. Action films screen Tues. at 8:30pm, while cultural films are shown on Fri. and Sat. at 8:30pm.

■ Near Ibarra

SAN ANTONIO DE IBARRA

With it's economy firmly rooted in its exquisite woodcarving, San Antonio de Ibarra isn't just another chip off the old block. The town has little to offer outside of its woodwork, but the work is of such quality that it has carved a place for itself among the South American *artesanía* elite. People from across the Americas migrate to San Antonio annually to witness the town's handiwork and often buy a piece or two. Only recently has San Antonio become known for its craft worldwide, but already many shops sell pieces overseas, and the influx of foreign visitors keeps increasing.

San Antonio is located west of Ibarra along the Panamerican Highway. Trips from Ibarra take longer than the normal 2km sprint due to the horrendous condition of that particular segment of the road. There are rumors that the highway will be smoothed within a year, but it's very likely that it will take longer. San Antonio's layout is simple—**Av. 27 de Noviembre** is the main street and runs from the town center, **Parque Francisco Calderón,** to the Panamerican Highway. Most of the woodcarving galleries are either around the park or along Av. 27 de Noviembre. **Trans Otavalo buses** drop off on the Panamerican Highway, at the edge of town (every 15min., 10min., s/300). From here, **taxis** go directly to the heart of San Antonio for around s/5,000. Alternatively, the uphill walk from the Panamerican Highway to the town center takes about 20 minutes.

The **Hosteria Nogales,** Sucre 11-85 (tel. 932-000), is the only place to stay in San Antonio. The lack of market competition reveals itself in their painfully basic rooms. Supposedly, they'll be refurbished soon. Plan on an intimate evening with your daily grime accumulation, because bathrooms only have hot water in the morning (doubles s/16,000, with bath s/20,000). The **restaurant** downstairs is decorated with local woodcarvings and a tiny fish tank, definitely the decorative highlight of the Nogales experience. *Almuerzo* runs around s/5,000, *a la carte* dishes around s/8,000 (open 7:30am-9pm). Only one other place in town serves food, the **Restaurante Fogon del**

Chief (no tel.), along Ceballon on the north side of Parque Calderón. Though not much to look at, it serves huge, reasonably-priced portions of Creole and Peruvian cuisine and provides peeks at Imbabura. The management is amicable and gregarious, and the food is a refreshing break from typical indigenous fare. Seafood Creole soup s/7,000, soup of the day s/3,000.

San Antonio's woodwork stands out because of its meticulous, stunning precision. The **Unión Artesanal de San Antonio de Ibarra,** at the south end of the Parque Calderón, is a set of 10 woodcarving workshops that sell pieces straight from the tables they're made on. This is the best place to watch the work in progress, and workshop #1 even offers classes in woodshaping. Many shops carry very similar carvings, but there are a few unique pieces waiting to be found. All the shops in the Unión accept Visa, but better discounts go to those who carry cash. To the east side of the park, the **Galería de Arte Luis Potosí** (tel. 932-056) has work that's a little finer and more detailed than in other shops. Five or six more galleries lie on the left side of Av. 27 de Noviembre towards the Panamerican Highway. These galleries, including the **Galería de Arte Ruben Potosí** (tel. 932-302), produce larger works, some as tall as six feet, and carry a multitude of abstract, modernist carvings. The furniture shops are farther down Av. 27 de Noviembre.

LA ESPERANZA

Strange things start happening as you head south out of Ibarra. Life slows down dramatically, hearts beat at a healthier pace, and buses will sometimes even decelerate as they attempt the rocky incline that is the road to La Esperanza. The town is situated 7km from Ibarra, at the foot of Volcán Imbabura. Its economic life is rooted in agriculture but, as a supplement, many of its inhabitants hand-embroider goods to sell in Otavalo. Although La Esperanza does not glitter with excitement, the views of Mt. Imbabura and the scenic countryside make it an idyllic getaway from Ibarra's hustle and bustle. La Esperanza's one road, which locals call **Gallo Plaza,** runs north-south past the two or three establishments in town, towards Imbabura.

Esperanza has the perfect location for outdoors-lovers—everything to see and to do is out in the fresh air. The walk down to the **Río Tajuando,** which leads to Ibarra, is painless and pleasurable. Head down Gallo Plaza from Casa Aida, take a right at the first cross street, and continue for a half-hour. Watch out for very big men with very big guns at the nearby military base; they don't like tourists getting in their way. For a more serious trek, try getting to the top of **Loma Cubilche** (3836m). Facing Imbabura, Loma Cubilche is the smaller mountain to the left. To get there, head up Gallo Plaza, cross the dry bridge, and take the road on the right all the way to the top. Expect a three-hour hike up and a two-hour return. Die-hard climbers can make a go at big, bad **Volcán Imbabura** (4609m). Leave early in the morning, as the climb takes over 10 hours. Directions to Imbabura are similar to those to Cubilche, but turn right on the street just before the bridge. This road goes most of the way up, and various paths lead to the very top. A small store on Gallo Plaza before the dry bridge sells bottled water, a necessity before attacking either Cubilche or Imbabura.

The excellent **Casa Aida** (no tel.) is located right in the middle of town. There is a sign you can't miss, but failing that, everyone knows where it is. This amazing four-person straw hut has two beds in a tree-fort-like loft, accessible only by a step ladder. Thick brick walls and blankets provide plenty of warmth on frigid nights. Two of the four common bathrooms have 24-hour hot water. Singles s/7,000; doubles s/14,000; triples s/21,000; quads s/28,000. The kitchen and bathrooms are probably clean enough to eat off of. There's no need, though—Casa Aida also has one of the only restaurants in Esperanza. Dine beside the cows and bulls, who chomp on the vegetable garden that likely produced your meal. Outdoor dining provides a view of the grand Imbabura in its entirety, as well as of a smaller volcanic chunk that was blown off in an eruption 120 years ago and landed in the hostel's backyard. A full vegetarian meal goes for s/4,000, fresh trout s/7,000 (open 6am-9pm). Otherwise, eat gargantuan indigenous meals off of tree stump tables at the **Casa de Don Eugenio,** just 100m from Casa Aida. Fried pork, potatoes, and corn (s/5,000). A jack-of-all-trades, Don

Eugenio also makes (and sells) the finely crafted leather that decorates the place (open 6am-4pm).

Buses from Ibarra to Esperanza (every 20min., 40min., s/500) can be picked up at the Parque Grijalva on the corner of Sánchez y Cifuentes and Toro Moreno, or at the southernmost end of Ibarra, on the corner of Torre and Retorno (Montalvo). **Taxis** from anywhere in Ibarra charge at least s/15,000 for the trip to Esperanza. If your boots are made for walking, the two-hour hike to La Esperanza is along Retorno, the same road the buses use. Exhaust fumes create unpleasantness from time to time, but if you bring your gas mask the scenic walk can be rewarding.

Tulcán

In Tulcán, everyone is always going somewhere. Whether it's travelers crossing the border into Colombia or those who have recently arrived, Tulcán's importance lies in its ability to transport visitors to their desired destinations. A large percentage of Tulcán's population is employed as taxi and *camioneta* drivers, and four or five different bus companies compete for travelers' sucres and Colombian pesos. People often rush to get in and out of Tulcán quickly, but if your bus doesn't leave for another hour, slow down and unwind at Tulcán's only tourist sight, the **topiary garden** within the cemetery at Av. 10 de Agosto and Esmeraldas. Filled with peculiar animals, geometric shapes, and carved crown bushes and trees, the garden is a magical respite from the rat-race to the border.

ORIENTATION

The two most happening streets in Tulcán, **Bolívar** and **Sucre,** run the length of this long, narrow town. Right in the center of things, the **Parque Principal** (sometimes called the **Plaza Central**) lies between Sucre and Olmedo, Ayacucho and Av. 10 de Agosto. The bigger **Parque Isidro Ayora** is northeast along Bolívar, 2 blocks southeast of the enormous **cemetery.** Head uphill along Bolívar, about 1.5km southwest of *el centro,* to get to the **terminal terrestre.** Counterintuitively, the **Colombian border** is south and east of town, about 6km down Av. Brazil, which leaves from the northeast end of town.

PRACTICAL INFORMATION

Tourist Information: CETUR, Pichincha 467 y Sucre, 2nd floor (tel. 983-892; open Sun.-Fri. 8:30am-12:30pm and 2-5pm).

Travel Agency: EccoTur, Sucre 51029 (tel. 986-468; fax 980-368), at Parque Principal. National and international tours and packages (open Mon.-Fri. 9am-4pm).

Banks: Cilanbanco, Sucre 5086 y Av. 10 de Agosto, has a 24-hr., Visa-accepting ATM and gives Visa cash advances. **Banco Pichincha,** Sucre and Av. 10 de Agosto, next door to Cilanbanco, changes cash and traveler's checks and has a 24-hr. ATM that only accepts American Express cards (open Mon.-Fri. 9am-2pm).

Currency Exchange: Casa de Cambio, Bolívar 52006 y Ayacucho (tel. 980-910; open Mon.-Fri. 8am-noon and 4-7pm), and **Casa Paz S.A.,** Ayacucho 373 y Bolívar (tel. 950-058; open Mon.-Fri. 8:30am-12:30pm and 2:30-5:30pm), both exchange Colombian pesos and U.S. dollars.

Telephones: There are 3 **EMETEL** offices in Tulcán, with national and international calling service: at the *terminal terrestre* (open daily 8am-10pm), at the border (open Mon.-Sat. 8am-6pm, Sun. 8am-1pm), and on Olmedo and Ayacucho (open daily 8am-10pm). There is a public phone for national calls at the corner of Sucre and Pichincha, in Parque Concordia behind the bust of Simon Bolívar.

Buses: Only taxis and *camionetas* go to the border from Tulcán (see below). All buses leave from the *terminal terrestre.* 3 bus companies go to **Quito** (every hr. 1:30am-10:30pm, 4½hr., s/11,500) and **Ibarra** (every 5min. 1:30am-10:30pm, 2hr., s/5,500). **Cooperativo de Transportes Expreso Tulcán** (tel. 214-680) sends the most buses throughout the day.

Local Buses: Trans Popular buses can be picked up across the street from the *terminal terrestre.* The 10-min. ride to the **Parque Principal** costs s/250.
Camionetas: Coop Carchi (no tel.), on Venezuela along the north side of Parque Ayora, goes to the border for only s/1,300. Leaves whenever vans fill up.
Taxis: The older-looking the taxi, the less expensive the ride. Some drivers try to pack people going in similar directions in the same cab, thus decreasing fares. Taxis can be picked up anywhere in town, but especially at the bus terminal and the Parque Principal. From the *terminal terrestre* to the border is around s/8,000.
Library: (tel. 980-487, ext. 34), at Olmedo and Av. 10 de Agosto, 3rd floor of municipal building (open Mon.-Fri. 8am-12:30pm and 2:30-10:30pm).
Pharmacies: Farmacia Americana, Sierra 7035 y Bolívar (tel. 984-854). Open Mon.-Sat. 7am-8pm, Sun. 7am-3pm. **Farmacia Moderna** (tel. 980-825), at Sucre and Ayacucho in Parque Principal (open Mon.-Sat. 8am-9pm, Sun. 7am-6pm).
Hospital: Hospital Luis G. Davilla de Tulcán, Av. 10 de Agosto 12051 y Esmeraldas (tel. 980-316 or 980-315). Emergency 24-hr. treatment is free.
Emergency: tel. 101.
Police: (tel. 981-321 or 980-345), at Manabí and Coral, on the northern outskirts of town (open 24hr.).
Post Office: Bolívar 53027 y Junín (tel. 980-552). Open Mon.-Fri. 8am-7pm and Sat. 8am-1pm.
Telephone Code: 06.

ACCOMMODATIONS

Unless you want to spend more than s/30,000 per person, the *habitaciones* in Tulcán are far from elegant. The constant influx of sucre-laden Colombians, exploiting the beneficial exchange rate, has upped the prices of the more refined hotels considerably. There are still plenty of affordable places to rest your head; just don't expect them to glow with ambience. Calle Sucre, just west of the Parque Principal, hops with lodgings—some ritzy, some reasonable.

Residencial Oasis, at Av. 10 de Agosto and Sucre. Footsteps away from Parque Principal and conveniently located for dining expeditions. Thick brick walls and windows facing into the courtyard create silent sleeping shelters. Doors made for munchkins, so crouch down to reach the 24-hr. hot water showers. Common bathrooms a tad dark and spooky, but once lighted they're grimeless and goblin-free. Singles s/10,000, with bath s/12,000; doubles s/20,000, with bath s/24,000.
Hotel Azteca (tel. 981-447; fax 980-481), on Bolívar and Atahualpa, a block west of Parque Ayora. The extra sucres go a long way; these are the cleanest, least depressing rooms in town. Wood-paneled walls resemble the inside of a sauna, but the A/C negates any other similarities. Carpeted floors plus fluffy beds and pillows make for plush slumber. Invest in earplugs; the weekend *discoteca* music below blares until 2am. All rooms have private bath, hot water, phone, color TV. Singles s/26,400; doubles s/45,000; triples s/58,000; quads s/70,000.
Residencial Sucre (no tel.), at Ayacucho and Sucre, in a cuisine-friendly locale. Windows face walls, when there are even windows at all, making rooms pitch-black. Creaky, old-style beds and stand-up coat racks round out the furnishings. Perk up in the lobby with the friendly staff, TV, and comfy chairs. Large bathrooms with 24-hr. hot water. Rooms cost the same with or without bath—it's all about luck. Singles s/8,000; doubles s/15,000; triples s/23,000.

FOOD

Colombian cuisine knows no boundaries, and a number of Colombian restaurants have made a place for themselves alongside the Ecuadorian establishments of Tulcán. To sample this international culinary excitement, make for the eateries along Sucre and Bolívar, to the west of Av. 10 de Agosto.

Restaurante El Patio (tel. 984-872), on Bolívar between Pichincha and Av. 10 de Agosto. Monstrous plates of Colombian cuisine, like the *Bandeja Paisa* (s/6,000), loaded with eggs, vegetables, rice, and meat, at minuscule prices. Antique gramaphones, sewing machines, and black-and-white photos provide glimpses of the Tulcán of old (open Mon.-Sat. 8am-9pm, Sun. 8am-4pm).

Europalace, Olmedo 50071 y Av. 10 de Agosto (tel. 983-950), bordering the central plaza. European posters and a wall-sized painting of the Swiss Alps bring the Old World to the New. Enchanting wide-window view of Parque Principal and fresh roses at every table. Russian and Italian salads s/4,000, goulash s/10,000 (open daily 9am-10pm).

Wimpy La Verdadera Hamburguesa (no tel.) at Sucre and Boyacá, around the corner from Hotel Azteca. This streetside cheapie cures late-night munchies and afternoon hunger pains alike. Even Popeye's burger-chowing buddy would be impressed. Set up like a bar, an L-shaped counter with 10 or 11 barstools creates a cheery atmosphere. Far from wimpy, the jumbo burger comes with fries and the works for s/3,000 (open daily 8am-midnight).

CROSSING THE BORDER

Crossing the *frontera* between Ecuador and Colombia is usually fairly straightforward. Tourists are required to present a **passport** for stamping at the immigration office of each country, and to turn in and/or receive a 90-day tourist card. Very few nationalities need a visa to enter Columbia. Those that need a visa to enter Ecuador are listed under Entrance Requirements (p. 5). Copies of passports, drivers licenses, birth certificates, and doctor's notes are not acceptable identification, and officials are fanatically strict about this. A **provisional passport** may be acceptable. Problems can sometimes occur on the Colombian side of the road. If crossing from Colombia into Ecuador, be sure to get your passport stamped inside the Colombian immigration office. There are plenty of thieves pretending to be border officers, offering to stamp passports and escort people across the border, but instead running off with travelers' bags and money. Occasionally, especially scruffy-looking tourists will be asked to prove that they have **sufficient funds** (US$20) for each day they plan to stay in the country (US$10 for poor traveling students). Officials may also ask to see a **round-trip ticket** proving that visitors intend to leave the country within **90 days,** the maximum amount of time a traveler can spend in either country in a one-year period. If you want to stay longer, you'll need to obtain a visa (see Entrance Requirements, p. 5). Tulcán's border and the **Ecuadorian immigration office** (tel./fax 980-704) are both open daily 6am-9pm. There are no taxes or fees at the border except for Ecuadorian residents, who have to pay a s/3,000 charge.

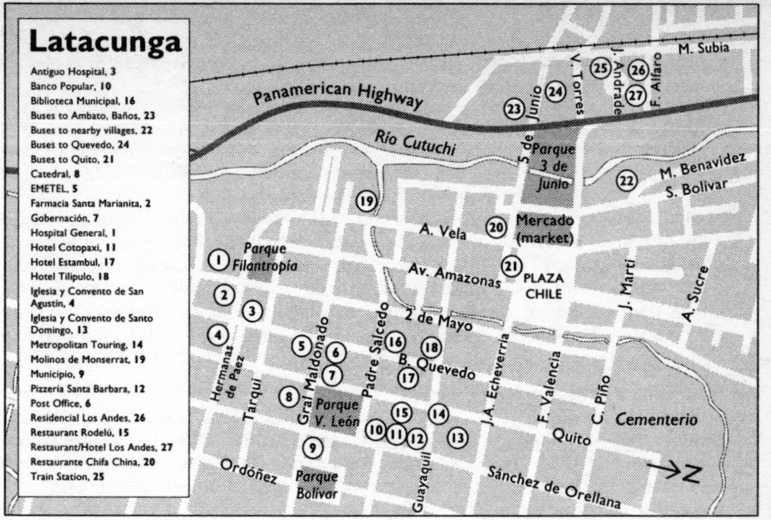

The Central Corridor

Dubbed the "Avenue of the Volcanoes" by German explorer Alexander van Humboldt in 1802, the strip of Andean highlands between Quito and Cuenca is Ecuador as its most geologically extreme. Some prominent snow-capped peaks assert their fire-spitting authority here—the towering cone of Volcán Cotopaxi (the tallest active volcano in the world), the angry spew of Sangay, and the sheer majesty of Chimborazo. But as intimidating as the volcanos may seem, the jaw-droppingly beautiful views from the misty Andean ridges somehow soften the sharp peaks. Natives in Andean dress move in and out of the fog and clouds, over rolling patchwork-quilt farmlands, often meeting at local weekly markets to sell handmade crafts. The natural hot springs at Baños relieve weary travelers—especially at sunrise, when the stunning dawn sky illuminates the lush valleys thousands of meters below. The 6310m Volcán Chimborazo, only a few easy hours from the capital, offers an adrenaline rush for the citied-out through its sheer altitude, and is easily accessible from the typically tranquil central highland city of Riobamba.

Latacunga

Between 1534 and 1949, the gigantic Volcán Cotopaxi, the tallest active volcano in the world, spewed its stuff nine times. Each time, the fire-spitter devastated and sometimes destroyed entirely the neighboring city of Latacunga. The citizens of Latacunga, which by one account means "land of my choice" in an indigenous tongue, always dutifully chose to return to their ruined home and rebuild virtually everything. This leads to one of the classic Ecuadorian mysteries—why the *hell* did they keep going back? Maybe it was the incredible panorama, with a crown of Andean peaks surrounding the 2700m-high town, and the proximity to natural wonders that has made it a popular tourist base today. Maybe it was all the gold and silver discovered and mined here, especially after the conquistadors arrived. It could have been the fruit, coffee, sugar, cacao, rubber, and herds of cattle that are sustained on soil made rich by millennia of volcanic ash. And then again, in some hypnotically masochistic way, perhaps it was Cotopaxi itself—its surreal, tranquil white cone in the northeast horizon—that drew the Latacungans to this spot, and like a spell cast by Pele himself, held them here for more than 450 years.

ORIENTATION

The most heavily-traveled part of Latacunga is along the Panamerican Highway. This strip has its selection of solid hotels and restaurants, but as the mechanic shops and Castrol oil center suggest, its main concern is the vehicular traffic passing through. On the other side of the **Río Cutuchi** lies the main part of the city, sloping up the mountainside in a grid-like fashion. Though hotels and restaurants are sprinkled throughout the streets, the main municipal and tourist section is on and near the **Parque Vicente León,** roughly along Quito and Quevedo. The market starts above the river and covers several blocks, including the **Plaza Chile,** between Av. 5 de Junio and F. Valencia.

PRACTICAL INFORMATION

Tourist Office: Latacunga doesn't really have a tourist office, but **Metropolitan Touring** (tel. 810-334), at Quito and Guayaquil, sells tourist maps (s/3,000) and reluctantly gives tips (open Mon.-Fri. 8:30am-12:30pm and 2:30-6:30pm).

Currency Exchange: The **Banco Popular** (tel. 810-179), at Sanchez de Orellana and Salcedo, will exchange cash or traveler's checks from dollars to sucres.

Telephones: EMETEL (tel. 810-128), at Quevedo and Maldonado, allows free calling card calls (open daily 8am-9:45pm).

Trains: The **train station** (tel. 800-700), at M.A. Subia and J. Andrade, is on the far side of the Panamerican Highway. Hardly running anymore, trains travel only to **Riobamba** (every Sat., 11:30am, 4hr., s/8,000) and **Quito** (every Fri., 3½hr., s/4,000). Schedule varies, so check at the station. Buy tickets at departure.

Buses: The most useful bus company is **Transportes Cotopaxi** (tel. 800-752). Main offices are on the Panamerican Highway across from Calle J. Andrade, but nearly all buses depart elsewhere, and only tickets to Quevedo need to be bought there. Buses to **Quito** (every 10min., 3:30am-7:10pm, 2hr., s/3,500) leave from a parking lot next to the market at Amazonas and Av. 5 de Junio. Buses to **Ambato** (every 10min., 5am-6pm, 1hr., s/2,000) and **Baños** (every Sun., 6:30am, 2hr., s/3,500) leave from the Panamerican Highway at Av. 5 de Junio. Buses to **Quevedo** leave from Av. 5 de Junio, 1 block west of the Panamerican Highway (every 1½hr., 5am-7pm, 5hr., s/8,500). Don't forget to buy a ticket in advance from the main office, adjacent to the bus stop. On its way to Quevedo, the bus stops in **Pujilí** (10min., s/500) and **Zumbahua** (1½hr., s/3,000). Buses to **Santo Domingo** (7am, 2:30pm, 3hr., s/6,000) leave from the Panamerican Highway at Jones. Buses to the loop of small **pueblos** surrounding Latacunga line up along Benavidez, next to the river, starting at Simón Bolívar: **Saquisilí** (every 10min., 5:30am-6:30pm, 20min., s/600), **Sigchos** (10am, noon, 2pm; 3hr.; s/3,500), and **Chugchilán** (11:30am, 4hr., s/4,600). If you're heading to Saquisilí on Saturday, expect a wait.

Library: The **Biblioteca Municipal** (tel. 800-849), at Quevedo and Salcedo, reflects the town's healthy reading appetite (open Mon.-Fri. 8am-12pm, 2-6pm).

Shopping: The **public market** is a required ingredient in the Latacunga experience. The *mercado* falls more or less between Av. 5 de Junio and Valencia, bordered on the east by Amazonas (open daily 7am-6pm, but Saturday's the big day).

Pharmacy: Farmacia Santa Marianita (tel. 800-728), at 2 de Mayo and Hmas. Paez, across from the hospital (open 7am-8pm).

Hospital: Hospital General (tel. 800-331 or 800-332), at Hmas. Paez and Av. 2 de Mayo, has ambulance service and is open 24hr.

Emergency: 101.

Police: The **police station** (tel. 612-666), is on General Proaño about 1km from the center of town.

Post office: (tel. 800-500), at Quevedo and Maldonado, a block from the Parque Vicente León, has a *Lista de Correos* (open Mon.-Fri. 8am-7pm, Sat. 8am-2pm).

Telephone code: 03.

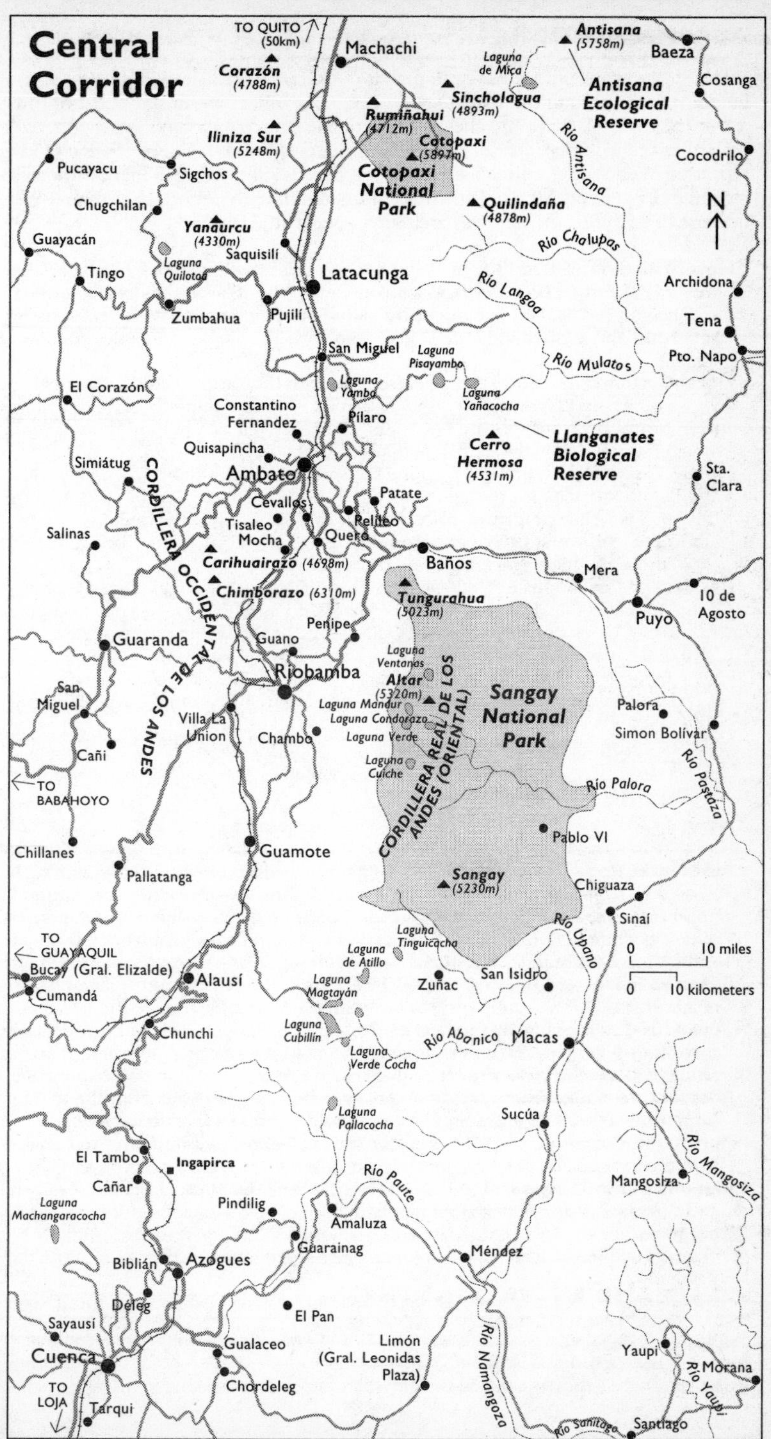

THE CENTRAL CORRIDOR

ACCOMMODATIONS

While Latacunga is not tourist-swamped, it does have its fair share of hotels. Several lie conveniently along the Panamerican Highway; others are in the midst of town across the river. All are pretty cheap, though some stretch down to the deepest, darkest realms of the budget world. Be sure to make reservations if you're coming to Latacunga on Wednesday; tourists always flock here for the Saquisilí market the next morning. In general, sleepy Latacunga shuts down early, never later than 10pm; because of its traffic, the highway area stays open a little later.

Hotel Tilipulo (tel. 820-130), at Guayaquil and Quevedo, one block north and then west of the Parque León. A brand-spankin' new place; its wood floors and furniture still gleam proudly. Not just rooms but actual suites, complete with bedroom, private bath, and a charming little living room with TV. Singles s/20,000, doubles s/40,000.

Hotel Cotopaxi (tel. 801-310), on Salcedo next to the Parque León, with excellent views of the park. As majestic as its namesake, comfort abounds; spacious rooms have restful beds and private hot water baths, as well as a helpful though somewhat erratic staff. Singles s/20,000, doubles s/40,000.

Hostal Quilotoa (tel. 800-099), on the Panamerican Highway between Eloy Alfaro and J. Andrado; look for the sign out front. Just a hop and a skip from the bus stop, this hotel is well-kept, private bathrooms and all. Satisfying as the quilt-like blankets are to the eye, you'll probably need more than one—ask for more before dark to avoid those late-night shivers. S/20,000 per person.

Residencial Los Andes (tel. 800-983), at Eloy Alfaro and the Panamerican Highway, enter on Alfaro side. Just look around ... there's no question that this place deserves its name. A block down from Hostal Quilotoa, it is a similar but cheaper alternative. S/10,000 per person, s/12,000 per person with private bath.

Hotel Estambul, Quevedo 73-40 (tel. 800-354), between Salcedo and Guayaquil. A travelers' favorite, with a TV in the *sala* (living room), but unpredictable in its availability. Rooms can get cold at night, but private baths have continuous hot water; like a Turkish bath, the steamy goodness of Hotel Estambul can warm your bones should they grow too cold. Secure luggage-storage room for guests heading up to Cotopaxi. S/15,000 per person.

FOOD

Restaurant Rodelú (tel. 800-956), on Quito between Salcedo and Guayaquil, in the hotel with the same name. Lonely for some English? Try this *gringo* meeting spot, popular for its warm, cozy atmosphere and warm, cozy pizza, hot out of their brick oven (medium s/11,500-16,500). Meat and chicken dishes s/8,000-11,000 (open daily 7:30am-2:30pm, 5:30-9:30pm).

Restaurant Hostal Quilotoa (tel. 800-099), on the Panamerican Highway underneath the hotel. The eatery stays warm with the heat and scent of the fire, as the chickens do their slow methodical dance, each on its own spit. Filling portions of *arroz con pollo* (s/6,000), or *almuerzo* (s/5,000). Especially convenient if you're on the far side of the river (open daily 8am-11pm).

Restaurante Chifa China, at Av. 5 de Junio and Vela, a block from the market. Copious quantities of chow in the *mein* dishes (chicken with vegetable s/8,000, beef with pineapple s/7,500), but the soups (wonton s/4,500) and rice dishes (*arroz chop suey* s/7,500) are meals in themselves (open daily noon-11pm).

Pizzeria Santa Barbara (tel. 810-790), on Sanchez de Orellana between Salcedo and Guayaquil, half a block from the Parque León. A low-priced option for indulging more conventional cravings. Pizzas s/4,500-6,500, hamburgers s/3,000, hot dogs s/2,000, milk shakes s/1,200 (open daily 8:30am-9pm).

SIGHTS AND ENTERTAINMENT

Admittedly, most tourists coming to Latacunga are here to see sights outside of town—Volcán Cotopaxi, Laguna Quilotoa, and various other highland destinations. However, there's more to see *in* the city than just the remarkable landscape outside

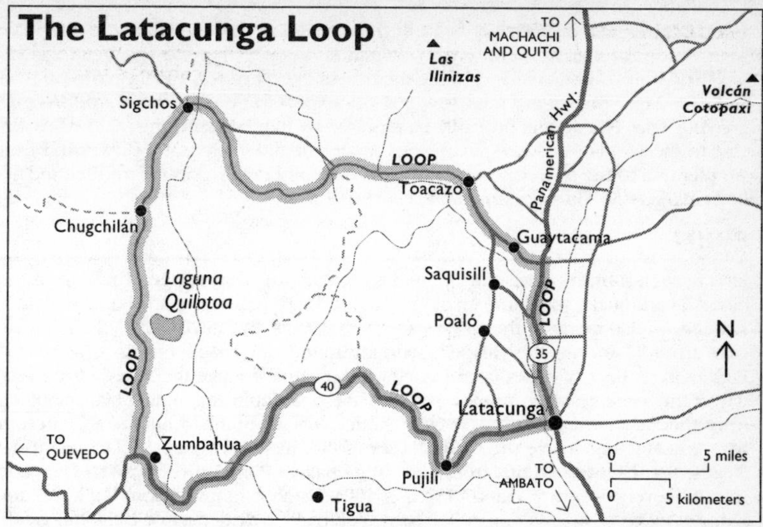

of it. The **Molinos de Monserrant,** next to the waterfall at Vela near Maldonado, is the center of the province's **Casa de la Cultura** organization. Built by Jesuits way back in 1736 and remodeled in 1967, it now houses (among other things) a museum of ethnology. Unsure of what that entails? Well, if you're interested in dolls and antiquated stone mills, this is your heaven (admission s/1,000; open Tues.-Sat. 9am-noon and 2-5:30pm). The city also has its fill of parks, the coolest of which is **Parque Vicente León,** located right in the tourist area at Maldonado and Quito. Bordering this clean, green, blooming machine are several buildings of note. The **Municipal Building** is the worn brown structure that looks like it has seen its share of volcanic eruptions, the rather unspectacular **Government Building** is across the way on Quito, and the city's **Catedral** is kitty-corner to the **Gubernación,** on Quito and Maldonado. The Catedral was first put up in the 17th century; after being slammed by many an earthquake and volcanic eruption, it was restored in 1973. There are other impressive churches in Latacunga, such as the **Iglesia y Convento de Santo Domingo,** near Quito and Guayaquil, the intersection of the metropolises. While you're there, check out the selection of colorful jackets and sweaters on sale at the artisan fair next door.

Which brings us to the next sight in Latacunga, by far the most noticeable: the **mercado.** The market's mammoth offerings takes up several blocks from the river to Avenida Amazonas, with bananas, super glue, Calvin Klein jeans, cow hooves, cow buttocks, cow heart, and (sorry, but there's no other way to describe it) yanked-open, spread-out, sledgehammered cow heads. The big day is Saturday, but this place is always busy from about 7am to 6pm.

Visitors here for November 3rd to 5th will have lots of stories to tell about the **Mama Negra** festival. The city's principal holiday, it's marked by the *macho* Latacunga men roaming the streets dressed up as black women. While you're at it, you might as well stick around for **Latucunga's Independence Day,** on November 11, commemorating the day Latacunga patriots defeated the Spanish royalists in 1820. Today this date is grandly celebrated each year with parades, fairs, and bullfights. The tradition of Ecuadorian partying can also be witnessed during the fiesta of **La Virgen de las Mercedes,** held September 23-24.

■ Near Latacunga: The Latacunga Loop

To the west of Latacunga, this loop of less-touristed towns are a postcard maker's fantasy come true. The small villages are hidden away among the patchwork farms and vast, undeveloped jagged-rock faces of the Andean peaks. Hidden is the operative word—populated almost entirely by indigenous people, these towns aren't exactly well-trod tourist destinations. Visiting them is an excellent way to take a trip off-road and submerge yourself in a foreign world, but expect to be a pioneer of sorts in figuring your way. Hiking will probably be required by more distant trips, as the bus service to these out-of-the-way places is inconvenient and inadequate. However, buses are plentiful to the two closest towns of Saquisilí and Pujulí, popular for their indigenous markets on Thursdays and Sundays, respectively.

PUJILÍ

Effectively a suburb of Latacunga, Pujilí is located just over a ridge of hills from the city. An earthquake shook the town in March of 1996; registering a 5.7 on the Richter scale, it leveled many of the town's adobe buildings. But never fear, when Sunday rolls around, so does the village's main attraction, the **market** at Rocafuerte and Pichincha. A fleet of buses from Latacunga perpetually make the speedy trip every day of the week, leaving from the corner of Av. 5 de Junio and M.A. Subia, one block from the Panamerican Highway (every 5min., 6:30am-8pm, 15min., s/600). Return trips to Latacunga leave the main plaza of Pujilí just as frequently. The less-usual **Transportes Cotopaxi** bus from Latacunga passes Pujilí on the way to Quevedo (roughly every 1½hr., 5:15am-7:15pm, s/500). Catch it to jump from Pujilí to Zumbahua, Quevedo, or anything in between. You may be denied a ride if the bus is full, but then again, full is a rather subjective term when it comes to Ecuadorian buses. Make calls from **EMETEL** (tel. 723-105). Pujilí's **hospital** is at Velasco Ibarra 698 (tel. 723-160); the **police** (tel. 723-164), are two blocks east on Ibarra. There are no accommodations in Pujulí; planning to stay in Latacunga is the best bet.

ZUMBAHUA

As you push further west from Latacunga, the rising road becomes a winding, cliff-hanging, and amazingly scenic roller coaster. Latacunga and Pujilí shrink in the enormous eastern panorama, and about one and a half hours later Zumbahua comes into sight. No more than a town square surrounded by a few buildings, the center of Zumbahua is a lilliputian speck among the Brobdingnagian Andes. Zumbahua's population is 90% indigenous, and these native Quichuas dress brilliantly in beads and bright cloth. Keep your ears open as you walk the streets and you'll likely catch a few snippets of Quichua conversation.

Zumbahua is not a particularly comfortable place for tourists, a fact that is doubly true on the **Saturday market** day. Market festivities include alcohol, bullfighting, alcohol, colorful clothing, more alcohol, thoroughly blasted Quichuas, and villagers being carried off because their legs no longer hold them up. What they do not include is a significant, or even visible, tourist contingent. The town is poor and when the people are drunk, the outsider is at serious risk of being harassed. A group may provide some protection, but always be on guard. There is one "hotel," the **Residencial Oro Verde,** above a restaurant near the plaza, that only has two rooms and a common bathroom (s/5,000 per person).

Get to and from Zumbahua on Transportes Cotopaxi's Latacunga-Quevedo bus, which passes every 1½ hours until 8pm (1½hr., s/3,000 back to Latacunga). Adventurous trekkers moving north along the loop to the crater lake of Quilotoa must catch the bus to Chugchilán, since no buses serve Quilotoa specifically.

LAGUNA QUILOTOA

Somebody could point out Laguna Quilotoa from the road and you still wouldn't notice the concealed lake. Now get a little closer and take another look. A 360-degree ridge towers over giant mountain slopes that plummet into a green-blue lagoon. Welcome to Quilotoa, the crater lake that remains where a colossal volcano once stood. A glance into this crater will probably justify whatever hardships you endured to get here, and then some. Hikes down to the lake take a half-hour or less, but the hike back up is quite steep and may take more than double that time. A walk around the edge of the crater reputedly lasts about five hours—halfway around, you're already well on your way to Chugchilán. "Halfway around" assumes you start at the road access at the top of the crater, where three "hotels" in a little settlement compete for the scanty overnight crowd. Each place is run by a family that has its home adjacent to its guest rooms; these hosts rely on rooming, tours, and artwork sales for their livelihood. **Cabañas Quilotoa** and **El Refugio de La Laguna** are the options; both charge s/5,000 for a bed, and food is negotiable, depending on the meal and portion size (s/3,000 for dinner is a good ballpark figure). The major consideration in choosing a place is *warmth,* since the temperature plummets at night; look for healthy fires and heavy blankets.

There are a range of options for getting to and away from Quilotoa, none of which is especially easy or convenient. The best option is to catch the Zumbahua-Chugchilán bus that passes right by Quilotoa. Failing that, a *camioneta* to Quilapungo will get you within a steep 3-km walk of Quilotoa for a reasonable s/3,000. Trucks from nearby towns will take tourists to Quilotoa, but rates start at s/30,000. Hiking all the way from Zumbahua takes about five to seven hours. The hike crosses through the **Río Toachi Canyon** and cuts the 22-km roadtrip between Chugchilán and Quilotoa significantly. Water and warm clothes are key on these walks—it gets cold up there, and the weather can change quickly.

CHUGCHILÁN

At the far end of the highland loop, the *pueblo pequeño* of Chugchilán explodes with quirkiness. Quiet and far from tourist-oriented, it has only one tourist accommodation, but what an accommodation it is! Like Quilotoa and the wild Sierra scenery, the **Black Sheep Inn** is another prime reason to venture into the villages west of Latacunga. This up-and-coming hotel/hostel, owned and operated by a young couple from Seattle who have ingratiated themselves with the locals, is more an experience than an accommodation. Dogs, ducks, and the mascot herself, an *oveja negra,* wander around the courtyard together; the indigenous townspeople stop to chat with the owners while alternative tunes play in the background; and the view—whoa, the view. Resting on a crop-green hillside, the Inn looks out at the canyon, Quilotoa, and a huge panorama of the mountains in the distance. Food is pay-as-you-take, including the communal s/12,000 vegetarian dinner feast. The shared bathroom doubles as a compost pile. Follow the road through Chugchilán, about 0.5km past the plaza towards Sigchos; the sign and steep driveway are on the left. No phone, no reservations, but owners promise they'll never turn people away. A bunk room costs s/15,500, with a 10% discount for guests over 50 and ISIC or South American Explorer's Club members. Private rooms brand-new and available.

The owners of the Black Sheep Inn can suggest some eccentric yet excellent excursions in the vicinity. Quilotoa is not far off, and the **Río Toachi Canyon** is even closer. But try following your nose in the other direction to a **European cheese factory,** established decades ago by a Swiss entrepreneur, though now run by local Ecuadorians. Some mysterious **Inca ruins** of the "circle in the ground" UFO variety lie three hours away by foot. For the more avid hiker, a one- or two-day trek leads into the **cloud forest** on the western slopes of the Andes, an amazing descent from about 12,000 to 2000 ft.

Chugchilán's location on the loop means that numerous buses pass through town and almost all of them stop. Several buses leave Latacunga for Chugchilán; the **La Iliniza** line has a bus leaving from Benavidez that goes via Sigchos (Sun.-Wed., Fri. at 11:30am; Sat. at 10:30am; 4hr.; s/4,600). These buses pass through Saquisilí and can be caught there about ½ hour after leaving Latacunga. On Thursday the bus departs directly from Saquisilí on account of the market (11am, 4½hr.). The **14 de Octubre** line goes to Chugchilán via Zumbahua and Quilotoa (Fri.-Sat., 10:30am, 4hr.). **Reina de Sigchos** also has another bus from Sigchos (every Wed. and Fri., 5am, 1hr.). To leave Chugchilán, simply hop on one of these buses as they pass through, or catch one of the painful early-bird buses (daily at 3am, Sun. at 6am; 3½hr.; s/4,600).

SIGCHOS

As yet, no liaison between the *gringo* traveler and the private world of the Andean people exists in Sigchos, so don't expect a cushion of hospitality. The village is a day's hike from the slightly smaller Chugchilán, and about the same distance from the cheese factory, though not in the vicinity of Quilotoa. Aside from all the bus routes to Chugchilán, most of which pass through Sigchos, the village has its own bus schedule (every day; 10am, noon, 2pm; 3hr.; s/3,500), leaving from Benavidez in Latacunga. There are two simple accommodations here, but if at all possible, it might be worth it to pass them up in favor of the Black Sheep Inn in Chugchilán. Sigchos's market day is Sunday.

SAQUISILÍ

The reason why hordes of people come to Latacunga in the first place is the acclaimed Thursday morning market of Saquisilí. Visit any other day of the week and find a quiet, ordinary village with no frills or bright hues. But come Thursday, and Saquisilí explodes in living color, splashing its goods out among the various town plazas. Buses leave daily from Latacunga at Benavidez (every 10min., 5:30am-6:30pm, 15min., s/600), but on Thursday mornings they fill to capacity. So do Latacunga's hotels each Wednesday night, not to mention the even higher-demand **Salón Pichincha** (tel. 721-247), at Av. Pichincha and Bolívar in Saquisilí. This cozy hotel has conscientious owners as well as hot water for its guests. Singles s/8,000, doubles s/15,000. Unexpected guests probably have a chance at a room any night but Wednesday. For the big night, it's probably more fruitful to concentrate efforts on securing a place near Latacunga. **Buses** arrive and depart in the area of Plaza La Concordia and the principal avenue, Bolívar. The **police** (tel. 721-101), **hospital** (tel. 721-015), and **EMETEL** office (tel. 721-105) are off Bolívar near the buses.

Parque Nacional Cotopaxi

Situated only 14km to the northeast of Latacunga and 60km southeast of Quito, Cotopaxi National Park is dominated by the snow-capped monster, **Volcán Cotopaxi** (5897m), the tallest active volcano in the world. While many visitors come only to scale this mammoth chunk of now-hardened lava rock, the park offers more subtle pleasures as well. The *páramo* (highland plain) surrounding the peak is home to many of Ecuador's most unique species of animal life.

The park was established in 1975 after a startling study concluded that there were fewer than 10,000 **llamas** left in Ecuador. Since that time, the park has struggled to nurture and preserve the llama population, along with the rest of the Ecuadorian *páramo.* The park is hopping with **white-tailed deer,** who have made an impressive comeback under the watchful eyes of park management. Hot on their tails, literally, are the **Andean pumas,** whose numbers have slowly but steadily climbed since a low point in the mid-1970s. Other mammal species, seldom seen but still alive and well in the park, are the **Andean fox,** the **Andean spectacled bear,** and the **knee-high red brocket deer.**

Though well recognized by ornithologists the world over, the winged population of Cotopaxi fights for the attention of everyday visitors. The park has received much attention as the last refuge of the endangered **Andean condor,** but also nests such rarities as the **Andean hillstar,** the **Andean lapwing,** the **Andean gull,** the **great thrush,** and the tongue-twisting **carunculated caracara.**

Also a sanctuary for a certain two-legged mammal, Cotopaxi satisfies adventure seekers who yawn at Quito's fast-paced life and bright lights. Without a doubt, the major adrenaline-inducing attraction of the park is the immense Volcán Cotopaxi. The first climber to reach Cotopaxi's rim was the energetic German Wilhelm Reiss in 1872. Since then, thousands of world-class mountaineers and adventurers have made the icy ascent to the snow-capped summit. The climb itself is not considered technically difficult—with a properly-qualified guide, that is. Even unexperienced climbers can reach the summit, provided they are strong-willed and in good shape. Despite the technical facility of the climb, experienced climbers can also benefit from a guide's knowledge of the particularities and peculiarities of the ascent.

Expeditions to the 5900-m summit begin from the **José Ribas refuge** (alt. 4800m) at around midnight or 1am, to insure hard-packed snow and safer conditions. It usually takes 6-7 hours to reach the top, but only about 2-3 hours to return to the refuge. Due to the necessity of an early start, it is imperative to stay in the refuge the night before. Though basic, the 70-person shelter has bunk beds, clean water, and a gas oven. Visitors must bring their own heavy sleeping bags and nourishment. For the climb, bring plenty of water and fruit for energy. The **absolute necessities** for the ascent are plastic boots, crampons, an ice axe, a harness, gaiters, windpants, a head lamp, a heavy waterproof jacket, gloves, and a wool hat. A good general rule for clothing: three layers of clothing for the legs, four layers for the torso. Acclimatization, another vital prerequisite, has nothing to do with age or the shape you're in, and should be taken seriously (see Hot, Cold, and High, p. 16). A good acclimatization for Cotopaxi is a week in Quito, but an even better preparation is a couple days of hiking around the national park, or even an ascent up one of the smaller peaks.

For more information on climbing Cotopaxi, check out one of the travel agencies in Quito, which are especially abundant along Av. J. León Mera. Make sure your guide is certified by the **Ecuadorian Association of Mountain Guides (ASEGUIM),** the most respected association around. **Compañía de Guias,** Av. 6 de Diciembre 425 y Jorge Washington (tel./fax 504-773), offers a two-day summit climb for around US$175 per person, complete with food, shelter, transportation, equipment, and an ASEGUIM-certified guide who speaks English, German, Italian, or French (open 9:30am-1pm and 3-6:30pm). **Safari Travel,** Calama 380 y León Mera (tel. 552-505; fax 223-381; e-mail admin@safariec.ecx.ec), also provides experienced, ASEGUIM-approved mountain guides equipped with more languages than the Tower of Babel. Their two-day summit package averages around US$145 per person and includes everything but the US$6.50 admission into the park (open daily 9am-7pm).

Vertigo sufferers and those sane enough not to climb a 19,000-ft. ice cube can safely enjoy the park's lesser-known hiking and camping opportunities. The two campgrounds within the park are both good four-hour hikes from the entrance gate. Just follow the main road as it winds through the imported Monterrey Pine forest for about half an hour. A sign for campgrounds will be on the left, and a short jaunt leads to a campsite fit for a king. Most people stay in tents, but there is a standing structure with four walls and a concrete floor that could, by some standards, be considered a cabin (a mere s/2,000 per night). At least it has running water. This campground is close to the shore of the immense **Lake Limpiopungo,** but don't get out the fishing rods—it's against the rules to fish in the park. Up the road another 15 minutes is a second sign for campgrounds on the right. This campground is about as big as the other, and provides a neck-bending, awe-inspiring view of Mt. Cotopaxi. There is a s/2,000 cabin here also, but it lacks running water.

A tiny museum on the path up to the campgrounds tributes the National Park, furnished with stuffed wildlife, a 3-D representation of the park, and wall-to-wall info on the history of Mt. Cotopaxi. Outside the museum, there is a helpful map of the park, which you can use to locate the park's other, lesser-known volcano, **Volcán Rumañahui** (alt. 4712m). There is a strenuous but rewarding four-hour hike from the museum to the base of Rumañahui. Head back up the road toward Limpiopungo. When you reach the lake on your left, you should see a stream running from the lake towards Rumañahui. Follow the hiking trail running along this stream until it becomes a heap of rocks: the top of the great Rumañahui. If you want to go further, you'll need a portable phone to call Safari or Compañía de Guias, because the rest of the way is treacherous. Although a shorter climb than Cotopaxi (only 4-5 hours), it is more technical and involves some rock climbing.

The best way to reach Cotopaxi is by bus from Quito. The *terminal terrestre* has various bus lines going past Cotopaxi, including **Transportes Latacunga Asofficiale** (every 10min., 6am-8pm, 1½hr., s/4,000). The buses will drop you off at the second, more southern entrance to the park, where there is a huge Cotopaxi sign. Those who hitchhike say that it is fairly easy to catch a ride into the park from this point. If you plan on walking in, expect a two-hour trek to the entrance along a dusty, lonely road. Or you can take the bus 10 minutes farther to Lasso, or 25 minutes farther to Latacunga. In Lasso, taxis and trucks take passengers into the park. If you want to go all the way to the refuge, it'll cost around US$30, and you'll still need to hike about 30 minutes up from the parking lot. From Latacunga, trucks go to the refuge for around US$35; pick one up at Hotel Estambul. Entrance into the park is s/20,000 for adults, s/ 10,000 for children under 13, and s/2,000 for residents. Parque Nacional Cotopaxi is open daily 7am-6pm.

Ambato

Nearly every Ecuadorian city claims to have miraculously survived some sort of natural catastrophe. Fires, earthquakes, volcanos—you name it, some town has lived through it. Ambato is no exception. In 1949, a serious earthquake shook the city into a pile of rubble. Instead of simply bouncing back to its previous glory, the new city far surpassed what it had been before. Many *ambateños* view the destruction of the old Ambato as the spark that fired up the spirit of the people. Half a century later, the modern mountain metropolis, resting at 2577m below the nearby peaks of Tungurahua and Chimborazo, still vibrates with this impassioned fresh start. *Ambateños* pride themselves on being productive, hard-working people who have continued the centuries-old tradition of farming the region's rich land, growing sugar cane, tobacco, coffee, and an extensive catalog of fruits and vegetables. Ambato's fertility has also broken ground in South American literature. Novelists **Juan Montalvo** and **Juan León Mera** hailed from here, as well as several other intellectual figures whose names now meet at the city's street corners and in its impressive museums. The development of tourism is evidenced by the recent proliferation of hotels all over Ambato, along with a sprawling yet surprisingly sparkling spectacle of offices, apartments, and highways. Fiestas every November 12 commemorate Ambato's independence. In the month of February, the week before Carnival, the city celebrates the Festival of Fruit and Flowers, a holiday that only dates back to 1951. Like the city itself, the event is spirited, bountiful, and has yet to celebrate its Silver Anniversary.

ORIENTATION

Ambato extends far beyond any visitor's interest or immediate comprehension. The **terminal terrestre** and **train station** are both in the northern end of the city, about 2km from the *centro*. Ambato's more congested downtown area is linked to the transportation hub via **Av. 12 de Noviembre,** which begins up the hill from the train tracks and runs south. A handful of hotels border the **Parque 12 de Noviembre.** Two other important parks are found in the downtown area: **Parque Juan Montalvo** (the center of the city's government offices and agencies) and **Parque Cevallos** (the departure spot for many local buses), bordered by a bustling commercial area. All of this is clustered within a five-by-five block area.

PRACTICAL INFORMATION

Tourist Information: The city is blessed with a **CETUR** (tel. 821-800), at Guayaquil and Rocafuerte in front of the Hotel Ambato. Located in an uphill, somewhat out-of-the way western corner, this office provides information on Ambato in a patient, light-hearted manner—but only in Spanish (open Mon.-Fri. 8:30am-5pm).

English-Speaking Language Association: Centro Ecuatoriano Norteamericano de Ambato, Egüez 383 y Vela, 4th floor (tel. 822-137).

Travel Office: There is a wide choice of *agencias de viajes,* but a popular and convenient one is **Metropolitan Touring** (tel. 824-084), at Bolívar and Castillo, across the street from the post office (open Mon.-Fri. 9am-1pm and 3-7pm).

Currency Exchange: Cambiato (tel. 821-008 or 828-059), at Bolívar and Mera.

Telephones: Two **EMETEL** offices (tel. 822-122), inside the post office, or a block away along Castillo towards Rocafuerte (open daily 8am-12:30pm and 1-10pm).
Trains: Terminal Ferroviaria, next to the bus station, has 2 trips every week: to **Quito** (every Fri., 12:30pm, s/2,000) or **Riobamba** (every Sat., 1:30pm, s/2,000).
Long Distance Buses: The **terminal terrestre** is to the north of downtown up Av. 12 de Noviembre. To **Guayaquil** (every ½hr., 7:15am-10:45pm, 5½hr., s/12,000), **Quito** (every 5min., all day, 2hr., s/6,000), **Santo Domingo** (every ½hr., 6:30am-6:30pm, 4hr., s/8,000), **Babahoyo** (every hr., 4am-4:15pm, 5hr., s/10,000), **Riobamba** (every 15min., 5:30am-7pm, 1hr., s/3,000), **Baños** (every 10min., 3am-9pm, 1hr., s/1,800), **Tena** (2pm, 8hr., s/17,000), **Puyo** (Tues.-Sat., 2pm, 10hr., s/22,000). On Sun. and Mon., when the Baños road is open to Puyo, a cheaper, faster bus runs from Baños out to the Oriente.
Local Buses: Buses to towns in the vicinity of Ambato depart from several places in the downtown area. From **Parque Cevallos,** buses depart every 15min. to **Ficoa, Atocha, Ingahurro,** and **Pinllo** (s/250). From **Parque La Merced,** at Av. Unidad Nacional and Colón a bit north of the *centro,* buses depart for **Píllaro** (every 15min., 6am-8pm, 30min., s/1,200). Buses to **Picaigua** leave from Av. Los Andes and Tomás Sevilla on the other side of Av. 12 de Noviembre (every 15min., 6:30am-6:30pm, 30min., s/250). The most popular nearby tourist destinations, Salasaca and Pelileo, are served from a "mini-terminal" on Carihuarazo in the suburb of Ferroviaria, farther up the hill from Av. 12 de Noviembre. To **Pelileo** (every 10min., 6:10am-6:10pm, 30min., s/800) via **Salasaca** (20min., s/600). Long-distance buses bound for Baños will also stop at these destinations en route.
Taxis: A trip across town costs about s/4,000. One taxi dispatch is **Cooperativa de Taxis Bolívar** (tel. 822-111).
Library: Biblioteca Municipal, at Bolívar and Castillo, in the Municipal Building (open Mon.-Fri. 9am-noon and 2:30-6pm, Sat. 9am-noon). Also libraries at **Casa de la Cultura,** on Bolívar next door, and **Instituto Técnico Superior Bolívar,** on Sucre near Lalama and Martínez (open Mon.-Fri. 8:30am-noon and 2:30-7pm).
Public Market: One of the biggest in Ecuador, held on **Mon.** Partly indoors on Av. 12 de Noviembre between Martínez and Egüez; also spread along Cevallos and into other nearby areas. Active all other days as well, especially Fri.
Laundromat: Química Automática, Vela 432 y Quito (tel. 822-888).
Pharmacy: Botica Bristol, Martínez 307 y Cevallos (tel. 822-015). Part of the *de turno* system; after-hours pharmacy listed in that day's *Herald.*
Hospital: There are two options, the **Hospital de IESS** (tel. 821-805 or 844-719 through 723), on Av. Los Capulies, and **Hospital Regional Ambato** (tel. 821-059), at Av. Pasteur and Nacional.
Police: Atahualpa 568 (tel. 843-656 or 846-400).
Post Office: Correos Ecuador (tel. 823-332), at Castillo and Bolívar. Has a *Lista de Correos* (open Mon.-Fri. 7:30am-7:30pm, Sat. 7:30am-2pm).
Telephone Code: 03.

ACCOMMODATIONS

Hotel San Francisco (tel. 821-739), at Egüez and Bolívar. Roomy rooms with choice of private or common bath, hot water gushing out of the faucets of both. The family's unceasing *salsa* music will either have you tapping your toes or tearing out your hair. S/12,000 per person, with bath and TV s/15,000.

Hotel Guayaquil (tel. 823-886), on Mera near Av. 12 de Noviembre, bordering on Parque 12 de Noviembre but hard to see from the sidewalk. Unlike the city of Guayaquil, the hotel is centrally located and conscientiously cared for, providing stark substance and comfort instead of flash. But similar to the coastal beaches, water is hot. S/7,000 per person, with bath s/15,000.

Residencial Laurita (tel. 821-377), on Mera between Vela and Av. 12 de Noviembre, a place that truly screams of simplicity. Arranged around a courtyard with a scenic vista of clothes hanging out to dry, these stripped-down rooms contain walls and, yes, beds. The cost is bare-bones, too: s/5,000 per person.

Residencial Nacional (tel. 843-820), at Lalama and Vela, near the indoor market. Separated from the more touristy part of the city, the Nacional is, quite simply, cheap. Padlocked doors open like castle entrances into less-than-royal rooms. Common bath with hot water, central lounge with TV. S/7,000 per person.

Hotel Colonial (tel. 827-134), on Martínez and Sucre, off Parque Cevallos. Slight splurge, anyone? Surrounded by trendy name-brand shops, the Colonial ascends into the world of the *nouveau riche.* The pink-and-white pastel decor has that yuppie feel, and what yuppie could live without a TV, hot water bath, and phone in every room? S/35,000 per person, discounts for more than 2 people.

FOOD

Restaurant Barcelona (no tel.), at Mera and Av. 12 de Noviembre, next to Hotel Guayaquil. Complete with posters of the Eiffel Tower, either to go along with the cosmopolitan European name or because the decorator never learned geography. The most expensive dish at this late-night *comedor* is the s/4,500 *arroz con menestra* (open until 4am).

Sweet (tel. 824-782), seated sweetly on Sucre between Martínez and Mera, serves gourmet *gringo* treats. Bigger and brighter, this snack bar is set in a nifty neon niche, serenaded by a sizeable screen showing MTV. Banana split s/3,000, hamburger s/2,000 (open 10am-8:30pm).

Restaurante Gran Alamo (tel. 820-806), on Montalvo and Sucre, near Parque Juan Montalvo. The elegant atmosphere, fine food, and of course the prices insure that you'll remember the Alamo. Filet mignon s/14,000, Jamaican-style chicken s/13,000, noodles and vegetables s/11,000 (open 11am-11pm).

Pizzería La Fornare (no tel.), at Lalama and Vela, near the central market area. A blast of heat from the brick oven greets guests to this economical Italian diner. Serves a selection of mini-pizzas (about s/5,000), and a good range of pasta, including spaghetti (s/5,500) and lasagna (s/5,000). Open daily noon-10pm.

Restaurante Vegetariano (no tel.), at Lalama and Bolívar, a block from Parque Cevallos. As usual, this vegetarian option is combined with a natural foods store. More of a snack bar than a restaurant, but a haven for fans of fruit, lovers of grains, and zealots of soy. Lunch s/3,500, fruit salad s/3,000, veggie-burger s/1,800.

SIGHTS

By far the most arresting sight is the **Museum of Natural Science** in the **Instituto Técnico Superior Bolívar (ITSB),** Sucre 839 (tel. 827-395), on the Parque Cevallos, between Lalama and Martínez. Though the museum's admission is a bit steep, the quality of the extensive exhibits rises to the occasion. It starts slow, with black-and-white photos of the Sierra way back at the beginning of the century (including a Cotopaxi eruption), a truly solid geology display, and some indigenous musical instruments and clothes. The highlight of the museum is its seemingly endless collection of preserved animals, all but two of which were found in Ecuador. Jaguars, birds, tarantulas, and snakes all preserve their final contorted poses, some from inside the murky confines of a glass jar. This excellent exhibit climaxes in the back with the stuff bad dreams are made of—unfortunate **freak animals** such as a two-headed goat and cyclops dog, whose frozen forms are definite nightmare material (open Mon.-Fri. 8am-noon and 2-6pm; admission s/5,000).

The city also provides plenty of opportunities to pay homage to its literary hero, **Juan Montalvo** (see Literature, p. 55). First there's the **park** that bears his name, well-groomed with bushes carved into topiary shapes. Next to the park, on the corner of Bolívar and Montalvo, is our hero's birthplace and lifelong home, the **Casa de Montalvo.** The various rooms of this open-air museum/mausoleum astound with the pure repetition of Montalvo renderings. On most walls is a painting of the man, next to it another, and next to that yet another. Interwoven with these images are long articles and captions with tons of interesting information about both Ambato's and Ecuador's past. And then there's the spacious room with the coffin, raised up on an altar-stage, marking the final resting place of the man, the myth, and the legend (open Mon.-Fri. 9am-noon and 2-6pm; admission s/1,000).

Don't worry—the Montalvo-fest isn't over yet. A couple of kilometers from the *centro* lies the **Quinta de Montalvo,** Juan's country residence. Located in the suburb of

The Trash Mouth

So you're finally starting to settle in. You've reluctantly accepted that three vehicles can fit across most any highway when necessary, and so you've relieved yourself of that vigilant, terrified gaze each time the bus driver moves to pass. But as a stranger in a strange land, the most violent culture shock probably still agonizes you: What is the *deal* with all those **clown trashcans?** In front of ice-cream shops, restaurants, and food stores, their eyes follow like a sinister painting, their gaping mouths hungry for more garbage. The original mastermind behind this ubiquitous shape lives just 7km south of Ambato. A self-proclaimed artist, 70-year old **Victoria Basmino,** the creator of the *basurero de payaso,* came up with the colorful trashcan some 25 years ago. Though her name is far from familiar, her art is arguably the most recognized in the country. Interested in starting a trend back home? Señora Basmino sells the clowns, as well as alligator and Mickey Mouse heads, for s/65,000 apiece. But make sure you're getting the real thing. By now, imitations of Basmino's genius are everywhere.

Ficoa, it can be reached by taking the bus marked with that destination, leaving from the Parque Cevallos every 15 minutes. This is only one of three such homes of dead *ambateño* celebs outside the downtown area. There's also the **Quinta de Mera** (home of **Juan León Mera**) and **Quinta de La Liria** (home of **Nicolas Martínez,** renowned mountain climber), located near each other in the suburb of Atocha (both open Mon.-Fri. 9am-4:30pm). Both can be reached by taking the Atocha bus from Parque Cevallos.

Ambato's headquarters for the arts, the **Casa de la Cultura** (tel. 820-338), on Bolívar between Montalvo and Castillo, is next to the Casa de Montalvo. The third floor houses free exhibits that change every other month (open Mon.-Fri. 9am-1pm and 3-6pm). It also organizes entertaining events, such as musical concerts, listed in the *Herald.* Across the way on Montalvo looms Ambato's **cathedral,** the eyesore of the city's skyline with a worn, dirty modern dome and jungle-gym spire.

ENTERTAINMENT

Once upon a time there were six movie theaters in Ambato. Then VHS took over, and slowly the theaters struck bottom and were converted into *iglesias evangélicas.* Listen to numerous *ambateños* recount this story, or go to the **Cine Sucre,** at Martínez and Mera, to witness the sad fate of the Ambato movie palaces. The city's only remaining theater, Sucre screens aged Hollywood flicks every Sat. and Sun.

Fortunately, Ambato's clubs haven't followed the same path. One popular nightclub is the **Disco Club Coyote,** Bolívar 2057 y Guayaquil (tel. 827-886), in the city's western corner. Usually a restaurant and bar, on weekends the Coyote powers up the disco ball and blasts everything from salsa to rap to techno for a young, somewhat wealthy crowd. Beers s/3,500 (open Fri.-Sat. 10pm-2am). The **Bufalo Cervecero,** Olmedo 681 y Mera (tel. 841-685), near Parque 12 de Noviembre, opens its doors to an 18-and-over crowd. Plays all kinds of music, but leans toward techno. Fridays and Saturdays are most crowded (open Mon.-Sat.; cover s/10,000). The **GCU** at Cevallos and Mera is also worth checking out.

■ Near Ambato

The road to Baños is so well-traveled that nothing remains untouched. Because of the tourist-magnet status of that hot springs hang-out, the innocent bystanding towns southeast of Ambato have also felt tourism's heavy hand. **Salasaca** is little more than a plaza along the road with an artisan fair (daily 8am-6pm), busiest on Sundays. The Quechua Indians who live here specialize in making woven ponchos and tapestries, with designs rich, attractive, and inexpensive enough to tempt the budget browser. The town has its own fiesta in January and a well-known Corpus Cristi celebration in early summer. **Pelileo,** a significantly larger town with a rather turbulent history, is 10 minutes farther east of Salasaca. Destroyed by earthquakes in 1698, 1797, 1840, 1859, and 1949, it now rests several kilometers from its original spot. After Ambato, it has the most important market in the province of Tungurahua, held every Saturday. Buses to Pelileo (every 10min., 6:10am-6:10pm, 30min., s/800) via Salasaca (20min., s/600) leave from the Ambato suburb of Ferroviaria. Baños-bound buses, leaving from Ambato's *terminal terrestre,* will also stop at these two towns en-route.

The smaller towns farther from Baños are less visited and more traditional. **Picaigua,** only a 15-minute bus ride southeast of Ambato, demands respect for the jackets that the locals sew and sell. The second half of January is a continuous party here, marking the festival of patron saint San Isidro. The town of **Patate,** 5km northeast of Pelileo, was founded in 1570, later destroyed by the 1797 earthquake, and finally canonized in 1973. Set in a fertile valley, the town is a fruit-producing marvel, chugging out grapes, peaches, and oranges, among other juicy fruits. Both villages can be reached via the Salasaca/Pelileo buses.

North of Ambato, the 2803m-high **Píllaro** looks down on its neighboring metropolis without any envy. This village of abundance bursts with agriculture, apples, and cattle galore. There's a big market on Sunday, but unlike other traditional villages, that's not even the most intriguing draw. Píllaro is the gateway to the Llanganates mountain chain, where the deceived emperor Atahualpa supposedly buried his treasure. Nobody has found it... yet. Less-materialistic travelers can simply enjoy the value of the landscape and wait for the brand-new **Parque Nacional Llanganates** to become more accessible to visitors.

Baños

The undisputed draw of this tiny highland town, the reason people flock here from all over the world, is the prospect of a leisurely soak in the legendary **baños**. These pools of water, some steaming and others just relaxingly warm, are geothermally heated by the same fiery god that created nearby **Volcán Tungurahua.** The baths have worked wonders for the town. Many locals and tourists alike sport the demeanor of a recently-emerged springs-soaker—loose, relaxed, indulged, and indulgent. Other aspects of the town only add to the already utopian ambience. A wall of neighboring green mountains, including Tungurahua, seem to shelter the town from the turmoil beyond. They loom so high and so close at night, the lights on top could easily be mistaken for planes flying overhead. As word spreads about Baños's stunning natural beauty, this quintessential Ecuadorian dazzler has adapted to harvest as many as possible of the tourist dollars that flow through its streets. *Gringo*-oriented American and European restaurants with multilingual menus are the norm. On every block, not only hotels but tour companies eagerly vie for attention, with postcard-perfect photos of past expeditions. Resting in the eastern flank of the Andes, the town's popularity comes not just from its own attractions, but from its status as a jumping-off point for jungle tours and other exotic excursions. The conveniences are here because the *gringos* are here, everywhere, walking the streets, bearing witness to the industry that over the decades has risen up to greet them. The industry has blossomed so fully that at times it is difficult to envision local life here. But there *is* a "normal" Ecuadorian town under the tourist Baños—it's just hard to see. Children head off to school in uniform, worshippers fill the *basílica* at mass, and yes, in this land of traveler's checks, people still beg in the streets.

ORIENTATION

Baños is a simple town to get the hang of. The main highway between Ambato and Puyo runs east-west across the northern end of town. From the bus station on the highway, it is about three blocks south along **Maldonado** to the **Parque Central,** which lies between the consecutive east-west streets **Rocafuerte** and **Ambato** (the principal street in Baños). These parallel ways also form the sides of the **Parque Basílica,** marked by the Lego-looking church on Ambato, and the **market area.** Lots

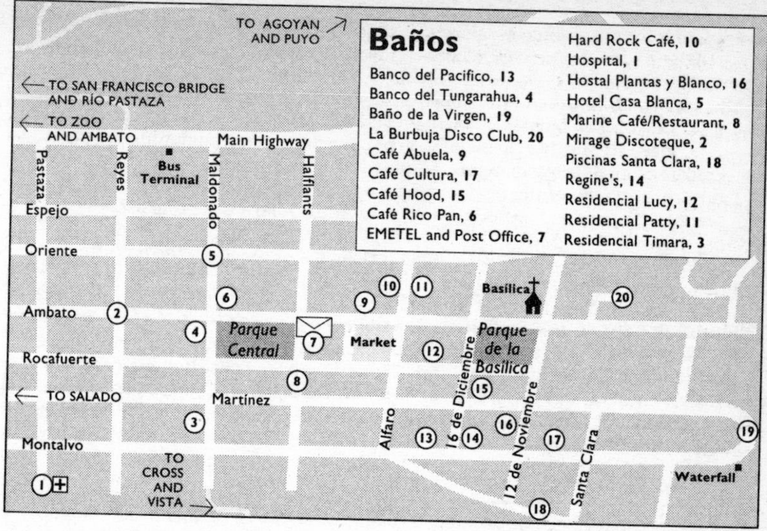

of the town's action is along **Ambato** between the two parks, though plenty of stores, restaurants, and hotels can be found several blocks away as well.

PRACTICAL INFORMATION

Tourist Office: There is no official CETUR in Baños, but if there were it would be superfluous. Numerous tourist businesses offer reliable info on what to do here.

Currency Exchange: Banco del Pacífico (tel. 740-162), on Montalvo between Av. 16 de Diciembre and Alfaro (open Mon.-Fri. 9am-5pm, Sat. 9am-1:30pm). **Banco del Tungurahua** (tel. 740-414), at Ambato and Maldonado, on the Parque Central (open Mon.-Fri. 9am-2pm, Sat. 9am-1pm). Both change cash and traveler's checks.

Telephone: EMETEL (tel. 740-104), at Rocafuerte and Halflants, on the Parque Central.

Buses: The **terminal terrestre** takes up a block between Maldonado and the main road to Ambato. Buses sally forth to several key destinations from the parking lot in front and from the station's border streets. To **Quito** (every ½hr., 3am-7:30pm, 3½hr., s/2,000), **Ambato** (every 10min., 3am-7:30pm, 1hr., s/1,800), **Riobamba** (every hr., 6am-5pm, 1hr., s/2,500). The scenic road to **Puyo** has been under construction for a while; the official date of completion is in early 1997, but locals aren't holding their breath. Currently, the road is open to buses on Sun. and Mon. only (every hr., 5am-9pm, 2hr., s/5,000).

Taxis: Baños is quite walkable, but a dispatch is **16 de Diciembre** (tel. 740-416).

Rental Info: Every hotel, café, drug store, and tour agency in Baños seems to rent some mode of transport for the tourist traffic. **Sierra Selva Adventures** (tel. 740-298), at Maldonado and Oriente charges the going rates in town (bikes s/10,000 per day; motorcycles s/100,000 per day; horses s/45,000 for 4hr., including a guide). **Café Hood** (tel. 740-516), on Av. 16 de Diciembre between Rocafuerte and Martínez, claims to have the only mountain bikes with suspension in town. **Hostal Plantas y Blanco** also rents bikes, jeeps, and motorcycles. For **horses,** check out **Isla de Baños,** the hostel on Montalvo near Alfaro. Be aware, though; some claim that Baños's horse selection is less than quality.

Luggage Storage: Because of all the tourist excursions offered from Baños, hotels are eager to watch your stuff for you, though some systems are more secure than others. **Hola** (tel. 740-923), on Montalvo and Espejo facing the bus terminal, has lockers (s/1,500 per day). The place advertises free information, but it's a private business, not a tourist office (open daily 8am-noon and 2-7pm).

English Bookstore: Buy or exchange used books in English at **Café Hood** (tel. 740-516), at Av. 16 de Diciembre between Rocafuerte and Martínez (open Wed.-Mon. 8:30am-9:30pm).

Library: The **Biblioteca Municipal** (tel. 740-458), in the **Municipio,** on Rocafuerte at Halflants (open Mon.-Fri. 8am-noon and 2-6pm).

Public Market: Mostly in a building boxed in by Rocafuerte and Ambato, Alfaro and Halflants (open daily 8am-6pm). **Sunday** is the biggest day.

Laundromat: One of the benefits of a town that caters to travelers is that laundry services are prevalent, especially in hotels. At the **Julio Verne** tour agency, washer-dryer service costs s/10,000 per load (open daily 9am-1pm and 3-7pm).

Public Toilets: At the Parque Central on Halflants, across from the post office.

Pharmacy: Farmacia Baños (tel. 740-237), on Ambato, centrally located between Alfaro and Halflants (open 8:30am-12:30pm and 1-9pm). Part of *de turno* rotation.

Hospital: (tel. 740-443), at Pastaza and Montalvo.

Police: (tel. 740-443), on Oriente, 3½ blocks west of the Parque Central.

Post Office: Correos Central (tel. 740-901), on Halflants between Ambato and Rocafuerte, bordering the Parque Central. Has *Lista de Correos* (open Mon.-Fri. 8am-noon and 1-6pm, Sat. 8am-2pm).

Telephone Code: 03.

ACCOMMODATIONS

Despite the high demand for lodging, Baños offers great budget accommodations. Lowest-end places have comfortable beds with shared baths. The tier above that includes private bath and several other spiffy services, like a complimentary breakfast. Hotels virtually pile on top of each other along Av. Ambato, and there are also dense patches on Montalvo in the direction of the pools.

Hostal Plantas y Blanco (tel. 740-044), at Martínez and Av. 12 de Noviembre, a block off the Parque Basílica. The French owner holds the secret behind this popular choice, and its name as well. Simply calling it a lodging would be a severe understatement. Aside from the good location, daily cleaning, and private hot water baths, there's a slew of other services. Rooftop terrace bar/restaurant (open 7:30am-10:30pm). Loads of American movies, with TV and headphones (s/2,000). Dollars exchanged from cash or traveler's checks at rates promised to be better than the bank's. Laundry service, phones, fax, luggage storage... the perks just keep on coming. Rooms s/15,000 per person; other services additional.

Residencial Tímara (tel. 740-599), at Maldonado and Martínez, 2 blocks south of Parque Central along Maldonado. A reliable hotel on the budget level, it includes plain rooms, a clean communal bath blessed with hot water, a sink for washing clothes, and a kitchen at your money-saving disposal. Owners are conscientious about maintaining their positive reputation. S/8,000 per person.

Residencial Patty (tel. 740-202), on Alfaro between Ambato and Oriente, ½ block from the market. Not only does Patty save you money, but her central location saves walking time around town. This climber hang-out sports comfortable beds in rooms bordering an inner patio, and an overhead deck for clothes drying. Shared bathrooms could be cleaner, but hot water flows. S/7,000 per person.

Hostal Los Nevados (tel. 740-673), 30 seconds from Parque Basílica; from Ambato, take the first left past Av. 12 de Noviembre. This hotel seems to have sprung up in the hopes of competing with Plantas y Blanco. It's got the same clean rooms, fresh decor, restaurant/bar on top, and laundry services. A room with private bath and hot water costs s/15,000 per person, including *desayuno.*

Café Cultura (tel. 740-419), on Montalvo and Santa Clara. Just a minute's walk with bathing suit and towel to the pool by the waterfall, this hotel-restaurant is a restful stay—and you get to look forward to the hearty complimentary breakfast in the morning. For s/30,000 per person, it better be hearty. Shared bath with hot water; always guarded at night.

Residencial Lucy (tel. 740-466), at Rocafuerte and Av. 16 de Diciembre, just west of Parque Basílica. Do you want to pet my monkey? That's the operative question at Lucy, where clean rooms come with or without private bath, hot water either way.

A restaurant runs out front, and in the courtyard Pepe the monkey yanks his chain every which way (but loose). S/6,000 per person, with bath s/10,000.

FOOD

Like the hotels and just about everything else in Baños, the restaurants have been molded especially for you, the tourist. You've got your *comedores,* your *chifas,* your *restaurantes típicos,* and they're all cheap! There are also several cafés with imported coffeehouse atmospheres and awesome food. Many restaurants reveal their German, French, or Italian roots in their titles and their menu translations. Here in Baños, restaurants are practically required to be multicultural.

Café Hood (tel. 740-516), on Av. 16 de Diciembre between Rocafuerte and Martínez. Your *gringo* radar will go apeshit in here. Patrons chill with various coffee concoctions and devour international cuisine. Omelette s/3,800, tacos s/5,500, "Hindu plate" s/5,500. The book exchange and alternative coffeehouse photos and posters complete the artsy experience (open Wed.-Mon. 8:30am-9:30pm).

Café Rico Pan (tel. 740-387), at Ambato and Maldonado, on Parque Central. Trying to beat other eateries as the most multicultural, the breakfast menu is in French, Italian, German, Spanish, English, and Hebrew. Popular pancake special s/4,000. Lunch and dinner menu puts the emphasis on the Italian. *Penne* with bacon, mushroom, and tomato s/7,000 (open Mon.-Sat. 7am-9pm, Sun. 7am-noon).

Mariane Café/Restaurant (tel. 740-911), on Halflants at Rocafuerte. The cordial French owner cooks up "sun-drenched cuisine" that might even tempt you back for a second helping. Cozy dining room decorated with *artesanía,* and plenty of *gringos* at night. Spaghetti s/8,500, trout s/13,000, beef stew s/13,000 (open Mon. and Wed.-Sat. noon-10:30pm).

El Marquez (no tel.), at Montalvo and Santa Clara. Enjoy some great Ecuadorian food, like spaghetti (s/8,000) or tacos (s/10,000). Well, maybe the food isn't typical, but the comfortable ambience is. Folklore music begins nightly at 8pm (open daily 8am-midnight; cover s/3,500 after 9:30pm).

Café Cultura (tel. 740-419), at Montalvo and Santa Clara, in the hotel by the same name. Multicultural in ownership as well as in menu, this restaurant has changed hands since its Danish days and is now owned by an Ecuadorian and partly run by an Australian. Lots of vegetarian dishes, though in this town that's no novelty. Lasagna s/6,500, potato soup s/3,800 (open daily 8-11:30am and 3-9pm).

Regine's (tel. 740-641), at Rocafuerte and Av. 16 de Diciembre, plus a café at Montalvo and Av. 16 de Diciembre 2 blocks away. The German magazines reveal the origin of the food and much of the clientele. Not surprisingly, German translations on the Spanish menu. *Asado de res* s/9,000 (open noon-3pm and 4-10pm; café open 8am-10pm).

SIGHTS

Baños is one big sight. The tourist magnets begin at the hot spring pools and radiate outwards to the volcanoes, the Oriente and beyond. There are three **baños** in town. The locals have the right idea—they soak themselves in the salubrious springs at sunrise. Tourists who take a dip later miss the splendor of daybreak over the Andes. The pools are quietest early in the week, busiest on Fridays and Saturdays.

The most heavily touristed *baño* is the **Baño de la Virgen,** at the eastern end of Montalvo (tel. 740-462). A waterfall cascades down the mountainside into this pool, but it's really the crowds and taxis that make it a bit conspicuous. Several murky brown pools, reputedly cleaned daily, are filled with the legendary hot healing waters (open daily 4:30am-5pm, everyone must leave by 6pm; admission s/2,000, children s/1,000). A block away, at Montalvo and Santa Clara, the **Piscinas Santa Clara** (tel. 740-915) are much more a local thing than their not-so-pure virgin neighbor. In addition to the warm or cool volcanic water, the complex also includes a gym, sauna, and a disco for dancing (all services s/8,000, pool only s/3,000). The third pool, **El Salado** (tel. 740-493), is a 15-minute walk or s/3,000 taxi ride from the *centro.* Head west up the hill on Martínez, then cross a creek and follow the road until hotel signs beckon you to take a left. That's El Salado, and the pools with the same name are at the end of the road. Cleaned each day, the six pools here include one cold, three hot, and two scalding (open 4:30am-5pm, must leave by 5:40pm).

If your skin has pruned beyond a healthy level, Baños has several other worthwhile sights. The **basílica** at Ambato and Av. 12 de Noviembre imposes its strange form upon the backdrop of the city. Inside, the famous murals display the devotion and faith that the Catholic population of Baños hold for the Virgin Mary. Lining the grand walls, the paintings display miracles in the city's history, each attributed to the grace of the Virgin. Car crashes, horse accidents, volcanic eruptions—she's there every time, as are the captions in Spanish that describe the stories. You will believe.

The **San Martín Zoo,** a 20-minute walk on the road west to Ambato, detains its animal residents on the mountainside above the **Cascada Ines María.** The magnificent entranceway is a short bridge under which canyon walls plummet. With a professed mission to conserve, educate, and rehabilitate, the private **Ecozoológico** houses condors, jaguars, roaming tapirs, and rock-like tortoises, among other animals (open 7am-6pm; admission s/2,000, s/1,000 for children). Buses to the zoo leave from Alfaro at the market (s/250).

Several cool **hikes** traverse the hills and valleys near Baños. The **Agoyán Falls** cascade past the road to Puyo, about 8km east of *el centro.* The river is held off here by the modern **Agoyán Dam.** For excellent **vistas,** follow Calle Maldonado toward the mountainside. Where the road ends, a path leads to the illuminated **cross** on top of the hill. From here you can count the number of *gringos* per city block.

For excursions to places both nearby and not-so-near, the **rental possibilities** are comprehensive and ubiquitous. Tour agencies, hotels, and restaurants all lease mountain bikes, motorcycles, jeeps, and horses. Transportation to specific destinations? Guides for a day, a week, or a month? No problem—everyone is eager and willing to take your money. Dozens of tour agencies pack the streets of Baños; just keep in mind that relatively few of these are legitimately registered agencies.

Numerous tour agencies also offer longer, more distant excursions (their major money-maker, as the prices show). Plenty of people are ready to bring you where you want to go, or tell you where you want to go, but not as many are qualified to do so. These trips can be a sizeable investment, and justifiably so, since they may be the highlight of an Ecuadorian experience. One reputable business is **Rainforestur** (tel. 740-743; fax 740-743), right off the Parque Central. General manager Santiago Herrera sets up trips to the mountains (Tungurahua, Cotopaxi, or Chimborazo), the Galápagos, and the Oriente. Jungle packages come in many shapes and sizes (US$45 per person per day for a minimum of 4 days). All tours are led by guides with specific experience on that particular river or mountain. Rainforestur also rents bikes and horses (open daily 8am-8pm). The **Varoxi** backpack store (tel. 740-051), on Maldonado between Oriente and Espejo, repairs backpacks and sells windbreakers, backpacks, and protective covers (open daily 8am-1pm and 2:30-7pm).

ENTERTAINMENT

Baños is not a fast-paced party town. With its 2am closing law, nightlife *can't* really get too wild. There is no guarantee that the *discotecas* will draw in crowds, even on weekends. The **Mirage Discoteque** (tel. 740-381) at Ambato and Reyes, one block from the Parque Central, plays "all types of music," though their classical and contemporary Christian collections are a bit weak (open Tues.-Sat. 8:30pm-2am; cover s/ 3,000). **La Burbuja Disco Club** (tel. 740-520), is a block east of the Parque Basílica on Ambato (open Wed.-Sat. 8pm-2am, Sat. "grand matinee" 3-7pm).

Plenty of bars provide the opportunity to meet other travelers or hang out with friendly Ecuadorians, minus the disco ball. One is **Tequila,** on Ambato between Alfaro and Av. 16 de Diciembre. Another, the **Hard Rock Café,** on Alfaro between Ambato and Oriente, probably awaits a lawsuit for copyright infringement. *Peñas,* like the one at the restaurant **El Marquez,** are excellent places to settle back and take in the authentic sounds of *música folklórica.* Like everything else that appeals to tourists, they line the streets of Baños.

Travelers in the mood for a movie can visit the **cine** on Av. 12 de Noviembre, next to the Basílica. Signs around town advertise the different flicks shown each day, some of which are mainstream American (screenings Wed.-Mon.). For other selections, the **video-and-headphone service** offered by the Hostal Plantas y Blanco (see above) is not limited to guests. The movie choices there are recent and extensive.

■ Parque Nacional Sangay

Come to Parque Nacional Sangay, where the tapir and lava streams run side-by-side. This unwieldy 517,765-hectare (over 5000km^2) park sprawls south from Baños through five Ecuadorian provinces, falling from jagged Andean ridges in the west to the Amazon River basin in the east. The mountainous portion of the park boasts three of Ecuador's 10 highest peaks, including two active volcanoes. Excursions to Sangay's snow-capped summits and virgin forests are less commercialized than those to Chimborazo or Cotopaxi, each a virtual pioneering expedition through relatively undiscovered and resplendent lands. With altitudes ranging from 5319m (17,446 ft.) on the peak of Volcán Altar, to 900m (3000 ft.) in the Amazon basin, much of the amazing landscape is simply impossible to traverse. This inaccessibility, combined with the park's main objective (to protect and conserve) bars visitors from reaching some of Sangay's more remote areas. First founded as a reserve in 1979, the park shelters a selection of flora and fauna almost as diverse as the geography, including rare and strange specimens such as the endangered **Andean tapir** *(Tapirus pinchaque),* also known as the *"canta de monte."*

INEFAN, the Parque Nacional's administration, is a tremendous resource for those planning to explore the park. In addition to providing information about the park, the helpful staff offers advice and suggestions for finding guides. They also give free rides from their Riobamba office to the three park entrances at **Alao, Pondoa,** and **Candelaria.** For more information, contact them at the Riobamba office, listed in Riobamba Practical Information, p. 121.

The park's unreachable areas may fascinate, but the accessible ones are nothing to scoff at. Sangay is divided into two sections—the *zona alta,* in the Sierra (with elevations from 1500-5319m), and the *zona baja,* in the Oriente (alt. 900-1500m). The *zona alta* contains the Parque Nacional's main attractions, and its entrance points are easily accessible from Baños or Riobamba. The four main sites in Parque Sangay's *zona alta* are the relaxing **El Placer** and the towering fire-spewers, **Volcán Tungurahua** (alt. 5016m), **Volcán Altar** (alt. 5319m), and the namesake, **Volcán Sangay** (alt. 5230m) itself.

One of least difficult snow climbs in Ecuador, the young **Volcán Tungurahua** is technically easy but physically arduous. This 10th highest peak in Ecuador was most recently volcanically active from 1916 to 1925. The two-day excursion begins at **Pondoa,** at the base of the mountain, from which it is about a four-hour hike to the **Santos Ocaña refugio** (alt. 3800m). The shelter is equipped with a gas stove and straw mats, but bring your own food, toilet paper, and matches (s/10,000 per person). If you're feeling generous, leave some for the next party. Staying in the *refugio* is imperative, as the four-hour ascent to Tungurahua's summit must begin at 2am, when the snow is hardest. Trails can be muddy, especially during the June-August rainy season. Crampons, ice axes, ropes, and experience are necessary for the climb. Non-climbers can make Tungurahua into a daytrip and simply hike to the *refugio* and back. From Riobamba, INEFAN has a one-hour free shuttle to Pondoa. From Baños, various tour agencies offer rides to the climb's starting point (s/5,000).

Among the most active volcanoes in the world, **Volcán Sangay** constantly spews ash and smoke into the air to make sure the world doesn't forget it. This lava-dripping peak has three deep craters way up top. The park's mammoth namesake requires a six-day trip at minimum: two and a half days hiking each way, and one day for the climb. Begin the hike up Sangay from the entrance at **Alao,** on the western side of the park. Hiring a guide is a must, at least for the start of the climb. In Alao, you can find a guide (s/20,000/day) and a mule for your luggage and equipment (s/15,000-20,000/

day). You'll also need all the proper hiking and mountain-climbing equipment, plus clothing and six to eight days' worth of food and water. Stock up in a Baños or Riobamba's supermarket; there's not much in Alao. It is dangerous to climb all the way up to Sangay's crater, as you might get in the fiery path of all that spewed ash and lava. Experience is a must, and only climb as far as the guides recommend. INEFAN rides from Riobamba to Alao leave as early as 4am—call in advance to check definite times. INEFAN officials can give advice on equipment and help you find a guide.

El Altar (Los Altares), the highest mountain in the park, collapsed in 1460 and is now partially covered in glaciers. Accessible from yet another park entrance at **Candelaria** (a 45-min. free ride from INEFAN in Riobamba), this eight-hour climb to the crater is similar to the two-day Tungurahua ascent, though there is no worthwhile daytrip to a *refugio.* Prices are similar to those of other trips and guides are readily available in Candelaria (INEFAN officials will assist you). Again, equipment is needed for the climb to the crater. Camping is possible in a cave near the crater (ask guides for help), or stay overnight at the park entrance near Candelaria.

El Placer is a relatively low, swampy area with *aguas temales* for bathing. There is a *refugio* with amenities for staying overnight, but most just make this into a long daytrip, departing for Alao at daybreak (INEFAN leaves at 4am) and returning at dusk. **Atillo,** a picturesque lagoon, is a two-hour drive (free from INEFAN, 8am), and also the head of a path crossing the park from the Andes to **Macas** in the Oriente, the best means for discovering the true diversity of the park's terrain. Some amazing species of plants and animals populate the Parque; the Andean tapir, visible at times from the Atillo and El Placer areas, is found nowhere else in the world. Plant and animal stalkers in the know head to **Playa de Sangay** and **El Palmar** for their observational kicks. Others take a walk on the wild side of the Oriente, by heading to **Culebrillas** and the **Lagunas de Sardmayacu** in the *zona baja* in the never-ending quest for still more jaguar and bear sightings. Both places are accessible from Palora and Macas (see Jungle Tours from Macas, p. 239).

The admission fee at any entrance to the park is s/20,000 for tourists, s/2,000 for locals. Suck it up—the pricing scale is discriminatory, but try as you might to blend, it's unavoidable. Once in the park, guides are a necessity for all climbs. The Riobamba INEFAN offers friendly and extremely useful assistance (as usual) in finding a guide, as does the South American Explorer's Club in Quito, which has trip reports and information on recommended guides (see Travel Organizations, p. 1).

Riobamba

Known as the "Sultan of the Andes," Riobamba (pop. 120,000; alt. 2750m) needs no orchidaceous show of regalia to prove that it is master of its domain. Tranquil and relatively tourist-free, this quintessential Andean city will allow you to immerse yourself in Ecuadorian life without the fast pace and possible dangers of a major metropolis. Cobblestone streets weave in and out of three plazas and five parks, including the **Parque 21 de Abril,** with its awe-inspiring views of snow-capped Volcán Chimborazo and neighboring El Altar and Tungurahua. These towering volcanoes keep watch over a city that bears the scars of its tremulous past. After an earthquake in 1797, the entire city, then the capital of Ecuador, was moved to its present site on a highland valley plain. As a result, the city's oldest architecture is *neo*-classical with one notable exception; the **catedral** on Velez and Av. 5 de Junio was transported stone-by-stone from its pre-quake location. The past 200 years have taken their toll on the grand old buildings that frame the streets and parks of Riobamba. Crumbling reminders of the town's former glory, many of the buildings have been taken over by *ferreterías* (hardware stores) and fast-food restaurants. The majestic **Colegio Nacional Maldonado** at Plaza Sucre is one of the few buildings that has managed to stay grease-free. It still serves its original purpose—as a local high school.

Most visitors, however, don't come for the parks, plazas, and architecture. The city is known primarily as a departure point for some of Ecuador's most thrilling sights and expeditions. Try a daytrip up Chimborazo, Ecuador's tallest peak, or experience

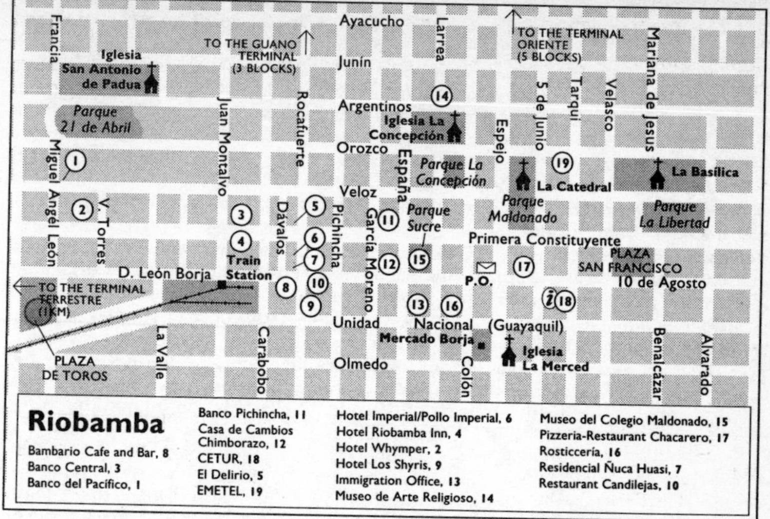

the jaw-dropping train ride to Guayaquil, which travels through every tropical habitat from highland *páramo* to coastal lowland. Visit nearby indigenous villages, or explore Parque Nacional Sangay, home of one of the world's most active volcanoes. Seated high on his Andean throne, the Sultan offers an array of experiences you won't find anywhere else.

ORIENTATION

Riobamba's straightforward grid layout and clear, consistent street signs make it one of the most navigable cities in Ecuador. Activity centers around the area squared off by **Argentinos** and **Olmedo** to the north and south, and **Av. 5 de Junio** and **Angel León** to the east and west. **Primera Constituyente** and **Av. 10 de Agosto** are the city's main thoroughfares. From the bus station, head east for 1km on León Borja; it turns into Av. 10 de Agosto. The train station is in the center of town at Av. 10 de Agosto and Carabobo. Out of the city limits and above the clouds, Chimborazo lies to the northwest, El Altar to the east, and Tungurahua to the northeast.

PRACTICAL INFORMATION

Tourist Information: CETUR (tel. 960-217 or 941-213), at Av. 5 de Junio and Av. 10 de Agosto, will amiably distribute city maps and brochures, as well as help any lost or querying souls. English spoken (open Mon.-Fri. 8:30am-5pm).

Immigration Office: España 10-50 and Guayaquil (tel. 969-844). For affairs relating to visas and tourist cards (open Mon.-Fri. 8am-noon and 2-6pm).

INEFAN: (tel. 963-779), at the **Ministerio del Cultura Agrícola (MAC)** on Av. 9 de Octubre near Duchicela. Super-helpful staff has information about Sangay and free rides to the park, leaving at 8am (open Mon.-Fri. 8am-4:30pm).

Currency Exchange: Casa de Cambios Chimborazo (tel. 967-427 or 940-545), on Av. 10 de Agosto between García Moreno and España, near the Parque Sucre. The only place in town, so lines move slowly. Dollars and traveler's checks exchanged at decent rates (open Mon.-Fri. 9:30am-1:30pm and 3-6pm; Sat. 9:30am-1pm).

Banks: Abundant in the main section of town—look up and chances are you'll see one. Large banks include the **Banco del Pacífico,** at Veloz and Angel León, and **Banco Pichincha,** at Primera Constituyente and García Moreno (both open until 6pm). Most banks are open Mon.-Sat. 9am-1:30pm and have lengthy lines.

ATM: BanRed ATM machines, available at many banks, take Cirrus/Plus cards and are open 24hr.

Telephone/Fax: EMETEL (tel. 969-816 or 962-001), at Tarqui and Velos, offers local, long-distance, and international calling services. Free local calls with an AT&T or MCI calling card. EMETEL also sends and receives faxes for a fee. Use a calling card, make a collect call, or receive calls at local upscale hotels such as the **Hotel El Galpón** (tel. 960-981), at Argentinos and Zanibrano; or **Hotel Whymper,** Angel León 23-10 y Primera Constituyente (tel. 964-575). Guests can receive international calls at virtually all hotels, usually a cheaper option than dialing home from Ecuador.

Trains: The **train station** (tel. 961-909) is at Av. 10 de Agosto and Carabobo (open daily 8am-noon and 2-5pm). The magnificent **Riobamba-Guayaquil** route was recently re-opened after over 10 years of repair to tracks, which had been destroyed by the catastrophic El Niño of 1982-83. Loads of tourists catch this train just for the scenery; if you've got the nerves, ride on the roof for the best views. The track runs south from Riobamba to Alausí, then cuts west to Guayaquil to the town of Bucay. The small **Alausí-Bucay** section is the most scenic, and some tourists only hop on for this portion of the ride. The last stretch from Bucay to the Guayaquil suburb of Durán is uneventful, and the train may arrive after dark. The train leaves from Riobamba quasi-daily (Fri.-Mon., Wed., 6am, 12hr., s/24,000-36,000 depending on how far and long you travel). Check the schedule, however, as it often changes. A **Riobamba-Quito** route (2 per week, 9am, s/30,000) also runs, offering fantastic yet frigid volcano views from the train roof. Buy a ticket at the station the day before you plan to travel and arrive for your ride by 5:15am on the date of departure. For more information, see The Riobamba-Alausí-Bucay-Durán Railway, p. 129.

Buses: The main **terminal terrestre** is on León Borja (the western part of Av. 10 de Agosto) and Daniela, about 1km to the northwest of the center of town. From there, buses head to **Quito** (18 per day, 3:15am-7pm, 3½hr., s/9,000), **Guayaquil** (6 per day, 5:30am-6:30pm, 4½hr., s/9,000), **Cuenca** (6 per day, 5½hr., s/18,000), **Huaquillas** (2 per day, 9hr., s/18,000), and **Machala** (every day, 9pm, 12hr., s/30,000). All buses except those marked "express" stop at all towns along the way, so take the Quito line for towns like **Ambato** (1½hr., s/4,500) and the Cuenca line for **Alausí** (1½hr., s/9,000). The **Terminal Oriental** (tel. 960-766), on Espejo and León Borja (north of town), sends buses eastward and on to the Oriente daily. Like most Ecuadorian buses, these generally do not run on strict schedules; rather, they either leave roughly every 30min. or simply depart when they're full. To **Baños** (every ½hr., 5am-7pm, 1hr., s/6,000), **Puyo** (every ½hr., 5am-7pm, 3½hr., s/14,000), **Tena,** and locations further east (every hr., 5am-7pm). The **Guano Terminal** on Rocafuerte and Nueva York (north of town) sends buses to **Guano** (every 15min., ½hr., s/1,500) and **Santa Teresita** (every 15min., ½hr., s/2,000). Buses for **Cajabamba, Laguna de Colta,** and **Guamote** leave from the area around Av. Unidad Nacional, Angel León, and Bolivia (every ½hr., ½hr., s/1,500). Additional buses leave on Thurs. for the Guamote market. Buses to **San Juan,** the closest town to Chimborazo, leave from Av. Unidad Nacional and Av. Prensa.

Local Buses: Unless you're in a big hurry, local buses are unnecessary; Riobamba is eminently walkable. There are two routes—"Control Norte," along León Borja and Av. 10 de Agosto, and "Control Sur," running through Orozco between Carabobo and Unidad Nacional on the other end of town. The fare is a paltry s/200.

Taxis: These ubiquitous nightcrawlers—they're everywhere, all night long—charge a reasonable s/2,500 to go between any two points in the city.

Pharmacy: Farmacia Perpetuo Socorro, next to the Hotel Zeus on León Borja toward the *terminal terrestre.* This perpetually helpful place is open 24hr.

Hospitals: The **Policliníco** (tel. 965-725), at Olmedo and Cuba, is the most modern and highly recommended medical facility in town (open 24hr.). The **Hospital del Seguro Social** (tel. 961-811), at Av. Unidad Nacional and Carlos Zambrano, is another option, as are the numerous private clinics.

Emergency: tel. 101. Lately, however, civil unrest among authorities has caused this line to be unattended.

Police: The police station (tel. 969-300), at Av. de la Policía and La Paz on the Vía a Chembo, is open 24hr.

Post Office: (tel. 966-066) at Av. 10 de Agosto and Espejo is now back at its grand old home. You can't miss it. Postcards and postcard envelopes are sold. Don't count on incoming mail (open Mon.-Fri. 8am-6pm, Sat. 8am-2pm).

Information/Directory: 104.

Telephone Code: 03.

ACCOMMODATIONS

Hotel Imperial (tel. 960-429), at Av. 10 de Agosto and Rocafuerte, is right in the heart of Riobamba. Relax in spacious, airy rooms or lounge on the balcony. Large beds with holey sheets are reasonably clean, but not quite divine. Bathrooms are puny but bearable. Singles and doubles have access to a shared bathroom; triples and quads have their own. Friendly management will arrange cheap Chimborazo excursions. A good deal at s/12,000 per person.

Hotel Los Shyris (tel. 960-323), at Av. 10 de Agosto and Rocafuerte, is a step above the Imperial in both sheet and overall room quality, but doesn't quite have the same warm, fuzzy atmosphere. The clean, telephone-equipped rooms (local calls s/1000 per 3min.) seem all the larger in comparison with the smallness of the bathrooms, which are tidy with so-so showers. S/15,000 per person.

Hotel Riobamba Inn, Carabobo 12-20 y Primera Constituyente (tel. 961-696 or 940-958), across from the Banco Central. It may have a redundant name, but that is because day after day it keeps repeating the same meticulous cleanliness. Sparkling private bathrooms and spotless rug-bearing bedrooms. Though the televisions in each room are black-and-white, the glare from the colorful phones and hot pink bedspreads more than make up for it. Hot water 24hr. At s/25,000 per person, it's a step up in price (though not necessarily in taste).

Hotel Whymper, Angel León 23-10 y Primera Constituyente, is a bit outside the center of town. Whimper with delight at the sight of the king-sized beds. With its green bedspreads and linoleum floors, it rivals Hotel Riobamba Inn for the "Best Decor from a Past Decade" award. Telephones and private bathrooms give each room an added bonus. S/24,000 per person. Breakfast at the cafeteria s/8,000.

Residencial Ñuca Huasi (tel. 966-669), on Av. 10 de Agosto between Rocafuerte and Dávalo, offers the budget-conscious a last resort—and a sexy palindromic phone number. Rumor has it that the once-grand building may be haunted; listen for ghosts in the nooks and crannies. The starkness of the huge, somewhat shabby bedrooms does little to quell fears aroused by these supernatural superstitions. Bare, hanging lightbulbs round out the ghostly decor. But for the price, rooms at the Ñuca Huasi have little competition: s/7,000, with bath s/10,000.

Hotel Humboldt, León Borja 35-48 y Uruguay (tel. 961-788 or 940-814). More expensive than its in-town counterparts, but what you get for the extra money could keep you amused for days. Bright, airy rooms with color TV, telephone, cheery color schemes, and knick-knacks galore—including candy bars and bags of chips on the bedside table. No, they're not complimentary. Private baths, but not quite the utmost in bathroom quality. Cafeteria downstairs (open 7:30am-8:30pm). Singles s/33,000; doubles (far larger) s/45,000.

FOOD

Riobamba, being the classic Ecuadorian city, has plenty of budget *almuerzo* stops, with meals for around s/3,000. Many eateries are virtually indistinguishable; choose based on cleanliness, recommendations from local patrons, or just personal preference. Come dinner time, locals crowd around outdoor stands that scoop various traditional stews and meat dishes out of steaming bowls lit up by little floodlights. The food can be good, but eat at your own risk—look for flies, and remember, no raw veggies. These stands cluster around Carabobo and Guayaquil, selling their goods for around s/1,500-3,000. The cheapest filler-uppers, though, are the ubiquitous bakeries *(panaderías),* which sell bread for s/210 and up.

Restaurant Candilejas (tel. 960-220), on Av. 10 de Agosto between Pichincha and Rocafuerte, secludes itself from the street with yellow curtains and a covered door. The elegant setting—with tablecloths, flowers, and chandeliers—is misleading given the budget prices here. The comprehensive menu includes Kodachrome pictures that preview your meal in living color—perhaps just a tad too vividly. Pizza s/6,500-13,000. Plenty of meat entrees (*bistek* s/5,000). Open Mon.-Sat. 7:30am-8:30pm, Sun. 7:30am-1:30pm.

Chifa Joy Sing, Unidad Nacional 29-33 y Carabobo (tel. 961-285). The huge portions of savory cuisine at this typical Ecuadorian *chifa* will have you singing with joy. Creative dishes as well as old favorites. Fried "wantans" s/4,000. Tasty *tallarin especial* (angel hair noodles with Chinese vegetables, chicory pork, beef, and shrimp; s/6,200). The large dining room is rather nondescript, but draws in crowds of Ecuadorians and Chinese (open Mon.-Sat. until 10pm).

Pizzeria-Restaurant Chacarero, Av. 5 de Junio 21-46 y Av. 10 de Agosto (tel. 969-292). An inexpensive Italian joint that serves with a smile. Chefs go above and beyond with abundant toppings; pasta dishes like the *putanesca* overflow with olives, garlic, onions, peppers, tomatoes, and more (s/6,000). Meat entrees s/6,000-6,500. Pizzas with your choice of toppings ("individual" s/8,000, medium s/16,000, large s/25,000). Open Mon.-Sat. 3-10pm.

Rosticcería (tel. 942-355), at Colón and Av. 10 de Agosto, is another in the Italian vein: pizza (slices s/2,500-3,800, individual pies s/7,500-13,000), lasagna (s/8,000), and spaghetti *capricho* (with ham, mushrooms, and cream, s/10,000) round out the menu. Don't spill the tomato sauce, though—meals served on white tablecloths, beneath white walls, on white plates (open daily 8am-8pm).

El Delirio (tel. 967-502), at Primera Constituyente and Rocafuerte, beautifully situated in Simón Bolívar's old house, a historical landmark. Outdoor tables in a charming patio garden under blossoming trees. If it was nice enough for the liberator of South America, it's probably nice enough for you. A slight splurge, but entrees like the *lomo al jugo* (tenderloin, s/9,500) aren't costly by foreign standards, and the hamburgers (s/4,500) are downright cheap. Pleasant indoor dining as well, with historic pictures decking the wooden walls and woven lanterns hanging low (open Mon.-Sat. noon-10pm, Sun. noon-3pm).

Bambarío Cafe and Bar (tel. 942-316), at Av. 10 de Agosto and Rocafuerte, across the street from Hotel Shyris, is the only place in town that caters to *gringos,* a rare breed in Riobamba. Gulp down tea, coffee (s/1,000), and alcoholic drinks (s/3,000-8,000) in a room so warm, friendly, and comforting that you may never want to leave. If on the other hand you prefer to shun comfort at the first prospect of adventure, Bambarío also arranges tours (open Mon.-Sat. 8:30am-11pm).

Pollo Imperial, on Av. 10 de Agosto and Rocafuerte beneath the Hotel Imperial, serves chicken in *all* its various forms (¼ chicken s/6,000, chicken soup s/4,000). Perhaps not surprising for a place called *The Imperial Chicken,* walls are a vibrant orange and a large-screen TV shows English-language subtitled movies until late into the night (open daily noon-midnight.)

SIGHTS

Riobamba's scenic parks just cry out to be strolled in. One of the most compelling pleas comes from **Parque 21 de Abril,** also known as **La Loma de Quito,** perched above the rest of Riobamba. Head to the northern part of town; the park is boxed in by Orozco, Argentinos, Grancia, and Juan Montalvo. Due to its auspicious position, Parque 21 de Abril monopolizes the best panoramic views and photo opportunities in the city. On a clear day, the vista captures not only Riobamba, but the surrounding peaks as well, with Volcán Chimborazo king of them all. Romantic and beautiful at sunset, the park also holds a church, **San Antonio de Padua,** with stone steps leading up to its picturesque patio gardens from every direction.

The **Parque Sucre,** in the center of town at España and Primera Constituyente, graces the inland city with the next best thing to the sea—a beautiful bronze **fountain** and **statue of Neptune.** Local old men gather on the palm-tree-shaded benches, engaged in the lost arts of socializing and people-watching. Within the park, the regal schoolhouse **Colegio Nacional Maldonado** takes up an entire block along Primera

Constituyente. The engaging **Parque Maldonado,** at Primera Constituyente and Espejo, next to the CETUR office, displays a monument to its namesake, Pedro Vicente Maldonado. This *riobambeño* historian and cartographer drew up the first political map of Ecuador. Big and bustling with weekend activity on its swings and play structures, **Parque Guayaquil,** at Unidad Nacional and León Borja, provides the perfect opportunity to let your inner child roam free. There's no end to Riobamba's peaceful parks and strolling spots; other halcyon hangouts include **Parque La Libertad,** across from the Basílica at Veloz and Benalcazar; and **Parque de la Concepción,** at Orozco and Larrea.

The city's various **churches** reveal the Riobamban penchant for atypical architecture. **La Basílica,** at Veloz and Benalcazar, gained its fame as the only round church in Ecuador, constructed from 1883-1915. The main **Catedral,** at Veloz and Av. 5 de Junio by Parque Maldanado, is the oldest building in town. The sole remnant of Riobamba's pre-earthquake site, it was transported, one stone at a time, in 1797. **La Concepción** (La Loma de Quito), at Orosco and Larrea, and **La Merced,** at Olmedo and Espejo, don't have such fascinating histories, but do open for mass Mon.-Fri. 6-8am and 6-8pm, Sat.-Sun. all day.

Two **museums** of note grace Riobamba. **La Concepción,** or the **Museo de Arte Religioso** (tel. 965-212), at Argentinos and Larrea, has a grand collection of religious art and artifacts (adults s/5,000, children s/2,000; open Tues.-Sun. 8:30am-12:30pm and 2:30-6pm). The **Museo del Colegio Maldonado,** also known as the *Museo de Ciencias Naturales,* is a tiny natural history and science exhibit inside the monumental schoolhouse at the Parque Sucre (open Mon.-Fri. 8am-1pm and 3-6pm; admission s/210).

ENTERTAINMENT

The **Saturday market** is literally a *huge* affair. The entire length of every street boxed in by España, Av. 5 de Junio, Guayaquil, and Argentinos—as well as all the space in-between—fills up with vendors, shoppers, and good old Ecuadorian energy. People from all the small surrounding villages come to join in the spectacle. Nearly *everything* imaginable is sold somewhere, from live chicks to toothbrushes, traditional Indian weaving to entire cow legs. More touristy items center around Parque La Concepción between Orosco, Veloz, España, and Colón; after all, customs has rules about cow legs, but woven bags and clothing are just fine. The market can be an exciting morning of bargains and discovery, but brace yourself—it's not a place for indecisive strollers.

Even on the weekdays, the shopping scene stays strong. Riobamba is famous for its carved **tagua nuts**, ivory-white, rock-hard palm tree nuts from the rain forest. Local craftsmen carve them into various gadgets and souvenirss; look for a super selection at **The Tagua Shop/Alta Montaña,** León Borja 35-17 y Uruguay (tel. 963-694 or 942-215). Tagua nuts and their various reincarnations are far from cheap by Ecuadorian standards (the smallest souvenirs start at s/4,000; chess sets go for s/50,000 and up), but that's not so surprising given that the store is an actual artisan's workshop where you can see the nuts being carved (open Mon.-Sat. 9am-1pm, 3-7pm). Another well-known form of local *artesanía* are the woven bags known as **shigras.** Market spots include Colón and Veloz, Junín and Av. 5 de Junio, and the area around the post office at Primera Constituyente and Espejo.

For the testosterone-abundant, **cockfights** can be seen Saturdays and Sundays in a house at Almagro and Chimborazo, or at the *Colizeo de Balles* at Ciudadela in the Barrio Tapi (ask at CETUR for details). After all, what could be more *macho* than a bunch of men watching roosters peck each other to death? Riobamba's biggest *fiesta,* **La Loma de Quito,** commemorates the city's founding. The actual holiday falls on April 21, but *riobambeños* know how to party—the celebration lasts from April 18-22, when fairs, bullfights, and parades swamp the streets.

By night, **The Bluff,** at Av. 10 de Agosto and Carabobo, is the hangout of choice for locals. This bar/*discoteca* features an indoor slide—just make sure you don't slip up and drink too much before you start slidin'. *Peñas* are ubiquitous in Riobamba; some of the best are **El Faraon,** León Borja 43-40 y 44 (tel. 963-488 and 968-161), near the *terminal terrestre;* **Ureja Guardea,** at Manuel E. Flor and Zambrano; and **Media Luna,** at Zambrano and Veloz. Most *discotecas* cluster around the same area—on León Borja between the *terminal terrestre* and Hotel Zeus at Duchicela—making a night of club-hopping all too easy. Some of the most dance-friendly *discotecas* are **Casablanca** and **Gems Chop,** which has a large dance floor and UFO-style flying colored lights. At the *terminal* itself, **La Casa del Billar** entertains with pool, ping-pong, and a disco. The nightlife gets going around 9-10pm and keeps on rollin' into the wee hours (usually until 2-5am).

■ Near Riobamba

GUANO AND SANTA TERESITA

Only a 30-minute bus ride from Riobamba, these tiny villages offer a close-up glimpse into a different sort of Ecuador, a rural Andean lifestyle that makes even tranquil Riobamba seem bustling. **Guano** specializes in rug-making and slow living, with a picturesque plaza in the hilly shadow of the Volcán El Altar. Numerous *artesanía* shops vend monstrous rugs, leather goods, and hemp items; sometimes the weavers display the creation of their craft outside, spinning intricate designs with their wooden looms. The simple pleasures of all Ecuadorian towns can be found here as well—only in a smaller, quieter version. The central square houses a lovely **park** with a garden in its center, and a small **church** stands at Colón and García Moreno. One of the only restaurants in town, **Los Fuentes** dishes out chow at Hidalgo and García Moreno, near the main plaza (hours erratic). *Panaderías* and small stands throughout town offer bread, soda, chips, and other snacks. It's hard to imagine an emergency happening in so placid a place, but in case of any sort of disaster, there's a **bank** across the street from Los Fuentes, and a **pharmacy** and **medical center** at García Moreno and Ramirez. To get here from Riobamba, catch the bus from Rocafuerte and Nueva York (every ½hr., 5am-7pm, ½hr., s/1,500).

The 5-6km walk down García Moreno to the town of **Santa Teresita** lasts about an hour. You won't see another tourist for miles as you walk through the rural valley, down dusty cobblestone streets, past shacks and sweatshops, small gardens and suspicious dogs. Except for Sunday market days, the towns are eerily silent, so expect stares. If you don't want to walk the whole way, buses rumble along García Moreno every few minutes, kicking up clouds of dust that linger in the silence. There's no way to get lost heading to Santa Teresita—absolutely nothing else is around. A **bus station** next to a 24-hour liquor store and another of those ubiquitous churches welcomes visitors to some of Ecuador's more remote **natural springs.** Take a right down the highway and walk for about 20 minutes to get to the *aguas termales.* The setting of these swimming pools, in a pasture against a mountainside, framed by Andean hills and Volcán El Altar, is better than the quality of the actual pools, but it's a refreshing plunge nonetheless. An s/200 entrance fee grants free rein to wander between two lower cool-water pools, and the warmer, larger upper pool. Located in a spooky, rundown building reminiscent of a suburban high school gym, the whole complex appears to be a mere shadow of its former self. You'll likely have a pool to yourself, so take a swim, but keep your mouth closed.

CAJABAMBA, LAGUNA DE COLTA, AND GUAMOTE

Aside from the Sunday Indian market a bit further down the highway, there's not much to see in **Cajabamba.** The village was devastated by a 1797 earthquake, but from the way this run-down industrial town sags, the tremblor might have happened last week. As a matter of fact, Cajabamba is an excellent place to leave—that is, it makes a good starting point for the scenic one-hour hike to the **La Balbonera church** and the lovely **Laguna de Colta.** Start walking uphill just after the road peaks—the hills and fertile valley spread behind while Chimborazo looms above.

In 1959, the conductor of a derailed train prayed to the Divine Lady of La Balbonera, and by an apparent miracle the train was saved. A painting of this crash hangs on the wall of Cajabamba's tiny, no-frills church. Basic wooden benches serve as pews, and a thatched roof and adobe walls shelter the interior of La Balbonera in darkness. Beyond the church to the left sits the large Laguna de Colta. While the lagoon is visible from the highway, there's also a small dirt road that meanders through several beautifully-framed rural villages to the backside of the lake. The backwoods route reveals charming rural settlements with Indian farmers working fields on the slopes of picturesque, clouded hills. The thousands of reeds growing out of the lagoon obscure the water from view; it's a surreal experience to watch the locals float through the reeds on their bamboo rafts. Eventually, after about a two and a half hour walk around the lagoon, the road bends back around to the highway (turn right at the end of the lake). There's a small store on the road where you can wait for buses back to Riobamba or forward to Guamote, both of which run until dark.

Guamote, about 45 minutes down the road, is a very high (alt. 3056m), very pretty town, but it's probably only worthwhile for the bustling and non-touristy Thursday market. The Riobamba-Alausí-Durán railway goes right by the basic *pensión* (s/10,000 per night) and a couple of restaurants.

Buses bound for Cajabamba, Laguna de Colta, and Guamote leave Riobamba from the area around Unidad Nacional and Bolivia every ½-hour, or as often as they fill up. More buses leave on Thursdays for Guamote's market.

■ Volcán Chimborazo

How fearful
And dizzy 'tis, to cast one's eyes so low!

—William Shakespeare, *King Lear*

Have you ever felt really, really tiny? Volcán Chimborazo (alt. 6310m) overwhelms even the most lordly with the powerful magnitude of nature and the relative helplessness of humanity. This dormant volcano is absolutely not to be missed if you're in the area. Topped by snow year-round, Chimborazo peeks above the clouds into the silence of space. The trip to the summit is breathtaking, due to both the unparalleled view and the lack of oxygen at these altitudes. Chimborazo's second refuge (alt. 5000m) offers stunning views as well, and can be reached in half a day, without any climbing experience, equipment, or extreme expense.

Superb scenery graces the ride to the rural *parrochia* of San Juan (s/1,500), the starting point for most trips up Chimborazo. *Comunas* and *caseríos*—tiny villages without any government administration—dot the fertile farmlands and the *cerros* (hills) in the shadow of Chimborazo. Tourists and local *indígenas* find each other equally foreign sights; schoolchildren in polychromatic shawls gape at visitors, and even the local cows stare. The rocky ascent passes through cloud forests lined with pines and then past tiny shrubs covering misty boulders, hills, and slopes. Suddenly, above the treeline, everything disappears—and only rocks, clouds, and snow remain. Clouds are a mixed blessing; while they curb visibility, they also add to the mystical wonder. Not surprisingly, Chimborazo was once believed to be the highest mountain in the world. Look further up than you imagine land could be, and there in the distance is the peak, enough to render anyone but an Everest-veteran speechless. Listen to the profound silence from this other-planetary position above all life.

A relatively cheap way to reach the second refuge is through the **Hotel Imperial** (tel. 960-429) in Riobamba. Tell them the night before, and they'll set you up with a driver who can take you on the two-hour trip to the 4800m-high Edward Whymper refuge. While you hike up to the second refuge, the driver will wait for a few hours, then take you back. The round trip runs s/35,000-45,000; trips generally leave at 7am and return between 1-2pm. Be careful climbing to the 5000m-high second refuge; though it's only an hour-long walk at most, it must be taken at a snail's pace. Frequent rest stops and water are a must, as your body will not be acclimatized to the altitude.

Going alone isn't the best idea; try to find a companion for the walk up, since it's always good to have a partner in case of emergency. The drive to Chimborazo can also be done by any 4WD taxi you find in Riobamba, or by guides arranged by any of the numerous but expensive travel agencies in town.

Most people stop at the second refuge, but experienced and adventurous climbers can take on the challenging ascent to Chimborazo's summit (a nine-hour ascent and four-hour descent at best). Though the summit does not have the highest altitude in the world, it is still the farthest point from the center of the earth due to the fact that the earth bulges at the equator. Crampons, ropes, and other standard climbing equipment are essential. Climbs leave at 1am from the second refuge, and a tour guide is a necessity; for information on guides see Mountain Climbing (p. 33). **Alta Montaña** (tel. 963-964 or 942-215), in Riobamba, can provide guides, but they're not cheap.

Both refuges on the mountain have basic food items and coffee, as well as tourist souvenirs (t-shirts s/22,000, postcards s/1,000). They also offer **sleep accommodations** (s/30,000)—but bring your own sleeping bag, and stock up on plenty of extra water and food. If you stay overnight at a refuge, arrange for the 4WD taxi to pick you up the next day (roundtrip around s/75,000). But beware—sleeping under a full moon high above civilization comes at a price. **Altitude sickness** can be a serious problem for those not acclimatized to heights above 3000m. For more information, see Hot, Cold, and High (p. 16).

Alausí

Alausí is a tranquil mountain stop in the central Sierra, where the general silence of the town's streets is disturbed only by the Sunday market and the regular chug-chugging of the train descending the "devil's nose" en route to Bucay. But with a towering, cloudy mountainside dominating everything, who has much to say anyway? At least the alpine overseer is a charismatic one, providing an amazing backdrop for Alausí's ancient buildings and sleepy streets. A beautiful setting and a slower pace of life make Alausí a worthy stop for weary travelers about to pick the devil's nose.

Orientation and Practical Information **Plaza Bolívar** and the **train station** are at the base of *el centro,* near Av. 5 de Junio and Sucre. It takes about five minutes to walk through the entire downtown area. The streets heading down the mountainside are Av. 9 de Octubre, De Loza, Ricaurti, and Sucre. Cross-streets are Bolívar, Villaluz, Av. 5 de Junio, and **García Moreno,** the main thoroughfare in town. **Buses** stop in the middle of Av. 5 de Junio between Av. 9 de Octubre and De Loza, and go to **Riobamba** (every 30min., 6am-6pm, 1½hr., s/9,000), **Quito** (2 per day, 5½hr., s/15,000), **Cuenca** (2 per day, 3hr., s/15,000), **Guayaquil** (3hr., s/15,000), and **Ambato** (every hr., 3hr., s/6,000). For **train** information, see The Riobamba-Alausí-Bucay-Durán Railway, p. 129. The basic **Farmacia Americano** sits under the Hotel Americano. Don't even try to make phone calls or mail anything from this small town. If you need **medical services,** you'd be better off heading up to Riobamba.

Accommodations and Food **Hotel Americano,** García Moreno 59 y Ricaurti (tel. 930-159), is located above the Farmacia Americano and run by the same management. In a town of unexciting hotel choices, this is probably the most appealing of the bunch. Clean and cozy rooms with wooden floors, street views, and good bathrooms cost only s/10,000 per person. The vista is more scenic from the balconies of the **Hotel Gampal** (tel. 930-138), on Av. 5 de Junio, but the private bathrooms are aging and the rugs unremarkable. Singles s/15,000; doubles s/24,000; triples s/30,000. Prices are lower off-season. **Hotel Panamericano,** near the bus stop on Av. 5 de Junio, may inspire a game of one-on-one with its parquet floors. Just be sure not to mess up the tidy rooms and well-washed sheets when dunking. Quality varies from room to room; ask for a bath with a gas shower instead of a dangerous electric one. S/10,000 per person with common bath. With bath: singles s/15,000; doubles s/25,000. The most appealing culinary choices in town are the hotel restaurants. Like the lodgings, the **Hotel Gampal Restaurant** (tel. 930-138), on Av. 5 de Junio, delivers the standard goods with minimal flair. *Corvina frita* s/6,500, *bistek* with fries, rice, and salad s/6,500 (open daily 7am-11pm). The **Hotel Panamericano Restaurant** has slightly cheaper meat entrees (s/3,500-6,000) and soups (s/2,000-4,000). Open daily 7:30am-9pm. Or eat under the stars while the buses whiz by at the **Parador Vera del Camino** (tel. 930-055), on the highway just past town. Climb up the steps to the highway, turn right, and walk five minutes. This late-night trucker stop makes its clientele feel comfortable with a choice of self- or full- (table) service. Fuel up on *almuerzo* (s/5,000) or *carne a la plancha* (s/6,000), indoors or out (open 10am-4pm).

■ The Riobamba-Alausí-Bucay-Durán Railway

The Riobamba-Alausí-Bucay-Durán Railway is one of the most exhilarating train rides in Ecuador, and the heart-racing stretch between Alausí and Bucay is the climax of the entire trip. A lengthy 464km, the line actually begins in Riobamba and snakes its way to the Guayaquil suburb of Durán. Some people go all the way; others, for lack of patience, only stick around for the quick thrills. From Riobamba, the train climbs along steep mountainsides and mounts the towering Andean cliffs, peaking at 3609m, then suddenly thrusting into the steamy jungle at Bucay. Many travelers ride on top of the train for the best views.

The tracks opened in 1908, but a large section between Guayaquil and Alausí was washed out by El Niño in 1983 and took 10 years to rebuild. In the first 26km, the train does nothing but build up altitude. Just before the **Sibambe** station, the tracks run straight into the rocky roadblock known as **El Nariz del Diablo (Devil's Nose),** where the train surmounts a perpendicular cliff by means of two amazing switchbacks—quite a feat of railroad acrobatics. In under 30km, it descends from 2347m to 1255m at the **Huigra** station. On each bend, heartstopping horseshoe twists and turns reveal magnificent views of the countryside. If you decide to get your adrenaline-rushing thrills on top of the train, be careful as there are no guard rails. Center your weight towards the middle of the train and hang on tight. Also try to get a car toward the rear to avoid the steam engine's constant spew of ash. Before you touch solid ground again, you'll have descended from snow-capped volcanoes and highland cloud forests to the sea-level, banana-growing tropics of the western lowlands.

Catch this famous train in **Riobamba** (Fri.-Mon., Wed., 6am; see Riobamba Practical Information: Trains, p. 122) or **Alausí** (Fri.-Mon., Wed., 9:30am). Arrive at least half an hour early to buy tickets. The train is unreliable, and the schedule often changes; don't plan your trip around its transportation. The uphill return trip from Durán is less popular (Sun., Tues., Thu., Sat., 6:25am). **Bucay** (also known as Gral. Elizalde) is not a pleasant place, and when the train arrives around 2-3pm, most catch the next bus to Riobamba, Guayaquil, or El Triunfo (for Cuenca). If you continue to Durán, you may arrive at night; ferries run to Guayaquil until 10pm. The total ride each way averages 12 hours, and depending on the length, costs US$8-12 for tourists. Yes, prices are in dollars, and you don't want to know how much less the locals pay.

■ Ingapirca

Ingapirca, or "Wall of the Inca," located two hours north of Cuenca just off the Panamerican Highway, is Ecuador's most notable Incan ruin site. Constructed over 500 years ago, the ruins are neither as impressive nor as important as those in Perú. But, set on a highland plain in the rural hills of the south central Sierra, they still make for a worthwhile daytrip from Cuenca or the nearby town of Cañar.

The **central structure** of the ruins is called the "Adoratorio," "Castillo," or "Temple of the Sun." Scholars speculate that this elliptical *usnu* platform was originally used to worship the sun, but may have had astronomical as well as religious uses. The impressively solid structure, 37.5m by 13.5m, is filled with small niches and windows. The **aposentos** (lodges) next to the Temple of the Sun were most likely used in the administration of Ingapirca's religious activity. Although the trapezoidal **plaza** is eroded almost to the ground, it still reveals a 20m by 10m building also believed to have been used for religious purposes. The **pilaloma** section to the extreme south of the complex has revealed the biggest collection of remnants from the **Cañari Indians,** who inhabited the area before the Incas. The **intihuayco, collcas** (circular receptacles for food), **incahurgana** (ceremonial spot), **bodega** (market), and many **stairways** are also worth checking out. The ruins are open daily 8am-5pm (admission s/12,000). There are free but not overly well-informed government-funded guides at the site.

There are two ways to get to Ingapirca by bus. One **direct bus** runs to Ingapirca from Cuenca's *terminal terrestre* (9am, 2hr., s/4,000). Alternatively, Cuenca buses leave more frequently to the town of **El Tambo,** on the Panamerican Highway between Cuenca and Riobamba (every hr., 6am-5pm, 2hr., s/3,000). From there, *camionetas* go to Ingapirca (every 45min., 7am-5pm, 1hr., s/2,000). For the return trip, there is sometimes a direct bus to Cuenca at 4:45pm. Otherwise, catch a *camioneta* back to El Tambo and flag down any bus traveling the Panamerican Highway. When visiting the ruins, it is good idea to bring enough food and water for the day, and don't plan on staying the night. One restaurant, **Posada Ingapirca,** is right at the ruins (tel. 838-508), but it aims to seat the well-off tourists willing to pay exorbitant prices for grub. Just down the road from the ruins, the small town of Ingapirca is home to **Señora Julia** and her basic chicken-and-rice restaurant.

Some visitors spend the night in the nearby colonial town of **Cañar,** south of El Tambo on the Panamerican Highway. While it may make a nice rest stop on the way to or from the ruins, there are better places to catch some shut-eye. The town itself has little of interest and only a sparse selection of hotels. Only one bus per day travels the rugged direct route to the ruins from the town plaza (6am, 45min., s/3,000), and is both less comfortable and more expensive than the normal route via El Tambo.

If a solo visit to Ingapirca sounds unappealing, several tour companies in Cuenca offer convenient but pricey daytrips that include transportation and more knowledgable guides. **Río Arriba Tours,** Hermano Miguel 7-14 y Pres. Córdova (tel. 840-031 or 883-711), charges s/115,000-135,000, depending on the number of people in the group (open Mon.-Fri. 9am-6pm, Sat. 9am-1pm). **Hualambari Tours,** Borrero 9-67 y Gran Colombia (tel. 842-693), charges s/115,000 per person, and **Santa Ana,** next to CETUR, charges s/120,000. There are several other tour companies as well, so it might be worth your while to shop around.

Azogues

Set in the rolling mountains north of Cuenca, **Azogues** (pop. 30,000) pales in comparison to its more cosmopolitan neighbor to the south when it comes to tourist-tempting attractions, but still radiates with charm. The humbly prosperous town and surrounding countryside are blessed with a number of saintly mountaintop churches, most notably Azogues's **Iglesia San Francisco** and neighboring Biblián's **Santuario de la Virgen Del Rocío.** The capital of the Cañar province, Azogues also hosts a bustling Saturday morning market and is a center of Ecuador's Panama hat industry (see Panama Hats are Not from Panamá, p. 182). So while it may not be the most visible shining star of southern Ecuador, Azogues does make a rewarding daytrip from Cuenca, an easy way to get a genuine glimpse of a busy but untouristed Ecuadorian city.

Orientation and Practical Information The **Panamerican Highway** doubles as **Av. 24 de Mayo** and forms the western boundary of town. The bus station is on Av. 24 de Mayo, two blocks north and two blocks west of the **main plaza.** The **market** is one block south of the plaza on Matovalle. Most activity centers around the plaza area at **Bolívar** and **Serrano.** The only *casa de cambios* in town is **Cambiara del Cañar** (tel. 241-925), on Bolívar between Sucre and Solano, with decent rates for cash or traveler's checks (open Mon.-Fri. 8:30am-1pm and 2:30-4:30pm, Sat. 8:30am-2:30pm). **Filanbanco** (tel. 240-332), on Bolívar and Sucre, will change traveler's checks but not cash (open Mon.-Fri. 9am-pm). **EMETEL** (tel. 240-590 or 240-515), at the corner of Bolívar and Serrano on the main plaza, dials national and international calls (open daily 8am-10pm). Numerous companies send out **buses** from the **terminal terrestre:** to **Biblián** (every 15min. during daylight or when full, 15min., s/400), **Santo Domingo** (5 per day, 7:45am-9:30pm), **Quito** (10 per day, 6:30am-11:30pm, 10hr.), **Loja**, and **Guayaquil** (10 per day, 7am-midnight, 6hr.) via **Cuenca. Super Taxis** also sends fancy buses to **Quito** (1:30pm and 10pm, 10hr.) and **Guayaquil** (12 per day, 5:30am-7pm, 6hr.) via **Cuenca** (1hr.). **Taxis** can be flagged anywhere in town, and the main office of "Cooperativa de Taxis Azogues" is on the main plaza (tel. 240-450). **Pharmacies** are all over town near the main plaza. The **Hospital Crespo** (tel. 240-600 or 240-502) heals across the river. The **emergency** number is tel. 101, and the **police** can be reached at tel. 240-289. The **post office** (tel. 240-380) is on Bolívar in the main plaza, across the street from the church (open Mon.-Fri. 8am-noon and 2:30-6pm, Sat. 8am-3pm). Azogues's **telephone code** is 07.

Accommodations and Food Though it's perhaps the best hotel in town, don't expect consistently cordial service at **Hotel Charles International** (tel. 241-210), on Serrano between Abad and Bolívar. Slide into the slippery wood-floored rooms and shining bathrooms through an airy, plant-covered lobby. S/20,000 per person. At the plain **Hotel Charles** (tel. 241-364), at Solano and Rivera, you lose that "international" flavor and save s/10,000. Clean sheets are the selling point of the very ordinary rooms (s/10,000 per person). The **Hostal Chicago,** Av. 3 de Noviembre 3-23 y Av. 24 de Mayo (tel. 241-040), captivated by the mobster image, tries to associate itself with the windy city. The rooms are clean and cool, the private baths acceptable, the water hot, and the whitewashed walls white. S/10,000 per person.

Restaurants in Azogues are two things: cheap and basic. Next-door neighbors **El Padrino** (the Godfather) and **El Gran Padrino** (the Great Godfather), Bolívar 60-11 between Sucre and Av. 3 de Noviembre (tel. 240-534), suffer from the same mafia obsession as Hotel Chicago. But where's the pasta? Both offer the same old traditional Ecuadorian menu, like *pollo* with potatoes and rice (s/6,000) and *caldo* (s/3,000). Open Mon.-Sat. 8am-9pm, Sun. 8am-10pm. Dripping with ferns, **Pollería 87,** at Av. 24 de Mayo and Av. 3 de Noviembre, serves chicken in an eclectic dining room with posters of Big Ben, the Golden Gate Bridge, horse pastures, and Jesus. *Pollo al jugo* s/7,000, *arroz con menestra y pollo frito* s/7,000 (open daily 8:30am-9:30pm).

Sights and Entertainment The **San Francisco Church** sprawls out over a hill to the southeast, and is visible from various places in town. A 45-minute climb pays off with a socks-knocking view of the surrounding hills and the town below. The ornate interior also delights the eyes. Down closer to sea level, Azogues's placid **main plaza** is a pleasant place to watch cool trees and kick back with a cup of coffee. A huge 1994 monument to Ecuador's working classes, **"El Trabajador,"** poses with mallet in hand. Though market day is Saturday, the fruity **main market** is active throughout the week. Azogues's nighttime entertainment leaves much to be desired. You might check out **Cine y Video Azogues** (no tel.), on Azuay between Bolívar and Ayacucho just east of the bus station. Movies, advertised in the main plaza and at the theater, are shown daily at 4:30pm (s/2,000) and 8:30pm (s/3,000).

Other than its inherent rural attractiveness, the nearby town of **Biblián** has one significant sight: the **Santuario de la Virgen del Rocío.** Its white turrets evoke images of fairy tale castles, and its steep hillside setting overlooking idyllic Biblián is the stuff postcards are made of. Biblián is a quiet, lonely town with virtually no tourists, so look forward to your shadow's company during the 45-minute haul up to the Santuario, past many isolated rural Andean huts and farms. At the top, you'll be treated to a panoramic view of the town and countryside. Nothing thrilling awaits inside the sanctuary, but drawer-type graves and an interestingly-shaped main chamber may pique your interest. If the walk up is not your speed, wait for the local *cooperativo* bus or pickup truck that occasionally travels the rough, steep road to the church. To get back to Azogues or Cuenca, flag down a bus along the Panamerican Highway; you may have to try awhile before one actually stops. Biblián is either a 10- to 15-minute bus ride from Azogues's *terminal terrestre* or a challenging, two-hour hilly walk.

Cuenca and the Southern Highlands

The southern tip of Ecuador's Sierra may be out of sight of the snow-capped peaks of the central *Cordillera de los Andes,* but the southern highlands' natural and architectural wonders leave little to be desired. The mild climates of alpine elevations cool their equatorial warmth, and the cloud cover that results lends a distracting, mystical quality to each of the bumpy bus rides on unpaved cliff-hanging roads (and there are *plenty*). Cosmopolitan yet charmingly colonial, Cuenca, the most brilliantly shining star of the region, is one of Ecuador's most bucolic environs, the nation's only true *city* that carries out all of its important business in its historic colonial center—and this in the shadow of the most beautiful cathedral in the country. Only a few hours away, the rugged cloud forest and alpine lakes of windy El Cajas mark the territory just before the western ridge of the Andes. Even farther south, Loja, smaller and more *tranquilo* than its northern neighbor, sprawls over a highland plain carved into a narrow valley; the "gateway to the Oriente" (a breathtaking two-hour ride from Zamora) is also a gateway to Vilcabamba, the sacred valley of longevity, and to Parque Nacional Podocarpus's wondrous mountain cloud forests. The ruins at Ingapirca—Ecuador's largest Inca site—call the southern highlands home as well, though veterans of travel through Perú will be less than stunned.

More interesting are the living villages and market towns that are to be found not far from the southern highlands' urban centers; they have all the charm of the Ecuadorian Sierra yet greater *tranquilidad* than northern tourist hotspots like Otavalo. The rolling, clouded countryside provides a perfect backdrop for lonesome strolls through silent thatched-hut villages like Biblián. But the southwestern ridge of the Andes range—as seen from the routes that descend from Cuenca and Alausí to the coast (El Triunfo and Guayaquil)—is home to the most spectacular scenery in all Ecuador. Roads and train tracks alike descend almost 3000m, hugging cliffs and deep ravines as they pass thorugh innumerable vegetation zones, from mountain *páramo* to coastal jungle wetlands, dipping into layer after layer of misty cloud cover en route to their muggy destinations. Gaping tourists scramble to keep their weight in the center of the passenger car as they strain to keep from falling off the top of the steam train that traverses *"El Nariz del Diablo"* from Alausí to Bucay. Thankfully, the view is too fantastic to worry seriously about matters mortal.

Cuenca

Ecuador's third-largest city, Cuenca (pop. 300,000) sits in the Guapondélig Valley (alt. 2530m), at the heart of southern highland culture and the hub of several wonderfully scenic roads. Once a prosperous indigenous city worthy of its original Cañari name, *Tomebamba* ("plain as big as heaven"), the city was more plain than heavenly by the time the Spanish arrived. When Gil Ramirez Dávalos re-founded Cuenca in 1557, the mysteriously deserted Tomebamba already lay in ruins, saving the Spanish the trouble of doing it themselves. Today, cobblestone streets, wrought-iron balconies, a famed cathedral, and ornate stone buildings ooze colonial influence. Unlike Quito, Cuenca is not a city divided between old and new, a temporal harmony central to its charm.

A lively locale bursting from the banks of the Río Tomebamba, cosmopolitan Cuenca offers travelers tasteful brown-roofed buildings, raging nightlife, and some of the finest international restaurants and museums in Ecuador. Life in this cultural mecca revolves around the old colonial center, Parque Calderón, where a beautiful, blue-domed cathedral towers over tree-lined benches. Despite it's relatively cool climate (average year-round temperature of 15°C), Cuenca is an artistic hotbed, nurturing communities of artisans renowned for their baskets, shawls, and Panama hats.

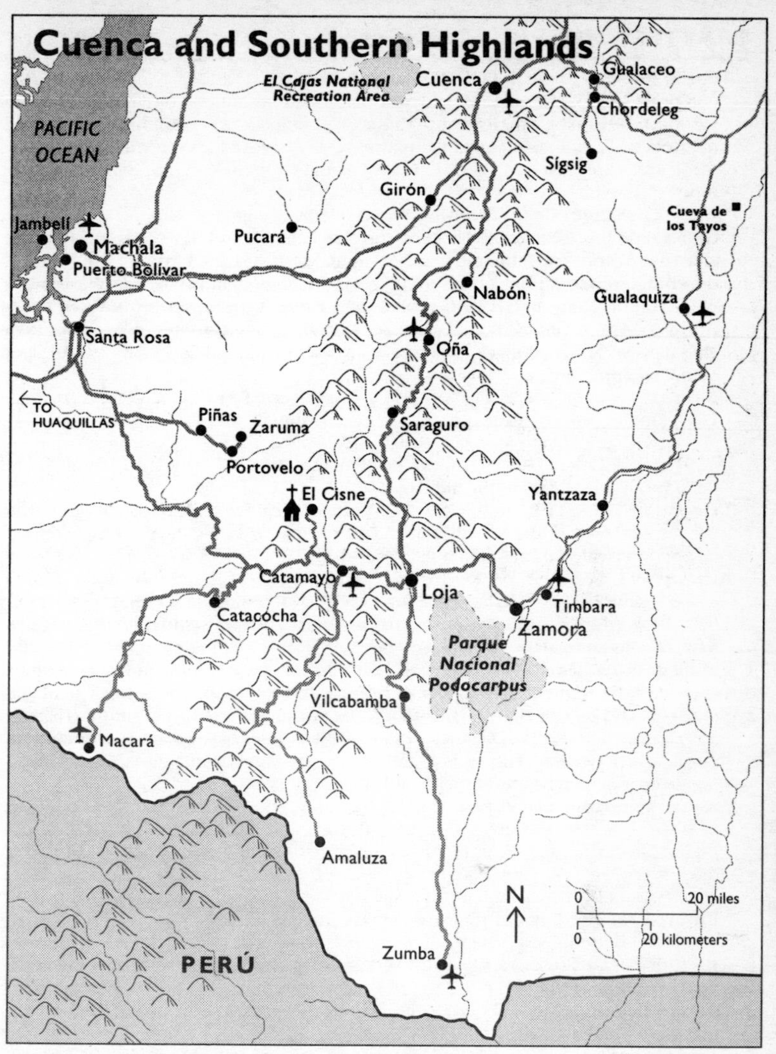

Cuenca's grace and charisma are powerful enough to overcome even its terrible traffic, a sure sign that even the most devoutly anti-urban travelers run the risk of falling under its spell.

ORIENTATION

Most of Cuenca's activity transpires in the area framed by **Mariscal Lamar, Honorato Vasquez, Tarqui,** and **Mariano Cueva.** The **Río Tomebamba** flows through town south of *el centro,* parallel to Calle Larga, and its grassy banks look anything but citified. Another respite from everything urban, **Parque Calderón** lies at the heart of the colonial center. The **terminal terrestre** is a 20-minute walk, s/4,000 taxi, or s/400 bus ride northeast of *el centro.*

PRACTICAL INFORMATION

Tourist Information: CETUR, Hemano Miguel 686 y Presidente Córdova (tel. 822-058 or 839-337), offers helpful advice, maps, and brochures (open Mon.-Fri. 8am-5:30pm). **INEFAN,** on Hermano Miguel and Bolívar, is the administrative headquarters of Ecuador's 14 national nature reserves. Provides information on all of these areas and gives maps of El Cajas (p. 141). Open Mon.-Fri. 8am-4:30pm, at times sporadically.

Money Exchange: Casa Cambios Yaz (tel. 833-434 or 832-795), on Cordero and Gran Colombia. Changes dollars and traveler's checks and has Western Union service (open Mon.-Fri. 9am-1pm and 3-5:30pm, Sat. 9am-12:30pm).

Currency Exchange: Banks are abundant in the center of town. **Filanbanco** (tel. 813-322), on Sucre between G. Torres and Padre Aguirre, **Banco La Previsora** (tel. 831-444), at Gran Colombia and Benigno Malo, and **Banco del Pacífico,** Benigno Malo 9-75, which gives MasterCard advances, are among the largest. All open Mon.-Fri. 9am-6pm, Sat. 9am-1pm.

Consulates: Colombia, L. Cordero 955 y Pasaje Hortencia Mata, 2nd floor (tel. 830-185). Open Mon.-Fri. 9am-1pm and 3-6pm. **Chile,** Tomás Ordoñez 327 (tel. 831-383 or 830-529). Open Mon.-Fri. 8:30am-12:30pm and 2:30-6:30pm.

Immigration Office: (tel. 831-020), on Benigno Malo between Juan Jaramillo and Calle Largo (open 8am-noon and 2-6pm).

Telephones: EMETEL, on Benigno Malo and Mariscal Sucre, less than 1 block from Parque Calderón, offers free MCI and AT&T calling-card calls and expensive domestic and international calls (open daily 8am-10pm).

Airport: (tel. 862-203), on Av. España, 15min. north of the city by taxi (s/3,000-4,000) or bus (s/250). Flights leave from the early morning until around 6pm (open 6am-1pm and 3-6pm). For reservations, go to the individual airline offices. **SAETA,** Benigno Malo 727 (tel. 839-090; fax 835-113), in Edificio El Galeón, next to the main cathedral. **TAME** (tel. 827-609, airport tel. 862-193), at Gran Colombia and Hermano Miguel, Pasaje Nieto Hermanos. **American Airlines,** Herman Miguel 8-67 (tel. 831-699 or 827-134). **LACSA,** Gran Colombia 12-18 y Tarqui (tel. 837-360). TAME flights out of Cuenca head to **Quito** (1 per day, US$86.50), **Guayaquil** (Mon.-Fri., 1 per day, US$64.50), and smaller national destinations. International flights generally head out of Quito and Guayaquil only.

Buses: The **terminal terrestre** (tel. 842-023), on España, is northwest of the center of town. It is a bit difficult to get to and from, and a taxi (s/3,000-4,000) may be preferable to the local buses (s/200), which are horribly overcrowded and don't go directly between *el centro* and the *terminal.* A huge number of bus companies operate out of Cuenca, and most passengers arbitrarily gravitate toward whomever happens to be yelling out their destination. If comfort is important to you, get on one of the better buses (usually the long-distance ones), even if you're only going a short distance. **Turismo Oriental** serves **Guayaquil** (every 40min., 1am-11pm, 5hr., s/15,000), **Quito** (6 per day, 7:30am-8:45pm, 10hr., s/25,000), **Macas** (5 per day, 10am-9pm, 13hr., s/23,000), and **Zamora** (9am, 7hr.). **Transportes Loja** has beautiful, brand-new Mercedes-Benz buses to **Loja** (noon, 5, 10pm, 5hr., s/15,000) via **Saraguro** (3½hr., s/10,000). **Express Sucre** goes to **Machala** (10 per day, 6am-6:45pm, 4hr., s/9,000), **Santo Domingo** (7:15am, 2:30, 7:30pm), and **Milagro** (1 per day, 5pm). **Azuay** buses go to the Peruvian border at **Huaquillas** (5 per day, 5:45am-11:30pm, 7hr., s/18,000).

Car Rental: Cuenca Rent-a-Car (tel. 825-318), at Pres. Cordova and Av. Huayna Capac, is affiliated with Budget. Charges an all-inclusive s/88,000 per day for the cheapest cars and s/160,000 per day for larger cars (open Mon.-Fri. 8am-noon and 2:30-6:30pm, Sat. 8am-noon). **Internacional Rent-a-Car,** Av. República 221 y Huayna Capac (tel. 801-892). **Oro-Rent** (tel. 831-200), on Av. Ordoñez Lazo at Hotel Oro Verde. **Localiza Rent-a-Car,** Av. España 14-85 (tel. 828-962).

Markets: Plaza Rotary, in the Machuca and Sangurima area northeast of *el centro,* hosts a huge market favored among locals, selling everything from animals to watches to clothing. A smaller, livestock-less market specializing in clothing and weaving dwells next to the Hotel Milan, at Pres. Córdova and Aguirre.

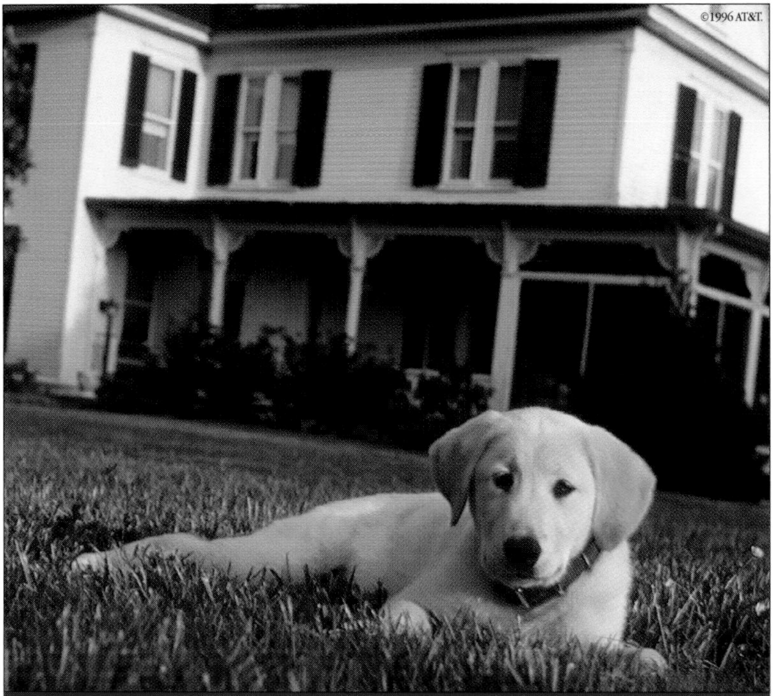

Photo: R. Olken

Greetings from LET'S GO

With pen and notebook in hand, a change of clothes in our backpack, and the tightest of budgets, we've spent our summer roaming the globe in search of travel bargains.

We've put the best of our research into the book that you're now holding. Our intrepid researcher-writers went on the road for months of exploration, from Anchorage to Angkor, Estonia to Ecuador, Iceland to India. Editors worked from spring to fall, massaging copy into witty and informative prose. A brand-new edition of each guide hits the shelves every fall, just months after it is researched, so you know you're getting the most reliable, up-to-date, and comprehensive information available.

We try to make this book an indispensable companion, but sometimes the best discoveries are the ones you make on your own. If you've got something to share, please drop us a line. We're Let's Go Publications, 67 Mount Auburn Street, Cambridge, MA 02138 USA (e-mail: fanmail@letsgo.com). Good luck and happy travels!

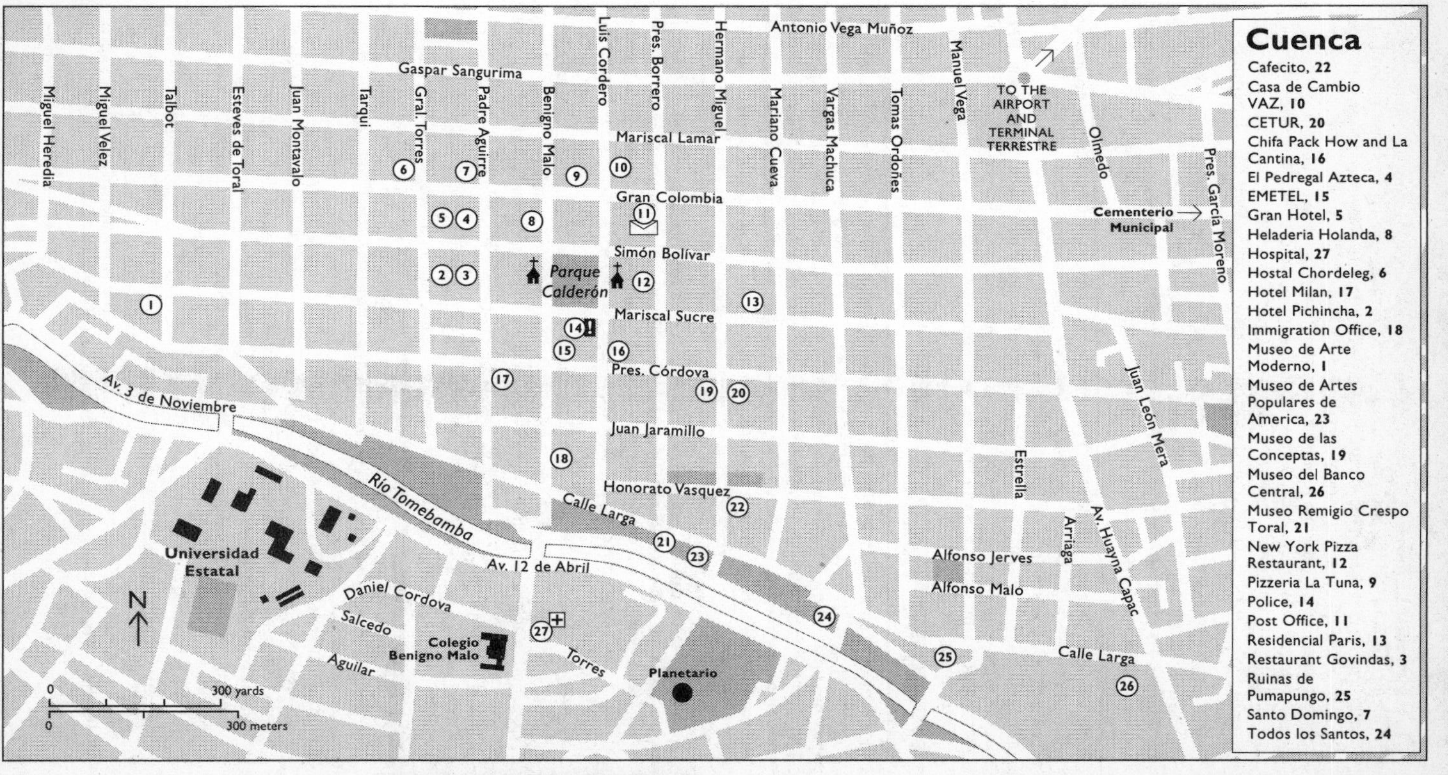
Cuenca
Cafecito, 22
Casa de Cambio VAZ, 10
CETUR, 20
Chifa Pack How and La Cantina, 16
El Pedregal Azteca, 4
EMETEL, 15
Gran Hotel, 5
Heladeria Holanda, 8
Hospital, 27
Hostal Chordeleg, 6
Hotel Milan, 17
Hotel Pichincha, 2
Immigration Office, 18
Museo de Arte Moderno, 1
Museo de Artes Populares de America, 23
Museo de las Conceptas, 19
Museo del Banco Central, 26
Museo Remigio Crespo Toral, 21
New York Pizza Restaurant, 12
Pizzeria La Tuna, 9
Police, 14
Post Office, 11
Residencial Paris, 13
Restaurant Govindas, 3
Ruinas de Pumapungo, 25
Santo Domingo, 7
Todos los Santos, 24
Antonio Vega Muñoz
Gaspar Sangurima
Miguel Heredia
Miguel Velez
Talbot
Esteves de Toral
Juan Montavalo
Tarqui
Gral. Torres
Padre Aguirre
Benigno Malo
Luis Cordero
Pres. Borrero
Hermano Miguel
Mariano Cueva
Vargas Machuca
Tomas Ordoñes
Manuel Vega
TO THE AIRPORT AND TERMINAL TERRESTRE
Olmedo
Pres. García Moreno
Cementerio Municipal
Mariscal Lamar
Gran Colombia
Simón Bolívar
Parque Calderón
Mariscal Sucre
Pres. Córdova
Juan Jaramillo
Honorato Vasquez
Calle Larga
Av. 3 de Noviembre
Río Tomebamba
Av. 12 de Abril
Juan León Mera
Estrella
Arriaga
Av. Huayna Capac
Alfonso Jerves
Alfonso Malo
Calle Larga
Universidad Estatal
N
Daniel Cordova
Salcedo
Aguilar
Colegio Benigno Malo
Torres
Planetario
0
300 yards
0
300 meters

Laundromat: Lavamás, Honorato Vásquez and Vargas Machuca (open Mon.-Fri. 8am-noon and 2-6pm, Sat. 8am-noon). **La Química,** Borrero 7-34 y Cordova (tel. 823-945 or 831-125). Not cheap, but same-day dry cleaning service offered (open Mon.-Fri. 8am-noon and 2-6pm, Sat. 8am-12:30pm).

Pharmacy: Local pharmacies work on the rotating *de turno* schedule, so one of them is always open 24hr. The schedule is published in *El Mercurio,* the local newspaper. **Farmacia International,** on Gran Colombia between Luis Cordero and Pres. Borrero, is large and centrally located (open Mon.-Fri. 8am-noon and 2:30-7pm, Sat. 8am-noon).

Hospital: Clínica Santa Ines, Av. Córboda Toral 2-113 y Av. Cueva (tel. 817-888), on the far side of the river, just south of Av. 12 de Abril. **Clínica Santa Ana,** Av. Manuel J. Calle 1-104 (tel. 814-068), southeast of the river, near Av. 12 de Abril and Calle Paucarbamba. Look for it behind the monument to José Peralta.

Emergency: tel. 101.

Police: The **Central Office** is on Pres. Córdova and Luis Cordero. Report crimes and stolen items to **OID** *(Organización de Investigación del Delito),* (tel. 831-041), on Benigno Malo and Torres, south of the river.

Post Office: (tel. 840-271), on the corner of Borrero and Gran Colombia. **EMS** (Express Mail Service), for expensive 3-day international mail, is next door. Both are open Mon.-Fri. 8am-6pm and Sat. 9am-1pm.

Telephone Code: 07.

ACCOMMODATIONS

Hotel pricing in Cuenca is a tricky business. Though accommodations are on the expensive side, at least by Ecuadorian standards, don't just make a mad dash for the cheapest place around. For only a few more sucres, hotel quality shoots up drastically. Avoid ritzy hotels in town unless you absolutely need their amenities: they charge tourists twice as much as locals (yes, it's legal), and they're not that outstanding for the price. For **camping** options, see Jaime at the Pizzeria (see Food, below).

Hotel Milan, Córdova 989 y Padre Aquirre (tel. 835-351), in the center of town. Rooms vary in quality, but if you strike it rich, you're living the good life. Live it up in commodious comfort with phone, color TV, and hot-water bath with wooden fold-out doors. Gaze lazily over your balcony into the noisy chaotic local market. But ask to see your room first, as there's not a pot of gold in every one. A good bargain at s/20,000.

Cafecito, Honorato Vasquez 7-36 y Hermano Miguel, is a classic *gringo* hangout. You won't find many Ecuadorians at this shared-room hostel, but you will find washed, warm, and well-decorated rooms with 3 or 4 beds. Bathrooms are as good as shared ones can get. Romantic café in an open-air covered courtyard below (see Food, below). S/15,000 per person per night.

Gran Hotel, Gral. Torres 9-20 y Bolívar (tel. 831-934 or 841-113). While the rooms offer everything a weary traveler could need, like private baths, color TVs, and lots of space, the real excitement emanates from the indoor courtyard. Festooned with bizarre, out-of-place trees and ferns, the yard can brighten a cloudy Cuenca day. Singles s/15,000, with bath s/25,000; doubles s/30,000, with bath s/40,000. Breakfast included.

Hostal Chordeleg, Gran Colombia 1115 y Gral. Torres (tel. 824-611 or 822-536). If you're going to spend a bit more, this would be a good way to do it. Everything looks so perfect, you might not even want to touch the lacquered-wood railings, the beautiful, fountained center courtyard, or your immaculate room with exhilaratingly comfortable beds, private bath, phone, and color TV. Choose between balconied street room or inner one. S/30,000 per person. Breakfast included.

Hotel Pichincha, Gral. Torres 8-82 y Bolívar (tel. 823-868). Dirt-cheap but dirt-free for strict penny-pinchers. For precious few sucres, settle down in the center of town. Only small sinks, mirrors, and large, clean-sheeted beds break up the whiteness of the walls. Sketchy toilet seats make electric hot-water bathrooms less-than-inviting. Friendly common lounges on each floor have huge Trinitron TVs. S/13,000 per person.

Residencial Paris, also known as **Hotel Paris,** Sucre 6-78 y Borrero (tel. 842-118 or 827-978). Don't be put off by the prison-gray corridors and their ghostly echo—they lead to simple but tasteful rooms. The better rooms have private baths, hot water, black-and-white TVs, and rugs (singles s/18,000; doubles s/32,000). Or save sucres and skip out on the TV and rug (singles s/16,000; doubles s/30,000). Go for it. Bust the extra s/2,000.

FOOD

With its attractive and diverse array of delectable diners, Cuenca is a great place to cure some hunger pangs. From the ubiquitous *almuerzo* stops with their traditional budget lunches, to the costly world-class cuisine at **El Jardín,** Cuenca satisfies even the most selective of stomachs. As usual, **panaderías** and **pastelerías** are the cheapest stomach-stuffers around, with tasty croissants *(canchos)* for a measly s/100. Pastry and candy vendors pack the sidewalks of Parque Calderón selling every sweet under the sun for a smattering of sucres.

Raymipampa Café-Restaurante, Benigno Malo 8-59 (tel. 827-435). This lively room, as bouncy as its name, absolutely hops with *gringos* and the local bourgeoisie. The view onto the Plaza Calderón complements the casual, coffee-shop feel. Enjoy scrumptious dinner *crepes* (chicken and mushroom s/6000, vegetarian s/4,500) and delectable cream soups (s/2,500), along with the requisite 3-course *almuerzo* (s/6,000). Open Mon.-Fri. 8:30am-11pm, Sat.-Sun. 9:30am-11pm.

Pizzeria La Tuna, Gran Colombia 880 y Benigno Malo (tel. 831-620). The delicious pizza smell draws both *gringos* and locals like moths to a mozzarella flame. House specialties include 'kabobs (s/6,300-6,500), *trucha la tuna* (trout with potatoes, ham, and cheese, s/1,900), and of course, pizza (medium s/18,000). Jaime Delgado, the friendly owner, offers advice to tourists and has a local campground (s/9,000 per night, including equipment). Inquire at the restaurant (open Mon.-Sat. 11am-11pm).

New York Pizza Restaurant, Borrero 8-38 between Bolívar and Sucre (tel. 842-792). A thin-crusted, tomato-coated break from traditionally thick, sauceless Latin American pizza. But New York pizza comes with inflated New York prices: large pies s/20,000-28,000, slices s/3,000, calzones s/3,500 (open Mon.-Sat. 10am-11pm, Sun. 10am-10pm).

El Pedregal Azteca, Gran Colombia 10-29 y Padre Aguirre (tel. 823-652), dishes out some of the best Mexican food in Ecuador. No bargain basement, but authentic *enchiladas* (s/11,000) and *burritos* (s/15,000) accompanied by ice-cold Pilseners (s/3,500) are well worth the price. Be prepared to dine in relative solitude, however—beyond the means of many locals, this dark, romantic setting can be sparsely populated.

Restaurant Govindas (no tel.) on Sucre behind the huge cathedral in Parque Calderón. Krishna consciousness Ecuadorian-style. Scrumptious and healthy vegetarian food, served by the local Hindu contingent, satisfies your hunger and your soul. Meditate on a bountiful vegetarian *almuerzo*, with fruit, cooked vegetable entrees, soup, and a yogurt drink (s/4,500). Open Mon.-Sat. 8:30am-6pm.

Chifa Pack How, Presidente Córdova 772 y Cordero. As with many spectator events, patrons of this Chinese joint have to pay a little extra for the chance to watch dinner swimming in cloudy, pre-death fish tanks in the window. Popular with the wealthier local crowd for its tasty fare (entrees s/9,000-12,000) and late hours (open daily 11am-3pm and 6pm-midnight).

Hostal Chordeleg Restaurant, Gran Colombia 1115 y General Torreo (tel. 824-611 or 822-536). Perfect for a cheap and convenient date, the hostel transforms into a romantic outdoor restaurant complete with courtyard tables, stone fountains, and a surprisingly reasonable menu. Filet mignon with mushrooms s/8,500, shrimp *al ajillo* s/7,500, *cordon bleu* s/8,000 (open 7am-11pm).

Cafecito, Honorato Vasquez 7-36 y Hermano Miguel (no tel.), serves up cheap food to hungry *gringos* in a straight-forwardly charming atmosphere: candles, outdoor tables, a courtyard, and the like. Daily special (usually vegetarian) s/5,000, *burrito* s/4,000, *sopa del día* s/2,000. Diners are enticed to wash dinner down with distinctively uncheap cocktails (*piña colada* s/7,000). Open daily 10am-10pm.

Restaurante Madre Tierra, Gran Colombia 14-35 between Talbot and Esteres de Toral (tel. 810-292). Just opened in June 1996, Madre Tierra is definitely a restaurant of the 90s. All-natural vegetarian victuals made with "safe, pure, and disinfected" fruits and vegetables. Meet scores of other health-conscious locals enjoying a cheap multi-course *merienda* (s/5,000) or *almuerzo* (s/5,000) in the attractive 2nd floor eating area (open Mon.-Sat. 8am-8pm).

SIGHTS

Though the area's most compelling sights are out of town—at Turi, Ingapirca, Baños, Biblián, and the nearby markets—Cuenca offers more diversions than simply fine dining. Rather than propagate gluttonous foreigners, the metropolis has begun to develop a more recreational tourist industry. With a booming *artesanía* community and almost too many museums to count on your fingers, Cuenca serves up cultural offerings as well as culinary ones. Fun-lovers also flock to Cuenca's two preeminent annual festivals. During the **El Septenario** (Corpus Christi) celebration in early June, the main plaza explodes with fireworks, music, and dancing. Drinks like the cinnamon- and *aguardiente*-filled *caneliza* help the Cuencans let loose for unusual games of chance and wild matches of the ever-popular foosball. The **Pase del Niño** festival on the Saturday before Christmas features fantastic and surreal parades celebrating the upcoming holiday.

Museums

Cuenca puts its museums where its mouth is, with enough galleries to support the city's claim to cultural significance and prove its sophistication. Founded in 1947, **Museo Remigio Crespo Toral** (tel. 830-499), at Calle Larga and Borrero, honors that eponymous Cuenca poet with unrhymed exhibits of miscellaneous historical items (open Mon.-Fri. 8am-4pm). **Museo del Banco Central** (tel. 831-255), at Calle Larga and Huayna Cápac, outside of the center of town at the ruins of Pumapungo, banks on drawing interested visitors with artifacts and archeological displays relating to the Incan civilization that once set up its accounts here. The museum also organizes children's events and art shows (open Tue.-Fri. 9am-6pm, Sat.-Sun. 10am-1pm; admission s/4,000). Just as Cuenca has more than one set of ruins, so does it have multiple museums to honor them. The **Todos los Santos** ruins support the next-door **Museo de Sitio de la Casa de la Cultura "Manuel Agustín Landivar"** (tel. 832-639), on Calle Larga and Manuel Vega, and its archeological exhibits. There's even a library to answer those more esoteric post-museum questions (open Mon.-Fri. 8am-noon and 2-6pm). For those who just can't get enough of those ancient *indígenas,* **Museo de las Culturas Aborígenes,** Av. 10 de Agosto 4-70 y J.M. Sánchez (tel. 811-706), sports an array of Cañari and Incan artifacts. Though the museum is a little out of the way in Ciudadela Santa Anita, it's accessible by a cheap taxi ride (open Mon.-Fri. 8:30am-12:30pm and 2:30-6:30pm, Sat. 8:30am-12:30pm; admission s/6,000).

But Cuenca's claim to cultural fame doesn't rely exclusively on the remains of the dead. Several museums promote livelier local arts and crafts. Founded in 1982, the **Museo de Arte Moderno,** on Calle Sucre and Col. Talbot., operating in the ancient House of Temperance, displays local modern art and hosts the *Biennial Internacional de Pintura* (open Mon.-Fri. 9am-1pm and 3-6pm, Sat. 9am-noon). **Instituto Azuayo de Folklore,** Cordero 7-22 y Presidente Córdova, third floor (open Mon.-Fri. 9am-6pm), and **Museo de Artes Populares de America** (tel. 828-878), on Larga and Hermano Miguel (open Mon.-Fri. 9:30am-1pm and 2:30-6pm, Sat. 9am-1pm), exhibit fascinating arrays of local and regional *artesanía.* El Instituto also runs programs to support Cuencan artisan traditions. For art with religious sensibilities, there's **Museo de las Conceptas,** on Hermano Miguel between Pres. Córdova and Jaramillo (tel. 830-625), in the 400-year old Monastery of the Immaculate Conception. Explore Catholic mysteries as you peruse pious art and Guayasamín lithographs (open Mon. 2:30-5:30pm, Tue.-Fri. 9am-5pm, Sat. 10am-1pm; admission s/5,000).

Churches

Cuenca's two most striking churches face each other across Parque Calderón in the heart of town. Built in 1557, the **Iglesia de Sagrario (Old Cathedral)** is rarely open nowadays, but back in the 18th century, it was the toast of the town. In 1739, a French geodesic mission used the cathedral's spire to measure the curvature of the recently unflattened earth. But out with the old and in with the new—across the street, the massively exquisite **Catedral de la Immaculada Concepción (New Cathedral)** towers over Parque Calderón and glows spookily by night. Designed by Obispo Miguel León Garrido but actualized by the German Juan (Johannes) Stiehle in 1885, the cathedral is one of the most recognized churches in Ecuador. Its ornate domes and brick face cover a cavernous marble interior, where brilliant angles of sunlight enter through the various windows and radiate off a four-column gold-leaf canopy. Another church, **Todos Los Santos,** on Larga and Machuca south of *el centro,* was the site of Cuenca's first outdoor mass. **Santo Domingo,** on Gran Colombia and Padre Aguirre, rose up along with the city in the 16th century.

ENTERTAINMENT

La Cantina, at Borrero and Córdova, serves beers to Cuenca's bourgeoisie (in a glass of course, s/3,000). After catching a few mellifluous notes and sneaking a peek into the beautiful, wood-paneled room lined with musical instruments, Andean-music lovers might want to stay, but proletariat wallets will not. Piping-hot *caneliza* (made with *aguardiente,* a local-firewater) s/3,000. Open daily 5pm-1am. Though not as enchanting as La Cantina across the street, **Picadilly Bar,** Borrero 7-46 y Pres. Córdova, has more of a no-frills, laid back, working-class feel, with lanterns and a pool table in back. Drinks still cost an arm and a leg, though. Bloody Marys s/6,400, beers s/2,800. Active weekends and weeknights alike (open daily 5pm-1am).

A haven for the performing arts, **Teatro Casa de la Cultura,** on Cordero and Sucre, shows movies and houses local events like *mariachi* concerts. **Cine 9 de Octubre,** at Cuerva and Lamar, and **Teatro Cuenca,** at Padre Aguirre between Lamar and Gran Colombia, advertise their cinematic screenings in *El Mercurio,* the local paper available all over town. The first of the daily double features starts 2:30pm, and the second film begins around 7:30pm. Admission is s/3,500 for all shows, good for both halves of a double feature.

■ Near Cuenca

MIRADOR TURI

Nobody navigates Cuenca better than the birds, and from Turi, a treacherously high lookout spot 4km south of the city center, you can experience that avian outlook as only the high-fliers do. A spine-breaking, 15-minute bus ride up a steep, pothole-ridden road pays off at the top, with a breathtaking panoramic view of all of Cuenca and its surrounding mountains. It looks like a map of the city laid out in front of you: closest are more remote rivers, while farther north flows the Río Tomebamba. The stadium and the city center, with the Old Cathedral's blue-and-white domes, are both clearly visible. A cartographic tiled painting of the city matches the view and provides a guide to the scenery. Pay-binoculars let you look closer (s/1,000). Even El Cajas Recreation Area inches its way into the view, in a notch to your left looking down. Turi is actually a little town of its own; sharing the hill are a quiet blue church, an orphanage, a few small grocery stores, and stairs that lead even further up the hill, past Virgin statues, to a radio tower. Charmingly-painted city scenes of children curiously adorn many of the tiny town's outside adobe walls. Turi attracts both local and foreign visitors, and it seems that only tourists break its silence.

Getting up to Turi means taking either a bus or a cab. The buses leave from Av. 12 de Abril and Fray V. Solamo, south of the river (every 3hr., 7:30am-4:30pm, s/250). Facing the river, wait on the right side of the wide Fray V. Solamo near the intersection. A taxi up is a more comfortable ride, but costs s/4,000-5,000. Getting down means waiting for the next bus (similar schedule) or catching one of the numerous cabs that drive by. Walking it one or both ways is also possible—allow about two hours for the climb and at least an hour for the descent.

THE MARKETS OF GUALACEO AND CHORDELEG

Every Sunday, the center of activity in the Cuenca area shifts. The weekly markets in these two tiny villages east of Cuenca draw in bargain-hunters from neighboring mountain towns and even more rural settlements. Indians from highland farms come to town to make their living for the week. Not only do they sell goods, but they barter and trade in exchanges of mutual respect between people whose foremost goal is to feed their children each night. Despite the outsiders who frequently discover these villages, the markets manage to maintain their local flavor and richness.

The market at **Gualaceo** is the most tantalizing taste-bud temptation around. The **main market** lies diagonally across from the town square. From the bus station, head down Cordero and turn right on Cuenca, or better yet, follow the herd. Only a couple of tourists can be spotted among the teeming masses of fruit- and vegetable-hawking vendors. Rows of outdoor eateries, selling every part of the pig but the squeal, make up a meat-lover's paradise. Whole pigs on spits, skewered with their heads at attention and ears pricked up, get ripped apart by numerous hands. Vendors drip flavorful pig fat onto delicious *llapingachos* (potato and cheese cakes, s/200) and talented chefs whip even those hard-to-find pork parts into culinary wonders. Try grilled stomach *(guatita)* or hoof soup *(caldo de pata)*... if you dare. If the vendor has washed hands (look for rags and soap) and the victuals are boiled and aren't surrounded by flies, then the food's probably fit for consumption. The **indoor food market,** toward the bus station on Cuenca, might look cleaner. Remember not to partake of any water, ice, or raw fruits and veggies (unless peeled), as tempting as they may be. The prices don't do anything to detract from the allure. Everything is cheap; a multi-course *almuerzo* for over s/3,000 is unheard of. Non-food items lurk around the edges of the market. Practical goods from watches to toothbrushes to Panama hats abound, but don't look for baskets and shawls of the tourist variety—that's not what locals come for.

If you must eat outside the market (you're not scared, are you?), **El Gran Chaparral** and **Santa Barbara** restaurants, across the street from each other at the *terminal terrestre,* both get high marks with the locals for their s/3,000-s/4,000 *almuerzos* (open daylight hours). Near the charming central park, **Bar-Restaurant Don "Q,"** at Av. 9 de Octubre and Gran Colombia, aims for more ambience than other restaurants in town, with an indoor, skylit courtyard and hanging plants. Entrees run around s/ 6,000 (open until 7pm). An acceptable place to stay, **Residencial Gualaceo** (tel. 255-006), on Gran Colombia, is one block from the main plaza (away from the market). Nondescript rooms have decent private baths, clean enough for a night's slumber. Lounge on a communal balcony out back. S/10,000 per person. The **Museo Artesanal de Gualaceo,** 1km south of Gualaceo off the highway toward Chordeleg, displays local artists' work. **Buses** from Gualaceo go to **Cuenca** (every 15min., 5am-7pm) and continue on to **Azogues** or **El Triunfo** and **Machala.** Don't just get on a Cuenca bus; buy tickets at the window beforehand. To get to Gualaceo, catch the bus at Cuenca's *terminal terrestre* (every hr., 6am-6pm, 2hr., s/2,500).

While Gualaceo's market specializes in the daily necessities, the market at **Chordeleg** has a lock on the luxuries. The main plaza is absolutely studded with **jewelry stores,** sparkling with good deals thanks to all the competition. Some artisan goods are also sold on the main plaza, but the best pottery shops, including the large and upscale **Centro de Artesanías,** are outside the center of town, toward Gualaceo on the main road. Everything in the smaller Chordeleg is quieter than in Gualaceo, including the **market.** While the plaza is generally silent, a little more activity goes on a few blocks down at the **market,** a small-scale version of Gualaceo. A modern **church** is on the main plaza. To the right, facing the church, three decent **comedores** of the local variety spoon out chow. The small but information-packed **Museo Communidad** is on the plaza diagonally across from the church.

Most **buses** heading back to **Gualaceo** and on to **Cuenca** or **Sigsig** leave across from the market (every 10min.). Buses depart for Chordeleg from Gualaceo's *terminal terrestre* as soon as they fill up (about every 5min., 10min., s/500). Buses coming from Cuenca to Gualaceo also generally continue to Chordeleg (s/3,000). The **walk** between Gualaceo and Chordeleg is a beautiful saunter past picturesque rolling countryside and farmland. The downhill stretch from Chordeleg to Gualaceo takes about an hour; the return uphill can take one and a half hours. On blind curves, be careful of cars hugging the right side of the highway.

Other market villages in the area, including **Sigsig** and **Paute,** are both accessible by one-hour bus rides from Gualaceo. Both are less touristy and more rural than either Gualaceo or Chordeleg. As with the other markets in the Cuenca area, the big activity is on Sundays. The **tour agencies** listed under Ingapirca and El Cajas offer day-trips for around s/120,000 per person to all of these markets. Their guides are not too useful, but you get the advantage of a better vehicle for the rough ride.

EL CAJAS NATIONAL RECREATION AREA

Taking the high road is easy on any trail through El Cajas National Recreation Area, a 28,808-hectare reserve that exemplifies the word "highlands" in its truest sense. Nowhere in the reserve does the altimeter dip below 3150m (10,330ft.), and the zenith, at Arquitectos, reaches a skyscraping 4450m (14,600ft.). Despite its accessibility from Cuenca, few have tried this Andean mountain high; established as a national recreation area in 1977, El Cajas remains a relatively unexplored natural wonder. Ancient glaciers carved boxlike, U-shaped valleys into the high rock ridges, lending the reserve its name (*cajas* means boxes in Spanish), while failing to explain its grammatical error. A geologically hip place for water to gather, the range hosts 232 lakes and over 750 ponds, distinguishing itself from its generally cold, rainy Sierra cousins with its aquatic take on alpine beauty. Not only does the water nestled in the barren mountains present a feast for the eyes, but it also provides life's sustenance for diverse flora and fauna. El Cajas is a haven to standard-issue wildlife like deer, foxes, and rabbits, as well as the more distinctive spectacled bear, llama, puma, *huagur,* and *tigrillo* (little tiger). Bird-watchers can feast their eyes on land, air, and lake as the Andean condor, highland toucan, and hummingbird are also regular tenants of "The Boxes." Those who prefer Flora to her sister Fauna will enjoy diminutive Quinua trees, the highest-altitude trees in the world, which sprout from the grassy humid *páramo* (highland plain) covering most of the park's area. El Cajas's unique climate makes it one of the few places where the rare *cubilán, chuquiragua,* and *tushig* plants flourish. Virgin humid mountain forests cover the east and west ends of the area. Offering more than just the wild plant and animal life of the present, though, the reserve also provides glimpses into the past. Pre-Columbian **indigenous ruins** lie scattered throughout, and the ancient Inca Road of **Ingañan** stretches for 4km between **Luspa Cave** and **Lake Mamamag** in the center of the park. The best preserved ruins are at **Paredonesñ,** but Lakes Luspa and Avilahuayco serve up similar slices of Inca history closer to the information center.

A would-be mountain oasis, the **Information Center** at **Lake Toreadora** (3810m; 12,500ft.) offers basic shelter and a cafeteria, but you need to bring your own sleeping bag, and might as well bring your own food (the cafeteria is often closed). There are two more basic shelters along the shores of Lake Toreadora. Temperatures drop to -5°C at night, and despite the humidity, daytime mercury can sink to 8°C. Warm, waterproof gear is a must, as is powerful sunblock (high Ecuadorian altitudes mean you're that much closer to the sun). A solid supply of bottled water can help with thirst, altitude sickness, and avoiding those pesky mountain water bacteria. Take extreme care wherever you walk in the park and pace yourself slowly (see Hot, Cold, and High, p. 16). The excellent hiking and mountaintop views are to die for, but not literally; deaths from overexertion in the harsh climate have been reported. For a somewhat less strenuous outdoor activity, **sport fishing** on Lake Toreadora is permitted. Tour agencies in Cuenca can provide necessary equipment rentals. Admission to the park is s/21,000.

From the Information Center, the only immediate recreation is a beautiful three-hour stroll around Lake Toreadora, replete with views of Volcán Chimborazo in the distance. The only way to make excursions beyond the lake is with a private tour. **Río Arriba,** Hermano Miguel 7-14 y Pres. Córdova in Quito (tel. 840-031, on Sun. tel. 883-711), offers daytrips (open Mon.-Fri. 9am-6pm, Sat. 9am-1pm). Edgar "El Negro" Aguirre is a well-known, recommended guide. Six-hour tours cost s/115,000-270,000 per person for the day, depending on group size. Río Arriba also sports two- to three-day trips with more ambitious routes, such as a walk on the Inca Trail and excursions to some of the ruins (s/120,000 per day). A similar outfit, **Santa Ana** (Quito tel. 832-340), right around the corner from CETUR in Quito, charges s/120,000 per person regardless of number, and transports people in a 4x4 Trooper with an English-speaking guide (open Mon.-Fri. 9am-1pm and 3-7pm, Sat. 11am-1pm). The best resource for El Cajas, hands down, is **INEFAN,** in Cuenca, which can provide a good map of the entire recreation area—a necessity, as it's easy to get lost. To contact INEFAN, see Cuenca Practical Information, p. 134.

Buses leave from San Sebastian Park at Talbot and Mariscal Sucre in Cuenca (Fri.-Wed., 1 per day, 6-7:30am, 1hr., s/4,500). Arrive well before 6am to assure a seat for the crowded and treacherous ride. The bus drops off and picks up at the Information Center. The return trip leaves between 2-3pm.

SARAGURO

Saraguro's population of 20,000 is deceptively large. A tiny stop on the Panamerican Highway between Cuenca and Loja, the town's main attraction, other than typical small-town charm and untouristed solitude, is the *artesanía* of the Saraguro Indians. With peculiar all-black shawls and dark knee-length shorts, these *indígenas* are a fascinating sight. The Sunday market brings the black-robed farmers into town from surrounding areas. In Saraguro, where millions of stars visit the unpolluted mountain sky on clear nights, you can truly feel a part of the Ecuadorian countryside.

Everything of any importance is located within two blocks of the **main plaza,** a pleasant garden with benches and trees, typical for a small highland village. By night, there is little to do but look up at the **starry sky** or have a beer at the **Gruta Azul.** Go to bed early, head to Loja (1½hr. away—buses run late into the night), or bring a good book. For a place with such a small-town feel, Saraguro has a large number of useful services. **Banco Nacional de Fomento** (tel. 200-109; open Mon.-Fri. 9am-2pm), **EMETEL** (tel. 200-104 or 200-105; open daily 8am-10pm), a good **general store,** and **Farmacia La Salud** (no tel.; open daily 8am-1pm and 2-10pm) are all located along the main plaza, across the street from the church. Buses pass by the **bus stop,** also on the main plaza across from the church, heading north (toward **Cuenca**) and south (toward **Loja**) every 15 minutes or so. **Pullman Viajeros** (tel. 200-165) runs north to **Cuenca** (10 per day, 6:30am-1am, 3½hr., s/10,000) and **Quito** (3 per day, 10:30am-8pm, 13hr.). **Transportes Sur Oriente, Transportes Union Carramanza,** and **Coop Loja** all go south to **Loja** (1½hr., s/5,000) and the **Oriente** (via **Zamora** and **Yantzaza**). The **post office** (no tel.) is on Av. 10 de Marzo on the main plaza (open Mon.-Fri. 8am-noon and 2-6pm). Next door reside more municipal facilities—the **police (Policía Municipal)** and the **public bathroom.**

There are two hotels and two restaurants in Saraguro—no more, no less. **Pensión Saraguro** (no tel.) might be a little hard to spot, since it's run out of a grocery store. From the plaza facing the church, head left one block and look for the *"Pensión"* sign diagonally across the street. Laundry facilities unsully guests' clothes and sheets. Simple rooms with shared baths (hot water 6am-6pm). S/7,000 per person. Its rival down the street, **Residencial Armijos** (no tel.), has slightly nicer rooms, but only cold water in the common bathrooms. Facing the church, head left one block, then turn right and walk half a block; it's on the left. There are no keys to the doors—but hey, it's Saraguro. Clean sheets, a mattress and pillow, and walls—what more could you ask for s/8,000 per person? The **Gruta Azul** restaurant-bar, on the main plaza on Eloro, across from the post office and police, serves some of the tastiest victuals in town. Get in some shopping time in this storefront setting while wolfing down *almuerzo* (s/3,000) or *merienda* (s/5,000), which will likely include chicken in some form (open daily 8am-10:30pm). The other dining choice, **Cristal,** is populated not only by hungry locals, but also by flies and naked pictures of Samantha Fox. Ask for prices—if you dare to stay (open daily 7am-9pm).

Loja

Always on the move, Loja (pop. 100,000, alt. 2100m) was relocated from the Catamayo area in 1548, rebuilt after earthquakes twice, and, as its first city to use electric energy, pioneered Ecuador into the Age of Electricity. A gateway to the Oriente, Loja sits only a stone's throw from the most seductive and secluded spots in the southern *cordillera*—Vilcabamba, Zamora, Parque Nacional Podocarpus. Beautiful and friendly, Loja boasts enough endowments to be a siren of the Sierra in its own right. The secret to Loja's allure lies in its balance between old and new. Home to two universities, a law school, and a musical conservatory, Loja has developed a sense of modern culture that many other towns in the area lack, while retaining ties to its rustic origins. No buildings rise past the fourth story, and the local **Saraguro Indians** in their traditional black dress are a strong presence throughout the city. No longer a mobile metropolis, Loja has comfortably settled into its mountain setting, offering visitors a rich combination of scholarly atmosphere, safe streets, traditional charm, and excellent restaurants.

ORIENTATION AND PRACTICAL INFORMATION

Loja lies along two rivers. The main one, **Río Malacatos,** runs between (and underneath) Av. Universitaria and Manuel Agustín Aguirre in town. **Río Zamora** parallels Av. 24 de Mayo, marking the eastern boundary of the city. The **terminal terrestre** is about a 15-minute walk north of *el centro* along Universitaria.

Tourist Information: CETUR, Valdivieso 8-22 y Av. 10 de Agosto (tel. 572-964), provides maps of Loja and other information (open Mon.-Fri. 8:30am-5pm). **INEFAN,** on Azuay between Olmedo and Bolívar, administers **Parque Nacional Podocarpus** southeast of town. Hours erratic.

Immigration Office: (tel. 573-600), on Argentina and Bolivia, next to the police station. Open Mon.-Fri. 8am-noon and 2-6pm.

Peruvian Consulate: Sucre 10-56 (tel. 571-668 or 579-068).

Banks: There are no *casas de cambio* in Loja, but banks perform the same money-changing feats. **Banco del Azuay** (tel. 570-262) and **Banco La Previsora** (tel. 572-733) share the corner of Av. 10 de Agosto and Valdivieso. **Filanbanco** (tel. 571-811), on Valdivieso between Av. 10 de Agosto and Eguiguren, changes traveler's checks only (open Mon.-Fri. 9am-2pm).

Telephone: EMETEL (tel. 573-050 or 573-990) has 2 branches in Loja: at Eguiguren and Valdivieso, and on Aguirre between Lourdes and Catacocha. Both allow collect and calling-card calls at no charge—important if you're heading to Vilcabamba, where calls cost an arm and a leg (open daily 8am-10pm).

Airport: The **La Tola airport** is a 30km, s/10,000 taxi ride out of town in Catamayo (p. 146). Loja's **TAME office** (tel. 570-248 or 573-030), is on the extension of Av. 24 de Mayo across the Río Zamora (open Mon.-Fri. 9am-5pm). Some advise against taking afternoon flights into Loja/Catamayo, as fierce winds blow through town and the airstrip is precariously wedged between several mountains.

Buses: Transportes Loja has some sparkling new Mercedes-Benz and Volvo buses, and some merely average ones. Buses go to **Cuenca** (1, 4:30am, 8hr.), **Gualaquiza** (4, 8am, 12:30pm, 8hr.), **Amaluza** (4am, 1, 4pm), **Cariamanga** (7 per day, 4am-6pm), **Machala** (9 per day, 4:30am-11:30pm, 8hr.), **El Pangui** (5am), **Zapotillo** (4 per day, 5am-11pm), **Guayaquil** (7 per day, 6:30am-11pm, 11hr.), **Macará** (6 per day, 7am-7:30pm, 7hr.), **Santo Domingo** (4pm, 7pm), **Huaquillas** (9:30, 11:15pm, 10hr.), and **Quito** (5 per day, 5pm-9pm, 18hr.). Some other Loja-based companies with similar routes are **Catamayo, Union Yantzaza, Loja, Sur Oriente, Cariamanga, Pullman Viajeros,** and **Ejecutivo.**

Taxis: Standard fare between locations in Loja is s/2,500. **Taxi Ruta** crams 5-6 people into their cabs bound for **Vilcabamba** (1hr., s/3,500). The ride is about twice as fast as buses to Vilcabamba, and costs only s/1,000 more. Taxi Ruta headquarters are on Av. 11 de Mayo; their stop is on Universitaria near the Gran Hotel Loja.
Supermarket: Tía, Av. 10 de Agosto and Bolívar (open daily 9am-8pm).
Pharmacy: Pharmacies are on the *de turno* schedule—check the local paper to see which one is open on any given night. **Farmacia Loja** (tel. 570-266), is on the corner of Bolívar and Rocafuerte (open daily 8am-9pm).
Hospital: Hospital General (emergency tel. 560-159 or 570-540), on Isidro Ayora and Kennedy. Far from *el centro,* so it's best to take a taxi. Free 24-hr. emergency treatment. **Hospital Militar de Loja,** Colón 13-28 y Bolívar (tel. 570-254 or 573-941), charges for its medical services.
Police: (tel. 115), on Argentina and Bolivia.
Post Office: Sucre 05-85 y Colón (tel. 571-600). Open Mon.-Fri. 8am-6pm.
Telephone Code: 07.

ACCOMMODATIONS

Hotel Acapulco (tel. 570-651), on Sucre between Av. 10 de Agosto and Eguiguren. Not quite Mexico's Pacific coast, but it does provide small, liveable, squeaky-clean rooms with color TV and lacquered desk set. Rooms on 2nd and 3rd floors escape noise from the indoor 1st floor corridor (strangely used as a driveway/parking lot). Many windows face the interior central hall; quieter back rooms have natural light. Singles s/20,000, with TV s/24,000; doubles with TV s/40,000.

Hotel Metropolitano (tel. 526-000 or 570-007), on Av. 18 de Noviembre at Colón. Creep around on sturdy wood floors and relax on comfortable wood-paneled beds before washing off in small but sanitary yellow-tiled private bathrooms. Color TVs and quiet surroundings. A good deal at s/18,000 per person.

Hostal International (tel. 570-433), on Av. 10 de Agosto, between Av. 18 de Noviembre and Sucre. For the price, bathrooms are surprisingly decent, and rooms aren't too shabby either. Centrally located, with a courtyard in the absolute center of it all. Old wood floors support the feet, and strange furniture holds the imagination captive. S/7,000 per person, with bath s/10,000.

Hostal Londres (tel. 561-936), on Sucre at Av. 10 de Agosto, next to Hotel Acapulco. Less comfortable than its neighbor, but the price is hard to beat. Showerheads curiously close to toilet seats make for a peculiar bathroom experience. At least the water's always hot. Padlocked rooms have that bare, hanging-lightbulb look, but they're very clean for the money. S/7,000 per person.

Hotel Chandelier, Imbabura 14-84 y Sucre (tel. 563-061 or 578-233). If only there really were chandeliers to spice up the sterile hallways and linoleum floors. Cleanliness is clearly a priority—walls are whiter than Snow White's epidermis. Request a bathroom with gas-heated water instead of a sketchy electric hookup. And hold out for a toilet seat. Some rooms have color or black-and-white TVs. S/12,000 per person, with bath s/15,000.

Hostal Carrión, Colón 16-36 y Av. 18 de Noviembre (tel. 561-127). Despite the evocative name there's no rotting flesh here. Basic shared-bath rooms satisfy fundamental living needs with a bed, table, and clean sheets (s/10,000 per person), while significantly snazzier private-bath rooms have color TVs (singles s/18,000; doubles s/30,000). Hot water, rooftop terrace, and helpful owner to boot.

FOOD

Benvenuto, around Av. 18 de Noviembre and Av. 10 de Agosto. Have your conversational Italian and your appetite ready. Even though this lunch stop is Italian-run and named, its menu is typically Ecuadorian. Inexpensive, tasty, and filling *almuerzos* (s/3,500). *A la carta* dishes, like *lomo picante* (s/1,500) and *espaguetis de camarón* (s/5,000), are just as welcoming (open Mon.-Sat. 8am-8pm).

Parillada Uruguaya (tel. 570-260), on Universitaria at Azuay. Flee yon vegetarian, hasten dear carnivore. It's a challenge to find a table and figure out the prices, but the likeable owner serves up some of the best grilled meat in the southern highlands. Try the outstanding *chuleta de chancho* (a huge pork chop, s/10,000), the

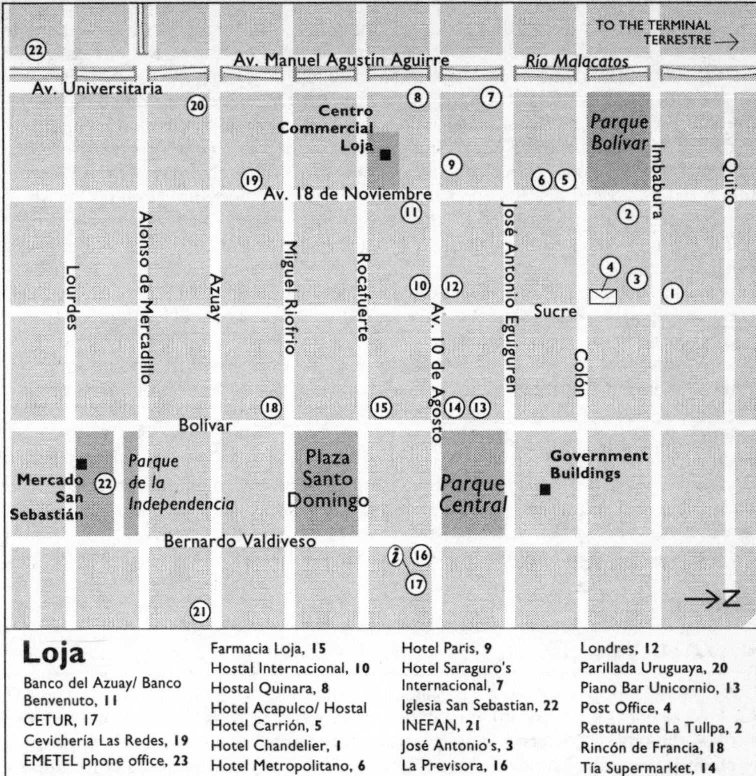

house specialty *lomo fino* (grilled beef, s/9,500), or a *parillada* (mixed grill, s/15,000 per person). Meat—it's what's for dinner.

La Tullpa, on Av. 18 de Noviembre at the Parque Bolívar. Fancy touches put other *criollo* restaurants to shame. Dishes aren't dirt-cheap, but they don't taste like it either. *Chuleta de chancho* (pork chop) s/6,500, *lengua a la española* (Spanish-style tongue) s/6,400. Scrumptious *almuerzo* (s/3,700) is quite a deal.

Cevichería Las Redes (tel. 578-787), at Av. 18 de Noviembre and Riofrio. This net-decorated seafood joint offers more than just your average *ceviche.* Breaded squid (s/7,800) and whole boiled crab (s/2,900) are among the specialties, but the *sopa de mariscos* (with octopus, squid, shrimp, crab, and more, s/7,500), big enough for a meal, swims above the rest (open Mon.-Sat. 8am-10pm, Sun. 8am-3pm).

José Antonio's, Imbabura 15-46, between Sucre and Av. 18 de Noviembre (tel. 577-274). One of the best restaurants in Loja, with filling meals under s/15,000. Begin with irresistible grilled bread, followed by *mar y tierra* ("surf 'n' turf" in dill sauce, s/10,500), served by tuxedoed waiters to tableclothed, crystal-laden tables. Shrimp dishes are right at home among sea-oriented wall decorations (open Mon.-Sat. 10am-3pm and 6-10pm, Sun. 10am-3pm).

Rincón de Francia (tel. 578-686), at Riofrio and Bolívar. For the cheap romantic in everyone. A dark room, candlelight, elegant French dining, soft music—the works. Filet mignon s/10,800, tongue s/9,000 (open daily noon-10pm).

SIGHTS AND ENTERTAINMENT

The area surrounding Loja is so amazingly scenic that every visitor ends up outdoors, whether it's trekking in the nearby hills or admiring the view from the **Virgen de Loja** statue. Guarded by a graffiti-laden stone lion below, the Virgin overlooks sprawling Loja from between the Andean hills. To get there, head east on Rocafuerte, go uphill past the river, and climb a few steps and a small hill.

The **Parque Universitario La Argelia,** run by the **Universidad Nacional de Loja,** is another outstanding outdoor experience. Full of beautifully-maintained hiking trails, it covers the campus hills a couple miles south of the town center (catch the "Argelia" or "Univ. Nacional" buses, or take a s/3,000 cab). While the start of the 45-minute climb passes typical countryside vistas, the top is pure *páramo.* Nothing but small shrubs keep you from blowing off the treeless ridge into the valley far below. There is a small museum and information center at the base of the trail, and a wooden sign outside illustrates the various hikes. Take the trail heading right for a complete two-hour loop through a flowered pine forest, full of tranquil mountain streams, and (depending on the time of year) squadrons of butterflies. The trail heading left passes a great picnic spot but eventually dead-ends, so you must retrace your steps to get back. On the way up, you'll pass the entrance of the University's other outdoor enterprise, the **Jardín Botánico,** which boasts a wonderful collection of blossoms and buds. Both are open daily during daylight hours and are free.

Entertainment is a bit scarce in Loja, but the decor alone at the **Piano Bar Unicornio,** Bolívar 7-63 y Av. 10 de Agosto (tel. 574-083), is amusement enough. They don't serve cheese, but they might as well—the bar is decked out from head to toe in velvet and red-and-white stripes. Mirrors, a disco ball, and a piano/mike set-up threaten at every moment to add to the 70s lounge atmosphere. Beer s/2,400, daiquiri s/6,000, ham sandwich s/2,000 (open Mon.-Sat. until 11pm).

■ Near Loja

CATAMAYO

Busy but uninspiring, Catamayo's main contribution to the traveler subculture is the **La Tola airport** (2.5km away), the nearest spot for flights in and out of Loja. Once the site for the city of Loja itself, Catamayo has been untroubled by major happenings ever since the better-known metropolis moved 30km east in 1548, two years after its founding. However, travelers with early-morning, late-evening, and standby flights can avoid complete boredom while passing through. They can stare at the cops in unusual straw cowboy hats striding along Catamayo's main street and social center, **Isidro Ayora.** And a sunny afternoon at the **Centro Recreacional Popular Eliseo Arias Carrión,** 5km away, is the perfect antidote to airport claustrophobia (s/500 by bus from Catamayo, s/2,500 from Loja). A popular spot for families on the weekends, Centro Recreacional Carrión has sports facilities, a large pool, fresh air, and appropriately enough, an airplane smack in the middle of the grounds (open daily during daylight hours).

Activity centers around the **Parque Principal** between the east-west Isidro Ayora and Bolívar and the north-south Av. 24 de Mayo and Catamayo. Cadillo runs north of the Parque, Espejo runs south, and Av. 18 de Noviembre runs west. Make calls from **EMETEL**, on Isidro Ayora across from the gas station (open daily 8am-10pm). **Cooperativa Transportes,** on Catamayo near Isidro Ayora and the Parque Principal, has **buses** to **Loja,** the only place to go (every ½hr., 45min., s/2,000). **Camionetas** go to **El Cisne** (every hr., 1hr., s/2,000). **Farmacia Macará** (tel. 677-149), at Bolívar and Av. 24 de Mayo, is on the Parque Principal (open Mon.-Sat. 7am-9pm, Sun. 7am-noon). Catamayo's equivalent of a hospital, the **Centro de Salud de Catamayo** (tel. 677-146) is at Av. 18 de Noviembre and Espejo (open Mon.-Fri. 8am-noon, and 2-6pm). Call the **police** at 677-101. The **telephone code** is 07.

There's not much reason to spend the night in Catamayo unless you have an early-morning flight and want to sleep in a bit, rather than catch a sunrise bus from Loja. The **Hotel Granada** (tel. 677-243), at Av. 24 de Mayo and Espejo, has snug, spic-and-span rooms ventilated with windows and balconies, all with color TV. S/7,000 per person, with bath s/10,000. **Hotel Turis** (tel. 677-126), on Ayora and Av. 24 de Mayo, is conveniently close to the bus stop. Dark, drab rooms surround a dingy, bird-filled courtyard. But Turis delivers the basic goods for a one-night stay, especially if you're leaving the next morning. S/5,000 per person, with bath s/10,000. The **Hostería Bella Vista,** 10 minutes out of town off Via a la Costa, is more posh, but you'll have to pay the price. Rooms are inviting and clean, just like you'll be after a soak in the Turkish bath and beautiful swimming pool, surrounded by mountains and an airy restaurant. All rooms have color TV and private bath. Singles s/25,000; doubles s/40,000. Restaurants in Catamayo are basic, so just choose a cheap *almuerzo* spot near the Parque Principal and hope it's clean. The **Embajador,** at Isidro Ayora and Catamayo, is near the Parque Principal and next to the Hotel Reina el Cisne. Its staple Ecuadorian grub comes recommended from frequent fliers (entrees s/3500-5000). Open daily 8am-10pm. **Hostería Bella Vista's restaurant** is on another level, both in price and food. Complex creations like *pescado al vapor* (s/8,000) are served in a dining room overlooking the pool. Beautiful mountain views from the bar (open daily 8am-10pm).

EL CISNE

For five days every summer (Aug. 16-20), a river of faith pours into Loja from El Cisne, led by a famous statue—**La Virgen del Cisne.** The local virgin, a common postcard image, floats on the shoulders of the hearty pilgrims who clog the 40km road to Loja. Not one to settle down, the Virgin stays in Loja for only a short while; on November 1, she begins her crowd-surfing return to El Cisne. A sign of die-hard Catholicism, the Chaucer-worthy pilgrims consider the trek almost enough to merit canonization. After all, for some of them, completing the 70km one-way trip amounts to a minor miracle in itself.

The easier, though less devout, route to El Cisne involves taking a 3-hr. bus ride from Loja's *terminal terrestre* (schedule erratic). Outside of the fascinating processions, the town's best offering is the sanctuary itself, a building gargantuan in both its scale and its reputation among Catholics. The Virgin, who is originally from Quito, may not get out much, but the presence of both her statue and her sanctuary have conspicuously moved the locals, even in Loja—especially when it came time to name buildings and buses. Despite regional Catholic significance, only the truly fascinated, the well-timed, and the imminently papal should bother with the long daytrip between El Cisne and Loja. Given that El Cisne has no hotels, lesser pilgrims have to proceed at least 40km back out of town to Catamayo for a bed.

Zamora

Maybe Coronado was looking too far north when he searched the American southwest in vain for the mythical golden city of El Dorado. According to some *indígenas,* El Dorado glistened right around here in the Amazon Basin. Ecuador's modern city of gold, Zamora (pop. 9000; alt. 970m) is a rustic jungle town that suddenly found itself in the center of things when the gold rush began in nearby **Nambija.** Situated just before the eastern Sierra becomes the southern Oriente, Zamora remains wonderfully untouristed, yet home to a comfortable hotel, decent restaurants, and easy access to primary tropical rainforest through the **Parque Nacional Podocarpus.** Some come to Zamora just for the ride; the newly-finished highway winds along cliffs on the side of the Río Zamora valley, descending from *páramo* highland cloud forests to the leafy, palm-laden habitats of the tropical Oriente. But all that's gold does not glisten. The industrial mining equipment and tin-roofed gold boom houses, haphazardly gripping the sides of tropical river-valley hills, stick up sorely through the palms, interrupting the jungle-town habitat.

Orientation and Practical Information Activity in Zamora, as in most Ecuadorian towns, centers around the town's main park and church. In this case, that center is **Parque Pio Jaramillo,** at the junction of **Tamayo** and **Diego de Vaca.** Other streets in town either have no names or no street signs. If you've been traveling much in rural Ecuador, you're used to it.

Essential for Parque Nacional Podocarpus excursions, **INEFAN** is up on the highway in Barrio 2 de Noviembre, across from the cemetery. **Banco del Azuay** (tel. 605-235), next to EMETEL, will change U.S. dollars but not traveler's checks (open Mon.-Fri. 8am-4pm, Sat. 9am-1pm). Make collect or calling-card calls from **EMETEL** (tel. 605-104 or 604-105), near Tamayo, one block from the main plaza away from the church (open 8am-10pm). The **terminal terrestre** is at the end of town, one block from Diego de Vaca. Facing the church, go left. **Cooperativa Loja** sends the best buses around to **Cuenca** (11hr., s/17,600) via **Loja, Gualaquiza** (6, 10am, 2pm, 5hr., s/7,000) via **Yantzaza** (1½hr., s/2,260) and **El Pangui** (3hr., s/5,000), **Loja** (5, 9, 11am, 1:30, 6pm, 2hr., s/4,600), and **Quito** (3pm, 18hr., s/35,000). **Transportes Pullman** sends the most buses to **Cuenca** (9:45am, 6:15, 10:30pm, 11hr., s/20,000) via **Loja**. **Union Yantzaza, Union Cariamanga,** and **Transportes Nambija** also send buses from Zamora. **Farmacia Santa Fé** (no tel.) is on Diego de Vaca toward the *terminal terrestre*. If facing the church, head left (open Mon.-Sat. 8:30am-noon and 2-6pm). **Hospital Julius Deepfuer** (emergency tel. 605-149) is two blocks left from the church (open Mon.-Fri. 8am-noon and 2-6pm). A private **medical clinic** is across the street. The **telephone code** is 07.

Accommodations and Food On Diego de Vaca, one and a half blocks from the plaza towards the river, **Hotel Maguna** (tel. 605-919), is by far the most comfortable spot in town to spend the night. Rooms, though a bit dark, have black-and-white TVs and the all-important fridge. Chill your beer and your mood on hot nights. Shared bathrooms with cold water, but not toilet seats. Singles s/25,000; doubles s/40,000. **Hotel Zanion** (tel. 605-253), at Sevilla de Oro and Pio Jaramillo near the plaza, offers simple but airy rooms with washed sheets. Unfortunately, cold water shared bathrooms are less than stellar. But don't worry about that gold you found—rooms are padlocked. S/8,000 per person. **Hotel Seyma** (tel. 605-583), is on Av. 29 de Mayo and Amazonas near the plaza. Seyma explores the fundamental essence of simplicity. In rooms this dark, it's hard to see more than the clean gleam of the washed sheets and cold-water shared bathroom. S/10,000 per person.

Restaurante Don Pepe, one-half block from the church, is popular with locals. Order the *almuerzo* (s/3,500) or *merienda* (s/3,500) if you want to fit in—it's what everyone else does. Or assert your individuality and get an *a la carte* dish, such as the whole grilled *corvina* (sea bass, s/7,000). Open daily 8am-10pm. **Restaurante Tropy Burger,** one block toward the river from the main plaza on Av.24 de Mayo, whips up a good *almuerzo* (s/3,500), featuring soup with unidentifiable but tasty pig parts. Apparently, flies enjoy the porcine goodies too. Two floors of fun, decorated with palm trees and larger-than-life food painted on the walls. If only the portions were that big.... The Tropy is open daily from 6am to 9pm.

Sights and Entertainment Zamora is a sleepy town, particularly at night. You might check out the unusually-shaped **church** in the center of town, the pleasant park, or the **market** on Diego de Vaca across from the bus station. When it gets dark, you could enjoy a beer on the corner of the plaza across from the church at **King Burguer.** Otherwise, hit the sack early and save your energy for the town's main attraction **Parque Nacional Podocarpus** (see below).

When the El Dorado myth died in the 16th century, **gold** fell out of both the conquistadors' minds and the Ecuadorian limelight. Few suspected that the hard-to-access area of the Oriente offered more riches than its oil and biodiversity. When gold was unexpectedly discovered in the Zamora area of the southern Oriente about 15 years ago, a **mining frontier culture** sprouted up alongside the Oriente vegetation and the **conservationist colonies** of the rainforest (see We Don't Need No Stinkin' Badges!, p. 151).

The gold-rush town of **Nambija,** four hours from Zamora near the road to Gualaquiza, has been a traditional Incan mining spot for hundreds of years, yet was unknown outside of *indígena* communities until the 1980s. Ever since Ecuadorian miners struck upon a rich lode here, Nambija has attracted hopeful adventurers with a pick-axe in one hand and a hard-hat in the other. The gold boom has transformed this formerly traditional, isolated village into an exceedingly dirty and unfriendly frontier town. However, in the past two years, the military presence has maintained a higher and higher profile, trying to prevent mining in restricted areas like the nearby Parque Nacional Podocarpus. Due to these bans, as well as quickly-flagging gold resources, Nambija is fast becoming a ghost town. Miners have started to head elsewhere in search of more fruitful and less vigilantly-guarded lands.

Signs of mining culture line the Zamora-Macas "highway," the southern Oriente's only road. **Gualaquiza, Yantzaza, Limón,** and similar villages play host to roving miners and oily mining trucks barreling through town. Machete-wielding prospectors venture deep into the untamed jungles in search of the next mother lode. The **Guadalupe** area, near La Paz and Av. 28 de Mayo, as well as areas to the north, are hotbeds of mining-development activity. Check out the many fascinating mining hardware and rifle stores in these towns, but don't get any funny ideas. For now, true lawless frontier towns exist, but their persistence depends on the how long it takes the military to get their act together and monitor them. One of the most popular ways to reach these towns is hiring a **cooperativa** truck in Zamora and asking to be taken to the latest popular lode.

Parque Nacional Podocarpus

ZONA ALTA (LOJA ENTRANCE)

Layer upon layer of rolling cloud forests obscure the misty mountain scenery in the high-altitude section of Parque Nacional Podocarpus. Miles of cliffside paths traverse this *"zona alta,"* a fairytale elfin forest that surges up to 3600m (11,800ft.) above sea level. Notorious and elusive high-flyers—the toucan *de altura,* the quetzal, and the Andean cock-of-the-rock—hide in the fingers of fog that cloud the Podocarpan sky.

There are four main *senderos* (paths) through beautiful mountain terrain, all of which leave from the main *refugio* at the park entrance. Mainly for children or families, **Sendero Oso de Anteojos** (Spectacled Bear Path) is a short 400m loop near the entrance. Although this trail gives a taste of the park's natural nirvana, only the paths that go onward and upward provide climactic vistas. **Sendero Bosque Nublados** (Cloud Forest Path) climbs higher through the clouds and offers slightly larger servings of the scenic delights below. This 700m trail is a bit more difficult and takes two hours to complete.

Sendero al Mirador captures the true essence of Podocarpus, revealing a veritable banquet of foggy soup vistas along the way. The view from the 3600m *mirador* astounds, and a post-peak picnic here is an excellent reward for a challenging uphill journey. Birdwatchers can observe a feathered cabaret, and lucky hikers who smell strongly of food might glimpse a spectacled bear, mountain tapir, fox, or puma. Don't get too comfortable, because half the hike is still to come. The 3.5km, medium-difficulty trail stammers along a precarious ridgewalk, obscured by a mystical mist in the summertime, but clear and dry in the winter. Less ambitious hikers, whether plagued by lethargy or a stone in the shoe, can opt out of the second part of the trail and do only the one-hour hike to the *mirador* and back.

If Sendero al Mirador is a banquet, **Sendero Las Lagunas del Compadre** is a culinary orgy worthy of the gods. The 14km trail leads to the jewel in the crown of Podocarpus—shimmering lakes buried deep in the mountain forest. The total excursion takes two or three days, and the absence of trail facilities makes proper camping equipment essential for this festival of scenery. With water, water everywhere, trails can be excessively muddy during the summer and steep parts are often slippery. Huge, waterproof rubber boots are the intrepid hiker's only defense against mud-soaked footwear and pants. The animals are already in the know when it comes to the well-hydrated climate, making the drier season best for fauna-watching. In January and February, the time is right to grab the nearest pair of binoculars and follow the circling birds. Spectacled bears and *dantas* (tapirs) prefer to romp during November and December. The plants, however, are less particular about road-conditions. The punk era never ends for the red-spiked bromeliads that line the trails; orchids and bamboo provide an off-setting floral chorus.

Staying in the park for more than a few hours? Drinking a lot of water? The *refugio* is the perfect refuge, with a bathroom, several beds, a kitchen, and an overnight staff. *Cabañas* near the *refugio,* farther into the forest, are an *au naturale* alternative. The trails begin at the Catanuma station, where a s/20,000 entrance fee buys access to the entire Sierra section, including the camping *cabañas* and resource-laden *refugio.* The station lies about 15km from Loja, off the road to Vilcabamba. Unfortunately, buses and shared taxis heading to Vilcabamba will drop you off on the highway, leaving a grueling 8km uphill hike to the station itself. A hired taxi can handle the road all the way there on good days (about s/30,000 round-trip), but 4WD vehicles are ideal. The **Arco Iris Foundation** in Loja (tel. 572-926), at Lauro Guerrero and Mercadillo, one block from the river, is a local, non-profit conservation group that frequently jeeps up and down the hill and offers guided park tours (free if you have a "special" purpose; otherwise, negotiate a price). Talk to director Fausto López for details (open Mon.-Fri. 8am-5pm). Local travel agencies also run daytrips with guides, but the hills aren't the only steep part of these packages (US$35). While a guide isn't necessary, hiking with at least one partner is advisable.

ZONA BAJA (ZAMORA ENTRANCE)

Tropical butterflies flutter across virtually every step of the trails in Parque Nacional Podocarpus *"zona baja,"* a primary tropical rainforest along the Río Bombuscara. Though lovers of the cloud forest might beg to differ, a consensus of local INEFAN officials and butterfly aficionados hold that the jungle section of Podocarpus outshines it's uphill counterpart. Beautifully kept trails wind past waterfalls and rainforest streams, creating an omnipresent chorus of rushing water to accompany the scenic symphonies of river views and jungle greenery. Budding botanists can explore the Universidad Nacional de Loja study area, home to a cacophonous diversity of plants. Highlights include over 40 varieties of orchids and the *cascarilla* tree, the source of quinine, a key ingredient in both malaria remedies and the Gin and Tonic. A colorful coalition of wildlife may accompany you on your journey through the Zona Baja: yellow butterflies fluttering with each footstep, spectacled bears rustling nearby trees, and toucans croaking through the air overhead.

Zona Baja's entrance fee reflects its good standing with the locals—twice as nice for twice the price, admission runs s/40,000. Buy tickets from the INEFAN office in Zamora (tel. 605-315), a 10-minute walk from town on the highway (open Mon.-Fri. 8am-noon and 2-6pm). Those looking to save some sucres can buy tickets from the INEFAN office in Loja for half the price—admission tickets for either part of the park are honored at all entrances. Inside the park, the station at the trail entrance is staffed 24 hours. Get a taxi from Zamora's *terminal terrestre* for about s/30,000 roundtrip (arrange a pickup time with the driver in advance). Even with a car, visitors must make a 2km uphill walk to the Bombuscara ranger station. INEFAN trucks also come and go periodically, but are often full.

Several *zona baja* trails start from the Bombuscara ranger station. A short trail from the station down a wooden staircase leads to the river itself, where you can **swim** in fresh water next to a **large waterfall.** Water clarity varies depending on recent rainfall, but under any conditions, take proper jungle-swimming precautions. **Los Helechos** is a trail so short that spending a half-hour on it requires self-control. INEFAN helps the time killing process with a brochure, available in Zamora, offering 11 points of interest along the trail. Among the labeled botanical attractions are the orchids, *guarumo, helechos* (huge trees), palms, and *cascarilla.* The longest path, **Sendero Higuerones,** is a two-hour round-trip trek along the Río Bombuscara, but the most welcoming adventure in the *zona baja* is unmarked. Bushwacking, backwoods camping, and general exploring away from trails are legal, allowing the more

We Don't Need No Stinkin' Badges!

Gold miners and conservationists have traditionally mixed about as well as mayonnaise and ice cream, and nowhere in Ecuador are the gold wars more heated than in Parque Nacional Podocarpus's primary tropical rainforest. In the years since the recent gold rushes in Nambija and the Zamora area, miners have viewed the government-protected national park as treasure just waiting to be dug up. Photos in Podocarpus's *refugios* show the San Luis, Cerro Toledo, and Río Numbala areas, dafaced and devastated by illegal mining excavations. In the high *refugio*, some of the chairs have holes in the upholstery, marks left by miners' knives in a 1996 vandalism of the INEFAN-run shelter. One conservationist was recently shot by miners in another scuffle.

As gunshots and illegal bulldozers echo through the leafy jungle grounds and drown out the gentle buzz of rainforest insects, INEFAN and other conservation groups' messages of ecological awareness, "Take only photos, leave only footsteps," have never been more pressing. While taking care to heed their warnings, try not to lose perspective of the miners' side of the battles. They deem conservationists rich kids with nothing better to do than impede the working class's honest attempts to support their starving families. Where conservationists see endangered species, miners see dinner for their children. A solution is not as simple as it might seem; the battle over mountains, valleys, and rivers is merely a symptom of class struggles that cut as deep as the Río Bombuscara itself.

outgoing to explore the rainforest more intimately. Bring a mosquito net if you plan to camp in the heart of the jungle's darkness. The less-intrepid can explore the *cabañas,* bamboo enclosures for sleeping, near the station. There are also accommodations in the station itself for one or two people on research excursions. If interested, make special arrangements with INEFAN in Zamora.

Another entrance to Podocarpus's *zona baja* is two hours south of Zamora at a tiny town called **Romerillos.** INEFAN officials staff a *refugio* similar to the one at Bombuscara, but much smaller. **Buses** head to Romerillos from Zamora each morning; check with the Zamora INEFAN office for details. The Romerillos entrance is certainly off the tourist trail, with less hand-holding than you'll find at the well-staffed Bombuscara; this is strictly for die-hard trekkers.

Vilcabamba

Gently resting in a rolling valley at the southern tip of the highlands, the hot, sleepy town of Vilcabamba offers Ecuador's most curious specimen of *gringo* subculture. The town's fame has its origins in the legends of residents who lived to ridiculously old ages, supposedly reaching 120 years or more. This phenomenon was attributed to the clean air, mild climate, and healthy food and water in this *"Valle de la Juventud Eterna"* (Valley of Eternal Youth). Its setting is surely idyllic, and its streets *tranquilas,* but Vilcabamba owes its reputation as an unforgettable trip to its flora, like the remarkable San Pedro cactus, often used as a hallucinogenic drug. Vilcabamba's *gringo* contingent is a mellow mix of merrymakers who ask nothing more than to lounge around and enjoy the countryside, perhaps on short hikes or longer journeys through the surrounding hills. Given such an atmosphere, it's no surprise that more than one weary tourist has come away from Vilcabamba with deeper understanding and broader perspective. No place captures the spirit of Vilcabamba like the **Hostal Madre Tierra,** a hilltop paradise offering gorgeous grounds, spectacular views, and enough diversions to entertain for days without even a glimpse of the town.

Orientation and Practical Information Every 15 minutes or so throughout the day, buses and shared "Taxi Ruta" cars cruise in from Loja. Along the road before reaching town, a little **wooden sign** marks the turn-off point for the **Hostal Madre Tierra.** If you're going to be staying there (and you probably are), ask the taxi or bus driver to let you off early at the turn-off. From there, it's a 20-minute walk on that road to the **center of town.** Streets are, for all practical purposes, unnamed in Vilcabamba. Activity in the center crowds around a **main plaza,** which is overlooked by a **church** on one side.

The **EMETEL** office, on the corner of the main plaza, does not allow anything but ridiculously expensive toll calls—no collect or calling-card calls. Calls to the U.S. cost s/27,000 per minute (open daily 8am-9pm). The **Hostal Madre Tierra** (tel. 580-269) is slightly more reasonable. You can call someone for about US$6 if you keep it under a minute, then receive a call back from them at normal rates. Calls within Ecuador cost s/5,000 for five minutes. Most **buses** stop near the main plaza in town. All buses pass through **Loja,** but **Sur Oriente** has the most buses that go directly there (17 per day, every hr., 5:30am-7pm, 1½hr., s/2,500). **Transportes Loja** goes to **Quito** (5 per day, 1-8pm, 13hr., s/24,000), **Cuenca** (4 per day, 4:30am-7pm, 5hr., s/12,000), **Ambato** (5 per day, 1-8pm, 10hr., s/20,000), **Macará** (6 per day, 6am-7:30pm), **Machala** (4 per day, 4:30am-11:30pm), **Huaquillas** (11:15pm, 6hr., s/11,000), and **Guayaquil** (6 per day, 6am-11pm, 9hr., s/15,000). **Transportes Viajeros** goes to **Quito** (9am, 6pm, 13hr., s/24,000), **Cuenca** (13 per day, 5am-11:30pm, s/10,000), and **Ambato** (9am, 6:30pm, s/22,000). Other *cooperativos* heading north are **Transportes Santa** and **Transportes San Luis.** The luxurious **Paramericana** buses, with food, toilet, A/C, and bus attendants, go to **Riobamba** (10hr., s/25,000) and **Quito** (13hr., s/35,000). **Cooperativo Nambija, Union Cariamenga,** and **Unión Yantzaza** all head to the Peruvian border. **Taxi Ruta Av. 24 de Mayo** cabs get to Loja in less than one hour, but cram up to six people in a small car. At s/3,500, it's not much more expensive than the buses. Taxis leave from the center of town. **Farmacia Reina del Cisne** (tel. 580-289) is one block from the plaza, near EMETEL on the corner. **Hospital Kokichi Otani** is three blocks away from the plaza opposite the church (towards Madre Tierra), then take a left (open Mon.-Fri. 8am-noon and 2-6pm). Better hope you don't get hurt on a weekend. The **police** are three blocks from the plaza in the direction opposite the church (open 24hr.). The **post office** is located one block from the plaza, two blocks opposite the church (open Mon.-Fri. 8:30am-6pm, Sun. 9am-1pm). Vilcabamba's **telephone code** is 07.

Accommodations Outside town on the road from Loja, a 350m walk from the turn-off with a wooden sign, sits **Hostal Madre Tierra.** An icon of the *gringo* culture that has sprung up in Ecuador and Perú, Madre Tierra is a trip of its own. In this social, international spot (especially popular with Israelis), summer-camp style communal meals make it easy to find friends even if you come alone. The rustic but well-kept cabins cover a large section of country farmland with wide-perspective views of the hills and *fincas.* The exceedingly beautiful main lodge has a restaurant, outdoor swimming pool, and garden with hammocks cradled between palms and psychedelically-colored tropical flowers. Some cabins are a 10-min. hike from the main building, but have better views of the Andean countryside. Somewhat like a health spa, Madre Tierra offers a huge variety of fee-based activities, from horseback riding (s/25,000 per 4hr.) to massages (US$25). The more daring can try "colon therapy" (s/16,000 per 30min.)—otherwise stick to a whirlpool bath (s/5,000 per 30min.), hot clay bath (s/12,000 per 30min.), or steam bath (s/9,000). Facials with clay and herbs or corn and honey s/7,000. Rooms cost s/31,000 or s/35,000 per person, depending on whether your shower is gas-heated or solar-heated (i.e. cold). Breakfast and dinner are normally included in the price of the lodging but can also be paid for individually (around s/8,000). Eaten communally on the Madre Tierra's beautiful outdoor terrace, the 3-course feasts please the palates of carnivores and vegans alike. Unlimited lemonade and chilled bottled water come with the deal.

Hotel Valle Sagrado, right on the plaza in town, is a basic and cheap alternative. Rooms are far from sacred; in fact, they're quite small, but clean enough to sleep in. Electric hot water flows from the showers in the communal bathrooms, though toilet seats are sketchy. Hammocks, ping-pong, a kitchen, and a laundry basin round out the facilities. S/5,000 per person. Horses rentals as well (10am-2pm, s/15,000, with guide s/20,000). The attached **vegetarian restaurant** has a simple atmosphere, but serves tasty *almuerzos* or *meriendas,* with soup, wheat bread, vegetable entree, and salad for only s/4,000. Breakfast s/3,000 (open daily 8am-10pm). **Hostería Vilcabamba** (tel. 580-271 or 580-273), is on the road toward Madre Tierra, closer to town. Though expensive, it offers outstanding facilities and beautiful rooms. A central pool is surrounded by idyllic tropical gardens. Sauna, jacuzzi, and exercise room are among the well-kept facilities. At these prices, you *should* be living in luxury—singles s/48,000, doubles s/72,000. An excellent but pricey **restaurant-bar** and **Spanish language school** are also on the grounds. The pool is available for use by non-guests for a small fee.

Most people dine at their hotels, but there are alternatives. **Restaurant Valle Eterna Juventud** is four blocks away from the plaza, on the street to your left as you face the church. Though it's Canadian-run and *gringo*-infested, the menu is still mostly Ecuadorian. You're guaranteed a clean and tasty meal, and it won't break the bank (entrees s/3,000-s/6,000). Open Mon.-Fri. 11am-9pm, Sat.-Sun. 3-9pm. For a zesty meal, **Pizzería Pepito's,** on the same street as Eterna Juventud, pumps out Italian food. So does the **Green Triangle Bar-Café,** three blocks from the plaza in the direction opposite the church, which doubles as a hopping night spot (open 7pm-1am). Two basic *almuerzo* restaurants on the corner of the plaza across from the church, serve up a quick, filling lunch.

Sights and Entertainment The countryside provides all the sights and entertainment most Vilcabamba-goers could ask for. The days are easily filled with leisurely strolls, heartier hikes, and horseback rides through the land's forested terrain. A number of trails criss-cross the hills near the town; one runs up from a left turn in the road just past the pizzeria—follow the river here up the mountain for awesome views. Or take the four-hour **river walk,** as described by a hand-out at the Madre Tierra. Gavilan's **Enchanted Excursions to the Edges of the Earth** (tel. 571-025) offers more structured three-day horseback tours into the nearby cloud forest. While many satisfied customers recommend the guide, his price is a bit steep, at US$75 per day. Ask how to find Gavilan at the Madre Tierra. **Orlando's Excursions** offers one-day cloud forest walks for US$15 per person, for groups of three or more. Tours can be arranged from the **Artesanal Primavera** shop in town near the plaza.

When the sun finally sinks below the Vilcabamban hills, nocturnal life begins to stir around town. A newly opened **discoteca** pumps techno beats to a small crowd into the wee hours on weekend nights. It's located at the turn-off to Madre Tierra (unfortunately for sleepers, a little *too* close). Another disco, with similar hours, has better bar service and a nicer, less garage-like atmosphere. Coming from Madre Tierra, it's a few hundred feet down the road to town. In town, the **Green Triangle** (open until 1am) and **J.J. Bar Café Peña,** one block from the plaza behind the church, are popular night spots. Another bar, **Rumors,** is near the river bridge, off the main street (open 8-11pm). **Max** offers a couch potato's dream. Veg out in front of a large-screen Sony color TV and grab a *Pilsener* (s/2,500), coffee (s/1,200), *Cuba Libre* (s/3,000), or basic food from the waitstaff. Max's video collection includes many English-language films on videotape, with subtitles in Spanish (s/1,000 per person). True to the Vilcabamba vibe, Max is decked out with Bob Marley propaganda (open Mon.-Fri. noon-2pm, Sat.-Sun. noon-11pm).

Machala

The self-proclaimed "banana capital of the world," the growing town of Machala (pop. 130,000) takes its peelable yellow fruit quite seriously. Located 200km south of Guayaquil, floating in a sea of banana trees, you can almost hear the banana laborer's soulful anthem, *Day-O,* echoing through the fields. Machala even greets entering visitors with a huge statue of **El Bananero,** a larger-than-life banana grower carrying a six-foot, seven-foot, eight-foot bunch. Locals extol the sacred fruit with a **banana festival** during the third week in September; rather than work all night, they take this chance to kick back and a drinka rum. The festivities include the selection of one lucky lady to receive the highest honor the city has to offer, the coveted title of Her Highness, the **Banana Queen.** Far from just tallying bananas, Machala is also capital of the El Oro province. Most of Ecuador's entrance formalities are carried out in the grimy border town of Huaquillas, 73km away, making Machala a more pleasant choice for a first or last night's lodging in Ecuador. Unless you hit Machala in festival season, however, most tourists will find little to amuse themselves here, and as soon as daylight come, they wanna go on.

ORIENTATION

Streets in Machala use both a naming and a numbering system, but locals in the know generally use the names. **Avenida 9 de Mayo** is the main north-south thoroughfare, running past the **market,** and, one block south of that, the **main plaza.** The **church** stands on the west side of the plaza; its spire can make a useful landmark. There is no *terminal terrestre,* so buses arrive and leave from various places around town.

PRACTICAL INFORMATION

Tourist Information: CETUR (tel. 932-106), at Av. 9 de Mayo and Pichincha, 2nd floor. Spanish-speaking staff answers questions and offers a booklet with helpful maps (open Mon.-Fri. 8:30am-5:30pm).

Peruvian Consulate: (tel. 930-680; fax 937-040), on Calle Bolívar near Colón, 2nd floor, room 102. Can supply visas, though most travelers who intend to spend less than 90 days in Perú don't need one (open Mon.-Fri. 9am-5:30pm, Sat. 9am-noon).

Currency Exchange: Casa de Cambio Ullauizi (tel. 931-349), on Calle Páez between Av. 9 de Octubre and Rocafuerte (open Mon.-Fri. 8am-noon and 2-6pm).

Telephone: EMETEL (tel. 931-515; fax 922-666), on Av. 9 de Octubre between Calle Velez and Anda de las Palmeras (open daily 8am-10pm).

Airport: Machala's **airport** is located a few blocks west of *el centro* on Montalvo. It is served mainly by TAME, which has one flight to **Guayaquil** (Mon.-Fri., 11:30am, 30min., s/65,500) that continues to **Quito** (3hr., s/135,900). The **TAME office** (tel. 530-139) is on Calle Juan Montalvo between Bolívar and Pichincha, next to the post office.

Buses: CIFA, at the corner of Bolívar and Guayas, across from the Rizzo Hotel, has 2 types of buses to the Peruvian border at **Huaquillas:** the direct (every 30min., 6:30am-7:30pm, 1hr., s/3,600) and the indirect (every 10min., 4:45am-7:45pm, s/3,200). The latter makes stops in **Arenillas** (25min.) and **Santa Rosa** (40min.). There are routine passport checks en route to Huaquillas. To make these as painless as possible, have your passport ready and carry minimal luggage. Various bus companies serve **Guayaquil,** leaving from Av. 9 de Octubre around Tarqui (every 30min., 3am-10:30pm, 3hr., s/8,000-10,000). A few *cooperativos* on Colón between Bolívar and Rocafuerte leave every hr. to **Piñas** (1½hr., s/3,000), **Portovelo** (2hr., s/4,000), and **Zaruma** (2½hr., s/5,000). **Coop Pullman Azuay** (tel. 930-370), on Calle Sucre between Junín and Tarqui, has buses constantly departing for **Cuenca** (43 per day, 1am-10:45pm, 4hr., s/10,000). Buses to **Quito** (via **Santo Domingo** or **Pallatanga**) depart from the **Panamerica** headquarters (tel. 930-141), on the corner of Bolívar and Colón (every 2hr., 8:30am-10:30pm, 10hr., s/24,000, 9:30pm bus s/27,000).**Trans-Loja Internacional** (tel. 932-030), on the corner of Bolívar and Rocafuerte, goes to **Loja** (9 per day, 4am-11pm, 6hr., s/13,500).

Pharmacies: Pharmacies are almost as common as armed guards in Machala. Coincidence? We think not. **Farmacia San Jose** (no tel.), conveniently across from the hospital; **24Hr. Farmacia** (tel. 939-035), next door to TAME. Neither is huge, but both are open 24hr.

Hospital: Hospital Teofilo Pavila (emergency tel. 937-581; fax 935-570), at Buenavista and Boyaca, in front of the Parque Colón (open 24hr.).

Police: (tel. 930-449, 933-391, or 933-392; fax 933-911), at Av. 9 de Mayo and Manual Serrano, about 3 blocks past CETUR (open 24hr.).

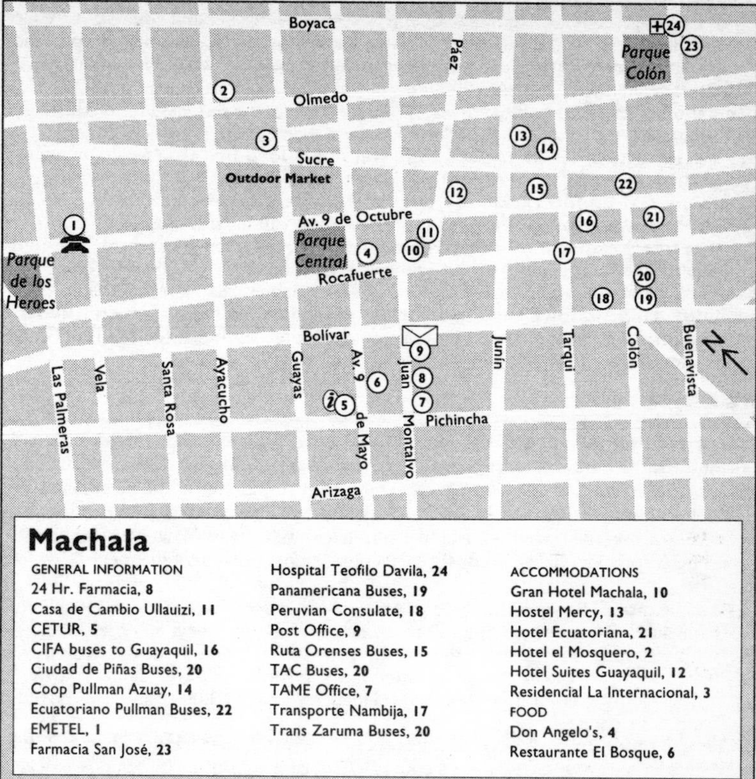

Post Office: (tel. 930-675; fax 931-908), at Bolívar and Calle Juan Montalvo (open Mon.-Fri. 7am-7pm).
Telephone Code: 07.

ACCOMMODATIONS

Because of the large number of tourists spending the night in Machala after shedding the shackles of Huaquillas, budget accommodations are usually easy to find. Anyone staying overnight in Machala should check for window screens or mosquito nets during the hot, wet months. Hotels closer to the center of town, while usually noisier, tend to be safer than those on the outskirts.

Gran Hotel Machala (tel. 930-530), on Montalvo at Rocafuerte. At first the centrally located hotel seems almost as boxlike as the town's forced street plan, but bedspreads peppered with flowers and cherubs keep the place cheerful. An impressive iron gate and 24-hr. security guard assure safety. Rooms for 1-6 people. S/10,000 per person, with bath and fan s/15,000.

Hotel Ecuatoriana (tel. 930-197), at Av. 9 de Octubre and Colón, above the Ecuatoriana Pullman bus station. Though above the bus station, this hotel isn't any noisier than other places, unless you count the chatty receptionists. Upper floors offer well-scrubbed rooms with fans, private baths, and A/C for the lucky few. 2nd-floor rooms share a large communal lounge with a TV and enough floral velvet to make Elvis feel welcome. S/14,500 per person.

Hotel El Mosquero (tel. 931-752; fax 930-390), on Olmedo between Ayacucho and Guayas. Shining but basic rooms all have private bathrooms and hot water. Some have TVs, a good distraction given the two-tone chartreuse-and-white walls, which give the feeling of being submerged in a bowl of pea soup. But hey, soup is good food, the staff is friendly, and most travelers don't get enough liquids anyway. With fan s/20,000, with A/C s/25,000.

Hotel Suites Guayaquil (tel. 927-570), on Páez between Av. 9 de Octubre and Sucre. Old but clean, it has harbored many a weary budget traveler. Marvel at that worthy accomplishment, but hope you don't get a bed that's equally accomplished. Rooms have private baths and either A/C or fan. S/15,000 per person.

Residencial La Internacional (tel. 930-244), on Guayas between Olmedo and Sucre. Diligent young sweeper ensures simple rooms and communal baths are dust-free. Nearby outdoor market makes this place noisier than others, but sturdy screens block brutal mosquitoes and fans keep a-whirrin'. S/9,000 per person.

Hostal Mercy (tel. 920-116), on Junín between Ouinde and Sucre. Tall plants thrive in the courtyard, well-tended by the sweet, grandparent-like owners. *Merciful heavens!* They sure do their best to make visitors feel at home. No-frills rooms with private baths and fans accommodate 1-3 people.

FOOD

Those in search of native flavor should head to Machala's **outdoor market,** mainly around (but not limited to) Sucre between Guayas and Montalvo. Fresh fruits and meats can be found at nearly any hour. The pricier restaurants at the nicer hotels are good for those special occasions. If it's seafood you're craving, join the locals at **Puerto Bolívar** (see below), only a five-minute cab ride away. Whatever you choose, don't be surprised if bananas constitute a considerable portion of the meal.

Restaurante El Bosque (no tel.), on Av. 9 de Mayo between Bolívar and Pichincha. Famished? Try the walloping *carne asado y patacones* (meat and fried plantains with steaming rice, beans, and tomato, s/7,000). So much food, you won't even have room for *ceviche* (s/6,000). Afterwards, relax beneath the bamboo awning, with a frothy glass of *jugo de mora* (blackberry juice, s/2,000), and watch all the animals in Machala's concrete jungle.

Don Angelo's (tel. 932-784), on the corner of Av. 9 de Mayo and Rocafuerte. Within sight of the Parque Central, it's a cool place to hang out during off-hours, especially since they'll never kick you out. Large portions of *comida típica* for around s/10,000. Open 24hr.

Panadería Buen Sabor (tel. 933-216), on Bolívar near Av. 9 de Octubre. This friendly, family-owned bakery cooks up excellent cakes, croissants, and pineapple tarts. Snag the banana turnovers when they're warm (open daily 6am-8pm).

■ Near Machala

PUERTO BOLÍVAR

So here's land-locked Machala, absolutely bursting with bountiful bunches of bananas, with no way to ship them out before they start rotting in the hot equatorial sun. Not to worry. Almost before the town could grasp the magnitude of its problem, the international port at Bolívar, 6km west of Machala, was born. A waterfront town of the Guayaquil genre, people don't come to Puerto Bolívar to sight-see nor to revel in the stench wafting through its waterfront streets. Though little more than Machala's cargo zone, Puerto Bolívar doubles as a savory spot where savvy locals come for **scrumptious seafood.**

Compared to the polluted ocean and streets, Puerto Bolívar's restaurants are refreshingly clean. Each tries to outdo its competition with a stronger superlative, but when multiple restaurants claim to make "the best *ceviche* in the world," it's hard to know where to turn. Actually, it doesn't much matter; seafood here is universally delicious, and meals everywhere usually run between s/6,000-12,000. The *ceviche de camarones* (shrimp *ceviche*) is especially popular. Friendly and family-run, the **Res-**

taurant Sarita (tel. 923-553) cooks up marine delights at the corner of Municipalidad and Apolinaeio Galvés, two blocks behind the waterfront police station. The *ceviche* here gives the competition a run for its money, and even comes with a bowl of tiny limes. If someone steals your limes, Puerto Bolívar's **police** (tel. 929-684) are located on the water, at the corner of Malecón and Municipalidad, in front of the piers (open 24hr.). The **EMETEL** office is next door (open daily 8am-10pm). Puerto Bolívar is not a safe place at night. Given the dreary selection of accommodations and the town's proximity to Machala, passing a night in Puerto Bolívar should be avoided at all costs. If you have to travel here after dark, by all means take a **taxi.** To get here, hop the #1 bus from Machala's Parque Central or anywhere on Av. 9 de Octubre (7min., s/400). Cabs cost around s/5,000.

JAMBELÍ

Though the Galápagos are prized for their endemic wildlife, they don't have anything on the small island of Jambelí, 20 minutes by boat from Puerto Bolívar. Don't come here looking for blue-footed boobies, however; Jambelí's wildlife consists almost completely of Ecuadorian daytrippers and vacationers. In fact, so few *gringos* come here that the ones who do raise quite a stir among the friendly locals. Jambelí's palm-covered food stands and bell-ringing ice cream vendors congregate around the miniature, tropical equivalent of Atlantic City's boardwalk, a cement and Spanish tile street that runs through the center of this small town. While music, swaying palms, and spirited volleyball matches give Jambelí a constant "spring break" feel, the atmosphere changes dramatically with the seasons. Hot summer months bring mosquitoes, so bring insect repellant and check hotel windows for screens. Peskier vermin, *los turistas,* come in droves from August to October and during holidays, causing prices to rise to as much as three times the normal rates.

Not all visitors are daytrippers, and Jambelí has several options for those looking for a place to hang their beach hats. Despite its fun-in-the-sun atmosphere, accommodations here are by no means Club Med. The popular **Las Cabañas de Pescador** (Machala tel. 937-710) offers doubles for s/20,000, but is often full. Next door, the older **Hotel María Sol** (Machala tel. 937-461) has basic rooms with private baths. Singles s/20,000; doubles s/35,000. The nicest rooms are at the pricier **Cabañas del Mar** (tel. 937-007, leave a message at the EMETEL office). Plan to share an adjoining shower with the adjacent room. Doubles s/60,000. Scrumptious seafood is almost always the specialty of the day in Jambelí. Restaurants **El Niño Turista** and **El Pinguino,** next door to each other on the boardwalk, both serve fantastic, fishy, and frugal meals running between s/7,000-12,000. After supper, grab a cool drink and watch the sunset from the awesome bamboo hammocks in front of El Pinguino.

To get to Jambelí during the week, take a **boat** from Puerto Bolívar (Mon.-Fri., 7:30, 10am, 1, 4pm, 20min.). The same boats also return from Jambelí (Mon.-Fri., 8:15am, noon, 3, 5:30pm). On weekends, boats leave whenever they're full, though the wait usually isn't very long (s/8,000 round-trip). Be prepared to pay the s/200 entrance fee on your way into town. Weekend or holiday travelers should find out when the last boat leaves, as some drivers like to start their own holidays early.

PUYANGO PETRIFIED FOREST

The Puyango Petrified Forest, near Ecuador's border with Perú, celebrates both the living and the dead. The park's few visitors roam under the towering palms and creep through the giant ferns that grow alongside Puyango's 100-million-year-old **Arcadia trees.** These stone-cold stumps have some of the largest fossilized trunks in the world, measuring 11m (36ft.) in length and over 1.6m (5ft.) in diameter. Though they'd be hard-pressed to nest in the Arcadias, over 130 bird species live in this small park. To fully appreciate and identify them, check out Dierdre Platt's *Puyango Bird Guide* (s/5,000), available from the park administration. The trail through the towering trunks is toilsome in places, with some tough terrain and river crossings. Gold panning and river rafting may also be possible—ask the park administration for more details. Camping is available for US$20 per person, or guests can stay in the much cheaper rooms at the center for s/10,000 per person. Friendly local guides cost another s/5,000. Park admission is US$10 for foreigners.

Puyango is a worthwhile site for those with plenty of time or genuine interest. Other travelers might find that the extended travel time outweighs Puyango's pleasures. No buses go to the small city of Puyango (pop. about 200), but **Cooperativa de Loja** gets you pretty close. From Machala, take the 9am bus #2 to Alamor. Ask the driver to let you off at the second security checkpoint at the entrance of the park. From here, either walk the 5.5km to the park's entrance (about 1hr.) or arrange for a car to meet you; try calling the **Puyango Administration Commission** in Machala (tel. 934-378 or 930-012; fax 937-655), at Boyaca and Novena Este. Rides cost s/10,000. Buses back to Machala or Loja pass by at frequent though uncertain times. Ask about return times when buying your morning bus ticket.

Zaruma

Founded in 1536, just after the arrival of the Spanish conquistadors, the mountainous, gold-mining town of Zaruma (pop. 7000) wears its age well. Most mines were believed to have been combed clean long ago, but the conspicuous number of *"Compro Oro"* ("I buy gold") signs still found around town threaten to give away Zaruma's secret. Yes, several active gold mines are located just outside of town, and with a little research and persistence, it is even possible to visit one of them. Despite the gold, Zaruma is not a rich town and its narrow streets are still lined with aging but beautiful wooden buildings from the turn of the century. One of the town's biggest festivals, the yearly **Expo-Zaruma,** is held during the second week of July.

Practical Information Zaruma is easily accessible by bus either from Machala or Piñas. **TAC** (tel. 972-156) and **Ciudad de Piñas** (no tel.) share an office on Av. Honoristo Márquez. Buses go to **Quito** (5:45, 6:30pm, 12hr., s/25,500), **Guayaquil** (midnight, 2, 8:45am, 6hr., s/14,500), **Cuenca** (12:30am, 6hr., s/15,000), **Loja** (4, 8am, 5hr., s/9,500), and **Machala** (every hr., 3am-7pm, 2½hr., s/5,800) via **Portovelo** and **Piñas. Coop de Azuay** (no tel.), down Márquez, has two additional buses to **Cuenca** (1:30, 7:30am, 6hr., s/14,500). The **post office, pharmacy,** and **doctor's office** are all located in the town plaza beside the church. The **police** (tel. 972-198), on Colón, are available 24 hours.

Accommodations and Food On the main road into town, **Hotel Rolando** (tel. 972-800) sits just above the gold mine. All rooms have private bath, hot water, and a TV. Get here early to snag one of few rooms not reminiscent of a mineshaft. The other quarters are underground and considerably darker. Singles s/25,000; doubles s/30,000, with two beds s/40,000. The **Hotel Municipal** (tel. 972-176), on Calle El Cesmo, is near the mountain ridge. Though you might grumble your way through the hike up, the view is without a doubt the best thing about this place. All rooms have private baths and warm water. Make sure your *cabaña* isn't musty. S/15,000 per person. Grub in Zaruma isn't scarce, and several good places can be found on Sucre. Near the top of the hill, the **Zamora Café** (no tel.), is a cool local joint. The big thing here is *tigrillo—plátanos,* cheese, and eggs all scrambled up together (with drink, s/3,500). Your arteries might not thank you for that one, but don't worry—tamer, healthier fare is also served. **Mimos,** the restaurant across the street, isn't afraid to experiment either. Try their banana leaf-wrapped cuisine, like the *quimbolito* (a sweet cake with raisins, s/700) and *umitas* (ground corn, sugar, and cheese, s/600).

Sights Grab a pick-axe and hard hat, cross your fingers, and hope to strike it rich. Just outside of town, a number of active **gold mines** inspire dreams of the sweet life. Those wishing to visit or learn more about the mines should enquire at the Municipio (tel. 972-121; fax 972-194), or talk to local historian German Gallardo Cabrera (tel. 972-113), who can usually be found at Farmacia Suiza in the central plaza. **Compañía**

Bira (tel. 972-766), a gold mining outpost on the road into town, has given tours in the past. Those overcome with gold-plated, greedy thoughts may want to absolve themselves of the deadly sin with a hasty retreat to the stunning **Iglesia de Zaruma** in the center of town (daily services 6:30am, more on Sun.). Started in 1912, this intricate chapel took over 18 years to build, and the decorating still isn't finished. Two surprisingly life-like series of paintings have recently been added to its ceiling. The first begins with the creation of Adam and Eve, the second chronicles the life of Christ. Both murals end above the two-story altar that gleams with a thin layer of the very best Zaruma's mines have to offer.

■ Near Zaruma: Piñas

In 1825, Spanish geologist Juan José Luis was given a large land grant for his work in the Ecuadorian gold mines near what is now the town of Zaruma. Eager to honor his homeland, the miner called his new ranch Piñas after his former home in Spain's pineapple region. Eventually, Piñas-the-big-ranch became Piñas-the-little-village, with a current population of about 10,000. Never ones to live in the shadow of Juan's pineapple-rearing kinfolk, the people of Piñas happily spend their time cultivating coffee and bananas. And as far as living in the shadows goes, they've chosen something altogether different. About 10 years ago, the people of Piñas erected a large but simple white cross on top of the mountain overlooking their town. From this vantage point, the town itself spreads out beneath determined hikers' sore feet and in the distance, countless mountains fade from deep green to even darker blue. If you talk to anyone in Piñas about their home, the word *tranquilo* will doubtlessly come up, as it is the town's universally agreed-upon adjective.

Maneuvering through Piñas is easy. The four or five main streets run parallel to each other. Cross-streets are rare; flower-strewn staircases take their place. The unhelpful **EMETEL** (tel. 976-105; fax 976-990), just up the street from the Soda Bar, does not allow collect or calling-card calls (open daily 8am-10pm). The two **bus** companies, **Ciudad de Piñas** (tel. 976-167) and **TAC** (tel. 976-151), share an office on Sucre near the center of town. TAC's buses to **Machala** (2hr., s/3,800), **Portovelo** (30min., s/2,000), and **Zaruma** (45min., s/2,000) leave every hour between 4am-6pm. Buses also go to **Loja** (7:45am, 5hr., s/10,000), **Cuenca** (1:30am, 5hr., s/12,000), and **Quito** (6:45, 7:30pm, 11hr., s/25,500) via **Santo Domingo,** with occasional service to **Guayaquil.** There is also daily **local bus** service to the **nearby villages** of Balsas, Marcabelí, Paccha, La Bocana, Moromoro, and Palosalo. **Policlínico Reina del Cisne** (tel. 976-689), on Loja near Olmedo, is a 24-hr. clinic.

Secure, padlocked doors are a must in any Piñas hotel, and the cheapest lodgings of this genre are located on Av. Bolívar and Loja. The **Residencial Dumari** (tel. 976-118) is a quality establishment with no surprises, no frills, and hot water all around. Ask about getting one of the two breathtaking terrace rooms for no extra charge. S/10,000 per person, with bath s/20,000. **Hotel Las Orquideas** (tel. 976-355), on the corner of Calderón and Montalvo, has simple, sunny sleeping spaces. Extras like color TVs are randomly dispersed through a few rooms, often at the expense of other amenities like toilet seats or shower curtains. Shop around and choose the extras that interest you most. S/6,000, with bath s/10,000. The orchidaceous **Orquideas Restaurant** is right next door to the hotel. All meals are *comida típica* (entrees s/3,500), and the locals are lovin' it. The spacious, sunny **Mundo Real,** on the corner of Juan León Mera and Sucre, second floor, leaves out no food group with its selection of meat, fish, chicken, and seafood, as well as a variety of grains, soups, and salads. Entrees s/6,000-12,000.

Huaquillas

On Ecuador's border with Perú, the small town of Huaquillas enjoys a fame that is strictly geographic. Unlike many of Ecuador's beautiful small towns, Huaquillas isn't a place where anyone uses up a whole roll of film, except perhaps for the obligatory

"Welcome to Perú" shot. In fact, when it comes to aesthetic value, Huaquillas's dusty streets simply disappoint. Because prices in Ecuador are lower than those in Perú, the main road becomes a virtual street market, swarming with Peruvian day shoppers, money changers, and ubiquitous mosquitoes. Travelers often swap horror stories about Huaquillas; mosquitoes certainly aren't the only thing to watch out for, as thieves lurk in the shadows. The border crossing is usually a painless affair, and most travelers opt to keep moving rather than loiter in Huaquillas.

Orientation and Practical Information Everything of any importance, including the bus stop, border, and immigration office, is along Huaquillas's one street, a nameless thoroughfare referred to here as the **main road. EMETEL** phones are located on the main road across from Ecuadorian Immigration (open daily 8am-10pm). The bus *cooperativo* **CIFA** (tel. 907-370), two blocks from the immigration office, just off the main road, goes to **Machala** (every 30min., 7am-7pm, 1¼hr., s/3,600). **Ecuatoriano Pullman** (tel. 907-025), a few blocks past the immigration office, has buses to **Guayaquil** (13 per day, 2am-6pm, 4½hr., s/10,500). **Panamericana** (tel. 907-695), at the corner of Cordovez and Santa Rosa, goes to **Quito** (10 per day, 6:30am-9pm, 11hr., s/25,000) via **Santo Domingo** (9hr.) or **Ambato** (9hr.). **Pullman Azuay,** next to Panamericana, has buses to **Cuenca** (6 per day, 1am-6:30pm, 5hr., s/12,000). **Trans Unión Carimanga,** two blocks away from the main road at the immigration office and one block to the left, goes to **Loja** (12:30, 5½hr., s/11,000). **Police** are ready 24 hours at their station near the border. Huaquillas's **telephone code** is 07.

Accommodations and Food Huaquillas is not a place where most budget travelers want to hang out, and incoming tourists often immediately catch an outgoing bus to Quito, Machala, Guayaquil, or Cuenca. Travelers arriving late in the evening, may find it more convenient to check into one of Huaquillas's several hotels, though those near the center of town can be noisy. **Hotel Guayaquil** (tel. 907-303), next to the immigration office, has tidy *habitaciones* as basic as they are inexpensive, with bare wooden floors, fans, and not much else. S/7,000 per person, with bath s/10,000. **Hotel Vanessa,** Av. 1 de Mayo 323 y Hualtaco (tel. 907-263), is slightly off the main drag but easily accessible. Though more expensive than some other places, it's one of the best guarantees in town for spotlessness and safety. All rooms have private baths, TVs, fridges, and phones. Singles s/33,000; doubles s/55,000; triples s/77,000.

For some sit-down budget grub, several of the larger restaurants in town have appended smaller, cheaper cafes. Locals recommend **Restaurante Flamingo** (tel. 907-876), on Calle Santa Rosa next to the Panamerican Bus Company. A sweeping selection of seafood, chicken, and rice meals range from s/5,000-16,000. The owners also operate an old fashioned ice cream shop next door.

Crossing the Border Ecuador and Perú are separated by the Río Zarumilla, which is crossed by an international bridge. In general, crossing the border in either direction is a painless process. Everyone leaving Ecuador must pass through the **Ecuadorian Immigration Office** *(Oficina de Migraciones)* (tel. 907-755), on the right side of the main road, about 200m before the border with Perú. It's a good idea to get there early as the lines get longer throughout the day (open daily 8am-noon and 2-6pm). All persons crossing the border in either direction must have a tourist **T3 card,** available at both Ecuadorian and Peruvian immigration offices, and a **valid passport.** Tourist can spend **90 days** in Ecuador within a one-year period. Anyone who wishes to stay longer must get a visa (see Entrance Requirements, p. 5). Citizens of a number of Eastern European, Asian, and African nations need a visa simply to enter Perú. Sometimes immigrations officials ask for a **return ticket** out of the country or for **proof of sufficient funds** for each day travelers expect to spend there, but this is rather uncommon. Customs prohibits bringing bananas, oranges, used cars, or large quantities of clothing for resale into Perú.

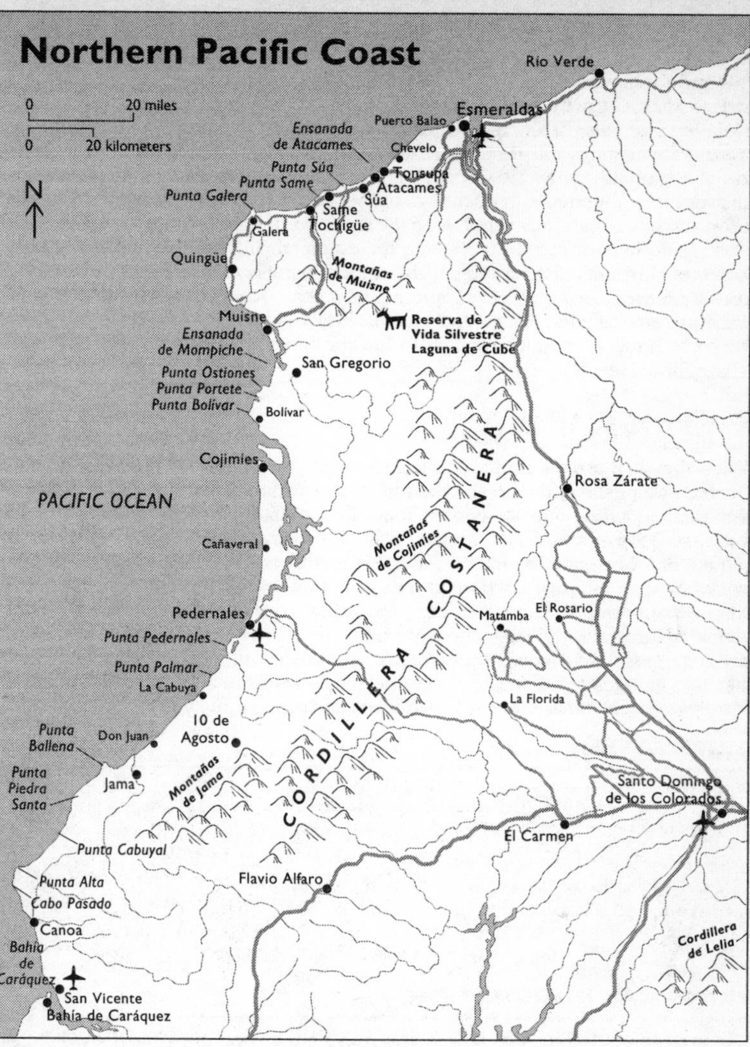

The Pacific Coast

Ecuador's convoluted Pacific coast, composed of a motley combination of beaches, mangroves, estuaries, and rocky shores, winds its way almost 3000km from the town of San Lorenzo in the northern province of Esmeraldas near the Colombian border to the Peruvian border town of Huaquillas in Ecuador's southern seaside province of El Oro. While weather patterns are quite similar down the length of the coast, with a rainy season from December to April caused by warm water currents offshore, the finer details of life vary somewhat with latitude. The African-influenced northern reaches of the coast mellow more to the beats of the *marimba*. The unpretentious resort center of Atacames sits on Esmeraldas's shores with an abundance of beach-side discos pumping late-night weekend jams to eclectic crowds of native Ecuadorians and foreigners alike. South of Atacames lie ever-so-sleepy Súa and almost-as-mellow-Muisne, towns that do more of nothing than anything else. South from here takes you past miles of lonely beaches and forgotten fishing towns, to the Metroplex of San Vicente and Bahía de Caráquez, towns which sit opposite each other across the gaping mouth of the Río Chone. Bahía sets the stage for the urban coastal cities that start to pop up more frequently to the south of it, including Manta and the ritzy resort town of Salinas. Sprinkled along the sands north of Salinas are the gems of the coast, sparsely populated beaches with recreation ranging from surfing the echoing barrels of Montañita to the testing the hammocks at the isolated resort Alandaluz. The nearby friendly town of Puerto López makes a good base for explorations of Ecuador's only coastal park, Parque National Machalilla. Wherever you decide to visit on the coast, bring your bathing suit and a healthy appetite for seafood, because... it's what's for dinner.

Esmeraldas

When they first arrived on the Ecuadorian coast, the Spanish conquistadors were greeted by emerald-clad *indígenas* and wrongly concluded that the land overflowed with that rare green gem. Despite the folly of its origin, the ensuing name stuck, and today the people of Esmeraldas regard it as a compliment to the beauty of their city and culture. Not quite the tourist town, Esmeraldas is an active hub of the fishing, banana, and oil industries, whose unseemly and malodorous by-products can sometimes detract from the waterfront experience. The bona fide gems of the city are the people of Esmeraldas, illuminating what would be a dingy port town with smiles and laughter, music and dancing. Every August 1st through 5th, the locals commemorate the city's independence and celebrate Esmeraldas's African ancestry with the music of the *marimba* and accompanying parading and dancing.

ORIENTATION

Buses from Quito usually drop off on **Av. 10 de Agosto,** the northern border of the central plaza. **Bolívar** borders the park to the east, and **Sucre** to the west. Bolívar becomes **Libertad** north of Pichincha, and leads to Esmeraldas's beach community, **Las Palmas.** Buses from neighboring towns drop off along **Malecón,** which runs parallel to the **Río Esmeraldas** and leads to the port in the north. Esmeraldas is fairly spread out, and it is difficult to quickly discern where the hub of the city is. Keep in mind that apart from Las Palmas, most of the city's attractions are between Rocafuerte and Canizares, along the parallel streets of Olmedo, Sucre, and Bolívar.

PRACTICAL INFORMATION

Tourist Information: CETUR, Bolívar 2-23 y Mejia (tel. 714-528). Open Mon.-Fri. 8:30am-1pm and 3-10pm. **Esmeraldas Tur,** Canizares 221 y Bolívar (tel./fax 712-142). Open Mon.-Fri. 8:30am-1pm and 3-10pm.

Money Exchange: Banco Pinchincha (tel. 728-743 or 728-748; tel./fax 728-745), at Av. 9 de Octubre and Bolívar (open Mon.-Fri. 8am-2:30pm and 3-8pm, Sat. 8am-2pm), and **Banco Popular** (tel. 725-391), at Piedrahita and Bolívar (open Mon.-Fri. 9:30am-4pm, Sat. 9am-2pm), both change money and traveler's checks and have 24-hr. ATMs.

Telephones: EMETEL (tel. 728-814), at Montalvo and Malecón, above the post office. S/500 per 3min. in a booth (open Mon.-Sat. 8am-4pm and 7-9:45pm).

Buses: Trans Esmeraldas, on Av. 10 de Agosto between Sucre and Bolívar. Buses to **Quito** (13 per day, 7:45am-12:55am, 5½hr.) come in 2 varieties: larger ones show movies and TV shows and have clean bathrooms (s/16,000), while smaller buses lack bathrooms and other luxuries (s/14,000). Buses to **Guayaquil** also come in degrees of luxury (13 per day, 7:20-12:15am, 12hr., around s/18,500). **Coup La Costenita** (tel. 713-552 or 712-846), at Malecón and Av. 10 de Agosto, has buses to **Muisne/Salto** (16 per day, 5am-8pm, 2hr., s/4,000), **Tola** (6, 7:30, 9, 11am, 1:30, 3pm, 4hr., s/6,500), **Borbón** (6:30am, 8, 10pm, 4hr., s/8,000), **Atacames** (every

15min., 5am-11pm, 45min., s/1,800), **Súa** (every hr., 5am-11pm, 1hr., s/2,000), and **Same** (every hr., 5am-11pm, 1¾hr., s/2,500). **Del Pacífico** (tel. 714-099), at Malecón and Piedrahita, transports to **Muisne/Salto** (10 per day, 5:30am-4:30pm, 2hr., s/4,000), **Borbón** (every 2hr., 5am-5pm, 4hr., s/8,000), and **Tola** (every 2hr., 4:30am-4:30pm, 4hr., s/7,500). Buses to **Atacames** (45min., s/1,800), **Súa** (1hr., s/2,000), and **Same** (1¾hr., s/2,500) leave at 5, 5:30, 5:45, 8:20, 9:15, 11am, noon, 1:20, 3:30, and 4:30pm.

Taxis: Cooperativa de Automoviles 5 de Agosto (tel. 710-033), at Av. 10 de Agosto and Bolívar in the northern corner of the park. **Cooperativa de Taxis Puerto Balao** (tel. 711-940), at Bolívar and Av. 10 de Agosto.

Library: (tel. 711-673), at Bolívar and Av. 9 de Octubre, 1st floor, in back of the Municipal Building (open Mon.-Fri. 8am-noon and 1-7pm).

Pharmacies: Farmacia Ortiz, Bolívar 2-00 y Salinas (open Mon.-Sat. 9am-6pm) and the simply-named **Farmacia,** Bolívar 5-19 between Av. 9 de Octubre and Pichincha (open Mon.-Fri. 7am-6pm).

Supermarket: Micromercado Imperial, Bolívar 2-40 y Mejia (open Mon.-Sat. 8:30am-1pm and 3-8:30pm).

Hospital: (emergency tel. 711-143, tel. 710-151 or 710-012), on the right-hand side of Libertad as you head towards Las Palmas. Free 24-hr. emergency treatment.

Police: (emergency tel. 710-055, tel. 711-484 or 714-510), at Bolívar and Cañizares (open 24hr.).

Post office: (tel. 710-140), at Montalvo and Malecón, 1st floor, in the same building as EMETEL (open Mon.-Fri. 8am-7pm, Sat. 8am-2pm).

Telephone code: 06.

ACCOMMODATIONS

If arriving from Quito or any other Ecuadorian city with decent lodgings, prepare to be underwhelmed. After researching the options, you'll be fortunate if you've found two or three suitable budget destinations. Most charge around s/20,000 for musty, cramped rooms dying for new paint jobs. No hotels offer hot water, which might be actually providential, in light of the city's unbearable humidity.

Residencial Zulema (tel. 710-910, 711-789, or 712-424), on Olmedo between Cañizares and Piedrahita, in the southwest part of town. One of the few budget hotels in town that isn't straight out of a Poe tale, thanks in large part to the almost comical green paint job. Supple mattresses laid down on just about anything from cots to slabs of concrete. Keep cool with ceiling fans and windows big enough to catch even the smallest breezes. Singles s/10,000, with bath s/15,000; doubles s/20,000, with bath s/30,000; triples s/30,000, with bath s/45,000.

Hostal Galeon, Piedrahita 3-30 y Olmedo (tel. 713-470, 713-116, or 710-861; fax 714-839). Avast, knick-knacks from the days of armadas and pirates. Lobby adorned with paintings of sea adventures, a ship's wheel, and a mysterious stand of toothbrushes (dirty dog, that's fer scurvy). Rooms resemble ship's compartments only in their simplicity. You can bounce a doubloon off the ship-shape beds. Private baths in all quarters. S/25,000 per mate.

Hotel Roma, Olmedo 718 y Piedrahita (tel. 710-136 or 713-872), just north of the Galeon. Rooms fit for a prince or a pauper—it's all a matter of luck. At best, breezy rooms have color TVs, polished hardwood floors, and the occasional oak dresser. Not so ideally, some walls could definitely use a paint job. All rooms have private bathrooms that may need new lightbulbs (make sure to check). S/25,000-35,000 per person, depending on "quality," which can be quite arbitrary.

Hotel Colonial (tel. 711-888), on Plata Torres, off Kennedy in Las Palmas. Follow Libertad north out of town; about 300m from the road's end, take a left on Plata Torres. Colonial is at the end of the street on the right. Saturated with coconut trees and grass hut quarters, Colonial is one of the few affordable places to slumber near the seashore, and is not bashful in its use of tropical motifs. Rooms are not much to look at, but the coastline is. All rooms have A/C and giant private bathrooms. Rooms for 1-5 people. S/30,000 per person, discounts for 4 or more.

FOOD

The major port town along the northern coast, Esmeraldas abounds with scrumptious seafood cuisine, served in both sit-down restaurants and tiny booths along the road. Typical regional dishes include *encocados* (seafood cooked in coconut milk), *tapaos* (meat or fish covered with plantains and wrapped in banana leaves), and *ceviche* (a raw seafood soup steeped in oil and vinegar). Av. Olmedo has an especially dense congregation of eateries with inexpensive sit-down meals.

Restaurant Las Vegas (no tel.), at Cañizares and Bolívar, 2 blocks south of the central plaza. No showgirls or slot machines here. Interior design looks like an immense double garage, but the food is unsurpassed in Esmeraldas. Ghettoblaster emits *discoteca* jams while ceiling fans provide a well-needed breeze. Gargantuan pasta dishes s/3,500-6,500, seafood s/8,500. When you're done, they'll bring toothpicks for your pearly whites (open Mon.-Fri. 7am-10pm, Sat. 7am-3pm).

Las Redes (tel. 711-739), on Bolívar facing the Parque Central. Bongo drums swing from fish-net ceilings over intimate fold-up picnic tables. Decorated with Nat King Cole albums and the Beatles's Abbey Road—they couldn't find Yellow Submarine, so they settled for an Octopus's Garden. Fish entrees right out of the nets (s/6,500). Don't miss the fried fish dish (s/8,000). Open Mon.-Sat. 7am-10pm.

Chifa China, Av. 9 de Octubre 3-20 y Olmedo (tel. 722-221). Providing much-needed variety, Chifa China breaks from typical regional cuisine. While you wait for the sometimes sluggish service, learn the Chinese characters for men and women magic-markered over the restrooms. If you gotta go, ask the management to interpret or hope for peaceful encounters. Massive rice dishes s/4,000-4,800. One of the least expensive lobster plates in town for s/13,000.

La Sultana del Valle (tel. 712-988), on Libertad just past Tello, at the northern end of town. If you're lucky, your place setting may be blessed with an entire flower. But given the charisma here, you could just get a leaf. Postered walls scream Colombia, but dishes are pure Ecuador. Enormous *arroz de la sultana* (rice with seafood, beef, and chicken, s/12,000) fills any stomach. The traditional *encocado*, filled with fish or beef, runs s/10,000-11,000 (open Mon.-Sat. 8am-10pm).

SIGHTS AND ENTERTAINMENT

Esmeraldas's **beaches** are less than picturesque, commonly cluttered with driftwood, stones, and a smattering of litter. The hard, smooth sand of the gray shore stretches for miles, the perfect surface for the **soccer games** played here daily but less than ideal for postcards and sunbathing tourists. The water temperature hovers around 21°C (70°F), ideal for a morning dip. At night, the beach becomes the center of the goings-on, with a few outdoor **bars** along Kennedy and a multitude of drinking and dining options down near the sand. **Keops,** one of the seven or eight *discotecas* along the seashore, rocks nightly to the rhythms of *salsa* and *merengue.* Both beer (s/3,000) and cover charge (s/5,000) are more or less standard (open daily 7pm-2am). For a more mellow night, there are two movie theaters in town. The **Cine Bolívar,** Bolívar 5-09 y Piedrahita, shows a wide variety of films, from American hits (yaaa!) to hardcore pornographic films (ooh-la-la), so make sure to check the signs outside that indicate the night's feature presentation (screenings Mon.-Sun., 5:30pm, s/4,000). **Cine Esmeraldas,** Bolívar 7-06 y Av. 10 de Agosto, shows only good, clean films (screenings Mon.-Fri., 6, 8, 9pm, midnight and Sat.-Sun., 2:30, 6:30, 9pm, s/4,000).

Atacames

They're coming. If they're not here yet, just wait until Friday afternoon, when the buses start to arrive. Each weekend, Ecuadorian merrymakers and large groups of high school students infiltrate this small beach town, 30km southwest of Esmeraldas. In droves, they descend on its restaurants, *cabañas,* and bars, filling each to the brim. Groggy visitors wake every morning to the sounds of reggae and dance music flowing nonstop out of local bars from 9am until as late as 3am. Blenders whipping up *batidos* (fruit shakes) from coconuts, pineapples, guavas, mangos, and oranges can be spotted on every street corner and bar stand. During the week, Atacames slows down a little; the blenders go at half-speed, the music dies down around 1am, and the partiers rest up for the weekend. Arrive on a weekday to situate yourself before the hordes of hyperactive sun-seekers assault the sands of Atacames.

Orientation and Practical Information The road from Esmeraldas runs through the center of town and continues on to Súa and Same. People refer to this road as **Principal,** but don't confuse it with the Principal that leads from the footbridge to the beach. Buses drop people anywhere along this main road, but it's best to get off at the center bus stop, recognizable by the long white bench in front of an *"helado bar"* and the sign that says *parada.* The road splitting to the right leads to the beach. To reach the center-of-beach action, walk along this road past the Nuevo Hotel and bear right as the road joins another. Cross the footbridge over the **Río Atacames** and take a right. The street that leads from the footbridge to the beach is **Calle Principal,** and the street that runs parallel to the beach is **Calle Malecón.** Malecón dominates Atacames, monopolizing most of the bars, *discotecas,* and budget hotels. **La Acacia** intersects the main road Principal a little farther south.

Banco del Pinchincha (tel. 731-052), on Principal just north of the central bus stop, changes cash or traveler's checks and has a 24-hour ATM (open Mon.-Fri. 8am-8pm, Sat.-Sun. 8am-2pm). Make national and international calls from **EMETEL** (tel. 731-104), one block south of the bank, opposite the park, first floor. The three booths cost s/500 per three minutes of usage (open daily 8:30am-10pm). Hire the **boats** scattered along the shore to take groups to **Súa** (15min., s/15,000), **Same** (1½hr., s/120,000), or **Muisne** (4hr., s/300,000). **Buses** run through the town center from about 6am-10pm, going to **Same** (½hr., s/1,000), **Muisne** (2½hr., s/4,000), and **Esmeraldas** (1hr., s/2,500). It is also possible to **walk to Súa** (1hr.), but only at low tide. At high tide, the water rises up against rocky cliffs, creating an insurmountable roadblock. **Taxis** are a scarce commodity in Atacames, since they are all based in Esmeraldas. You can get to Esmeraldas from Atacames for as low as s/3,000, but from Esmeraldas to Atacames bargaining starts at s/30,000. **Micro Mercado,** south of the bus stop but north of the basketball/soccer area, sells water, toilet paper, and other staples (open Mon.-Sat. 9am-noon and 3-10pm). **Farmacia Popular** (no tel.), at La Acacia and Malecón, is on the south end of the beach (open 24hr.). **Farmacia** (tel. 731-253), on the corner by the basketball/soccer area, meets pharmaceutical needs, changes dollars, and has a phone for international calls. Resident doctor also provides **emergency medical service** (open Mon.-Sat. 24hr., Sun. until 1pm). **Dr. Vinizio Díaz** (tel. 731-504 or 731-463; fax 731-504), 40m north of the central bus stop, can also provide 24-hour emergency medical attention. Another option, the **medical attention office** (tel. 731-204), is just north of Dr. Díaz (open 24hr.). The **police** (tel. 731-410), on the corner of Acacia and Principal, near the beach, are south of town in a blue and white building. The **post office** is north of EMETEL, facing Banco del Pichincha (open Mon.-Fri. 8:30am-noon and 3-5pm).

Accommodations Atacames possesses a wealth of accommodations, but the riches are quickly devoured when the busloads of high school students and other Ecuadorian beach-goers descend on the town. The sand-sprinkled Calle Malecón has the most places to stay, and almost every establishment ranges between s/18,000-25,000 per person. The benefit of Malecón's beach proximity is somewhat negated by the nuisance of noise from the street's assortment of bars, *discotecas,* and stereo-thumping automobiles. A suitable escape from Malecón is **El Nuevo Hotel** (tel. 731-020 in Atacames, 714-459 in Esmeraldas), at the center of town, 30m west of the bus stop. Pleasantly removed from the fanfare of Atacames nightlife, this brand-new establishment is still only a five-minute walk from the sand. Still reeking from new paint jobs, spotless rooms beckon with multiple-speed ceiling fans and resort names like Honolulu and Acapulco. Palm trees hang lazily over the walls of the courtyard, which contains a volleyball court and a guests-only bar with TV. Unwind until the painful

8am check-out time. Singles, doubles, triples, all with private bath; S/25,000 per person, discounts for groups of four or more. Back on the beach, **Hotel Galeria Atacames** (tel. 731-149), on the north side of Malecón, is just south of Hotel Tiburon. Straight out of *Swiss Family Robinson,* this 31-room hotel/restaurant appears as if it were built as a gigantic tree house. Rooms sport sheet-metal ceilings, wood-plank floors, and mosquito screens on windows. Quarters smell a little musty, but floors are well-swept and bathrooms well-kept. All rooms have private bath, and the hotel offers book swapping, money exchange, and a safety deposit box for valuables. Singles s/22,000; doubles s/33,000; triples and quads s/44,000. **Hotel Tiburon** (tel./fax 731-145), along Malecón, lies just north of Galeria Atacames. Simple, whitewashed rooms are concentrated toward the back to muffle the street sounds. Concrete floors and high-speed ceiling fans assure a chilly night's rest. All rooms have private baths, with soap and clean towels, that emit a reassuring lime cleaning fluid odor. Second-story restaurant, festooned with seashells on strings, provides quality food and ocean views (meals s/7,000-20,000). The café downstairs serves juicy hamburgers (s/3,000) and hotdog-with-fries plates (s/3,000). Rooms for up to 6 people; s/20,000 per person. **Hotel Rodelu Cabañas** (tel. 731-033 or 713-713; fax 714-714) is on Principal near Malecón. *"Cabañas"* are really just hotel rooms that can hold hordes of people. Ceiling fans and tiny radio systems for those who can't bear to leave the disco behind. Narrow beds with thin sheets, cold showers, and dusty wood floors combine for an unexciting but comfortable stay. Rooms hold four to eight; refrigerators s/3,000 extra. Rates start at s/22,000 per person (the more people, the cheaper the per-person price).

Food Most of Atacames's dining options are pressed from the same mold, serving a monotonous but enjoyable selection of rice dishes accompanied by seafood, beef, or chicken. Sidewalk chefs cook up beef shish kebobs and corn-on-the-cob at a number of cheap and savory pit stops along Malecón. **Marco's Restaurant** (tel. 731-541), on Malecón north of Hotel Tiburon, conforms to the popular tree house theme, perched just above the sidewalk on a foundation of second-story branches. Enjoy ocean views and ventilation while voraciously devouring various vitalizing victuals, including fried calamari (s/7,500), fresh fish dishes (s/7,500-8,000), and shrimp (s/9,500). Open daily 8am-11pm. **Comedor Pelicano** (tel. 731-260), on Malecón south of Hotel Tiburon, is a local fluorescent hangout, dazzling with vibrant orange-and-blue place settings and classy yellow light bulbs slung from the rafters above. Boombox beats out *salsa* and *discoteca* rhythms as patrons sip 22-ounce beers (s/3,000), wondering how much longer the thatched roof is going to hold out. Fish soup (s/4,000), *encocados* (s/10,000). Yellow bulbs blaze from 8am to 10pm. At **Restaurant Karina,** on Malecón between Hotels Pelicano and Tiburon, eye-catching decor keeps patron from noticing the dogs that occasionally waltz through. Monstrous servings of seafood and rice more than make up for the lack of character. Color TV and stereo entertain from the corner. Feast of rice, shrimp, clams, oysters, and fried fish (s/10,000). Breakfasts run around s/4,000, lunches around s/6,000. **Restaurante La Ramada** (tel. 731-207), on Malecón about 50m south of Principal. Set back from the sand and pleasantly removed from the *discoteca* music, the secluded picnic tables please intimate couples. Seat yourself in bamboo surroundings under grass-thatched roofs. King-Arthur-style round tables could seat all of Camelot. Fried shrimp plate (s/10,000), fish soup (s/4,000), *encocados* (s/10,000), goldfish crackers at the bar (free). Open 8am-10pm.

Sights and Entertainment Lined with nearly 50 grass-hut bars, Atacames's well-maintained shore bursts with diversions. Though dull and gray, the beach itself is actually unsullied and soft, sprawling far enough for 45-minute walks in either direction. First-rate views of **Punta Esmeraldas** to the north and the jagged **Isla de Pájaros** to the south frame this enormous expanse. Though competing for the same prime beachfront space, sunbathers and local soccer players coexist peacefully, while jet skis (s/100,000 per hour) and banana boats (s/5,000 per person) buzz by on the gray-green water. Though the beach is generally safe in the resort area, exercise caution if you decide to explore less populated stretches. Also be careful when swimming in the surf, as the undertow can be quite strong at times.

As the sun sets over the Pacific horizon, the grass-hut bars come alive with lights and music. Welcome to Atacames's nighttime carnival. Packs of teenagers stroll the boardwalk, blushing and making eyes at each other. Adults with beers in hand attempt local moves on the sandy dance floors between the bars. Older visitors catch their breath, sip margaritas, and enjoy the ocean views. The seaside bars, with their identical bamboo structures and woven thatched roofs, all compete for the most complex tropical fruit arrangements. **Nagiba Bar,** just north of Principal along the sand, strives for individuality by presenting two or three different Ecuadorian dance and song teams who put on lively Afro-Ecuadorian performances. Just north of Nagiba Bar along Malecón, partiers of all ages cram into the brand-new **Discoteca Ludos,** jammin' to the vibrations of Latin and American dance beats (open 8pm-2am; cover s/5,000). Even late into the night, Malecón is well-lit, populated, and generally safe. The beach is more dangerous, and late-night walks are strongly discouraged. Pool sharks swim away from the fanfare of Malecón to the mellow billiard hall, **El Gato Wilh,** on the street just before the footbridge to the beach. Each of the three pool tables cost a trivial s/4,000 per hour (open daily 10am-2pm).

■ Near Atacames

TONSUPA

Following in Atacames's footsteps like an admiring younger brother, Tonsupa quietly mimics the boisterous performances of its elder sibling. Grass-hut bars line the beach, virtually identical to those of Atacames—save the glitz, glitter, and heart-pounding music. Tonsupa's major draw is its lack of space-filling, sun-stealing crowds. Its smaller but still sizeable beach is trash-free, but can be shabby in spots. Lest tourists become bored by the absence of other visitors, frivolous beach activities like banana-boating and jet-skiing aim to entertain.

While Tonsupa makes for a quick and painless daytrip escape from Atacames, few accommodations merit a night's stay. One commendable hotel is the brand-new **Cabaña Turística Doña Emerita** (tel. 711-407 or 711-757), at the far south end of the beach. Situated on an empty stretch of sand, the *cabañas* enjoy a solitude unmatched in the area. Spotless white tile floors, whitewashed walls, and sophisticated floor fans add modernity to an otherwise traditional, grass-roofed, cracked-coconuts-in-the-courtyard establishment. All rooms have private baths. Quads s/70,000; sexes s/80,000. There are a couple of places to eat north of the *cabañas,* near the center of Tonsupa. The **Hotel Miramac** (tel. 731-585) has ambrosial, affordable food despite its costly rooms. Two fans struggle to cool off customers as they down fish and shrimp *encocados* (s/7,000-8,000) and icy drinks (s/1,500). Open 7am-10pm. The **Bar/Restaurant Los Corales,** 100m farther north along the beach, brightens up early mornings with breakfasts of eggs, juice, bread, and coffee (s/4,000). Lunch and dinner of the day s/9,000 (open 7am until whenever customers leave). To get to Tonsupa from Atacames, take the **bus** (every ½hr., 10min., s/1,000) or **taxi** (s/3,000). The wide mouth of the Río Esmeraldas prevents walking between the two towns along the beach.

SÚA

Surrounded by bountiful green hillsides, Súa is a tiny fishing village nestled in a shallow valley, a 15-minute drive south of Atacames. The beach is set in a **halcyon** cove with rocky edifices to the north and south. **Still** and gray, its waters are home to a number of **quietly** anchored fishing boats. Occasionally the cove's **pacific** waters are rippled by a returning vessel burdened with nets of squirming sea life. While the beach is rather dark and dirty, strewn with fishing nets and equipment, the picturesque bay and its surroundings make Súa a top-notch setting for **tranquil** hiking and photos. A **calm** half-hour hike leaves from the south of the bay, climbing a winding dirt path up the side of the green bluff that **coolly** dominates the cove. From the top, there is a **serene** panoramic vista of Súa and Atacames to the north and the **quiescent** coastline extending to the south. The bay's waters are most **placid** at dawn, but to witness this you have to pass an **easy-going** night in Súa. The **Hotel Chagra Ramos** (tel. 731-006 or 731-070; fax 731-025), located on the far north side of beach, provides **restful** hillside villas and *cabañas* (s/18,000-22,000 per person, depending on the age of the quarters). Set high upon the hillsides, the villas have private baths and patios with hammocks for **reposing** before scenic sunsets. The basic but blemish-free rooms boast screens on the windows to provide a cool, itch-free, and **untroubled** sleeping environment. The Chagra is also one the few quality places to eat in Súa. Relish the **relaxing** view of the bay under the shade of droopy palm trees as you gobble up chicken salad (s/7,500). American (s/4,500) and fried-fish (s/8,500) breakfasts. The French-owned **Hotel Súa Café/Restaurant** (tel. 731-004) is 50m south of Chagra Ramos. Though few ne'er-do-wells wander into this **hushed** neighborhood, Hotel Súa takes safety seriously. Sturdy door locks and strongboxes for valuables are found in each room. Sleeping spaces are a little musty, with worn floorboards and old wooden dressers, but each has a patio facing the sea, providing **refreshing** sea air and aromas. For now, all living quarters have private baths with cold water, but management promises warm water within a year. The cosmopolitan restaurant downstairs serves French, Italian, and local cuisine. Menu is in French and prices are listed in francs. Shrimp dish sauteed in a **smooth** mystery sauce, made nowhere in the world but here (a hefty s/19,000), pasta with seafood (a more reasonable s/12,000), chocolate mousse (s/6,000). Open daily 7am-9:30pm. To get to Súa from Atacames take a **bus** (every ½hr., s/1,000), a **taxi** (s/3,000), or **walk** south along the beach (1hr., only possible at low tide).

SAME

A honeymooner's paradise, the soft shore of Same waits each day to be deflowered by the first footprints to mark its untouched sands. Same's virtually uninhabited beach, 6km southwest of Súa, is trimmed with bountiful palm trees and tastefully commercialized with only a handful of low-key establishments. Though never more than 20m wide, the beach stretches to the south for a couple of miles. Its greenish surf is said to be the best in the Atacames area, and lingers at a refreshing 25°C (75°F) year-round. Same has many wealthy inhabitants, and its semi-resort status means prices are jacked up a bit more than at other local beaches. The charming seafront *cabañas* of **La Terraza** (tel. 544-507) sit right on the sand, but porch chairs and hammocks mean you won't have to. Built on stilts, each *cabaña* comes equipped with private bath, fan, and window screens. Singles s/20,000; doubles s/40,000; quads s/70,000. Built around a tree trunk, La Terraza's excellent **restaurant** is in touch with its natural side, adorned with giant turtle shells and deserted dugout canoes. The macho *parillada de mariscos* (a feast of lobster, shrimp, calamari, and conch with a helping of rice and fries, s/29,000), is large enough to fill two stomachs. Smaller seafood plates run around s/13,000 (open 9am-3:30pm and 7-9:30pm). For simpler fare, try the **two tiny comedores** opposite the Terraza that serve up seafood cuisine to outdoor diners for around s/7,000. Next door to La Terraza, the **Hotel/Restaurant Seaflower** has expensive meals starting at s/20,000, but lodgings are more reasonable. In the lobby, jazz and local music float past a decor of tapestries and straw couches. The vivacious monkey hops around as freely as the hotel's adorable puppies. Immaculate rooms embellished with seashells and ornate stones, replete with fans, mosquito nets, and well-kept private bathrooms. Doubles s/50,000; quads s/70,000. Get to Same by bus or boat from Atacames or Muisne.

Muisne

Quarantined from the epidemic of tourism that is sweeping the rest of the coast, the quiet island of Muisne, situated about 35km southwest of Atacames, remains ignorant of other beaches' touristy ways. Without cars and telephones, days on the island are as carefree as the inhabitants that walk barefoot through the streets. The lack of badgering tourist crowds allows the gregarious locals to take the time to befriend the visitors they do receive. A few days in Muisne and you'll probably know the names of all of the beach's restaurant owners. If you've got an affable disposition and a few words of Spanish under your belt, they may even remember your name. Sun, quietude, and hospitality unite here to create an experience of overwhelming leisure, contained only by the island's watery borders.

Orientation and Practical Information The **bus stop** is in the mainland town of **Salto,** just footsteps from the docks. From the dock, it is a thrilling three-minute, s/400 crawl across the 200m waterway that makes Muisne an island. On the docks of the island, boys on bicycles offer rides to the **beach** for s/1,000; otherwise, it is a 15-minute walk with a couple of bicycle boys in tow. The road directly perpendicular to the docks leads to the beach.

There are no official money-changing facilities here, so bring some sucres with you. Transport to other destinations leaves from the mainland docks. **Buses** run to **Esmeraldas** (5:30am-9:30pm) via **Same** (1hr.), **Súa** (1¼hr.), and **Atacames** (2hr., s/4,000). **Boats** run to **Cojimíes** from the dock to the right of the main one (10am, 1pm, or as soon as they fill up, 1½hr., s/15,000). It pays to get there on time, and be ready to get wet (see Near Muisne: Cojimíes, p. 170). The **EMETEL** office and **hospital** are on the road from the docks to the beach. EMETEL is often closed and not usually useful, but the hospital is open 24 hours. A **pharmacy** is on the road parallel and to the right of the main road as you go from the docks to the beach. The **police** are down the first cross street to the right as you go from the docks to the beach.

Accommodations While Muisne has few hotels, there's nearly always something available since so few tourists visit the island. All rooms come equipped with mosquito nets (an absolute must) and not-so-reliable cold water. Perhaps the biggest problem hotels here have is keeping wet sandy feet from creating indoor beaches. With the sand come the crabs, and eventually the palm trees start growing. The newly renovated (but far from finished) **Hotel Plaza Paraíso** is at the far south side of the beach. Sherry, the Texan proprietor, treats every guest like family with her unbeatable tourist information and tips. Enveloping love chairs, reed mats, candled tables, board games, self-serve beer in the fridge ... no wonder she called it paradise. Windowsill collections of seashells and stones show only rudimentary forms of an indoor beach, and the obligatory mosquito nets should obstruct any further progress. Communal but well-scrubbed toilets and showers. S/10,000 per person, but prices may rise with the arrival of a bar and international chef. The **Cabañas San Cristóbal** are at the far north end of the beach. Musty wooden floorboards whisper tales of bygone days, but fresh air flows through front and back windows. Doors open right onto the sand, equipped with good-sized locks to prevent unwanted visitors. All rooms have private baths. Showerheads curiously similar to toilet seats make for a peculiar bathroom experience. S/10,000 per person. On the sandy road that runs from Cabañas San Cristóbal into town, **Hotel Galápagos** takes the classic Muisne approach of relative isolation. It's more removed from beach life, plus the amicable management is conscientious about cleanliness, so no need to worry about sandy floors here (nor crabs nor palm tree saplings nor giant tortoises...nor damned sea lions). Immaculate, well-ventilated rooms sport pink-and-yellow mosquito nets, and all have private bath. S/20,000 per person.

Food Dining on this coastal isle is an exercise in patience. The typical selection of seafood dishes is served up at a predictably lackadaisical pace. But laid-back dining does have its advantages. Most restaurants sit right on the beach, and mellow Muisne's unofficial mantra reads, "No shirt, no shoes, no problem." So as you wait for your food, sneak a nap or sip a beer and have faith. Eventually the food will come, and when it does ... ooooh, doggey! **Restaurante Mi Delfin,** next door to Hotel

Paraiso, fits the Muisne restaurant profile to a tee. Slow cooking has its mouth-watering rewards here. Shrimp *encocado* comes with a kick (s/9,000). Similarly kickin' fish soup (s/2,500). Open daily 8am-10pm. **Restaurante Suiso-Italiano,** another Muisne mainstay, is on the main road about 100m from beach. Daniel, the Swiss owner, speaks Italian, German, French, Spanish, and English, and can entertain with a game of checkers and friendly conversation. He'll also share the secret of the fly-repelling water bags overhead. The dishes are a welcome respite from seafood. Veggie pizza (small s/9,000, large s/14,000). Mammoth spaghetti dish topped with mozzarella, parmesan, and a local cheese (s/13,000). Open Wed.-Sun. 10am-9pm. **Comedor Rosita,** on the beach north of the main road, cooks an atypically quick breakfast, complete with eggs, bread, coffee, and assorted juices (s/5,000). Wash it down with a banana milkshake special. Rosita also serves assorted seafood dishes (s/8,000). Imagine, all this under rainbow-colored umbrellas and a grass roof (open daily 8am-9pm).

Sights and Entertainment Muisne's shores are endowed with heaps of soft, unspoiled sand, strong surf, and gobs of solitude. The immense **beach** provides one and a half hours worth of walking room in either direction, and the difference between high low tides can be as great as 70m. In an effort to realize their dreams of a palm-fringed beach, the locals have planted palm trees all along the beachfront, with fences to protect the tender young saplings. For the time being, straw-reed umbrellas and avocado branches provide shade until the trees reach maturity. The surf can be rough at times, especially since it is home to tiny stinging jellyfish. The stings can be healed immediately with a dab of vinegar; ask for some at the local *cevicherías.* Occasionally, small sea snakes get washed up on shore. Local children aren't afraid to kill them with rocks, but *Let's Go* recommends steering clear of these venomous creatures of the sea. While the beach is generally quite safe, at night it's best to stay near the lights of the hotels and restaurants. The **Habana Club** is a nice place to rest your weary traveling soul with a chilly beer (s/3,000) or margarita (s/6,000). Huge selection of classic rock and reggae CDs, and amusing posters advocating the use of marijuana, including a never-before-seen version of the Mona Lisa chillin' with a spliff. Management is gregarious, and can provide tons o' info on the destruction of the local mangrove forests (open daily 8pm until closing).

■ Near Muisne: Cojimíes

For most, Cojimíes is little more than a necessary stop in a journey along the coast. The town itself isn't much of a beachy paradise due to the clutter of boats, shacks, and fishing gear covering the sand. The most exciting thing about Cojimíes is the 1½-hour wet-and-wild **boat ride** between here and Muisne. Sailing the open sea, a motorized dugout climbs seven- to 10-foot swells as buckets of saltwater splash into the boat, inevitably soaking passengers to the bone. The boats that make the trip have a storage compartment for bags and other necessities that absolutely can't get wet, but they won't let people in there, so bring some kind of rain gear. Departures from Muisne are roughly scheduled for 10am and 1pm, and boats from Cojimíes leave at 7am, 9am, and sometimes 1pm (s/15,000 each way). To ensure a seat, get to the docks early. **Camionetas** to Pedernales (1½hr., s/5,000) leave all day from the large plaza that doubles as a basketball court, near the dock.

Though there's little reason to spend much time here, if you need to make a phone call or require medical attention, Cojimíes does have an **EMETEL** (open daily 8:30am-9pm) and a **24-hour pharmacy/clinic** (ask for Dr. José García), located across from each other on the town's main street. If somehow you get stuck in Cojimíes, you'll definitely save money on accommodations, but the same can be said for getting thrown in jail. To be fair, Cojimíes's accommodations do provide mosquito nets and lightbulbs, luxuries not enjoyed by Ecuadorian convicts. The **Residencial Manuelita,** with its cramped, dingy rooms and sturdy locks, is on the main street, a couple of minutes down from EMETEL. Singles s/5,000. Farther down the main road is the **Residencial Popular,** which closes guests in with thick brick walls and wood-plank floors that don't quite fit together. The dining options in Cojimíes are limited, but of a much higher quality than the lodgings. Directly across the plaza from the docks is the **Marisquería El Cangrejo.** The grass hut is held up by scrawny bamboo branches, but diners come anyway for delicious s/7,000 dishes, including shrimp and calamari (open daily 7am-10pm).

Pedernales

This tranquil seaport, approximately 70km north of San Vicente and 40km south of Cojimíes, takes advantage of its position in the center of things. Pedernales hosts the largest market on the northern coast, and serves as an important center for the shrimp industry. But while locals may consider Pedernales crucial, travelers searching for the perfect *playa* paradise normally look elsewhere. The town is only significant to coastal visitors as a crucial link in the coastline's chain of transport. The famous *camionetas* to Cojimíes travel north up the coast from here, and several bus companies link Pedernales with inland and southern coastal towns.

Orientation and Practical Information Pedernales's **central plaza** is on the corner of the town's two most important streets: **López Castillo** runs north-south and **Eloy Alfaro** runs east-west. The town's lackluster **beach** is at the west end of Alfaro. Due to free-wheeling cars and industrious fishing boats, the sand retains a grimy appearance and a potent, fishy aroma. The dirty-brown surf is solid, rolling in two- to five-foot waves—fine for swimming, but not much to look at. The town's **EMETEL,** Alfaro 5-10 (tel. 681-105), east of the plaza, cannot make international calls (open daily 8am-1pm, 3-6pm, and 7-9pm). The town's **bus companies** are on López Castillo, south of the plaza. **Cooperativa Costa Norte,** López Castillo 5-28, and **Coactur Bus Company,** López Castillo 5-06, send buses to **San Vicente** (3hr., s/10,000), **Portoviejo** (5hr., s/15,000), **Manta** (6hr., s/16,800), and **Guayaquil** (9hr., s/25,500), approximately every hr., 4am-5:30pm. **Cooperativa Trans Santo Domingo,** López Castillo 5-07 (tel. 681-049), goes to **Santo Domingo** (approximately every hr., 4:30am-6:30pm, 3hr., s/8,000), where connections can be made to other inland destinations. **Camionetas** make the trip to Cojimíes (all day, 1½hr., s/5,000), leaving from the north side of the plaza. The trip begins on a dirt highway, but at low tide the trucks take to the sand and the joyride quickly becomes an off-roading adventure, filled with high-speed glimpses of the surrounding coastline and heart-pounding races to beat the rising water.

Accommodations and Food Given its transportation-hub status, Pedernales has a few suitable accommodations that don't exactly enchant with their ambience, but are decently-maintained and safe. If you arrive late at night, find a place in town rather than stumble around in the dark down by the beach. The **Hotel Pedernales,** Alfaro 6-18 (tel. 681-022), is three blocks east of the plaza. Tiny frames, poppy posters, and brightly painted rooms bring back the angst and trauma of painful kindergarten days. Flowery bedsheets battle the drab forces of concrete walls and floors. Rooms have refrigerators and color TVs. S/10,000 per person, with bath s/20,000. **Aire Libre** (tel. 681-237), on the beach 200m south of Alfaro, supplies 23 unembellished rooms at spare-change rates. Communal bath without showers. Two beds s/15,000, four beds s/30,000. If it's food you're hungry for, Pedernales bursts with bland eateries, both up in town and down on the sand. **Los Frailes** (tel. 681-212), on Alfaro by the beach, is named for the two rocks off Pedernales's jagged ocean cliffs. This place specializes in delicious *ceviche* dishes with fish (s/5,000) or calamari (s/6,000). Turtle shells, flowering plants, and framed photos of the monolithic namesakes cheer patrons on as they down some of the town's best seafood (open 8am-6pm). **El Rocio,** Alfaro 6650 (tel. 681-337), east of the plaza, is across from Hotel Pedernales. The pink rose settings on glass tables make it look expensive, but prices actually rival those of the sidewalk vendors. Soft leather chairs give your legs and eyes a rest from the oft-repeated white-plastic-chair motif. Breakfasts of eggs, bread, juice, and coffee (s/4,000), basic *almuerzos* and *meriendas* with soup, rice, entree, and juice (s/5,000-6,000). Open 7am-11pm.

Bahía de Caráquez

Glittering like a boardwalk in the rough, the *nuevo*-Miami highrises lining Bahía de Caráquez's shores spare no expense in catering to Ecuador's swanky elite. The trouble is, Ecuador doesn't have much of a swanky elite, and most of Bahía's true locals live in metal shacks hidden in the hills behind the city. The government pumps a portion of its mysteriously disappearing funds into making sure this home of ex-president Sixto Durán Ballen remains exactly as its opulent occupants like it. The immaculate streets battle trash with the ubiquitous, hypnotizing town slogan, *"Bahía no tiene una copia, cuidésela"* (roughly, "There's only one Bahía; take care of it"). You can be sure Big Brother is watching in Bahía, and he has placed garbage cans on every corner. Bahía's one insufficiency is in its want of beach space. Built on a rocky peninsula, neither the Río Chone nor the Pacific Ocean allow room for frolicking in the sand. The 10m of sludge-sand that appears at low tide is best used as a boat dock, not a tanning salon.

Orientation and Practical Information Boats from San Vicente drop anxious visitors off along the muddy shore near the intersection of **Aguilera** and **Malecón** (also referred to as Alberto F. Santos), the main street in town. Malecón parallels the **Río Chone,** running north around the peninsula and south towards the bus station. The **Guacamayo Tourist Office** (tel. 690-597), is at Bolívar and Arenas (open Mon.-Sat. 8am-7pm, Sun. 9am-5pm). Calls from **EMETEL** (tel. 690-020), at the corner of Malecón and Arenas, cost s/1,500 per three minutes (open daily 8am-10pm). Change money and traveler's checks, or just get some cash out of the 24-hour ATM at **Filanbanco** (tel. 691-096, 691-102, or 691-053), at Aguilar and Malecón, next to the post office (open Mon.-Fri. 8:45am-4pm, Sat. 10am-2pm). **Coactur buses** (tel. 690-014), on Malecón just past Minveza, at the south end of the boardwalk, go to **Pedernales** (every hr., 4:30am-6pm, 5hr., s/15,000) and **Portoviejo** (every ½hr., 4am-10pm, 2hr., s/4,000) via **Manta** (3hr., s/5,600). Feeling ill? Go to **Farmacia San Gregorio,** at Ascazubi and Montufar (open Mon.-Sat. 8:30am-1:30pm and 2:30-10pm). Feeling *really* ill? **Hospital Miguel H. Alcivar** (emergency tel. 690-002, 690-006, or 690-008, tel. 690-712 or 690-046), at Rocafuerte and Cruzan at the end of town, gives free treatment (open 24hr.). The **police** station (tel. 690-045), at Sixto Durán Ballen and Av. 3 de Noviembre, is open 24 hours. The **post office,** Aguilera 108 y Malecón (tel. 691-177), is open Mon.-Fri. 8am-5:50pm, Sat. 8am-1pm.

Accommodations Just look around—Bahía wasn't built for the budget traveler. While blessed with numerous waterfront establishments suitable for *Lifestyles of the Rich and Famous,* Bahía doesn't brag about its cheaper hotels. The sketchier, shoddier low-rent accommodations are concentrated a couple blocks back from the beach, along Montufar between Ante and Riofrio. The frighteningly expensive accommodations begin to pop up farther north along the peninsula. Luckily, there are a few places that offer something in between these extremes, combining affordable prices with decently-kept premises. **Hotel Palma,** on Bolívar between Arenas and Riofrio, around the corner from EMETEL, is just one block up from Malecón. Sure you came here on vacation, but think of how fun it would be to live in a stranger's madhouse for a couple of days. Kids run everywhere, the playful monkey tied to a pole in the lobby screeches, and the family's clothes dry from the lobby's ceilings. Despite the ruckus during the day, it's quiet at night. Most importantly, though the common baths could look better, the establishment is clean. S/10,000 per person, with bath s/15,000. **Hotel Bahía** (tel. 690-509 or 690-823), on Malecón near the bus stops. As whitewashed as the city's highrises, secure rooms offer little excitement unless you pay s/10,000 extra for color TV. Bring a paperback and enjoy the quietude supplied by the immense hotel's thick walls. All rooms with private bath, scrubbed until sparkling. S/20,000 per person, with hot water and color TV s/30,000. **Hostal Los Caras** (tel. 690-280), at Montufar and Riofrio, three blocks north from the docks and two blocks west along Riofrio. Closer to the beach than most other hotels in this price range, Los Caras even gives ocean glimpses from its fourth-story rooftop terrace. The name comes from an ancient indigenous label for the peninsula, but everything else about Caras is modern. Newly constructed, it comes equipped with all the amenities—private bath, hot water, A/C, and color TV. S/20,000 per person.

Food There are plenty of excellent dining opportunities in Bahía, and even the cheaper places along the Río Chone won't leave you feeling like you've been ripped off. Expect to be inundated with typical coastal entrees—*ceviches,* fish plates, rice and seafood dishes—but along with the meal, enjoy views of the marina and bluffs of San Vicente. **Pablo's Restaurant,** Malecón 11-20 y Ascazubi (tel. 690-529) serves common seafood dishes with uncommonly efficient service. Customers could eat off of the glittering floors of this brand-new establishment, but management likes them to stay in their chairs. Gawk at an impressive beer bottle collection and at the amazing lunch special (soup of the day, entree of choice, and freshly squeezed peach juice, s/6,000). *Ceviche* s/7,500-8,500. Snack on *plátanos* sliced paper-thin (open daily 9am-10pm). Look to your left along Malecón as you step off the docks: **Muelle Uno** (no tel.), on Malecón along the riverfront, is across from Banco Manabí and Restaurant Genesis. This riverfront bamboo shack serves the cheapest, greasiest food in town. Red faux carnations embellish the six undersized tables, each of which is always filled with ravenous locals. Grab an artery-clogging but appetizing breakfast of eggs, cheese, coffee, and fried bananas (s/5,000) or a lunch feast of soup, rice, salad, and a side of beef (s/5,000). Open Mon.-Sat. 8am-3pm. **Restaurant Genesis,** on Malecón along the riverfront, is just south of Muelle Uno. Genesis defines its image with its waterfront patio seating. Pastel umbrellas and sun-beaten deck are as close as it gets to the beach. Choices range from fried chicken to rice with calamari, but prices always hover around s/8,000. Management patiently serves s/1,500 coffees to visitors who enter under the guise of diners, but really come to snap river photos from the back deck (open daily 8am-10pm).

Sights and Entertainment The inhabitants of this sedate coastal city tend to be older, wealthier businessmen who have done their darndest to keep Bahía clean and quiet. They've succeeded—the streets are reasonably safe, spotless, and supremely strollable. Signs remind inhabitants of the prohibitions against soccer-playing on the shore, sidewalk vending, and loud music. All of this gives Bahía a certain peaceful quietude, but let's face it, its conservative creed also makes it a tad stuffy and boring. A **walk along Malecón** is a good way to get a feel for Bahía; it runs the length of the city and passes some of its more interesting attractions. As the road winds around the peninsula to the western side, the waves begin to crash violently against the rocky perimeters, catapulting water onto the streets and sidewalks above. On the western side, along Versillio Ratty, there is an excellent break for **surfing.** Although there isn't a beach, waves form so far out that surfers can get in good rides before they have to bail out to avoid a rocky conclusion. To get in, they stand along rocks to the left of the break and courageously leap into the murky depths, boards in hand. The waves roll in along a jetty, causing them all to break leftwards. During the summertime, the swells are 2 to 3 ft., but in the winter they get up to 5 or 6 ft. Rides are relatively short due to the dangerous shoreline. If you don't surf, it's almost as much of a rush to watch these talented daredevils challenge Mother Nature for quick thrills.

■ Near Bahía de Caráquez

CANOA

Canoa's broad, deserted sands sit 17km north of San Vicente. Free from the tumult of tourist traffic and sedulous seafolk, only the sounds of the waves crashing against the cliffs to the north and the occasional crab scuttling across the sand upset Canoa's calm. The waves that swell the muddled green water are wicked enough to bring a professional surfing competition here every February. Buses to San Vicente pass every half-hour (20min., s/1,000).

For a few surfing tips, try knocking on the gates of the **Hosteria Daniel Potosi** (tel. 691-201), 300m from the beach along the main road. Daniel, an aspiring young surfer who speaks decent English, often obliges guests by showing them how the waves were meant to be ridden. Daniel also offers daytrips to a mammoth cave hidden in the treacherous cliffs of Canoa, free to hotel guests. His newly-constructed cabins, mounted on hillside stilts, overlook the crashing waves. Guests can also stay in an older house with well-kept rooms and astoundingly high ceilings. Soft leather couches and a healthy scattering of paperbacks, magazines, and board games turn three breezy living rooms into chummy hangouts. S/15,000 per person, with bath s/20,000; two-person cabin s/50,000, four-person cabin s/60,000. For surfer's sustenance, the best bet is the **Restaurante Costa Azul** (tel. 690-075), on the main road, 10 steps from the sand. Painted a gutsy purple, Azul amazes with decor and ocean views, not to mention its battered fish dish (s/6,000). Open 7am-7pm.

SAN VICENTE

San Vicente's site at the mouth of the Río Chone prevents it from developing into a beach community, but its sheltered marina is home to a healthy fishing industry. Across the river from Bahía de Caráquez, San Vicente seems to stare in adoration at its wealthier, more pristine neighbor. Virtually every shop along the boardwalk faces Bahía, and boats leave hurriedly every five minutes to cross the river. Visitors escape across the river as well, but those who need to pinch pennies often find themselves crawling back to San Vicente's cheap beds.

San Vicente is basically just one road, **Malecón,** which runs right along the waterfront. All of the bus companies have their offices at the northern end of this street, and go to **Portoviejo** either hourly or bi-hourly (6am-8pm, 2¼hr., s/4,000-5,000), often continuing from there on to **Manta** (3hr., s/6,800-7,500). **Cooperativa Costa Norte** also goes to **Pedernales** (every hr., 6:45am-5:30pm, 3hr., s/10,000) and **Canoa** (every 20min., 7am-6pm, 20min., s/1,000). **Reina El Camino** passes through Portoviejo on its way to **Jipijapa** (6:45, 11am, 3, 10:15pm, 3hr., s/7,500). The blue-roofed **ferries** go to **Bahía de Caráquez** (every 5min., 6am-6pm, 10min., s/700). At low tide, they leave from the sands just north of the car ferry dock, but at high tide (usually afternoon), they depart from the nearby pier. The **police** (tel. 674-202) are at the north of the boardwalk, where Malecón splits at the rotunda. **EMETEL** is next to the police station, but only makes local calls (open Mon.-Sat. 9am-noon and 3-6pm, Sun. 3-6pm). **Farmacia Mayte,** Malecón 29 (tel. 674-245), is open 24 hours.

There are only a handful of places to stay in San Vicente, and the cheapest ones are clustered at the south end of the boardwalk. The **Hotel Narciso de Jesus** (tel. 674-514) uses anything it can to prop up the ceilings, and the beds may put a knot in your back, not a spring in your step. Ceiling fans, mosquito nets, decaying walls, and communal bathrooms complete this shoddy, s/7,000 per person package. The nearby **Hotel San Vicente** tries to sweep guests off their feet with crooked sinks, cracked headboards, and mildew-lined bathrooms. Just think of the money you're saving as you stare out the window you don't have. S/7,000 per person, with bath s/15,000. San Vicente offers very little in terms of dining options. There are a few unremarkable establishments near the bus stops, but you'll have to struggle to find one that's open due to an epidemic of quirky business hours. **Chifa Chunking** (tel. 674-160), at the southern end of boardwalk near the hotels, seems to be the only reliable eatery in town, serving gigantic rice dishes (s/5,000-6,000) and delicious chop suey (s/8,000).

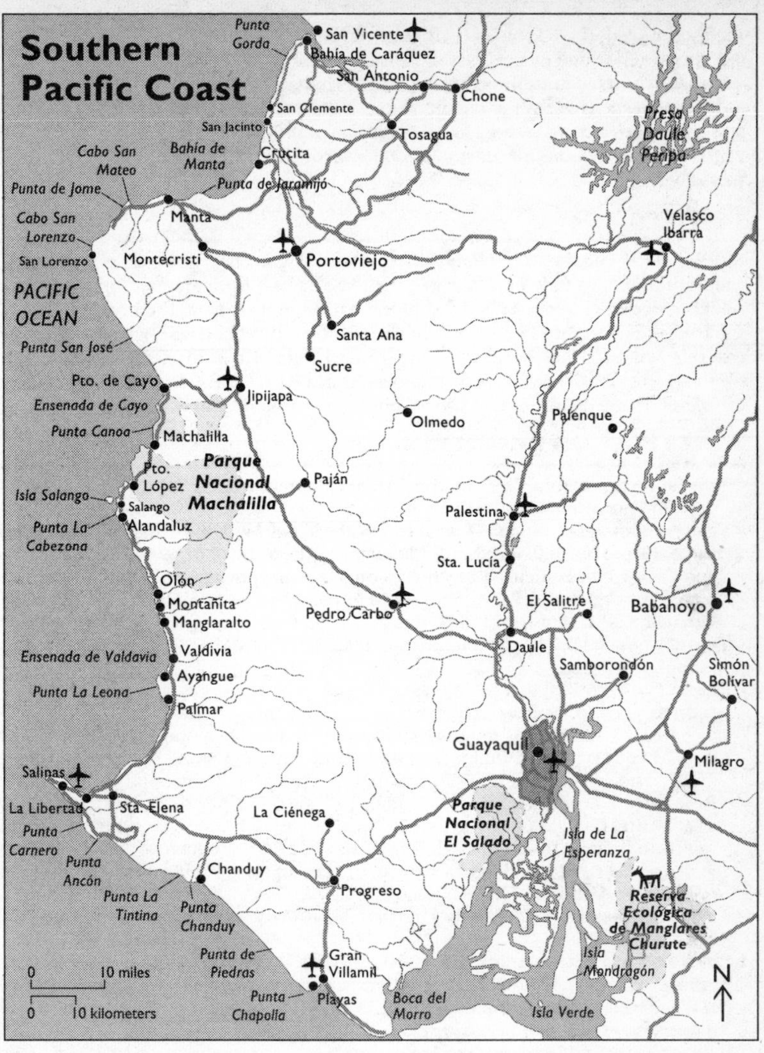

Chinese-owned and run, you can be sure the cuisine's authentic (open daily 10am-10pm).

Manta

Dominated by its immense harbor, Manta has long been a hub of seafaring activities. Known as Jocay ("fish house" in Quechua) prior to Spanish intrusion, Manta was home to a hedonistic community distinguished for its maritime accomplishments. Voyaging the high seas in balsawood rafts and dugouts, the Jocay made frequent excursions to Panamá and Perú, and some zealous scholars of the ancient culture assert they navigated as far as Mexico and Chile. Irrespective of the actual distances the Jocay sailed, the import of their adventures lies in their legacy of reliance on the sea for existence and entertainment, still a prominent reality today. Manta is a far cry from a lazy beach resort; the gritty trade of the industrious sea-faring inhabitants often induces visitors to deem the city filthy and impoverished. Closer to the truth, Manta is a hard-working city whose mirthful inhabitants spend their limited free hours engrossed in spirituous merriment, unconcerned with their sometimes begrimed surroundings.

ORIENTATION

Buses enter Manta by way of **Eloy Alfaro,** presenting fleeting glimpses of **Tarqui,** the southern beach, as they cross the inlet that separates it from Manta proper. The **terminal terrestre** is located just west of the harbor, not far from the bridge. North of the bridge, Eloy Alfaro becomes **Malecón,** running parallel to the water as it passes east of town and leads north to Manta's **Murciélago** beach. In Manta *centro,* north-south streets are **Avenidas,** with numbers increasing as the streets get farther from the water. East-west streets are **Calles,** numbered beginning at the bridge.

PRACTICAL INFORMATION

Tourist Information: CETUR, Av. 3 1020 y Calle 11 (tel. 622-944). Open Mon.-Fri. 8:30am-5pm, but known to close at 4pm.

Travel Agencies: Delgado Travel (tel. 620-046), at Av. 2 and Calle 13 (open Mon.-Sat. 8:30am-1pm and 3-6:30pm). **Manatours** (tel. 621-020 or 621-026), at Malecón and Calle 13, in Edificio Vigía. Open Mon.-Fri. 8am-1pm and 2pm-7pm. **Metropolitan Touring,** Av. 4 1239-45 y Calle 13 (tel. 623-090 or 622-366; fax 611-277). Open Mon.-Fri. 9am-1pm and 3-7pm.

Telephones: EMETEL (tel. 622-700), at Calle 11 and Malecón (open daily 8am-10pm).

Buses: The **terminal terrestre** is along Av. 24 de Marzo just past Av. 4. **Coop Montecristi** goes to **Montecristi** (every 6min., 6am-7pm, 45min., s/1,000). **Coactur** (tel. 620-036) has buses to **Guayaquil** (every 45min., 4am-6pm, s/10,000), **Bahía de Caráquez** (every 30min. starting at 5am, 3hr., s/5,500), **Portoviejo** (every 5min., 4am-10pm, 1hr., s/1,500), and **Jipijapa** (every hr., 4am-6pm, 1hr., s/1,500). **Reina del Camino** (tel. 620-963) goes to **Quito** (12 per day, 4am-10:30pm, s/17,000) and **Guayaquil** (every hr., 2:30am-7:30pm, s/10,000). **Coop Manglaralto** travels to **Jipijapa** (every 2hr., 4am-4pm, 1hr., s/2,000), **Puerto López** (every 2hr., 4am-4pm, s/5,000), **Salango** (every 2hr., 4am-4pm, s/5,000), and **La Libertad** (every 2hr., 4am-4pm, 5hr., s/13,000).

Taxis: Cooperación Ciudad de Manta (tel. 610-704). Taxis congregate around the bus terminal.

Pharmacies: Farmacia Rex (tel. 620-690), at Av. 2 and Calle 9 (open daily 8:30am-1pm and 3-6pm). **Farmacia** (tel. 610-638), at the corner of Calle 7 and Av. 24 de Mayo, in the municipal building (open Mon.-Sat. 8am-7:30pm). There are also 5 or 6 pharmacies adjacent to the hospital.

Hospital: Hospital Rodriguez Sambraho de Manta (emergency tel. 611-849, 621-595, 625-603, 625-602, 612-014, or 625-610), at Av. San Mateo and Calle 12 in Barrio Santa Martha. Free 24-hr. emergency treatment.

Emergency: tel. 101.

Police: (tel. 920-900), on Av. 4 de Noviembre at Calle 104 (open 24hr.).

Post Office: Av. 4 and Av. 24 de Mayo (open Mon.-Fri. 7:30am-6:30pm, Sat. 8am-1pm).

Telephone code: 05.

ACCOMMODATIONS

Manta's plethora of hotel options are mostly situated in Tarqui, not in Manta proper. Don't dream of charming beachside villas—you're likely to find unimaginative concrete highrises, all built in the late 70s and 80s. Malecón, Tarqui's beachfront avenue, monopolizes the accommodations market. A five-minute walk along its sand sidewalk is an expeditious way to land yourself a comfortable room for the night.

Hotel Miami (tel. 611-743), at Calle 108 and Malecón. Welcome to the Museum Miami, where living quarters are included with the price of admittance. Artifacts from the indigenous cultures of Manta, Jipijapa, and Bahía de Caráquez clutter the walls and floors. The bellboys and receptionist double as exhibit guides. Rooms haven't been preserved as well as the exhibits, but offer clean private baths and an occasional bamboo bed. S/15,000 per person.

Hotel Mantamar (tel. 624-670), at Malecón and Calle 103. Floors are wet but policy is dry–absolutely no alcohol on the premises. Basic rehab-style cement cells have high-speed fans to keep you on the wagon. Soberly dangle your arms and legs over toy-sized beds. All rooms have private bath, except the s/7,000 shoebox downstairs. S/10,000 per person, with ocean view and color TV s/15,000.

Panorama Inn (tel. 611-552 or 612-996), at Calle 103 and Av. 105. So the ceiling fans have cracked bulbs and the bathroom lights require 2min. and a little patience to rev up. Cleanliness and big window views of the harbor make up for this highrise's lack of charisma. All rooms have private bath and black-and-white TV. S/20,000 per person.

Hotel Pacífico (tel. 622-475 or 623-584), at Av. 106 and Calle 101. Greet world's smallest goldfish on the way in; maybe he'll lend you an oxygen mask and bottled water for the strenuous climb up. The name of this high-rising highrise is visible from almost anywhere in Manta. The nearby inlet's stench can be asphyxiating, but rooms smell oh-so-fresh. All have private bath, and that tiny red box that displays only a white line could be your color TV. S/20,000 per person.

Hostal El Talento (tel. 612-186, 626-730, or 626-830), at Av. 1 and Calle 13. A budget hotel in Manta proper must feel lonely this side of Tarqui. Though this colonial home has baroque touches like high ceilings and grandiose double doors, sparsely-decorated rooms only come with the bare necessities—a bed and a fan. No private baths. Singles s/8,000-10,000. Truly multitalented, it's also got a superb restaurant and a Euro-hip nightclub downstairs.

FOOD

Comedor Estrella del Mar, at Malecón and Calle 106, in Tarqui. A grass-hut restaurant in a deluge of grass-hut establishments, Estrella's the sore thumb with a bright yellow paint job (like us), cluttered Pilsener propaganda, and plastic tables on the sand. A shoes-and-shirt-optional kind of place, where guitar strumming isn't uncommon. Prices conveniently left out of the English-translated menus. Fried seabass s/12,000, clam and rice dishes s/9,000 (open daily 7am-11pm).

Cheers (tel. 620-779), Malecón and Calle 19. Sometimes you want to go where everybody knows your name. Well, nobody here will know it, but they'll greet you with an enthusiastic *gringo* shout as heartfelt as any of Norm's stormy entrances. The gang is all but gone, but somebody will be around to serve you *ceviche* (s/5,000-8,000) or asparagus soup (s/4,000). Open daily 11am-1am, bar open Wed.-Sat. 9pm-4am.

Restaurante Carlos Escalante, Av. 6 8-16 y Calle 8 (tel. 612-722). Carlos never intended it to be a restaurant; he just let some locals in for lunch and suddenly his living room became one of the most popular diners in town. The tiny concrete room fits 6 tables at most, so partake of homecooked local dishes in close company. Fried fish, rice, salad, and fried bananas s/6,000, *ceviche* s/4,000 (open Mon.-Fri. 8am-2pm, Sat. 8am-noon).

Topi TV Pizza (tel. 621-180), at Malecón and Calle 15. Gaze at the one-of-a-kind view of the harbor and the monstrous ships that inhabit it. Equally diverting scenery inside, with a boundless beer display—Heineken, Corona, and Miller (s/5,000-6,000) as well as the usual Pilsner and Club (s/3,000). Go tropical with the Hawaiian pizza (large s/28,400). Simple pepper-and-onion pizza costs s/12,000 for a large (open Mon.-Fri. noon-1am, Sat. 11am-2am, Sun. noon-midnight).

Yambou (tel. 612-186), in the parking lot for Murciélago beach, with a decent view of the shoreline. Palm trees grow up and out of the cement walls and roof, as popular beachy *discoteca* jams pump out of humungous speakers. Somehow it gets around the set government price limits, serving s/2,500 Pilsener and s/2,000 Club. Cheap fish and calamari *ceviches* s/4,500, shrimp *ceviche* s/8,000 (open Tues.-Sat. 8am-2am, Sun. 8am-8pm).

SIGHTS AND ENTERTAINMENT

There are two stretches of beach in Manta. **Murciélago** is located in Manta proper, while **Tarqui** includes the shores farther south. A five-minute drive north of *el centro,* Murciélago clamors with the typical assortment of *cevicherías* and *peñas.* Cut short by a breakwater to the north, the beach has a good deal of soft sand, but is often spoiled by the presence of overturned garbage cans and scattered litter. Murciélago receives the Pacific's currents unfettered, and hence is inundated with signs warning of strong currents. The powerful currents also create fair-sized surf, often dormant during the summer but active with three- to four-foot swells in wintertime.

Tarqui's beach, on the other hand, hibernates all summer, only to wake in winter, turn over its pillow, yawn, and go back to sleep. Placid as a lake at dawn, Tarqui's waters are a playground for pelicans and frigates, but offer little excitement for human folk. Still, it is amusing to observe the breakneck, dive-bomb landing tactics of the sea birds. Scattered with its share of soft sand, Tarqui is smaller than Murciélago, cut short by a breakwater to the south and the byproducts of the fishing industry to the north.

If you're tired of shaking the sand out of your clothes, you can always take a walk around **Manta's harbor.** The busiest port on the central coast, Manta's harbor teems with Old-World fishing vessels and gargantuan navy ships docked for refueling. Just over the bridge into Tarqui, across from Hotel Pacifico, is an oddly placed **statue of a Manabí fisherman.** It's hard to imagine how workers first erected the statue, since these days the stench is so pungent that it's impossible to stay in the area for more than five minutes. The **Museo del Banco Central,** at Av. 4 and Av. 24 de Marzo, in back of the Banco Central, has a diminutive but worthwhile collection of indigenous artifacts accompanied by scores of information on culture and history. The black-and-white photographs of an earlier Manta show it less densely populated, but as dependent as ever on the sea (open Mon.-Fri. 8:30am-4:30pm).

■ Near Manta: Bahía de Manta

On weekends, Manta residents drop their nets en masse and head to the tiny fishing villages situated between there and Bahía de Cáraquez. Collectively known as Bahía de Manta, these towns have beaches with sand that's no whiter nor more picturesque than the sands of Manta ... there's just more of it. While beach space in Manta is limited, Bahía lays endless, uninhabited sands under the feet of any visitor looking for a more secluded escape. **Coactur** buses from Portoviejo go to San Clemente and San Jacinto, two larger Bahía villages (every ½hr., 5am-9:45pm, 1hr., s/2,500).

San Clemente, the northernmost of the two towns, lies roughly 30km north of Manta and 20km south of Bahía de Cáraquez. Buses stop on the highway, five minutes from the beach. The San Clemente beach has limited space, but as you walk south toward San Jacinto, the sands get wide and expansive. Aggressive tides keep the beach smooth, damp, dark, and firm—an excellent combination for games of pick-up soccer, but a terrible one for casual lounging. Still, the beach is usually empty, so you won't have to worry about anyone stealing your sun. The waters are gentle and the mild current will have trouble storming even the most rudimentary sand castle walls. For a post-frolic, pre-bus meal, **Restaurant Gemita,** on the highway five minutes from the beach, serves s/5,000 fish plates over the sounds of passing cars and buses. Scarf down enormous pieces of fish, rice, beans, and thinly-sliced banana chips, while keeping your eyes peeled for the bus back to Portoviejo. Scarf it down—they don't do doggy bags, and buses won't wait for you to clean your plate (open daily 6am-7pm).

A 15-minute walk along a dirt road, Av. Quito (also known as Malecón), leads to the beach at **San Jacinto,** 3km south of San Clemente. If you arrive from Portoviejo, the bus will drop you off along the highway. Walk straight along what's referred to as "Calle Principal," which will reach Av. Quito in five minutes. Here, beach-going has become a spectator sport. Similarly dark, damp, and solid sands often host a fascinating display of tuna fishing. Chains of seven or eight residents line the shore, holding ropes and playing tug-of-war with huge tuna nets. When the nets are finally dragged onshore, the people descend on the them, tossing the fish into the truck beds as quickly as possible, while seagulls and pelicans make kamikaze descents for scraps. Like a mediocre action movie, the performance is amusing and even somewhat educational at first, but ultimately the catching of the tuna makes for a disturbing beach experience, especially when San Jacinto's sands become a thoroughfare for vehicles loaded with dead sea life.

The beaches here are longer and wider than those of San Clemente, and the establishments near the sand seem less destitute. There are a number of food stands and restaurants along Av. Quito. The bar-restaurant **Copacabana,** wedged between a couple of other *comedores,* serves speedy seafood dishes to pacific ocean-watchers. There's more than just music and dancing at this Copacabana. There's also the cheapest *langostino* (jumbo shrimp) plate on the coast (s/15,000 for those battered exotica), as well as *ceviche* (s/5,000-7,000) and rice dishes (s/7,000). Start the morning off with a spartan *pan y leche* breakfast (s/2,000) or a shrimp omelette (s/3,500). Open daily 7am-9pm. A few minutes north of Copacabana, along Av. Quito, the **Hotel San Jacinto,** does its duty decently. Located close to the sand, it's protected from the tides by a vision-obstructing slab of concrete, but who cares? Windowless rooms don't have views anyway. All rooms have private baths, but you'll need a shoe-horn to fit into them (s/20,000 per person, shoe horn not included).

Portoviejo

Originally situated on the coast, Portoviejo (literally, "old port") moved 40km inland to its present land-locked locale due to continual pirate attacks. Now situated 95km southeast of Bahía, Portoviejo preserves its ironic appellation, but the distance from the coast has become cultural as well as geographic. While its maritime neighbors rock to the rhythms of the *marimba,* Portoviejo's population plods along to the drone of its serious-minded tasks—commerce, industry, and education. Although often regarded as the stiff-necked, straight-laced capital of an informal province, Portoviejo commands respect along the coast as a center of business and education.

ORIENTATION

Portoviejo seems oversized at times because everything is so spread out. Buses enter the city along **Avenida Universitaria,** making stops along Universitaria and the perpendicular **Pedro Gual.** The final bus stop, the **terminal terrestre,** is on Pedro Gual, on the western outskirts of town. The east-west Pedro Gual is one of the busiest and most important streets, possessing most of the banks and other necessary services. The other major street, Universitaria, becomes **Morales** south of *el centro.*

PRACTICAL INFORMATION

Tourist Information: CETUR, Pedro Gual 234 y Montalvo (tel. 630-877), 3 blocks east of Morales (open Mon.-Fri. 8:30am-5pm).

Banks: Filanbanco (tel. 630-532, 630-456, or 637-550), at Pacheco and Pedro Gual, has a 24-hr. ATM and exchanges dollars and traveler's checks (open Mon.-Fri. 8:30am-4pm). **Banco del Pichincha** (tel. 630-800), on Av. 9 de Octubre and Olmedo, doesn't change traveler's checks, but has the best hours in town. Exchanges cash and has 24-hr. ATM (open Mon.-Fri. 8am-8pm, Sat. 8am-2pm).

Telephones: EMETEL, at Av. 10 de Agosto and Pacheco. To make long-distance calls, buy a token, or *ficha para larga distancia* (s/600), from a sidewalk vendors outside, and use it at one of the blue phones inside (open daily 8am-10pm).

Buses: 3 bus companies transport to nearby coastal towns: **Carlos Aray** (tel. 932-269), **Reina del Camino** (tel. 932-377), and **Coactur** (tel. 931-069 or 931-287). They have the same prices, but Carlos Aray buses generally leave more frequently. Buses go to **Manta** (every 5min., 4am-8:30pm, 1hr., s/1,500), **Guayaquil** (every 45min., 2am-midnight, 3½hr., s/10,000), **Santo Domingo** (every ½hr., 4:30am-10:45pm, 5hr., s/12,000), **San Vicente** (every hr., 4am-7:45pm, 2½hr., s/5,000), **Pedernales** (every hr., 4am-5pm, 6hr., s/15,000), **Jipijapa** (every 45min., 4am-9:30pm, 3hr., s/2,500), and **Bahía de Caráquez** (every 40min., 5am-9pm, 2hr., s/4,000).

Pharmacies: There are a ton of pharmacies here, but the 2 most centrally located are **Farmacia Americana,** Av. 9 de Octubre 6-16 y Olmedo (tel. 652-967; open Mon.-Sat. 8:30am-8pm, Sun. 8:30am-noon) and **Farmacia Portoviejo** (tel. 652-344), at Av. 9 de Octubre and Ricuarte (open Mon.-Sat. 8am-7pm, Sun. 8am-1pm).

Hospital: Regional Hospital de Portoviejo (emergency tel. 630-555, 630-087, 630-525, or 636-520), at Rocafuerte and Av. 12 de Marzo. Free 24-hr. emergency treatment.

Police: (tel. 630-345), 3km outside of town along Via Crocita.

Post Office: Correos del Ecuador, Ricuarte 217 y Sucre (tel. 632-384). Open Mon.-Fri. 7:30am-7pm, Sat. 8am-1pm.

ACCOMMODATIONS

As in many other coastal cities, visitors have to search long and hard to find a place that balances quality and economy. Most of the prize budget establishments are situated in the eastern half of the city along Universitaria/Morales. The more expensive places are located along Pedro Gual, especially toward the western end of the city.

Hotel Paris (tel. 652-727), at Sucre and Olmedo. This townhouse has collected some dust over the years, but still sparkles with antique architecture and charming family management. Immense rooms are properly ventilated with lofty, ornate ceilings and gigantic windows looking out on the street. All have decent private baths, despite patchy tile work and some mildew. Stay in shape on the family weight bench, but don't disturb their meals at the kitchen table nearby. S/13,000 per person across the board.

Hotel Portoviejo Plaza, Morales 304 y Pedro Gual (tel. 634-442). No, you haven't checked into a hospital, but Portoviejo Plaza's white walls and narrow cots might have you thinking that you did. Apart from an occasional crooked mirror or political sticker, the walls are silent and unadorned. Rooms are well-swept, bathrooms well-kept. Pipes sticking out at random angles pass for shower heads. Singles s/8,000, with double bed s/12,000, with bath s/12,000, with both s/15,000; doubles s/20,000, with window and bath s/25,000; triples with bath s/30,000.

Hotel Pacheco (tel. 631-788), at Av. 9 de Octubre and Universitaria. This enormous maze of hallways and rooms has at least 70 sunless sleeping chambers. Colored circus sheets and tiny skylights battle the darkness. But alas, it's a losing battle for luminosity, and victory will likely go to deep slumber. Vanity is the management's pet peeve, so they've removed all mirrors from the premises, even in bathrooms. S/10,000 per person, with bath s/15,000, with bath and TV s/20,000.

FOOD

The cuisine of Portoviejo is slightly different from that of its more maritime neighbors. Though Portoviejo's *comedores* still offer many of the typical fish dishes, they concentrate more on beef entrees like *carne asada* or fowl plates like *seco de gall-*

ina. Yogurt has become a wildly popular snack food, and the demand for the sweet bacteria has placed a late-night quasi-fast-food yogurt shop on every corner.

July's, Sucre 8-17 y Av. 18 de Octubre. A local favorite, July's delivers heaping portions, but not hefty prices. Mickey Mouse mirror says that *seco de chivo* (s/5,000) is the house specialty, but a breaded cod dish (s/7,000) begs to differ. Break the Coca-Cola monopoly with either a Pepsi or 7-Up. Or defy the soda powers altogether and wash down a giant, s/6,000 plate of rice, beans, and beef with a pulpy melon juice (seeds optional). Open daily 8am-10pm.

Restaurant Palatino, at Av. 10 de Agosto and Chile, 2 blocks east of EMETEL. Serving much of the business community, Palatino attempts to imitate them with efficient service and anal neatness, like plastic-covered furniture. Fans are powerful enough to keep the tie-choked clientele from fidgeting. One of the few places in town with shrimp (s/12,000). Heaping rice dishes (S/6,000) could feed the whole office (open Mon.-Fri. 7am-4:30pm, Sat. 7am-noon).

Fuente de Soda "El Arabe," Rocafuerte 903 y Pedro Gual. Greasy treats done dirt cheap until the wee hours. Owner Magno Balcázar tempts loiterers inside with banana yogurt shakes (s/1,500). One whiff of the mayonnaise-heaped fries and chicken (s/3,500) and you'll be a goner. As if that's not enough, El Arabe serves exotic beers like s/2,000 Miller, s/2,000 Schlitz, and s/3,000 Budweiser (open daily 8am-1pm). Ahh, nothing like a carefully-crafted, slow-brewed beer at 8am.

SIGHTS AND ENTERTAINMENT

For a capital city, Portoviejo has a sad scarcity of stuff to see and do. The **Casa de Cultura** (tel./fax 631-753), on the left side of Calle Sucre, just past García Moreno, is a culture-enhancing excursion. At present, it only offers the occasional theater, dance, and music performance, but there are plans to expand its horizons. By late '97, it hopes to include an annual series of orchestral concerts (open daily 8am-noon and 2-6pm). The president of the Casa de Cultura, Wadía Lavando, is a published poet who may read you some of his work if he's not too busy. Pick his brains for cultural and historical information about the province, as he's a fountain of knowledge. **The Cine Victoria,** Cordova 512 y Olmedo, is devoid of couplets, unless James Bond happens to seduce a maiden by dropping a few lines of Byron. Offering American action films, international soccer matches, and late-night pornography, Cine Victoria appeases an eclectic movie-going audience (tickets s/3,000). They don't have a phone, so check postings out front for shows and showtimes. *Fútbol* fanatics might want to catch a live **soccer** match while in town. The local professional team, **Liga de Portoviejo Universitaria,** is competitive within Ecuador's premier league, drawing large, vivacious crowds (admission s/10,000). Games are scheduled throughout the week, so check the paper. The stadium is located on the right-hand side of Universitaria as you head north, about 0.5km outside of town.

■ Near Portoviejo: Montecristi

Between the hurly-burly giants of Manta and Portoviejo lounges mellow Montecristi, patiently churning out its world-renowned and sadly-misnamed **Panama hats.** Though these high-grade hats have long been made in Montecristi, most of the ears that their woven brims shelter haven't heard the name. Montecristi's obscurity stems from the same reason Columbus thought he'd disembarked in India: *gringo* confusion (see below). *Montecristianos* do not appear overly obsessed with their industrial anonymity, though for obvious economic reasons, they'd probably endorse efforts to educate misinformed *sombrero*-seekers. Still, namelessness has its privileges. The town's streets are tranquil and uncommercialized, with only a light traffic of lethargic burros and wandering pigs.

Shopping in Montecristi is about as fast-paced as a ride atop one of the town's many donkeys, but (thankfully) a great deal smoother. **Av. 9 de Julio,** Montecristi's principal street, presents four or five different *sombrero* shops, all selling similar items at comparable prices. *Superfinos,* the highest quality Panama hats, start at around s/70,000 apiece, but can be "discounted" down to s/50,000. Prices drop steadily the more hats you promise to buy. Along with the famed Panamas, most of these shops sell collections of straw handbags, backpacks, and baskets. Wickerwork has also become a popular pastime in Montecristi, and shops selling items from baby cribs to baskets also lie along Av. 9 de Julio.

After shopping, pay a visit to Montecristi's impressive house of prayer, the church of **La Virgen de Montecristi.** Located on the corners of Sucre, Av. 23 de Octubre, and Av. 9 de Julio, this striking edifice is home to the venerated Virgin of Monserrat, rumored to have miraculously cured various sickly *montecristianos* on a number of occasions. Along with her medical practice, the Virgin is also known to be an avid walker, and legends describing her perambulatory jaunts around Montecristi circulate through the town. Apparently there's a shortage of quality hats in the hereafter, and Mary got stuck with the cumbersome task of shopping for the entire kingdom.

Excellent hats *and* quality budget accommodations would be far to much to expect from one town. Montecristi doesn't even offer many places to eat either. **Pollos y Algo Más,** Av. 9 de Julio 404 y Olmedo, manages both quality fare and friendly local atmosphere. Typically provincial, Pollos is decorated with mounted Panama hats and wickerwork tablesettings. Lounge outside, adjust your newly-purchased, slightly stiff (and consequently silly-looking) hat, and munch a s/6,500 serving of rice and fish (open Mon.-Fri. 8am-9pm, Sat.-Sun. 8am-11pm).

Buses arriving in Montecristi drop passengers off along the highway just north of town. A walk up Av. 9 de Julio leads to the town center at the intersection of San Andreas and Av. 23 de Octubre. The **central plaza,** a tiny, shade-filled park facing the adjacent church, is home to Montecristi's practical establishments. The **Banco del Pinchincha** (tel. 606-10111 or 606-105) changes money, but doesn't exchange traveler's checks, nor does it have an ATM (open Mon.-Fri. 8am-8pm, Sat. 8am-2pm). The **EMETEL** office, on the central plaza at the corner of Av. 9 de Julio and Av. 23 de Octubre, has three booths that make national calls only (open Mon.-Sat. 8am-1pm and 2-8pm, Sun. 8am-noon). The **post office** (open Mon.-Fri. 8am-noon and 1-6pm) and **police station** (open 24hr.) are in the same building at Sucre and Av. 23 de Octubre, directly opposite EMETEL.

Panama Hats Are Not from Panamá

Forget the name, forget your other misconceptions, **Panama hats are made in Ecuador.** Born of economic necessity, the Panama descended from the ancient straw hats of the pre-Columbians in the Manabí province. The industry got its start in the 1830s, when the poverty-stricken inhabitants of Cuenca were forced to make hats for a living. Exports got a major boost from a major monarch at the 1855 World Expo, when King Napoleon III (and subsequently the rest of Europe) fell in love with the hat. Fifty years later, the craze hit the States. During construction of the Panama Canal, American workers found the hats perfect protection from the scorching sun and dubbed them with the misnomer that stuck. Gangsters began wearing the hats in the 20s; to this day, a certain model is called the Capone. The industry reached its peak in 1946, when 5 million hat exports accounted for 20% of Ecuador's earnings. Presidents and Hollywood stars alike sported the stylish, exotic hat—an integral part of 30s and 40s American fashion.

Meanwhile, poor Ecuadorians worked for pennies, making hats that sold for a hefty profit in the States. The middlemen, processing factories, exporters, and retailers all took their share, leaving little for the actual artisans. These days, the hats are less popular and imitation paper hats have taken a substantial bite out of the market. The master artisans of Montecristi may soon cease to practice their art because it no longer supports them. So while you're in the neighborhood, help save a dying art, and pay your respects to the real creative geniuses; buy yourself an Ecuador Hat.

Jipijapa

Most of the fun associated with Jipijapa (pronounced "heepy-hoppa"), 60km south of Manta, comes from its bouncy, fun-to-say name. Otherwise, despite its abundance of Panama hats, the town has little of its northern neighbor's charm. Shopping here is as bountiful as in Montecristi, but far less concentrated, with hat shops scattered throughout town. Situated between Manta and the southern coast's primary beaches, Jipijapa's chief function (outside of hat-making) has been shuttling eager sun-seekers and anxious surfers to the sandy shores of communities like Puerto López, Salango, and Montañita. Most travelers stay long enough to get their shoes polished in the shade of Parque Simon Bolívar, before stepping on a bus headed towards for the coast. Shiny-shoed, beach-bound travelers, be warned: there are very few, if any, places to change money or cash traveler's checks between Jipijapa and La Libertad. Stock up on sucres in Jipijapa while you can.

Orientation and Practical Information Much of what you'll need while you're in Jipijapa is located near its central plaza. The plaza consists of **Parque Simon Bolívar** and a concrete area adorned with an anonymous female statue. East-west streets **Sucre** and **Bolívar,** and the north-south **Colón** and **9 de Octubre** border the central plaza. **Coop de Transportes Turismo de Manta y Jipijapa (CTMS)** buses, arriving from the north, drop off along Av. 10 de Agosto near Santistevan, one block north and one block east of the plaza. **Cooperativa de Manglaralto (CITM)** buses, arriving from the south, let their passengers out along Sucre near Av. 9 de Octubre, a half-block east of the central plaza.

Banco del Pinchincha, Sucre 503 y Av. 9 de Octubre (tel. 600-472; fax 600-800), changes money, but doesn't accept traveler's checks (open Mon.-Fri. 8:30am-8pm, Sat. 8:30am-2pm). **Filanbanco** (tel. 600-345 or 601-620; fax 600-455), at Bolívar and Av. 9 de Octubre, takes traveler's checks but not cash, and has a 24-hour ATM (open Mon.-Sat. 8am-4pm). The **EMETEL** office, at Bolívar and Av. 9 de Octubre, across from Filanbanco, has two booths, neither of which can make international calls (open daily 8am-10pm). The primary bus companies in town are located near the central plaza. **Cooperativa de Transportes Turismo de Manta and Jipijapa,** at Av. 10 de Agosto y Colón, sends buses to **Puerto López** (every hr., 4:30am-5:30pm, 1¼hr., s/3,000) and **Manta** (every 15min., 5am-9pm, 1¼hr., s/2,500). **Cooperativa Manglaralto,** Sucre 604 y Av. 9 de Octubre (tel. 601-000), runs to **Manta** (every 2hr., 5:15am-5:15pm, 1hr., s/2,500) and **La Libertad** (7 per day, 7:45am-7:45pm, 4hr., s/11,000) via **Puerto López.** The principal pharmacy is **Farmacia Corazón de Jesus,** Bolívar 301 y Santistevan (tel. 601-648; open daily 7am-9:30pm). If you're still aching, **Hospital Cantonal Jipijapa** (tel. 600-377), at Espejo and Av. 12 de Octubre, is open for emergency treatment 24 hours, but only Monday through Friday. The **emergency** telephone number is 101. The **police station** (tel. 600-444) is several blocks east of the plaza on Bolívar at Antepara. Jipijapa's **telephone code** is 05.

Accommodations and Food The inexpensive sleeping options in Jipijapa are limited and shabby. Though it calls itself a hostel, the **Hostel Jipijapa** (tel. 601-365 or 600-522; fax 600-783), at Santistevan and Eloy Alfaro, more resembles an upper-class hotel. Depending on how much you value impeccable cleanliness, accompanied by a remote-control color TV, the s/38,000-per-person charge could either seem outrageous, or a small price to pay for a night of immaculate laziness. For more inexpensive lodging, march over to the dungeonesque **Hostel Mejia,** Mejia 324 y Colón (tel. 600-387). Endowed with poorly-lit hallways and low concrete ceilings, Mejia plunges you back in time to the Middle Ages. A bare, solitary bulb in each room reveals adequate concrete cells equipped with metal beds, naked walls, and well-swept floors. Bathrooms are clean enough, but crowded toilet, shower, and sink squeeze out into the bedroom. S/8,000 per person, with bath s/12,000. A couple of unremarkable restaurants adorn Av. 9 de Octubre near the plaza. One satisfactory establishment, **Comedor La Rochelle,** at Av. 9 de Octubre and Sucre, serves adequate *ceviches* for a s/3,500 drop in the bucket. Benches may leave you walking funny, but not before you've been able to devour a plate of rice and fish for s/5,000 (open daily 7am-11pm).

Puerto López

Blessed with tranquil waters and picturesque, looming bluffs, Puerto López is a fisherman's—and a photographer's—paradise. Unlike the coast's other fishing epicenters, Puerto López has somehow kept itself unsullied, boasting well-swept streets and immaculate sands, devoid of the usual unsavory by-products of an intense fishing industry. Inevitably, though, the odor of the fish trade permeates the aesthetic airs of the sheltered cove. Resting their weary wooden hulls after a grueling day of pounding the waves, high-seas fishing rigs saturate the harbor, neatly anchored as if posing for cameras. The fish may have brought the boats, but it's the nearby Machalilla National Park and its famed Isla de la Plata that reel in travelers from around the world. As a result of this almost cosmopolitan flare, travelers tired of struggling with Spanish can seek refuge in the restaurants and bars, which murmur with enough languages that at least one is bound to sound familiar.

Orientation and Practical Information **Machalilla,** the principal road in town, runs north to Jipijapa and south to La Libertad. **Malecón,** the street closest to the sand, runs parallel to Machalilla two or three blocks to the west. **Machalilla Tour Agency,** Malecón 119 y Julio Izurieza (tel. 604-206), has whale-watching and Isla de la Plata tours (open daily 9am-1am). **Mantaraya** (tel. 604-233), on Malecón, north of Machalilla Tour Agency, also has whale-watching and Isla de la Plata packages, and rents scuba equipment as well (open daily 7am-6:30pm). The **Machalilla National Park Headquarters,** at Eloy Alfaro and Machalilla, back 50m from EMETEL and on the left, has information and a park museum (open daily 7am-noon and 2-5pm). There are no **banks** in Puerto López, so load up on sucres before you arrive. The **Hotel Pacífico** occasionally gives sucres in return for traveler's checks, but only in rare, desperate situations. **EMETEL,** at Machalilla and Atahualpa, only makes calls within Ecuador (open Mon.-Sat. 8am-noon, 2-5pm, and 7-9pm). The **bus stop** is located at the southern end of town, on the corner of Machalilla and Cordoba. Northern-bound buses go to **Manta** (every ½hr., 4:45am-6pm, 2hr., s/8,000) via **Jipijapa** (1¼hr., s/3,000). Buses going south run through town (every 20min., 4:45am-6pm), then continue to **Salango** (10min., s/1,000), **Alandaluz** (15min., s/1,500), **Montañita** (45min., s/3,500), and **Manglaralto** (50min., s/4,000). Puerto López's favorite pharmacy, **Farmacia Edicita** (tel. 604-600), at Av. Machalilla and Atahualpa, is across the street from the post office in the center of town (open daily 7:30am-8:30pm). And its most helpful hospital, **Centro de Salud de Puerto López,** is at the end of Machalilla, seven or eight blocks north of *el centro.* There is a sign, but it only faces north (open Mon.-Fri. 24hr.). The **police** (tel. 604-101), are at Machalilla and Atahualpa, next to EMETEL (open 24hr.). Around the corner stands the old reliable **post office,** at Atahualpa and Machalilla (open Mon.-Fri. 9am-noon and 3-5:30pm, Sat. 9am-noon). Puerto López's **telephone code** is 05.

Accommodations Of the few places to stay in town, only one is in immediate proximity to the beach. The others are on the eastern side of Machalilla, scattered among the modest homes of the town's inhabitants. Though shacking up near the beach makes swimming convenient, visitors can feel isolated from the town. Two or three days east of Calle Machalilla, on the other hand, leaves guests feeling right in the swing of things. **Villa Colombia,** off Cordoba, is off the first right from Cordoba to a basketball court, onto a wide dirt road. The hotel is the second or third building on the left, but you have to walk down the alleyway just beyond it to get to the entrance. Weary visitors are welcomed with a hot cup of coffee and an enthusiastic lick from Tyson, the owner's rambunctious black lab. Known by tourists for his Colombian hospitality, Jaibel the owner opens his heart and his kitchen to all guests, providing use of stove, oven, and fridge, and plenty of conversation. If you're lucky, he may help you fry something up or just take you out for a beer. Modest, multi-media rooms are constructed in a hodgepodge of concrete, wood planks, and bamboo. S/9,000 per person, with bath s/12,000. **Hostel Tuzco** (tel. 604-132), on Cordoba, is two and a half blocks east of Machalilla. Like clones in a sci-fi movie, these identical *Twilight Zone*-esque rooms are eerily new, sparkling, and white. Sleep on pliable mattresses laid on raised cement slabs. A giant painted map of the region, paired with each room's cantonal name, can be used to decipher the aliens' attack plan (see aliens on the cover). Quarters fit up to six, all with private bath. S/15,000 per person. The one beachfront lodging, **Hotel Pacífico** (tel. 604-147), at Suarez and Malecón, is only 50m from the sand at the northern end of Malecón. Lush courtyard is laden with hammocks that swing from sun-fighting palms. *Cabañas* have dusty floorboards and ample beds with woolen blankets. Impeccable common baths flow with invigoratingly frigid water. S/20,000 per person. Rooms at Pacifico provide pristine tile in place of wooden floorboard, and transform your communal ice bath into a warm private shower for only double the price—s/40,000 per person.

Food Relax. Puerto López has plenty of seafood to go around. Various restaurants scattered throughout town cook up the traditional coastal dishes: *ceviche,* fried seafood, battered seafood (ouch), invariably accompanied by a portion of rice. Due to the strange dearth of sidewalk vendors, most dining occurs in formal restaurants. If you want seconds, be economical about it and visit the **indoor food market,** diagonally across from the bus stop at Machalilla and Cordoba. **Spondyllus Bar and Restaurant** (tel. 604-128 or 604-108), at Malecón and Cordoba, dishes outstanding eats in an international Latin milieu. Burlap ceiling looks like it was just shipped in from Colombia, brimming with coffee beans. Owner plays anything from bootlegged Bob Marley to sauntering *salsa.* Munch on *ceviche de spondyllus* (s/10,000) and savor your bitter-sweet Sol beer (s/3,000), imported from Mexico (open daily 10am-10pm, though it sometimes stays open until 4am). **Restaurante Acapulco** (tel. 604-206), at Machalilla and General Cordoba, not only has the best cheap eats in town, but also boasts an unbeatable view of the bus stop. Bamboo motif complemented with a splash of conversation from the gregarious management. Gratify taste buds with icy blackberry juice, accompanied with rice and beans, an egg tortilla filled with shrimp, and an immense bowl of soup—all for only s/4,500 (open daily 6am-10pm). **Urña del Mar,** Malecón 123 y Julio Izurieta (tel. 604-206), is the source of those smells wafting next door to Machalilla Tour. Grab something to eat so you'll be nice and full for the long whale-watching trip. Cozy outside seating provides ocean views and liberation from indoor wooden benches. Full breakfast (eggs, bread, juice, coffee) s/5,000, shrimp *ceviche* s/8,000 (open daily 6:30am-4:30pm).

Sights and Entertainment Puerto López is an ideal port from which to explore the marvels of **Parque Nacional Machalilla** (see p. 186), and the town knows it. Multiple tour companies battle for tourists' bucks with bigger and better bargains, especially with **whale watching** tour packages to the notorious "poor person's Galápagos," **Isla de la Plata,** situated 40km off of Puerto López. The boat ride out takes two solid hours and the high sea swells are tremendous, so anyone even slightly susceptible to seasickness should take precautionary measures. Before you fully realize that the waves are bigger than the boat, numerous humpback whale sightings attest that *everything* in the sea dwarfs your tiny craft. Various agencies in Puerto López offer the same boat trip to Isla de la Plata for similar prices. **Machalilla Tour Agency,** Malecón 119 y Julio Izurieza (tel. 604-206), offers a four- to five-hour, s/75,000 per person whale-watching trip. The price includes lunch, but not the s/40,000 park entrance fee (open daily 7:30am-7:30pm).

If you'd rather keep your feet on solid ground and your insides at peace, Puerto López's own **beach** meets the challenge quite suitably. Soft, unspoiled sands make the shore an enjoyable spot for sunbathing or just gawking at the magnificent harbor.

Bring your camera and capture a maritime still-life, or test the lukewarm, tranquil waters with a swim.

■ Near Puerto López

SALANGO

Situated 5km south of Puerto López, Salango sits patiently, like an old man with a story to tell. Salango's tale comes whispering up from beneath its sands, which are home to a massive collection of **archeological artifacts.** Dating back almost 5000 years, six different pre-Colombian communities thrived here, leaving behind scatterings of everyday life as well as jewelry and artwork. Many of the pieces have been excavated and now fill Salango's archeological museum, but a large number remain trapped in the silence of the sand, buried beneath Salango's fish factory. Or, at least, the factory *used* be Salango's. After a strike over low wages in 1989, the plant's foreign management fired its Salangan workforce and employed people from more impoverished neighboring towns. Salango has been hit hard by the lay-offs, and most locals have returned to unpredictable, and often unprofitable, fishing careers. The fish factory plods along like a fat cat, stretched out over a gold mine of historical evidence, smothering the economic life of Salango's people.

Only 10 minutes and a s/1,500 bus ride separate Salango from Puerto López. The main reason to make this convenient half-day trip is the **museum,** whose well-presented and informative collection chronicles the six cultures found at the site. Valdavian culture is the oldest, subsisting from 3000-2000 BC, followed by the Machalilla (2000-1500 BC), Chorrera and Foriguroy (1500-500 BC), Guangala/Bahían (500 BC-500 AD), and Manteño (500 AD). For more information, see The Earliest Ecuadorians, p.37. Each culture has separate glass encasements labeled with Spanish descriptions, which present various artifacts from religious, artistic, and daily life found at the site. Knowledgeable museum guides will show you around, gladly answering any questions. The museum also has artists who create reasonably priced replicas of the artifacts (open Wed.-Sun. 9am-5pm; admission s/3,000, children s/1,500). You can also visit on Mon.-Tues. between 8am and 4pm; the door will be locked, but just knock.

Salango lacks accommodations, but it does support a couple of restaurants. The oft-praised **Delfín Mágico,** roughly 200km south of the museum, looks rather nondescript, with the usual bamboo motif and white plastic furniture, but just wait for the remarkable food. Deliciously affordable jumbo shrimp dishes (s/18,000-19,000), fresh shrimp and fish *ceviches* (s/6,000-10,000). Open Mon.-Fri. 9am-8:30pm, Sat.-Sun. 8:30am-11pm.

Salango's beach is small but uncluttered, laden with clean, soft sand and a spectacular view of the diminutive **Isla Salango,** 2km off the shore. Waves get uppity in this sheltered cove only during *temporada* (Dec.-April). The beach's only sour note is the murmuring **fish factory,** at the south end of the shore. Incongruous with Salango's natural beauty, this drab, gray processing plant puffs miasmic wisps of smoke into the sea breezes. It is a five-minute walk south along the beach, and worth taking a look at, even if only to cheer on the frigates and pelicans as they snatch bits and pieces of the factory's profits.

PARQUE NACIONAL MACHALILLA

Spanning over 35,000 hectares, with climates ranging from tropical dry forests (Salaite and Aguablanca) to a tropical cloud forest (San Sebastian), Parque Nacional Machalilla has all the diverse wildlife one comes to expect from forested coastal national parks. A poor person's Galápagos, the 1200-hectare Isla de la Plata, 40km from the shores of Puerto López, swarms with animal life, accessible for a mere fraction of the cost of a trip to the more illustrious islands.

From the main gate, a dirt road winds 5km to the diminutive hamlet of **Aguablanca.** A languid, dusty one-hour trail through the lowland dry forest allows for careful study of the varied flora. Figs, laurels, and Kapok trees are scattered loosely, while the lush beanstalks of the pea-like, perennially-verdant *algarrobos* pierce the dry wasteland. Those dry-climate staples, cacti, abound in the arid terrain. The tall spindly cactus, the prickly pear, and the *pitahaya* (which sprouts a delectable red fruit during February and March), are well-represented among the spines. Aguablanca provides an interlude to the wilderness education, with both an archaeological museum and the ruins of the **Manteño,** an indigenous group who resided here from the 6th century AD until the Spanish conquest. The museum brims with Manteño artifacts, including art, jewelry, pottery, religious pieces, and miniature replicas of their **balsa rafts.** For a faint idea of what a labored task it must have been to build the real things, try one of the do-it-yourself raft replica kits for sale. The park does not allow visitors to hike to the sites on their own, due to the complexity of paths and dangerous surroundings, but instead offers affordable guided tours. The giant **pottery urns** on the way to the ruins were used as tombs for Manteño dead. Claustrophobes and the faint of heart beware—many of the skeletons have been left in the urns, painfully crouched in the fetal position, strewn with ceramic offerings from their loved ones. A half-hour walk uphill, the anticlimactic **ruins** themselves are only the basic foundations of the Manteño's homes and places of worship. Rumor has it that a dip in the **sulfur pond** on the way back to town does wonders for illness, soreness, and clogged nasal passages, but common sense maintains that these murky waters may cause your skin to take on a raw-sewage stench and emit a strange green glow. The entire two-and-a-half-hour guided package tour runs s/5,000 per person; museum admission alone costs s/3,000.

To explore the cloud forests of **San Sebastian,** visitors must hire a guide for the five to six-hour round-trip trek (s/30,000-50,000, depending on group size). During the course of the hike there, the vegetation makes a striking transition from dry to cloud forest. San Sebastian sports many an exotic animal species, including tarantulas, giant centipedes, scorpions, and coral snakes, as well as less-intimidating armadillos, howler monkeys, *guantas* (agoutis), anteaters, and numerous bird species.

For still more environmental contrast, the secluded shores of **Los Frailes,** 2km north of the Aguablanca gate, include three beaches: La Playita, La Tortuguita, and the star of the sand-show, Los Frailes. **Buses** from Puerto López make the 9km trip to the Los Frailes gate (s/1,000). About 100m past the gate, the road bends left at a *cabañita,* while a smaller dirt path leads to the right. Like reading the last page of a novel first, you can skip the other two beaches' prologue and go straight to Los Frailes on the left road (30min.). However, park rangers recommend the road more traveled, the dirt path to the right, which arrives at Los Frailes only after passing the other two beaches. The tiny rock cove of **La Playita,** a 25-minute walk from the *cabañita,* is layered with black sands and lapped by calm waters perfect for waders and young children. Walk five minutes farther and reach a cove festooned with curious rock configurations, **La Tortuguita**. Though its ankle-deep, soft, whitish sand won't harm a soul, the chaotic swirling waterway, caused by two swells breaking toward each other, can be a danger. Despite its tremulous waters, La Tortuguita is a popular snorkeling spot, especially just off the rocks that separate its two sand plots. Swimming is not advised at the second beach, as there is a low line of rocks where the waters break. The immense, almost perfectly symmetrical, rocky cove of **Los Frailes** lurks behind La Tortuguita's second sand plot. Uninhabited except for a lining of greenery, the beach stretches in a golden arc of pure, solitary sand facing tranquil waters, perfect for sun-worship and cool dips.

Known as the "Poor Person's Galápagos," the prized **Isla de la Plata,** 40km off the shore of Los Frailes, delivers the wildlife goods without the sky-high prices. A monolithic fortress visible on the clearest of days, its looming cliffs rise 90m above the ocean surface, launch pads for the island's **masked booby** population. As its name might suggest, the masked booby is easily recognizable, sporting a black feather-mask around its distinctive yellow eyes. Other boobies thrive here as well, including the abundant and cartoonish **blue-footed booby** and the pint-sized **red-footed booby.** Tropical birds build their precarious nests on the island's cliff edges, and the largest colony of **frigatebirds** in the world also calls La Plata home. From April to November, the rare **waved albatrosses** wing in for fly-by-night mating season affairs. The boobies and the other birds aren't the only wildlives of this island party. A small offshore colony of generally elusive **sea lions** is occasionally spotted sun bathing, and from July to September, the waters teem with humpback whales. Like the albatross, the whales prefer big love on the run, migrating here from the Antarctic to mate in the warmer waters. These amorous aquatics are best seen during the rollicking boat rides from Puerto López to the island. The only park office is at **Bahía Drake,** the island's only inlet and the docking point for mainland boats. Snorkeling and diving are possible here, but equipment rentals must be arranged in Puerto López. Camping is strictly prohibited, and bring your own food and water.

For more information on Machalilla National Park, visit the **headquarters** in Puerto López, at Eloy Alfaro and Machalilla, 50m from the EMETEL office. In addition to pamphlets, maps, and English brochures, the office has a museum featuring stuffed versions of park wildlife and a huge map of the park, great for orienting yourself before any expedition (open daily 8am-6pm). The **main entrance** to the National Park sits 7km north of Puerto López, off the coastal highway to Jipijapa. **Buses** leave Puerto López every half-hour; specify to the driver that you want to be let off at the main entrance at Aguablanca (s/1,000). Park **admission,** good for five days, runs s/40,000 (s/4,000 for travelers with visas). Admission tickets are available at the Aguablanca main gate at the southern end of the park, the western gate at the shores of Los Frailes, and the park's headquarters in Puerto López. Services within the park are extremely limited. There is a primitive campground in San Sebastian with no facilities (s/5,000 per person). Before heading to into the park, be sure to purchase bottled water and food, as they are almost impossible to find inside the park.

ALANDALUZ ECOLOGICAL TOURIST CENTER

Announcing itself with two enormous, palm-thatched bamboo houses, among a collection of more diminutive cabins, the **Alandaluz Ecological Tourist Center** seems more like an indigenous village nestled in the jungle than a tourist resort. In truth, Alandaluz has never been merely a resort. Whereas most resorts aim only to please their paying visitors, Alandaluz tries to appease Mother Nature as well. Constructed wholly of rapidly-growing, easily replenishable materials, Alandaluz is a temple of bio-friendliness, making daily offerings to an afflicted environmental goddess. Comically, visitors can make their contribution simply by frequenting the bathroom, where waste is mixed with sawdust and dried leaves to speed up the decomposition process. The decomposed waste is then applied to the soil in the nearby vegetable gardens, which were moved off-site recently due to salt-water intrusion.

While Alandaluz's shoreline locale is counter-productive for vegetable growing, it multiplies the beauty of the resort ten-fold. The beach has impeccable and uninhabited sands fingered with palm-thatched umbrellas. The surf is monstrous, far too dangerous for swimming. But if you have a surfboard, and you know how to use it, the water is ideal. Generally slow-breaking, crumbling waves with six- to seven-foot faces in the summer and 10- to 12-foot faces in the winter break in both directions. Arguably Ecuador's premier surfing locale, Alandaluz doesn't always have the echoing barrels of Montañita, but it also doesn't have the crowds.

The resort itself is set up like a tiny village. In addition to the two main buildings with regular rooms, there are three individual cabins right by the sand, complete with bamboo patio-decks and ocean views (another set of more luxury cottage-like cabins is under construction). All of the pristine bamboo quarters are festooned with cheerful, multi-colored curtains and mosquito nets and equipped with bamboo bed frames and mounted bamboo water bottle holders for your complimentary bottles of Guitig water. The one exception is the *Cabaña del Arbol,* the honeymoon suite. Built into the structure of a live tree, you can feel the tree sway as you climb the tree-branch ladder into your lofty love nest. One of the most luxurious tree houses ever built, it also includes a private bathroom.

The complex boasts plentiful amenities. Don't pay for a whale watching tour; instead try the four-story *mirador* (lookout tower). Relax at a cozy bamboo **bar,** furnished with cushioned straw couches and an outdoor furnace (open daily 8:30am-midnight). Alongside the bar, a first class **restaurant** specializes in vegetable and seafood dishes. The chef uses an oven constructed of hardened fecal matter to create his pride and joy, the *vivado de pasado* (an enormous serving of baked shellfish served inside a bamboo cane; s/14,000). Open daily 8:30am-9pm.

Eco-conscious extravagance has its price, though. The most affordable accommodations are the **hammocks** (s/15,000), which hang from underneath the stilted main house, safe from surprise tropical rainstorms, and come equipped with thick, hand-woven blankets and mosquito nets. Impeccably-maintained common bathrooms scattered around the grounds have both hot and cold water. From there, the prices climb: **cabins** s/39,000 per person, with bath s/48,000 per person, with second floor terrace facing the sea and solar-powered lighting s/70,800 per person.

Alandaluz is 6km south of Salango, a 15-minute, s/1,500 **bus** ride from Puerto López, that is practically impossible to miss on the west side of the road. Even if you don't have time to spend the night, a 10-minute walk through the well-kept gardens along stone paths provides an excellent feel for the place. For reservations, call 505-084 or Quito tel. 604-103.

Montañita

Situated 45 minutes south of Alandaluz, and a solid 65km north of La Libertad, Montañita is undoubtedly the most popular surfing spot in Ecuador. Hopping with surfers from all over Latin America, the streets of Montañita are a barefoot parade, flowing with bronzed, unclad torsos, long hair, and surfboards. Many surfers live here year-round, sticking out the down-season from June-October, while others trample in around December, boards in hand, and stay until June. The town has an atmosphere as laid back as the waves themselves. Selling surf t-shirts and fruit to visitors constitutes the primary method of surfer survival; other than that, the surfing life consists of early morning (pre-breakfast) surf sessions, mid-afternoon sessions, and a possible dusk session, ending just as the sun dips below the Pacific horizon. A grueling regimen, to be sure, often followed by nights of beach parties, bonfires, cocktails, and general debauchery by the sea. Legends of revelry in Montañita that are too intriguing to ignore permeate much of Latin America, and hundreds of non-surfers also wind their way to Ecuador's an all-around party town.

Orientation and Practical Information There are two separate and quite distinct sectors separated by a mile and a half of parallel beach and highway. The **pueblo** to the south houses all of Montañita's practical resources, as well as its small population of Ecuadorian inhabitants. Here, **Calle Rocafuerte** runs from the highway to the sand, while **Av. 15 de Mayo,** perpendicular to Rocafuerte, is the last street before the sand. **La punta,** the other sector to the north, is named for the rocky bluffs that loom over its famous barreling brake, and has a handful of hotels and restaurants. Surfers and sunbathers spend their lazy days here, visiting the *pueblo* only for practical purposes. Although most of the area's practical resources (including the post office, hospital, and police station) are in the nearby town of Manglaralto, Montañita does have a **pharmacy,** at Av. 15 de Mayo 836 y Rocafuerte. Like all good Ecuadorian towns, it also has an **EMETEL** office, along Calle Cheribogo, 50m from Restaurante El Chivo. On the left, the **Casa Communal** houses the phones (open Mon.-Sat. 8am-noon, 2-5pm, and 7-9pm, Sun. 8am-noon and 7-9pm).

Accommodations Loaded with cheap places to stay, Montañita is an easy town to settle into. An alternative to hotels, beach houses often offer rooms for rent. The *pueblo* has a few budget rooms, but most establishments are concentrated near *la punta.* **Rincón del Amigo,** at the end of La Punta Road, is the epicenter of the surfer and backpacker scene. Exotic quarters in this palm-thatched hotel come with all the tropical necessities: bamboo ceilings, mosquito nets, and rickety homemade beds, adorned with sea shells and coral. S/10,000 per person, with bath s/15,000. Sporty restaurant-bar downstairs, with billiards and foosball (open daily 9:30am-10pm). Rincón also offers bike rental for daytrips to the Machalilla National Park (s/30,000 per day, s/15,000 per half-day). A hippie commune of sleepy surfers and moon-children alike, **El Pelicano** embraces all toward the end of La Punta Road, on the right. The two-story cobblestone hotel has a palm-thatched roof strewn with tie-dyed curtains and much-needed mosquito nets. Flowers from the garden make garlands for newly-grown mops of hair. S/10,000 per person, with bath s/15,000. Those who would just as soon sleep on the sand should check out **Vito's,** along La Punta Road on the left. Though it tends to be disheveled, its prime beach location provides pole position for anxious board-riders. Brimming with arched palms, the relaxed, sandy courtyard houses a hammock-hanging hut. Bright, blue-walled quarters sport cartoon surfing and diving scenes. Singles s/12,000; doubles with bath s/40,000; triples with bath s/50,000. Vito's relaxed restaurant is also popular (open daily 8:30-9pm). Away from the surf crowd in the *pueblo,* **Hostal de Lucho,** Rocafuerte 830 y Av. 15 de Mayo, appeals to the Spanglish-fluent with a sign that reads *"rento habitaciones."* Rooms have musty floorboards and square foam blocks for pillows, but prices are unbeatable. Lucho's kitchen is open to all, a 24-hour diner equipped with stove and refrigerator. Communal scruffy-looking toilet and mildewy shower. Singles s/8,000; doubles s/15,000.

Food Surfing's hard work, so Montañita makes sure to feed its visitors well. Occasionally, you'll stumble upon beach bonfires cooking up fresh oysters and fish, but not as often as you might like. In *la punta,* most people frequent the cheap, reliable hotel restaurants (see above), but there are other delectable options. **Restaurant El Chivo,** at Calle Chiribogo and Rocafuerte, offers cheap eats, town gossip, and a heavy dose of surf videos on the immense color TV. Marvel at haphazardly-lying surfboards and the wall mural depicting a dreamy, flowered vision of Montañita. Mouth-watering rice and seafood dishes go for around s/8,000, and vegetarian entrees for around s/10,000. Chivo also sells and fixes surfboards (open daily 7am-midnight). **Las Olas,** on the right-hand side of La Punta Road before El Pelicano or Rincón, is run by Chivo's mother. Decor consists of a five-foot, painted surfboard sign mounted on the ceiling, and a smattering of surfing stickers on the tabletops and roof supports. *Pescado al ajillo* s/7,000, inedible postcards s/1,000. Rent surfboards (also inedible) from the same window that takes food orders (s/15,000 per day, half-day s/8,000). Open daily 7am-9pm. The *pueblo* also has a handful of dining options popular with surfers and locals alike. **Restaurant La Punta,** at Av. 15 de Mayo and Rocafuerte, has sidewalk seating shaded by palm-thatched umbrellas. In a professional employment of nature, chairs are made of tree branches, table legs are tree trunks, and ashtrays are conch shells. Veggie-and-rice dishes s/4,000, veggie spaghetti s/5,000, pancakes s/1,000 each. Standard *desayuno* of eggs, bread, juice, coffee s/3,000 (open daily 8am-10pm). **La Quilla,** Av. 15 de Mayo 832 y Rocafuerte, is a standard hole-in-the-wall with stools much shorter than the bar top. Quick eats won't weigh you down in the water. *Tostadas* come in the unfamiliar form of cheese sandwiches filled with tomatoes, onions, and peppers (s/1,000). Wash it down with a fruity *batido* (s/1,000), often refilled for free as you slurp it up (open daily 7am-10pm off-season, 7am-1am during *temporada*).

Sights and Entertainment Visitors flock to Montañita for one reason: the **surf.** The beach stretches endlessly south, but looming, jagged cliffs with peculiar rock formations contain it to the north. These cliffs are responsible for the consistent four- to five-foot swells with echoing barrels that always break right, away from the point. During the off-season, the waves struggle a bit, offering two- to three-foot apologies whose barrels whisper like the inside of a seashell. Aside from the surfing, Montañita is a well-known party spot, where **beachside bars** open at around 6pm and don't close until everyone's lying face-down in the sand. Though the area is overrun with men who love to surf (and the women who love them), you don't necessarily have to be a card-carrying member of either party to enjoy yourself here. The sun shines all day, and ocean acrobatics provide constant entertainment. Montañita's nighttime party scene is dark and spirited, with bonfires, sandy dance floors, and tropical drinks to provide strength, social courage, and merriment for all.

■ Near Montañita

MANGLARALTO

Five minutes south of Montañita and 60km north of La Libertad, an adequate surf taps the beach of Manglaralto. Practical resources line the wide pebbled streets, so well-kept they look untouched. Quieter and gentler than Montañita, Manglaralto grows shady, sweet-smelling, orange-blossoming trees that add to the tranquility.

The main entrance to Manglaralto is along **El Oro,** marked by a liquor store on the south side and a small shop with a billiards table on the north. El Oro runs east-west, and the entrance is four blocks from the sand. **EMETEL,** at Los Ríos and Av. 24 de Mayo, makes cash-only international calls (open Mon.-Sat. 8am-9pm, Sun. 8am-4pm). A 24-hour **pharmacy** (tel. 901-172) occupies the corner of Malecón and Azuay. **Hospital al Manglaralto** (emergency tel. 901-192), at Av. 24 de Mayo and Av. 10 de Agosto, provides free 24-hour treatment at the south end of town.

Alegre Calimar, along Constitución at the northern end of town, is an acceptable hotel/restaurant, decorated with a poster of the Last Supper and a creative arrangement of painted tuna, octopi, squids, and lobsters. Unfortunately, the food selection is less exotic: fried fish s/7,000, shrimp s/8,000, or calamari with rice (open daily 7am-8pm). Basic rooms have scruffy green-marble floors, but well-polished oak beds and desks. Common bath is clean enough. Singles s/15,000; doubles s/25,000.

VALDIVIA AND AYANGUE

Just south of Montañita and Manglaralto, these two diminutive fishing villages eagerly pursue the ones that don't get away. **Valdivia** is farther north, 50km above La Libertad, just over an hour away from Puerto López. The town wastes no time with formalities, choosing instead to announce its main tourist attraction with a sign for the **Museo Las Calaneras.** The museum is on the west side of the road, just off the highway. Home to artifacts of the area's oldest culture, the **Valdivians,** the museum looks like little more than a camper from the outside, but inside it's loaded with religious, funereal, and ceremonial artifacts that will tell you everything you ever wanted to know about the people who lived here from 3000-2000 BC (admission s/1,000). From the town's main entrance, a few minutes farther along the highway, the road heads straight towards a sizeable statue of an anonymous woman and child, then continues to the sand. While the calm waters make for easier swimming than at other nearby beaches, the main occupants of Valdivia's beach are obnoxious telephone poles, giving the littered stretch of sand a dead-in-the-water atmosphere.

Although **Ayangue** is only 5km south of Valdivia, only mountain goats ever manage the walk. With a monstrous rocky point separating the two towns, the bus provides the only feasible inter-village transport, dropping passengers off along the highway near a cluttering of "Welcome to Ayangue" signs. The paved road heading west leads into town, a five-minute drive or a half-hour walk. This road leads directly to Ayangue's beach, a small, protected cove reputed to be a dangerous swimming hole. Instead of risking life and limb for a dip in the ocean, walk along the street leading to the beach, where street vendors sell gigantic pieces of coral and sizeable sea shells, and a caged howler monkey named Rocky will shake your hand, then steal anything in it. There are a few hotels on the street parallel to the beach. The friendliest of these, **Hostal Un Millón de Amigos** (tel. 916-014), can't help but surround guests with lots and lots of love. Eclectically-postered rooms sport posters of Schwarzenegger, the Beatles, naked people, and various American cities. Beds can be either regal wooden frames or raised slabs of concrete. All rooms have spotless tile floors and private baths. S/20,000 per person. The best **restaurant** in town also calls Un Millón de Amigos home. There are hardly a million menu items, but those that exist are certainly friendly. Boneless fried fish, shrimp, or *ceviche* each s/1,000. One of the few places on the coast serving affordable *langostino* (jumbo shrimp); munch this delicacy for only s/12,000 (open Mon.-Fri. 7am-9pm).

Salinas

In the hedonistic city of Salinas, BMWs cruise the streets, yachts rip across the harbor and night greets the morning with the pounding sounds of the *discoteca.* Charged with affluence, the town is home to (that is, second or third home to) many of South America's wealthiest folks. At the westernmost tip of the Santa Elena Peninsula 150km due west of Guayaquil, the white high-rise skyline towers over the rubble of La Libertad. With well-to-dos from Chile, Colombia, Perú, and of course, Ecuador attracted to its streets and sands, Salinas cannot help but adopt a cosmopolitan air. Yet somehow it has ended up less sophisticated than perhaps it should be. People come to Salinas not for highbrow culture but to play with their money, patronizing bars and *discotecas* and frolicking in the surf.

ORIENTATION

The **beach** cuts across the northern end of town. The only straightforward street names belong to the roads running north-south, perpendicular to the water; these **Calles** are numbered in order from lowest to highest, from west to east. The east-west streets, however, are a complete mess. Most have two names—the one on the street sign and the one most people use. **Malecón,** the closest parallel road to the water, offers most of the dining, nightlife, and expensive lodgings. **Buses** from La Libertad enter Salinas along **Av. 3 (Tercera),** parallel to the beach, three blocks inland. At about Calle 26, Av. 3 becomes Av. 7; catch a bus here for La Libertad.

PRACTICAL INFORMATION

Tour Agency: Pescatour, Malecón 577 y Rumiñahui (tel. 772-391; fax 443-142) leads 9½-hr. deep-sea fishing adventures for 1-6 people (US$325). Lunch is included, but bottled water is not (open daily 8am-noon and 2-6pm).

Banks: Filanbanco (tel. 773-640 or 773-431), at Enriquez Gallo and Las Palmeras has a 24-hr. ATM and changes traveler's checks, but not cash (open Wed.-Sun 8:45am-4pm). **Banco La Previsara** (tel. 773-092), at Enriquez Gallo and Leonardo Avilles, has a 24-hr. ATM, and changes cash, but not traveler's checks.

Telephones: EMETEL, at Rumiñahui/Calle 23 and Enriquez Gallo. Buy s/700 *fichas* (tokens) from the police station next door to make international calls. You have to keep plugging tokens in just to keep the line alive, even after you're connected with an operator (open daily 8am-10pm). Most of the **ritzy hotels** in town have public pay phones that accept calling cards.

Buses: The town of **La Libertad,** a few kilometers to the east, is the peninsula's transportation hub. Buses from Salinas to La Libertad leave every few minutes 'round the clock, or take a taxi or *camioneta* to La Libertad's *terminal terrestre*; get any of these on Av. 3. In La Libertad, **Coop Libertad Peninsular** (tel. 785-85[illegible] or 786-433), **Coop Trans Esmeraldas** (tel. 786-670), and **Coop Intercantonal Costa Azul,** are all at Av. 9 de Octubre and Calle Guerra Barreiro. Libertad and Costa Azul go to **Guayaquil** (every 15min., 3:30am-8:10pm, 2hr., s/6,500) via **Progreso** (1hr., s/3,000), and Esmeraldas goes to **Quito** (8, 9pm, 9hr., s/25,000).

Library: Biblioteca Municipal, at Los Almendros and Eloy Alfaro (open Tues.-Fri. 8:30am-12:30pm and 1-4:30pm, Sat. 8:30am-2pm).

Pharmacy: Farmacia Central, Malecón 331 y Calle 23 (open daily 9:30am-1pm and 2:30-10pm). **Farmacia Adreita** (tel. 774-194), at Av. 7 and Calle 18 (open daily 8:30am-9pm).

Hospital: Hospital Jose Gaurez (tel. 776-017), 3 blocks south of Espinoza, well past the police station in Ciudadela Frank Vargas Pazoz. The emergency room around back is open 24hr.

Police: (tel. 778-699), at Espinoza and Calle 57, on the east end of town.

Post Office: On Las Palmeras at Enriquez Gallo, diagonally across from Filanbanco (open Mon.-Fri. 8am-noon and 2-5pm, Sat. 9am-noon).
Telephone Code: 04.

ACCOMMODATIONS

Salinas's budget accommodations are few but not far-between. Most congregate between Calle 22 and Calle 27, on the parallel roads south of Malecón. You won't find anything lower than s/15,000 per person, but almost all rooms are well-maintained and have private bathrooms.

Hostal Las Rocas (tel. 774-219), on Calle 22 at Enriquez Gallo, 2 blocks from the beach, with white stucco and blue trim. 2nd-story rooms have lounge chairs and a breezy patio, good for admiring the harbor. Tidy blue curtains in the immaculate rooms match the exterior trim. Well-scrubbed private baths and oft-ignored ceiling fans, unnecessary when sea breezes waft through open windows. English-speaking management provides helpful information and serves hot cups of complimentary Colombian coffee all day. S/15,000 per person.

Hotel Oro del Mar (La Libertad tel. 783-110), at Av. Segunda and Calle 23. Dilapidated, time-worn curtains redeemed by sizeable windows and ocean glimpses. Spacious rooms seem sterilized with chlorine; lipstick kisses adorn otherwise stark walls. The brown tile in the narrow-showered private bathrooms masks the spots not hit by the chlorine. S/20,000 per person.

Residencial El Refugio, at Calle 27 and Av. 7a. Take Calle 27 away from the waterfront; 7a is the street after Av. 7. Off the beaten path, the "refuge" is a haven for travelers weary of Salinas's glitz and glitter. Among the city's more humble abodes, it offers private baths and ceiling fans. Beds have about as much give as the red-and-white checkerboard floor. S/15,000 per person.

Hotel Albita (tel. 773-211), at Av. 7 and Calle 23, around the corner from Las Rocas. Choose red-and-white checkerboard or speckled concrete floors in your windowless cubicle. Floor fans work desperately to rid rooms of the musty smell. Private baths sparkle with cleanliness. S/15,000 per person.

FOOD

Salinas's seafood is excellent, but not necessarily good enough to justify these prices. Even sidewalk booths are on the expensive side. If you like *ceviche,* however, you've come to the right place. **Cevichelandia,** at the corner of Luz de Serrano and Las Palmeras, may just be your wildest fantasy come true—a plaza containing 15 separate outdoor *cevicherías,* all fresh, all delicious. *Ceviche*-land continues along Enriquez Gallo, beginning at Las Palmeras and running until Calle 18, where another plaza of outdoor *cevicherías* awaits. Malecón is loaded with places to eat, but like the beachfront hotels, restaurants tend to overcharge.

Restaurant Herminia, at Malecón and Calle 28. One of the few relaxed joints along the waterfront, Herminia's decor seems to have accrued effortlessly, like dust, over time. An empty box from a Miller 24-pack shares the wall with a giant painting of the sneering Barcelona bull, mascot of Guayaquil's ever-popular *fútbol* club. Admire the harbor from the straw hammock or pick at your paint-chipped Coca-Cola tabletop while awaiting a plate of fried fish and rice (s/5,000) or a *churrasco* feast (s/8,000). Open Sun.-Thurs. 9am-midnight, Fri.-Sat. 9am-1 or 2am.

Comedor and Cevichería Jully, at Calle 18 and Enriquez Gallo. Served in an open-air roadside stand, the cheapest eats in town come complete with a smile and a chat. Everything is cooked 4ft. from where you sit on the L-shaped tile bartop, laden with blenders and surrounded by wooden bar stools. Fish-filled *almuerzo* (s/5,000). Break the nightly fast with a s/4,500 breakfast of coffee, eggs-as-you-like-'em, bread, and one of Jully's *batidos* (open daily 7am-4pm).

Restaurante Los Helechos (tel. 773-984), at Malecón and Calle 28. *Los helechos* (the ferns) hang everywhere in this simple, shady, breezy diner, strewn with fishing nets and wood carvings. A feast of the senses; feel the scattered pebbles and seashells that rustle and chime as you step over them. Admire the various fish tanks as you enjoy chicken salad (s/10,000) or battered trout (s/8,000). Gaze at the yachts in the harbor and delve into a s/8,000 plate of steak, rice, and potatoes (open daily from 8am, usually until very late, depending on the clientele).

Comedor y Cevichería Carmenita, along Las Palmeras at Luz de Serrano, in *Cevichelandia.* The closest thing to fast food in Salinas, but easier on your arteries. Open-air sidewalk stand has 3 long benches and a white sheet-metal roof providing shade. Smiling women serve delicious *ceviche* (s/10,000), fresh from Salinas, otherwise imported all the way from La Libertad (open daily 7am-5pm).

SIGHTS AND ENTERTAINMENT

Salinas has two beaches, divided by a small peninsula that houses the **Salinas Yacht Club.** Salinas's main beach covers the stretch of sand to the east of the Yacht Club. Palm-laden and relatively unlittered, the sands are packed to capacity with sun worshippers. The water is even more congested, teeming with every kind of watercraft imaginable: expensive yachts, luxurious sailboats, time-worn fishing dugouts, banana boats, paddle boats, and jetskis. Shallow water is safe for children and timid swimmers; the surface only stirs when a boat motors through. Join in the water diversions, like a **banana boat** ride for s/5,000. **Paddle boats** fit up to four (s/10,000 per hr.). The chronically lazy can rent junior **motor boats** to go around the harbor (s/100,000 per hr.). If you don't want to lift a finger, **tour boats** cruise the harbor as well (s/3,000 per person for the 30min. excursion). Never fear, high-speed enthusiasts, the sea's the limit on **jet skis** (s/100,000 per hr.), and boats can take you **waterskiing** (s/120,000 per hr.). The less-crowded beach on the western side of the Yacht Club doesn't offer any of the aforementioned diversions, but it does offer peace and quiet on its tranquil, protected shorebreak. Although this beach manages to avoid the crowds and the carnival-like atmosphere, the tacky white high-rises still loom inescapably in the background.

When the sun goes down, Salinas's sandy carnival moves inside, infiltrating the city's bars and *discotecas.* Nightlife in Salinas means bar-hopping; just follow the teeth-rattling *discoteca* music. **Flintstone's Rockabar** (tel. 774-144), at Enriquez Gallo and Rafael de la Cuadra, somehow combines American cinema, a sports bar, and a *discoteca* in a tribute to pop culture. DJed dance floor covered with a strange collection of James Dean, Marilyn Monroe, and American football posters. Clumsy folk can pretend to rest on tree stumps covered with faux dinosaur hide, and really just watch cutting-edge sports on the TVs above. Billiards-and-foosball saloon upstairs provides a good dance floor scoping spot. Beer s/5,000-7,000, whiskey s/10,000 (open Thurs.-Sat. 9pm-4am; cover s/10,000). **El Patio,** at Calle 27 and Enriquez Gallo in Hotel Salinas Costa Azul, is another popular dance bar that really gets going after 10pm. You could lose yourself in the soft velvety couches, especially with lighting this dim. A disco ball rotates while the DJ spins *merengue, salsa,* and dance-hall hits. (open Thurs.-Sun. 8pm-around 4am; cover s/10,000). **El Tobaco,** at Malecón and Suastegur, has inside and outside dance floors under palm-thatched roofs. Spins the usual toe-tapping Latin and foreign hits (open Fri.-Sun. 9pm-late, with a s/10,000 cover).

Playas

As the closest beach resort to Guayaquil, Playas inevitably receives masses of *guayaquileños* during the sweltering weekends. And because it's cheaper than the other major beach resort at Salinas, Playas is the sunbathing spot of choice for most of the southern Sierra. The regular weekend invasions by fervent Ecuadorian tourists have given Playas the feel of a rental car—handled without care and left in disrepair. The beach is strewn with litter, evidence of the comings and goings of visitors who knew they wouldn't be around to clean up on Monday. But as an affordable and almost effortless escape from the city, Playas will do you right.

ORIENTATION

Buses from Guayaquil enter from the north along **Pedro Hernandez Gilbert**, and exit Playas for Guayaquil north out **Calle Paquisha,** parallel to Gilbert, two streets east. Passengers are dropped off along east-west **Av. 15 de Agosto,** Playas's main street. All of the town's practical facilities are located along this street, as is the triangular **central plaza. Calle 9** runs south from the central plaza to east-west **Calle Malecón,** Playas's shoreline drive. **Avenida 2,** also called **Calle Jaime Roldos Aguilerra,** runs parallel to Malecón, one street north.

PRACTICAL INFORMATION

Currency Exchange: Multibanco Banco de Guayaquil (tel. 760-040), on Av. 15 de Agosto at Gilbert, exchanges traveler's checks only (open Mon.-Fri. 9am-6pm).

Telephone: EMETEL (tel. 660-104 or 660-105), on Av. 2/Aguilera, 800m west of town, is the place to go for international calls. S/5,000 to talk to an operator from AT&T, Sprint, or MCI (open daily 8am-10pm).

Buses: Coop Transportes Villamil, at Pedro Menendez Gilbert and Av. 15 de Agosto goes to **Guayaquil** (every 20min. 4am-7pm, 2hr., s/4,800) via **Progreso** (30min., s/2,000). Wait for buses at the station or at the **bus stop** on the right hand side of Paquisha at Av. 15 de Agosto.

Pharmacy: Farmacia Villamil (tel. 760-159), on Av. 15 de Agosto between Gilbert and Paquisha (open daily 8am-10pm).

Hospital: Hospital General Villamil Playas (emergency tel. 660-238), on Av. 15 de Agosto, 1km east of town. Free 24-hr. emergency treatment.

Police: (tel. 764-145), on Calle Asiselo Garay at Av. 15 de Agosto, on the right hand side of the street as you head north.

Post Office: On Calle Asiselo Garay and Av. 15 de Agosto, next to the police station (open Mon.-Fri. 9am-1pm and 2:30-6pm, Sat. 9am-1pm).

Telephone Code: 04.

ACCOMMODATIONS

Most establishments in Playas have been around a while and show visible signs of their age. But don't discount them yet—the management certainly hasn't. While hotels may appear tumbledown from the street, they often retain a time-worn charm on the inside. Many congregate in the western end of town, along Malecón and Av. 2, but there are a few others dispersed along Av. 15 de Agosto.

Hotel Miraglia (tel. 770-154), on Av. 2, 3 blocks west of Hotel Acapulco. Weather-beaten on the outside, this monstrous colonial home has a made-over interior. The wood plank walls in the high-ceiling rooms have been painted multiple times, and the wooden bed frames, desks, and chairs look brand-new. Breathe the ocean air in the wide breezy hallways, or relax in a rope hammock, eyeing the water from the 3rd story patio. All rooms have hot-water private bath and mosquito nets. Foreigners s/12,000 per person, Ecuadorians s/15,000. Go figure.

Hotel Playas (tel. 760-121 or 760-611), at Malecón and Jaime Roldos Aguilera. Not only is it across the street from the sand, but constant breezes keep mosquitoes minimal. Fans in immaculate quarters seem almost unnecessary. Rooms sprinkled with a faint scent of potpourri, a woodsy complement to narrow wooden beds and straw nightstands. All rooms have private bath. S/15,000 per person.

Hotel Acapulco (tel. 760-343), at Av. 2 and Calle 9. Generally spooky atmosphere, with ample but empty quarters except for the bed and a dangling, solitary lightbulb. Mysterious stains on the scruffy walls and creaky wooden floors. Pray for a room with a window facing the sea breezes, as mosquito nets are conspicuously absent. Common baths are clean but a bit decrepit. S/15,000 per person.

FOOD

For seaside views, a series of four or five nondescript seafood establishments sits down on the sand, serving standard coastal dishes for typical prices. The best food in town, however, is found along Paquisha near Aguilera, where a collection of *cevicherías* use the freshest of shellfish the sea offers.

Cevichería Doña Gladys, at Paquisha and Aguilera. Part of the *ceviche* streetside mall, complete with palm-thatched roof and screaming Coca-Cola billboard. Various exotica laid out for your appraisal: conches, oysters, clams, and *patomulas* all begging to become your *ceviche* dinner. Shellfish *ceviche* s/6,000, shrimp *ceviche* s/8,000, basic plate of fried fish, rice, and veggies s/6,000 (open daily 7am-9pm).

Comedor Sabor Criollo, at Jaime Roldos Aguilera and Calle 9, diagonally across from Hotel Acapulco, a couple of blocks from the beach. The "Criollo" comes from the smiling owner's last name, as well as the secret spices that give the food that New Orleans twang. Streetside tables and benches, spiced with creative sugar containers and cotton swab faux-roses. *Churrasco* s/7,000, fried filet s/6,000, *corvina* s/7,000 (open Mon.-Fri. 8am-8pm, Sat.-Sun. 8am-noon).

La Cabaña Típica (tel. 760-464), at Malecón and Jaime Roldos Aguilera, on the beachfront, across from Hotel Playas. Tree-branch seats ground the bamboo surroundings. In a biblical tale with a twist, fishing nets entangle both a likeness of Christ and an assortment of wood-carved sealife. Ugly metal bars on the windows don't stop the cool breezes. Monstrous plate of rice and calamari, shrimp, conch, and fish s/10,000 (open daily 9am-8pm).

SIGHTS AND ENTERTAINMENT

The name says it all: people come for the **playas.** Most visitors spend the weekend either sweating in the sun or sprinting to the ocean in a quest for relief. Far from picturesque, the vast, treeless, litter-sprinkled sands of Playas are popular because there is plenty of room for everyone. While Playas Beach (or the sing-song *Playa Playas*) offers no shade, many sunbathers bring immense canvases to create shady tents over the sand. The surf is weak and relatively harmless, perfect for wading and dog-paddling. If the sun's getting to be too much, duck inside the Playas **cinema,** at Av. 15 de Agosto and Asiselo Garay. Films screened in English and Spanish; ask the ticket seller the language of the night. Adult films featured Thursdays and Fridays; Hollywood hits Sundays and Mondays (screenings 9:30pm; tickets s/2,000).

■ Near Playas: Baños de San Vicente

Situated 15km southeast of Santa Elena, the Baños de San Vicente offer a filthy good time. A miracle of nature, San Vicente's muddied volcanic crater is a natural panacea for such ailments as arthritis and rheumatism. Sufferers of these afflictions, as well as health-conscious pleasure-seekers, flock to San Vicente to experience this alternative physical therapy and enjoy extras like massages, steam baths, and health food.

General admission to the park (s/6,000, children s/3,000) includes access to the **mud bath,** where you can wallow the day away, as well as the three indoor pools, one of which is a natural hot spring. Further indulgences wouldn't be indulgences if they didn't cost more. **Massages** using mud or *savila,* a natural aloe, relieve about s/15,000 of tension, while **hydra-massages**—20 minutes of high-powered jacuzzi jets—soak you for s/10,000. The jets bombard bathers with surges of water that activate the surface of the skin, relaxing muscles while at the same time improving circulation. The park also offers **internal purification,** which involves sweating away the evil build-up of everyday life in the s/6,000 steam bath.

After indulging in these pleasures of the flesh, healthful gastronomic therapy awaits at the park's **restaurant.** Tuna or ham sandwiches s/3,000, all-natural juices (s/2,500-3,000). **Hotel Florida** (tel. 785-020), a two-minute walk behind the park, offers rooms with private baths, metal cot-beds, and scruffy blank walls. The top-notch **restaurant** downstairs serves truly full meals. S/50,000 per person, including all three meals.

Buses from Progreso to La Libertad run past San Vicente. Ask the driver to drop you off at Los Baños de San Vicente. From the highway, it's 15km to the park. You can walk, but it could take up to two hours. Many choose to hitchhike.

Guayaquil and the Western Lowlands

Fertile plains sitting at the western base of the Andes, the lowlands have long played a pivotal role in the country's history. It was here that the first banana and cacao plantations were planted during the 17th century, crops that would later take over the majority of this low, flat, well-irrigated land. The endemic forests that once shaded the fertile soil here were pushed farther and farther towards the perimeter of the lowlands, in many cases pushed all the way out of their habitat and into extinction. Today, Río Palenque Science Center, to the north, shelters a small patch of what was once an expansive lowland forest.

Such is the price burgeoning Ecuador was willing to pay to develop its most prosperous industry. Coming into its own during the youthful era of independence, the liberal port of Guayaquil was the luckiest benefactor of the newly booming agricultural industry. The profits that poured into Guayaquil made it more and more of a commercial city, and in turn further fueled the development of the industry that had already given it so much. This self-perpetuating cycle of industrial, commercial, and urban development continued well into the 20th century. The discovery of oil in the Oriente in the 1970s took some wind out of their agricultural sails, but Guayaquil and the lowlands cannot change what they are today: a gritty commercial capital and the agricultural machine that fuels it.

Guayaquil

Once an indigenous settlement, this coastal city was conquered by the Spanish in the 16th century. Legend has it that before surrendering their pride and their beloved home, the native prince and princess committed suicide. His name was Guayas, her name Quil, and from their martyrdom was born the name of the most populous city in Ecuador, with a population of over two million.

The suffering of this couple lives on in its residents. While many cities seclude their shantytowns from the public eye, Guayaquil has little to display but an unglamorous array of urban squalor and pollution. From the day Francisco de Orellana landed here in 1537, this crowded port has been bombarded by commerce from the sea. Industry exploded in the early part of this century, establishing the nitty-gritty disposition that dominates Guayaquil's character to this day. Trash-paved streets lead down to a stinking, murky river, and the occasional squashed rat is a more common sight than the healthy palm tree. Women beg on corners with their children, often sick and starving, on their backs.

But while some eyes follow foreign tourists as they would a money roll wearing a backpack, most *guayaquileños* are kind, proud, and eager to show you why their "Pearl of the Pacific" is worth visiting. Aside from being a convenient stop on the way to the coast or Perú, Guayaquil offers the dense, winding, 400-year-old **Las Peñas** neighborhood, as well as a collection of museums and very old but restored churches. But that's just the downtown. What seems like a whole other world—Mercedes Benzes, *Beverly Hills 90210* billboards and all—is found in *el norte:* not the U.S., but the suburbs of **Urdesa** and **Alborada** to the north of the city. Here, the people and the sidewalks are whiter, and everyone is healthier and better dressed. The insane crowds and numerous clubs in these areas have given Guayaquil's nightlife a reputation as the wildest, most memorable around. Perhaps the nightlife helps the affluent forget the tiny children on the street selling roses and bubble gum far into the night, struggling to be noticed.

ORIENTATION

Guayaquil sprawls, but the gridlike downtown, or *centro,* next to the river, is easy enough to navigate. **El Malecón Simón Bolívar,** called **Malecón** for short, is a busy thoroughfare with many hotels and offices that follows the waterfront. **Avenida 9 de Octubre,** the main east-west boulevard in the city, starts at Malecón where **La Rotonda** stands and passes through the central **Parque del Centenario.** In general, the farther north and south you head from Av. 9 de Octubre in *el centro,* the more dangerous the area will be. **Guayaquil is not a safe city:** watch where you walk and who's walking with you. Take caution if you find yourself on an abandoned street. Eyes will be on you, especially if you're carrying a lot of baggage. The most common tourist area is along **Pedro Carbo** near the **Hotel Doral** and **Parque Bolívar.** This municipal area is generally safe for walking, alone or in groups. Taxis are helpful, even though the downtown area is almost small enough to cover by foot.

To get to the nearby suburbs, though, taxis or buses are a must. **Urdesa** and **Alborada** are north of *el centro,* in the same direction as the airport and bus station. Worlds apart from downtown Guayaquil, these bourgeois suburbs are cleaner, safer, and strikingly more healthy-looking. The main strip in Urdesa, **Victor Emilio Estrada,** is packed with restaurants and shops and is *the* place for nightlife in Guayaquil, and probably in Ecuador. The **Las Peñas** neighborhood is to the east, near the **Río Guayas.** This river, which runs east of *el centro,* is spanned by the largest bridge in the country, the **Bridge of National Unity.** On the other side of the river is the run-down suburb of **Durán,** home to the train station. A ferry from Malecón also goes to Durán.

PRACTICAL INFORMATION

Tourist Offices: CETUR (tel. 328-312 or 531-794; fax 531-044 or 329-377), on Malecón and Aguirre, 3 blocks south of La Rotonda. Tucked next to a pharmacy on the corner, it's up the stairway entrance on the 2nd floor. The staff wants to help, but lacks organization and resources. Mediocre photocopied maps and other information materials provided. One employee speaks English (open Mon.-Fri. 8am-5pm). **Airport Kiosk,** in the middle of the larger terminal room, near international departures. English is spoken, and they have more experience in offering assistance (open daily 7am-7pm).

Consulates: United States (tel. 323-570; fax 325-286), Av. 9 de Octubre and García Moreno (open Mon.-Fri. 8am-noon and 1:30-5:30pm). **U.K.,** Córdova 623 y Padre Solano (tel. 560-400 or 563-850; fax 562-641 or 322-062). Open Mon.-Fri. 9am-noon and 2:30-5pm. **Canada,** Córdova 810 y V.M. Rendón, 21st floor, office 4 (tel. 563-560 or 566-747; fax 314-562). Open Mon.-Fri. 9:30am-1:30pm. **Australia** (tel. 298-823; fax 298-822), San Roque and Av. Francisco de Orellana (open Mon.-Fri. 9am-1:30pm). **Perú,** Av. 9 de Octubre 411 y Chile, 6th floor (tel. 322-738 or 327-639; fax 325-679). Open Mon.-Fri. 8:30am-1:30pm. **Colombia,** Córdova 812 y V.M. Rendón, 2nd floor, office 11 (tel. 563-308; fax 563-854). Open Mon.-Fri. 9am-12:30pm and 2:30-4:30pm.

Currency Exchange: The first several blocks of Av. 9 de Octubre, starting from the waterfront, are loaded with banks and *casas de cambio.* Swapping cash or traveler's checks is no problem during business hours, but afterward the search becomes a challenge. **Cambiosa** (tel. 325-199 or 325-284), on the 1st block of Av. 9 de Octubre, has good dollar-to-sucre rates.

American Express: Av. 9 de Octubre 1900 y Esmeraldas, 2nd floor (tel. 394-984 or 286-900). Offers travel information and receives mail without charge for card members (open Mon.-Fri. 9am-1pm and 2-6pm). Send mail to: Ecuadorian Tours, American Express, Av. 9 de Octubre 1900, Guayaquil, Ecuador.

ATMs: Most are located on and around Av. 9 de Octubre, near the waterfront.

Western Union: (tel. 561-364; fax 564-986), at Malecón and P. Icaza.

Telephones: EMETEL, at Pedro Carbo and Ballén, in the same building as the post office. The place to go to make international calls, but be careful. Calls over longer distances are charged by the minute, so be prepared to pay for operator problems, dialing mistakes, and especially the incompetence of the cashiers. Local and long-distance national calls and telegram service are also available (open daily 8am-

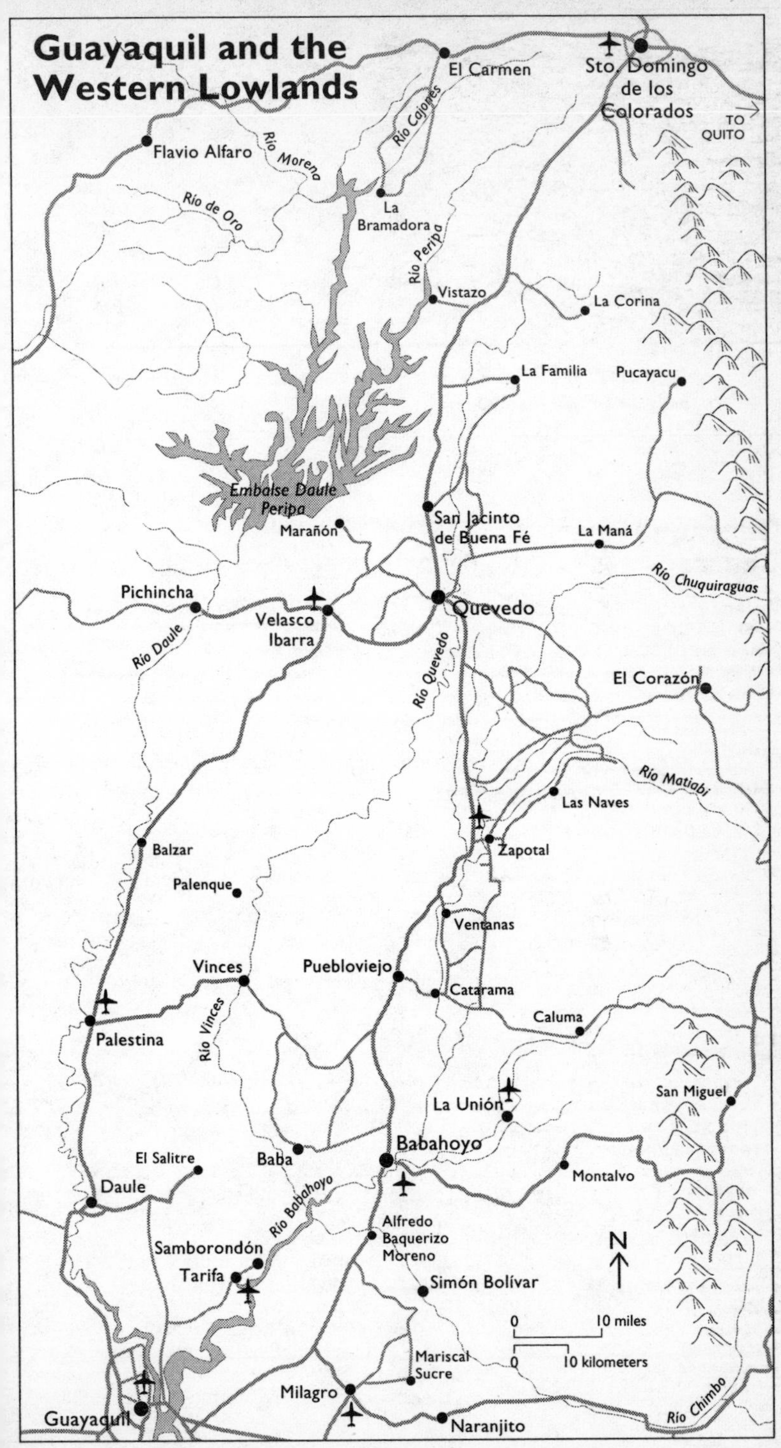
Guayaquil and the Western Lowlands
El Carmen
Sto. Domingo de los Colorados
TO QUITO
Flavio Alfaro
Río Morena
Río Cajones
Río de Oro
La Bramadora
Río Peripa
Vistazo
La Corina
La Familia
Pucayacu
Embalse Daule Peripa
Marañón
San Jacinto de Buena Fé
La Maná
Río Chuquiraguas
Pichincha
Velasco Ibarra
Quevedo
Río Daule
Río Quevedo
El Corazón
Río Matiabi
Las Naves
Zapotal
Balzar
Palenque
Ventanas
Vinces
Puebloviejo
Catarama
Caluma
Palestina
Río Vinces
San Miguel
La Unión
Babahoyo
El Salitre
Baba
Montalvo
Daule
Río Babahoyo
Alfredo Baquerizo Moreno
Samborondón
Tarifa
Simón Bolívar
N
0
10 miles
0
10 kilometers
Mariscal Sucre
Milagro
Guayaquil
Naranjito
Río Chimbo

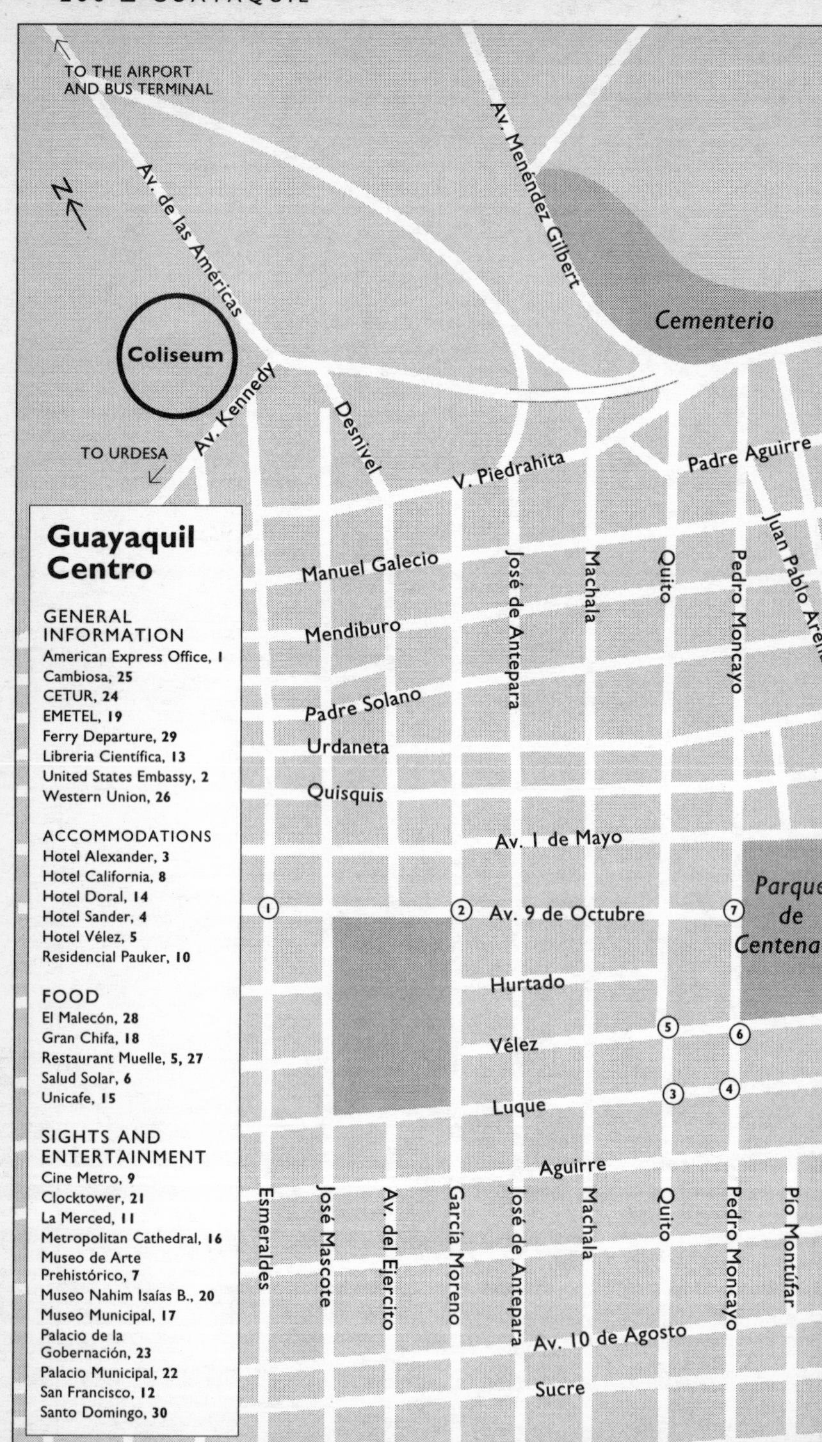

Guayaquil Centro

GENERAL INFORMATION
American Express Office, **1**
Cambiosa, **25**
CETUR, **24**
EMETEL, **19**
Ferry Departure, **29**
Libreria Científica, **13**
United States Embassy, **2**
Western Union, **26**

ACCOMMODATIONS
Hotel Alexander, **3**
Hotel California, **8**
Hotel Doral, **14**
Hotel Sander, **4**
Hotel Vélez, **5**
Residencial Pauker, **10**

FOOD
El Malecón, **28**
Gran Chifa, **18**
Restaurant Muelle, **5, 27**
Salud Solar, **6**
Unicafe, **15**

SIGHTS AND ENTERTAINMENT
Cine Metro, **9**
Clocktower, **21**
La Merced, **11**
Metropolitan Cathedral, **16**
Museo de Arte Prehistórico, **7**
Museo Nahim Isaías B., **20**
Museo Municipal, **17**
Palacio de la Gobernación, **23**
Palacio Municipal, **22**
San Francisco, **12**
Santo Domingo, **30**

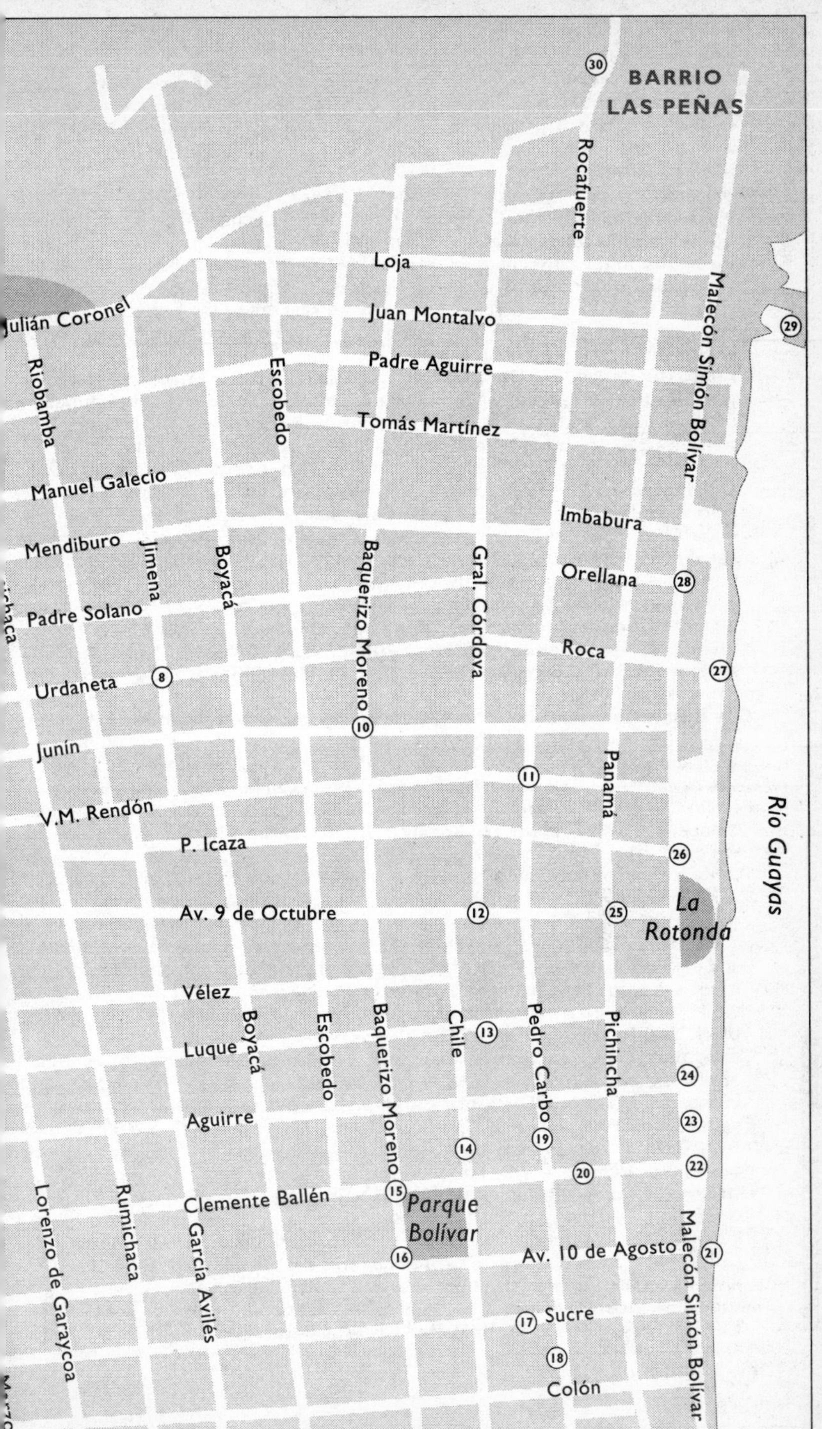
BARRIO
LAS PEÑAS
Rocafuerte
Loja
Julián Coronel
Juan Montalvo
Padre Aguirre
Riobamba
Escobedo
Tomás Martínez
Malecón Simón Bolívar
Manuel Galecio
Imbabura
Mendiburo
Jimena
Boyacá
Baquerizo Moreno
Gral. Córdova
Orellana
Padre Solano
Roca
Urdaneta
Junín
Panamá
V.M. Rendón
P. Icaza
Río Guayas
Av. 9 de Octubre
La
Rotonda
Vélez
Boyacá
Escobedo
Baquerizo Moreno
Chile
Pedro Carbo
Pichincha
Luque
Aguirre
Clemente Ballén
Parque
Bolívar
Lorenzo de Garaycoa
Rumichaca
García Avilés
Av. 10 de Agosto
Malecón Simón Bolívar
Sucre
Colón
30
29
28
27
8
10
11
26
12
25
13
24
23
19
14
22
20
15
16
21
17
18

12:20pm, 1-6pm, and 7-9:30pm). For calls on public payphones, tokens are sold all over by street vendors. The number for **information** is 104.

Airport: Simón Bolívar International Airport (tel. 282-1000; fax 290-018), on Av. de las Américas, about 5km north of the city. The airport has 2 terminals separated by less than 1km. The larger one houses national and international flights. The smaller is the place to catch one of the more frequently departing *avionetas* to a national destination.

National flights: To **Quito** (s/98,000), **Cuenca** (s/82,000), **Loja** (s/76,500), **Machala** (s/65,000), **the Galápagos** (s/247,000 for Ecuadorians, a much higher US$167 for foreigners). **Taxis** wait out front, but prepare to be ripped off. From the airport to the city center, a taxi ride should cost no more than s/7,000. If you are headed to the nearby outgoing bus station, argue the taxi driver down to around s/6,000. Avoid exorbitant prices by walking out to the highway and catching a taxi there, or taking a bus. However, if you're bursting with baggage or it's after nightfall, this is probably not safe.

Trains: The station is in **Durán,** about 2 blocks from the ferry landing. Head left, then down to the street that runs along the tracks. The train is not as popular a mode of transportation as buses. It runs only to **Riobamba** and in-between locations, leaving daily at 6:25am (11hr., s/8,000 for Ecuadorians, US$14 for foreigners). Since the first ferry leaves Guayaquil at 7am, to get to the station before departure you'll have to either take a taxi or stay overnight in Durán.

Regional Buses: Jaime Roldos Aguila Terminal Terrestre (tel. 297-574), on Av. de las Américas, a few km past the airport. A veritable food court of ticket counters and different *cooperativos,* the main room seems to go on forever, as do the departure times and destinations of the bus lines. Consistent prices to the same destinations spare you the task of shopping around. To **Quito** (every 30min., 7hr., s/20,000), **Cuenca** (roughly every hr., 4½hr., s/14,000), **Salinas** (every 15min., 2¼hr., s/6,500), **Babahoyo** (every 10min., 5am-10:20pm, 1¼hr., s/2,200), **Ambato** (roughly every hr., 6hr., s/12,000), **Huaquillas** (roughly every 2hr., 4½hr., s/10,500).

City Buses: These ubiquitous vehicles are usually cramped with locals. Their cheapness is the key to their popularity. A bus ride is around s/600, so if you have the time and skill to analyze the system, by all means wave one down. Be careful if you're carrying excessive luggage; crowded buses can be hotspots for thievery.

Ferries: To get to **Durán,** a boat leaves from the waterfront at Malecón and Juan Montalvo, 9 blocks north of La Rotonda. Departs for the other side of the Río Guayas every ½hr. from 7am-6:30pm, except from 9am-noon and 2-4pm when departures are only on the hour. Returns to Guayaquil are equally frequent.

Taxis: Once you get used to the currency, you may develop a deep resentment for your first few taxi drivers. Guayaquil drivers are notorious for taking advantage of "new arrivals" and tourists in general. The meter comes to mean almost nothing, and it is best to decide on a fare before getting into a vehicle. Be pushy and willing to let a taxi go. Taxis between 2 places in *el centro* shouldn't cost more than s/2,000-3,000. Taxis between the airport and the city run s/5,000-7,000. Try the dispatch **Taxi Paraíso** (tel. 201-877 or 204-232).

Car Rental: These are relatively expensive. Considering the other options, it may not be the best idea. **Avis** (tel. 285-498), **Budget** (tel. 284-559 or 288-510), and **Hertz** (tel. 511-316, 327-895, or 293-011) all have offices in or near the airport.

English Bookstore: Librería Científica, Luque 223 y Chile (tel. 328-069 or 328-569). Have the urge to study up while in Guayaquil? Need a modern English novel? This is the place (open Mon.-Fri. 9am-7pm, Sat. 9am-3pm).

Library: The Guayaquil Municipal Library is at Sucre and Pedro Carbo (tel. 515-738). Open Mon.-Fri. 9am-5pm, Sat. 10am-2pm.

Pharmacy: Street-level pharmacies are scattered throughout the downtown area. One popular chain is **Fybreca,** with a branch at V.E. Estrada 609 y Las Monjas (tel. 881-444 or 381-468), in the suburb of Urdesa (open 24hr.).

Medical Services: Two reputable hospitals are **Clínica Kennedy** (tel. 286-963) and **Clínica Guayaquil** (tel. 563-555). **Red Cross** ambulance service can be reached at 560-674.

Emergency: 199.

Police: (tel. 101), on Av. de las Américas, several kilometers towards the airport.

Post Office: (tel. 514-713), on the west side of Pedro Carbo between Aguirre and Ballén. Has a *Lista de Correos* (open Mon.-Fri. 8am-6pm, Sat 8am-2pm).

Telephone Code: 04.

ACCOMMODATIONS

Ecuahogar (tel. 248-357 or 240-388; fax 248-341), on Av. Isidro Ayora, across from the B.E.V. bank. About 10km north of *el centro,* near the airport and bus terminal. All 4 floors of this breezy, relaxed hacienda are open to the residential suburban air. A hammock and panoramic city view give the top floor rooms an especially lazy ambience. International crowd drawn to the European *dueña,* who speaks Spanish, English, German, and French. Hot water Fri., Sat. only. Laundry and phone services. Reservations suggested. US$8, HI/ISIC members US$7; with private bath US$10, HI/ ISIC members US$9. Light breakfast included.

Residencial Pauker, Baquerizo Moreno 902 y Junín (tel. 565-385). This dank establishment is at the top of the lower-end motels, so don't be too alarmed that most guests don't stay the night. Staff is eager to please. All rooms have beds, some even 3 or 4, for groups. Some private baths (but no hot water), and all except the cheapest rooms have A/C or fans for those sweaty nights. Can often be noisy. Mattresses and sheets look well-worn. Some rooms have balconies, reception/TV room in front. Singles and doubles s/12,000, with A/C s/15,000, with A/C and bath s/20,000.

Hotel Sander, Luque 1110 y Pedro Moncayo (tel. 320-030 or 320-944). The "Nuevo Sander" is a budget travel gem. Though plain as hell and slightly bug-infested, this place rocks because the price is right. Sure, rooms have no carpet or hot water, and A/C is extra *dinero,* but Sander is bright and clean enough. The bug community seems to prefer the bathroom to the vast beyond. Singles and doubles s/24,000, with fan and TV s/26,000, with A/C s/30,000.

Hotel Alexander, Luque 1107 (tel. 532-000, 532-651, or 532-652; fax 328-474), between Quito and Moncayo. Almost attached to the Sander, the Alexander could be that hotel's more expensive, carpeted, less-bug-infested twin. The multiple floors rise above a busy, generally safe part of Guayaquil. Some rooms have A/C and a hot-water private bath; a few even have eye-jolting fluorescent comforters covering soft, heavenly mattresses. Awesome staff stores guests' valuables in a safe in the main office. Elevators provide wheelchair access. Reservations suggested. Singles s/40,000; doubles s/55,000, plus 10% service tax.

Hotel Vélez, Vélez 1021 y Quito (tel. 530-256, 530-311, 530-292, or 532-430). So close to the Parque del Centenario you can almost hear the masses congregating. The Vélez is a comfy cradle for the weary traveler, without any padding. All rooms have private bath and A/C, but if you fall you *will* hit something hard (the mattress isn't necessarily an exception). No hot water, and staff is less than eager to help. No matter, though; for the price, this ascetic place does its job. Rooms begin at s/30,000, with A/C s/33,000, with 3 beds and a window view s/50,000.

Hotel California, Urdaneta 529 y Jimena (tel. 302-296, 302-376, 302-406, or 302-484; fax 562-548). The rifle-toting guard at the door is a good hint that the area is not a safe place to frolic with a bevy of luggage, but he also insures that the inside is plenty safe. It's also much more luxurious than other similarly-priced places in Guayaquil. All rooms have A/C, private bath, and cable TV. Phone services, including international. At the *"moderada"* level: singles s/40,000; doubles s/50,000. *"Superior"* rooms add carpet, refrigerator, phone, hot water: singles s/50,000; doubles s/60,000. Cafeteria downstairs (open 7am-11:30pm).

FOOD

Along the sidewalks of Guayaquil, locals in the know frequent the anonymous one-room restaurants whose few tables spill out into the streets. These *comedores,* so similar to one another that it's difficult to tell them apart, serve cheap *almuerzos* and *meriendas* of the day. Often, though, the food quality reflects the roughly s/3,000 price tag attached to most meals. Fancier restaurants come complete with names, a bigger selection of food, and of course higher, but still reasonable, prices.

Salud Solar, Pedro Moncayo 1015 (tel. 519-955), between Luque and Velez, a few stores away from Parque Centenario. Compact and a bit dim, this 1-room sidewalk restaurant offers healthy vegetarian options for around s/6,000 a meal. Shhhh, the secret of the food is in its soy beans. Vegetarians in town might not find many other options (open daily 7am-10pm).

Restaurant Muelle 5 (tel. 561-128), on the waterfront at Malecón and Roca. If the city's cramping your style, escape to this restaurant—literally *on* the water. Muelle 5's wooden planks are supported by pilings on the bank of the Río Guayas. Appropriately, the menu includes plenty of seafood dishes as well as other tasty Ecuadorian-style grub (s/8,500-10,500). Get a sunny table at the end of the deck and watch banana branches and blobs of fuel float toward the Gulf of Guayaquil. Or maybe eating inside the mess-hall like interior is better. That way you smell the food, not the river (open daily 11am-11pm).

Restaurant Manantial (no tel.), at V.E. Estrada and Monjosa, a lively, patioed place on the Urdesa strip. Loud, young, and often visited by travelers, this restaurant and bar is an escape from the humdrum of many Guayaquil eateries. Wood interior is packed with beer-guzzling *jóvenes* chatting above the general roar. Come for a drink or a meal (a mere s/8,000-12,000) and lounge out front on the covered deck. This is Urdesa for you (open Mon.-Sat. 9am-2am, Sun. 9am-1am).

Gran Chifa, Pedro Carbo 1018 (tel. 530-573 or 530-784), near Sucre. There are many *chifas* in Guayaquil, but none like the great one. Stroll in on a boardwalk, past trimmed bushes and genuine Chinese decor. With the mood convincingly set, enjoy an awesome gourmet meal (s/12,000-20,000). English translations on the menu are a blessing, and the kitchen is spacious and clean (open Wed.-Sun. 11:30am-2:30pm and 6:30-10pm).

Unicafe, Ballén 406 (tel. 327-100, ext. 1420), between Carbo and Chimborazo, on the 1st floor of the Unihotel shopping mall. Jungle scenes dot the walls, so vivid that painted parrots seem to fly out of the glass doors into the Parque Bolívar. Polite, helpful waitstaff serves Ecuadorian dishes as well as reliable favorites, like killer cheeseburgers (s/12,000-18,000). A window to the kitchen assures that all is clean (open daily 6am-midnight).

La Nuestra, Estrada 903 y E. Higueras (tel. 386-398 or 882-168), on the Urdesa strip. Pressing the limits of budget dining, this suburban restaurant is well-known for its excellent offering of Ecuadorian edibles. The owners of the place present their own in an intimate, elegant, and carefully-created ambience. Wandering serenaders sometimes included in the s/15,000-25,000 prices (open Mon.-Tues. noon-midnight, Fri.-Sun. 7am-3am).

El Malecón, Malecón 606 y Orellana (tel. 565-555). So you've just returned from the jungle and you're ready to let loose a ferocious appetite. Or maybe you're sick of budgeting yourself on food that satisfies your cultural conscience but not your hunger. The buffet here will have you drooling: pastries, fruit, french fries, and several juicy meat dishes, among other creatively arranged options. Eat 'til you're sick to justify the s/34,800 splurge. Entree prices are less outrageous (s/10,000-20,000), with plenty of chicken, beef, and seafood favorites (open daily 7am-7pm). Go ahead, you deserve it.

SIGHTS

The most impressive tourist sight in the city is probably the most dangerous (after all, this is Guayaquil). The **Las Peñas neighborhood,** climbing the hills that begin at Malecón's northern end, contains the oldest houses in the city. The product of over 460 years of development, this area shows its age with its almost complete lack of empty land. Tin-roofed homes pile onto each other, some rising majestically at the water's edge. The higher up you go, the more spectacular the views of the city and the river become. Watch for cars as you ascend, and keep an eye out for the house of the musician who composed the Ecuadorian national anthem. Before the road's end, a series of stairs towers up to the left. If you decide to climb them, expect an incredible view—but also get ready for lots of stares, and remember that these are people's homes all around you. It's a good idea to travel through Las Peñas in a group. The veritable maze of houses closes in and if you run into trouble, you're effectively trapped. Various parts of the area are frequented by thieves, and the deeper in you go, the less possible it becomes to escape their threats.

Down at sea level, a **clocktower** rises at Malecón and Av. 10 de Agosto, on the waterfront. Inside, a friendly woman eagerly shares the history of Guayaquil with anyone willing to listen. Struggling if necessary to speak English, she will break her back to accompany you to the top, ascending stairway rooms right out of an Escher drawing. The climb is one of those strangely satisfying things that people do for the mere pointlessness of it all. At the top, you get to look through the guestbook to see who else did it too. The mayor of the city rules from the ornate, gray **Palacio Municipal,** across the street and up a bit from the clocktower. Next to this stands the smaller, peachier **Palacio de la Gobernación,** the headquarters of the provincial office. If this guide fails to answer all questions about this site or about Ecuador in general, visit the top-notch public relations staff on the second floor.

The **waterfront** itself, stretching along Malecón from roughly Av. Olmedo to the foot of the Las Peñas neighborhood, *could* be considered a tourist attraction. Various historical plaques, statues, and fountains decorate the nearly 20-block stroll. In between, though, a community of homeless people naps under the banyans, amid trash-strewn sidewalks and patches of grass. The river smells rancid, and if you fall into a fountain you've probably gotten yourself a case of salmonella. High points? The above-mentioned clocktower, a strange bronze statue of a boar, and the august **Rotonda** at Av. 9 de Octubre. It's hard to miss this last landmark—at the edge of the water, a row of columns rises from a curved marble base. In front of this, the great liberators Bolívar and San Martín shake hands, commemorating their secret 1822 Guayaquil meeting in a vaguely homoerotic pose.

Travelers seeking still more in the way of standard, or at least photogenic tourist sights can look to Guayaquil's churches to satisfy that hunger. Just past the end Malecón near Las Peñas, **La Iglesia de Santo Domingo** rests comfortably at the end of Calle Rocafuerte, secure with its title as the oldest church in Guayaquil. After all, it's been around since way back in 1548. When younger, better-looking churches sprung up, it fought back with facelifts, the most recent of which was in 1938. This area of the city should be approached with caution. The church of **La Merced,** about 10 blocks farther south on Rocafuerte, dates back to 1787, but the present version was constructed during the flurry of church renovations in 1938. Today, in homage to Guayaquil's commercialization, it is glued to an office building. Where Rocafuerte becomes Pedro Carbo, at Av. 9 de Octubre, *el centro* opens up to a plaza dominated by the façade of the church of **San Francisco.** A number of handicapped and homeless people gather in front of this graceful building, originally constructed almost 300 years ago. The **Metropolitan Cathedral** is even farther south on Chimborazo, between Ballén and Av. 10 de Agosto. The original wooden building, built in 1547, would have beat Santo Domingo out as the oldest *guayaquileño* church, but it burnt down. The current stained-glass splendor was built in 1948.

The Cathedral overlooks the **Parque Bolívar,** also called the **Parque Seminario.** In June 1996, a crew of workers began restoring this gated, manicured square of land, which meant that they had to gate up the hundreds of iguanas that have scampered around in this garden for decades. The homesick iguanas were moved to another park, but don't worry—when renovations are completed, they'll be brought back to their original home here at Chile and Av. 10 de Agosto. Not ready for the Galápagos splurge? Find these fellows—they're almost as fun as sea lions!

Several of the museums in Guayaquil are worth at least a cursory visit, especially the free ones. The **Museo Nahim Isaías B.,** at Pichincha and Clemente Ballén (tel. 329-099), has one large square-shaped hall, housing works from the Quito School of Art. Paintings range from religious Baroque to modern abstract, with little in-between. The kind staff goes out of its way to help the English-speaking (open Mon.-Fri. 10am-5pm; free). The **Museo Municipal** (tel. 531-691), on Sucre between Chile and Pedro Carbo, is a slightly larger set of rooms attached to the library. Aside from the works of some modern Ecuadorian artists, it features paintings done in a special program for deaf-mute Guayaquil children (open daily 8:30am-12:30pm and 1-4:30pm; free). Across town, the **Museo de Arte Prehistórico** (tel. 300-500 or 300-586), at Av. 9 de Octubre and Pedro Moncayo, is perched on the sixth floor on the western side of the Parque del Centenario. Unlike the other museums, this display of regional archaeological finds can only be seen at a cost (open Tues.-Fri. 10am-5:30pm, Sat. 9am-3pm; admission s/5,000).

Morbidly spectacular, Guayaquil's hillside **cemetery** faces the city from the north. Mausoleums and elaborate tombs crowd the slopes of this virtual city of the dead like mini high-rises, and pathways wind like streets through the resting sites. The cemetery is located on the far side of a highway, past a rough part of the city, so going in a group might be a good idea. Inquire for more information at the gate.

ENTERTAINMENT

As the saying goes, spend your days in Quito and your nights in Guayaquil. Like the rainforests of the Oriente, this urban jungle goes wild after dark. Clubs and *discotecas* in *el centro* light the sky in shades of neon until sunrise, but the downtown area can be dangerous and considerably unpredictable. Instead, head to Urdesa, the wealthier suburb to the north. A parade of suped-up sports cars cruises the main strip here, each competing for the loudest stereo system (especially Thurs. through Sun.). They're all heading to the scores of nightclubs—some let in anyone who pays the cover charge, others admit members *(socios)* only, meaning you have to look good to get in. In its quest to become an official South American party mecca, Guayaquil shocks visitors from even the most festive cities of the world with its **chivas.** These huge trucks carry at least 100 revelers, whose bodies hang out the windows, on the hood, and off the roof where the Latin band plays. The vehicles shuttle their passengers all night from hotspot to hotspot throughout the city, including downtown, for a price. Go to Infinity (below) to find out how to be a part of the drunken caravans. As for the clubs themselves, they're nothing to complain about either. Guayaquil is tough during the day—enjoy it at night.

The Wall, on Estrada near Guaycán, and **Falls,** Estrada 612 (tel. 881-352), spin the latest in techno and house. Young crowds swamp The Wall, but not *that* young—the drinking age is 18 (open Thurs.-Fri. 10pm-5am; cover s/25,000, free before midnight). Down the street, Falls lures slightly older mobs (cover s/20,000).

Infinity, Estrada 505 y Ebamos (tel. 389-390), across the street from Falls, attracts an eclectic crowd of travelers, perhaps because of its equally eclectic musical offerings. Techno and house in the front room, more sultry Latin tunes in the back. Or come not to stay, but to hop onto one of Guayaquil's infamous party *chivas* (open Tues.-Sat. 9pm-4am; cover s/10,000, free before 11pm).

Metropolis, Estrada 302 (tel. 884-026), further down the strip near Cedros. Where Guayaquil's beautiful people flock. The bouncers at this elitist *socios* club ensure that only the most glamorous are admitted, but George the *dueño* will grant concessions to those who identify themselves as travelers. The interior could be straight out of a Madonna video (open Thurs.-Sat. 11pm-5am; cover s/40,000).

Amen, Av. Francisco de Orellana 7-96 (tel. 298-276; fax 298-963). A departure from the strip, the oversize Amen is reputed to be one of the largest clubs in South America. Young and old congregate in a sunken dance floor as the crowd bumps and grinds to Latin dance mixes early into the morning (open Tues.-Wed. 9pm-3am, Thurs.-Sat. 9pm-7am; cover s/30,000).

Clubs are certainly the highlight, but not the entirety of the Guayaquil entertainment experience. While Guayaquil isn't known for its artistic and cultural achievements (that's Quito up north), it does have plenty of cinemas showing slightly dated Hollywood films. The most comfortable, and therefore most expensive, of these are **Alborines** (tel. 244-986), at the C.C. Plaza Mayor in Alborada (tickets s/15,000); the **Maya** (tel. 386-456), at Avenue Las Lomas and Dátules in Urdesa (s/15,000); and

Multi-Cines (tel. 831-230), in the acclaimed new Riocentro Shopping Plaza between the bridges to Durán. Avoid taxi fees at the **Cine Metro** (tel. 322-301), downtown at Boyacá and Vélez (s/10,000). Aside from movie theaters, the **Teatro del Angel,** Bálsamos 602 y Ficus (tel. 382-056), in Urdesa, presents a variety of live shows.

Babahoyo

Today's Babahoyo began in a blaze. When the original city burnt down in the mid-19th century, then-president Jerónimo Carrión moved the public offices across the river and founded the new-and-improved Babahoyo on May 27, 1869. Today, that date is wildly celebrated in a not-so-new Babahoyo, which has since endured the extraordinary El Niño flooding of more than a decade ago (see graybox below). About an hour northeast of Guayaquil by bus, this capital city of the Los Ríos province is surrounded by rich agricultural fields. But in Babahoyo's streets, only dust and dirt seem to flourish. People here use their gutters as trash receptacles, tossing most anything out of their shops and houses into a moat of wrappers and other refuse. Locals are not used to seeing tourists; as the stares show, the arrival of a *gringo* is a bona fide event. Relax in Babahoyo, and take a look at the river homes that rode out the flood. But use caution in this less-than-touristy city, as some people may be interested in more than just your goofy foreignness.

Orientation and Practical Information Although Babahoyo spreads away from the river for at least 15 blocks, only the first five closests to its bank are vital for navigation. These streets, from the waterfront **Malecón 9 de Octubre** to **García Moreno,** form the grid that is "downtown" Babahoyo. The name doesn't lie—the **Plaza Central,** bounded in part by **Sucre** and **General Barona,** really is the center of town. It is a block from the **Río Babahoyo,** a block in the opposite direction from the buses, and directly adjacent to the government building and the Church.

Banks will exchange cash but not traveler's checks. **EMETEL** phone offices are located in several spots, including Av. 5 de Junio and Rocafuerte (2 blocks down from Sucre), General Barona near Flores (a block up from the police station), and across from the FBI bus stop on Bolívar (open daily 8am-10pm). Most **bus lines** have offices and stops around Av. 5 de Junio and García Moreno, near Sucre. The busiest station is the **Flota Babahoyo Interprovincial (FBI),** with buses to Guayaquil (every 15min., 4:30am-9pm, s/2,000). Ticket office open daily 6am-9pm. **Taxis** are common, and a

The Watery Child of Death and Destruction

There are some things on this earth that cannot be controlled, things that cannot be understood, things that leave us helpless and dumbfounded with their awesome power to destroy. The devastating **El Niño** is one of those things. A warm water current born off the Pacific coast of Panamá, it brings the rainy season to Ecuador's coastal region and Galápagos Islands. Because the current arrives annually around the time of Christmas, it has been given the deceptively diminutive name El Niño (The Child). Most years this restless child stays well-behaved, arriving in December and leaving on cue in late April or early May. However, in those fateful years when the child decides to act up, havoc ensues. The warm waters stick around longer than usual, continued rainfall causes floods in the lowlands, and tidal waves formed offshore race inland, destroying everything in their path. Many aquatic plants and animals can't take the abnormal heat; it's as if Mother Nature forgot to regulate properly the temperature in her giant aquarium. The last misbehaved child arrived in 1982, and when it finally receded in 1983, a crippled and broken Ecuador was left in its wake. Babahoyo and the rest of the lowlands were devastated by torrents of muddy floodwaters. On the coast, fisherman returned with empty nets, and the national economy suffered. A certain species of green algae in the Galápagos was killed off, and an endemic marine iguana population dependant on that algae was decimated. This disastrous phenomenon is still not fully understood.

ride across the downtown area should cost s/4,000 or less. There's a friendly self-service **laundromat** (tel. 734-212) on Olmedo between Av. 5 de Junio and Moreno (open 7am-9:30pm; s/3,000 to wash or dry). There is a crowd of **pharmacies** and **clinics** near the hospital. Pharmacies in the city operate on the *de turno* system, so at least one is always open. The **Hospital Martín Icaza** (emergency tel. 730-181), is at the Malecón and Ricaute, 2 blocks from the police station. Five blocks down from the Plaza Central, the **police station** (tel. 730-020), at Olmedo and Barona, is open 24 hours. The **post office,** at Barona between Sucre and Bolívar, in the government building, has a *Lista de Correos* (open Mon.-Fri. 8am-7pm, Sat. 8am-2pm). The **telephone code** is 05.

Accommodations and Food You'll find a handful of hotel choices in Babahoyo: the dirt-cheap ones a strain on the back, and the more comfortable ones a strain on the wallet. Most are on the blocks between Sucre and Pedro Carbo. **Mesón Popular** (tel. 730-068), is at Sucre and Av. 5 de Junio, across from the church. The cells, complete with fan, dented mattress, internal bar lock on the door, and three bathrooms down the hall, couldn't be cheaper (s/6,000 per person). **Hotel Capitol** (tel. 730-907), at Sucre and Moreno, is two blocks from the plaza. Well-lit rooms have private baths, but you might not be sleeping alone—the cockroaches have rights too. All rooms are singles, s/15,000 per person. More in the mood for semi-luxury? Try the sequel by the same management, **Hotel Capitol 2** (tel. 733-138), at Av. 10 de Agosto and Martín Icaza, a notch up in terms of comfort (with hot water, A/C, and TV) and price (s/40,000 per person). **Hotel Cacharí** (tel. 731-205), at Bolívar and Barona, is right off the plaza next to the government building. Perfect for pampering, this waterfront establishment has hot water, private baths, TV, and some rooms with A/C and phone. Don't miss the goldfish pond at the base of the stairs. Singles s/25,000-s/40,000; doubles s/50,000-80,000.

Comedores are the cheapest options, and those with rotisserie chicken may just provide the best meal deals. From there the prices rise. **Pizza Restaurante** (tel. 732-998), at Av. 10 de Agosto and Rocafuerte, is two blocks down from Sucre. First, try to get over the incongruity—a pizza joint surrounded by Ecuadorian rice paddies and banana plantations? You bet. This spot's got definite hang-out potential. Pizza slice s/6,000, hamburger s/4,000. The mouth-watering tomato pie aroma is free (open Mon.-Thurs. 4pm-10pm, Fri.-Sun. noon-10pm). **Típico Esmeraldeño** (tel. 733-646), on Av. 5 de Junio between Icaza and Flores, about three blocks from Sucre. An about-face from the pizza-and-burger alternative, Esmeraldeño fills the belly with typical Ecuadorian dishes from chicken to specialty seafood. Most dishes under s/10,000 (open daily 9am-10pm). **El Chifa Atlántico** (no tel.), on Barona between Av. 27 de Mayo and Calderón, about three blocks from Sucre, serves savory Chinese food in the fresh Babahoyo air for around s/7,000 (open daily 8am-9pm).

Sights and Entertainment At night, smooching couples haunt the **waterfront.** If in a voyeuristic mood, watch them; if in a romantic mood, join them. Otherwise, come during the day to see the **floating houses (casas flotandas)** on the banks of the Babahoyo. Built atop virtual rafts, these homes are still functional and ready to rise with the next flood. The first-ever *casa flotanda,* still inhabited by its original owner, has its own set of stairs leading to the bank, named in his honor. Other floating houses are reputed to now be part of the sex trade.

The **church** on the plaza houses a huge interior behind a mural of the Madonna and her child. Surprisingly grand for such a gritty town, the building apparently doesn't get much respect from the locals. Ironically, hot and heavy couples use the dark corners and even the confession booth to make out. After about 8pm, Babahoyo's many *discotecas* crank up the volume, turn down the lights, and pour techno into the streets. **Genesis,** in the Hotel Cachaú at Bolívar and Malecón, is a safe second-floor dance club that looks onto the plaza. Several blocks up from this area are **La Noche es Mía,** at Av. 5 de Junio and Av. 27 de Mayo, and **D' Cache,** at Av. 10 de Agosto and Av. 27 de Mayo. The air-conditioned **Cine Continentale** at Av. 27 de Mayo and García

Moreno (tel. 734-419) screens Hollywood flicks, generally from the past year (tickets s/3,000). Popular **shopping areas** are around Av. 10 de Agosto and Av. 27 de Mayo, and along Calderón near Av. 5 de Junio.

Quevedo

If you're in Quevedo, then where you're going and where you've been are most likely more important than where you are. People and bananas pass with indifference under the cinder-block skyline of this cross-roads town. Going from Quito to Guayaquil? Santo Domingo to Babahoyo? The coast to the Sierra? There's a good chance you'll pass through. Don't expect a fascinating historical journey, a mosaic of artistic possibilities, or even a lively night on the town. Before and after its October 7, 1943 canonization, this agricultural hub has simply plowed ahead, growing with the practical needs of an expanding Ecuadorian economy. Quevedo is not a tourist town. Concentrated in a *centro* of four-story dilapidated buildings next to the Río Quevedo, the city has an industrial, raw, and somewhat unsafe feeling. Its collection of hotels and plentiful *comedores* are conspicuously geared toward locals and travelers from other provinces. Your uniqueness in Quevedo is a reason for caution, especially if you're traveling alone.

Orientation "Downtown" Quevedo is a narrow few blocks between the river and the roughly parallel hill. The more the streets slope, the more strange looks you'll get, so stay close to **Malecón Eloy Alfaro** along **Río Quevedo.** The next two avenues—**Simon Bolívar** and **7 de Octubre**—are the principal commercial, hotel, and restaurant-swamped walkways. Perpendicular to these, the **Calle Primero** (1st) begins at the **Plaza de la Madre,** where the only vehicle-ready bridge crosses into the city; you'll most likely cross it if coming from Babahoyo. This triangular intersection is where the buses board and let off, and not coincidentally, it's also known for its thievery. Take care here and spend as little time as possible this far west. Heading east, the streets ascend in ordinal numbers to **Decima Quarta** (14th). There's a **central plaza** between Quinta and Sexta, but it's seedy and rather unwelcoming.

Practical Information **Banco Internacional** (tel. 751-910), at Av. 7 de Octubre and Quarta (open Mon.-Fri. 9am-3pm), and **Filanbanco** (tel. 755-344), a block away at Bolívar and Quarta (open Mon.-Fri. 9am-4pm), exchange cash dollars and traveler's checks. The **IETEL office** (tel. 754-223), at Av. 7 de Octubre and Decima Tercera, offers telephone and telegram services (open daily 8am-10pm). **Buses** in this transportation hub are generally located near or in the Plaza de la Madre. **Transportes Interprovincial Asouado (TIA)** (tel. 750-565), at Av. 7 de Octubre and Tercera, has buses to **Guayaquil** (every 30min., 4:30am-6:30pm, s/6,000). **Transportes Valencia** (tel. 750-177), at Bolívar and Segunda, serves **Babahoyo** (every 20min., 6am-7:30pm, s/3,500). **Transportes Macuchi** (tel. 750-820), at Bolívar and Primera, transports to **Quito** via **Santo Domingo** (every hr., 2am-5pm, s/3,500 to Santo Domingo, s/10,000 to Quito). **Cooperativa Transportes Ambato** (tel. 750-134 or 753-085), at Bolívar and Primera, goes to **Ambato** (8:30, 10, 11:30am, 1, 5pm; s/14,000). **COTUR Taxis** (tel. 750-328) generally charges s/2,500 and up to get around town. Meet your worldly pharmaceutical needs at **Botica International** (tel. 750-480), Av. 7 de Octubre and Novena (open 7:30am-10:30pm). **Hospital Centro de Salud de Quevedo,** Av. Guayaranes 400 (tel. 750-373), is slightly east of *el centro,* with limited ambulance service. The **police** (tel. 750-361), are on Novena near Progreso. For **emergencies,** tel. 101. The **post office** (tel. 751-888), on Decima Segunda between Av. 7 de Octubre and Bolívar, is tucked inside a hallway-like mall (open Mon.-Fri. 8am-6pm). Quevedo's **telephone code** is 05.

Accommodations and Food Like the town, hotels in Quevedo are gritty but serve their purpose. Try to stay around the safer Malecón, Bolívar, and Av. 7 de Octubre area. **Hotel Imperial** (tel. 751-654), at Malecón and Septima, overlooks the market. With additional views of the river and nearby footbridge, its location *almost* creates the illusion that you've escaped the grime of the city. Rooms provide low-end private baths, sexy high-powered fans, and concave beds. The chatty patriarch downstairs will eagerly smooth over any problems. S/12,000 per person. **Hotel Continental** (tel. 750-080), on Av. 7 de Octubre between Septima and Octava, second floor, ½ block east of the market, occupies a prime location along the busy strip. The Continental prices its rooms according to the creature comforts it throws in; presumably, they cover the well-worn form of what's there when the rooms are bare. A/C and private bath in all rooms. Locker-room style showers (spigot on the wall, no curtain). S/ 12,000 per person, with black-and-white TV s/15,000, with color TV and exterior view s/20,000, with hot water also s/30,000. The business-class **Hotel Olímpico,** about 0.5km east of Decima Quarta, pampers the city's successful corporate travelers. Filled with businessmen rather than backpackers, this place ain't budget, but could be considered a tourist sight in itself.

The sizeable Chinese community in Quevedo dominates a whole chunk of the restaurant selection. *Chifas* are frequent, cheap, and generally dependable, as well as being some of the only full-fledged restaurants in town with actual menus. Most *comida típica* is taken in local *comedores.* **Restaurant Columbus** (no tel.), at Av. 7 de Octubre and Decima Segunda, is a quality *comedor* with dedicated staff. *Desayuno* s/5,000, *almuerzo*, and *merienda* s/4,000. Sympathetic to Spanish-impaired customers (open daily 7am-10pm). **Chifa China** (tel. 751-343), at Av. 7 de Octubre and Decima Quarta, next to IETEL at the end of the main strip. A tasty local fave, though maybe not the best service in town. Chicken or beef dishes s/6,000, rice dishes s/5,000 (open daily 11:30am-5pm and 5:30-10pm). **El Fruital Soda Bar** (tel. 756-332), on Av. 7 de Octubre between Decima and Decima Primera. So cheap that the menu may cause you to double-take, this diner serves common favorites. Hamburgers s/2,000, chicken sandwiches s/2,000 (open daily 9am-11pm).

Santo Domingo de los Colorados

Before the roads and the buildings, Santo Domingo was home to the *indígenas* who give the city the second part of its name—the Colorados. The scant clothing and punch-red bowl cuts of this tribe are commonly exploited on postcards, and statues in traffic circles commemorate the days when they really looked that way. Now, only a costly cab ride and a tourist's eager bribe can buy a glimpse of the tribe's customary *traje* before the juggernaut of Westernization overtook them. Near the foothills of the Andes, Santo Domingo is a cool, fresh break from the rest of the western lowland area, its climate in-between that of hot, sticky Guayaquil and chilly Quito. Only 130km west of the latter, Santo Domingo's tourist industry and sizeable selection of hotels cater to tourists from Quito and beyond. The growing area spreads across gentle slopes at the confluence of several spoke roads, with downtown Santo Domingo crammed into the hubcap. Its suffocating exhaust, random sidewalk pits, and mud-litter-detritus concoction are cogent reminders that Ecuador is still a developing nation.

Orientation and Practical Information Santo Domingo is laid out in a rather irregular pattern. The grid form exists in a small area along the busiest two downtown streets, the parallel **Avenidas 29 de Mayo** and **3 de Julio.** There's at least one budget hotel on each block, and Av. 29 de Mayo, in particular, is replete with *comedores.* The blocks near **Ambato, Latacunga,** and **Cuenca** are packed with booths that make up the market. From the eastern end of the *centro,* the **Avenida Sáchila** takes off to the north, past the post office, to the **terminal terrestre**—not a distance conveniently walked. For some breathing room, follow the **Avenida Quito** out to the northeast, where open space awaits.

No CETUR here, but **0049 Club de Viajes** (tel. 760-772 or 760-637), at Av. Quito and Río Toachi, in the San Francisco de Asis building, is an alternate travel office (open Mon.-Fri. 8:30am-1pm and 3pm-6:30pm, Sat. 8:30am-1pm). Make phone calls or send telegrams from **IETEL** (tel. 750-083), on the second floor of the San Francisco de Asis building at Av. Quito and Río Toachi (open daily 8am-10pm). **Banco Internacional** (tel. 750-503 or 750-603), at Av. Quito and Río Blanco, changes cash US$ to sucres. Across the street and up some, **Produbanco** (tel. 751-616), at Av. Quito and Chorrera del Napa, exchanges traveler's checks. Santo Domingo is a busy bus transport hub between the coast and the Sierra. The **terminal terrestre** is out on Sáchila. **Transportes Macuchi** goes to **Quito** (every 30min., 2am-5pm, 3hr., s/6,000), **Quevedo** (every 30min., 8:30am-6:30pm, 1½hr., s/3,500), and **Esmeraldas** (8am, noon, 4, 6pm, 5hr., s/10,000). Because of its popularity, Quito is served by numerous carriers, so compare the options. **Transportes Ambato** heads to **Ambato** (every hr., 7:30am-6:45pm, 4½hr., s/8,000) via **Riobamba** (3½hr.). **Transportes Zaracay** goes to **Guayaquil** (every 30min., 3:20am-6:30pm, 4½hr., s/10,000). **Transportes Panamericana Internacional** goes to **Huaquillas** (2, 6, 8:30pm, 7 hr., s/21,000). **Taxis** within the city run from s/2,500-4,000; one dispatch is the **14 de Febrero** company (tel. 751-218). **Local buses** run along major streets for s/250. The fresh-smelling **public market** bustles between Av. 29 de Mayo and Av. 3 de Julio, near Ambato and Cuenca (open daily 8:30am-6pm). The local pharmacy is **Farmacia Chone** (tel. 750-336), on Av. Sáchila next to Parque Principal (open daily 8am-10pm). **Hospital Santo Domingo** (tel. 750-336), is off Av. Quito on a short street, past the traffic circle and across from Banco de Pichincha. Ambulance service available. The **police** (tel. 750-225) are headquartered on Sáchila next to the traffic circle, across from the terminal. In **emergencies,** call 101. The **post office** (tel. 750-303), on Av. Sáchila and Clemencia de Mora, about a 10-minute walk from Av. 29 de Mayo on Sáchila, has a *Lista de Correos* (open Mon.-Fri. 8am-9pm). Santo Domingo's **telephone code** is 05.

Accommodations and Food Hotels are densely packed in the downtown blocks, especially near Av. 29 de Mayo. Those along Av. Quito cost a couple sucres more. Discriminatingly decorated in colorful weaves and paintings, the stylin' rooms at **Hotel La Siesta,** Av. Quito 606 y Pallatanga (tel. 751-013 or 751-860), border an equally polychromatic garden. TVs, phones, and hot water expected soon. Singles s/22,000, with bath s/33,000; doubles s/33,000, with bath s/49,500. **Hotel Lucy** (tel. 750-265), on Quito at the traffic circle, is next to a motorbike shop. Borderline-clean rooms are simple and bare, so it's a good thing guests have the private baths and fans to get excited about. S/15,000 per person, with TV s/24,000. Despite its name, there's nothing mythical about the **Hotel Unicornio** (tel. 760-147), downtown at Av. 29 de Mayo and Ambato; its prices are deservedly low. Try to ignore the cacophony of traffic and a less-than-aromatic odor; ample rooms, arranged around an open-air balconied atrium, are comfy nonetheless. All rooms have private bath. S/13,000 per person, with TV s/18,000. Make a few sacrifices to sleep on the cheap at **Hotel Amambay** (tel. 750-696), at Av. 29 de Mayo and Ambato. Hallways are dim, but you'll still be able to see the sewing factory on the second floor. In the light, rooms are clean. S/10,000 per person, with bath s/12,000 (BYO shower curtain).

Restaurante La Siesta, Av. Quito 606 (tel. 751-013 or 751-860), has the same aesthetic charm as the attached hotel, and doesn't snooze in its efforts to prepare savory food for all meals. *Desayuno* s/6,000, steak s/12,000, chicken s/10,000. English menu translations suggest that foreign visitors aren't strangers here (open daily 7am-10pm). The choices of pizza toppings astound at **Pizzeria Orégano's** (tel. 759-729), on Av. Quito, 1.5km from *el centro,* next to Banco del Pacífico. Combos of ham, salami, ground beef, olives, pineapples, onions, peppers, veggies... It isn't Italian gourmet or even Chicago pies, but it's pizza. Small s/12,000, medium s/19,000, large s/24,000 (open Tues.-Sun. noon-midnight). **Fruti Deli** (tel. 755-622), at Av. 29 de Mayo and Julian, downtown. Despite the idiotic name, the food is both fresh and refreshingly mainstream. Vegetarians can dig into a fruit salad for s/3,500. Hamburger s/3,000, *almuerzo* s/4,500, *merienda* s/4,000 (open Tues.-Sun. 11am-7pm).

Sights and Entertainment The **market** here is popular, safe, and ripe for the browsing. There are also some movie theaters, including the **Cine Ambato** (no tel.), at Ambato and Av. 29 de Mayo, for not-so-recent Hollywood movies (s/2,500).

And then there's what Santo Domingo is famous for: the **Colorados.** In the nearby village of **Chihuilpe,** members of the Sáchila tribe don their postcard apparel for a price, letting salivating camera shutters snap them up. Traditional medicine men *(curanderos vegetalistas)* will also do their stuff if you pay them. To witness the Santo Domingo traveler's rite of passage, head south on Av. Quevedo to the 7km mark, then take a left on a dirt road. Taxis charge a heavy s/15,000 or so for the trip, but other options are scarce. Sights are behind the tall brush that lines the dirt road. Follow any turn-offs with "Tourists Welcome"-type signs.

If you're down for a raging party, the fiesta celebrating the **canonization of Santo Domingo** on July 3 draws enormous crowds. The usual extensive, lively, and bargain-crazy markets become even crazier, and the cock-fighting coliseum right outside the city puts on a grand show of killer poultry. As the nearby Colorados must be thinking, this is what you get when civilization comes to town.

■ Near Santo Domingo: Río Palenque Science Center

The Centro Científico Río Palenque not only preserves dying breeds, it is one. The last tropical wet rainforest reserve in the western Ecuadorian lowlands, this terrain doesn't contain just the same old flora and fauna found in the Oriente. Researchers travel to the reserve to study what can be seen only here, including the 100 plant species first discovered within the reserve's boundaries. More than 3km of trails meander through the home of 360 species of birds, 350 different butterflies, and over 1100 catalogued plant species. Of these, more than 30 species of flowering plants claim their last remaining home in these tiny 200 hectares. Don't expect to see herds of animals swarming the forest here. Though a family of monkeys makes its home down by the river, the pressure of deforestation around the sanctuary has virtually wiped out any extensive mammal population. But the reserve does offer a number of trails that meander through the sanctuary of humid, thriving plant and insect diversity, and an enthusiastic host who will help make the less-than-luxurious accommodations more comfortable. While the trails and facilities have lately suffered from a lack of care, a recently-arrived, enthusiastic Peace Corps volunteer has vowed to turn this around.

First organized 12 years ago by a group of American scientists, the tiny forest sanctuary then consisted in 200 hectares (around 500 acres), a little less than it is today. For a while, the center was run by the University of Miami, but the university eventually pulled out, leaving the research facility to its handful of owners. Presently the whole reserve is owned by Dr. Carl Dodson, who has had to cultivate 100 hectares in order to fund the place. Dr. Dodson has been involved with the reserve from the beginning and now lives in a house on the far edge of the land. The Science Center, a research-hotel facility for scientists and visitors, is 1km away.

The **Center-Hotel** is a true hike from the bus drop-off on the highway. Head up the path, take a left at the fork, and expect to walk a good 25 minutes. One night's lodging costs s/45,000 (US$15) if you bring your own food to cook in the kitchen facilities, s/90,000 (US$30) with meals included. A day's hiking fee, without staying over, is s/9,000. Overnight guests should arrive before 9pm (a nighttime hike is not advisable anyway). Bring repellant—creepy-crawlers are everywhere, especially at night (after all, that's the whole purpose of the reserve). Although the place rarely fills up, it's a smart move to call ahead to the Center's office in Santo Domingo just in case (tel. 561-646; fax 225-468). For visitation requests or other information, write to: Río Palenque Science Center, Santo Domingo de los Colorados, Ecuador.

To get here, take a bus from either Santo Domingo or Quevedo to the entrance along the highway. Coming from Quevedo, the entrance is at turn 58, past a farm called Tío Coco. From Santo Domingo, the entrance is 47km south, 2.5km past a town called Patricia Pilan. Be sure to let your bus driver know that you want to stop here ahead of time. To get back, just wave a bus down as it passes on the highway.

Oriente

THE NORTHERN ORIENTE

The northern Oriente is Ecuador's last, but fast disappearing, frontier. It stretches away unhampered from its easternmost urban outposts, Coca and Lago Agrio, for more than 100km, past thousands of acres of nationally-protected lands, to its remote borders with Perú and Colombia. This jungle, much of which consists of primary growth, is home to an immense diversity of fauna and flora. Countless plant and insect species thrive here, as do larger, rarer animals, like jaguars, sloths, monkeys, and *cocodrilos* (crocodiles).

The human history of the northern Oriente bears a striking resemblance to the stories told by many other former frontier lands in this part of the world. For centuries, even after the arrival of the Spanish, the indigenous people of the jungle lived in complete isolation, save for the occasional wandering missionaries. Only at the beginning of this century did colonists from the highlands descend upon the jungle and begin to clear plots of farmland, hunting the wildlife and generally intruding upon the *indígenas* who were already living there, including the Huaorani, Secoya, Siona, and Shuar peoples. The industry growing around the 1970s discovery of oil poses the greatest threat yet to these pristine natural areas and indigenous communities. The oil companies cut roads deeper and deeper into the jungle every day, not only destroying the forest as they go, but opening it up for colonization and consequent deforestation and habitat destruction. Like the biodiversity, the indigenous communities are threatened by encroaching civilization. Keep these things in mind when you venture into the endangered jungle during your time in the northern Oriente.

Puyo

In Puyo, civilization is still negotiating its lease. At the eastern foothills of the Andes, a two-hour ride from the verdant valley of Baños, the Río Puyo passes through the town that bears its name and the sweeping Amazon rainforest materializes. Whether out of heartfelt pride or simply as fuel for tourism, Puyo nurtures its jungle-town image. River scenes adorn the walls of virtually every hotel and restaurant, while most shops sell wood-carved parrots and postcards of exotic jungle fauna almost exclusively. But the town's image is more than imaginary. Puyo itself is no more than a cluster of urban blocks that surrenders quickly to the surrounding wilderness; a very real, untamed rainforest canopy stretches east from town.

While wilderness has the earliest and strongest claim on Puyo, human beings go back pretty far as well. Archeological evidence indicates that people lived in the area as long ago as 4000-3500 BCE. By the time the Spanish arrived, local tribes had united into a group called the Náparos. But in the years that followed, diseases that did not speak their language decimated the Náparos to one-seventh of their previous population. Originally a missionary site, this present-day capital of the Pastaza province now has a population of over 15,000, a large part of which is Quechua. While it has hotels and few restaurants, most people simply pass through on their way into the heart of the Oriente.

ORIENTATION

The road from Baños, **Ceslao Marín,** flows in from the west, past the high-class Hotel Turungia, past the **terminal terrestre** (a bit south of the highway), and smack into the **main plaza.** Just west of *el centro,* **Atahualpa** diverges from Marín at a slight angle and becomes another principal east-west thoroughfare. Hotels, *comedores,* and various shops cluster in the area of **Av. 9 de Octubre** and Atahualpa.

PRACTICAL INFORMATION

Currency Exchange: Banks in town may exchange dollars, but **Casa de Cambios Puyo** (tel. 883-064), at Atahualpa and Av. 9 de Octubre, changes traveler's checks as well as U.S., Canadian, British, German, Swiss, French, Spanish, and Colombian cash at very competitive rates (open Mon.-Sat. 8am-8pm, Sun. 8am-midnight).

Telephone: Call home from **EMETEL** (tel. 883-104), on Orellana and General Billamil, 1 block west of the market (open daily 8am-1pm and 1:15-10pm).

Buses: The **terminal terrestre** (tel. 885-480) is about a 20-min. walk or a s/2,500 cab ride west of *el centro.* Take Av. 9 de Octubre south past the market to a traffic circle with a bronze bust. Take a right onto Alberto Nambrano and follow it about 1km. Serves arrivals and departures until 6pm, after which buses begin to drop people off downtown. Evening and night trips leave from **Transportes Touris San Francisco,** on Marín about 10m west of where Atahualpa joins it. Due to construction, the Baños-Puyo road is only open to traffic on Sun. and Mon., so many routes change and take much longer on Tues.-Sat. Most buses heading west, therefore, pass through Baños on Sun. and Mon., and go through Tena all other days. Buses run to **Ambato** (Sun.-Mon., every hr. 6am-6pm, 3hr, s/6,000; Tues.-Sat., 9pm, 10hr., s/22,000), **Quito** (Sun.-Mon., 2, 9, 10am, 3, 5:45pm, 5hr., s/11,000; Tues.-Sat., 7, 8:15am, noon, 3:30, 9, 11pm, 8hr., s/18,000), **Coca** via Tena (every day, 8pm, 8hr., s/20,000), **Tena** (every day, 7, 8:15am, noon, 3:30, 8, 9, 11pm, 2½hr., s/6,000), **Guayaquil** (Sun.-Mon., 9, 11pm, 8hr., s/17,000), **Macas** (every day, 3, 8, 10am, 12:45, 2, 5:45, 6, 8pm; 5hr., s/11,000), **Palera** (noon, 3:30pm, 2hr., s/4,000). **Local buses** to **Shell** leave from the south end of Av. 27 de Febrero, near Av. 24 de Mayo (every 15min., 5:45am-8:45pm, s/500).

Taxis: They can be scarce; try calling **Cooperativa 12 de Mayo** (tel. 885-185).

Laundromat: Clean your smellies at **Lavanderías Familiares** (tel. 885-242), at Av. 9 de Octubre and Av. 24 de Mayo. S/500-s/3,000 per piece, and if you drop clothes off in the am, you can get them back in the pm (open daily 8am-7pm).

Library: Biblioteca Municipal (tel. 885-245), on Orellana between Av. 27 de Febrero and Av. 9 de Octubre, on the 2nd floor of the Municipal Building. It also has a number of computers (open Mon.-Fri. 8am-noon and 2-6:30pm).

Red Cross: Sucre 1540 (tel. 885-214).

Pharmacy: Farmacia Atahualpa (tel. 885-544), at Atahualpa and Av. 27 de Febrero, is part of the *de turno* system (open 9am-1pm and 3-10pm).

Hospital: Hospital de la Brigada 17 (tel. 883-131 or 885-541), at Alfaro and Pino. Many locals recommend the hospital in nearby Shell, **Hospital Vozandes** (tel. 795-172), on Asunción.

Police: (tel. 883-101), on Av. 9 de Octubre.

Post Office: (tel. 885-332), at Av. 27 de Febrero and Atahualpa. Check the *Lista de Correos* here (open Mon.-Fri. 8am-6pm).

Telephone Code: 03.

ACCOMMODATIONS

Hotel Europa Internacional (tel. 885-220 or 885-228; fax 885-120), on Av. 9 de Octubre between Atahualpa and Orellana. On its way to becoming a Puyo institution, this trustworthy hotel rents rooms with hot-water private baths. Quaint quotations reassure, *"El hotel es un lugar para descansar ... favor, no hacer ruido."* They'll take care of you here, and they'll feed you well in the restaurant downstairs. S/15,000 per person.

Hotel Granada (tel. 885-578), at Av. 27 de Febrero and Orellana, 2 blocks south of Atahualpa next to the market. Management could stand to scrub the place down a bit. Patrons can scrub themselves down too, but only with cold water. Singles s/5,000, with bath s/9,000.

Residencial Ecuador (tel. 883-089), at Av. 24 de Mayo, between Av. 9 de Octubre and Av. 27 de Febrero, just below the market on the south side of *el centro.* A charmer for those who like shadows and a bit of dirt. Shower-goers should be flip-flop equipped. Bathrooms on each floor. Second-floor rooms (s/8,000) are newer and cleaner than third-floor rooms (s/6,000).

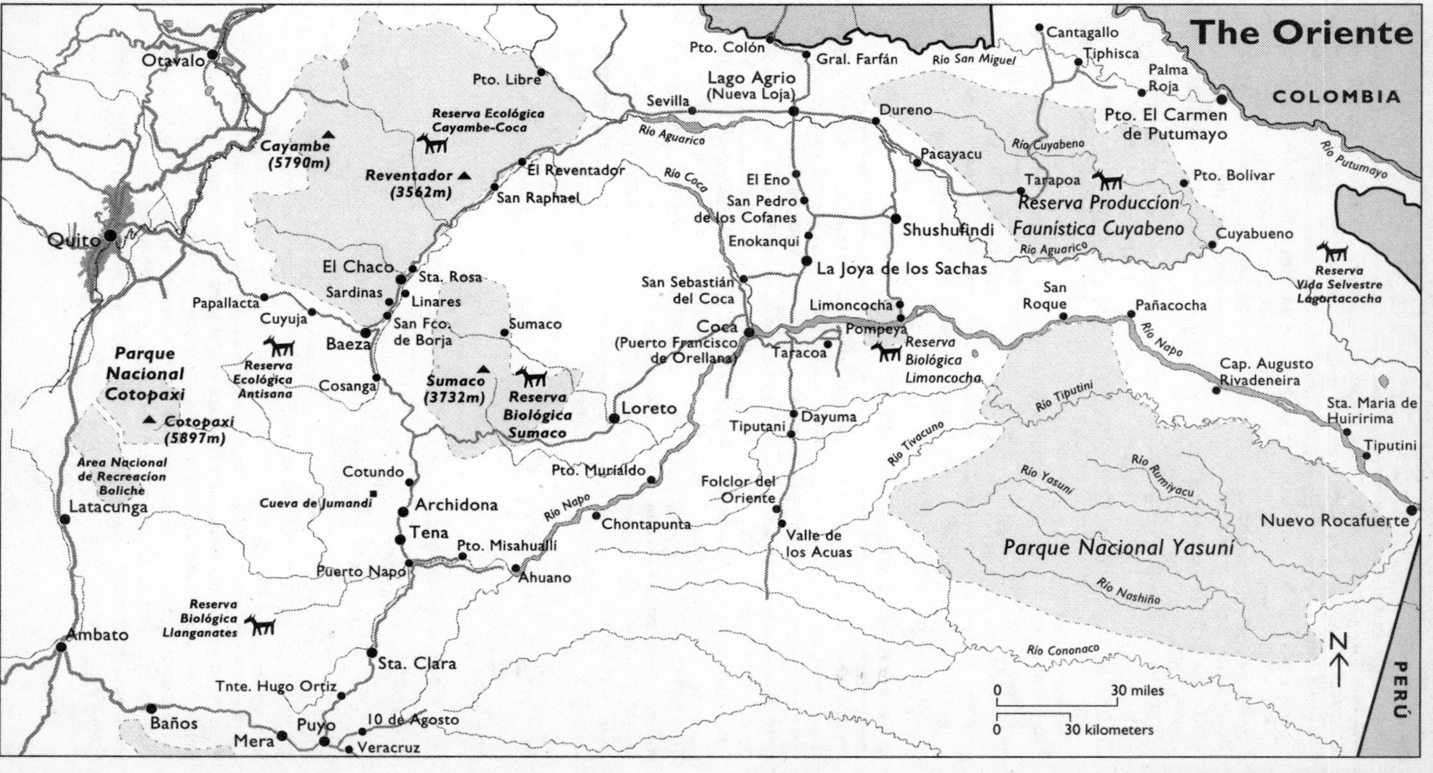
The Oriente
COLOMBIA
PERÚ
N
0 30 miles
0 30 kilometers
Otavalo
Pto. Libre
Reserva Ecológica Cayambe-Coca
Cayambe (5790m)
Reventador (3562m)
El Reventador
San Raphael
Quito
El Chaco
Sta. Rosa
Sardinas
Linares
Papallacta
Cuyuja
San Fco. de Borja
Sumaco
Baeza
Parque Nacional Cotopaxi
Reserva Ecológica Antisana
Cosanga
Sumaco (3732m)
Reserva Biológica Sumaco
Cotopaxi (5897m)
Área Nacional de Recreacíon Boliche
Latacunga
Cotundo
Cueva de Jumandi
Archidona
Tena
Pto. Misahuallí
Puerto Napo
Ahuano
Reserva Biológica Llanganates
Ambato
Sta. Clara
Tnte. Hugo Ortiz
Baños
Mera
Puyo
10 de Agosto
Veracruz
Pto. Colón
Gral. Farfán
Río San Miguel
Lago Agrio (Nueva Loja)
Sevilla
Río Aguarico
Río Coca
El Eno
San Pedro de los Cofanes
Enokanqui
La Joya de los Sachas
San Sebastián del Coca
Coca (Puerto Francisco de Orellana)
Loreto
Pto. Murialdo
Río Napo
Chontapunta
Dureno
Pacayacu
Shushufindi
Limoncocha
Pompeya
Taracoa
Reserva Biológica Limoncocha
Dayuma
Tiputani
Folclor del Oriente
Valle de los Acuas
Río Tivacuno
Cantagallo
Tiphisca
Palma Roja
Pto. El Carmen de Putumayo
Río Cuyabeno
Río Putumayo
Tarapoa
Pto. Bolívar
Reserva Produccíon Faunística Cuyabeno
Río Aguarico
Cuyabueno
Reserva Vida Selvestre Lagartacocha
San Roque
Pañacocha
Río Napo
Cap. Augusto Rivadeneira
Río Tiputini
Sta. Maria de Huiririma
Tiputini
Río Yasuní
Río Rumiyacu
Nuevo Rocafuerte
Parque Nacional Yasuní
Río Nashiño
Río Cononaco

FOOD

Mesón Europeo (tel. 883-919), on Nambrano, 200m east of the *terminal terrestre.* Set on the outskirts of town with an eye-catching name for foreigners, some have mistaken it for a jungle mirage. This open-aired *hacienda* restaurant sports fancy aesthetics; the cost is included in the price of the meal. *Almuerzo* (11am-3pm) s/9,000, fried chicken s/9,000, banana split s/4,000 (open daily11am-10pm).

Chifa Oriental (tel 885-113), at Marín and Av. 27 de Febrero. Chomp cheap Chinese cuisine at this popular place as you ponder a peculiar poster of a rough-'n'-tough toddler on a Harley. Beef dishes s/5,500-s/7,000, rice entrees s/5,000 (open daily 11am-3pm and 6pm-midnight).

Cha-Cha-Cha Pollo a la Braya (tel. 885-208), on Marín just past the Hotel Turungia. Say it out loud, and this time feel the rhythm ... *Cha-Cha-Cha Pollo a la Braya.* If the name alone makes people this happy, imagine them after they get the food. Enjoy pizza, chicken, and sparkling welcoming smiles. *Merienda* with rotisserie chicken s/5,000 (open 10am-10pm).

Restaurant Hostelería Turungia, Ceslao Marín 294 (tel. 885-180), on the western edge of town. While the exorbitant rooms are out of most budget travelers' reach (s/50,000 a night, *ouch!),* come as a spectator and visit the hotel's garden, pool, pet snake, and gourmet food. Polish up your hiking boots—this is the fanciest place in town. American breakfast s/8,500, breaded steak s/10,000, pineapple chicken s/10,000 (open daily 7am-9pm).

SIGHTS AND ENTERTAINMENT

A good place to catch up on that novel you've been carrying, Puyo isn't exactly the amusement capital of the world. The **Parque Pedagógico Etno-Botánico Omaere** (tel 883-001), north up Av. 9 de Octubre, is one worthwhile walk (or s/2,500 cab ride). Locals can point the way if you stray, but it is mostly straight ahead, along bumpier streets through a residential neighborhood. The Parque itself lies on the Río Puyo, across a roped footbridge, and includes a botanical garden with medicinal plants and several traditional Quechua homes. One house contains exactly one *shaman* (warning: use only as directed). A two-hour tour explores the forested extent of the park. If you want to swim, the river awaits your plunge.

Closer into the city, the **catedral,** on the main plaza at Av. 10 de Agosto, between Sucre and Bolívar, may sate your sightseeing hunger. Failing that, there are some **waterfalls** outside of town; the better hotels can give information on how to get to there. Some even offer jungle tours of the Oriente, but options are much more extensive elsewhere, like in Baños or Tena.

Tena

East of Tena spans the jungle. Just 197km southeast of Quito, Tena sits at the fast-flowing union of the Ríos Tena and Napo, part of the headwaters of the Amazon, and the jagged silhouette of the mighty Cordillera de los Llanganates dominates its western panorama. Tena's auspicious location has always been apparent; even the Spanish realized the geographic potential when they founded the city in 1560 as an ambitious reach into the Oriente. Today this provincial capital stands above the other towns in the Napo Province, developing quickly and eagerly to become the real, live tourist center that its location facilitates. What was once a Spanish reach into the jungle has now become a *gringo* one, and a budding industry of tourist possibilities has risen up to meet the traveler traffic. Tena's entrepreneurs have developed a kind of jungle playground here, with bamboo *cabañas,* cave spelunking, white-water rafting, kayaking, and any other adventure a weary urbanite could hope for. But as more established tourist destinations like Baños attest, Tena still has a ways to go. Hotel and restaurant choices are sadly limited, and menus have yet to include English translations. Give Tena a couple years, it might just start to catch up.

ORIENTATION

If the mountains to the east are visible, use them for navigation. The most important parts of Tena are on either side of the area where the Ríos Napo and Tena merge. To the west, Tena *centro* spreads as an irregular grid, from **García Moreno,** on the riverfront, to **Montalvo,** two blocks west, and from the **Main Plaza** along **Mera** to **Bolívar,** four blocks farther north. A pedestrian bridge crosses the river from Mera. East-west **Olmedo** becomes a vehicle bridge that takes a right on the other bank and becomes **Av. 15 de Noviembre.** This principal strip houses the best hotel and restaurant selections, as well as the **terminal terrestre,** about 1km south of the bridge.

PRACTICAL INFORMATION

Tourist Information: CETUR (tel. 886-418), on Bolívar near Amazonas in *el centro.* Not well-known by the locals, and usually not too busy. Brochures on Ecuador and the Oriente in various languages (open Mon.-Fri. 8:30am-5pm).

Currency Exchange: Banco de Pinchincha (tel. 887-600 through 602; fax 887-603), at Amazonas and Mera, exchanges cash or traveler's checks at good rates (open Mon.-Fri. 9am-1:30pm). In an emergency, ask around—several stores also offer exchanging services, though not at very favorable rates.

Telephones: At the ever-ringing **EMETEL** (tel. 886-105), at Olmedo and Montalvo (open Mon.-Sat. 8am-10pm, Sun. 8-11am, 2-5pm, and 7-9pm).

Airport: The airstrip is 3 blocks uphill from Olmedo behind Bolívar, and offers flights to Coca or Puyo-Pastaza. The problems are the frequency and prices: to **Coca** (every Mon. and Wed., 9-10am, 30min., s/20,700 for nationals, 75% more for foreigners). While severe, it may well beat the bumpy 7-hr. bus ride. The flight to **Puyo** depends upon the demand for flights back from Coca, since it's the same plane. Connections are therefore much less reliable.

Buses: The **terminal terrestre** can blend in with the buildings around it, so look closely along the west side of Av. 15 de Noviembre, about 1km south of the bridges. Plenty of destinations, mountain and jungle, are offered, and some are affected by the road closure between Puyo and Baños. To **Quito** (2, 3, 6:30, 8, 10am, noon, 2, 4, 9, 11, 11:45pm, 5½hr., s/12,000) via **Baeza** (3hr., s/6,000), **Puyo** (Tues.-Sat., every hr., 5am-9pm, 2½hr., s/6,000; Sun.-Mon., every hr., 5am-midnight), **Ambato** (Sun. and Mon., every hr., 5am-midnight, 6hr., s/12,000) via **Baños** (5hr., s/9,000), **Riobamba** (Sun. and Mon., 2, 3, 4, 9am, 3, 6pm, 6hr., s/12,000), **Coca** (8, 9, 11am, 12:30, 7:30, 8, 10, 11pm, 7hr., s/16,000). Beware of the bad road between Tena and Coca. Buses to **Misahuallí** leave from Amazonas and the road adjacent to the airstrip, 1 block from Bolívar (every 45min., 6am-7pm, 1hr., s/1,900). From Amazonas and Olmedo, buses go to **Archidona** (6am-7pm, every 15min., s/700), and **Ahuano/La Punta** via **Puerto Napo** and **Jatún Sacha** (every hr., 6:30am-5:30pm, 1½hr., s/3,000) making several stops along Av. 15 de Noviembre on the way out of town.

Taxis: Taxis in this part of the jungle are not the familiar yellow boxes, but rather brawny white pick-up trucks. They're all over, and prices are comparable.

Public Market: There are several market areas, but one of the biggest and most constant is at Amazonas and Bolívar (open 6am-6pm).

Pharmacy: Farmacia Amazonas (tel. 886-495), is at Amazonas and Calderón in *el centro,* and a part of the *de turno* network (open daily 8am-9pm).

Hospital: Hospital José María Velasco Ibarra (tel. 886-302 through 305), on Av. 15 de Noviembre outside of town.

Police: (tel 886-425), on García Moreno next to Main Playa.

Post Office: (tel. 886-418), at Av. Olmedo and Amazonas, with a *Lista de Correos* (open Mon.-Fri. 8am-6pm, Sat. 8am-4pm).

Telephone Code: 06.

ACCOMMODATIONS

Hostal Traveller's Lodge, Av. 15 de Noviembre 438 (tel. 886-372), next to the footbridge landing. Welcome to *gringo*-central (as if the name didn't give it away). Attached to a restaurant and tour agency, this reputable complex has private baths, hot water, fans, and back-friendly beds in all rooms. *Dueño* Don Mario loves his guests with big love, and boasts plans of luxury rooms in the future. A good place to catch the word on what to do in the area. S/15,000 per person.

Residencial Alemana (tel. 386-409), at Dias de Pineda and Av. 15 de Noviembre, next to the vehicle bridge. A quiet sanctuary across from the Traveller's Lodge, Alemana is worn but friendly, like a favorite t-shirt, though a slightly bug-infested one. All rooms have private bath, but no cold water. Singles s/15,400; matrimonial (2 people, 1 bed) s/22,000; doubles s/26,400.

Hotel Amazonas (tel. 886-439), at Mera and Montalvo, just off the main plaza. This enthusiastic budget choice has breezy, open-aired rooms. You could lick tile cleaner off the immaculate communal bath—licking is *always* fun! An awesome s/6,000 per person.

Hotel Turismo Amazónio (tel. 886-508), at Amazonas and Calderón. As usual, throw in the word "Turismo" and the prices go up, as do the amenities. All pads have telephone, television, fridge, and private bath (with only room-temperature water). S/30,000 per person.

FOOD

Restaurant Cositas Rios (tel. 886-372), on Av. 15 de Noviembre, next to the footbridge. The alimentary sequel to Hostal Traveller's Lodge, this open-aired hangout often crowds to capacity with tourists. Mmmm, slurp up yummy food. Veggie spaghetti s/9,000, choice-beef cheeseburger s/3,500 (open daily 7am-10pm).

Restaurante Servi-Pan, at Diaz de Pineda and Av. 15 de Noviembre, under Residencial Napoli. A tranquil place to scarf down breakfast (s/3,5000), lunch (s/4,500), or dinner. The baked goods are delicious; add jelly and you won't be able to control yourself (croissants *increíbles* s/500). Open daily 6:30am-9pm.

El Descanso del Viajero (tel. 887-156), on Av. 15 de Noviembre, about 0.5km from the bridges. Another welcoming budget choice, this siren of casual *comedores* calls out, "Eat my *almuerzo* (s/4,000)! Eat my *merienda* (s/4,000)! Eat my spaghetti (s/4,000)!" Listen closely; you will hear (open daily 7am-11pm).

SIGHTS

Tena is the jungle gym of the Ecuadorian playground. Visitors swing from adventure to adventure, reveling in the junglescape. While some of Tena's attractions may exist Oriente-wide, others can be found nowhere else. Probably the biggest adrenaline-rush in Tena—and maybe all of Ecuador—comes from its killer **whitewater rafting.** Barely discovered by the world's whitewater enthusiasts, the region around Tena in the western Oriente is a truly amazing find. These rivers are the headwaters of the Amazon, rushing through canyons, over waterfalls and past rocky banks. While downstream piranha-filled currents run muddy and slow, near Tena the water flows fresh from the heights of the Andes mountains. The density of whitewater rapids is higher here than almost anywhere else in the world—and what's even cooler, it's always high season. East of the Andes, the whitewater rapids churn year-round.

Like much of Ecuador, this whitewater mecca has gone relatively undiscovered ... until now. **Ríos Ecuador** (tel. 887-438), in the Hotel Cambahuasi near the bus terminal, runs trips out of Tena, under the watchful eye of its owner, Gynner, a 25-year old kayaking and rafting pro with five years of guiding experience on rivers around the world. The sincere, congenial entrepreneur is a native Ecuadorian, but he speaks better English than most Americans. Using professional guides and equipment from the U.S., the company leads knowledgeable, energetic, and safety-conscious trips for travelers eager to feel the cold spray of whitewater in their faces. A one-day rafting trip is US$50 per person for Class II and III rivers (novice/moderate skill level), US$60 for the more challenging trips. Kayaking expeditions are also available for a day at US$60 per person. These prices include transportation from Tena, the guide's services, and a beachfront picnic along the way. Kayak rentals are US $15 per day, US$80 per week, or US$30 and US$160 with all equipment included. Ríos Ecuador also offers a five-day kayak course, teaching all the funky maneuvers, for US$300. Reservations can also be made at **Safari Tours** in Quito, Calama 380 y Juan Leon Mera (tel. 552-505), or through the Tena number above.

For a more tranquil wilderness experience, try spending a day or more in one of the many **cabaña** complexes scattered along the rivers. These basic, family-run thatched-roof resorts offer the "unembellished" experience of living in the jungle, including authentic food, well-informed guides, and peaceful settings off-the-tourist-track. The best-known of these *cabaña* operations in Tena is **Amarongachi Tours,** Av. 15 de Noviembre 438 (tel./fax 886-372), which works out of the **Hostal Traveller's Lodge.** A hefty book contains rave reviews from an international posse of satisfied customers from Luxembourg, Malaysia, France, Australia, Canada, England, and the U.S., to name a few. US$25 per person per day, all-inclusive. Other lesser-known *cabañas* are often just as honest and knowledgeable, and may even be a little quieter. Several hide behind the trees along the whitewater routes, and a brief stop or night's stay may even be incorporated into a day on the rapids. For more information, contact Gynner at Ríos Ecuador or ask at Safari Tours in Quito.

You don't even have to roll the dice to get to the **Cuevas de Jumandi,** gigantic caves that lie between Archidona and Cotundo, north of Tena. A resort has recently been established here, a convenient base for daytripping tourists who wish to explore the natural formations. Take a bus to Archidona from Amazonas and Olmedo (every 15min., 6am-7pm, 20min., s/700), then catch the bus from Archidona to Cotundo and ask to be let off at *las cuevas,* about 10 minutes from Archidona. Buses to Coca, leaving from Tena's *terminal terrestre,* also pass the caves.

More a safari than a daytrip, the strangely misplaced **Volcán Sumaco** rises out of the damp, densely-vegetated hills northeast of Tena. With patience and persistence, you may be able to spot the peak through cloud breaks in the streets of Tena. With even more patience and persistence, you might even be able to reach the mountain itself, though guides and machetes are a must. For more leads, ask around in Tena or head to the town of Loreto, about three hours away by bus along the Tena-Coca road.

One of the most impressive municipal parks in the county, the **Parque Amazónico La Isla** occupies 2200 hectares between the Ríos Tena and Napo. Clearly visible from the city, it connects to Tena via a bamboo bridge about 50m upriver from the main footbridge, behind the Hostal Traveller's Lodge. Monkeys and birds live freely in the park's sprawling forest, which merges with the greater jungle in the distance. Several closed-in pools and cages house animals recuperating from injuries or waiting to be moved into larger habitats, including alligators, capybaras, tortoises, boas, and the occasional guinea pig curiously placed in the boa cage. (Perhaps the boas are connoisseurs of *cuy.*) Various swimming areas dot the bordering rivers, and a look-out tower provides a panorama of Tena (open daily 10am-5pm; admission s/3,000, nationals s/1,000).

For even better views of Tena and the surrounding jungle, Señor Jorge Lara (tel. 887-160) offers **super-lite plane flights** over the area (US$15 per 15min.).

ENTERTAINMENT

On Friday, Saturday, and Sunday nights, Tena goes disco. Travelers who haven't had all their energy sucked by the myriad jungle activities are welcome to take part. Join the visiting U.S. soldiers as they let loose at **La Gallera,** a well-lit bar and dance club playing Latin tunes and techno favorites. Follow Av. 15 de Noviembre to the vehicle bridge, then veer right to the waterfront—if it's after 10pm on the weekend, you'll hear it. **Tattoo's** overlooks the water on the other side of the river, between the vehicle and foot bridges. Its stilt-supported bamboo structure has a bar and a second floor loft, all open-aired and cozy. A popular dance club called **El Rodeo,** opposite La Gallera on the river, plays similar toe-tapping tunes.

The Tailbone Terror

Why, one might wonder, does a 130km (82mi.) bus jaunt take nearly seven hours? Your backside, your tailbone, and in fact your whole body will know the answer soon after the experience. The "road" to Coca from Tena is a tribute to linguistic flexibility. It is hard to call something a road when at times it's a stream, at times a waterfall crossing, and usually just a trail of rocks and potholes. With all of its darting and weaving, the drive seems like a video game with the most advanced virtual reality sensations in the world. Sooner or later (though probably later), after trundling through the towns of Archidona, Cotundo, Guamaní, and Loreto, after cramming more and more bodies and boxes inside, after the driver stops to grab a meal while the patient passengers hungrily guard their seats, the bus really will arrive in Coca.

Misahuallí

The jungle port of Misahuallí is the only town downriver from Tena known for its tourism. But tourism here is on the wane, and the cause, indirectly, is the tourism itself. Years ago, when the town first started growing on the north bank of the Río Napo, its claims of sandy beaches attracted jungle-hungry tourists. These outsiders were most fascinated by the **Huaorani** Indians, whose exotic, elaborate traditional body jewelry and clothing provided the perfect gawking material. Surprise, surprise, eventually the Huaorani developed a resentment for the ubiquitous, camera-toting visitors and the local guides who exploited their native villages. As the Huaorani's passive welcomes were worn thin and their open statements of resistance went ignored, they escaped the uncomfortable situation the only way they could—by moving farther east into the Oriente, away from the tourist industry that had thrived off their presence.

Today Misahuallí is still a hub for many guided tours and the *gringos* who have come to experience them. The town, for better or worse, grew around its heyday of tourism, and the mark left on this compact Oriente community is definitely permanent. Everybody and his mother runs hotels and gives tours into the *selva.* With the absence of the significant indigenous population, these tours have transformed into canoe cruises to *cabaña* complexes built to fill the Huaorani's void. Native food and jungle surroundings mimic what was once the genuine experience. Gold-panning and other such extras are artificially packaged, while equally-contrived canoe excursions slip off the sandy Napo banks. By taking a tour straight from Quito or an Oriente town farther east, you may be able to skip Misahuallí altogether. And you may not miss much.

Orientation and Practical Information The road heads into town from the west. A sign greets you to Misahuallí, and you've pretty much seen the whole place. Some hotels, restaurants (more like acceptable *comedores),* and shops congregate around the plaza. The best advice for **changing money** in Misahuallí: do it somewhere else. If in need, though, the general store **Don Alonzo Guevara,** close to the beach at the corner of the plaza, changes dollars (in cash and traveler's check form) at sad rates (open daily 7am-9pm). The only phones in town are at **EMETEL** (tel. 584-964 or 584-965), down the Pununo road about three blocks, on the left. The town secretary at EMETEL answers the town's only two phone numbers (open daily 8am-noon, 3-5pm, and 8-9pm). **Buses** go to **Tena** from the central plaza (every hr., 5am-6pm, 1hr., s/2,000). You can also come and go from Misahuallí by **motorized dugout canoe.** Because the options aren't dependable or affordable, bus travel is much more common. Prices and frequency depend on demand; be careful you're not getting ripped off. Approximate per person costs are s/9,000 to **Ahuano,** s/59,000 to **Coca.** If you're lucky, you may happen upon one of the passenger boats that go to and from Ahuano for around s/5,000. The blue-and-white Registro Curl office houses vestiges of a **police** force and a **mail-drop box,** but don't count on anything mailed from here ever arriving. Around the corner in the same building, the **Centro de Salud** functions somewhat erratically. **Doctora Mercedes Alcivar,** at the dead-end of the Tena road, has permanent hours and runs **Farmacia Misahuallí,** half a block before the plaza (open 8am-8pm).

Accommodations and Food For the most part, hotels in Misahuallí seem to have a s/15,000 price floor. Challenge this. Needy hotels make a habit of over-pricing, but they're also competing for business. For food, you'd almost be better off foraging in the jungle. If your hunter-gatherer instincts have waned, either chow at one of the hotel restaurants or resign yourself to the sometimes-overpriced *comedores* near the plaza.

The two most professional, comfortable budget accommodations emerge over on the right just before entering town. First looms the **Hotel Albergue Español,** P.O. Box 15-01-254 in Tena (Quito tel. 02-221-626 or 553-857). This "jungle lodge" has spacious, spotless rooms that include private bath with the elusive, rarely found jungle species, Spanish name *agua caliente.* Lobby decor includes a huge black dog that looks like Marmaduke. (Here boy. Roll over. Speak. *Rrruff.* Sit, Ubu, sit. Good dog.) S/ 20,000 per person. The **restaurant** here specializes in high-class dining. But hey, who doubled all the prices? (Spanish omelette s/9,000, steak s/18,000.) These folks sure know how to settle *gringo* anxieties—a sign assures that all water is boiled before use. **Hotel Dayuma,** mailing address Casilla 220 in Tena, is camouflaged down the road 50m, in a four-story building. Immaculate rooms have stained-wood furniture, hurricane-powered fans, mini-bar fridges, pay-as-you-go snacks, and kick-ass comforters. A quality set-up, but try to negotiate the s/18,000 per person price tag. Down the street near the plaza, some slightly less glamorous options await. The **Hotel La Posada,** on the corner at the plaza, is nearest to the river beach. In addition to well-kept rooms with private bath, it provides a laundry service and a locked area for jungle-goers' valuables. (S/15,000 per person, with hot water s/20,000.) Below the s/ 15,000 mark, **Hotel El Paisano,** a block down the road to Panuno from the plaza, on the left, aims to please penny pinchers. Dwellings are more rustic, sheets more worn, but baths still private. If you're looking to chill, head to the hammocks outside (S/ 12,000 per person). The **restaurant** downstairs cooks the basics, along with some *gringo* favorites thrown in (*desayuno* s/3,000, hamburger s/5,000). The vegetarian-friendly **restaurant** below Hotel Jennifer, on the plaza, keeps prices low and food simple. (*Desayuno*, *almuerzo*, and *merienda* for s/4,500, plus some other *a la carta* options.)

Sights There's really only one reason to go to Misahuallí: the jammin' jungle tours. Tours down the river can last from a day to a week, and include two people or twenty. Packages are flexible, but the important part is getting a satisfactory guide. Key guide qualities include language ability (if you don't want a tour in Spanish) and wilderness experience. While a good number of the guides in Misahuallí have the experience under their belts, their language range is usually limited. If you've accepted this, along with the reality of the not-so-pristine jungle just east of Misahuallí, there are a few reliable tour agencies to pick through.

Cruceros y Expediciones Dayuma, out of the Dayuma Hotel, is one of the biggest tour agencies in Misahuallí, operated by Marena and Douglas Clarke, along with an army of other tour guides. Dayuma has three- to six-day expedition packages, custom-designed to your needs. The trips zoom you downriver on motorized canoes to thatch-roofed jungle *cabañas.* Meals are cooked using *yuca* and other native foods; exploratory hikes pass oodles of waterfalls, squadrons of birds, and a few indigenous jungle-dwellers. Hopefully they'll be glad to see you. If the itineraries originate and end in Quito, they also throw in excursions to Baños and the hot pools near Baeza (for 1-8 people, US$35 per person per day for 3-5 days; for 8 or more, US$30). Some guides speak some English, but this is *not* a given. **Ecoselva,** across the street from Dayuma, leads similar trips into the jungle. Pepe Tapia González, who runs the place, reputedly speaks English, as his recent rainforest talks in British public schools indicate. Tours include cascades, lagoons, hopefully some alligators and piranha, and other assorted jungle stuff. Other guides work for him, but if possible, try to snag the man himself (for 5-15 people, US$25 per person per day for 1-3 days). Trips of more than three days may venture into Yasuní or Cuyabeno parks (US$40 per person per day, minimum 6 people). **Sacha Tours,** very visibly next to the beach, is owned by Hector Fiallos. Hector has been around awhile and speaks some English. If you have the time to spare, his trips head deep into the jungle. Again, try to get the man himself. Their mailing address is Casilla 225, Tena.

Entertainment Go play with the big black dog that looks like Marmaduke at the Albergue Español. *Rrruff.*

■ Near Misahuallí

JATÚN SACHA

Big forest. That's what you'll find at the Jatún Sacha Biological Station, and coincidentally, that's the Quichua meaning of the name. Located 8km east of Misahuallí, right off the south bank road of the Napo River, this 1437-hectare (3300-acre) tropical wet forest reserve is still 70% primary growth. Refreshingly enough, Jatún Sacha is completely Ecuadorian owned and run, and in 1993 was named the world's second International Children's Rainforest.

This is the stuff bumper stickers are made of. The rainforest has tons of medicinal plants, a canopy of hillside trees, plenty of reptiles, and an alien empire in the form of insects galore. Founded in 1986, Jatún Sacha's aims both to conserve the incredible biodiversity of the land and to provide a window to it for researchers, especially Ecuadorian ones. Thus, as **Alejandro Suárez,** the long-haired, English-speaking administrator and co-founder, will readily tell you, tourists are not invited to spend the night or even the day if they arrive in large herds. The forest is first and foremost for scientific study. The facilities at Jatún Sacha can accommodate 35 visitors and 13 long-term residents at once. A new part of the complex, the dining hall offers three meals each day. Bunk beds in screened *cabañas,* with nearby latrines, showers, and a supply of rainwater for hand-washing round out the amenities. These facilities are open only to "scientists," but you may want to ask Alejandro how broadly that word can be interpreted—sometimes the worldly contributions of college students fall under the name of science. **Buses** running between Tena and Ahuano can drop visitors off right in front of Jatún Sacha (from Tena, 1¼hr., s/2,500). The **entrance fee** is US$6 for foreigners and s/6,000 for nationals. Meals cost s/5,000 for everyone. One night's stay, including three meals and the reserve entry fee, is US$20 for foreigners, s/20,000 for nationals. To contact the reserve or make research reservations, the **Quito address** is: Fundación Jatún Sacha, Casilla 17-12-867 (tel./fax 441-592; e-mail dneill@isacha.ecx.ec). The **Tena address** is: Casilla 15-01-218. Crafts and t-shirts sold on-site support the reserve.

But there's more than one way to support the biological station. Rejected non-"scientists" and travelers seeking more comfortable accommodations can head to the downright luxurious **Cabañas Alinahui**, 3km down the road to the east of Jatún Sacha (follow the signs; a 1-hr. walk). With an office in Quito, Río Coca 1734 y Isla Fernandina (tel. 253-267; fax 253-266), the Cabañas help fund the reserve. The eight spacious cabins are raised on stilts above a hammock-blessed patio area. Each cabin has two rooms that share a bathroom below, one of which has hot water. Conference room, bar, library, and top-notch view are all part of the package. (US$45 per cabin per night, plus 20% in taxes; 10% discount for nationals).

LA PUNTA AND AHUANO

In mathematics, a point is a location that contains nothing at all. The Ecuadorian equivalent, **La Punta,** lies on the southern bank of the Río Napo about 10km east of Jatún Sacha, along the same dirt road. The tranquil *pueblito* of **Ahuano,** down the river and around the bend, can be accessed from here by motorized canoe for s/ 2,500. Boat drivers often ask more from *gringos,* but hold out for the fair price.

With no road access nor tour industries, there is actually little reason to visit Ahuano itself—it's the nearby resorts that really attract visitors. **Hotel Anaconda** and **Hotel Jaguar,** two moderate options upstream, feed on the reputations of the least common and most exotic animals of the Oriente. But Ahuano's most conspicuous specimen is **Hostería La Casa del Suizo.** You'll catch your first jaw-dropping glimpse when your canoe rounds the bend to Ahuano. There, on a bluff overlooking the Amazon, rests the decadent splendor of this wealthy traveler's paradise. Use of the topaz blue pool, polished bamboo doors, and winding wooden staircases costs over s/ 145,000 a night. The well-monied can make reservations in Quito, at Reina Victoria 1235 y Lizardo García; post address Casilla 17-21-1608 (tel. 509-115 or 508-871; fax 508-872). Visitors rarely stay in Ahuano, but **accommodations** are there for the taking. **La Posada de Mama Aida** is on the road adjacent to the spot where the boats from La Punta pull up. The namesake is an endearingly protective old woman who has four immaculate beds upstairs, above the family's *comedor.* For a bed and three meals Mama Aida asks s/30,000, but negotiating downward is not only possible but probable. **Lojanito,** two doors inland, offers beds in much darker, cell-like rooms at s/ 10,000 per person.

Coca

The easternmost urban outpost of the Napo province, Coca (also known as Puerto Francisco de Orellana) has two histories that add up to one identity crisis. The first settlement was a tranquil jungle town seated 260m above sea level, where the Ríos Napo, Payamino, and Coca come together. This original Coca developed in the early 20th century, when its pioneer residents built a hospital, schools, and churches, and prospered to a whopping population of 300. Then it happened. In the pivotal year of 1969, foreigners from the north found banks of bubbling ooze underground. With an eye for the black gold, oil tycoons decided not to sip but to chug this Texas tea. Within a few years, Coca's population doubled and its landscape changed forever. Roads tore into the jungle and newly-erected pumps drained the land and filled the pockets of the oil entrepreneurs.

Exploitation or sound economics? Whatever the judgment, outsiders have transformed Coca into a gritty, dirty, riverside pit. Recently, the unmarked streets have been muddy disasters—the soggy, sticky result of an ambitious water-purification project. While it's impossible to tell when the project will be over, or if locals will ever get to remove their rubber boots to walk two blocks, some things will never change. Regardless of the city's aesthetic, Coca is significant for travelers because tours often begin and end at this Oriente outpost. Guides and tourists zip from the airport and bus terminal to the river bank, without stopping to consider the city at all. Maybe they've got the right idea.

ORIENTATION

The roughly gridded city has no street names or helpful vantage points, so orientation is a challenge. From the bus terminal in the north, **Calle Napo,** the principal mud-laden tourist drag, extends eight blocks to the **Río Napo,** the town's southern boundary. Another important road perpendicular to the riverfront, **Amazonas** dead-ends at the dock a block east of Calle Napo. The parallel **Tena-Lago Agrio Road** enters the town from the north, curves around, and eventually straightens out one block east of Amazonas. It then crosses the river to the **military camp** on the other side. The **Hotel El Aura,** north of the river on Calle Napo, six blocks south of the bus terminal, is a helpful landmark.

PRACTICAL INFORMATION

Tourist Office: Coca doesn't have a CETUR, but it does have an **INEFAN,** or *Instituto Ecuatoriano Forestal de Areas Naturales* (tel. 880-171), at the northern end of Amazonas bordering the airfield. Helpful information on nearby parts of the jungle, in Spanish only (open Mon.-Fri. 9am-1pm and 2-5pm).

Currency Exchange: Hotel El Aura exchanges cash, but traveler's checks are trickier matter. Ask around, but don't hold your breath.

Telephones: EMETEL (tel. 880-104), 1block south and 3 blocks west of Hotel El Cluca, is under the big tower. Unfortunately, there's no long-distance service, even with toll-free access numbers. The same applies for the rest of Coca as well (open Mon.-Sat. 8am-11am, 1-5pm, and 6-9pm, Sun. 8-11am and 6-9pm).

Airport: The airstrip is on the highway, about 1km north of the river. It is also accessible by walking across the runway from behind the municipal building on Napo, 7 blocks from the river. **AEROGAL** offers flights to **Quito** (Mon., Wed., Fri., 8am, 10:15am, US$52.60). **TAME** (tel. 880-046) also flies to **Quito** (daily, 9:30am, 12:30pm, US$52.60), with **Guayaquil** connections from there. **Air Force planes** (FAE) takes civilian passengers to Tena or Nueva Rocafuerte if sufficient demand exists, i.e. approximately 19 people. Flights leave between 10am and noon; to **Tena** s/20,700, to **Nueva Rocafuerte** s/34,500, 75% more for *extrañeros.* Inquire at airport office for the most current information.

Buses: The **terminal terrestre** is on Calle Napo, 8 blocks north of the river. **Transportes Jumandi** (no tel.) heads to **Tena** (8, 10am, noon, 6, 10pm, 6hr., s/16,000). **Transportes Baños** (tel. 880-182) runs 2 routes to **Quito;** one going north (7, 10:15am, 2, 6pm, 12hr., s/20,000) through **Lago Agrio** (2hr., s/6,000), the other going south (9am, 7, 8, 9, 9:30, 10pm, 10hr., s/20,000) through **Loreto** (2hr., s/6,000). Buy a ticket beforehand for the trip to Quito only. **Transportes Petrolera Shushufindi** (tel. 839-310) goes back and forth to **Lago Agrio** (7am, 8am, 10am, 1:30pm, 2:30pm, 3hr., s/6,000). Only the 7am trip is in a bus; the others are in less comfortable, open-air *rancheras* (farm vehicles). **Trans Esmeraldas** (tel. 881-309) goes to **Quito** (8:20, 9:15pm, 9hr., s/25,000) via **Loreto** (2hr., s/5,000) and **Baeza** (7hr., s/20,000); ticket necessary only for Quito. **Transportes Zaracay** (tel. 881-191) goes to **Guayaquil** (3:30pm, 15hr., s/35,000) via **Santo Domingo** (10hr., s/24,000) and **Quevedo** (12hr., s/30,000).

Boats: Also known as the marina of Puerto Francisco de Orellana, Coca sees its share of boat traffic. Most tourist traffic on the river comes from organized tours, so travelers don't have to worry about prices or times. All traffic on the river, whether coming or going, must record the names and passport numbers of all foreign passengers at the **Capitañia,** a government office right on the water at the end of Amazonas. Motorized canoes head downriver on Mon. and Thurs. at 8am, and return on Sun. and Wed. Destinations are **Hacienda Primavera** (s/13,200), **Pompeya** and **Limoncocha** (s/18,700), **Panacocha** (s/39,600), and **Nueva Rocafuerte,** near the Peruvian border (14hr., s/40,800). Prices listed are for foreigners (Ecuadorians get cheaper rates). Schedules may change due to variation in demand and water conditions.

Taxis: White jungle trucks, rather than normal taxis, reign supreme, but they are virtually impossible to get late at night.

Library: On the 4th floor terrace of the municipal building, 7 blocks north of the river on Napo (tel. 880-148 or 880-445). Open 8am-noon and 2-6pm.

Pharmacies: If you're near the river, the **Farmacia Oriental** (no tel.), on Espejo between Amazonas and Napo, is a block from the waterfront (open 7am-8pm). **Farmacia Bristol** (tel. 881-260), is next to Hotel El Aura on Napo (open 8am-1pm and 2-10:30pm).

Hospital: Hospital Francisco de Orellana (tel. 880-139, 880-468, or 880-469), on the road to Tena/Lago Agrio, a 20-min. walk from the river. The emergency room facilities and medical treatment are not up to Western standards. Try not to get sick in Coca.

Emergency: (tel. 880-101). The police reached at this catch-all emergency number aren't always helpful. The word *"emergencia"* is sometimes the only way to get attention, and even that doesn't get anyone too excited.

Police: Policía Nacional (tel. 880-525, 880-101), at Napo and Rocafuerte.

Post Office: At the southern end of Av. 9 de Octubre, by the river, 3 blocks west of Napo (open Wed.-Fri. 8am-4pm, but the hours aren't too reliable).

Telephone Code: 06.

ACCOMMODATIONS

A few respectable hotels cluster on Calle Napo around the Hotel El Aura. Other dank, simple cheapies hover close to the waterfront. The only other frequented tourist area of the city is just down the tiny street, Malecón, that veers off to the left from before the bridge, where the **Hotel Oasis** and top-of-the-line **Hostería La Misión** set up their quarters.

Hotel El Aura (tel. 880-127), on Av. Napo at García Moreno, 6 blocks south of the *terminal.* A married couple runs this commune of red-roofed bungalows. Spider monkeys and parrots with excellent Spanish accents inhabit the garden courtyard. While it's *the* place for backpacking budget travelers to gather in the morning to form tour groups, El Aura refreshingly does not run its own tour operation. *Cabañas* vary in size, but all have private bath. Singles s/26,000-s/30,000; doubles s/46,000-s/53,000.

Hotel Oasis (tel. 880-164; fax 880-206), on the Malecón on the river, 50m down the narrow left branch before the bridge. Climb up to the 2nd story of this getaway to escape the muddy quicksand of the rest of the city. Beds are fluffed, floors swept spotless, and private baths (in all rooms) well scrubbed. Fans in all rooms. Often houses pre-packaged tour groups from Quito. S/15,000 per person.

Residencial Lojanita (tel. 880-032), on Calle Napo and Cuenca, 1 block from El Aura. Enter through grocery store below. Lojanita cuts cost at the expense of quality. Of the *real* budget accommodations in town, it's one of the cleanest—which isn't saying much. Mud tracks through the communal bathrooms are true to Coca form; don't forget shower sandals. Midnight curfew. S/8,000 per person.

FOOD

Restaurant Dayuma, in Hotel El Aura, invites guests and anyone else in the area to grab a sound portion of *comida típica.* Slightly inflated prices and brusque, efficient service reflect its mainstream tourist status. American breakfast s/5,000, shrimp cocktail s/12,000, *arroz con legumbres* s/10,000, *arroz con pollo* s/13,000 (open daily 6:30am-10pm, closed mid-day on Sun.).

Restaurant Hotel La Missión (tel. 880-260 or 880-261), on Malecón next to Hotel Oasis. Higher-priced than other local eateries; after all, it's *the* gourmet experience in Coca. Dine in high-ceilinged comfort in the dining room, or on the bamboo patio by the river. All entrees s/16,000, including pepper steak and country chicken. At s/14,000, the *almuerzo* must be gold-plated.

Restaurant La Jaiba (no tel.), at Quito and Alfaro, 1 block south of El Aura, then 2 blocks west. Not just a typical old comedor, but a nicer, newer one. Well-intentioned and engaging staff entertains customers. Vegetarians will feel at home too. *Desayuno, almuerzo, merienda* s/5,000. Entrees around s/10,000 (open 7am-3pm and 4-9pm).

JUNGLE TOURS FROM COCA

Coca's location, farther *al oriente* than Tena or Misahuallí, makes it a good base for trips to the more isolated parks, reserves and deep-jungle communities of the indigenous **Huaorani.** The still-untamed region east of Coca is home to some of the most isolated indigenous communities and densest biodiversity in the world, but in an ironic misfortune, it's also home to Ecuador's most lucrative natural resource in the technological age—its oil. Both the *indígenas* and the wildlife thrive in isolation, but exploitation of the oil reserves inevitably puts an end to this confinement. On top of the toxic waste spills common to the region's waterways, oil companies are responsible for most of the road construction that continues to open the land up to further "development."

Industry and nature have always been quarrelsome neighbors, and the tourist industry is no exception. Despite universal claims of ecologically responsible tourism, the tours that stream into the jungle and down rivers and industry-made roads have had ill effects on the area (see Environmentally Responsible Tourism, p. 56). While the amazing flora and fauna of the Amazon may benefit from conscientious exposure, the same cannot necessarily be said for the Huaorani. While some Indian communities have signed contracts with specific guides, allowing tourists to come along for a glimpse of their blow-dart hunting and other customs, others have made overtly anti-tourist statements. When deciding which places will be included on your tour itinerary, recognize that the Huaorani live far out in the jungle for a reason, and frequent visits from tourists are bound to disturb their cultural environment.

A handful of villages and natural areas down the Río Napo are favorite tour destinations from Coca. A relatively short distance downstream, the **Reserva Biológica Limoncocha** and the mission towns of **Pompeya** and **Limoncocha** often make their way onto tour groups' itineraries. These days you don't even have to float to get there, courtesy of the road that the oil industry that has cut past Limoncocha into "pristine oil country." Further downriver sits **La Selva Jungle Lodge,** a pricey resort whose facilities and excursions are among the best around. Well-funded guests generally fly in to Coca and get escorted straight to the lodge. **Pañacocha,** another nature reserve on the Río Napo, about halfway between Coca and Nueva Rocafuerte, is an especially popular tour destination. *Cocha* is Quechua for lagoon, and *paña* means piranha; that should give an idea of what's there. The sprawling swamp has enough plant and animal species to make any biologist's day. Canoes wind their way through murky waterways and hikers wind their way through murky trails. **Cabañas Pañacocha** offers housing for tours to the area. Entrance is s/40,000, standard for all nature reserves in the area. Even farther downriver, accessible only on longer tours, lurks the immense, isolated **Yasuní National Park** (p. 227). To the south of Coca, the village of **Tiputini,** on the Río Tiputini, is one of the closest Huaorani communities to Coca and consequently one of the most touristed.

Tours offered from Coca vary greatly in price and quality. Part of the expense is the s/40,000 **entrance fee** for each protected natural reserve on the tour. Some guides calculate their prices with this amount included, while others clearly state that it is additional. Either way, the INEFAN office in Coca strongly suggests that at least one person from your group accompany the guide to INEFAN to pay the required amount. It's a jungle out there, and INEFAN can't easily know how many people enter each area. By fudging the numbers, guides have been known to embezzle sucres meant for the reserves and parks. Check out a number of tour companies and make sure you find one that seems reputable.

Selva Tour (Coca tel. 880-336, Quito tel. 659-311). Easily contacted through Hotel El Aura, experienced director Whymper Jones leads his own tours to Pañacocha, Limoncocha, Yasuní, and wherever else. As long as the group is between 5 and 10 people, and the duration is more than 2 days, he won't leave you jonesin'. US$45 per person per day, including food and transportation.

Ejarsytur (tel. 880-251), across from the Hotel Oasis near the bridge. Another branch located in Quito (tel. 569-852; fax 223-245), at Jorge Washington and Amazonas. The owner, Julio Jarrín, and his team of guides bring groups to Pañacocha, Yasuní, Tiputini, Cuyabeno, and other jungle locations, depending on the duration of the trip. Boat transport, cabins, food (vegetarian possible), and hikes included in the hefty US$80 per person per day.

Yuturi Jungle Adventure operates out of Hotel Oasis. Another location in Quito, Amazonas 1324 y Colón (tel./fax 504-037, 503-225, or 544-166). Organizes 4- to 5-day jungle tours that leave from Quito. Enthusiastically recommended for its tasty food, comfy lodging, and guiding expertise. Price per person increases as group size decreases and/or number of days increases. The season is an added variable (Dec., July, and Aug. are busiest). A 5-day, 4-night tour for 7-10 people in peak season runs around US$290.

Amazon Jungle Adventures (Coca tel. 880-606; fax 880-451). Operated out of Pappa Dan's bar on the waterfront, this English-speaking agency has built up years of experience in Pañacocha and other popular parts of the Oriente near Coca. One of the North American owners, Michael Muzzo, is the son of Pappa Dan himself. Trips can be ½-day or full-day, and appropriate meals are always included. Mailing address: P.O. Box 17-21-841, Quito.

■ Near Coca: Parque Nacional Yasuní

Coca is the push-off point to mainland Ecuador's largest national park, the 982,000-hectare Parque Nacional Yasuní. This is river country, **Amazon River** country, with the Tiputini, Nashiño, Cononaco, Yasuní, and other tributaries coursing through the park's enormous expanse. Yasuní has three major habitats: dry land, sometimes-flooded land, and always-flooded land. While the rainforest is understandably wet year-round, the region's seasons still alternate between dry (Dec.-Mar.), rainy (April-July), and unstable (Aug.-Nov.). Founded in 1979, Yasuní includes the greatest biodiversity in the country. The **Huaorani Indians** are as natural a part of the park as the wildlife; hunting and living off the land, they call this protected tropical jungle home. They are not alone; boa constrictors, alligators, jaguars, eels, parrots, toucans, piranhas, capybaras, monkeys, and sloths are just a few of the animals that share Yasuní's abundance. In spite of this biodiversity and the park's legally-protected status, the government has chosen to ignore the recent proliferation of a newly introduced species, *Oilus maximus,* which flattens paths across pristine jungle, then plunges its trunk-like mouth deep into the earth, sucking petroleum pools dry.

So far, INEFAN has yet to organize a management system for the Parque Nacional Yasuní; it's simply way too massive. A force of only 10 rangers controls activity within the sprawling park. Because of this ridiculously inadequate situation, INEFAN recently closed the park from tourists, temporarily—not in an attempt to discourage visitation, but to prepare the park for more orderly tourist traffic. Despite the closure, tour guides continue to penetrate the park, and there is a good chance that it will soon legally re-open. To find out if tourists are permitted into the park, call or visit the Parque Nacional Yasuní's **INEFAN** office in Coca (tel. 880-171), on the north end of Amazonas, next to the airport.

Lago Agrio

A young city with a story, Lago Agrio is testament to exactly what is in a name. Way up north in Texas, an American city exists with its English translation, Sour Lake, as a name. That spot brought the Texaco conglomerate its first oil fortune, so it was only fitting that in the 1960s, when Texaco struck a jackpot at this location in Ecuador, they named it Lago Agrio. Though a community of Loja pioneers existed here prior to the oil pipes, Lago Agrio was very little before it was an oil town, and not surprisingly, the name has stuck.

Ask locals nowadays, and many will claim that the source of the title is a nearby lake with green waters like a bitter lemon. This type of mix-up epitomizes the confusion of an Ecuadorian city developed by outsiders for foreign reasons, foreign buyers, and foreign motivations, despite whatever existed here previously. Since 1989, Lago Agrio has been the capital of the Sucumbíos province, an area that has been home to the Confane, Siona, Secoya, and Shuar Indians long before Texaco, or any other oil interest, claimed a stake here. But despite a history of indigenous influences, oil transformed the city into what it is today—strips of three-story banks, hotels, restaurants, and grocery stores, not to mention plenty of tour agencies and services. Close to the Colombian border and Parque Nacional Cuyabeno, Lago Agrio is more often a base for jungle tours or a destination en route than anything else. Its petroleum rewards and rumored drug activity have clearly given it a more urban reputation, but haven't made Lago Agrio any more exciting or attractive.

ORIENTATION

Lago Agrio's main road is the east-west **Av. Quito.** This artery runs in from the **airstrip,** 5km to the east, and forks at the market, forming the southern branch of **Av. Río Amazonas.** The **market** is a triangular area formed by the fork of Quito and Amazonas, and the north-south **Av. 12 de Febrero,** one block west. **Francisco de Orellana** is parallel to and one block west of Av. 12 de Febrero. In the absence of a bus terminal, most bus *cooperativos* line up on Quito, to the east of the market; this is the most bustling area in town.

PRACTICAL INFORMATION

Tourist Information: INEFAN (tel. 830-129), at Manabí and Av. 10 de Agosto (open Mon.-Fri. 8am-noon and 2-6pm).

Immigration Office: In the police station, at Quito and Manabí, across from the market. Has information about crossing the Colombian border.

Colombian Consulate: Av. Quito 441 (tel. 830-084). Along with the immigration office, the consulate also has information concerning the dangerous Colombian border crossing 20km north of Lago Agrio. Most Ecuadorians recommend against crossing the border there, clearly communicating the danger with a sharp, quick hand gesture across the throat.

Currency Exchange: Banco de Prestamos (tel. 830-582), on Quito about 100m east of the fork, changes cash or traveler's checks at good rates (open Mon.-Fri. 9:30am-3pm). In an off-hour emergency, check out streetside change stands.

Telephone: EMETEL (tel. 830-104 or 830-040), at Quito and Orellana (open Mon.-Sat. 8am-10pm, Sun. 8am-noon and 8-10pm).

Airport: Located 5km east of the city center, a s/5,000 taxi ride away. TAME has flights to **Quito** (Mon.-Sat., 11:30am, 30min., s/167,200 for foreigners, s/82,000 for Ecuadorians). Return flights from Quito to Lago Agrio every Mon.-Sat., 10:30am. For more information, the **TAME office** (tel. 830-113), is at Av. 9 de Octubre and Manabí.

Buses: For some reason, long-distance buses from Lago Agrio are more luxurious than others in the country, and companies are sometimes reluctant to sell tickets for intermediate spots en route to the final destination. Even if you don't plan to ride a bus to its last stop, be prepared to pay for the entire distance.**Transportes Esmeraldas** (tel. 830-161) has luxury buses with bathroom, TV and videos, and snack to **Quito** (1:35, 9:30pm, 8hr., s/20,000) via **Baeza** (hopefully only s/15,000). **Transportes Occidental** (tel. 830-736) also goes to **Quito** (7:45am, 12:30, 9:20, 9:45, 10, 10:15pm; 8hr.; s/20,000), **Guayaquil** (8pm, 16hr., s/30,000) via **Santo Domingo** (10hr., s/20,000), **Quevedo** (12hr., s/25,000), and **Babahoyo** (13hr., s/28,000). **Transportes Baños** (tel. 830-330) serves **Coca** (approx. 5, 11am, 3, 6, 7:30, 8pm, 2hr., s/6,000). **Transportes Putumayo** (tel. 830-034), in the deep garage where Av. 12 de Febrero hits Amazonas, runs *rancheras* (open-aired farm vehicles with rows of benches) to **Coca** (6, 6:45, 9, 10:40,11:30am, 3hr., s/6,000) and deep-jungle locations like **Palma Roja** (5hr., s/11,000) via **Tarapoa** (2hr., s/5,000), the **Cuyabeno** bridge entrance (3hr., s/7,000), and **Tipishca** (4hr., s/8,500). **Transportes Zaracay** runs to **Esmeraldas** (6:45pm, 13hr., s/28,000), **Guayaquil** (14hr., s/32,000), and **Santo Domingo** (4:30pm, 11hr., s/22,000) via **Quito** (8hr., s/20,000). **Cooperativa Loja** heads to **Loja** (1pm, 24hr., s/55,000), **Guayaquil** (4, 7pm, 18hr., s/32,000), and **Quito** (10:45pm, s/20,000).

Taxis: Cabs take the form of yellow trucks and congregate at the fork.

Library: Casa de la Cultura (tel. 830-624), on the northwest corner of Av. 12 de Febrero and Jorge Añasco, 1 block from Quito, hiding behind a fence (open Mon.-Fri. 8am-5pm).

Pharmacy: Attached to 24-hr. clinic, **Farmacia International** (tel. 830-038), on Quito near Av. 12 de Febrero (open daily 7:30am-10pm). Part of the *de turno* system, so there is always a pharmacy in town that is open late.

Hospital: Hospital Lago Agrio (tel. 830-198), on Quito about 0.5km west of the market.

Police: (tel. 830-101), at Quito and Manabí, across from the market.

Post office: (tel. 830-115), on Rocafuerte just off Av. 12 de Febrero. Has a *Lista de Correos* (open Mon.-Fri. 8am-noon and 1-6pm, but not always punctual).

ACCOMMODATIONS

Hotel D'Mario, Quito 175 (tel. 830-172; fax 830-456), about 50m east of the fork. The street-level restaurant makes this hotel a tourist hive. Rooms are all refreshingly clean and obviously well-cared for, with private baths and fans. Call for reservations, as it sometimes fills up. Singles s/15,000; doubles s/25,000, with A/C, TV, and an extra-big bed s/30,000.

Hotel Willigran (tel. 830-163), on Quito just before the fork. It rocks because of its prices, but not necessarily its roaches (unless, of course, you like roaches). Rooms have comfy beds and grated windows that let in hallway breezes. Bathrooms, especially communal ones, need a good mopping. Don't be overcharged; try to get rooms at s/10,000 per person, s/15,000 with bath.

Hotel Oro Negro (tel. 830-174), on Quito across the street from D'Mario. Named for the town's crude sustenance, this hotel houses mainly tourists, not drillers. Beds draped lavishly in grand mosquito nets; each floor fitted with communal bath, with toilets and shower stalls galore. S/10,000 per person.

Hotel Secoya, Av. Quito 222 y Amazonas (tel. 830-451), at the fork. Head up a vertiginous spiral staircase, then re-orient yourself on the 2nd-floor landing with patio TV area and 2 rows of spacious, fan-equipped rooms. Singles s/15,000, with bath s/20,000, with TV s/25,000. It's worth bargaining.

FOOD

Pizza Restaurant D'Mario (tel. 830-172), on Av. Quito in the eponymous hotel. With the professionalism of its tourist-trodden hotel home, this sidewalk restaurant feeds most of the *gringos* in town. White and sanitary decor reflects the food quality. Small pizza with chicken, ham, and salami s/10,000, fried chicken s/10,000. *Desayuno, almuerzo, merienda* each s/6,500 (open 7am-11pm).

Restaurante Típico La Picarjua, Av. Quito 414 y Orellana (tel. 830-177). The name means "canoe," and the excellent, inexpensive food is just as quintessentially jungle. Serves some wild stuff, like tortoise, *chili con carne, burrito* (s/2,500), *plato vegetariano* (s/8,000). Open Mon.-Sat. 7:30am-9:15pm, Sun. 7:30am-noon and 6-9pm.

Restaurante Alexander (tel. 831-468), on Quito near Av. 12 de Febrero. A bit dim, this spacious *a la carta* restaurant also cooks up the ubiquitous *desayunos, almuerzos,* and *meriendas* for s/6,000 each. *Arroz con pollo* s/12,000 (open daily 6am-midnight).

Araza Hotel Restaurant (tel. 830-223), on Av. Quito at Guayaquil. These overpriced dishes are probably the best in town, considering the extravagant clients who dance daintily around the place, tossing money to and fro. *Arroz con camarón* s/19,000, *pollo apanado* s/19,000. Care to dance? Open daily 7am-9pm.

JUNGLE TOURS FROM LAGO AGRIO

For most foreigners, Lago Agrio's charm lies not in its black, sticky oil, but in its mind-boggling natural surroundings. To the east of town, vast expanses of jungle resonate with the cries of monkeys, calls of birds, and chirps of so many insects that their diversity leaves the most ardent bug enthusiasts speechless. Rivers flow silently throughout the rainforest, swallowing the ripples left by alligators and monkey-munching anacondas. Unlike other parts of the Oriente, the area around Lago Agrio sees little hunting, despite the fact that several native and still-traditional tribes (like the colorful Cofanes and the formerly head-shrinking Shuars) continue to make a natural living off the jungle. Some of the tours that leave from Lago Agrio visit these native communities; as in other parts of the Oriente, each tourist must make the difficult decision whether or not to take part in this interesting but unavoidably invasive practice. Jungle tours often cruise the **Río Aguarico,** which runs near the city and on to more remote areas, passing some Indian villages along the way. The lagoons of **Lagartacocha** ("alligator lagoon"), **Limoncocha,** and **Pañacocha** please visitors particularly interested in experiencing oodles of wildlife; the last two are also accessible from Coca. The **Reserva de Produción Faunistica Cuyabeno,** the mother of all wildlife areas in the Ecuadorian Oriente, lies two and a half hours east of Lago Agrio by truck (see below).

The most dependable way to plunge into the jungle east of Lago Agrio is to hire a tour guide from a reputable agency in Baños or Quito. This expensive proposition often disheartens budget travelers. Many cheaper tour operations are based in Lago Agrio, but most haven't yet organized themselves to properly satisfy the requirements issued by INEFAN (the government's park management agency). Though technically illegal, many of these unauthorized tour groups operate out of Lago Agrio. However, INEFAN officials have been known to check for credentials when tour groups enter nationally protected areas, and in these cases, unapproved tours are routinely turned away. Check the list of the INEFAN-approved agencies in the appendix (p. 284). Many tour agencies advertise along Av. Quito, often in connection with *gringo*-frequented hotels. For help deciding on a tour agency, members of the South American Explorer's Club in Quito can consult trip reports for jungle tours in the Sucumbíos province. For the most up-to-date information and additional questions, INEFAN has offices in Lago Agrio (see Practical Information, p. 228), in Tarapoa en route to Cuyabeno, and at the bridge entrance to Cuyabeno.

■ Near Lago Agrio: Reserva de Producción Faunística Cuyabeno

When God created the animals of the earth, He must have stopped for a picnic in Cuyabeno. He looked at what He had made—giant armadillos, boa constrictors, electric eels, alligators, freshwater dolphins, spiders, monkeys, tapirs, land tortoises, piranhas—and it was good. Far to the east, past the Limoncocha mission and the Pañacocha lagoon, this 603,400-hectare wildlife reserve claims a proliferant chunk of the Sucumbíos province.

The reserve was established in order to give Mother Nature some living space. Cuyabeno's organic orchestra perpetually plays a screeching symphony; the sounds of howling monkeys and buzzing bugs replace dog barks and engine roars. Though silent, the flora blooms and thrives as well, from joltingly colorful fruits and splashy flowers to enormous green leaves and fronds. A network of tributaries stem from Cuyabeno's **Río Aguarico** and **Río Cuyabeno,** and parades of wildlife follow the rivers as they flow into the reserve's **14 lagoons.** The park also encloses the homelands of various Indian communities, such as the **Siona, Secoya,** and **Shuar.** The *other* human presence in the reserve came as a consequence of the oil industry. Over the last 30 years, oil companies have been having their way with the land despite its protected status. The damage here is reportedly less severe than in Parque Nacional Yasuní to the south, though.

There are several ways to approach the park from Lago Agrio. The drive by truck or bus through Tarapoa to Puente Cuyabeno is a rough and dusty two and a half hours. This entrance is often used to access the popular lagoons deep in the bush. Other tours launch into the Río Aguarico, then travel by water through the upper or lower regions of the reserve. Sun block and bug repellant are necessities; exchange leather hiking boots for the big, tough, goofy yellow boots supplied by many guides. If traveling by river, it's a good idea to do part of the tour by paddle canoe, since motors chopping through the rivers seem like little earthquakes to animals up ahead. For information on arranging a tour see Jungle Tours from Lago Agrio, p. 229.

Baeza

Officially a part of the Oriente, Baeza's puts on the convincing façade of a Sierra hamlet. The quiet village lounges in a cushion of green mountains at the junction of three roads, known as the **Y de Baeza.** One road leads west to Quito, one south to Tena, and the other east to Lago Agrio. Though it elicits objections from red, blue, and yellow, green is the primary color here; green hills and mountains dominate even the concrete main highways. The town itself sits along a snaking segment of the Tena road, so those traveling between Quito and Lago Agrio don't even see Baeza itself. Not far from Quito and a step up (in altitude) from the jungle, Baeza is a pleasant stop on the way to or from the Oriente. Here, away from crowds, there's nothing to do but enjoy the coolness and scenery of the mountains.

Orientation and Practical Information As the Tena road slips away to the south, it curls around a hill to the old city, **Baeza Vieja,** which simply consists of a peaceful verdant plaza surrounded by a square of dilapidated buildings. The road continues a little ways, crossing over a stream, then rises slightly and straightens out to become **Avenida de los Quijos,** the principal avenue in **Baeza Nueva. EMETEL** (tel. 580-651), at Av. de los Quijos and Av. 17 de Enero, on the north end of Baeza Nueva, has the only phone number in town, but is fully equipped to make international calls (open Mon.-Sat. 8am-noon, 2-4pm, and 6-8pm, Sun. 6-8pm). Getting to and from Baeza is a cinch; just head to the "Y," about 25 minutes downhill from the new town, and flag down a **bus** heading in the right direction. Traffic is fairly constant from 7am-midnight, with early buses to **Quito** (3hr.) passing through at 3 and 5:30am. Buses pass about every half-hour, but keep in mind that they may be full and simply pass you by. To **Tena** (2hr.), to **Lago Agrio** (6hr). The **Hospital Estatal Baeza,** 30m east of the *colegio* on Avenida de los Quijos, is always open for emergencies. The **pharmacy** is next door (open daily 7am-noon and 1-5pm). The **police** are at the "Y," and always on-call. Baeza does not have a **post office.**

Accommodations and Food Happy, homey, hospitable hotels have popped up in both old and new Baeza, all either on or within 50m of the road to Tena. **Hotel Samay,** in the new Baeza strip, on the right side on the way out of town towards Tena, is perhaps the best choice in this part of town. The staff won't tuck you in, but the snug blankets on the wooden beds are enough to keep you roasty-toasty on cool nights. The otherwise stark rooms are clearly well-acquainted with many a mop and broom. Communal baths have hot water. (S/10,000 per person.) Across the way in Baeza Vieja, **Hostal El Nogal de Jumandy** is above the Tena road, up the second right if you're coming from the "Y." Rooms might get a little colder at night than at Samay; not everyone can have such warmhearted blankets. If it gets really chilly, get clean—shared bath supplies hot showers for an extra s/500. (S/8,000 per person.) **Hostal Mesón de Baeza,** about 50m up the first right coming from the "Y," is also run by kindhearted, helpful folk. Set across from the town's old plaza, the walls boast horse pictures. Like a stable, rooms are wooden and simple, but unlike equestrian abodes, bathrooms are impressively clean. (S/10,000 per person, with bath s/12,000.) **El Restaurante Gina,** the choice dining spot in Baeza, is on the same street as Hostal Jumandy. Run by the people from the Mesón, the atypically savory and elegant *desayunos, almuerzos,* and *meriendas* are all s/4,000, and noodles with vegetables s/7,000 (open daily 7am-10pm). In Baeza Nueva, **Restaurante El Viejo,** on Av. 17 de Enero just off of Av. de los Quijos, gives extra-special attention to travelers. Glowing wicker lamps illuminate each table in a slightly Polynesian setting. Those three daily staples each cost s/3,500, *churrasco* s/7,500.

■ Near Baeza

VOLCÁN REVENTADOR

As Ecuadorian peaks go, Volcán Reventador is a baby giant. While more dormant volcanoes long ago settled into their habitat grooves, this hybrid of highland and jungle just recently experienced some maturing eruptions in the late 1970s. The burst of magma shook the mountain so hard that it broke open, leaving behind slick beds of hardened lava on the floor of the wet, muddy jungle that line its slopes. The 3562-m green cone rises symmetrically between two mountain ridges, visible from Baeza, some 50km to the southwest.

Like its jungle companion, the isolated Volcán Sumaco, Volcán Reventador guarantees a strenuous, messy climb through thick vegetation and slippery dried lava. Just finding the trailhead is confusing. The climb begins along the Baeza-Lago Agrio road, about two hours northeast of Baeza or four hours west of Lago Agrio by bus, just to the east of the **Río Reventador bridge.** Usually hidden by clouds and nasty weather, the volcano lies to the north of the road. Ask *Señor Conductor* to let you off the bus when you approach the **oil pipeline** that crosses the highway. Walk to the pipeline and follow it left, up to a set of **wooden steps.** After the steps, keep on the path to the left until it reaches a hut; from there, go around to the right. This well-marked trail continues to the **refuge,** about a three-and-a-half-hour walk. The refuge has no mattress, satellite dish, or Internet hook-up. From the refuge, find the **river** and follow it upstream for about a minute; this is another hard path to find. Look for a **faint trail** heading toward the forest. The angry volcano seems eager to keep the **crater** to itself; after all, it takes a six-hour hike on this trail to reach it.

The journey to the summit of Volcán Reventador is a non-technical climb that takes two to four days. Bring lots of water—at least four liters per person. Boots, machetes, and raingear are key, as is a sleeping bag if you plan to spend the night near the top. Despite the fumaroles, it gets frigid up there. The **South American Explorer's Club** in Quito can supply complete, current information about the experiences of members who have scaled the peak. Guillermo Vasquez, from the town of Pampas, 3km from the bridge, has been recommended as a guide. He can reportedly be found near the town's school; ask around.

SAN RAFAEL FALLS

Though less intense, the **Cascadas de San Rafael,** or San Rafael Falls, are another impressive display of natural beauty on the Lago Agrio-Baeza road. The falls dive down a little west of the starting point of the Reventador climb, about one hour east of Baeza or four hours west of Lago Agrio. Bus drivers generally know where to let you off if you ask for *las cascadas;* it should be right near an **INECEL hut** along the highway. The trail descends from there, continuing past an ancient INECEL building that reputedly has been transformed into a lodge. If it's during office hours and there's an attendant on duty, he may charge s/10,000 for you to proceed. The hike to the waterfall cuts through thick jungle. It's some stunning stuff, so you might want to spent the night at the campsite nearby.

Papallacta

It's been exhausting and messy wherever you've been; dirt-smeared and drained, you're ready for Papallacta. The baby-Baños of Ecuador, this steaming sanctuary hides away in a spectacular Andean valley, one hour to the west of Baeza and two hours to the east of Quito. The town itself is nothing to look at, sloping downward from the road and eventually settling in a basin. But Papallacta's only sight isn't meant to be seen; it's meant to be plunged into. The hotels don't have it, but the pools do—that steaming, screaming-ly hot water! When the air is slightly chilled, make for the spiffy, clean, modern-looking **blue pools** in downtown Papallacta. The water is piping hot, a virtually orgasmic experince for the mountain-weary body (admission s/5,000). Changing stalls and mandatory hot-water showers provided (open Tues.-Sun. 8am-5pm). But the genuine hot springs, the **Termas de Papallacta,** are a challenging hike on a dirt road that ramps off the Quito highway, 100m west of the Hotel Quito. Tucked in an amazing corridor of mountains, these brown-water *piscinas* simmer in a resort-like atmosphere that caters to vacationing *quiteños.* A sign and restaurant mark the beginning of this sweat-inducing 1km trek to the hot springs. These pools are the town's secret, and most of the clientele are native Ecuadorians in-the-know. The four or five brownish pools inside line up next to a rocky stream that also steams with hot water. Compared to the blue pools, this place has fancier facilities, a more isolated and natural location, and higher prices (open daily 5am-10pm; admission Mon.-Sat. s/8,000, Sun. s/6,000).

The collection of buildings that makes up Papallacta includes a **police station,** a gray-and-blue checkpoint on the road to the bottom of the slope. The **centro de salud** is down near the blue pool area, but the best idea is to stay healthy in Papallacta. Papallacta has no post office, nor telephones. Getting to and from Papallacta means hopping a bus in the right direction between Baeza and Quito. The waiting is the hardest part. Ride the roof if you get the chance.

The **Hotel Quito,** along the highway, is budget choice *numero uno* if you get Papallacta-ed for the night. Its stark, cozy rooms aren't the kind of thing you'd want every night, but they're a relief in light of the situation, like candles during a power outage. A handful have breathtaking views. The acceptable, cheap rooms cost s/8,000; choicer rooms are s/15,000. If Quito is full, head west up the highway a couple minutes to **Residencial El Viajero.** At the *Termas de Papallacta* hot springs back behind the mountains, **Hostal de Montaña** charges higher prices for their *cabañas'* proximity to the springs. Hopefully they have higher quality as well, because they get away with s/50,000 per person per night. True to their jungle roots, the Papallactan wildlife feeds by the water. The blue pool in town gravitates towards the **snack bar** vein, with a food hut that'll trade you a s/1,000 for a Coke (fried trout special runs s/5,000). Up at the real pools, the **Café Canela** impresses with well-ironed tablecloths and a gourmet poolside feast. (American breakfast s/10,000, rump roast with baked potatoes and seasoned vegetables s/12,000.) Outside of the pools, the **Restaurante La Quiteñita,** under the Hotel Quito, is plain old *típica. Desayuno, almuerzo,* and *merienda* all go for s/5,000.

THE SOUTHERN ORIENTE

In the shadow of the sharply-sloping eastern edge of the southern Andes, leafy palms hide the hot, humid clusters of flat concrete buildings and tin shacks that make up the tiny and hauntingly exotic villages of the Southern Oriente. As Ecuador's frontier has moved eastward, many of these towns have only recently popped up—and utility has governed their architecture. One road connects all: the single treacherous "highway" of the Southern Oriente traverses the land at approximately 1000m of elevation, linking the working-class jungle communities with the rural charm that embeds them. These cities and hamlets dot a region blessed by thousands of square miles of lush primary tropical rain forest and all the glorious wildlife that goes with it. Unfortunately, the land has been equally "blessed" with a swath of gold deposits which have in recent years brought on the destruction of some of its most precious natural treasures. The struggle between miners and conservationists takes on its bleakest incarnations on the battlefields of Parque Nacional Podocarpus and the mining areas near Zamora and Nambija. Meanwhile, a more international conflict broods in the nearby borderland of eastern Morona-Santiago, where a 50-year-old border dispute culminated in a 1995 skirmish between Ecuador and Perú. The turmoil cost Ecuador few lives but much pride (Macas, the province's capital, was evacuated two years ago during an especially violent chapter in this conflict).

Meanwhile, connected to the rest of civilization by little more than deep bush trails, the Shuar Indians, former headhunters and headshrinkers, must now content themselves merely to keep alive a liminal form of their distinct version of polytheistic animism. The Shuar still live in traditional log huts deep in the jungle, with little more than bamboo reeds for shelter and dugout canoes for locomotion. Lightweight aircraft carry some of the Southern Oriente's few tourists into Shuar villages from Macas and Sucúa for a glimpse at lives that have remained essentially untouched by technology for the past 500 years. But it does not take an airplane for the observant *gringo* to glimpse the essence of this hinterland. A good look at the rural highway-stop towns of Gualaquiza, Limón, and Mendez will reveal a lifestyle which is perhaps most foreign to the tourist for its friendliness to the outsiders they see so few of: you will not walk past a rugged local without being stared at, but then greeted politely—and for God's sake, say "Buenos días" back! If you're willing to endure grueling bus trips over roads more rugged than any terrain on 4WD commercials, in the same bus you once rode to grade school in the 70s, a more penetrating—if lonely—glimpse into the land and people of Ecuador cannot be found.

Be aware that during the rainy season, from June to August or so, landslides and their ilk torment the narrow, bumpy, and unpaved roads of the southern Oriente. Don't plan too tight a schedule for yourself; buses are sometimes forced to stop and let their passengers walk a few kilometers to firmer ground. In rare cases, you may end up stranded in a town for a couple days, waiting out torrential rains.

Gualaquiza

Hibernating deep in the heart of the southern Oriente, the forgotten jungle town of Gualaquiza lies buried in a den of dramatic tropical hills. Curious stares from the villagers bombard the occasional deviant tourists; surprised at the sight of strangers, the locals eagerly wonder who has distubed their slumber. The most common tourist route through the southern Oriente, from Cuenca down the eastern slopes of the Andes and then up to Macas, doesn't go through Gualaquiza. In fact, this remote and fascinating town has no true tourist sights. Die-hard off-road travelers are attracted to Gualaquiza's remoteness; the town itself and its stunning setting are an added bonus. Watch the operations of daily life go by with an interested outsider's eye. Nearby, the surrounding mountains offer some interesting daytrips to a **Salesian mission** in Bomboiza, forgotten **Inca ruins** in Aguacate, and **caves** at Nuevo Tarqui.

Orientation and Practical Information It doesn't take long to get a feel for Gualaquiza; within an hour or so, you'll probably know its layout by heart. The lovely **main plaza** houses a fountain and a church. **Av. 24 de Mayo** and **Domingo Comín** run the length of the park on either side, and **Pesantez** and **Ciudad de Cuenca** run its width. Parallel to Comín are García Moreno, Alfaro, and Atahualpa.

Make calls from **EMETEL,** on Ciudad de Cuenca and García Moreno, one block from the park (open Mon.-Sat. 8-11am, 2-5pm, and 7-9pm, Sun. and holidays 8-11am and 7-8pm). **Buses** leave from the **terminal terrestre,** on Pesantez and Alfaro, two blocks from the plaza. Some run north to **Macas** (6am, 6pm, 8hr., s/15,200), stopping in **Limón** (4hr., s/10,200), **Méndez** (6hr., 2/11,200), and **Sucúa** (7hr., s/13,200). Two buses go directly to **Cuenca** (9, 9:30pm, 8hr., s/14,700). Buses heading south go to **Loja** (2:30, 3, 4, 6am, 12:15, 9:15, 10pm, 7hr., s/11,200) via **El Pangui** (1½hr., s/2,000), **Yantzaza** (3½hr., s/5,000), and **Zamora** (5hr., s/7,000). Buses also service **Chuchumbletze** (midnight, 6pm) and **Valle del Quimi** (5am, noon). Be forewarned that the bumpy Gualaquiza-Limón ride travels over roads that are horrible in some stretches—not for the weak-stomached. The Oriente version of **taxis**, 4WD pickup trucks, make slightly smoother and much faster trips to **Limón** (about s/120,000), **Macas** (about s/200,000), and just about any other destination. Gualaquiza's pharmacy, **Farmacia Central** (tel. 780-203), is on Pesantez and Alfaro (open Mon.-Sat. 8am-10pm, Sun. 8am-1pm). The **hospital** is up toward the church, near the school (open Mon.-Fri. 8am-noon and 2-6pm). The **police** (tel. 780-101) are located on Pesantez and Alfaro. Only extremely unimportant parcels should be mailed from the **post office** (tel. 780-119), on Ciudad de Cuenca and Atahualpa, five blocks away from the park (open Mon.-Fri. 8am-noon and 2-5pm). **Jota Be Travel,** Av. 24 de Mayo 08-08 (tel. 780-236), at the main plaza, also sends letters and packages to the United States (letters s/4,000, packages s/14,000 per pound. Open Mon.-Sat. 9am-11:30am and 2-5:30pm, Sun. 10am-2pm.) The **telephone code** is 07.

Accommodations and Food Just so that you don't get your hopes up, accept it now: no hotel in Gualaquiza has hot water. (Take a cold shower, deal with it, and move on.) On Pesantez and García Moreno, **Hotel Turismo** (tel. 780-277), is the best-equipped hotel in town. Revel in the rotating fans and private bathrooms, which even include those elusive toilet seats. Somewhat clean but basic rooms have a mysterious, slightly unpleasant odor. (S/8,000 per person, with bath s/10,000.) **Residencial Amazonas** has cleaner, airy rooms, but suffers from communal bathrooms with dirty showers and a toilet seat deficiency. Unfortunately, the spartan white-walled rooms lack fans. Singles s/6,000.

At mealtime, head to **Cabaña Los Helechos,** at Av. 12 de Febrero and Orellana. There's probably not much demand for exotic circus animals in the middle of the jungle, because this bizarre circular *cabaña* houses a good, cheap eatery instead. Serves *almuerzo* or *merienda* (s/3,500), with fine views of the bus station across the street (open daily 8am-10pm). Also near the station, the **Bar/Restaurant Oro Verde** offers similar meals, similar views, and similar prices (around s/4,000). When it comes to ambience, you can't lose; choose a pleasant, polished room or outside on the sidewalk (open daily 8am-10pm). The **Restaurant Sabor Latina** (tel. 780-113), serves traditional Latin food in the same building as Hotel Turismo. Locals laud the *almuerzos* and *meriendas* (s/3,500), as well as *a la carta* entrees (open daily 5am-11pm).

Sights and Entertainment Admire Gualaquiza, but don't expect it to satisfy much more than your eyes. Moderately interesting both culturally and architecturally, the local **church** stands one block up from the main plaza. Diversions by night are sparse unless there's a street *fiesta* or school celebration in town. Overlooking the plaza next to the school, the **Teatro 16 de Agosto** houses occasional movies and events. **Memo's Bar/Cafeteria,** on Pesantez at the plaza, is a late-night hangout where the food and beer (s/3,000) glow in the aura of a huge 30-inch Sony TV, which blazes nightly until 10pm or 11pm.

But why sit around inside when there are nearby hills to be explored? Don't get lost in the **deserted caves of Nuevo Tarqui,** 15km west of Gualaquiza. A taxi or *camioneta* can take you here from Gualaquiza, or you can lace up your walking shoes and make the long jaunt by foot. Ask around Gualaquiza for more specifics about exploring the caves. Visit the **Salesian Mission of Bomboiza,** a bastion of New World civilization that holds its own against the jungle. This easy-to-reach daytrip lies just off the highway to Zamora. Buses traveling this road can drop you off and often stop to pick passengers up. Become the new Indiana Jones for a day with one last crusade, the relatively unexplored **Inca ruins** in the nearby town of **Aguacate.** A guided cab tour costs s/50,000, but that's not how Indy would explore the ruins. Ask in town for directions if you want to make the more active half-day walk.

The Road from Gualaquiza to Macas

LIMÓN

Just north of where the road from Cuenca comes in from the west, Limón serves as a common pit-stop for industrial trucks and buses running from Cuenca, Loja, and Zamora north to Macas. Also known as General Leonidas Plaza Gutiérrez, this tiny town lies on the southern Oriente's single so-called highway, explaining why its muddy streets are strewn with hardware and rife with auto-body shops. Removed from the typical tourist track, the sleepy jungle town doesn't have much in the way of typical beauty, but the settlements down by the river offer some intriguing sights. Tiny, tin-roofed houses stick up through the palms and tropical flowers, and precariously balconied houses pile over the river's bank. The houses along **Calle Quito,** the town's main street, are a creative mix of barn wood and cement.

The two streets of any importance in Limón, **Quito** and **Av 28 de Mayo,** both run parallel to the river. **Av. 12 de Diciembre** and the **highway** are across the river. **EMETEL** (tel. 770-104), on Quito next to Hotel Turismo, uncharacteristically will allow calling-card or collect calls (open Mon.-Sat. 8-11am, 2-4pm, and 8-9pm, Sun. and holidays 8-11am). To get to the **bus stop** from *el centro,* cross the bridge across from the long wooden building and the Parque Central. Turn right on the other side of the river, and continue five minutes down the road until you reach the restaurants and police station. Buses rumble by daily, heading north to **Méndez, Sucúa,** and **Macas.** Coming north from Gualaquiza, buses pass by most frequently from 10am-1pm; coming east from Cuenca, they pass from 8pm-1am. Buses also head south to **Gualaquiza, Zamora,** and **Loja** (similar hours) and west to **Cuenca** (more overnight buses). Back in town, the small but pleasant **library** on Av. Quito has a TV and a small scale model of the Parque Central across the street (open Mon.-Fri. 8am-noon and 2-5:30pm). **Farmacia Limón** is on Av. 28 de Mayo (open daily 7am-9pm). The **hospital** (tel. 770-738), to the right of the main bridge if you're facing the river, can give 24-hour treatment, but only in emergencies (open Mon.-Fri. 7:30am-12:30pm and 1:30-4:30pm).Across the river, the **police** are occasionally found in a guardhouse building on Av. 12 de Diciembre, near the highway next to the bus stop. The **post office** is in a family's house on Av. 12 de Diciembre (open Mon.-Fri. 7am-noon and 2-6pm, Sat.-Sun. when the family is home).

Perhaps the one hotel in Limón that makes for a pleasant night's stay, the **Residencial Limón,** on Quito, surrounds its garden courtyard with spotless rooms sporting soft, spacious beds. Although they usually perform admirably, shared bathrooms sometimes lose running water (and the water's never hot). More basic hotels in town include the **Dominguez** across the street and the **Santo Domingo** down the street, a much less comfortable, s/6,000 per person package. An attractive restaurant with well-washed wooden tables, **Chifa Rincón de Taiwan** is on Quito, across from Hotel Turismo. Enjoy complex Chinese dishes like *pollo saltado a cinco sabores* (chicken sauteed in five flavors, s/7,500; open daily 11am-9pm). The many *almuerzo/merienda* pit-stops along Quito and Av. 28 de Mayo may be cheaper, but their sanitary standards aren't quite as reliable. **Catilio's Restaurant,** on Quito, whips up *almuerzos* and *meriendas* (each s/4,000), as well as *a la carta* dishes like *trucha* (trout, s/7,000) or *chaulafan* (fried rice, s/7,000). (Open Mon.-Fri. 8am-9pm, Sat. 9am-4pm, Sun. 9am-2pm.)

MÉNDEZ

Méndez, another rarely-visited pit-stop along the highway, is even more *tranquilo* than its southern neighbor Limón, worthy of a visit only if you're charmed by a place that hasn't seen a tourist in months. Here is an opportunity to see life in a part of Ecuador where catering to *gringos* is as foreign a concept as a hot shower. As in the rest of the Oriente, the roads that tenuously connect Méndez with the rest of the world probably couldn't be much worse. Hard on the tailbone any time of year, they sometimes completely wash out during the rainiest months (June through August). The view from behind the bus station captures Méndez perfectly: an industrial village amid tropical jungle hills, drinking from the banks of the muddy **Río Paute.** Legend has it that a treasure of gold lies in a cave in the nearby hills, but as luck would have it, access is impossible due to swarms of bats.

Everything of interest in this town predictably centers around the typically verdant, picturesque **main plaza.** Adjacent to the plaza on **Calle Cuenca,** the church is modern and strikingly angular. One major road, **Domingo Comín,** is on the left if you're standing in the park facing the church. **Guayaquil** runs parallel to Comín on the other side of the plaza, and the river runs parallel to Cuenca two blocks away. **Banco Nacional de Fomento** is on Cuenca, one block from the plaza. The **bus station** is at the **Turismo Oriental** office (tel. 760-126), at Cuenca and Guayaquil, on the corner of the plaza. Buses head north to **Macas** (5:30, 8pm, 3hr., s/8,000) via **Sucúa** (2 hr., s/5,000), and south to **Cuenca** (1:30, 9:30pm, 6hr., s/13,500) via **Limón** (2 hr., s/5,000). If buses aren't running, **camionetas** can make the same journeys (about s/70,000). **Farmacia Botica Méndez** is on the same corner of the plaza as the bus station (open daily 8am-6pm). All municipal offices, such as the **post office** and **library,** are on Comín at the plaza. In general, it is worthwhile to take care of things in the more "metropolitan" towns of Sucúa and Macas.

If you decide to spend the night in town, **Hostal Los Cerbos** (tel. 770-133), is a first-rate choice. Chock full of homey atmosphere, rooms have clean sheets and ceiling fans to boot. Shared, cold-water bathrooms are as spotless and painless as that deadly combination can get. The upstairs terrace's lovely view of Méndez makes a perfect place to while away those lonely southern Oriente afternoons. S/15,000 per person. More primitive pensions line Cuenca, a block or less from the plaza. Eating in Méndez is easy (chew, savor, swallow ... chew, savor, swallow), but don't expect the savoring to be the highlight of the experience. **Turismo Oriental** is a spanking clean exception, as well as a bus stop and an office. You wouldn't know its non-culinary alter-egos from the delicious *almuerzos* and *meriendas* (each s/6000), or their *pollo frito* (s/8000). Color TV and ice-cold beverages also help brighten any traveler's day (open daily 7am-10pm).

SUCÚA

One last pit-stop on the infamous southern Oriente highway, the typically placid Sucúa, about an hour south of Macas, is distinguished as the seat of the Shuar Federation and home to a Shuar cultural center. An aboriginal group of the central and southern Oriente, the **Shuar** lived in relative isolation until the beginning of this century. Long considered a "savage" people because of their head-hunting and head-shrinking habits, the Shuar no longer practice these legendary acts. As missionaries, colonists, and oil companies moved in on their territory, the Shuar were forced to make the abrupt transition to life in the modern world, or risk losing their land and their culture all together. As a result, Sucúa does not manifest as many signs of "traditional culture" as one might expect of an indigenous capital. A visit to the cultural center provides a better understanding of the Shuar than a simple walk through its streets ever could. For more information on the Shuar and their Federation, see Indigenous Identity, p. 47.

Sucúa's main street is **Domingo Comín,** and the **Parque Central** lies along it. Other buildings of importance, as well as most of Sucúa's accommodations, lie further up along Comín. Across the park and parallel to Comín runs **Carbajal.** Most **buses** leave from Comín, near the Shuar Federation, about four blocks from the main plaza, running to **Macas** (every ½hr., 1hr.) and, slightly less frequently, to Oriente towns to the south. Sucúa's **terminal terrestre,** a 10-minute walk down Comín (take a right at the fork), seems to get little action, since most buses go through town. Buses go to **Morona** (10am, 5pm, 6:45pm, 8hr.), **Gualaquiza** (1:45, 4:30pm, 8hr.), **Cuenca** (8 per day, 6:30am-10:30pm, 8hr.), and **Puyo** (8, 9, 10, and 11pm, 5hr.) sometimes continuing to **Ambato** and/or **Quito**, depending on the status of the Puyo-Baños road.

■ Macas

As the cosmopolitan capital of the rural Morona-Santiago province, Macas outpaces other booming townships in the southern Oriente, which isn't saying much. But this urban enclave loses some of its quaint beauty with its bustle, and travelers seeking a taste of rural Ecuador might consider spending their time in pristine Gualaquiza, tribal Sucúa, or fascinating Limón as well. Though Macas is one of Ecuador's premier jungle tour launch-pads, boasting large stretches of primary forest, the cavernous **Cueva de los Tayos,** and a number of nearby traditional **Shuar villages.** With visions of jungle-resort grandeur, Macas makes a concerted effort to become a tourist destination in itself. Lined with small CETUR-sponsored information booths, the town's main street, Domingo Comín, aspires to become a *paseo turístico,* and Macas counts a huge bus terminal, a number of tour operators, and even a semi-high-rise hotel among its worldly assets. Macas's struggle epitomizes that of the entire southern Oriente—to attract genuinely interested travelers without contaminating the city's tranquility.

ORIENTATION

The **airstrip** forms the western boundary of the town. Macas's main north-south road, **Amazonas,** runs one block east of it. The **terminal terrestre** is just west of Amazonas, on the east-west **Av. 10 de Agosto.** North of Av. 10 de Agosto run the east-west streets **Comín, Bolívar, Sucre,** and **Cuenca,** in that order. East of Amazonas run the north-south **Soastri, Av. 24 de Mayo,** and **Av. 9 de Octubre.** The **main plaza** is between Comín and Bolívar, east of Av. 24 de Mayo, but the real center of activity is actually around the intersection of Amazonas and Comín.

PRACTICAL INFORMATION

Tourist Information: There is no CETUR in town, but there may be one soon. **ETSA** (tel. 700-550), in the bus terminal, and **Ikiaam** (tel. 700-457), across the street, can supply tourist information (open sporadic hours). They also arrange tours (see Jungle Tours from Macas, p. 239). **INEFAN,** on Av. 29 de Mayo, has information on Parque Nacional Sangay and other nationally protected areas.

Telephone: EMETEL (tel. 700-104), on Av. 24 de Mayo between Cuenca and Sucre. Free collect, calling-card calls (open daily 8am-noon, 2-6pm, and 7-10pm).

Airport: TAME (tel. 700-162), at the airport on Amazonas and Cuenca, has flights to and from **Quito** (Mon., Wed., Fri., from Quito at 2pm, from Macas at 3:05pm, 30min., US$50 for foreigners). Open Mon.-Fri. 8am-noon and 2-4pm.

Buses: Macas's **terminal terrestre,** on Av. 10 de Agosto just west of Amazonas, is large and in charge. Various companies go to **Cuenca** (10am, 5:30, 6:30, 8, 8:30, 9, 10pm, 10hr.), **Morona** (7, 9am, 4, 5:45, 7:30pm, 9hr.), **Gualaquiza** (12:45, 2, 3:30, 5pm, 9hr.), and **Puyo** (every hr., 7am-6pm, 6hr). **San Francisco Tours** sends high-profile, long-distance buses to faraway places like **Quito** (4 per day, 3am-11pm, 18hr.) and **Guayaquil** (6pm, 21hr.) via **Riobamba** (14hr.). The quickest route to Quito, via the Puyo-Baños road, is presently under construction and only open Mon. Buses travel via Tena/Baeza all other days.

Taxis: Coop. Taxis 24 de Mayo (tel. 700-056). Cabs hang out all over Macas.

Pharmacy: Farmacia Central (tel. 700-388), on Amazonas near Comín (open daily 8am-10pm).

Hospital: (emergency tel. 700-904). Otherwise, there are a number of private **medical clinics** on Amazonas near Comín.

Police: emergency tel. 700-101.

Post Office: (tel. 700-060), on Av. 9 de Octubre near Comín, 1 block from the central plaza. Relatively reliable *Lista de Correos;* fax service to the U.S. (s/22,200 per page), Europe (s/27,400 per page), and within Ecuador (s/3,000 per page). Open Mon.-Fri. 7:30am-6pm.

Telephone Code: 07.

ACCOMMODATIONS

Hotel Splendit (tel. 700-734), at Soasti, with "hotel" entrance on Comín, "residencial" entrance on Bolívar. "Hotel" sports a range of brand-new rooms, all with private bath, all splendit-ly clean and comfortable. They may have spelled the name wrong, but they know what it means. Hot water, color TV, and freshly-painted everything (s/25,000 per person). Slightly older rooms run s/15,000 per person, with hot water s/20,000. "Residencial" has aging rooms with shared bathrooms that must be scrubbed before they can be used (s/8000 per person).

Hotel La Orquidea (tel. 700-970), on Sucre at Av. 9 de Octubre. Crisp, clean rooms that entice with their value and simplicity. They're not orchidaceous, but quality doesn't need to make a fuss. Good private bathrooms, always a plus. S/14,000 per person, with hot water s/16,000.

Hostal Esmerelda (tel. 700-160), on Cuenca and Soasti, 1 block from the airport. Great values seem to be a trend here. Rooms come fully-equipped with a nice TV, hot (electric) water in private baths, and immaculate maintenance. Modern building has a good café downstairs. S/12,000 per person, with hot water s/16,000.

Hotel Peñon del Oriente, at Amazonas and Comín. As the tallest building in Mácas, it's a town landmark. Rooms aren't the best values in town, but the rest is heavenly.

Rooms are physically higher (thus closer to heaven), and residents benefit from their proximity to the Christian radio station that broadcasts from the roof. Comfortable beds, picture windows with good views on higher floors, black-and-white TVs, and plenty of religious propaganda, from booklets strewn across the room to biblical passages plastered on the walls. Singles s/21,000; doubles s/40,000. Color TV s/30,000 extra.

FOOD

Macas's restaurants, while plentiful compared to the rest of the southern Oriente, are sparse at best compared to most provincial capitals. A fine seafood or Cuban meal provides a welcome break after weeks of *almuerzos.* The best deals in town are at the simple lunch stands in and across from the market, near Hotel Peñon del Oriente, where s/2,000 *almuerzos* are the norm. But while pesky flies may spoil the mood at the market, a couple of cleaner places on nearby streets are nearly as cheap.

Bar-Restaurant La Randimpa (tel. 700-696), at Bolívar and Av. 24 de Mayo. Cool, any way you cut it. Cuban music and food (including Cuban pizza, s/6,000) are as mesmerizing as the modern art on the walls. Sit at a tasteful wood table and be chilled by the breeze *and* the atmosphere (open daily 8am-10pm).

Café El Jardín, on Amazonas across from Hotel Peñon del Oriente. Delicious *almuerzos* (s/5,000) in a non-*comedor* setting, classier than other cheap cafés in both taste and ambience. Swanky *a la carta* options, like *pollo al vino* (chicken made with wine, s/7,500) and *lomo fino* (steak, s/8,500). *Meriendas* (s/5,000) are wonderfully worth it (open Mon.-Sat. 7:15am-10pm, Sun. 8am-3pm).

Adonde Ivan (tel. 700-826), Amazonas and Av. 10 de Agosto. Where did they go? Probably to this delightful thatched-roof bamboo hut. Opened in 1996, this restaurant is *very* tropical and *very* different. Seafood eaters sit at wooden picnic tables, cheered on by 2 huge squawking parrots. *Almuerzo* (s/5,000), *ceviche de camarones* (s/8,000). Open Sun.-Fri. 8am-5pm. *Peña* on Friday nights.

JUNGLE TOURS FROM MACAS

Macas is the most developed and convenient town in the southern Oriente from which to begin a jungle jaunt. While the northern Oriente sees more tourists, the jungle east of Macas provides some unique opportunities. As in the north, hundreds of thousands of hectares remain undeveloped and large tracts of primary forest still grow intact. Some of the more staggeringly beautiful areas remain untouched with the help of government protection, like Parque Nacional Sangay's *"zona baja,"* the ecological reserve near Santa Rosa, and the caves at Cueva de los Tayos.

This area is also home to Ecuador's second-most-populous indigenous group, **the Shuar.** While many Shuar around Macas and Sucúa have changed their traditional ways, more isolated communities in the jungle east of Macas continue to live more or less as they have for centuries. Some tours from Macas visit these isolated Shuar communities. While the Shuar have not expressed as much distaste for this kind of tourism as the Huaorani and other *indígenas* to the north, the visits cannot help but affect their traditional way of life. If you do decide to visit one of these communities, prepare yourself for **culture shock.** The Shuar are usually friendly, welcoming hosts, but accommodations are basic to say the least, and food is traditional. That means rice, and lots of it. You may even be offered **Chicha de Yuca,** an alcoholic drink made from the yucca plant, fermented with the saliva of an older Shuar woman. Your hosts will have precious little experience with the amenities of modern life, something you could either find refreshing or a bit unsettling. Visitors must also be sensitive to issues of Shuar religion and customs. All but the most isolated parts of Ecuador have been proselytized by Catholics trying to integrate indigenous polytheism with the New Testament. In these communities, beliefs about **shamanism** and spirits still thrive; you may even witness the **rites of the war spirit, Aratum** or receive a **ritual purification** at the **Cascadas Sagradas** (Sacred Waterfalls).

For a less people-oriented experience, try a trip to the **zona baja** at **Parque Nacional Sangay** (Macas entrance). One of the most jungle intensive excursions around, its trails climb hills and weave through primary tropical rainforest. At one point in the journey, cable cars cross the otherwise impassable Ríos Sangay and Upano. At least one trail actually traverses the park, crossing over into the *zona alta* in the highlands near Baños and Riobamba (see Parque Nacional Sangay, p. 119). If all you're dreaming of is jungle, jungle, and nothing but jungle, a trip to Sangay could be the ideal excursion. While some praise this tour as fascinating, others warn that after a few days of nothing but green, and lots of it, the park can get a bit monotonous. Some tour companies also make excursions to an **ecological reserve** near the town of Santa Rosa, about two hours from Macas. Jungle adventurers sleep in cabins and explore by horseback and canoe, with stints of tubing and swimming.

Another commonly visited sight in the jungles near Macas, **Cueva de los Tayos** is an enormous (85m deep), pitch-black cave that can only be explored with a guide. Its name comes from the large colonies of oilbirds *(tayos)* that reside in the cavern. These unusual birds have picked up some telltale habits from their neighbors in the darkness, the bats. Not only are they nocturnal fruit-eaters, they also use sonar to stake out their location in the pitch-black environs. The drillers don't extract all the underground oil in the Oriente; these *tayos* used to be captured and boiled for the oil harvested from their fat-rich flesh. Many tours leaving from Macas pencil Cueva de los Tayos onto their itineraries, but it can also be explored from **Morona,** a village on the Peruvian border with neither restaurants nor accommodations.

The many **tour companies** leading trips from Macas offer a wide variety of packages that include one or more of the above attractions. Most companies offer pre-set itineraries, but these can often be customized to accommodate individual interests. The price per-person per-day varies depending on the duration of the tour and the number of people in the group. Another important consideration is the type of transportation used. Some companies use small (and sometimes nausea-inducing) planes to conveniently and quickly transport people to remote parts of the jungle. Others tours include horseback rides, canoe trips, and varying amounts of walking. Before you leave, make sure the mode of transport suits your needs and desires.

Ikiaam (tel. 700-457), across from the *terminal terrestre.* Run by friendly, knowledgeable Shuar tour guides (Ikiaam means "jungle" in Shuar). Trips usually last 1-6 days, but can be longer. A popular 4- to 6-day trip begins with a flight to the indigenous community of Yaupi, followed by 2 days of **rainforest trekking** around the Wompak lake and the Río Wampisa, a **horseback ride** to the Shuar community of Tsawantas, a canoe trip with fishing, and a visit to the **Cueva de los Tayos** (US$60 per person for 2 people, US$45-50 per person for 3-4). Other 2- to 4-day trips visit Parque National Sangay and the ecological reserve near Santa Rosa (about US$35 per person). Daytrips include jungle walks and introductions to Shuar culture (around US$20 per person). Meals and equipment included on all tours. Office hours are sporadic, since the guides may be out touring.

ETSA (tel. 700-550), in a building that is part of the *terminal terrestre.* Associated with Huasca Agencia de Viajes, this company is also run by Shuar Indians. Offers similar trips to Ikiaam's at similar prices (see above), including canoe trips, horseback rides, piranha fishing, and visits to Shuar villages. ETSA's Marcelo Churunio Saryo also offers trips to the Cuevas de los Tayos only. Longer excursions possible to the most rural and geologically-endowed parts of Ecuador, near the disputed border with Perú (a suspiciously low US$15 per person per day).

The Galápagos Islands

The Galápagos Islands lie nearly 1000km off the Ecuadorian coast, but instead of simply crossing the Pacific Ocean to reach these 19 islands and 42 smaller islets, visitors penetrate an entirely new world, where everything you've come to expect on the mainland metamorphosizes. As if a smoky screen were lifted from your eyes, colors suddenly illuminate—from the verdant scalesia forests to the luminous turquoise waters and even the lustrous black volcanic rocks lining the shores of some of the islands. The hierarchy of people and animals disintergrates as spunky sea lions swim alongside snorkelers and intrepid iguanas nap on tourists' shoulders. Climb majestic volcanoes rising up out of shark-infested bays; pet giant Galápagos tortoises who live the placid life in wildlife reserves like the Charles Darwin Research Station. When most people think of the Galápagos, Darwin jumps to mind, but there are more birds in the Galápagos than just his finches. Frigatebirds, Galápagos penguins, and three comically-colored species of boobies are only a hint of the wildlife that has spawned in this breeding ground of common and endemic biodiversity.

When to Go

You can have a rewarding experience in the Galápagos any time of the year, but climate-wise, the Galápagos only have two seasons. Warm ocean currents cause hot, rainy weather from January through April, while the rest of the year is relatively dry and a bit cooler. Neither season is completely ideal—during the rainy months, the ocean water refreshes at a comfortable 75°F (24°C), but heavy rain showers often disturb the tropical tranquility. Likewise, while rain may fall rarely during the dry months, the sky is often overcast, the water a chilly 70°F (21°C) or lower, and the waves choppy from sporadic winds. The ideal visiting months, therefore, are between seasons—March and April, when rain begin falling less frequently, and November and December, as the climate warms up.

Visitors, however, do not always pay attention to these Galápagos seasons. Tourist traffic is heaviest during vacation times—Easter week in the spring, June through August, and December and January. In fact, August and December can get so busy that finding a boat becomes challenging, bargaining is nearly impossible, prices rise significantly, and flights need to be booked well in advance. October is not a busy month, but precisely for this reason many boat owners choose to make repairs then, so many vehicles are out of commission.

Useful Organizations

Charles Darwin Foundation, Inc., 100 N. Washington St., Ste. 311, Falls Church, VA 22046, USA, and P.O. Box 17-01-3891, Quito, Ecuador. A non-profit membership organization dedicated to promoting conservation, education, and scientific research in the Galápagos Islands. They publish a newsletter, the *Galápagos Bulletin,* 3 times a year.

Corporación Ecuatoriana de Turismo (CETUR), Eloy Alfaro 1214 y Pasaje Carlos Tobar, Quito (tel. (02) 229-330; fax 507-560). The government-run tourist information agency, with valuable facts about hotels and transportation. Provides maps and info as specific as animal mating seasons and the best sites to spot various types of wildlife. There are CETUR offices in all major cities in Ecuador, including one on Av. Charles Darwin in Puerto Ayora (tel. 526-179).

South American Explorers Club (SAEC), 126 Indian Creek Rd., Ithaca, NY 14850 (tel. (607) 277-0488; fax 277-6122; e-mail explorer@sameplo.org; http://www.samexplo.org), and Jorge Washington 311 y L. Plaza, Apartado 17-21-431, Eloy Alfaro, Quito, Ecuador (tel./fax (02) 225-228; e-mail explorer@saec.org.ec). A non-profit organization with extensive information of all kinds on traveling, work-

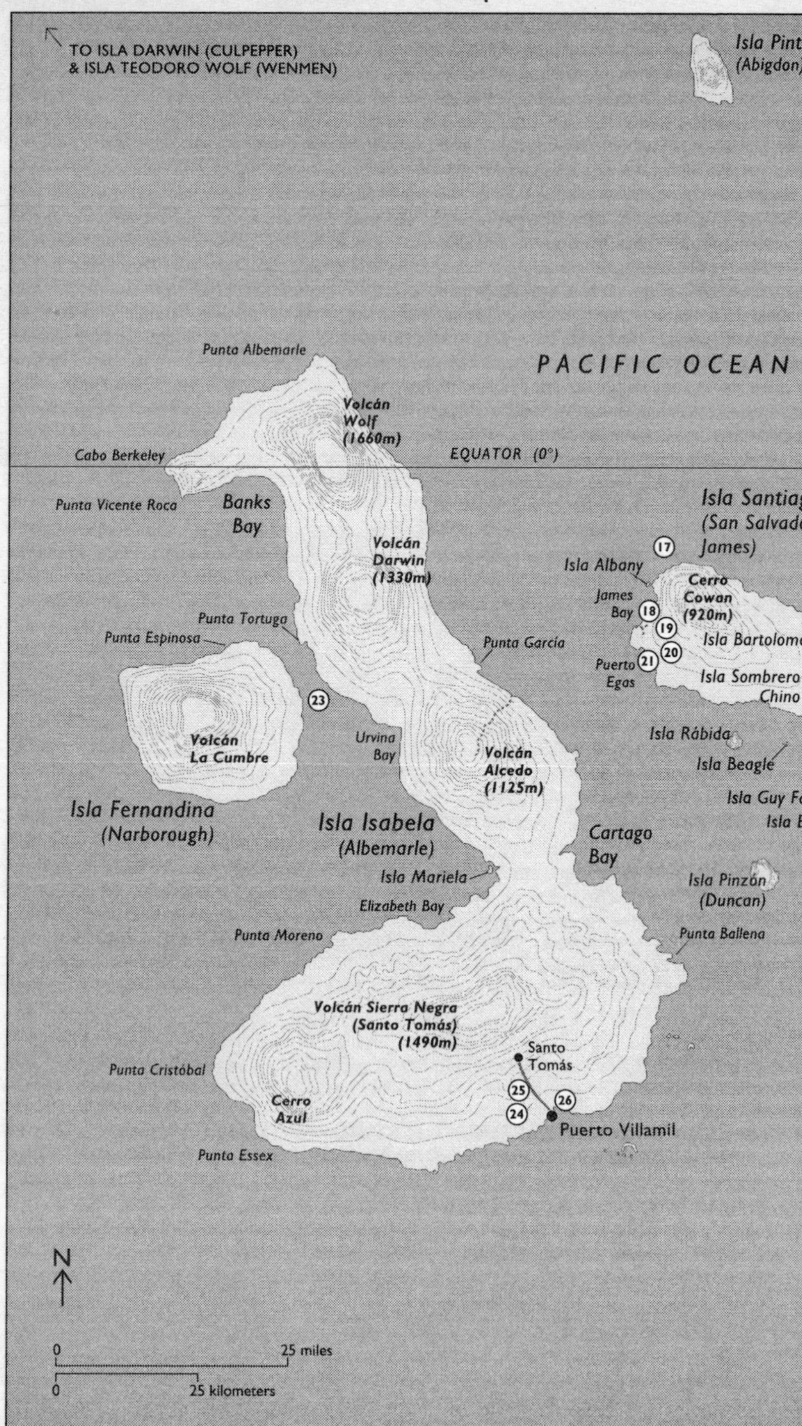
TO ISLA DARWIN (CULPEPPER)
& ISLA TEODORO WOLF (WENMEN)
Isla Pinta
(Abigdon)
PACIFIC OCEAN
Punta Albemarle
Volcán
Wolf
(1660m)
Cabo Berkeley
EQUATOR (0°)
Punta Vicente Roca
Banks
Bay
Volcán
Darwin
(1330m)
Isla Santiag
(San Salvador
James)
Isla Albany
James
Bay
Cerro
Cowan
(920m)
Puerto
Egas
Isla Bartolomé
Isla Sombrero
Chino
Punta Tortuga
Punta Espinosa
Punta García
Volcán
La Cumbre
Urvina
Bay
Volcán
Alcedo
(1125m)
Isla Rábida
Isla Beagle
Isla Guy Fav
Isla Fernandina
(Narborough)
Isla Isabela
(Albemarle)
Cartago
Bay
Isla Mariela
Isla Pinzón
(Duncan)
Elizabeth Bay
Punta Moreno
Punta Ballena
Volcán Sierra Negra
(Santo Tomás)
(1490m)
Santo
Tomás
Punta Cristóbal
Cerro
Azul
Puerto Villamil
Punta Essex
N
0
25 miles
0
25 kilometers

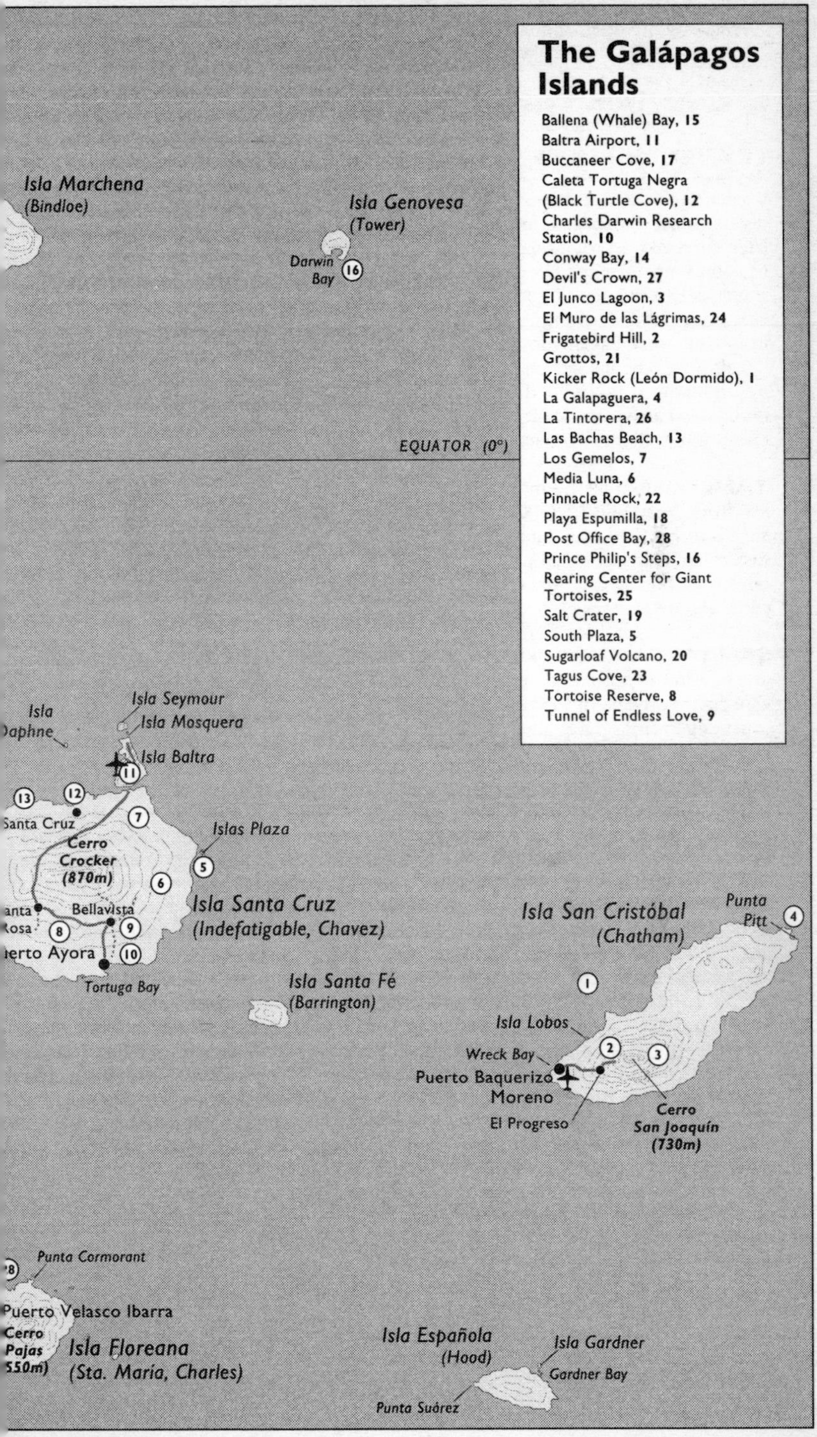

The Galápagos Islands

Ballena (Whale) Bay, **15**
Baltra Airport, **11**
Buccaneer Cove, **17**
Caleta Tortuga Negra (Black Turtle Cove), **12**
Charles Darwin Research Station, **10**
Conway Bay, **14**
Devil's Crown, **27**
El Junco Lagoon, **3**
El Muro de las Lágrimas, **24**
Frigatebird Hill, **2**
Grottos, **21**
Kicker Rock (León Dormido), **1**
La Galapaguera, **4**
La Tintorera, **26**
Las Bachas Beach, **13**
Los Gemelos, **7**
Media Luna, **6**
Pinnacle Rock, **22**
Playa Espumilla, **18**
Post Office Bay, **28**
Prince Philip's Steps, **16**
Rearing Center for Giant Tortoises, **25**
Salt Crater, **19**
South Plaza, **5**
Sugarloaf Volcano, **20**
Tagus Cove, **23**
Tortoise Reserve, **8**
Tunnel of Endless Love, **9**

Isla Marchena (Bindloe)
Isla Genovesa (Tower)
Darwin Bay 16
EQUATOR (0°)
Isla Daphne
Isla Seymour
Isla Mosquera
Isla Baltra 11
13 12
Santa Cruz
7
Islas Plaza 5
Cerro Crocker (870m)
6
Isla Santa Cruz (Indefatigable, Chavez)
Santa Rosa 8
Bellavista 9
Puerto Ayora 10
Tortuga Bay
Isla Santa Fé (Barrington)
Isla San Cristóbal (Chatham)
Punta Pitt 4
1
Isla Lobos
Wreck Bay
2 3
Puerto Baquerizo Moreno
El Progreso
Cerro San Joaquín (730m)
28 *Punta Cormorant*
Puerto Velasco Ibarra
Cerro Pajas (550m)
Isla Floreana (Sta. María, Charles)
Isla Española (Hood)
Isla Gardner
Gardner Bay
Punta Suárez

ing, volunteering, and researching in Latin America. Their "Galápagos Packet" of practical information about the islands is updated every few months.

Getting There and Back

TRAVEL BY PLANE

Ecuador's two national airlines, **TAME** and **SAN/SAETA,** provide the only available flights to the Galápagos. All flights originate in Quito, stop in Guayaquil one hour later, then take an additional 90 minutes to reach the islands. Both airlines have similar round-trip fares, but prices fluctuate depending on the season. During the highseason (December-August), round-trip tickets run around US$375 from either Quito or Guayaquil; low season fares dip to approximately US$280 from Quito and US$260 from Guayaquil. Passengers can pay for tickets either in dollars or in sucres; compare the airline exchange rate and the street rate to determine which is the better bargain. All flights must be booked at least one day in advance. Flights are routinely overbooked, so arrive at the airport at least an hour in advance to secure a seat and recheck return flight information a day or two before departing the islands.

TAME TAME runs the most flights to the Galápagos, with planes departing Mon.-Sat. from Quito at 8:30am, Guayaquil at 9:30am. Planes land on Isla Baltra, with easy access to Isla Santa Cruz and Puerto Ayora, the largest town on any of the islands. Returning flights leave Baltra at 11:30am. TAME also offers a 15% discount to students who hold both a valid university ID and an international student ID (ISIC student cards are not accepted).

SAN/SAETA SAN/SAETA flights take off every day except Thursday and Sunday, at 11am from Quito, noon from Guayaquil. They arrive on Isla San Cristóbal, not an especially convenient location unless you have a tour leaving from that island. Most tours depart from Isla Santa Cruz, so check your itinerary before making reservations with a particular airline.

TRAVEL BY BOAT

Although sea travel isn't necessarily any cheaper than an airplane, sailors-at-heart can opt to breathe in the salty air, face the open waters, and leave the land-lubbers behind. There are three ways to get to the Galápagos nautically. Voyage by **cargo ship,** while strictly a no-frills experience, is the cheapest way to go. The three-day, two-night journey costs about US$150 each way, but cabin space is limited and meals are strictly Bring Your Own Food. Arrange passage at the TRAMSFA office in Guayaquil (Av. Baquerizo Moreno 1119, 6th floor, at the corner of 9 de Octubre), or just ask for the *capitano* of the port along the Guayaquil *malecón.* Some ships only leave once a month, though, so be ready to be flexible with departure dates. **Cruise ships** are by far the most comfortable and luxurious option, but loungers definitely have to pay for that luxury, often over US$100 per day. Those with the money to spare should contact a travel agent; some ships include benefits such as spacious cabins, bilingual naturalist experts and guides, and a professional staff. **Military ships** used by the Ecuadorian Navy are another option, though they charge more (US$300) and take longer (11 days) than cargo ships.

ENTRANCE REQUIREMENTS

When arriving on Isla Baltra or Isla San Cristóbal, everyone must immediately pay a US$80 park entrance fee, which must be paid in cash, whether in dollars or sucres (traveler's checks and credit cards are not accepted). Sorry, but there is no getting around this charge, and it's a good idea to keep the receipt if you'll be traveling between islands. Visitors continuing onto Isla Santa Cruz must pay an additional US$12 "entrance tax," also in cash only. A passport is required to enter the island.

Getting Around

PACKAGE TOURS AND CRUISES

Travel agencies worldwide can arrange tours of the Galápagos, but the general trend is that the cost of the trip goes up as the distance between the agency and the islands increases; thus, the cheapest tours can be arranged within Ecuador or even on Isla Santa Cruz. The South American Explorers' Club recommends the following tour companies, all based in Quito:

Angermeyers Enchanted Excursions, Foch 768 y Amazonas (tel. (02) 569-960; fax 569-956).
Andes Discoveries (tel. (02) 228-591; fax 550-952), at Amazonas and Davalos.
Galasam, Pinto 523 (tel. (02) 561-470 or 567-662).

INTER-ISLAND TRAVEL

Instituto Nacional Galápagos (INGALA), the government-run public transportation system, offers shuttle boats between the archipelago's three most populated islands in various exciting combinations:

San Cristóbal to Santa Cruz	Mon. and Wed., 10am
Santa Cruz to San Cristóbal	Tues. and Sat., 10am
Santa Cruz to Isabela	Thurs., 8am
Isabela to Santa Cruz	Fri., 10am

While INGALA is the most reliable means of inter-island travel, it gives preference to island residents and charges *extrañeros* inflated rates (adults s/110,000 each way, children under 12 s/55,000). Tickets must be purchased at least one day in advance.

Private boats also transport adventurers for about the same cost. Some run on schedules as regular as the ferries; the *Estrella Mar* always leaves at 10:30am, traveling from Isabela to Santa Cruz on Tuesdays and returning to Isabela every Wednesday. Just track down Captain Marcos Martínez at Hotel Salinas in Puerto Ayora on Tuesday evening to buy a ticket. Other private boat owners run daytrips from Puerto Ayora or Puerto Baquerizo Moreno to some of the closer islands: South Plaza, Bartolomé, Seymour, and Santa Fé. Daytrips generally include transportation to and from the dock, breakfast, lunch, and a guide and cost in the neighborhood of US$45. Just make sure that you and your guide speak a common language—some have only a rudimentary mastery of English at best. Visit **Coltur** in Puerto Ayora for a list of boats and owners, as well as information about which are available and where they can be found.

RENTALS

Sailboats are difficult to find, but can be a valuable resource. They only carry about five passengers (at US$65-80 per person per day) and travel more slowly than larger boats, but are sometimes the best way to visit outlying points. **Bicycle** and **horse** rentals are also available on the larger islands.

Practical Information

ACCOMMODATIONS AND CAMPING

While high-paying visitors on package tours and cruises sleep in cabins on their boats, land-based accommodations are readily available for the budget traveler. Puerto Ayora (on Isla Santa Cruz) has a plethora of lodgings, while Puerto Baquerizo Moreno

(Isla San Cristóbal) and Puerto Velasco Ibarra (Isla Floreana) are also home to a few budget hotels. **Camping** is allowed at designated sites on Isla Santa Cruz for a fee.

MONEY

Ecuadorian sucres are the common currency, but U.S. dollars are sometimes accepted. There are a few money-changing facilities on the islands, mostly in Puerto Ayora, but exchange rates are much lower in the Galápagos than on the mainland. Rather than get ripped off, it makes more sense to change dollars and traveler's checks to sucres back in Quito or Guayaquil.

TIME DIFFERENCE

The Galápagos Islands are one hour behind the Ecuadorian mainland, or six hours behind Greenwich Mean Time. As on the mainland, the Galápagos do not observe Daylight Savings Time.

WHAT TO BRING

There aren't many stores in the Galápagos, so buy everything you'll need beforehand, either at home or in Quito or Guayaquil. Footwear is one of the most important parts of a trip to the Galápagos. Think about it—how could you climb volcanoes or wander among the tortoises if you've got mega-blisters on your feet? **Hiking boots** or **sturdy shoes** are a must if you plan to anything more active than lounging on the beach. Of course, if you plan to do that as well, bring along a pair of **waterproof sandals** or **flip-flops.** Insect bites can also bring you down, so bring along some **insect repellant.** Even if it's the rainy season, the sun's rays can still be killer, so stock up on **sunscreen** and bring a **rimmed hat.** Likewise, it gets nippy in the evenings no matter what the season, so keep cozy with a **sweatshirt** and a pair of **pants.** It's best to prepare for any kind of weather with a couple of **t-shirts,** a pair of **shorts,** and a **light raincoat.** The latter is an absolute necessity during the rainy months, January to April. Finally, if you plan to do any snorkeling or scuba diving (which is *highly* recommended), invest in a **short-sleeved wetsuit** to keep you warm in the chilly waves.

SCUBA DIVING

Despite the word on the street, there are several full-service dive shops in Puerto Ayora. **Galápagos Scuba Iguana** (tel./fax 526-330; fax 934-564), is located at the Hotel Galápagos. Daytrips span between 3-8 hours and prices range between US$75-110 (trip price includes dive gear, tanks for two dives, a divemaster guide, and a box lunch). Divemaster Mathias Espinosa is a certified divemaster/instructor and naturalist guide who speaks Spanish, English, and German. Also nearby is **Galápagos Sub-Aqua** (tel. 526-350; fax 526-350, international fax 593-4-314-510), on Av. Charles Darwin, 800m from the Darwin Center. Diveleader Fernaldo Zambrano is also a naturalist guide and the first actively-teaching dive instructor on the islands. Daytrips and prices similar to Scuba Iguana. Sub-Aqua also offers "all inclusive dive packages" (US$135 per day, up to 8 days), which includes accommodations, three meals, and diving, as well as introductory scuba courses for non-certified divers. Full certification courses are also available, but take seven days.

History

All the flora and fauna on the Galápagos miraculously, mysteriously crossed almost 1000km of ocean to get the islands, and the first human inhabitants arrived with the help of auspicious waves as well. Pottery shards found on various islands suggest that pre-Inca *indígenas* spent some time on Santiago, Santa Cruz, and Floreana, likely the result of their balsa rafts floating astray. But the first Galápagos tour to be recorded in the annals of history set sail around 1485, when legend has it that the Inca prince Tupac Inca Yupanqui either sent his army or accompanied them on an exploratory expedition of the islands. Like all Galápagos visitors, they returned loaded with souvenirs, though the gold treasure, bronze seat, and horse's skin and jaw that they brought back aren't sold in any of Puerto Ayora's gift shops today.

The first Europeans on the islands were also accidental tourists; at the time, however, Fray Tomás de Berlanga, the archbishop of Panamá, and his Peruvian-bound ship didn't think it too propitious when a week-long storm and a six-day drift carried their boat so far off-course. In fact, although Berlanga's 1535 jaunt is often considered the official "discovery" of the Galápagos, the man himself was actually a bit put off by the remoteness of islands (though he did note the amazing tameness of the wildlife). When the islands were first included on maps about 35 years later, they were given the name Galápagos (Spanish for "tortoise") after the enormous shelled specimen that Berlanga described.

For the next few centuries, pirates used the islands (most notably Isla Santiago's concealed Buccaneer Cove and James Bay) as hideaways and launching pads for surprise sea attacks. Raiding and pillaging can be hard work, and when hungry pirates discovered that the Galápagos tortoises could survive for months with little food or water, they began storing them in their ship hulls to use as a fresh meat source on long voyages. When this trend caught on, it was disaster for the tortoises, who dwindled at astonishing rates; in fact, if Charles Darwin had arrived on the islands much later than he did (see below), he might not have considered the Galápagos so pristine. But his 1835 arrival *was* early enough, and this famous naturalist's visit changed the course of the archipelago's history.

Although Darwin only stayed in the Galápagos for five weeks, the archipelago's important role in his development of the theory of evolution gave the islands a high profile worldwide. Ecuador had claimed the islands only a few years before Darwin arrived, and used them as a penal colony at first. But due to the Galápagos's fame and importance in the scientific and ecological world, a few areas were declared wildlife reserves in 1934, and in 1959 all non-colonized areas officially became the Parque Nacional Galápagos. In the following decades, tourism steadily increased; in 1994, the islands hosted 54,000 visitors, 76% of whom were foreigners.

Geology

The first Galápagos island was formed over 4 million years ago, and new islands have been forming ever since. The islands were never part of the mainland, but instead have been formed by underwater volcanoes that keep on spitting out lava, building themselves higher and higher until they finally break the surface of the ocean. Well, that's the simple version of the story.

A more in-depth understanding of how the Galápagos Islands formed requires a review of tectonic theory, the generally accepted belief that the surface of the earth is made up of a number of **tectonic plates** that are suspended on the **magma** (molten rock) that lies below them. These tectonic plates are constantly moving, each one being pushed and pulled by the plates around it. The Galápagos are located on the **Nazca plate,** which is being pushed towards the southeast by plates to the north and west of it. The volcanoes that formed and continue to form the Galápagos are the result of a "hot spot," a stationary area beneath the Nazca plate that is hot enough to melt the plate above it. This melting causes magma to be released onto the surface of the earth, usually in the form of a volcano. Other famous hot spots are responsible for the formation of the Hawaiian Islands and the geothermal activity of Yellowstone National Park in the United States.

While the Galápagos hot spot remains stationary, the Nazca plate is moving to the southeast, taking the older islands with it and leaving the hot spot to form new islands to the northwest. This agrees with the finding that Isla Española in the southeast is the oldest island in the archipelago, while Fernandina and Isabela to the northwest are the youngest and most volcanically active.

While most people come to the Galápagos to see the unique wildlife, the geology is some of the most interesting in the world. Very young geologic formations abound,

Darwin's Inspiration

The natural history of this archipelago is very remarkable: it seems to be a little world within itself; the greater number of its inhabitants, both vegetable and animal being found nowhere else.

— Charles Darwin, *Voyage of the Beagle*

Once upon a time, Charles Darwin was an English naturalist also studying to be a clergyman. Before settling down for a quiet life as a man of God, he decided to broaden his horizons and signed on as naturalist of a ship setting out to sail the world. That ship was the famous *Beagle,* and it was the things he saw on that voyage that inspired his theory of evolution by natural selection.

Darwin's travels brought him to the Galápagos in 1835, where he marveled at the geological newness of the islands and the biological uniqueness of its inhabitants. He presumed the plants and animals to be relations of mainland species, but it was not until he discovered the great variety of species *within* the Galápagos islands themselves—13 species of finch and 14 sub-species of tortoise—that he began to ponder the mechanisms behind speciation, or the evolution of different species. In conjunction with other discoveries, this led Darwin to postulate that speciation can occur within an isolated group that is separated from others of its kind, as in the Galápagos. This idea blended with others and matured to finally become his famous *On the Origin of Species,* the book that laid out his theory of evolution by natural selection. His ideas were ridiculed as blasphemous at first, but more than 100 years later we consider him a genius of his age, one of the most brilliant minds of all time. His notebooks later revealed these cryptic words: "In July opened first book on 'transmutation of species'—Had been greatly struck from about one month of previous March—On character of South American fossils—and species on Galápagos Archipelago—These facts (especially latter) origin of all my views."

since the islands themselves are so young (4 million years is a blink of the eye, geologically speaking). The volcanoes of the Galápagos were formed by basaltic lava, which has a relatively fluid consistency. For this reason, the Galápagos volcanoes are more inclined to vent their fury in the form of lava flows than enormous explosions. This is also the reason they tend to look more like domes than the perfectly shaped, conical volcanoes most people know and love.

There are many volcanic phenomena you might come across during your travels through the enchanted Galápagos. On the island of Santa Cruz, you can lose yourself in the **lava tunnels** of love (p. 260). These were formed by lava flows that hardened on the outside but remained liquid and continued to flow on the inside, eventually forming a rocky hollow tube. On Isabela, visit one of the largest **calderas** in the world (10km in diameter) on the summit of Volcán Sierra Negra (p. 272). Also on Isabela, witness the steamy, vaporous emissions of the **fumaroles** of Volcán Alcedo (p. 271). The 6.5km-wide and 900m-deep *caldera* of Volcán La Cumbre is the fiery heart and soul of Isla Fernandina (p. 273). The island grows larger and larger with every eruption; a 1975 eruption caused the uplift that formed Punta Espinosa to the northeast, and an eruption in February of 1995 caused a lava flow that resulted in the formation of a new cape on the island's southwest end. While this recent flow is not yet open to visitors, many slightly older **lava flows** are, including the beautifully sensual *pahoehoe* flows at Sullivan Bay on the island of Santiago (p. 276).

Fauna and Flora

Just over 4 million years ago, the Galápagos were born. Newly-formed islands composed entirely of volcanic matter—barren, desolate, and devoid of all life—the Galápagos waited patiently, 1000km from the nearest landmass. One day, some debris washed up on the island, and among the debris were some seeds, extremely hearty seeds, resistant to salt water, and able to go great lengths of time before germinating. A little later, a flock of birds flying by on their way to Chile spotted the islands and decided to rest awhile. A few stayed behind, excited by the prospect of a new beginning. Creatures began to crawl out of the sea as well. Voyaging turtles washed up on shore and decided to stick around. A few stalwart finches were blown off course somewhere near Costa Rica. Lost without hope of finding their way home, they did the best they could to make it on the islands. The volcanic rock turned into fertile soil with the gradual processes of erosion and the action of colonizing plants. Marine life started to gather around the islands as well; coral reefs sprung up in the shallow waters, providing food and shelter for smaller fishes. Bigger fishes then came to eat the smaller ones. The only large mammals to find the islands were the marine mammals. Frenetic seals took over the beaches and whales fed on the nutrient rich waters off-shore.

Thus, the animals on the Galápagos are the only ones that could survive the long voyage and manage to eke out a living once they arrived. Birds could fly in; reptiles made it because of their watertight skin and low-water needs. Today these species live on, though many have adapted to better cope with the challenges posed by life in the Galápagos. In many cases, this adaptation has progressed to the point of speciation, so that today many of the animals on the Galápagos are found nowhere else.

No land mammals have made the trip to the islands until the humans (aside from mice that are thought to have floated across the ocean on debris), and since then we have managed to do some serious damage. With humans came goats, horses, cats, dogs, and rats. These new arrivals have upset the ecological balance considerably, both by consuming the food of the aboriginal animals and by consuming the animals themselves. Humans have done their share as well, feeding on the large, meaty, and helpless tortoises that inhabit many of the islands.

Still, many species remain and their diversity and uniqueness are worth the trip. One of the most remarkable things about the animals of the Galápagos is their indifference towards humans. Seals perform for tourists while birds perch arrogantly on the heads of passersby. While the animals seem quite accepting of people, keep in mind that you are just a visitor here. In such a rare and fragile place, it is important that you follow guidelines set up by park officials and enforced by the tour guides. Hopefully, the above will help you appreciate the things you see, and convince you of the importance of preserving this one-of-a-kind exposition of nature.

BIRDS

The Galápagos are well-known for their birds, the most prominent and diverse type of animal on the islands. The different species of birds found in the Galápagos are presented here grouped by habitat, the first group being birds of the **sea.** Undeniably a seabird, the endemic **Galápagos penguin** is an aberrant member of its cold-water family. Long-lost relatives of the penguins of southern Chile and Antarctica, these shy birds live mainly around the Bolívar Channel between the western coast of Isabela and Fernandina. They are also found in various places near the island of Santiago. Another famous endemic seabird, the **flightless cormorant** is found only on the westernmost islands of Fernandina and Isabela. These cormorants have lost their ability to fly due to the lack of predators in the Galápagos, and have instead developed powerful legs and webbed feet for swimming through the water in search of fish, eel, and octopus. They nest in small colonies on sheltered shorelands. Some of the largest and most notable birds on the islands are the black **frigatebirds.** Both humble species (the Great and the Magnificent) are **cleptoparasites,** which means that they make a living by stealing the food of other birds, usually harassing them in midair, and forcing them to give up their catch. Since they spend so much time in the air, their wingspans grow up to 2.5m. Their cleptoparasitic ways have pre-empted the need to get their feathers wet, and they have therefore lost the ability to produce the oily secretions that protect the feathers of other seafaring birds. One of the most outstanding features of the frigates is their enormous red pouch beneath the beak that males inflate when courting. To witness this sensual display, visit the colonies on San Cristóbal and

Genovesa during the mating season (March and April), or visit North Seymour Island anytime. Some of the most well-known birds in the Galápagos are the **boobies,** of which there are three types: the blue-footed, the red-footed, and the masked. The boobies, like the frigates and cormorants, are related to the pelican, members of the order *Pelicaniformes.* They use their large and sometimes colorful feet to incubate their eggs and to swim through the water after dive-bombing fish. Red-footed boobies are the most common in the islands, with the highest concentration of birds on Genovesa. They are the only boobies that nest in trees or bushes. Blue-footed and masked boobies nest right on the ground, surrounding their territory with a circle of *"ejecta"* (bodily waste). While the masked boobies cannot be recognized by the color of their feet, they are easily identified by the black mask that contrasts with their otherwise white bodies. Perhaps the rarest bird in the Galápagos, the **waved albatross** is endemic not just to the Galápagos, but specifically to Isla Española. The largest bird in the archipelago, weighing over 4kg with a wingspan of 2.5m, they only stay on the island from April to December; they spend the rest of the year in various places around the South Pacific. Other seabirds include five kinds of **petrel** and two endemic **gulls,** the swallowtail and the lava gull.

Of the **shorebirds,** the **flamingos** are by far the most well-known. These guys are fairly rare, inhabiting only a few lagoons around the islands. They feed on small animals living in the silt and shallow water, and build nests of mud on the shores of the lagoon. They can be seen on Isla Rábida, in lagoons near Puerto Villamil on Isabela, at Punta Cormorant on Floreana, and at Espumilla beach on Santiago. A much more common shorebird is the **heron,** of which there are three types in the Galápagos: the great blue, the lava, and the night heron. These long-legged waders feed on all kinds of small animals, from beach creatures to lagoon-dwellers. A more specialized shorebird is the **oystercatcher.** About the size of your average heron, this bird is not quite as common due to its particular habits. It is mostly brown, with a black head and red eye ring and feeds primarily on shellfish, such as abalone and sea urchins. The Galápagos has a number of other shorebirds including **egrets, gallinules, turnstones, stilts,** and **whimbrels.**

The **landbirds** of the Galápagos, because of their isolation from other landbird populations, include the greatest percentage of endemic species (76%). Most famous are **Darwin's finches,** of which there are 13 types. Tiny sparrow-sized birds, they all look extremely alike and can only be differentiated by beak morphology and feeding habits. While some live simply on seeds or fruits, the carpenter finch uses a stick to dig insects out of trees, and the "blood-sucking" finch of Wolf Island actually uses its sharp beak to suck the blood of red-footed and masked boobies. There are also several endemic species of **mockingbird,** all of which are descended from a species native to mainland Ecuador. These brown and white birds are carnivorous, eating insects, lizards, and even small finches. Extremely social and territorial, they are often seen in large numbers and are not afraid of humans. Other notable endemic landbirds include the Galápagos **hawk,** the Galápagos **dove,** the Galápagos **martin,** and the Galápagos **rail.** Some of the more striking land birds are non-endemic. The **vermillion flycatcher,** a red and black bird found in the humid highland forests of the central islands, is a favorite, as is the nearly universal **yellow warbler.** Lastly, as surprising as it may be, some pioneering, adventurous owls must have made the trip form the mainland long ago; the islands are now populated by two subspecies of **barn owl** and **short-eared owl.**

REPTILES

The namesake of the islands, the undisputed king of the Galápagos reptiles, is the **giant tortoise.** Famous since the time of Darwin and even before, these are the animals that really set the islands apart (only one other island in the world has a tortoise population). How the tortoises first came to inhabit the islands is to this day a mystery. Their closest relative is a species of tortoise native to Argentina, but with males weighing up to 250kg, it is hard to imagine creatures so big coming so far across the ocean without swimming. Whatever their origin, the anomalous giant tortoises have been appreciated for centuries. Back in the day, whalers and pirates cruising the Pacific used to visit the islands to stock up on these defenseless but hardy animals, piling them in their holds for months at a time to use as a fresh meat supply. As a result, the tortoises aren't quite as plentiful as they once were. Three of the original 14 subspecies are now extinct, and introduced animals such as rats and dogs continue to threaten the population. While each animal can live to be over 150-years old, they do not reproduce very often, and when they do, it is not guaranteed that the vulnerable hatchlings will ever reach maturity. The Galápagos National Park and the Darwin Research Center are doing what they can to prevent predation and boost the population by harvesting eggs, raising the hatchlings to four years of age, and then releasing them in their original habitat. The largest tortoise population is found on Isabela, predominantly concentrated around the crater of Volcán Alcedo. Other islands where wild tortoises can be observed are the Tortoise Reserves on Santa Cruz and Española. Captive tortoises can be observed at the Darwin Research Center on Santa Cruz, and the Rearing Center for Giant Tortoises on Isabela.

Back in the sea and on the beaches, **marine turtles** are also commonly found. These animals float easily on the water's surface and can therefore travel great distances across the seas with the greatest of ease. Four of the eight species of marine turtle have been seen on the Galápagos, and none of them are endemic (which makes sense, given their great mobility). The black turtle, a sub-species of the Pacific green turtle, is the most common. They lay their eggs in nests on the beach, burying them to incubate in the hot sun. While they can lay their eggs year-round, it is most common from January to June. For a day or two after the eggs are laid, visitors may observe tracks leading from the sea to the nest and back again. Night visitors may even catch a turtle in the process of laying. In these cases, it is fine to watch quietly, but do not disturb the animals, especially not with the beam of your flashlight.

One of the most bizarre and unique reptiles of the Galápagos is the **marine iguana,** the only aquatic iguana in the world. Related to the land iguanas of the American mainland, marine iguanas have evolved to eat green algae that grows underwater. For this purpose they have evolved a tail tailored for efficient swimming, the ability to swim up to 60 ft. deep, the capacity to stay under the water for up to one hour at a time, and the bizarre tendency to shoot excess absorbed salt out of their unusually square noses at great speed. The largest marine iguanas (on Isabela) can grow up to 1m long. Like other reptiles, these strange creatures are ectothermic, meaning that their body temperature is determined by the temperature of their environment. As a consequence, they can often be seen sunning their big, black, spiny bodies on the rocks, piled on top of each other in big groups.

Land iguanas also inhabit the islands; while their genus is endemic to the Galápagos, they are not quite as unusual as their marine counterparts. They can also reach up to 1m in length, but their noses are more characteristically pointed. Their diet varies depending on their particularly habitat. They eat insects and scavenge for other meaty meals, but also love to eat grasses, cacti, fruits, and flowers, particularly the big yellow blossoms of the **opuntia** cactus.

On a smaller scale, seven species of **lava lizard** are also endemic to the islands. Reaching up to 250cm, they feed primarily on plants, with the occasional insect thrown in for good measure. They are gray, and females typically have eye-catching red-orange throats. While they are very territorial, most confrontation takes the form of bouncing up and down on the forelegs; fights are seldom serious.

Long ago, through some heroic feat of seamanship, **snakes** also reached the islands. On land, the non-poisonous Galápagos **land snake** slithers hither and yon in search of small prey that it can crush with its 1m length of constricting power. Found on all but the northernmost islands, these brown or gray snakes have yellow stripes or spots.

MAMMALS

The most prominent and strangest mammals of the Galápagos inhabit the islands of Santa Cruz, San Cristóbal, Isabela, and Floreana, though some may be found on other islands from time to time. Social animals, they live in big groups, primarily by the ocean, but also in more fertile and moist regions of the islands. Their bodies are quite strange in form, and vary greatly in size. They all have oversized heads and most commonly support themselves on only two of their four limbs. They travel in groups from island to island, curiously observing the things around them. There often seems to be a leader that communicates with the rest of the group using strange sounds emitted from the mouth. At night these creatures gather once again, usually around unknown sources of strange rhythmic sound, and consume various quantities of liquid that alters their behavior dramatically, causing some of them to start making more noise and causing others to regurgitate and eventually lie prone, presumably in a state of dormancy. While these **Homo sapiens** have arrived only recently on the islands, they have had a great impact on the ecology. The number of individuals in the population fluctuates regularly, but continues to rise steadily. It is unclear whether the population can continue to grow at this rate without damaging the islands beyond repair. It appears that the homo sapiens are aware of this, but it remains to be seen whether they choose to do anything about it.

Another large mammal found in astonishing abundance in the Galápagos is the endemic **Galápagos sea lion.** Relatives of the sea lions of California and Perú, they live in colonies on the beaches of most of the islands. Males are much larger than females and can reach up to 250kg. They are very territorial, holding territories for about a month at a time, defending them from any kind of intruder (usually from other males). Mating occurs in the ocean, but females give birth on land. Pups are suckled for up to two years before being weaned. The animals are playful and are commonly seen surfing or showing off for tourists in other ways. Another related but quite distinct species found in the Galápagos is the **fur sea lion.** The endemic Galápagos subspecies is the only non-antarctic fur sea lion. They were once on the brink of extinction due to hunting by fur traders. They can be easily differentiated from normal sea lions by their furry skin, smaller size, pointed nose, and larger eyes.

The only other mammals on the islands that were not introduced by man are the **rats** and the **bats.** Two species of bats comb the islands of Santa Cruz, Floreana, Isabela, and San Cristóbal for insects, while six species of brown rice rat scurry across the majority of the islands in search of a tasty vegetarian meal. Lately, the rat population has been decreasing in number due to the introduction of the black rat, which competes with the rice rat for food.

MARINE LIFE

The waters of the Galápagos are truly tropical, teeming with just about every kind of marine life. The islands are fed by three nutritious currents: the Humboldt, the Cromwell, and the El Niño, which bring a bounteous supply of species and nutrients from all over the Pacific. Sixteen species of **whales** and seven species of **dolphins** have been sighted around the Galápagos, with a particularly high concentration of sightings off the west coast of Isabela where the Cromwell current brings plankton and other delectable organisms to the surface. Whale species include sperm, humpback, blue, and killer whales. The most prevalent species of dolphins are the common and bottle-nosed dolphins. Twelve species of **shark** also inhabit these waters. By far the most common is the white-tipped reef shark, but black-tipped reef sharks, hammerheads, Galápagos sharks, and tiger sharks are common as well. Also sharing these waters are five species of **rays,** including stingrays, eagle rays, and manta rays. Hundreds of species of smaller fish also make their home here, both in the open water, and in the **coral reefs** and isolated coral heads near several of the islands. Lobster, crab, squid, octopus, starfish, sea cucumber, and shellfish of all kinds add to the **submarine extravaganza.** Because of this great diversity, the waters in and around the Galápagos, an area of 70,000km^2, are part of a marine reserve established in 1986. Snorkeling and scuba diving are possible at numerous sights throughout the islands. If you want to go snorkeling, just let your boat captain know. Scuba diving requires a bit more preparation and planning (see Scuba Diving, p. 246). While the area is protected, regulated commercial fishing of certain species is still permitted. But before snagging a salt-water snack for yourself, consult the locals or your trusty tour guide.

FLORA

The Galápagos have seven vegetation zones that are home to over 600 species of plants, approximately 170 of which are endemic. The zones range from dry and low to high and moist. The area right on the coast is the **littoral zone** and is dominated by plants that have adapted to the presence of salt, such as **mangroves.** The **arid zone** is the driest region and comes just above the littoral in altitude. Generally on the side of the island opposite the prevailing winds, this region is dominated by cacti and other dry-weather plants. The **opuntia cactus** with the yellow flowers is the only endemic species of cactus and also happens to be the most common. It often grows like a shrub, except on islands where it is threatened by herbivorous animals; there these cacti can grow trunks up to 5m tall. The **Palo Santo** tree is also native to this zone. Producing only small leaves during the wet season, the branches of these stark gray trees are often burned for their incense-like odor. The next highest zone, which is also less dry, is the **transition zone.** The most common inhabitants are the Palo Santos again and the **pega pega,** or "stick stick" tree, that has spread-out branches and a short trunk. The next zone is very humid and has been called the **scalesia zone** for the endemic **scalesia trees** that are so common here. In addition to scalesia trees which can grow up to 10m, there are many mosses, ferns, and grasses. The scalesia forest of the Santa Cruz highlands is the best place to see this kind of vegetation. The three remaining zones are the **brown, miconia,** and **pampa zones.** The brown is named for the prominent **brown liverwort mosses** found here. The miconia zone gets its name from the endemic and shrubby **miconia plants** that look somewhat like a flowering cacao plant. The highest and wettest vegetation zone is the **pampa,** dominated by mosses, ferns and grasses; very few trees or shrubs grow in this hyper-humid region.

ISLA SANTA CRUZ

Known also by its English name of Indefatigable, Isla Santa Cruz's never-ending diversity—its myriad of wildlife, radically varied geology, and scores of international visitors—is indeed tireless. As Santa Cruz lies geographically in the center of the archipelago, tourism in the Galápagos revolves around this hub. Nearly every visitor inevitably stops here, whether to schmooze with the sea lions or just to stock up on supplies. After all, **Puerto Ayora** (on the southern shore) is the largest and most developed town on the islands, and Santa Cruz is a conveniently close first stop if you arrive at nearby **Baltra Airport.**

The scenic trip from the airport to Puerto Ayora serves as the perfect introduction to the islands. Baltra looms barren and powerful, the entire landscape covered with lava rock, cacti, and wind-blown trees. After a short boat ride across shimmering turquoise waters, visitors enter the central highlands of Santa Cruz, where the bus jostles its way through vegetation that seems all the greener in comparison to the desertscape before it. From there the bus descends to the cool, relaxed port town.

Good news for landlubbers—Santa Cruz is one of the few islands in the Galápagos where you don't need a boat to see all the sights. The intellectually curious should make for the **Headquarters of the Galápagos National Park** and the nearby **Charles Darwin Research Station** just outside of Puerto Ayora. At the station, visitors can get up close and personal with the undisputed star of the island, the giant Galápagos tortoise. Those with more time on their hands can journey into the lush scalesia forests of **Santa Cruz's highland region,** where you can rent horses or hike into the **Galápagos Tortoise Reserve** to interact with these friendly giants in their natural habitat. After exploring the island, rest your bones on the white sands of **Tortuga Bay,** a relaxing 3km walk from town.

Puerto Ayora

The Galápagos Islands prove that Mother Nature has a unique ability to roll with the punches. Over the years, the plants and animals of the archipelago have managed to adapt to fill virtually every unexploited niche. The wings of the flightless cormorants on Isabela have gradually grown short and stumpy because the lack of predatory animals renders flying pointless; the previously arctic penguins on Bartolomé and Fernandina (like so many Floridians) have happily given up their frigid ways to adapt to life under the hot equatorial sun. Not to be outdone by other Galápagos phenomena, the seaside settlement of Puerto Ayora eagerly rises to the archipelago's call for a "developed port town."

Santa Cruz's central location and Puerto Ayora's beautiful bay firmly ground this haven of hospitality on nearly everyone's itinerary. Visitors stroll up and down the settlement's main thoroughfare, escorted by representatives of the island's large marine iguana population. While the first group patronizes the town's scuba shops and restaurants, the latter prefers sticking almost exclusively to seaweed beds just beneath the surface of Pelican Bay.

A local custom illustrates the hospitality of the town: shop owners will often collect small piles of coconuts from nearby trees. If you get a hankering for one of these island treats, don't try to buy one—the town's juicy supply of coconuts comes from the land, making it a commodity most islanders refuse to sell. If there is an extra 'nut lying around it will, of course, be free—a gift from both the island and the islanders.

ORIENTATION AND PRACTICAL INFORMATION

While nearly all of the islands in the Galápagos archipelago have three or four names, many of the streets in Puerto Ayora have yet to receive even one. Don't fret, though—Puerto Ayora is one of the few sites in the Galápagos where a native guide isn't needed. Virtually everything of importance is located on the city's one major street, named **Avenida Charles Darwin** (what else?).

Tourist Information: For all those pesky questions regarding everything from hotels to heron-mating seasons, visit the **CETUR information office** (tel. 526-179), on Av. Darwin next to the Geminis 2 souvenir shop. CETUR's answers are always up-to-date and always *en español.* The office also provides informative (albeit blurry) town maps, as well as information about INGALA, the Galápagos's public transportation system. (See "Inter-Island Travel" on page 245.)

Bank: El Banco del Pacífico (tel. 526-282 or 526-365), on Av. Darwin just beside Hotel Sol y Mar, changes traveler's checks and cash for more sucres than other restaurants and shops around town, though rates still lag behind those on the mainland (open Mon.-Fri. 8am-3:30pm, Sat. 9:30am-2:30pm).

International phone calls, faxes, and telegrams: Do it all from **EMETEL** at the **Central Telefónica de Puerto Ayora** (tel. 999-170), on Calle Charles Binford (open daily 7am-9pm).

Airport: Getting to Puerto Ayora from the **Isla Baltra airport** is easy enough. Buy the requisite 2 tickets at the airport (the first covers the combination bus/boat trip to Isla Santa Cruz, the second is for the 1½-hr. bus ride to Puerto Ayora; each ticket s/6,000). The **shuttle** back to the airport leaves from the center of town in front of the CITTEG sign at 8am (but getting there early is recommended). Buy the ticket to Baltra at the **CITTEG office** (s/6,000-10,000), and the second ticket to the airport at the **TAME office** (tel. 526-527), on Av. Darwin (open Mon.-Fri. 7am-noon and 1-4pm; s/6,000).

Market: Mini Bodega Santa Cruz, just up the street from Central Telefónica, is one of many convenient stores around town that stock those essential groceries.

Restrooms: If you find yourself stranded far from the restroom of your hotel or boat, **public restrooms** are located on Av. Darwin near the park. If you don't manage to make it to the restroom in time...

Laundromat: Services available at **La Lavandería,** near the bed and breakfast, for cheap rates by the kilo.

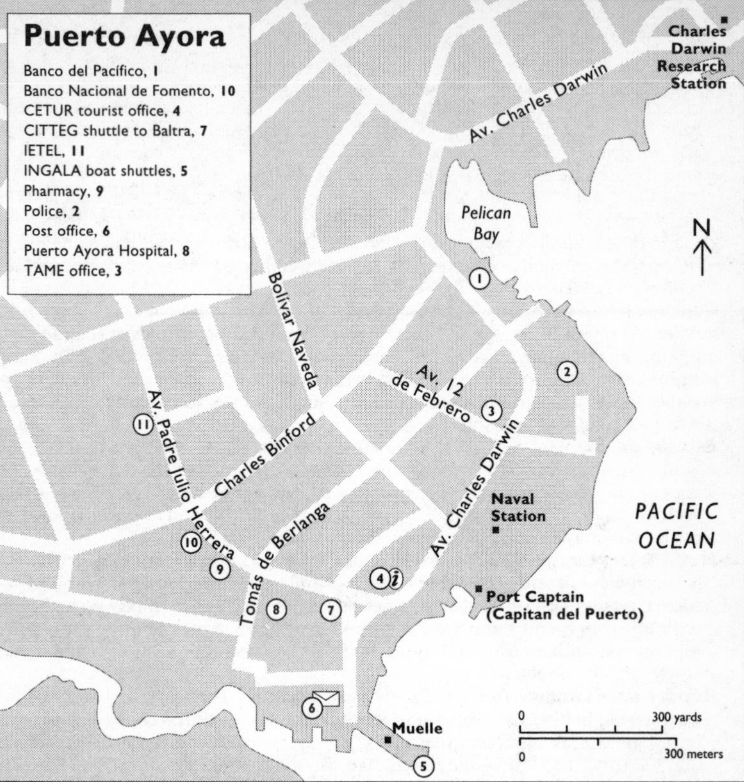

Pharmacies: Farmacia Edith (tel. 526-487; open daily 8am-11pm), and **Farmacia Vanessa** (tel. 526-392; open daily 8am-10pm), can be seen from the hospital.

Hospital: Puerto Ayora Hospital (24-hr. emergency tel. 526-103) near the corner of Av. Padre Julio Herrera and Pelicano Rd.

Police: (tel. 526-101), by the water off Av. 12 de Febrero, at their headquarters beside the Estrella del Mar. On duty daily from 8am-6pm.

Post Office: The **Correo Central** (tel. 526-575), on Calle Charles Binford, 3 blocks beyond Av. Darwin. Postcards and stamps are available here; the post-mistress promises (perhaps vainly) that mail will get to the U.S. in 10 days (open Mon.-Fri. 8am-noon and 2-6pm).

Telephone Code: 05.

ACCOMMODATIONS

The Galápagos are home to 13 different kinds of finches and even more hotels, though the large price discrepancies leave visitors wondering if they really could have evolved from a common ancestor. Accommodations in Puerto Ayora change hands often, so always ask to see a room before sleeping in it. Besides doing a quick cleanliness check, look for netting or window screens to keep out mosquitoes—while not usually a problem, they can be murder during the wet season. Without those precautions, sleepers are in a no-win situation: either suffer through the mosquito warfare, or close the windows and suffer through the heat. In general, you pay for luxury, leaving budget travelers more likely to hear the sounds of the local disco than waves gently lapping outside their door. Some gems, however, are still hidden alongside Puerto Ayora's increasingly busy streets.

Bed and Breakfast Peregrina (tel. 526-323), off Av. Darwin, just behind Pipos Restaurant. Lodgers at this B&B feel like they've come home—the manager, Columbia, is even more caring than the mother hen out front. She'll make sure you have a clean bed and a hearty complementary breakfast (homemade bread and jam, eggs, fruit, and coffee or tea). S/15,000 rooms fit up to 4; some have a private bath, and all are secure and have ceiling fans. Unlike most mothers, Columbia will still do your laundry, no matter how old you are (s/3,000 per kilo).

Hotel Lirio del Mar (tel. 526-212), near the corner of Tomás de Berlanga and Bolívar Naveda. 3 stories high with 2 breathtaking terraces that overlook Pelican Bay, the harbor, and the restaurant/bar below. Rooms are sparkling and safe, and the owners as warm and accommodating as the weather. All rooms have private baths with solar-heated water. S/20,000 per person.

Residencial Los Amigos, near the corner of Darwin and Av. 12 de Febrero. The island's answer to the youth hostel, with communal bathrooms and large dorm-type rooms that may have to be shared when the place is crowded. The college atmosphere often spills like an overflowing beer into the courtyard, where people gather to discuss animal encounters, swap scuba gear, or just to play cards. Rooms start at s/10,000 per person.

Estrella del Mar (tel. 526-427), at the intersection of Av. 12 de Febrero and Av. Darwin. Though it seems to cower behind larger buildings, Estrella del Mar has nothing to hide from—its position gives it typically scenic Puerto Ayora views. A room with a balcony view costs a little more. Cross your fingers and hope for a group discount, which is occasionally offered. Rooms start at s/15,000.

Hotel Sol y Mar (tel. 526-281; fax 471-701), on Av. Darwin overlooking Pelican Bay. A bit pricier, but you get what you pay for. And in this case, you pay for clean, safe rooms; dining with sun-soaked iguanas on the oceanfront patio; private bathrooms with hot water; and the priceless company of hotel owner Jimmy Pérez. Full of information on boat trips and tours, Sr. Pérez can also tell many an island legend. Singles US$15; doubles US$20.

Residencial Flamingo (tel. 526-526), on the corner of Tomás de Berlanga and Bolívar Naveda, behind the skeleton of a larger hotel. Budget travelers flock here like long-legged pink birds, settling in the sunny, overflowing floral courtyard. But don't squawk too loud—the doors, like the mattresses, are stick-thin. All rooms have private bath. Prices start at s/10,000.

Hotel Palmeras (tel. 526-139), on the corner of Bolivar Nevada and Tomás de Berlanga, just past Lirio del Mar. A notch above the bare-budget, this family-run joint sports stark but spacious rooms, spotless private bathrooms, rotating fans, and comfortable beds. Restaurant and bar downstairs. Singles s/20,000; doubles s/35,000, triples s/45,000, quads s/60,000.

New Hotel Elizabeth (tel. 526-178), conveniently located right on Av. Darwin, is run by the friendly couple Vilma and Victor. Modest rooms all have private bath, but some lack shower curtains. Flashers may enjoy the one suite with an all-glass door. Rooms start at s/4,000 per person.

Hotel Darwin (tel. 526-193), on Av. Herrera, 1 block from the ocean. Passersby love Hotel Darwin's laid-back look, with its weathered sign jauntily tied to a palm tree, but potential patrons may want to wait for Hotel Darwin to evolve a little bit more. Bathroom fixtures and thin mattresses betray their years, despite their cleanliness. Singles s/12,000, s/10,000 each additional person.

FOOD

The two most common sights on Av. Charles Darwin are the diving pelicans and the seaside restaurants. The eateries on this main drag are moderately priced; a bare-bones meal goes for s/6,000-12,000. Perhaps because these places tend to attract the timid tourists fresh off the boat, the patio furniture has become a great spot to meet other visitors and arrange boat tours. Travelers looking for more endemic fare should check out the **open-air market** on Av. Charles Binford, where meat, seafood, and fresh produce are sold from small wooden shacks.

Restaurante El Sabrosán (tel. 526-262), on Calle Julio Herrera across from Mini Bodega Santa Cruz. Cooperative chefs and good food on a bamboo-covered patio. Watch super-friendly Ramón make *chuzos* (steak, onions, and peppers on a stick, s/6,000) over an open fire. Conch and shrimp *chuzos* on days when there's a good catch. All meals served with beans and rice. Open for lunch and dinner.

The Tropic Bird, on Av. Herrera, just up from El Sabrosán. A big place by Puerto Ayora standards, its six plastic tables are often full of locals and tourists in the know. Come early to get a popular table by the television, though the scene that surrounds the tables near the street is entertainment enough. Heaping portions of excellent local food served daily for breakfast, lunch, and dinner. If you're famished, try the special: *chuzos,* steaming rice, beans, roasted corn on the cob, and a drink for about s/9,000.

Media Luna Pizza (no tel.), on Av. Darwin past Hotel Sol y Mar, features homemade pizzas *a la Galápagos,* with fresh and fishy toppings such as shrimp and blue crab. Assortment of sandwiches like the top-notch avocado sub, plus a fun, easy-going crowd. Pizzas s/10,000-52,000, sandwiches s/9,000. Open for lunch and dinner.

The Iguana Café (no tel.), on Av. Floreana. Walk down Av. Darwin towards the research station, turn left at the big turtle statue, and continue up Floreana about 50m; it's on the left. On the way in, stop to pet the iguana statue. Friendly management serves up huge, hot sandwiches on homemade bread (s/9,000). After eating, kick back against the beautiful *cascarilla* wood columns with a savory slice of homemade cheesecake (s/3,000). The most philanthropic place on the island to get a drink, a portion of alcohol sales goes to the island's school system.

Restaurante Gaviota, on Av. Herrera towards the post office, this place needs no sign; just follow your senses towards the seducing smells and the sounds of salsa. A favorite with the Puerto Ayorans, come here to fill up on more than just seagull seeds; local chow includes corn soup, salad, meat, rice, and fried bananas. Quite a deal at s/4,000 a meal. Open three meals a day.

La Panera (no tel.), on Binford past the hospital. A bakery whose bread rises with the sun. Grab a bite here before an early morning boat trip. Breads and pastries are as tasty as they are cheap. Milk, yogurt, cheese, and cola on sale too. Open daily at 6am.

El Rincón del Alma (tel. 526-196), facing the park on the waterfront, with both indoor and patio seating. Open bar reveals juxtaposing decorations from a choral trophy to distracting mugs in the shape of female breasts. Upon inspection (of the menu, not the mugs) the restaurant offers food as eclectic and erotic as its decor. Entrées cost around s/15,000, but come heaped so high they're hard to finish. Meal of the day s/5,000.

Playa Sol y Mar, on Av. Darwin across from the park. Dine in true budget style—on plastic lawn furniture under huge, shady trees. If you don't immediately enjoy the relaxed atmosphere, you'll have time to get used to it; food may take a while if you don't order the special. Traditional breakfast, lunch, or dinner s/5,000. Menu items, which include pasta, cost a bit more.

Chifa Asia, on Av. Darwin in the center of town. No wonder this is where all the wheeling and dealing with tour operators occurs; speedy service and cheap eats make this Chinese restaurant perfect for grabbing a bite and schmoozing in the center of it all. Well, all five blocks, anyways (open daily 8am-11pm).

NTERTAINMENT

ollow the loud music to the best bar in town, **El Bar de Frank,** on Av. Darwin past inford. The cold beer (s/5,000) keeps a-flowin' as long as the electricity does, usually ntil around midnight. The crowd is usually sunburnt and very friendly. For those ho haven't seen enough mating displays during the day, Puerto Ayora has still more ightlife options. **Panga,** a *discoteca* at Av. Darwin and Tomás de Berlanga, attracts oth endemic and migratory Galápagos residents. Another option is the **Discoteca ive Fingers,** just down Av. Darwin. Both discos sell cold drinks, have pool tables, nd stay open into the wee hours of the mornin'.

■ Near Puerto Ayora

For most, a visit to Puerto Ayora is rushed, so much so that a visit to yet another site named after Charles Darwin might not sound like a worthwhile way to spend a morn- ing. Wrong, it is. Instead of drinking that cold pineapple juice in the shade of Puerto Ayora's busy streets, get it to go and head down Av. Charles Darwin to the **Charles Darwin Research Station,** 20 minutes from town on an easy trail, just past Hote Galápagos. The trail leads past both a **national park information center** and the **park's administrative headquarters** (tel. 526-189; fax 526-190). Information on the islands' natural history, as well as Darwin Station education and conservation pro grams, can be found in the nearby **Van Straelen Exhibit Hall.** The station is run by a small but enthusiastic staff. Feel free to poke around the other buildings if no one is there to answer your questions. An explanatory film is supposedly shown twice daily but because of uncertain visitor numbers it rarely runs.

Just beyond Van Straelen is the station's **tortoise rearing center.** A shady path leads past pens containing miniature giant tortoises, fresh from the egg. The big boys are just around the corner and their pen is open to all. For many, this is the only chance to see and interact with a "tame" Galápagos tortoise. The animals in this area were originally kept by islanders as pets, so they really do like people and very rarely retreat into their shells like the wild ones do. Some even stretch out their necks in hopes of getting a nice scratching; even tortoises have those "hard-to-reach" places While in the tortoise pens, however, be careful not to walk across or stand on the tor toise feeding platform, as this may contaminate their food with harmful organisms For more information about the Galápagos, the Darwin Station, and its projects, visit the station's library in the area behind the Exhibit Hall. If you have a specific interest or question, this is a good place to find Gail Davis, a delightful and extremely helpfu staff member who came to the islands years ago on a research project and never left

If it is leisure and not enlightenment that you seek, head to **Tortuga Bay.** Consid ered by many to be the most beautiful beach in the Galápagos, the picturesque white sand beach is accessible to anyone anytime, even without a guide. The beach gets its name from the large number of sea turtles that come to lay their eggs. Other species roost in the nearby lagoon as well—pelicans, flamingos, and other feathered folk roost high in the mangroves on the water's edge. Sharks and marine iguanas have also been known to call Tortuga Bay home. When swimming, be careful of the unusually

Lonesome George

Lonesome George is a large tortoise who lives at the Charles Darwin Research Center... but George isn't like all the other tortoises. He isn't like any other tortoise anywhere—George is a sad tortoise, the last of a dying race.

Found in 1971, George was the first **Pinta tortoise** *(Geochetone elephantopus abingdoni)* seen in 65 years. Tragically, the story of George's race is all too reminiscent of other tales of endangered species the world over. When pirates and whalers discovered that the tortoises could survive long periods of time without food or water, they rushed to store the animals on their ships as a fresh meat source. The dwindling tortoise population of Pinta suffered another blow when goats drastically affected the island's ecological habitat, further contributing to the demise of George's tragedy-stricken race.

Some think he should live out the remainder of his days on his home island of Pinta, now goat-free. Currently, George remains at the research center, comfortably housed with two lovely lady turtles from Isabela, genetically his closest relatives. But sadly, it appears that George is far too depressed to think about sex; the females just don't arouse his interest. Researchers are offering a US$10,000 reward to anyone who can supply a female Pinta tortoise, so keep an eye out.

Unfortunately, the Pinta is not the only tortoise species in danger. Of the 14 species that originally inhabited Isla Santa Cruz, five others are in danger and may soon join the three species that are already extinct.

strong currents, and if you go snorkeling, bring a buddy; there's no lifeguard on duty to save yo' booty.

To get to the beach from the town park, walk past the hospital to Calle Charles Binford, turn left and follow the dirt road out of town for about 200m. Beyond the interesting assortment of island houses stands a sign welcoming visitors to the **Galápagos National Park.** Check out the observation tower standing high on a sheer rock cliff; Tortuga Bay is a pleasant 2½-km stroll from the tower. The path is good for bird-watching and meeting other travelers.

The Highlands of Santa Cruz

For those who haven't quite gotten their sea legs, never fear—the interior of Santa Cruz offers a plethora of land-based outings. One of the best things about these day-trips is that many of them can be visited independently of tour groups or guides. The towns of **Bellavista** (about 6km north of Puerto Ayora) and **Santa Rosa** (8km north-west of Bellavista), though sans hotels and almost everything else, do allow camping and are ideal departure spots for nearby hikes. Two popular hiking peaks are **Media Luna,** a cresent-shaped volcanic cinder cone about 5km from Bellavista, and **Cerro Crocker,** about 3km beyond Media Luna.

Buses serve the highlands from Puerto Ayora, leaving at 6:30am, 12:30pm, and 4:30pm. The bus stop is on Charles Binford Rd.; from the Parque Central, walk four blocks away from the ocean. Tickets may be purchased onboard (s/2,000). The buses follow a circular route, traveling to Bellavista, on to Santa Rosa, then returning to Puerto Ayora via Bellavista once again. Passengers may get on and off at any point on the route. Though *Let's Go* does not recommend hitchhiking, it is not unusual for trucks to stop and pick up passengers for a fee similar to that charged by the buses. It is a good idea to head out early in order to ensure catching a ride back into town before dark. While there are currently no hotels or hostels in the highlands, **camping** is available in Bellavista and at the Tortoise Reserve near Santa Rosa. To camp in Bellavista, contact Spanish-speaking Eddie Gallardo (tel. 526-532) or send a fax to his English-speaking brother, Marcello, at the same number. To arrange camping in the tortoise reserve, contact the National Park system (tel. 526-189).

The Tortoise Reserve

No trip to the highlands is complete without visiting the tortoise reserve just outside Santa Rosa. The tortoises here are noticeably different from those found at the "interaction area" of the Darwin Center—these guys are as wild as 200-lb. tortoises can get, so watch out. Because of its distance from Puerto Ayora, the reserve is not often included in large tour itineraries, which gives the trek a truly off-beat aura.

Because the reserve isn't in a regulated section of the park, visitors are not required to be accompanied by a guide. However, a knowledgeable guide can greatly enrich the experience; tortoise sightings, for instance, cannot be guaranteed, but a good guide will know where to look. The trails also can be confusing and many lone tourists have lost their way—one even died before he was found.

Luscious but lengthy, the 1½-to-2-hour hike to the reserve can be a challenge through all the dense, low-growing vegetation. Highland tortoises have gradually developed large dome-shaped shells that enable them to burrow through Santa Rosa's plant growth. Since our own evolution has unfortunately deprived us of exoskeletons, the best way to overcome the navigation problem is on horseback. Mario Ramón outfits visitors with guides and horses to their liking (ask for his house at the Santa Rosa bus stop); each costs s/20,000. Riding to the reserve also gives the bonus of better views of the surrounding landscape, but if you decide to use a guide, you'll have to rent a horse for him or her as well.

The reserve itself offers a feast of sensation. Depending on the time of your visit, the reserve may be a celebration of blooming flora, nothing brighter than the flowering hibiscus. Red, yellow, and orange *pajaritos* (little birds) dart to and fro, dive-bombing unsuspecting tortoises and occasionally perching on the heads of passing tourists. No festival would be compete without the food, so appropriately the reserve bears many fruits as well, all yours for the taking: bananas, coconuts, Galápagos oranges, as well as an abundance of more exotic fruit. *Guayabanas* are yellow on the outside with a pink fleshy inside, about the consistency of a fig; *maracuyas* are yellowish-orange, filled with a tasty green pulp.

At the end of a day at the Tortoise Reserve, hungry hikers may direct their noses towards one of the two restaurants back in Santa Rosa. **Jolita's** serves up native cuisine in a thatched-roof bamboo hut for only s/5,000 a meal.

■ Los Gemelos

These "twins" are a pair of craters, each approximately 30-m deep, on either side of the road to Baltra, just outside of Santa Rosa. Their origin remains mysterious; the holes may have been caused by a volcanic explosion, or they may simply be caved-in magma chambers. But the craters themselves are not the only attraction; the walk through the mist-enshrouded forest can be rewarding on its own. Bird life abounds; witness species such as the vermilion flycatcher, yellow warbler, cattle egret, and the occasional short-eared owl. Yet while birds may be easy to spot, the trail to Los Gemelos from the road is not, especially during the rainy season, when vegetation begins to grow over the path. To ensure your very own encounter with these concave beauties, consider hiring a guide, or get very detailed directions from someone who knows what they're talking about (try Jolita's in Santa Rosa).

■ The Lava Tunnels

The island of Santa Cruz is riddled with **lava tubes** *(los tunneles)*, the remains of ancient magma flows that helped form the Galápagos Islands. The outer crust of these molten streams hardened as it cooled, but the liquid magma within continued flowing. When it ceased, these empty tubes were left behind.

There are several tunnels around the island, but the most frequently visited is Bellavista's **"Tunnel of Endless Love,"** named not for the Casanova-type guides but rather for the heart-shaped hole in the roof. Though the tunnel is only 800m long, it does begin to seem endless the further you explore. The entrance to the tunnel is a gaping black hole, in sharp contrast to the lush growth around it. A rickety banister provides support, but visitors may choose to take their chances or to hold onto the nearest tree for support. Much like the endless love it is named for, the pathway inside is generally smooth—except for the occasional pile of rubble. The exit, in the spirit of romance, is draped with leaf-covered vines that filter the rays of the sun and the idyllic singing of the birds outside.

The number of tubes and caves open to the public varies. To get there, follow the Carretera al Cascajo out of town for 1km to a large sign announcing the tunnels. Admission is s/6,000 and the caves are always open. If you need a flashlight, Sr. Antonio Gallardo in Bellavista rents them for s/6,000 and provides guides (though none is needed) for s/15,000.

■ Other Sites on Santa Cruz

The far northwest side of Santa Cruz boasts beauteous bays and beaches that can be reached by boat. In the past, daytrips to these areas left from Puerto Ayora, but now most people visit them as part of larger multi-day boat tours and scheduled daytrips are no longer offered. Special day tours, however, can be arranged for groups.

The best of the sights is **Caleta Tortuga Negra** (Black Turtle Cove) on the northern side of the island. Visitors float in *pangas* (motorboats) or kayaks through silent mangrove inlets (all three mangrove types are found here) and experience Galápagos nature at its best. Gradually, dark circular shapes start swimming under the boat—the first glimpse at the Galápagos green sea turtle. Yes, the turtles really are green, not black as the name of the location and the view under the water imply. Turtle encounters are especially frequent during breeding season, from September to February. Visitors watch turtles mating, and some see intense, multiple-hour underwater turtle embraces. The elegant sharks and rays darting around in the water also make Black Turtle Cove an excellent introduction to the Galápagos animal kingdom.

Not far from this site, **Las Bachas Beach,** near the Baltra Airport, makes for a refreshing swim. **Conway Bay** and **Ballena (Whale) Bay** lie on Santa Cruz's west coast, though neither is often visited. Whale Bay gets pointed out from passing boats, and Conway is a good place to see sea lions.

Islas Plazas

Of the tiny twin islands, only **South Plaza** (a mere 13km^2) is open to visitors. **North Plaza** remains off limits due to mysterious scientific research. While one can only guess what goes on over on the north island, the flat, desert-like interior of South Plaza can be viewed from the rocky trail that circumscribes the island. Reddish vegetation carpets the ground and overgrown **prickly pear cacti** dominate the landscape. Much larger than those found elsewhere in the world, the colossal cacti soar over 8m tall. The Galápagos have no large native trees, so over the years the prickly pears have grown unchecked, assuming the domineering role usually reserved for water-guzzling hardwoods. But the burgeoning cacti also have an evolutionary history that would have made Darwin proud. Suspiciously colored the same bright yellow hue as the prickly pear's flowers, the gargantuan South Plaza marine iguanas often lurk shamelessly beneath the plants. Centuries ago, these reptilian culprits voraciously devoured low-growing flowers. The only cacti able to reproduce were the taller, tree-like plants with large trunks that the chubby iguanas weren't able to climb. Now the skyscraping prickly pears prevail, and the shrunken dragons must wait for their succulent treats to fall to the ground.

On the south side of South Plaza, a set of **cliffs** towers over the ocean waves. These sheer rock palisades provide a bird's eye view of seagulls returning to their nests, wings fully extended, after a hard day of fishing. Blue-footed and masked boobies, frigatebirds, and lava gulls reside here as well. Keep a sharp lookout for the rarer swallowtail gull, with its striking white-and-gray body and large orange eyes. Glance over the cliff to see just how easy it is for diving birds to spot schools of colorful fish in the translucent water; sometimes even sharks and eagle rays lurk below. Don't get too close to the edge, though—even the best boots don't grab limestone the way boobies do. The cliffs are also home to the island's colony of bachelor seals, who wrestle and tumble over each other all day. Come nightfall, these slippery mountaineers scale the steep rock wall to reach their refuge above the sea.

When you land on the beach, expect a warm welcome from the unofficial greeting squad of female sea lions and pups that crowd the shores, basking in the sun and frolicking in the surf. Galápagos sea lions bear little resemblance to their rather docile cousins often seen in zoos; these gregarious animals become visibly excited when human guests arrive. As if to keep the exuberantly immodest female greeters in check, the colony's dominant male, a mammoth bull named Charlie, often keeps an eye on his brood from the visitor's dock. Most sea lions love to interact with humans, but large bulls such as Charlie, like most jealous husbands, are best left alone. In fact, sea lions bite several tourists each year, making these furry frolickers statistically more dangerous than sharks. If Charlie doesn't seem particularly excited about letting your group pass through, a few loud hand claps will generally persuade him to move away.

By all means bring a snorkel and mask to South Plaza—few animals make more exciting swimming partners than sea lions. It is easy to lose oneself in the sea lion experience, so bathers should swim with a human buddy too. The furry torpedos literally surround bathers and swim straight toward them at full speed, only to spiral downward in a series of somersaults at the last second. Because of their location on the equator, the sea lions notice none of the subtle changes in seasons and breed year-round; playful pups always pack the waters. If you encounter Charlie underwater, don't be alarmed—he's only patrolling his territory. Give him room by swimming *away* from the island; ignore the impulse to make a quick dash for land. Disposable underwater cameras are now cheap and universally available—consider bringing one along. With their amazingly large, deep, liquid eyes, about the only thing sea lions like more than being watched is having their picture taken.

Isla Santa Fé

Isla Santa Fé doesn't believe in ostentation; she keeps her treasures well-hidden. Like many of the islands, this one teems with life both above and below sea level, but this type of wildlife doesn't exactly hit tourists over the head. Though the sprightly sea lion colony couldn't be discreet if it tried, the elusive Galápagos hawks and snakes, as well as the endemic land iguanas and rice rats, don't often advertise their presence. Not for the impatient or goal-oriented, exploring Santa Fé can either be a rewarding adventure or a day of pure frustration.

One of the more concealed island creatures, the crested *Conolophus pallidus* subspecies of **land iguana** is found nowhere in the world but here on Santa Fé. A mere visit to the island, however, doesn't guarantee a sighting. Hide-and-seek champions with a little patience and time to spare stand the best chance of spotting one. The prickly pear iguanas found on South Plaza also call Santa Fé home, but here they are a richer, more golden color than those found on other islands; maybe Santa Fé's prickly pears are especially sweet. These behemothic reptiles commonly measure over three feet long, and some giants even break the four foot mark.

To experience Santa Fé to the fullest, take one of the two easy hiking trails. There is a short 300m path and a longer 1.5km trail that extends all the way into the highland region. Both are somewhat rocky but definitely accessible to most visitors. The longer trail has more to offer: there's a better chance of spotting the iguanas, and it passes the **Galápagos' largest prickly pear trees,** which at a towering height of 10m couldn't hide even if they wanted to. The trail is also an excellent place to birdwatch and to look for the **Galápagos snake** and **rice rat.** Most rats have a bad rap due to their evil sewer cousins, but this tiny brown breed has adorable, oversized Mickey Mouse ears. Large **Galápagos hawks** and curious **Galápagos mockingbirds** also frequent the area, and have been known to land on startled visitors' hats.

Undoubtedly one of Santa Fé's best features is the beautiful, sheltered **cove** in its northeast bay. Snorkeling here is no more difficult than hiking, though to be safe you should bring a friend for both. Some groups make sightings before they even enter the water—keep an eye out for large schools of **eagle rays,** often seen "flying" in perfect synchronization just under the water's surface. **Hawksbill** and **green sea turtles** also hang out in these parts. The latter is endangered in much of the world, but abundant in the Galápagos.

Isla Seymour Norte

North Seymour is the thrifty corner store in the midst of the glitzy outdoor bazaars that make up the Galápagos. Convenient and dependable, it delivers the basic wildlife staples—frigatebirds and boobies, sea lions and iguanas—without much fuss or flash. And it's certainly no secret around town—Seymour's central location makes it easily accessible to daytrippers from Santa Cruz. Its proximity to Baltra (which used to be called *South* Seymour) makes it a favorite last stop for boat tours as well.

After making a somewhat slippery dry landing on a set of natural steps, visitors are greeted by hordes of sea lions and swallow-tailed gulls, who love to watch the activity surrounding the landing site. Once on shore, take the red, sandy 2-km trail that loops around the island to Seymour Norte's nesting colonies of blue-footed boobies and frigatebirds. Amid impressive amounts of hooting and whistling, the **boobies** strut their stuff across the rocky path, making every effort to draw attention to their technicolor feet. The only sight more amusing than the booby mating dance is that of less-coordinated humans imitating them; even the proudest visitors may find it impossible to resist.

The inflated red pouch of the **frigatebird** is a common sight on most islands, but Seymour Norte is one of the few places where these sleek black birds form large colonies, and one of the only spots where both fabulous subspecies (the Magnificent Frigate and the smaller Great Frigate) nest side-by-side. At first glance it's almost impossible to tell these two birds apart, and after a quick look at a bird manual it's still nearly as difficult (see Fauna and Flora, p. 248). Like many Magnificent or Great humans in history, the tyrannical frigates prove that they can bully the smaller and weaker like the best of the despots. Because their feathers aren't waterproof, frigates don't dive down into the sea to collect fish. Instead, they harass smaller diving birds as they return from the sea; when a startled booby or gull drops its fish, the speedy frigates zoom down and scoop it up. Nesting mothers are also favorite targets—frigates will wait for the birds to begin feeding their wide-mouthed babies, and then swoop down and stick their large beaks right into the booby's mouth to snatch a regurgitated fish.

■ Isla Mosquera

So small that it's often referred to by the diminutive "islet," Mosquera hides quietly between Isla Baltra and Seymour Norte. However, its prime location and proximity to Baltra Airport cause Mosquera to lose any potential anonymity. The first island excited visitors see as they arrive, Mosquera is a common starting point for departing boat tours. Reached via a wet landing, the island contains no visitor trails, so many tourists simply soak in the warm water with the sea lions. Others sprawl across Mosquera's shimmering white sand beach. While the attention-starved sea lions would never admit it, Mosquera really does have more marine life to offer—just take a look at its many tidal pools, each a separate world of activity.

ISLA SAN CRISTÓBAL

The easternmost and oldest of the islands, San Cristóbal was formed by the towering volcano **Cerro San Joaquín** (over 700m high) and low-lying lava flows that filled out the southern regions of the island. The northern part of the island is dry and rather barren, but the lowlands are kept moist by humid winds from the south. The island's first settlers founded the towns of **Puerto Baquerizo Moreno** and **El Progreso** to take advantage of the fertile soil and favorable climate. Today the island is the administrative capital of the Galápagos, boasting a naval base and the islands' only radio station. While San Cristóbal is not as centrally located as Santa Cruz, and therefore does not see as many tourists, there's still lots to see and do here. Puerto Baquerizo Moreno has lots of comfortable places to stay, and an unusual number of sites can be reached from town by foot and without a guide. There are also a number of intersting daytrips that can be made by *panga* to **Isla Lobos, Leon Dormido,** and the easternmost point in the Galápagos, **Punta Pitt.**

■ Puerto Baquerizo Moreno

San Cristóbal has always had to work just a little bit harder to attract people. After all, its first residents were ex-convicts who revolted and killed their overseer, and it's always hard to correct a bad first impression. Such violence today would be unthinkable, as well as far too strenuous, for the nearly 3000 laid-back residents of Puerto Baquerizo Moreno, who pride themselves on their town's small size, safety, and peaceful disposition. Even the town's pet giant tortoise, Pepe, is *tranquilo.*

Though the rambling Puerto Baquerizo Moreno is the political capital of the Galápagos, it's far from a major metropolis. Many of the island's most important officials live and work here, but the townies still know how to take it easy. Having a drink has become an art form and failing to take an afternoon *siesta* is tantamount to breaking the law. You can't beat them, so you might as well join them for conversation and a cold one while overlooking **Wreck Bay,** a misnomer for this beautiful idyll.

PRACTICAL INFORMATION

Tourist Information: CETUR, on Av. Charles Darwin at the center of town. Just keep an eye out for the unmistakable square pink box topped by the life-sized smiling gray whale (open Mon.-Fri. only intermittently, so consider picking up a map of Puerto Baquerizo Moreno at the CETUR office in Puerto Ayora).

Bank: El Banco del Pacífico (tel. 520-365; fax 520-368), on Av. Charles Darwin near Av. Jose de Villamil, next to the ocean between the police station and post office. Changes dollars and traveler's checks, though rates are higher than on the mainland (open Mon.-Fri. 8am-3:30pm, Sat. 9:30am-12:30pm).

Telephone: Central Telefónica San Cristóbal (EMETEL) (tel./fax 520-104), on Av. Quito, 4 blocks past Darwin. If you're not already wearing sunglasses, put them on and look for the yellow building with blaring blue windows. Probably the cheapest place to call home or fax in town (open daily 7am-9pm).

Airline: SAN/SAETA office (tel. 520-156), on Av. Charles Darwin at Av. Teodoro Wolf, in the string of shops on the left. SAN offers flights to Quito via Guayaquil (Mon.-Sat., to Guayaquil s/166,500, to Quito s/188,500).

Buses: All buses leave from *el muelle* at the end of Av. Darwin. **Airport** buses depart several times a day (ask at the SAN office for details). Several buses travel to the **highlands,** daily at 10am, 12:30pm, and 4:40pm (s/2,000).

Shuttle Boats: INGALA travels to Puerto Ayora (every Mon. and Wed., 10am); arrive at least ½hr. early. Tickets are sold the morning of the trip at 7:30am from the ticket counter at the corner of Av. 12 de Febrero and Ignacio de Hernandez, under a large fluorescent green sign advertising the Banco Nacional.

Pharmacies: Farmacia Tabavi (tel. 520-235), on Av. 12 de Febrero (open 8am-8 or 9pm). **Farmacia Jane** (tel. 520-242), on Av. Darwin next to the SAN office (open 7:30am-9:00pm). **Farmacia San Cristóbal,** on Jose de Villamil, 1½ blocks up from El Banco Pacífico (open daily until 10pm).

Hospital: Hospital Oskar Jandl (24-hr. emergency tel. 520-118), on the corner of Quito and Alsacio Northia, next to the Catedral and museum (open daily 7:30am-noon and 1-4:30pm). A doctor and one or more nurses are supposedly on duty 24hr. One doctor speaks some English.

Police: Policía National (24-hr. emergency tel. 520-101 or 520-129), on the corner of Av. Darwin and Española. It's the blue and grey building just before the post office and naval base (open 24hr.).

Post Office: (tel. 520-373; fax 520-373), at the end of Av. Darwin, in the string of shops just past the police headquarters. All mail comes through this office since Puerto Baquerizo Moreno is the provincial capital of the islands, so it's the safest bet for your postcards. Fax service (open Mon.-Fri. 8am-noon and 2-6pm).

Telephone Code: 05.

ACCOMMODATIONS

While luxury visitors stick to the cramped quarters of their boats, Puerto Baquerizo Moreno has several more spacious (and more stationary) options. Don't just dash into the first accommodations you see upon disembarking; most small hotels and hostels are clean and inexpensive, but more interesting options exist elsewhere. **Camping** is sometimes permitted on the beaches surrounding Puerto Baquerizo Moreno and in the highlands at El Junco Lagoon. Natives assure that no permission is necessary, but truly law-abiding campers should inquire at the CETUR office or the Park Information Site, just out of town on Av. Alsacio Northia.

Hotel Mar Azul (tel. 520-139 or 520-107), on Av. Alsacio Northia; turn right at the museum and continue to the end of the street. All rooms have ceiling fans and private baths with hot water, but some lack toilet seats. Two shady courtyards filled with large, old trees. Singles s/14,000; doubles s/24,000; triples s/30,000.

Cabañas de Don Jorge (tel. 520-208; fax 520-100), on Av. Alsacio Northia on the east side of town; turn left at the CETUR office and take Av. Darwin towards the edge of town. Walk up a large set of white stairs, turn left at the flamingo statue, and follow Av. Alsacio Northia out of town. After the 5-min. walk, Las Cabañas are a sight for sore eyes. Each cabin is different and surrounded by palms, cacti, and hibiscus-draped seating areas. Private bathrooms have hot water. One cabin even has a kitchen, but if cooking isn't on the agenda, try the restaurant with its sunken "conversation pit." Singles s/25,000; doubles s/20,000-28,000. Patrons are encouraged to rent for longer stays. In busy seasons, call for reservations.

Hotel San Francisco (tel. 520-304), on Av. Darwin, just across from El Banco del Pacífico. One of the best cheap places to stay, Hotel San Francisco has a rambling indoor courtyard filled with murals, plants, and staircases somewhat reminiscent of the set of Sesame Street. The prices are also likely to take you back to the childhood days of old. Individual rooms with fans, TVs, and clean private bathrooms are just s/10,000 per person.

Grand Hotel (tel./fax 520-179), on Av. Alsacio Northia past Cabañas de Jorge, just outside of town. Built years ago as a self-contained tourist destination, the Grand Hotel has recently lowered its prices into the budget traveler realm. The friendly cocker spaniel leads guests to commodious rooms with private baths, warm water, and ceiling fans. Singles US$12; doubles US$21. Locals love the Grand Hotel's restaurant, but if you plan to dine, tell them in advance. Breakfast s/8,000, lunch and dinner s/15,000. The beach out front is beautiful, open to the public, and a great place to watch the sunset.

FOOD

Puerto Baquerizo Moreno may suffer from a lack of many things, but good food it has in abundance. Seafood lovers can sample the island's *ceviche* from just about any restaurant, or head straight to the *cevichería* in the northeast corner of the town. Great island barbeque can be had on most Sunday nights at the **Soda Bar de Nathali.** Those with less meaty appetites can pick up a juicy morsel or two from one of the many fresh fruit stands scattered across town.

La Zayapa (no tel.), on Av. 12 de Febrero, one block up from *el muelle*. The nearly universal local consensus is that this is the best place in town. Enormous portions of fish, shrimp, and chicken (s/12,000-15,000) served beneath gently rustling palm fronds in the romantic yellow glow of insect-repelling lights. Feel free to grab an after-dinner nap in the hammock (open daily until 9pm).

Genoa (no tel.), near the end of Av. Darwin across from *el muelle;* just follow the music and colored lights. Almost as highly recommended as La Zayapa, this tin-roofed comfort zone is a great place for *comida típica,* and also sports an exotic assortment of fresh juices. Orchidaceous posters and strangely appropriate tinsel round out the decor.

Restaurante Rosita (tel. 520-106), on the corner of Villamil and Ignacio de Hernandez. Approaching near cult status in town, Rosita is known for her fantastic fish. Vegetarians can opt for the *arroz con vegetales* (rice and vegetables; not on the menu, but made to order). Dine indoors or outside under the palm-frond awning. Daytrips and island tours can also be arranged; ask for Gustavo.

Restaurante Ninfas, on Av. Darwin across from the bank. An inexpensive favorite, Ninfas has it all, including a full bar, gift table, and motorcycle in the corner. Music ranges from Japanese to classic opera. Though the surroundings are eclectic, the food is basic and tasty. Open daily for breakfast, lunch, and dinner (each around s/5,000). Ask about specials.

Galapan (tel. 520-292), on the corner of Av. Darwin and Av. 12 de Febrero. One of the town bakeries, come here for some bready, doughy goodness. Great cookies as well. Run by the friendly owner and her 3 daughters, all of whom are named María (open Mon.-Sat. 9am-1pm and 3-8pm).

SIGHTS AND ENTERTAINMENT

A cold drink under a palm tree is all most tourists experience of this small town. You might consider getting your drink to go and taking a walk up to the **Museum of Natural History,** on Alsacio Northia next to the cathedral, for a look at Galápagos wildlife in various stages of preservation. There are living inhabitants as well; a visit with town mascot Pepe the Tortoise is well worth the s/2,000 admission fee (open Mon.-Sat. 8:30am-12:30pm and 3:30-5:30pm).

The best disco in town is the **Blue Bay** near the center of town. Blue Bay cranks out a loud Latin/techno beat every night except Sunday, though groovesters with any pride wait until after Wednesday to bust their moves. Friday and Saturday nights are best, and with a little Club beer (s/5,000), things can get pretty wild. The nearby **Neptunus,** next to *el muelle* in the large white house, attracts an older, more touristy crowd. But they still know how to get down (perhaps helped by the slightly more expensive selection of American and European brews).

■ Near Puerto Baquerizo Moreno

Most of the sites on San Cristóbal can only be reached by boat, but the few listed below are accessible by foot or by a short truck ride from Puerto Baquerizo Moreno, and can be visited without a guide.

FRIGATEBIRD HILL

Breathe in the fresh air, lace up those hiking boots, and head on up to Frigatebird Hill. The hike up the hill is by no means easy—the trail misleadingly begins with a pleasant walk along a shady, pebble-lined path, and by the end visitors scramble over large boulders in the hot equatorial sun. The view from the top is breathtaking (both literally and figuratively)—the red roofs of Puerto Baquerizo Moreno stretch out to one side, with beautiful views of bright white sand and lava rock beaches on the other. Aside from the view, the main attraction is the big, black birds for which the hill is named. Both narcissistically-named species of **Frigatebird** nest here: the Magnificent Frigate and Great Frigate. With wingspans of about 2.3m (7.5 ft.) and bright red, inflatable pouches, they actually do live up to their names. Since these birds only frequent the hill at certain times of the year and certain hours of the day, there's no guarantee you'll spot one. To better your chances, consult a guide before leaving town. While hiking, also watch out for the endemic **Chatham Mockingbird,** the only type of mockingbird on San Cristóbal.

Though this site is accessible without a guide, it might be a good idea to bring one along. The terrain is rough, and the familiar black-on-white indicator sticks and direction arrows are often hard to spot, leaving hikers to navigate by looking for lava rocks placed in trees. Since the trail is not clearly marked, don't be tempted to take a quick look on the other side of the hill, where the trail seems to lead. The path actually ends mysteriously just past the rocky beach, and if you stray too far from it, you might not be able to find your way back. To get to Frigatebird Hill, start at the Grand Hotel and continue along the same dirt road for five to seven minutes. The trail head is at the end of the road. Although only 3.5km long, allow two hours for the challenging hike. Be sure to wear good hiking shoes and bring plenty of water.

LA LOBERÍA

La Lobería isn't on any tour company's "must see" list and snooty cruise ships don't come here, which is precisely what makes this secluded beach so special. Located just outside of Puerto Baquerizo Moreno, only the natives seem to take advantage of it—many maps don't even label it. But its not a secret to everyone—be prepared to share the shore with the oodles of sea lions. Those who choose to linger until sunset can watch the water darken from crystal clear to bright blue to deep purple. As the sky above starts to dim, the stars emerge; make sure you've got a flashlight for the trip home. To get here, follow directions to Hotel Mar Azul, then take the road out of

El Progreso's Progress

The first settlement on Isla San Cristóbal, El Progreso was founded in the 1880s by **Manuel J. Cobos.** Cobos imported a group of ex-convicts to serve as laborers on his sugar plantation, halfway between the highlands and the current capital of Puerto Baquerizo Moreno. His ruthless overseeing practices and slave-labor policies quickly incited an infamous mass-mutiny in which rebellious workers took his life. These days the memory of Cobos lives on, immortalized by the numerous street signs around the island that bear his name.

The small agricultural town he founded also survives, easily accessible by hike or taxi from Puerto Baquerizo Moreno. El Progreso boasts one of the best highland restaurants around, **Quita d'Cristhi.** Never a dull moment, come to enjoy great meat and chicken, stroll through the forest, or nap in a hammock beneath the orange blossoms. Particularly active on weekends, Quita d'Cristhi usually has soccer games, arm-wrestling matches, and particularly heated card games. For a sleeping experience only Walt Disney could equal, try **La Casa del Ceiba** (tel. 520-248), a large bamboo cabin built 12m (40 ft.) off the ground in a gigantic *ceiba* tree. Visitors enter via a hanging bridge made of vine-covered bamboo. The two-story house is completely furnished with two beds, a bathroom, hot water, music, television, a refrigerator, and a complete bar. Take a picture; your friends at home won't believe it. US$10 a night, tours US$1.

town (about a 30-min. walk). Keep left though, as an unfortunate right turn will lead you into the restricted naval base. When you reach the beach, turn left at the Galápagos park sign. When returning to town, use the same road and walk toward the airport signal tower.

EL JUNCO LAGOON

Most tour companies describe El Junco simply as the largest freshwater lake in the Galápagos. Sure, they're correct, but these words hardly do justice to San Cristóbal's beautiful highland lake. At the mountain's summit, which can now be reached by car, a mist-enshrouded pool encircles a fertile volcanic rim abounding with vegetation. It seems somehow fitting that the lagoon formed when hundreds of years worth of rainwater collected in the mouth of an extinct volcano—the perfect reconciliation of earth and sky.

A narrow trail winds its way around the perimeter of the rim, past numerous land and sea birds, and overlooks nearly all of San Cristóbal (including León Dormido to the north and Punta Pitt to the northeast). A small portion of the coastline is obstructed, however, by the looming **Cerro San Joaquín** (at nearly 900m, the highest mountain on San Cristóbal). Despite rumors to the contrary, visitors do *not* need to be part of a tour group to visit the highlands. While tours can be arranged in town (ask at Restaurant Rosita or any hotel), the highlands can also be reached by foot or by hiring a truck in town (prices are bargainable, but it should never cost more than US$20). To reach the lagoon, first head 8km east of Puerto Baquerizo Moreno to the town of **El Progreso,** which is itself an experience not to be missed (see graybox). From here, it is 10km farther to El Junco.

■ Other Sites on San Cristóbal

These nearby sites are accessible only by boat, either as daytrips from Puerto Baquerizo Moreno or as longer tours from other islands. The most popular excursion is to the islands of **Isla Lobos** and **León Dormido** (also called **Kicker Rock**) off San Cristóbal's western shore. Lobos, the first of the two islands, is about one hour northeast of Puerto Baquerizo Moreno. Separated from San Cristóbal's shore by only a small channel, the tiny, rocky island has a white sand beach where blue-footed boobies nest and sea lions sunbathe. Humans, however, only observe the habitat from the 300m trail that cuts across it from east to west. León Dormido, another hour northeast of Lobos, gets its name from its resemblance to a sleeping lion. But whoever named it must've had one mighty imagination; it looks more like a monstrous rock sticking straight up out of the ocean, with a gigantic splinter to one side. Unlike Aesop's lion, you don't need to remove the splinter to tame this lion and its waters; adventurous captains smoothly sail through the small channel between the sliver and the mother rock. Scuba diving here is prime, but watch for dangerous currents.

The easternmost point in the archipelago, **Punta Pitt,** is another of San Cristóbal's notable sites. Located on the far northeast corner of the island, it takes quite a while to reach from Baquerizo Moreno. But booby fanatics probably won't think twice about making the trip; red-footed, blue-footed, and masked boobies all call Punta Pitt home. After the landing in a sandy cove, a trail leads up into the mountainous terrain, weaving through prime booby territory and providing good views of the rocky shore below and the sea beyond.

One final site in the mountains of San Cristóbal, **La Galapaguera** is just down the shore from Punta Pitt. Giant land tortoises roam free at this site, which is very similar to the Tortoise Reserve on Isla Santa Cruz, but not nearly as convenient to reach. As with the Tortoise Reserve, the site is large, trails are badly marked, and tortoises may be hard to come by. An experienced guide is a must.

ISLA ISABELA

Though Isabela is the largest of the Galápagos Islands, making up over 58% of the archipelago's entire land mass, it is one of the most rarely visited. Its distance from the other islands and the fact that most of its visitor's sites are on its far western side make a trip to Isabela more a struggle than recreation. But don't get duped into thinking there's less to see here; to the contrary, Isabela has quite a few unique sites. One of the most volcanically active islands, it was once six separate volcanic isles, but lava flows united them into one landmass. Few of these volcanos have lost their steam; eruptions have occured on **Volcán Wolf, Cerro Azul,** and **Sierra Negra** in the past 20 years, and in 1991 earthquakes shook **Volcán Alcedo.** The towering shield volcanos are truly mastodonic, dominating Isabela's skyline. Those sailing to the western side of the island pass through the narrow **Bolívar Channel** separating Fernandina from Isabela. Steaming volcanic fumaroles sometimes flare up, and some groups get distracted by the dolphins and whales that also pop out of the water.

■ Puerto Villamil

As of yet, the southern-tip town of Puerto Villamil (pop. well under 1000) is untouched by commercialization. There is no tourist office, no phone book, and in lieu of a newspaper, people make announcements from a loudspeaker in the center of town. Prickly pears substitute for fence posts and disco lights struggle to compete with the stars above. Like many small towns, Villamil gossips and gawks. Don't be surprised if an islander invites you in for a bit of conversation; everyone's got a story to tell. Residents already know all about each other and will quickly learn all about their visitors as well. More than any other town, Villamil makes visitors realize that the Galápagos are not like any other nature reserve in the world. Here mankind and nature come together in a pleasantly confusing jumble of palm trees, chickens, sea lions, and *guayabana* pie.

Practical Information As far as tourist services go, helpful town information books are sold at the **Hotel Ballena Azul** (s/10,000). Phone calls can be made from the **EMETEL** office, on Calle Las Escalecias, three blocks away from the beach (just head towards the big orange antennae). **Buses** leave from the Municipio for the highlands (7am, 2pm, s/3,000-5,000; return trips 7:30am, 2:30pm). **INGALA** (tel. 529-157), travels to Puerto Ayora (every Fri., 10am). Tickets can be bought after 2pm on

Thursday at the INGALA office, 200m past Hotel Ballena Azul on the right. Captain Juan Mendoza takes passengers to Puerto Ayora each Tuesday morning on the privately-owned **Estrella Del Mar** for about the same price as INGALA. Purchase tickets in the municipal offices on Mondays. If you have to get back quickly, **EMETEBE** flies to Puerto Ayora on Tuesday, Thursday, and Saturday mornings. To buy tickets, ask for EMETEBE agent Emma Ramón at the Hotel Ballena Azul. There is no hospital on Isabela, but Puerto Villamil does boast a **health center** (open 8am-noon and 2-5pm), on Av. 16 de Marzo, across from El Municipio. In case of an emergency after hours, try calling Dr. Bazan's **private practice** (tel. 529-165), or go to her house in the INGALA compound, 200m past Hotel Ballena Azul. The **Policía Capitania** (tel. 529-101), in the center of town across from El Municipio, is supposedly open 24hr.

Accommodations Lodging in Villamil is good, verging on excellent. **Hotel Ballena Azul** and the adjacent **Cabañas Isabela del Mar** (tel./fax 529-125 for both), on Calle Conocarpus at the edge of town, are easily two of the best places to stay in the Galápagos. The large, airy rooms of Hotel Ballena Azul, with hot water baths, wooden walls, mosquito netting, and ocean views, would have made Hemingway's old man content to simply *look* at the sea. S/10,000 per person, with bath s/15,000. The Cabañas Isabela del Mar are spacious and spotless. Each private cabin fits two or three people, with a ceiling fan to ward off mosquitos and a private bathroom where hot water flows. The owners are outgoing and friendly; Dora loves to sit down and chat (in English, Spanish, French, German, or her native Swedish). S/20,000 per person, singles s/28,000. Another quality place is the nearby **Hotel Terro Real** (tel. 529-106), conveniently located on Calle Terro Real—just look for the red roofs. Two-story, triangle-shaped bungalows with refrigerators and private baths house four to five people each. Friendly management included in the s/15,000 per person cost. For **longer stays,** Marita Zecchettin (tel./fax 529-238) rents both a guest house with kitchenette and a guest room. Both have private baths and hot water, but you have to share the palm trees. Awesome family, and a beach that spans for miles. Minimum stay one week. **Hotel San Vicente** (tel. 529-140 or 529-180), offers free **camping** space in the front yard.

Food If you aren't invited to eat in someone's house, the restaurant at the **Hotel Ballena Azul** is the next best thing. Join Antonio and Dora for great local and international food that borders on the gourmet. Breakfast of fresh fruit, bread, homemade jam, and coffee s/4,500, with eggs s/6,000. Lunch and dinner go for s/10,000, and include rice, meat, salad, and vegetables. Soup and dessert each s/2,000 extra. For smoother sailing, let your hosts know in advance if you plan to have lunch or dinner. For a markedly different experience, try the **Restaurant Iguana,** between the disco and the ocean. This informal nightlife center serves up tasty treats in an atmosphere that can't be beat. Pull up a chair beside the Bob Marley poster and try the tuna pizza (s/10,000). For local food, try one of the small restaurants near the Municipio. Many recommend **Ruta,** which serves hot food and ice-encrusted drinks (meals s/6,000) but there's usually only one choice of entreés. For a little more selection, head to the nearby **Costa Azul.** Meal of the day s/6,000, just like Ruta. *A la Carta* items cost a bit more (mixed *ceviche* s/12,000), but the food is good, and yes, the purple tentacles are octopus.

Nightlife Come weekend, *villamileños* love to drink and dance with the best of 'em. To accomodate these passions, they've built a lagoon-shaped dance floor, complete with driftwood columns. The men arrive early and nurse their buzzes until the *chicas* arrive. Some guys sip exotic drinks at the bar, but many more go across the street to the **Iguana Bar** (the after dark alter-ego of Restaurant Iguana) for a cold beer. There, fluorescent animal figures lounge outside while a school of pufferfish lights swim over patrons' heads on waves of music and MTV videos. Try a cold Pilsener and watch the sleepy town wake up for the weekend. The town's power shuts down at

11pm, but the Iguana's prized generator keeps its school of pufferfish lights up and swimming until midnight. The disco stays open as long as the scene is still hoppin'.

■ Near Puerto Villamil

The marine site **La Tintorera** is about a five-minute *panga* ride from Puerto Villamil. Ask in town to see who's going, or walk past Hotel Ballena Azul to the docks and bargain with one of the *panga* owners. After a short walk, the rocky black lava trail approaches a large channel beside a lagoon. Small fish swim around the narrow channel entrance, but farther up lurks a bigger catch—white-tipped reef sharks. Bilingual marine experts will know that these sharks give the site its name. Far from aggressive, these docile creatures glide in and out of the channel in groups. Only two feet from the trail, cliques of 30 or more often bask in the shallows. Some daredevils jump in with the sharks; while this is not dangerous for the humans, it is for the sharks. They scare easily, sometimes cutting themselves on the sharp lava rocks in their attempt to avoid running into clumsy tourists. Best to take a dip in the large, adjacent lagoon, where sharks swim among smoother rocks. If you're lucky, you could also spot a sea turtle or spotted eagle ray.

For more wildlife encounters, the **Rearing Center for Giant Tortoises** (tel. 529-178), run in conjunction with the National Park Service, provides up-close looks at Galápagos tortoises in all degrees of giantness (open until 4pm). The center focuses on the rearing of two breeds of Isabelan tortoises from eggs to adulthood. To get there, follow Av. Antonio Gil past the health center to the edge of town, where a sign points to the station, another 1km past the stadium on the right.

One last visitor's site near Villamil, **El Muro de Las Lágrimas (The Wall of Tears)** commemorates Isabela's past as a penal colony. In June 1946, then-President José María Velasco Ibarra decided to move 300 prisoners and 30 guards from Guayaquil to the base of "La Orchilla," about 5km outside of Puerto Villamil. With no other means of employing the prisoners, the chief of the penal colony decided to begin construction of a jail, with the only substance available: lava rocks. Because of the lack of building materials, the wall was constructed without cement, by simply piling the rocks on top of each other. The extreme variety in the shapes of the rocks prevented efficient stacking. The result was a long pile of rocks, 2-3m high with sloping sides. The grueling hours in the hot sun and back-breaking labor also broke many men's spirits, stealing away their will to live. Over time, it came to be known as the place "where the cowards died and the brave wept." Construction of this "wall of tears" ceased when the sadistic chief was transferred and the colony moved to the highland agricultural area, where it was later abolished in 1959.

To get there, follow Av. Antonio Gil past the health center to the outskirts of town. From there, signs guide the way. The walk takes about two hours and there are several nice lagoons and beaches along the way (including the particularly secluded and aptly named **Playa de Amor**). **Horses** can be rented in town.

ELIZABETH BAY

Elizabeth Bay is a marine visitor site on the western side of Isabela, rife with marine and bird activity. There are no landing sites, so get out those binoculars and hope for a clear day. To the north of the bay lie the **Mariela Islets.** A landscape of rugged cliffs and gnarled trees, these islands are frequented by penguins and *pangas* alike. Be quiet when observing the penguins; despite their formal attire, these birds are quite shy and will turn their backs to approaching boats if startled. Like ostriches who stick their heads in the sand, penguins seem to think if they can't see you, you won't be able to see them. Be especially careful during molting season; their feathers are not yet waterproof and they really don't enjoy getting wet, so try not to scare them into the water.

At the other end of the bay, a labyrinth of channels and lagoons snake in and out of an aquatic **mangrove forest.** Clear blue water provides contrast to the sinister-looking roots of the red mangrove. Far from sinister in reality, the mangroves serve as breeding grounds for several types of fish and green sea turtles. Rays and white-tip reef sharks often make rounds in search of a quick meal. Some tours provide small kayaks that make for a more personal mangrove experience; ask about it before leaving.

PUNTA MORENO

On the western side of Isabela, Punta Moreno can be one of the most memorable sites of an entire tour. The juxtaposition of jagged lava rocks and small, idyllic lagoons scattered across the landscape is unforgettable. All varieties of birds flock to these watering holes, including blue herons and flamingos. It is especially mesmerizing to see these amazingly sleek and serpentine birds in flight. If you visit around mating season, the coloration of the flamingos is particularly vivid, with some birds sporting an uncharacteristic dark red color. The journey to the watering holes from the landing site traverses fields of jagged lava rocks. The black rocks reflect heat and the air is often very dry. Bring plenty of water and sturdy hiking shoes; sandals definitely won't do for this one.

Near Punta Moreno some groups might visit a series of coastal pools, one of which is known as **Derek's Cove.** While it is illegal to go ashore, these pools are an excellent place to observe sea lions and large numbers of sea turtles.

URVINA BAY

Urvina is one of the most surreal sites in the Galápagos. After a wet landing on an otherwise normal-looking beach, a trail leads a short ways to a bizarre, unnatural dreamscape. Coral heads seem to sprout from the sand, and where fish should be swimming, cormorants and iguanas make their homes. This entire area used to be underwater, but was completely uplifted due to volcanic activity by the nearby giant, **Volcán Alcedo,** in 1954. Though no one was present at the time, skeletons of marine turtles, sharks, and even entire schools of fish were found here when a crew of Disney filmmakers arrived on the scene a few days later. The fast-moving animals didn't even have time to escape, testimony to how quickly the uplift occurred.

VOLCÁN ALCEDO

The hike up Volcán Alcedo is the most difficult one in the islands (3-6hr. of rough uphill terrain), but the hard work pays off. Starting at a sandy volcanic beach on Isabela's east side, the trail leads 10km up to the *caldera,* past lots of lava rocks and scrubby bushes. Invest in a hat and sunscreen; there is little shade to protect from killer solar rays that you'll endure along the way. The 7-km *caldera* itself, filled with rocks and scruffy vegetation, is home to the largest turtle population in the islands, over 4000 strong. During the wet season (Jan.-June), the turtles wallow in mud puddles to cool off and rehydrate, while in the dry season they keep mostly to the bushes. The crater also has several active fumaroles that can be reached by hiking a few more kilometers around the crater. Perhaps the hike's most gratifying reward is the view; on clear days, the vista encompasses the entire volcano-studded island of Isabela. Be sure to note and admire the long, recently conquered trail to the ocean.

Reaching the summit of Alcedo requires advance planning and will most likely include an overnight stay, either at the landing site or on the peak. The site has been closed for the past year due to an extensive goat eradication program, but it is expected to re-open in September of 1996. To arrange a trip, contact a tour company or a boat captain in Puerto Ayora. The trip is very difficult, if not impossible, to arrange from Puerto Villamil.

PUNTA GARCÍA

One of the few sites located on Isabela's eastern side, Punta García used to be one of the best places to see flightless cormorants without traveling to Isabela's western side. Now... well, judge for yourself. Lately the birds have become rarer and rarer, and the number of visitors has declined along with the cormorants. The site also has a small mangrove forest, but who are you kidding—there are mangrove forests all over the place. Lava herons have been also spotted from time to time. The terrain is primarily sharp lava rocks, so good shoes are a necessity.

PUNTA ALBEMARLE

Punta Albemarle stands guard over the remote northern tip of Isabela. Passing boats can see the abandoned water towers of a defunct United States radar base from World War II. Because of the rough sea here, few boats go ashore. Wildlife on Punta Albemarle includes flightless cormorants, fur sea lions, and the largest species of marine iguana on all the islands.

PUNTA TORTUGA AND TAGUS COVE

A young visitor's site on the northwestern side of Isabela, **Punta Tortuga** is the result of volcanic uplift that occured in 1975 at the base of Volcán Darwin. Like the goddess Venus, this natural beauty was borne from the sea. The mangroves that surround the swimming area here are home to the tool-using mangrove finch. Endemic to Isabela and Fernandina, these talented birds explore tree bark using sticks or cactus spines held in their beaks. After some digging, they usually score a tasty grub or two. When they find a particularly good tool, they stash it away for later use.

South of Punta Tortuga, **Tagus Cove** bears the unmistakable mark of man, like Post Office Bay and so many other Galápagos sites. The "historical graffiti" here dates back to the turn of the century, when sailors scratched their ships' names on the cave walls. Current travelers are encouraged *not* to add their own mark. Instead, follow the trail to the nearby **Darwin Lake,** a saltwater-filled crater. Again due to volcanic uplift, the lake actually lies above sea level. Later, enjoy a *panga* ride along the cliffs of Tagus Cove past flightless cormorants, penguins, and blue-footed boobies.

VOLCÁN SIERRA NEGRA (SANTO TOMÁS)

Volcán Sierra Negra doesn't like to have its picture taken. The oldest and largest of Isabela's six volcanos, this one can afford to be a little proud. When seen from the *caldera* rim, the ominous, dark crater extends in all directions, refusing to fit in even the widest angle lens. With a diameter of 10km (6 mi.), Sierra Negra is the second-largest volcanic crater in the world.

A bus from Puerto Villamil stops about 10-20 minutes away from the **crater rim.** The crater itself is often filled with mist and can be rainy during the wet season. For better views and less chance of rain, there's another trail leading around the crater rim to **Volcán Chico,** on the north side of Sierra Negra. Just about a two-hour horseback ride from the bus stop, it offers excellent views of the crater and even more impressive panoramas of the rest of the island.

More adventurous travelers should consider following the trail westward along the crater rim to the **sulphur mines.** Just inside the crater, three levels of sulphur formations bubble and steam. Over the years, the geothermal activity has created a landscape of strange formations. Is it just the fumes, or are those really sulphur castles and flowers? Keep an eye out for a hole full of boiling mud that gurgles by onlookers' feet. Visitors should be in good physical condition, with some riding or hiking experience. Because of the distance (2½hr. by horse), you'll be hard-pressed to make it to and from this area in time to catch the afternoon bus back to Villamil. More often people hire private cars to come to the restaurant near the top of the mountain at an appointed time for the return trip to the village. A cheaper and more hard-core option is camping at the crater rim, which allows unlimited time to see all the sites. Before camping it's a good idea to talk to the park officials in Puerto Villamil (tel. 529-178), on Av. Antonio Gil. Remember, fires are not permitted and trash must be carried out. Tents can be rented from Hotel Ballena Azul, though other items (including rain gear) should be brought along.

To get to Sierra Negra independently, take the bus to the highlands that leaves from the Municipio (every day, 7am). On Saturday and Sunday, trucks also leave at 6am and 8am. The cost varies unpredictably between s/3,000 and s/5,000. Catch the bus home between 2:30pm and 3pm. A semi-autonomous option is to arrange for a guide and horses to meet you at the bus stop by radio-ing ahead from one of the hotels in Villamil (try Ballena Azul). The bigger your group, the less expensive the service (bulk price is around US$90, not including horse). Alternatively, you can join an already existing tour group. Tours leave town about three times each week.

OTHER ISLANDS

Isla Fernandina

An island of superlatives, Fernandina is the newest island in the archipelago, the westernmost link in the Galápagos chain, and the most volcanically active. The last eruption was in January 1995, and experts say **Volcán La Cumbre** could perform again anytime. Perhaps most impressive is Fernandina's lack of non-native plants and animals, a distinction that prompts many to award it the sought-after title of "the most pristine island in the world." In light of the fact that the rest of the islands in the Galápagos have been colonized by new species from rats to goats, Fernandina's purity is surprising. Visitors must be extremely careful not to accidentally transport plants, seeds, or nasty flesh-eating microorganisms onto the island. You may be asked to strip down and stand naked before high pressure water jets in the decontamination tank before stepping into the *panga.* In most cases, however, you will just be asked to wash your feet.

Fernandina has only one visitor's site, **Punta Espinosa,** a geologic baby formed by tectonic uplift in 1975. The dock here is an outcropping of lava that only allows dry landings during high tide, so be prepared for wet shoes. Snorkelers and scuba divers can explore underwater, and some tours will go sea kayaking around the *punta* to a lagoon surrounded by jagged black lava spires and green mangroves. The lagoon is frequented by white-tipped sharks, rays, turtles, and schools of glimmering fish.

On land, the visitor's trail branches in two directions. To the left, the path winds its way over dry fields of *pahoehoe* and *aa* lava, which take their names from similar flows in the Hawaiian islands. Although this walk takes longer, it passes through more interesting and recent lava formations, which guides can often discuss in great detail. Be careful of the *aa* flows, however, as these formations are *very* sharp—wear sturdy, closed-toed shoes.

If your time is limited, try taking the road *more* traveled, on the right. Make your way past all the barking sea lions onto a narrow sandy trail. Afternoon trekkers will likely encounter hoards of **marine iguanas** basking in the sun after a lunchtime feed. Marine iguanas are voracious eaters—after gorging themselves on a meal of seaweed and algae, these social animals stretch out next to (if not on top of) their neighbors to dry out, warm up, and digest their food. These reptiles are excellent swimmers; if forced, they can stay underwater for over an hour. Darwin's "Imps of Darkness" have one more trick up their scaly sleeves. They have evolved a unique way to excrete the salt they unavoidably consume from their seaweed main courses—they blow it out of their noses in a sneezing action. Years ago, pirates thought this "poisonous spit" was an acid; even though it's only salt water, it can pack quite a punch—the excreted salt often shoots three or four feet.

The iguana nests lie on either side of a very narrow sandy path, where blue herons, Galápagos hawks, and other predatory birds look to make a quick meal of their hatchlings. Be careful—any visitor that strays from this path will kill the iguanas before the birds even get a chance. Nesting sites are well concealed and quite fragile; the weight of a human being could easily crush an entire nest. Not too many visitors seem to have strayed from the straight and narrow, though, as just beyond this trail hundreds of iguanas are often to be seen dozing in the sun. This Malthusian outpouring of animals is due to Fernandina's lack of introduced predators—this is what all the islands must have been like years ago.

Punta Espinosa also offers the opportunity to see the rare **flightless cormorant.** This strange-looking subspecies is only found in the Galápagos; one of the rarest birds in the world, only about 800 pairs exist. For centuries, the birds have had no predators on the islands and thus no need to fly, so while most cormorant wings are large and impressive, those of the flightless cormorants have grown short and stubby. The birds instead rely on their powerful legs for swimming and catching fish. The cormorants have odd nest-building habits too: every time a bird returns to the nest, it brings some new sort of decoration. By the time the chicks are grown, the nests are eclectic masses of seaweed, stones, and shells. Before returning to the boat, stroll past the mangrove forest just beyond the shore. This shaded area sometimes acts as a nursery for sea lion pups while their mothers fish.

Isla Santiago (James, San Salvador)

To put it bluntly, Santiago rocks. In the face of catastrophe, this resilient island has triumphed time and again over the destructive forces of volcanic activity and mankind's unwelcome influence. Its volcanic cones, beach-front lava spires, gentle *pahoehoe* flows, and black sand beaches are reminders of the island's explosive past. The first humans to inhabit the island were 16th-century pirates who used the island's canopied coves as hideouts. But it wasn't until the 1880s that the most irreparable damage was done, when four rather amorous goats were abandoned on the island. The goat population soon ballooned to over 100,000 and the gluttons ate everything in sight. Since then, environmentalists with voracious appetites for conservation (and goat stew) have managed to keep the introduced population in check. The island was further sullied in the 1920s and 60s by two commercial salt mines that unsuccessfully attempted to profit from the island's salt-lined crater. Several rusty buildings built during these periods still stand near the western shore; tearing them down would cause more damage to the island than letting them stand. Despite its turbulent past, there is much to see and do on Santiago. Its central location makes it easily accessible, and its four visitor sights are among the best in the Galápagos. The island is a destination on nearly all tour itineraries.

Puerto Egas

Some say that life imitates art, but no human artist has ever come close to matching the scale of Mother Nature's sculpture. Over the years, wind and currents have carved unique sand formations in the black sand beach of Puerto Egas in Santiago's **James Bay.** Apertures, crevices, and natural bridges form a natural masterpiece at the island's most impressive visitor sight. These alcoves form perfect nesting spots for sea lions seeking refuge from the glaring equatorial sun.

A short trail from the beach leads to one of the best tide pool areas in the Galápagos. Gleaming sandy beaches contrast with black lava towers, basins, and craters, filled with crystal-clear sea water. Scattered over the coastline like dozens of tiny oceans, each pool really is its own universe, teeming with numerous schools of tiny fish, sea anemone, oysters, and hermit crabs. Lucky groups might even see large Galápagos eels and beautifully colored octopi. Sea birds also abound; lava herons, ruddy turnstones, oyster catchers, terns, and other birds often gorge enthusiastically near the tide pools. Look under warm rocks for the small Galápagos scorpion. These little fellows aren't really a threat, but the slippery lava rock along the tidal area is, so be very careful when walking.

Past the tide pools visitors come to what, for many, is the highlight of a trip to Isla Santiago: the **grottoes.** These pools, formed by the island's numerous lava flows, are constantly filled and refilled by the open sea. One pool, appropriately dubbed **Darwin's Toilet,** fills with a particularly noisy flushing force. Clear, gently circulating waters surrounds swimmers, while lava arches and natural bridges tower overhead. Fish, seals, and sea lions swim in and around these pools. Disney got many of its ideas for characters and scenery from the Galápagos; one almost expects singing fish and crustaceans to line the rocky walls, welcoming guests into a cartoon dance.

Snorkeling and scuba diving are popular activities around these parts, but check with your guide before taking a dip, as a swim in the grottoes at the wrong time is anything but idyllic. Currents and tides rush through quickly, and unlucky swimmers may find themselves at the mercy of the sea. If the tide is changing, it's best to watch from the side and let the seal and sea lion experts do their thing. The ocean teems with turtles, tropical fish, eels, and sometimes even sharks, rays, and **Galápagos fur seals.** Technically fur seals are not seals at all, but rather a different species of smaller sea lion with pointed ears and more fur. The rich pelt of these animals was once very much desired and hunted by humans; one boat in the Galápagos killed 50,000 in a period of three months. For obvious reasons, fur seals aren't quite as trusting or gregarious as their larger relatives.

NEAR PUERTO EGAS

A 2-km path from Puerto Egas leads to the summit of San Salvador's **Sugarloaf Volcano (Pan de Azúcar).** Because of the challenging rocky terrain and the heat absorbed by the black lava, this short distance can become an exhausting two- to four-hour hike. Water and sturdy shoes are a must. Up on the 395m summit, where the entire island stretches out below, views of James Bay and the two tuff cones at Sullivan Bay simply stun.

A less strenuous 3km trail leads to the **salt crater.** There is a good view from the top, but the walk there is not quite as aesthetically pleasing as the hike up Sugarloaf. Remnants of human presence are juxtaposed with the otherwise pristine area. Houses and leftover equipment from the salt mines mar the landscape; introduced cats, pigs, rats, and goats have also caused obvious damage. The thin gray branches of the gnarled *palo santo* ("holy stick") trees are often used as incense in Ecuadorian churches. Sniff the sap to experience wholly the tree's divine aroma.

At the north end of James Bay, visitors have the chance to see a slightly different type of wildlife—ducks and flamingos at **Playa Espumilla.** The site is accessible via a wet landing on a sandy beach. Be careful where you step, however, as sea turtles often lay their eggs here. There is a 2-km bird-watching trail into the interior that passes one of the island's inland lagoons. These lagoons bustle with activity; be quiet and you might come across a few flamingos. They aren't hard to spot—Galápagos flamingos are among the most colorful in the world because of the keratin in the bright pink shrimp they eat.

■ On Isla Santiago

BUCCANEER COVE

An impressive reminder of the renegade pirates that used to dwell here, **Buccaneer Cove** is located at the northwest end of Isla Santiago. After climbing volcanos, swimming with sharks, and hiking across lava fields, a visit to Buccaneer Cove is a pleasant change of pace. The site is best seen from the ship, as its landscape and sheer cliff walls are most impressive from the sea. But the underwater scuba and snorkeling views aren't too shabby either.

Pirates frequented this cove in the 1600s and early 1700s, later followed by visiting whalers. Today it is populated by feral goats that do as much damage to the landscape as the pirates did to the high seas. Needless to say, plant and animal diversity is not Buccaneer Cove's strongest attraction, but the cliffs themselves are amazing and have a lore as colorful as the island's history. Apparently, sailors watched the passing pinnacles and rock formations with the same imagination many people use when they look at clouds. Watch out for "The Monk" and "Elephant Rock".

SULLIVAN BAY

Santiago's final visitor's site is the unique **Sullivan Bay,** on the east coast of Isla Santiago. The most interesting part of this bay is not the water itself, though snorkeling is decent. Rather, its "beach" is completely unlike the typical sandy specimens lining most shores. Sullivan Bay's solid black fields were formed by a *pahoehoe* lava flow, and there's not a grain of sand in sight. This flow is only about 100 years young (new by geological standards), and a walk across it can be a sizzling experience, especially for those interested in volcanos and island formation. Pockets of water and gases trapped under the lava, known as *hornitos,* exploded to form the wrinkles breaking up the smooth black span.

Be sure to notice the "islands within the island": two tuff cones that were once their own autonomos rocky isles—before the sudden attack from all sides by Santiago's quick-flowing lava. The one- to one-and-a-half-hour trail loops around the bay. As with all lava walks, proper footwear is necessary, and water and sunscreen are equally important. For those who don't have time to visit Sullivan Bay, the view of it from Isla Bartolomé's visitor's site is almost as rewarding. The key word is "almost."

Isla Bartolomé

With a land surface of only 1.2 km^2, Bartolomé is one of the smallest islands in the archipelago, yet it has one of the most drop-dead, stunning vistas. The island itself is striking as well—deep reds, blues, and shimmering blacks mingle and shift over each other, creating a kaleidoscopic landscape, the majesty of which is impossible to capture even with a panoramic lens. Dominated by an ancient volcano of stark and imposing beauty, this barren island consists of ash and porous lava rock on which colonizing plants are just beginning to grow. The *isla* boasts two visitor sites: the **summit** of the volcanic cone and the **twin crescent beaches,** with the only colony of Galápagos penguins this side of Isabela (a wet landing site).

The easily climbed trail to Bartolomé's summit begins as a set of natural stairs that are a favorite sunbathing spot for marine iguanas. Farther up, lava lizards dart back and forth, rarely stopping long enough to allow spectators to get a good look—it's easy to miss small pleasures like these little guys. Though the view from Bartolomé's peak is unsurmounted, don't rush to the top; go slowly so as to appreciate how the island's appearance changes with altitude. On a clear day, the view from the summit enables climbers to grasp the immensity and uniqueness of the archipelago. North Seymour, Daphne Major and Minor, Santa Cruz, Sombrero Chino, Isla Sin Nombre, and Santiago are all visible from here; some, like Santiago, appear truly mastodonic, while others are simply tiny knolls sticking out of the water. From here it is easy to understand why Bartolomé is often compared to the surface of the moon—unearthly craters coated with black ash surround the volcano and fill the shallow beaches.

On the way down, take time to notice colonizing plants, such as the prickly pear, growing on the island. The **lava cactus** (*Brachycereus nesioticas*) has developed a unique method of forming its own soil. These spiny banana-shaped plants grow bright green arms from a central stalk, and as older growth decays, it falls to the side, generating its own organic fertilizer. A much less inspiring sight is the erosion on either side of the trail. This gradual destruction is the result of the large number of boat-tours and daytrippers who visit the island each year. If it continues, it will eventually seriously damage the fragile landscape. Not just for your own safety, but also for the safety of Bartolomé, it is imperative that you stay on the path.

Bartolomé's **twin beaches,** lying on either side of the island, are its other main attraction. Before landing at the beach, it is advisable to change out of hiking boots into something more beach-and-seaworthy; some brave souls try to go barefoot, but quickly discover the error of their ways when they step onto the hot island sand. Swimming is only permitted on the North Beach. Powerful tides and currents, as well as wandering sharks and stingrays, make the South Beach worse for swimming, but still top-notch for nature-watching. Look for nesting sea turtles from late December to early March, and keep an eye out for great blue herons year-round.

On the North Beach, the massive **Pinnacle Rock** points majestically to the sky. This "rock" is made up of tightly packed sand shaped by the wind and sea. As with everything in the Galápagos, Pinnacle Rock is still changing; the Swiss cheese holes caused by the wear-and-tear of the elements will eventually cause the Rock to crumble into the sea. The oceanside base is a popular place to try to spot the Galápagos penguin *(Spheniscus mendiculus),* an endemic bird markedly smaller than its Antarctic cousin. Though shy when it comes to nesting, the birds will let people get quite close to them in the water; snorkelers in the bay have gotten used to the sight of these slippery little sun worshippers swimming by.

Isla Rábida

As if embarrassed, the sheepishly small island of Rábida constantly blushes, its beaches glowing with maroon and deep scarlet hues. Also known as Jervis, the island is about one and a half hours by boat from Isla Sombrero Chino, near the exact center of the Galápagos archipelago. After a wet landing, visitors usually encounter a number of animals resting in the shade of nearby caves or under mangrove trees. Here's a shocker—sea lions top the list of beach bums. Past the mangroves lies a small lagoon where flamingos occasionally dwell. This is also one of the island's few nesting sites for the brown pelican, among the largest birds in the Galápagos. Some travelers may want to lace up some sturdy shoes and continue along the walking trail to a small cliff overlooking the inlet. Others might slip out of their shoes altogether and go for a swim—Rábida's excellent snorkeling could turn you rabid with excitement.

Isla Española (Hood)

The southernmost island in the archipelago, Española's distance from the rest of the chain may well be its greatest asset. The secluded wildlife has gone to evolutionary lengths never imagined—most people couldn't come up with such wild coloration and species diversity in their dreams. On most of the Galápagos, visitors have to climb mountains, scale cliffs, or snorkel their way into the heart of it all, but Española presents nature at its in-your-face best. Don't let Española's distance deter, as a visit to this remote island is the highlight of many an island tour. Not all boats go here though, especially not those departing from Santa Cruz, so travelers should take special care to make sure Española is on their itineraries. Upon landing at **Punta Suárez,** visitors are immediately besieged by barking sea lions hungry for attention (as if the spoiled suckers don't get enough). Go ahead, indulge yourself, but don't spend too long, as Española has much more to offer.

On Isla Española

PUNTA SUÁREZ

Boats reach Española via one of the more exciting soaking-wet landings, on Punta Suárez, a visitor's site covering the island's western tip. They anchor rather far out, so you'll have to take a *panga* to the island, riding waves and dodging large rocks (not to mention those increasingly annoying sea lions). When disembarking a *panga,* especially on Española, grab your guide hand-to-elbow. This grip gives a stable hold—*pangas* tend to jostle and a mere hand clasp just doesn't cut it.

One of the trails from Punta Suarez provides a prime view of the island's famous **blowhole.** A seaside cliff on the south end of the trail, provides the perfect vantage point from which to watch wave-powered spray soar over 25m (82 ft.) into the air. Incoming waves rush through a lava tube and get forced out of narrow volcanic fissures at the end, producing a geyser effect powerful enough to make the folks at Yellowstone nervous. A trail leads down to the blowhole; here, the unstoppable force of the ocean meets the volcanic shore in a fantastic face-off.

Perhaps alerted by the squabbling sea lions, the endemic **Española Mockingbird** curiously observes most groups. Slightly larger than its relatives on other islands, the Española subspecies also has a longer, curved beak. A communal bird, it travels in small tribes called "family groups." Don't be surprised if these tricksters land on your head or shoulder and try get a look at the contents of your knapsack.

A short ways down the visitor's path, proudly strutting **blue-footed boobies** have claimed the trail for themselves. With their squatty, duck-shaped bodies, graying hair, and bright blue feet, the boobies are almost as strange as their name. The newly renovated Punta Suárez trail winds its way into one of the archipelago's primary booby nesting grounds. These birds normally raise two eggs annually; parents take turns standing over them for incubation, encircling each egg with bright blue, webbed blankets. Male and female blue-footed boobies look quite similar but there are ways to tell them apart. Female boobies have larger eyes and voice their opinions by honking, while beady-eyed males answer with an unmistakable whistle. Sex distinction becomes crucially important when watching the boobies' mating dance, which not surprisingly focuses on those unforgettably sexy feet.

However, the most significant wildlife spot on the island is the nesting area of the **waved albatross,** the only one on the planet. They breed here between mid-April and mid-December. This striking bird, who has made guest appearances in Disney flicks like *The Rescuers Down Under* and *The Little Mermaid,* combines elements of grace and ungainliness in a way only the albatross can. Majestic in flight, the stately bird is a creamy blend of brilliant white and bright yellow, with gray wings. However adept in flight, these birds have a hard time getting it together enough to land on their small island. Don't pull out the crossbow just yet—be patient as the albatrosses glide to the cliff's edge, put their feet down, and stumble to a halt. Albatrosses mate for life but romantically renew their vows each year, re-performing their complex mating dance, a five-day spectacle involving a little more strutting, stumbling, honking, and a good deal of beak-fencing. Hey, they have to let out their marital frustration somehow.

GARDNER BAY

White sand, white sand, and more white sand. Though that's the majority of what you'll find here, the beach is far from humdrum. Waves crash and sea lions dance themselves into a frenzy in desperate competition for an audience. Divided into two sections by an outcropping of lava rock, the long, open shoreline is one of the few places in the Galápagos that is completely safe to explore without a guide. Visitors planning to walk the entire length of the beach should bring sturdy shoes. This type of independent, Darwinesque exploration is often the most rewarding—look for an endangered species, or maybe even discover a new one. Snorkeling is possible in Gardner Bay, but is usually more rewarding nearby at the aptly named **Turtle Rock.** Aside from turtles, you might also spot white-tipped sharks cruising the shallows.

Isla Floreana

The Galápagos have always seduced the disenchanted. Anything can happen—the islands have their own set of rules and nothing, least of all the animals, behaves conventionally. A universe in itself, the Galápagos's lush jungles and barren lava deserts evoke images of both Eden and the underworld. Separated from the motherland by nearly 1000km of open ocean, the islands are only superficially a part of Ecuador. It is this holistic separation that has always drawn people to the islands, particularly the far-flung island of Floreana.

The town of **Puerto Velasco Ibarra** is sometimes visited by tourist ships, particularly the Tip Top 11, owned and operated by Rolf Wittmer, one of the first natives of Floreana. Rolf's mother, Margret (see Murder in the Galápagos, below), runs the small **Pensión Wittner** (tel. 520-150, in Guayaquil 04-244-506), the only place to stay on

Murder in the Galápagos

Isla Floreana received its first residents in 1929, and hasn't been the same since. **Friedrich Ritter,** a German doctor and devoted follower of Nietzsche, retreated from society with **Dora Strauch,** his patient and lover. Their goal: to create an untainted community of two, dedicated to the healing powers of the mind. Before coming to the island, Ritter insisted that both he and Dora have all their teeth removed and **stainless steel dentures** made; one pair was soon lost, so the couple had to share. Over the next five years, more and more goofy Germans moved to the isolated isle. The temperamental **Baroness** von Wagner de Bosquet blew into Floreana like a hurricane, dressed in riding pants and tall leather boots, with a revolver in one hand and a **whip** in the other (presumably to keep her own two lovers in line). Of course, she could have used it to crack the tension in the air when she proclaimed herself **"Empress of Floreana,"** a declaration that went over big with Ritter and his dreams of intellectual isolation. But in 1934, the baroness suddenly disappeared with one of her lovers, and the mutilated body of the other was found on the beach of a distant island, mummified by the sun. Moreover, Dr. Ritter, a vegetarian, mysteriously died from poisoned chicken. Onlookers say he cursed Dora with his dying breath; she lived only long enough to write the book *Satan Came to Eden* before falling victim to that curse. Today, one of the less eccentric of Floreana's original residents, **Margret Wittmer,** still lives on the island. Nobody ever proved any foul play, but ask Margret if she ever picked up on any fishy smells during the whole sordid mess.

Floreana. Rooms with private baths, hot water, and an ocean view go for s/20,000; breakfast s/10,000; lunch or dinner s/15,000. Pensión Wittner also sells autographed copies of Margret's book, *Floreana,* and stamped letters for the post office barrel.

■ On Isla Floreana

POST OFFICE BAY

Sometime in the 18th century, a British whaling captain erected a post office barrel on the quiet bay of an uninhabited island. The island was later named Floreana, and for a long time its barrel was the only postal facility for hundreds of miles. Whaling ships from around the world left their letters in the barrel and picked up those addressed to their next destination. Although the first post-barrel is now long gone, the tradition is kept up by the island's many visitors every year.

Today's visitors get to the post-barrel via a wet landing at a brown beach on Floreana's northern shore. From there, the barrel is not far away. Today's barrel is quite different from the original, bare-bones one left by the British whaler so long ago. No longer content with simply leaving letters, numerous visitors have added their own tributes to this growing piece of public art with signs, pictures, and other wooden messages. Drop off a postcard or two and see if any are addressed to an area near you. When you get home, drop it in the mail, or if possible, deliver it personally. Who knows, maybe it could lead to a sordid romance in the spirit of Floreana.

PUNTA CORMORANT

Floreana's colorful history is notorious around these parts, full of wacky stories about meat-eating vegetarians and communal dentures, but Punta Cormorant takes on more conventional hues—red mangroves, gray hillsides, pink flamingos, white sands, blue waters, and glistening green stones. Visitors arrive at this sight via a wet landing at the northern end of the island, on a beach littered with thousands of small, green beads. This unique crystal, known as olivine, was formed centuries ago as a volcanic by-product. A short walk through several different regions of vegetation leads to one of the few colorless sites at Punta Cormorant—a dark, murky, mangrove-encircled lagoon. Flashy, filter-feeding, flourescent-feathered flamingos add life to these subfusc waters. While captive flamingos are fed a mixture of shrimp and red dye to achieve thier characteristic color, the coloration of the **Galápagos flamingos** is naturally maintained by their diet of bright pink shrimp. The graceful flamingos stand in sharp contrast to the gnarled, gray palo santo trees on the hillsides surrounding the lagoon.

Another site at Punta Cormorant, **Flour Beach,** may have the softest, cleanest sand ever to grace the human foot. Visitors who fail to take off their shoes might never forgive themselves. Shadowy, gray ghost crabs and green sea turtles frequent this beach. The latter come at night to lay eggs, but only one out of 100 survive as frigates, sharks, and other predators anxiously await the turtles' birth. Finally, keep an eye on the shallow waters of Flour Beach's quiet cove; large numbers of sting rays come here to feed. If you enter the water when the rays are around, shuffle your feet as you enter to give these barbed creatures ample time to squirm away. Snorkeling and swimming here are pretty good, but if possible, don't miss a chance to snorkel at **Devil's Crown.**

DEVIL'S CROWN

At one time, this underwater visitor's site just off the coast of Punta Cormorant was a submerged volcano. Subsequent eruptions and the power of the open ocean eroded the cone into a jagged ring of black lava spires rising from the sea floor. But to truly appreciate this imposing site, it must be experienced underwater. Devil's Crown offers some of the best snorkeling in the islands, thanks to currents that bring in tons of fish and coral. Snorkelers should be cautious, as these same currents can be dangerous if ignored. Listen carefully to the guide's instructions and use common sense.

The island's morbid history often prompt potential swimmers to joke about the odds of a close encounter with a shark. The chance of seeing these elegant creatures is actually very real—both white-tipped reef sharks and hammerheads frequent the area. Despite their incredible speed and fierce appearance, these animals are not aggressive; the skittish hammerhead rarely approaches if snorkelers are in the area. For the best odds of seeing a shark, remain calm, quiet, and close to your guide. Enjoy the lava rocks and fish below, but keep an eye on deeper waters, where groups of sharks sometimes cruise past. While the chance of seeing something big gets the adrenaline flowing, the often-ignored world of the small is amazing as well. Starfish, sea cucumbers, sea urchins, and eels have all been spotted here.

■ The Northern Islands

The distant northern islands (**Pinta, Marchena,** and **Genovesa**) are rarely visited by one-week touring boats, as the sail here takes about eight to 10 hours and the seas are usually rough. Marchena Island offers excellent scuba diving, but has no land visitor sites and is therefore only visited by diving tours. Pinta, with its collapsed volcano, is closed to the public as well. A visit to Genovesa Island (often known as **Tower Island**) is particularly rewarding for those salty enough to make the trip. Genovesa has two visitor sites, both accessible via **Darwin Bay** on the east end of the island. At the wet landing site, the bright coral of **Darwin Beach** contrasts sharply with the bay's deep green color. After passing a tidal pool section, the trail enters a wooded area of salt-bushes and mangroves where a red-footed booby colony builds its nests (the only Galápagos species to nest in trees). In addition to boobies, visitors to this island often see frigatebirds, Galápagos doves, and the beautiful red-billed tropic bird. Genovesa's other visitor site, **Prince Phillip's Steps,** is also an excellent birdwatching area. The rocky trail winds its way through several colonies of nesting sea birds to a wooded area (keep an eye out for short-eared owls and red-footed boobies), on to a large lava field where hundreds of storm petrels dwell, and finally to the cliff's edge. Don't think that all life on Genovesa is avian. A look from the cliffs into the bay might offer a glimpse of another animal often spotted here: the hammerhead shark.

Appendices

Glossary

abanico	fan
aduana	customs
aire acondicionado	air-conditioned (A/C)
albergue (juvenil)	(youth) hostel
alcaldía	mayoral district or headquarters
almuerzo	lunch, midday meal
amigo/a	friend
arroz	rice
artesanía	arts and crafts
avenida	avenue
bahía	bay
baño	bathroom or natural spa
barato/a	cheap
biblioteca	library
borracho/a	drunk
barrio	neighborhood
bocas	appetizers, at a bar
cabina	cabin, often just used to refer to a hotel room
calle	street
cambio	change
camino	path or track
camioneta	small, pickup-sized truck
campamento	campground
campesino/a	person from a rural area
cantina	drinking establishment, usually male dominated
caro/a	expensive
carretera	highway
carro	car, or sometimes a train car
casa de cambio	currency exchange establishment
casado/a	married
caseta de larga distancia	long-distance phone booth
catarata	waterfall
cena	dinner, a light meal usually served after 8pm.
centro	city center
cerca	nearby
cerveza	beer
ceviche	fish marinated in lemon juice, herbs and vegetables
chifa	Chinese restaurant
coche	car
colectivo	municipal transit bus
colonia	neighborhood in a large city
comedor	small, informal local restaurant
comida corrida	multi-course *á la carte* meal
consulado	consulate
corvina	sea bass
cruz roja	Red Cross
cuadra	street block
cuarto con dos camas	a room with two beds; **con una cama:** with one bed

desayuno	breakfast
descompuesto	broken, out of order
de turno	a 24-hour rotating schedule for pharmacies
discoteca	dance club
embajada	embassy
emergencia	emergency
farmacia	pharmacy
ferrocarril	train
finca	a plantation-like agricultural enterprise or a ranch
ganga	bargain
guayaquileño/a	a native of Guayaquil
herbido/a	boiled
indígeno/a	indigenous, refers to the Indian population (noun/adj.)
kilo	kilogram
ladrón	thief
lago/ laguna	lake
larga distancia	long distance
lavandería	laundromat
lejos	far
lista de correos	the general delivery system in most of Ecuador
lomo	hill
malecón	pier or seaside thoroughfare
maneje despacio	drive slowly
menú del día	fixed daily meal often offered for a bargain price
mercado	market
merienda	late afternoon snack
mordida	literally "little bite," bribe
muelle	wharf
oficina de turismo	office of tourism
panadería	bakery
páramo	highland plain
parque nacional	national park
parroquia	parish
peligroso/a	dangerous
peña	folkloric music club
piropo	jibe, verbal wolf-whistle
policía	police
quiteño/a	a native of Quito
Quitos	nickname for Marcos (not the capital of Ecuador)
reloj	watch, clock
riobambeño/a	a native of Riobamba
ropa	clothes
sala	room
salida	exit
seguro/a	noun: lock; adj.: safe
semana	week
Semana Santa	Holy Week
SIDA	the Spanish acronym for AIDS
solo carril	one-lane road or bridge
terminal terrestre	bus station
tienda	store
tipo de cambio	exchange rate

Notes About Language

Even if you speak no Spanish, a few basics will help you along. Any attempts at Spanish are appreciated and encouraged, and you'll find that many people in larger cities understand some English. You are likely to hear *indígena* languages as well as Spanish. Those who already know Iberian Spanish will find that many common nouns and expressions are different in Ecuador.

Pronunciation is very regular. Vowels are always pronounced the same way: *a* ("ah" in father); *e* ("eh" in escapade); *i* ("ee" in eat); *o* ("oh" oat); *u* ("oo" in boot); *y*, by itself, is pronounced like i. Most consonants are the same as English. Important exceptions are: *j*, pronounced like the English "h" in "hello"; *ll*, pronounced like the English "y" in "yes"; *ñ*, which is pronounced like the "gn" in "cognac"; *rr*, the trilled "r"; *h* is always silent; *x* has a bewildering variety of pronunciations.

Let's Go provides phonetic approximations for particularly tough town names. Stress in Spanish words falls on the second to last syllable, except for words ending in "r," "l," and "z," in which it falls on the last syllable. All exceptions to these rules require a written accent on the stressed syllable.

Useful Phrases

No hablo español.	no AHB-loh eh-spahn-YOHL	"I don't speak Spanish."
¿Habla Usted inglés?	AHB-la oo-STED een-GLEHS?	"Do you speak English?"
¿Puede Usted ayudarme?	POOEH-deh oos-TED a-yoo-DAR-meh?	"Can you help me?"
¿Cuánto cuesta un cuarto para x personas?	KWAHN-toh KWEH-sta oon KWAHR-toh PAH-rah x PEHR-soh-nahs	"How much does a room for x person(s) cost?"
¿Dónde hay un hotel, restaurante?	DOHN-deh aie oon oh-TEL, res-taw-RAN-tay?	"Where is there a hotel, restaurant?"
¿Dónde está el hotel x?	DOHN-deh es-TAH el oh-TEL x?	"Where is the hotel x?"
¿Puedo ver un cuarto?		"May I see a room?"
¿El cuarto tiene agua caliente, baño privado, un abanico?		"Does the room have hot water, a private bathroom, a fan?"
¿A qué hora sale el autobús a Vilcabamba?		"At what time does the bus to Vilcabamba leave?"
Hola.		"Hello."
Yo me llamo...		"My name is ..."
¿Cómo se llama Usted?		"What is your name?"
Mucho gusto conocerlo/la.		"Pleased to meet you."
¿Qué hora es?		"What time is it?"
¡Déjame (en paz)!		"Leave me (alone)!"
¡Ayúdame!		"Help me!"

Learn the vocabulary of courtesy as well; you'll be treated more kindly if you can be polite to those around you:

Con permiso	con pehr-MEE-so	"Excuse me," an important phrase used more frequently than its English counterpart, whether on a crowded bus or to excuse yourself from someone's company.
Perdón	pehr-DOHN	"Pardon me"
¿Qué pasa?	keh PAH-sah	"What's up?"

Por favor	pohr fah-VOHR	"Please"
Gracias	GRAH-seeahs	"Thank you"
De nada	deh NAH-dah	"You're welcome" ("It's nothing")

Learn the numbers, if only to bargain and to reassure yourself that you're on the right bus. 1: *uno;* 2: *dos*; 3: *tres;* 4: *cuatro;* 5: *cinco;* 6: *seis;* 7: *siete;* 8: *ocho;* 9: *nueve;* 10: *diez;* 11: *once;* 12: *doce;* 13: *trece;* 14: *catorce;* 15: *quince;* 20: *veinte;* 30: *treinta;* 40; *cuarenta;* 50: *cincuenta;* 60: *sesenta;* 70: *setenta;* 80: *ochenta;* 90: *noventa;* 100: *cien*; 1000: *mil.* Adding units to these base numbers is as simple as saying "and" (*y*); *diez y seis* is 16, *diez y siete* is 17, etc. Similarly, numbers in the twenties are *veinte y*-plus the units, in the thirties are *treinta y*-plus the units, and so on. Over 100, the *y* is no longer necessary for adding units; just say *ciento*-plus units or *mil*-plus units, for instance 157 is *ciento cincuenta y siete.*

No offense is meant if you are called a *gringo/a.* You may offend, however, if you call yourself an *americano/a*; as "Americans" themselves, South Americans resent monopolization of the term by the U.S. Instead, refer to yourself as a *norteamericano/a. Güero/a* (light-haired or light-skinned person) and *moreno/a* (dark-skinned person) are common forms of address among strangers in the streets. The most appropriate term for the descendants of the Inca is *indígena* or indigenous, the term that *Let's Go* uses; the only term that is guaranteed to be offensive is *indio.*

THE CALENDAR

Months: enero, febrero, marzo, abril, mayo, junio, julio, agosto, setiembre, octubre, noviembre, diciembre

Days of the week: (starting with Monday) lunes, martes, miercoles, jueves, viernes, sábado, domingo

Climate

Temp in °C Rain in cm	January Temp	 Rain	April Temp	 Rain	July Temp	 Rain	October Temp	 Rain
Seymour Island, Galápagos	30/22	2.0	31/24	1.8	27/21	0.0	27/19	0.0
Guayaquil	31/21	23.9	32/22	11.7	29/19	0.5	30/20	0.8
Quito	22/8	9.9	21/8	17.5	22/7	2.0	22/8	11.2

INEFAN-Approved Tour Companies

INEFAN, the government's National Park Administration, has approved the following tour companies for these protected areas through February 1997. Once agencies are approved, they tend to maintain that status. To check whether a company is still approved, or whether a company not listed has since been approved, contact Edgar Rivera at the INEFAN office in Quito (tel. (02) 506-337; open Mon.-Fri. 8am-4:30pm).

Reserva Faunistica Cuyabeno: Jungaltur, Kempery Tours, Turisamazonas Turismon, Transturi , Native Life Travels, Nomadtreck, Selvanieve Expediciones, Crucero Fluvial Harpia, Rainforestur, Etnotur.

Parque Nacional Cotopaxi: Exploratur, Agencia de Viajes Surtrek, Etnotur, Cretertur, Pamir Adventure Travels, Aventura Flying Duthcman, Expediciones Andinas.

Parque Nacional Machalilla: Agencia de Viajes Pacarina, Agencia de Viajes Surtreck, Señor Elpidio Parrales Caiche

Parque Nacional Sangay: Expediciones Andinas, Exploratur

Reserva Faunistica Chimborazo: Expediciones Andinas, Exploratur

Holidays and Festivals in 1997

NATIONAL HOLIDAYS

January 1	New Year's Day
January 6	Festival of the Three Kings (Epiphany)
February 10-11	Carnival
March 27	Holy Thursday
March 28	Good Friday
March 29	Easter Saturday
May 1	Labor Day
May 24	Battle of Pichincha (Independence Day)
July 24	Birth of Simón Bolívar
August 10	Independence of Quito
October 9	Independence of Guayaquil
October 12	Discovery of America
November 1	All Saints' Day
November 2	All Souls' Day
November 3	Independence of Cuenca
December 6	Foundation of Quito
December 25	Christmas Day

OTHER COMMONLY OBSERVED HOLIDAYS

January 15	Dances of the Innocent (Quito-Chillogallo)
February 12	Discovery of the Amazon River
February 27	Commemoration of the Battle of Tarqui (1829), National Unity Day
March 4-10	Peach Festival (Gualaceo)
April 19-25	Farming, cattle, handicraft, and industrial fair (Riobamba)
May 2-3	Festivals of La Cruz (Quito)
May 11-14	Fair in Puyo and the Amazon region
June 10	Corpus Christi
June 24	Saint John the Baptist's Day Corn and tourism festivals (Sangoloqui) Rodeo Day (Calpi)
June 29	Saint Peter and Saint Paul's Day
July 16	Celebration of Virgen del Carmen (Ibarra)
July 22	Canonization anniversary in Pelileo
July 23-25	Celebrations commemorating the foundation of Guayaquil
August 3-5	Esmeraldas's Independence Day celebrations
August 10	San Lorenzo festivities (Pillaro) San Jacinto festivities (Yaguachi)

September 1-15	Fiesta de Yamor (Otavalo)
September 6-14	Fiesta de Jora (Cotacachi)
September 20-26	Banana's World Fair (Machala)
September 24-28	Festival of the Lakes (Ibarra)
November 11	Independence of Latacunga
December 28	All Fool's Day
December 31	New Year's Eve

Recalibration

WEIGHTS AND MEASURES

The metric system is used almost universally throughout Ecuador. For help with conversion:

1 millimeter (mm) = 0.04 inches	1 inch = 25mm
1 meter (m) = 1.09 yards	1 yard = 0.92m
1 kilometer (km) = 0.62 miles	1 mile = 1.61km
1 gram (g) = 0.04 ounces	1 ounce = 25g
1 liter = 1.06 quarts	1 quart = 0.94 liters

To convert from °C to °F, multiply by 9/5 and add 32.
To convert from °F to °C, subtract 32 and multiply by 5/9.

°C	-10	-5	0	5	10	15	20	25	30	35
°F	14	23	32	41	50	59	68	75	86	95

TIME DIFFERENCE

The Ecuadorian mainland is five hours behind Greenwich Mean Time, the equivalent of Eastern Standard Time. The Galápagos Islands are an additional hour behind. There is no change for Daylight Savings, as the days and nights are always the same length due to Ecuador's location on the equator.

ELECTRICAL CURRENT

110 volts, 60 cycles, AC is the standard voltage in Ecuador. This is the same as in North America, but is not compatible with Europe and Australia. Ask first, though, as some places might have alarm-clock-melting 220 volt outlets. If you're planning to rely heavily on electricity, bring ample adapters and converters, including one for converting three prongs to fit two-prong outlets. Many hotel rooms won't have outlets, or will have only one (which is taken by the fan).

Telephone Codes

02: Pichincha (Quito)
03: Cotopaxi, Tungurahua, Pastaza, Chimborazo, Bolívar
04: Cuenca, Loja, Macas
05: Galápagos, Manabí, Los Ríos
06: Esmeraldas, Ibarra, Lago Agrio, Coca, Sucumbíos, Imbabura, Carchi
07: Cuenca, Loja, Macas

APPENDICES

Index